INTERNATIONAL POLITICS SINCE WORLD WAR II: A SHORT HISTORY

INTERNATIONAL POLITICS SINCE WORLD WAR II: A SHORT HISTORY
SECOND EDITION

Charles L. Robertson
Smith College

John Wiley & Sons, Inc.
NEW YORK LONDON SYDNEY TORONTO

Copyright © 1966 and 1975, by John Wiley & Sons, Inc.

All rights reserved. Published simultaneously in Canada.

No part of this book may be reproduced by any means, nor transmitted, nor translated into a machine language without the written permission of the publisher.

Library of Congress Cataloging in Publication Data:

Robertson, Charles L
    International politics since World War II.

    Includes index.
    1. World politics—1945–   I. Title.
D843.R63 1975   327′.09′04   74-23998
ISBN 0-471-72743-1
ISBN 0-471-72744-X pbk.

Printed in the United States of America
10 9 8 7 6 5 4 3 2 1

To Katy, Jenny, Heidi,
Christina, and Angelika

PREFACE

This book is a survey of international affairs since the end of World War II. It is primarily intended for students, but it also will be of interest to other people who have lived through these times. Almost 30 years have passed since the end of World War II and, to many students, what I consider to be current events—the Marshall Plan, the Korean War, and the Cuban Missile crisis—are only vague history; Churchill, Dulles, and Khrushchev might as well be Napoleon, Wellington, or Charles V. Indeed, friends whose adulthood spans this period often have forgotten much of what passed or the changes that have taken place.

This book, then, is a summary and synthesis, drawn mainly from secondary sources, but also from the memoirs and document collections on the period. It indicates the broad sweep of historical change and recalls numerous specific events that brought about the change. The treatment will not satisfy everyone. There is much controversy over this period and, because I have had to select and summarize, some readers will object to what I have selected and how I have summarized it. Therefore, although I have tried to be fair and "objective," I have a point of view, and I have stated it.

International politics differs from domestic politics chiefly because the power to make authoritative political decisions is decentralized among several distinct geographical units. We may therefore assume the existence of an international system in which these units—which we call "states"—coexist and conflict in regular patterns. All states, large or small, "developed" or "undeveloped," insist on what they call "independence" and "sovereignty." Independence and sovereignty may have resulted from objective conditions of the seventeenth century, as John Herz argued cogently in *International Politics in the Atomic Age,** when monarchs were first able to acquire centralized power and defend the borders of their states. But independence and sovereignty are still clung to as both the concept and reality necessary to create and maintain viable political societies, despite the challenges of modern warfare, economic interdependence, ideological movements, or corporations commanding vast economic resources. States, with their own bureaucracies, armies, laws, and currencies, still interact through the traditional means of diplomacy, war, trade, or intervention. They cooperate, coordinate their activities, or en-

---

* Columbia University Press, New York, 1959.

gage in a variety of conflicts. Defensive measures by one state are constantly viewed as aggression by another.

The outlines of the present international system—despite continuous change and flux—arose from a vast historical process beginning with the decline of feudalism and extending over several centuries, and the system cannot easily be altered. The number of "independent, sovereign states" has increased from 50 to more than 130 in a quarter of a century; "great powers" have collapsed and new ones have risen; mass weapons, mass communications, and the growth of an enormous international market have all undermined the nineteenth-century, Europe-centered, balance-of-power system. Yet, in the "bipolarism" of 1947 to 1955 and in the growing complexity of a militarily bipolar and politically multipolar system since 1955, "balancing" in the interest of security has remained a constant mode of conduct; when two giant Communist states like Russia and China are in conflict, they seek allies and support the opponents of the other: because Russia supports India, China backs Pakistan. China tacitily supports a United States presence in Europe to give Russia two fronts.

If decentralization of the international political system leads inevitably to the balancing process, it also ensures that the states composing the system will show uncertainty and indeterminacy in the conduct of their foreign policies. Policymakers act on the basis of assumptions, not truth. Therefore, in describing major events, I have spent considerable time surveying the assumptions on which policymakers acted, and I am frequently unable to make a judgment about the validity of these assumptions. Another consequence of decentralization is that the patterns that do emerge are a result of the separate actions of many states. Generally, none of these states, alone, can create the political pattern of the world (although several may cooperate to try). Thus the pattern of world politics often will be quite different from what the policymakers of a single state worked for or foresaw, and they cannot be blamed for this.

Finally, in justification of the title, the twentieth century has witnessed a complex interaction between international *relations* and international *politics*. Diplomatic history no longer can be written without considering the direction of trade, domestic and transnational groups, domestic and international opinion, and international institutions that play an important role: the international oil market or the office of Secretary-General of the United Nations. The environmental or background factors—economic, demographic, and ecological—must always be considered when political events are studied.

The years since World War II seem to fall into fairly logical divisions, as I have indicated in the text. The first two years after the war differed sharply from subsequent years; a second great break occurs in 1955, when the development of thermonuclear bombs and the means for delivering them gave policymakers a new set of assumptions and slowly moved the world from bipolarism to a far more complicated pattern. Within these broad spans of time, I also found several quite natural divisions, which constitute chapters. Occasionally, however, events did *not* fit within these divisions and, for this, I make no apology.

Although many readers will find slight mention of their own countries or interests, I do not consider them unimportant. To the people living in these countries, the events that I have passed over often have supreme importance. But I have selected topics on the basis of what has most affected the entire international political system—the whole world— and I have tried to do this honestly.

Soon after the second edition was completed, war again broke out in the Middle East, when Egypt and Syria initiated hostilities. This time Israel suffered heavy casualties in a contest that proved indecisive; Egypt and Syria gained an initial advantage and, although Israeli forces regained the initiative, they were forced to halt short of victory. A threatened Soviet intervention was prevented by an American alert, and the United States, playing down the damage to detente, began to take a much more forceful role through the personal diplomacy of Secretary of State Kissinger. He succeeded in devising complicated plans for a cease-fire that included a pullback of Israeli forces; Israeli acquiescence to another United Nations peace force was secured primarily by United States pressure plus guarantees. President Sadat's prestige rose in the Arab world; he had gone beyond words to action and secured American support for the Israeli withdrawal; he reestablished relations with the United States, which once more appeared as an important influence in the Middle East.

Meanwhile, however, trends mentioned in the text were heavily accentuated: Western and Japanese dependence on Middle East oil was underlined when the Organization of Petroleum Exporting Countries seized the occasion to quadruple the price of oil and use it as a political weapon. Western inflation, hastened by food shortages in the previous year, now increased greatly, and cooperative efforts to deal with these problems and the immense trade crisis that would ensue in subsequent years met with only limited success as states tried to preserve the health of their own economies through special deals. Less-developed countries felt the effect of petroleum price rises even more, but at least some of them hoped to emulate the oil-rich states by forming export cartels for other raw materials and commodities and by nationalizing more foreign-owned properties within their borders. Nationalist solutions to growing interdependence threatened to be the order of the day.

I thank many people who have helped me: Mrs. Marge Erikson, Miss Ciba Vaughan, Mrs. Norma Lepine, and Mrs. Agnes Shannon, who typed and retyped so much for me, and Peter Rowe who, after reading the manuscript, convinced me that the book could be useful.

Charles L. Robertson

Northampton, Massachusetts, 1974

CONTENTS

the 1952 Political Campaign—The Death of Stalin
and Soviet Foreign Policy—The Far East and
Southeast Asia—Geneva, 1954: The Far Eastern
Settlement—Taiwan and KOTO: The United States
Extends Its Alliances—More Stirrings in the
Non-Western World: Iran, Egypt, Africa—Latin
America Enters the World Stage—Europe, 1950–1955
—Developments in the United Nations—Conclusion.

PART I
BACKGROUND

ONE
THE BREAKDOWN OF THE
BALANCE OF POWER

With the advent of mass communications, everyone today is subjected to a flood of information on world affairs—sometimes detailed, sometimes oversimplified and distorted, frequently heavily biased. Most of us receive a hazy day-to-day impression of what is going on in the world around us. Too often, however, it comes in the form of suddenly finding out that there is a new crisis in some far-off spot: names of new places, names of new people compete for our attention. Sometimes the crisis drags on and we see its importance. Sometimes it disappears, along with the people involved. Which crises are "important"? Can we ever decide? Is it possible to see the forest and not merely the trees, to determine how events fit in to broader patterns of change? Is there, in fact, any pattern at all, or merely chaos and absurdity?

The "facts" rarely speak for themselves; interpretation is all-important. The account of international affairs in this book reflects a conviction that there are indeed discernible patterns and valid ways of making these patterns clear, that they result in large part from the interplay of current revolutionary developments in technology and ideology with persisting elements of the centuries-old balance of power system, and yet that the patterns are in part influenced by the very large measure of indeterminacy always present in human affairs.

In few other spheres of human endeavor does indeterminacy play a larger part than in the conduct of foreign policy. Those who formulate and carry out foreign policy for the states that make up the international community must constantly make assumptions about how their strategies will serve their various ends of security, economic welfare, or ideological expansion. In so doing they must constantly make assumptions about the aims and strategies of other states, or the implications of changes in background factors, such as the development of new weapons, the growth of multinational firms, or scarcities in world supply of raw materials or foods. And although policy-makers may try to equip themselves with as much intelligence and analysis as possible, they will always act on the basis of much speculation and hypothesis.

Thus, for the period immediately after World War II American policy-makers assumed that the Soviet Union would be too busy with internal reconstruction to set out upon a deliberate path of expansion. By 1947 this assumption had been revised, and a largely ideological explanation for Soviet hostility had replaced it. In 1950 the Korean War led to the assumption that the Soviets were now prepared to use force to expand. Yet all these views were essentially unprovable and, while always subject to question, have in recent times come to be roundly repudiated by numerous Western historians.

Time may give the historian perspective to make judgments, yet the writing of history is a constant dialogue over just such matters. In the meantime, the policy-makers of states must act on the basis of these views whether they are correct or not. Furthermore, in the post-war period, there were people in every country ready to dispute these particular assumptions about the Soviet Union and to make far different ones, whereas a close reading of Soviet discussions of military strategy reveals some startling assumptions about the possible hostile moves the United States might make and which the Russians must be ready to counter. The North Atlantic Treaty of 1949, with its subsequent rearmament of Europe, was based on the view that the Soviet Union might at any time overrun Western Europe. Billions of dollars were spent in strengthening the alliance, and yet many people in Western Europe felt no such military intentions existed on the part of the Soviet Union. The statesman might argue that he could take no chance and *must* be prepared for the worst. Yet he could be answered that the very act of such preparation would in turn stimulate the Russians to strengthen their own military capacities in ways they had not previously wanted, setting off the vicious circle of an unwanted arms race. At the moment of major policy decisions accurate judgments can rarely be made about such matters, although policy-makers are always called on to justify their actions—to themselves, if not to others.

A narrative of international relations, though limited to telling *what* has happened, must tell something of *why* it happened; for what men think they must do is a part of what they do, and their views of the world around them and their responses to these views are necessary parts of the story. At all times this view is subject to dispute, and in this lies the inevitable indeterminacy of international affairs.

Yet the past always sets the stage and the limits within which current actions can take place. The international events of the last three decades can be understood only if seen in the context of radical change in the balance-of-power system which had bequeathed to the contemporary world the sovereign, independent nation-state and the methods of maintaining some kind of order in a political system lacking any central political authority.

THE BALANCE OF POWER

The balance-of-power system arose out of the ruins of the preceding system, feudalism. Three hundred years of intermittent but often savage warfare ended with the Peace of Westphalia in 1648. The new system meant that kings and princes had successfully repudiated the superior authority of Pope and Emperor and substituted the idea and reality of the sovereign independent state which commanded the loyalty of all inhabitants within its territorial limits. States might differ in size, power, and geographical location, but on the basis of the idea of absolute sovereignty and the concomitant rejection of the authority of anyone outside the territorial borders of the state, each state also claimed equality with all other states.

For the first century and a half of its existence the system rested upon dynastic legitimacy; sovereignty—though sometimes disputed—was represented by a hereditary monarchy. The French Revolutiom decisively challenged the dynastic principle, which was eventually supplanted by ideas of nationalism and liberalism. The ensuing half-century was a struggle between those who believed that the state should be composed of any group of people who felt that they constituted a separate nation, reflecting the principle of self-determination and those who clung to the idea that the state could properly and legitimately be ruled only by members of one ruling family. Almost everywhere the struggle ended in the triumph of liberalism and nationalism. The new middle classes came to share political power in the state. Petty principalities in Italy and Germany united into national states, and multinational dynastic states like Austria-Hungary and Turkey experienced the increasing pressure that ultimately led to their breakup in World War I. Yet the struggle remained within the confines of the balance-of-power system.

There really was a "system" in the sense that the states of Europe, though lacking any superior authority or law, regularized their inevitable contacts with one another. They developed systematic methods of coexistence, of decreasing the frequency of their conflicts, and of controlling conflicts when they did occur.

When Thomas Hobbes, the seventeenth century English political philosopher, analyzed what would happen to any political system that had no absolute, central political authority, he argued that inevitably the units composing it would have to constantly strive to increase their power, fearful of the *potential* power of other members. Since each would calculate in this fashion, each would therefore be correct in his calculations. The result was bound to be a war of all against all unless an all-powerful sovereign could be installed to reassure individuals that they need not fear others. Machiavelli, writing a manual for Princes in 1513, argued that common, everyday morality could never apply to the actions of sovereigns. It was moral for them to do anything and everything necessary to strengthen the state against all its *potential* opponents.

Yet the balance-of-power system never fully assumed the characteristics attributed to it by Hobbes. Each state, of course, had to fend for itself, and the tendency toward arms races and the constant maneuvering for security inevitably made stability precarious. But the search for security or power rarely led to Hobbes' "war of all against all." The idea of preserving the balance of power as a means of security was sufficiently accepted to allow the creation of a crude international system in the sense that common rules of behavior were developed and observed. When one power threatened to become too strong, other states allied against it and, if necessary, fought against it. But if one of the allied states in turn emerged too strong, alliances shifted and it found itself facing a new alignment. When one state gained territory (and resources and population, the bases of power), there was general agreement that other states should obtain territory in compensation to maintain the balance. There was little regard for the wishes of individuals when one piece of territory was traded for another. When Europe discovered the rest of the world, the principle of compensation was further extended; much of the pattern of imperialism can be explained as the result of occupation of territory by one country in order to keep other countries from acquiring strength by occupying it, and of the other countries receiving compensation in the form of other territories. With the exception of the Napoleonic period, wars remained generally limited, the independence of most of the major states of Europe was maintained, and despite injustices, a general order was preserved.

Several factors helped maintain this decentralized system. Until the full impact of the industrial revolution was felt, the technology of destruction that had ended the supremacy of the armored knight and fortified castle of feudal times had remained static. The weapons used in the Napoleonic wars were scarcely different from the ones used two centuries earlier. It still required a massive effort to kill many people. Moreover, the states of the European system had a common cultural foundation. Their ruling classes intermarried and, perhaps most important, their diplomats came to think of themselves as an international class defending the *vital* interests of their countries but also willing, as European diplomats, to compromise and accommodate to maintain the peace.

In one way, liberalism helped buttress the balance-of-power system. The new bourgeoisie, as it rose to political power and vastly increased the productivity of state economies, instituted a relatively free and multilateral trading system based on greater specialization and exchange. Gold served as the currency of the new trading system, London as its financial center, and men, money, and goods flowed far more freely across national frontiers than in the days of the dynastic period when the prevalent trading pattern, known as mercantilism, had dictated close state control of the economy in order to develop a "favorable balance of trade." The strict controls of the mercantile period were designed to ensure an inflow of gold the new monarchs needed to pay for their new mercenary armies and centralized administrations; it had served its purpose. Proponents of the new liberalism not only argued that mercantilists had confused gold with wealth, but they also claimed that the increased links created by international trade would ensure perpetual peace. To a limited extent they were right; the international bourgeoisie, eager to ensure the security of investments and trade, developed a vested interest in peace. Members of the new class frequently pressed governments to forego strategic interests, confident that their counterparts in other countries would also renounce attempts to achieve military or political predominance. International law —previously concerned with defining boundaries, diplomatic immunities, and matters of citizenship—now reflected the common interests of the commercial classes in new rules to facilitate trade and communication.

Yet the whole international system had a more precarious base than most people realized and, later in the nineteenth century, the full impact of political liberalism and nationalism and their economic counterpart, industrialization, undermined it more. Increased reliance on trade and specialized economies made states more vulnerable to economic blockade. Now belligerents might be more tempted to carry war home to the mass of the population. The industrial revolution sparked the rapid development of weapons and communications technology that revolutionized warfare. A preview of modern war came in the American Civil War of the 1860s; North and South used magazine-loading rifles, crude machine guns, torpedoes, land mines and submarine mines, the field telegraph, wire entanglements, hand grenades, armored trains, and balloon observation of artillery fire. On February 17, 1864, a man-propelled Confederate submarine sank the U.S.S. Housatonic.

Then a few years later the Franco-Prussian War showed that the mobility provided by new railroads could have a decisive effect on hostilities. By World War I the modern submarine and torpedo were developed sufficiently to have as revolutionary an effect on naval warfare as the increased firepower provided by semiautomatic rifles, carbines, machine guns and rapid-fire artillery had on land warfare.

While the technology of destruction developed at such a rapid pace, the changed social structure of the new industrialized states presaged an equally important revolution in the conduct of foreign policy. Increased suffrage meant popular demands on government and a restricted freedom for negotiation by diplomats. In 1898 popular pressures brought about an American war with Spain that traditional diplomacy could easily have avoided.

Diplomacy failed to prevent the outbreak of World War I in 1914 and the carnage of the next four years revealed how much the old balance-of-power system had been undermined. Blockade *did* bring the war home to the mass of the people, and the new weapons produced the stalemate of trench warfare, the awesome casualties of the Western front, and unrestricted submarine warfare. All of these led to increased public pressure for a victory in which the vanquished would truly pay for the fantastic hardship that total war had brought. It was impossible to settle for a negotiated peace without victory.

The war had numerous consequences for the international political system. The stable basis for trade was gone; governments had learned that they could finance the war by inflation, and with fiscal policies conducted independently of the balance of payments, they resorted increasingly to tariffs, quotas, bilateral trade agreements, and exchange controls to channel the flow of trade. All of these made trade a more political matter; the war itself had showed that trade could be a weapon. War debts and reparations payments added to the burden on world trade and led to even more bitter quarrels. People held on to supplies of gold as a hedge against inflation, and by doing so limited its availability as an international currency. The war led to an increase of manufacturing outside of Europe and to liquidation of European investments abroad, further unbalancing trade and making the United States and Japan powerful competitors with Europe. On the other hand, Europe was forced to limit its imports; its economic decline *vis-à-vis* the rest of the world began.

The war brought revolution and the Communists to power in Russia. Except for its fruitless efforts to sponsor world revolution, the new Communist government withdrew from the world scene. A host of weak successor states emerged in Eastern Europe: Poland, Czechoslovakia, Austria, Hungary, and Yugoslavia joined Rumania and Bulgaria, and to the north, Finland, Latvia, Estonia, and Lithuania became independent. The French, deprived by the Communist revolution of their ally in the East turned to the weak new states on the other side of a Germany whose power they still feared. But England, distrusting France's attempts to keep Germany weak, dissociated itself from its wartime continental ally. The United States, refusing to join the League of Nations, participated on the international scene only to bring about a temporary stabilization of the Far East, to press for disarmament, and to attempt to buttress the German economy with short-term loans in the late 1920s.

The network of international short-term loans contributed materially to the spread of the depression from one country to another in the 1930s. As internal financial collapse took place in one country, it would call back its loans from another, thus causing internal financial collapse there. People who learned another hard lesson about the interdependence of the modern world tended to stress economic self-sufficiency and nationalism even more.

The depth of the changes in the international economy as well as in the distribution of power among European states and between Europe and new powers was hard to appreciate. But the war had emphasized how the balance of power could degenerate into arms races; it gave rise to demands for modifications of the whole international system. And so, at Versailles, the League of Nations came into being with three conscious attempts at major change.

The first involved an attempt to institutionalize the balance of power in a system of "collective security," under which every country would have the legal obligation to come to the aid of any country attacked by another. The uncertainty of the balance of power would be replaced by the certainty that overwhelming power would be brought against an aggressor.

The League of Nations incorporated a second major change in the international system though the creation of the Permanent Mandates Commission. The victors in World War I had wanted, in traditional fashion, to annex overseas territories taken from the vanquished, but they were forced to bow to the view that simple annexation was no longer possible. Instead, the victors were to act as trustees for the international community which would carry out a limited measure of supervision through the Mandates Commission. Mandatory powers were committed to goals of welfare and of development of the peoples within the mandate.

The mandate system was limited, incorporating within it only the territories lost by the Central Powers and Turkey. Only one mandate, Iraq, became an independent state during the life of the mandate system. Yet the attempt revealed a consciousness that people outside Europe could no longer simply be traded as pawns in the European balance of power; colonialism, with all its attendant evils, had brought stability and literacy to colonial areas and had begun to create the demand for independence and sovereignty modeled on the European pattern.

Finally, the League set up not only a Council in which the great powers would assemble as they frequently had in the past but also an Assembly. Here all countries, large or small, would have equal representation and could discuss world affairs. It was an unprecedented step, and no one was quite sure what the Assembly could do.

The 1930s gave the answer. Institutional modification of the international system was insufficient to cope with the challenge posed by states that repudiated the entire system—Nazi Germany, Fascist Italy, and Communist Russia—and a state like Japan that tried in the mid-twentieth century to do the kind of empire building Europe had done in the nineteenth. This challenge came at the same time that a world-wide depression cast doubt on Western society's ability to deal with its own problems and at the same moment that the bombing plane was developed. The challengers found an international system whose members had neither the will nor wit to respond. European states were still pervaded by memories of the horrors of the World War. The United States, disenchanted, had legislated itself into neutrality so that France and Britain could not look to it for help, and its Secretary of State preached a futile doctrine of free trade as the cure for all the world's ills. Collective security, as some statesmen had foreseen, proved a hollow promise. Countries were unwilling to take action against a distant state that seemed to threaten no vital interest of theirs. The aggressor of today might be the needed ally of tomorrow; it might be better to allow him to have his way.

The governments of Britain and France tried to offer the dictators limited gains, but they only grew more demanding. The Soviet Union, seeing the threat in Nazi expansionism, tried to return to membership in the international system and sought a rapprochement with the Western powers. But the effort to build a new coalition was doomed. The French, willing to use any means to avoid mass attacks against trenches, had adopted a strictly defensive strategy behind the massive defenses of the Maginot Line and could offer no real aid to the Soviet Union if the Nazis attacked. Moreover, both France and Britain failed to make a really serious effort to work out cooperation with Russia. Their leaders doubted the effectiveness of the Soviet Union as an ally, especially after the widespread purges of the late 1930s had liquidated the vast majority of the top rank of the Russian officer corps. They distrusted the Communist *volte face* and were afraid, too, of what Communist Russia might gain in Eastern Europe in a war. On the other hand, the Nazis could point out to Stalin that while the Western powers could not help him in a war Germany could offer the Soviet Union a buffer zone in Eastern Europe. Stalin decided to cooperate with the Nazis and on August 23, 1939, signed a nonaggression pact with Adolf Hitler, giving him the green light to go to war.

By the end of 1939, the Western powers that had dominated the world for the past three centuries were demoralized and unhappy and faced a situation in which they could only lose; neither alternative was attractive. On the one hand, German-Italian-Japanese victory seemed probable if the three could cooperate with Russia. Their defeat appeared assured only if Russia split off and joined the war against them, but this, the alternative to defeat by the Fascists, promised a much larger expansion of Soviet influence.

A series of lightning wars brought Nazi victory over Poland, Norway, Denmark, the Lowlands, France, and the Balkans. But the courage of a handful of British pilots, German strategic mistakes, and the unsuccessful German submarine attempt to cut British overseas communications were factors in the Germans' failure to win the Battle of Britain. Hitler mistakenly turned against the Soviet Union, leaving England as a strategic base from which attack could be brought both against his lines of communication and eventually against Fortress Europe. Meanwhile in the Pacific, the Japanese, faced with stiffening American resistance to expansion of empire, calculated that an internally divided United States would sue for peace after a series of quick defeats. They struck at Pearl Harbor and the Philippines, crippled a large part of the American Pacific fleet and moved rapidly through Southeast Asia. Within a few months they threatened Australia and New Zealand. On the mainland they moved through Burma toward India, at the same time cutting off land communications to China.

Early in 1942 the Axis was triumphant everywhere and the Western world was at its lowest point. German forces, moving through North Africa toward the Middle East, threatened to join the Japanese in India. Although they had suffered reverses in Russia, their spring campaign looked as though it would be successful.

By the end of 1942 the picture had changed. In the Pacific the Japanese fleet suffered a decisive setback in the Battle of Midway on June 4, 1942, and America had a breathing spell during which it could begin to draw upon its enormous latent industrial capacity and gradually to force the Japanese back from their extended conquests. On October 23, 1942, Field Marshal Montgomery turned back the German forces in North Africa at the decisive battle of El Alamein and began to chase them to ultimate defeat in Tunisia. Within a few months German forces surrendered at Stalingrad, marking the turning point in the German campaign in Russia. But it took two and a half more years before the Axis powers were finally defeated and World War II ended.

WORLD WAR II AND THE MAP OF THE POSTWAR WORLD

Military strategy had much to do with the shape of the postwar world. The basic decision to attack the most dangerous enemy—Germany—first, and then Japan, meant that only limited resources could be devoted to the Pacific and Southeast Asian theaters of war. As a result, the American commander in the Pacific, General Douglas MacArthur, developed an "island-hopping" strategy that bypassed China and brought it little support. Chiang Kai-Shek's Nationalist government therefore emerged from the war in a weak position, with its future in doubt. And Russia's late entry into the Pacific war, after years of neutrality vis-a-vis Japan, brought Russian power into Korea and Manchuria, from which the Russians stripped industry, blocked Nationalist Chinese troops' return, and regained port and railway rights extracted from Imperial China in the nineteenth century that had been lost to Japan in 1905. Considerations of grand strategy had thus fatally weakened the Chinese Nationalist cause and, unwittingly, strengthened the chances of the Chinese Communists in Manchuria and North China, while installing a Communist government for the northern half of Korea.

The Southeast Asian theater was put under British overall command, thus symbolically reasserting European interest, and at the end of the war the United States did, indeed, allow the Dutch, French, and British to reoccupy the territories from which the Japanese had driven them. The Americans held undisputed sway in the Pacific itself, in Japan, and in the southern half of Korea.

In the European theater, the decision to attack across the Channel rather than through what Winston Churchill called the "soft underbelly" of Europe meant that by the end of hostilities the Russians occupied all of eastern Europe while British, American, and French troops regained western Europe, Italy, and Greece. Austria and Germany were jointly occupied by all four.

Military strategy, however, was only part of the story. Diplomacy was supposed to play a large role, and all through the war diplomats exerted their efforts to delimit the boundaries of the postwar world in ways that would not necessarily reflect simply the raw facts of military power. In this they proved to be singularly unsuccessful; military occupation came to mean—by and large—political domination.

Although they suffered the greatest damage, the main victors were the Russians. Military power enabled them to regain the old Czarist-controlled states of Latvia, Lithuania, and Estonia, as well as portions of Poland and Czechoslovakia and Pacific Islands to the north of Japan. Reluctantly, Western states gave legal sanction to the acquisitions, agreeing to compensate Poland with a large slice of Germany.* In September

* In this way Stalin retained the fruits of the Nazi-Soviet pact of 1939. There is much argument over how war-born suspicions colored later relations. Recent revisionist historians have stressed that the delay in the cross-channel invasion reinforced Stalin's distrust of Western powers and made him seek a protective zone in East Europe. They discount the effect of the efforts made to supply him through Murmansk, enormously

1943 Stalin signed an armistice with the Finns, far to the north, and foregoing an occupation of Finland, made it cede important territory that protected western approaches to Leningrad. Subsequently, playing upon Western divisions, he received Churchill's agreement to respect Soviet zones of influence in eastern Europe, obtained Allied consent to prior Russian troop movements into Czechoslovakia, and to withdrawal of Western troops from areas of Germany that had previously been assigned to Russian occupation. To reassure the western Allies, he disbanded the old Communist International, through which Russia had exerted an iron control over Communist parties abroad. But he was blocked both from participation in control over liberated or occupied territories such as Italy, the rest of Western Europe and Japan, from joint control over the great iron and steel complex of the Ruhr, in western Germany, and from obtaining a trusteeship over Libya that would have brought Russian power directly into the Mediterranean.

If Stalin seemed to feel his way to whatever gains military power and diplomacy might secure for him, the western Allies were far less single-minded, and divisions between Britain, France, and the United States were matched by divisions within the American government. Churchill saw distinctly the relationship between military occupation and subsequent political influence, and had no illusions that spheres of influence or balance of power politics would ever be abolished. He therefore felt it incumbent upon himself to secure the best possible position for Britain at the end of the war and to accept the fact that Russia would emerge with a greatly enlarged sphere. He recognized that Russia had legitimate security concerns in eastern Europe; it would be necessary for him to persuade Stalin to accept certain limits to the Russian sphere of influence, and get him to accept that the English had certain interests, too. He maintained doubts about whether such interests could be reconciled with the Russians' continued ideological drive toward world revolution, but felt that Stalin, the realist who had opted for "socialism in one country" in an earlier period of struggle over Russian policy, would accept such arrangements.

Although Roosevelt was quite realistic about such matters, most Americans hoped that the war would indeed bring a worldwide move toward democratization, and create an international system in which there could be no repetition of either the events that had led to World War I or

---

costly in both ships and manpower, and his refusal to allow "shuttle bombing" in which Allied bombers would be able to fly across Germany to land in Russia and then fly back. But they also fail to mention Stalin's unequivocal determination to reincorporate parts of the Czarist Empire regardless of the wishes of their inhabitants. It laid the basis for later Western suspicions about Russian expansionism.

World War II. They shared Hull's abhorrence of spheres of interest and his distrust of the English allies. They condemned British methods in Greece and Italy, and were unhappy about the prospect of restoration of European empires.* But worse yet were the brutal methods employed by the Russians in the wake of their advancing armies, and the treatment of Poland and of non-Communist Poles who had resisted Hitler was particularly despicable (and had political repercussions in the United States during 1944, an election year). It was for this reason that at the great wartime meeting at Yalta in February 1945, the Americans tried to persuade Stalin to agree to free elections in eastern Europe, and to convince him that free governments there would be less of a problem in the future than subject ones. Persuasion was the only weapon they could bring to bear. It resulted in a Declaration on Liberated Europe that promised free elections—and sowed the basis for later dissension when Stalin, of course, failed to live up to it.

It was also at the great wartime heads of state meetings at Tehran, Yalta, and Potsdam that other hard decisions were hammered out, revealing that what bound the Allies together was unity against the enemy —and little else. When it came to Germany, everyone wanted it disarmed and "denazified." But the Russians, understandably, were insistent upon a high level of reparations for the immense damage done by the Germans. The Western allies agreed, yet as time wore on began to doubt that a battered Germany could provide the level the Russians demanded. They had in mind the malign effect that the whole reparations–war debt issue had had after World War I, and tried to persuade the Russians not to ask for too much. In addition, as German refugees from all over eastern Europe joined the millions who began to flee the Polish-occupied area that Poles simply assumed was now theirs, the westerners began to see themselves simply supporting a destitute Germany's payments to Russia. The issue was joined to questions about the level of industry to be allowed Germany after the war, about the treatment of war criminals, about occupation zones (which, as it turned out, came to mean spheres of influence again).* It was at Yalta that Stalin agreed, finally, to come

---

* It was here that Roosevelt parted company with Churchill. He felt that all the prewar empires would soon have to be liquidated, while Churchill—like de Gaulle— knew that only the resources, bases, and manpower of empire had enabled them to hold off the enemy during the two world wars.

* Planning for Germany was suspended after Roosevelt and Churchill agreed to the "Morgenthau Plan" for Germany, which would have reduced it to an agricultural state. Mindful of an immense error that would lead to economic chaos in Europe, they reversed themselves, but Roosevelt, abashed at the mistake, held up all further planning.

into the war against Japan after the German defeat, but at the price of obtaining substantial territorial gains and the recapturing of Czarist rights in China.

As the armies moved forward Churchill grew gloomier. Everywhere he saw the western Allies in discord. De Gaulle, who had been a thorn in the British and Americans' side, continually pressed both countries for material support and political recognition. What impelled the singlemind-ed Frenchman was the view that only if he developed the prestige of his government-in-exile and his armed forces could he take over and provide a peaceful transition in France. Without this, contending forces would soon be shooting at each other and civil war would result. But if the Americans and British would not provide sufficient support he would seek it elsewhere; in 1944 he flew to Moscow and signed a 20-year non-agression pact with Russia. It seemed to Churchill imperative to establish a British-American concord with which to face the spread of Russian power. When Harry Truman became President upon Roosevelt's death on April 12, 1945, the new President sent Joseph P. Davies, former American Ambassador to the Soviet Union, to talk to Churchill, and the latter seized upon the occasion to review events for Davies. The Russians had consolidated their hold on eastern Europe; Tito had taken Yugosla-via into the Russian orbit; Czechoslovakia, thanks to American willing-ness, had come under heavy Soviet influence. Western troops' presence in Austria had blocked the Russians, but American insistence on with-drawing to the pre-arranged zonal boundaries had enabled the Rus-sians to penetrate deep into Germany, and the Americans had permitted Russian troops to take Berlin. (Churchill, ever mindful of power realities, had wanted the Allies to use their advanced troop position in Germany to bargain for Russian concessions.) Tito's Yugoslav troops had almost come to blows with Anglo-American forces when he had tried to seize the Trieste area between Yugoslavia and Italy. The United States had al-ready begun to reduce its commitments in Europe by diverting Lend-Lease shipments and troops to the Far East; French and British troops had fought each other when Churchill blocked de Gaulle's efforts to rein-stall France in Syria. Everywhere, he told Davies, division existed among the Westerners in the face of the strong possibility that Stalin would use the opportunity to dominate all of Europe, especially if, as Roosevelt had told him earlier, the Americans were not prepared to keep troops in Eu-rope more than two years.

Davies' response could not have cheered him. The American sarcasti-cally asked him if he was now willing to admit that he had been wrong not to support Hitler. "For," Davies said in reporting the conversation, "as I understood him, he was now expressing the doctrine which Hitler and Goebbels have been proclaiming and reiterating for the past four years in an effort to break up Allied unity and divide and conquer. Exactly the same conditions which he described and the same deductions were drawn from them as he now appeared to assert."* Davies interpreted Churchill as trying to get the Americans to help him in "preserving England's position in Europe."

The carnage ended in Europe on May 8, with Hitler dead in his Berlin bunker. In the Far East events moved faster than foreseen, as Japan's capability to make war crumbled before the American aerial onslaught. American military men now questioned the advisability of Russian participation, but the wheels were already turning, and when the Japanese approached the Russians to ask them to act as peace intermediaries with the Americans, the Russians instead denounced the old neutrality treaty and declared war. In America men squabbled over whether the Japanese should be allowed to keep the Emperor or not—the one condition the Japanese insisted upon. During the delay, and still expecting heavy resistance from fanatical Japanese fighting men if an invasion proved necessary, the Americans dropped the first atomic bomb on Hiroshima. Five days later, to hasten the decision, they dropped the second one on Nagasaki. Despite a last minute attempt by an army clique to prevent the surrender, the Emperor recorded and broadcast an Imperial declaration of surrender to his troops, and World War II came to an end.

NEW ORGANIZATIONS FOR A NEW INTERNATIONAL POLITICS

The League of Nations had failed as an attempt to patch up the old sovereign state system. During World War II planners determined that they must not fail again and, amid much argument over the shape of post-World War II international institutions, arrived at a comprehensive plan, whose design, however, was more suited to preventing World War II than to coping with post-World War II realities. It drew heavily upon the experience of the League, but embodied changes that would, hopefully, make it more effective. In an attempt to revive the concept of collective security, the Security Council, where the supposed Great Powers were made permanent members, was given greater authority for taking economic or military measures against potential aggressors. Since aggressive action by one of these powers would be tantamount to war, however, each could veto enforcement action by the Council. It was hoped that this

* Quoted in Herbert Feis, *Churchill, Roosevelt, Stalin* (Princeton: Princeton University Press, 1957) , pp. 650–652.

would keep the powers from voting either ineffective resolutions opposed by one or more of them, or voting for action against one what would be equivalent to war. Instead, the requirement of unanimity would force them into seeking the agreement necessary to joint action, and force them into accommodation. The Security Council was to have armed forces at its disposal, and while it would first have recourse to traditional diplomatic means, it could, in the final analysis, use the kind of joint economic and military sanctions that might have stopped Italy, Nazy Germany, or Japan in the early 1930s if opposing powers could have agreed on such joint action. Delegates to the San Francisco Conference, where the Charter was signed in June 1945, expressed hope that the veto would be used sparingly. But they all realized that discrepancies in power could not be done away with and that the United Nations, at best, could only provide a modicum of standards for international action, and channels through which diplomacy could take place.

The General Assembly was given broad powers of discussion of virtually all matters that might concern the United Nations. All states—small or large—would be represented, but unlike the Security Council, the Assembly would only have powers of recommendation, not binding decision. Like the Security Council, it abandoned the old voting rules of the League of Nations, where, since all states were sovereign, voting had been by unanimity. Like the Security Council, it was a political organ that could help to resolve conflicts between states, thus providing the possibilities for peaceful change necessary for any political system; the collective security system under the Security Council would maintain order.

The Trusteeship Council, an outgrowth of the League Mandates Commission, would also provide for peaceful change. With strengthened powers for supervision, it would help provide the transition from a world of Europe-based empires to one of nation-states. The Secretary-General of the new organization, formerly merely an official who provided meeting space, translating facilities, and paperwork, was given enhanced powers to bring matters to the attention of the organization and to suggest solutions. Even more important, the Economic and Social Council was given status as a principal organ of the United Nations system, at the insistence of the smaller states at San Francisco. Their argument was simple: any political system must have healthy economic and social underpinnings; the collapse of the international economy in 1929 was what brought the Nazis to power in Germany and the militarists in Japan. The new United Nations must take an active part in rebuilding a functioning world economy. The Economic and Social Council would oversee action by various other agencies charged with promoting human rights, higher

standards of living, full employment, communication, economic development, health, and cultural and educational cooperation. The new International Bank would not only stimulate the flow of capital that had dried up
in the uncertainties of the thirties, but would also aid reconstruction, and
alleviate some of the strains that postwar reconstruction had caused in
the twenties. The new International Monetary Fund and the projected International Trade Organization would prevent the economic warfare into
which international trade and finance had degenerated in the interwar
years. In the meantime, the United Nations Reconstruction and Rehabilitation Administration, created in 1943, provided relief to wartorn areas.

Taken together, the organizations would be able to help the international system cope with some of the new developments that had under-
minded the old balance of power system, yet preserve the basic political
unit, the nation-state.

There was much optimism about the new system. Unlike the League of
Nations, whose Covenant was a part of the Versailles Treaty, it would
not be burdened with the peace settlement, and could, over time, modify
it. But many diplomats were not so sanguine. They were sure the organizations would not eliminate international politics, but merely channel
them. Moreover, they sensed fatal weaknesses, particularly in a security
system that precluded effective action against the great powers and was
premised upon their cooperation. It seemed dubious, too, that the new
economic organizations would have the resources to deal with the economic dislocations caused by the war. And what effect would the new su-
perweapon—the atom bomb—have upon United Nations? Was the
Charter not a pre-atomic document?

CONCLUSION

From the point of view of international politics, the nineteenth century ended in 1914: World War I exhibited once more the inherent
instabilities of the balance-of-power system and proved how much the
economic, political, and social factors sustaining the system had changed.
The dislocations produced by World War I seem to have led almost inexorably to the next act in the drama, World War II. The outbreak of this
second, disastrous war meant that the Western powers' efforts to rebuild
a more stable world through the League of Nations had failed. But the
war also ended Nazi, Fascist, and Japanese attempts to build their own peculiar type of world system on the ruins of the nineteenth-century system.

What did it mean for the future? What sort of world political system
could possibly emerge from this even more destructive holocaust?

Among the few certainties one stood out: Europe, which had dominated the world system in the past, would have a hard time doing so in the future. Germany and Italy lay shattered; de Gaulle appeared to have ambitions overreaching French capacities; it would be difficult for the Dutch to reinstall themselves in Southeast Asia. Only Britain appeared to have emerged capable of carrying out worldwide responsibilities. But even for Britain, appearances were deceptive, and perceptive observers could note her wornout and badly damaged industrial plant, and her radical shift from world creditor to world debtor. This new position would make any expenses incurred overseas in support of her far-flung responsibilities a terrible strain. On the other hand, Russia, though sustaining such enormous losses that most observers thought all her efforts would have to be turned to rebuilding, nevertheless occupied all of Eastern Europe, where even greater weaknesses existed, as well as an improved power position in the Far East. The United States, which had not suffered bombardment or occupation, emerged with a tremendously enlarged industrial capacity, new prestige, and greater resources for action.

The war also produced the shifting and shadowy outlines of a new political map of the world, in which—at least temporarily—the spheres of influence of the two new major powers were delimited, along with the more traditional English and French ones. The future of certain areas remained in doubt: China, it was hoped, would emerge as a reunited power to take Japan's place in the Far East. In Southeast Asia the nationalism that had been fanned by Japanese occupation was a force that opposed the efforts of weakened European powers to reassert their power under Anglo-American protection.

The war also left a legacy of doubt about the aims of the two new major powers and of the three other powers that joined them in permanent membership on the Security Council. The United States had thrown all its energies into prosecuting the war. Would it now withdraw from the vast area that it had come to occupy as a result? Would it participate in world reconstruction, and if so, how? Would it accept or contest Russian domination of large parts of the world? Would it use its power for its own narrowly conceived purpose? And how much did Stalin's foreign policy depend on the way the United States acted?

Some of Roosevelt's old advisers felt that Stalin faced a difficult reconstruction situation, was insistent on securing a protective zone around Russia, and would react only brutally if he were thwarted. He was counting upon American credits for reconstruction purposes; all through the war there had been talk of these, and Roosevelt, against Congressional reluctance, had used Lend-Lease to furnish the Soviet Union with nonmilitary materiel. Only in continued cooperation could peace and goodwill be assured. Others had come to share Churchill's view that Stalin was brutally expansionist and must be given no concession *except* in return for Russian concessions. President Truman was faced with conflicting pressures and advice.* And insofar as the Far East was concerned, no one was sure of what Chinese capabilities might be, nor what China's aims would be if Chiang were able to consolidate his government.

If these questions about individual countries' aims indicated an extraordinary uncertainty about the future and therefore about what policies to follow, there was also uncertainty about the new international institutions that had been created with such fanfare. Presumably these were meant to reshape the international system after the crisis that had convulsed it from 1914 to 1945. The sovereign state of the earlier system was still retained as the basic unit, and the new institutions even reflected a desire to break up empires and add to the number of sovereign states, each claiming to control its own affairs, its own borders, and its own armies. In the 1930s collective security principles had clashed with balance-of-power principles; on the basis of the former, England should have acted energetically against Italy when the Fascists invaded Abyssinia, and against Japan when the Japanese invaded Manchuria. On the basis of balance-of-power principles, however, England had still hoped to keep Italy from a firm alliance with Germany, which would have been the inevitable outcome of collective security action, and similar considerations played a part in lack of action against Japan. Only if collective security could really provide a firm guarantee could nations afford to ignore balance-of-power considerations. Did the new United Nations Charter provide the basis for such confidence? Did it rectify the weaknesses of the League? Many observers were already willing to answer that the existence of the veto—necessary, to be sure—proved that collective security could have only limited effectiveness. Russia's concern for securing strategic frontiers, France's search for military alliances, and the interest evinced by American military men in retaining islands captured from the Japanese in the Pacific for security reasons, all seem to show that no one was willing to trust collective security measures completely. In addition, questions were raised about the possibility of collective security in the atomic age: what would be the relationship of such security measures to national ownership of nuclear weapons? In comparison to the League Covenant, the Charter said little about disarmament, reflect-

---

* The advice included strong suggestions—especially from Churchill—that United States troops stay in their advanced positions in Germany and not be withdrawn back to the zonal boundaries until certain issues were settled with the Russians. Truman was not about to reverse Roosevelt's policies of trying to reach accommodations with the Russians and therefore refused.

ing the general feeling that a weak, disarmed West had invited the aggression by the Nazis and Japanese. Did the new weapon not require a complete reassessment of this position?

Would the other organizations and institutions such as the IMF, the IBRD, the ITO that clustered around the United Nations serve the functions assigned to them? They were based on reading of the past and a desire to avoid the disasters of the 1920s and 1930s. But could the new organizations cope with the economic and social legacies of World War II? And what would be the effect of defeat of the major powers, Germany, Italy, and Japan? De Gaulle, the British, and the Russians were determined that these countries would never again be allowed to disturb the peace. But was this to be done by keeping them divided and impotent, in the manner envisaged by the French—or by the American Morgenthau Plan? Or was it to be done by restoring the countries so that the kind of grievances that led their peoples to select leaders like Hitler and the Japanese militarists would not arise?

In the face of such uncertainties, conflicts and disagreements were inevitable, and the thousands of individuals trying to devise policies and carry out day-to-day operations faced extraordinarily difficult tasks. Grappling with these uncertainties and over whelmed by immediate necessities, what kind of answers could they provide? What patterns would emerge?

Underlying the political enigmas arising out of the immediate situation were all the fundamental changes that had already served to destroy the old nation-state balance of power system: the changes in the technology of destruction, in the internal character of the states composing the system, and in the membership of the system. They meant that no state was truly sovereign, no state truly independent; many analysts concluded that the era of the nation-state had finally come to an end. The nascent United Nations *must* result—sooner rather than later—in world government. And the changes have, in fact, speeded up in the period since World War II.

The speedup is most noticeable in the field of weapons technology and communications. The rickety 90-mile-an-hour bomber of World War I with its load of several hundred pounds and range of a few hundred miles became, by the end of World War II, the B-29 that devastated Japanese cities, flying at 300 miles per hour with a range of 4000 miles and dropping a load of 10 tons of TNT. By the mid-1950s the American B-52 could travel to any point in the world at 600 miles per hour; by 1963 it had been almost superseded by intercontinental rockets that could travel at 18,000 miles per hour up to 9000 miles. The latest of these were solid fueled and took only minutes to fire; they were protected against attack

by being placed in deep underground concrete silos or by being fired
from submarines cruising below the ocean surface.

More impressive were the developments in weapons that these carriers
could deliver. During the terrifying blitz on London, the Nazis dropped
12,000 tons of bombs, killing 30,000 people and injuring more than
120,000. In World War II the Allies bombarded Germany with a total of
two million tons of TNT. Then, in August 1945, the United States
dropped a single five-ton bomb over Hiroshima that released the explosive power of 20,000 tons of TNT that killed 78,000 people and injured
45,000 more. By the mid-1950s the atomic (fission) bomb had led to development of the hydrogen (fusion) bomb; its explosive power could be
measured in millions of tons of TNT equivalent (the term used was "mega-
tons"). In October 1961, the Russians exploded a 50-megaton hydo-
gen bomb. The new term, megaton, made people forget that this single
weapon had an explosive power 25 times that of all bombs dropped on
Germany during World War II. Moreover, such weapons have heat and
radiation effects in addition to their blast effects. A 10-megaton weapon
exploded 30 miles above the surface of the earth would sear an area of
5000 square miles, producing massive fire storms. An all-out attack on
either the United States or the Soviet Union would cripple the economy
and society of the countries involved for an indeterminable period.

Other weapons showed comparable development. During World War
II the vulnerable, thin-skinned submarine was increased in range and firepower and equipped with the "snorkel," a device that enabled it to stay
underwater while renewing its batteries and air, thereby decreasing its
vulnerability. By 1960, atomic-powered submarines could cruise underwater for weeks without refueling. A decade later both the Soviet Union
and the United States had such submarines in service equipped with solid-fueled missiles carrying thermounuclear warheads. Every few years
brought new developments: enormous extension of the range of the missiles, or development of multiple, independently targeted warheads, capable of vastly increasing the destructive capacity of each missile. The electronics associated with these and other developments achieved the realm
of the fantastic. By the early 1970s both super-powers were deploying
antiballistic-missile missile systems supposedly capable of searching out
and intercepting in-coming missiles despite their enormous velocities and
consequent short warning times.

Modern bombers and missiles also made it possible to kill from a dis-
tance and despite any squeamishness; it appeared that another restraint
of the balance-of-power period had disappeared. The pre-World War I
code had reflected in law and morality the political fact of limited war,
making distinctions between combatant and noncombatant that had now

simply evaporated. The strategists who devised deterrence by threats of massive retaliation paid little attention to the fact that their success lay in the assured capacity to destroy whole populations.

Finally, the prevalence of the new weapons led to a continuous debate about their implications—did they make total war more likely or did they reintroduce a period of limited war; could nations now withstand total war; did disarmament take on a new urgency or would the presence of these new weapons for the first time guarantee peace; were small states outmoded or, in a reversal of the trends of the past century, had they been given a new freedom and a new lease on life under the umbrella of a nuclear stalemate that prevented the major powers from resorting to use of their fearsome weapons?

But if the revolution in weapons development was striking, the effects of accompanying political and social revolutions were equally great. World War I destroyed the last dynastic states within Europe—Austria-Hungary, Ottoman Turkey and Czarist Russia—and enshrined the nation-state. It also weakened Europe's hold on the rest of the world: if nationalism and national self-determination were proper for Europe, then why not for the peoples of Africa, the Middle East, and Asia? Emancipation of peoples from European and American domination has proceeded at an everquickening pace: in 1945 the United Nations had a membership of 51 and in 1972 it had 132 member states. Each of these new states claims the attributes of sovereignty and independence, derived from the reality of the balance-of-power system, at the very time that these concepts seem to have lost much of their meaning. Equally important, while the European-centered balance-of-power system rested on relative cultural unity, the new world system is composed of culturally divergent states, whose leaders find diplomatic communication far more difficult.

Moreover, since matters outside its borders greatly affect affairs within the state, mass pressures on national political leaders have also increased. Whether the flow of influence is primarily upward, as in essentially democratic states, or whether the process is one of attempted manipulation from the top, as in authoritarian states, mass opinion must be taken into account in various ways. Policy-makers defer not only to political pressures within their states, but to a shadowy, hard-to-determine world opinion. Complicating this is the incidence of political instability within states both new and old, and a resultant constant turnover in political leadership that makes valid assessments of one state's relations with another hard to arrive at, and stable relations almost impossible.

If the number and variety of states in the international system has increased along with the scope of internal mass political pressures and the number of political participants, the current revolution has also produced another new phenomenon: the existence, side-by-side, of rich and poor states. Modern communications mean that their peoples know of each others' existence, and as a result those who lead the poor states have insistently demanded that something must be done to help relieve their poverty. Across the years, more and more, the United Nations family of organizations has come to be the setting for presentation of these demands. The wealthier states have responded to a certain extent, sometimes cooperatively, sometimes in a competitive spirit, when they felt that aid must be used to win the allegiance of the poorer peoples. But the complexities of development have become more apparent and the analyses of the causes and cures of poverty more divergent. Economic development and modernization have been seen to generate their own new problems, instabilities, and resentments, and conflict is endemic in a situation further complicated by population increase and ecological considerations.

Modern medicine and transportation were the two main factors in the population explosion. A world population of 500 million in 1600 doubled to one billion in 200 years. It took only 100 years to double again. The two billion of 1900 became the three billion of 1960; by 1990 there would certainly be five billion. If current rates of increase were to continue for 150 years—a clear impossibility—world population would reach 150 billion. But by 1970 people had become aware of some of the implications of geometric increase on both national and international levels. Whether they would be able to cope with it remained an open question.

On the international level, the main problem lay in the uneven distribution of the increase. Europe, the United States, and Japan have been able to cope in their fashion; production has increased faster than population, resulting in a generally high standard of living and a sharp drop in population growth rates. Resolution of the population problem, however, has been at the expense of a rate of consumption of raw materials that may not be able to continue for long—particularly if other areas begin an industrialization that will bring them into competition for the resources. In non-Western countries the situation varies. In some, a rising standard of living may produce the same phenomenon of declining birth rates; in many areas the rate of economic growth barely holds its own; in others population appears to have outstripped economic development. There, the situation is explosive and the potential for further tragedy enormous. The harshest of measures may become necessary, as even Marxists have had to recognize. For years, in the United Nations, Communist and Catholic states were aligned against population control measures, on the basis that only maldistribution under capitalism caused poverty. The "population problem" was a capitalist bogey designed to keep Asians and Africans weak. In the last decade they have abandoned the position, and Maoist China, for example, has had a thoroughgoing population control program.

But what is far from clear is the effect of the combination of continued poverty and population increase for one part of the world when other parts continue to increase in wealth. The poor may not unite and march against the rich as some have surmised, but unless the situation changes, the potential for conflict and upheaval would appear to remain vast.

If increase in population has finally been accepted as a problem requiring both national and international action, the ecological consequences of increased population coupled to high consumption has also come to public attention: the UN-sponsored Stockholm Conference of 1972, called to stimulate international action to deal with it, was the largest international conference ever held. On one level, the problem has been viewed as one of pollution and the simple husbanding of resources. But there are analysts who argue that the whole modern period dating from the start of the Renaissance in the West and leading, finally, to the unevenly industrialized, high-growth, twentieth-century world, is but a brief passing chapter in the history of mankind. While people concentrate on day-to-day political scandals and crises, and produce makeshift policies to deal with evanescent problems, they ignore the far more pressing international action that must be taken to avert a catastrophic collapse of the entire industrial system early in the twenty-first century. The analysis has opened substantial new areas of debate about what can be considered "development"—but the analysis itself is debatable.

All of the developments cited taken together combine to put into question national frontiers at the very time when the creation of eighty new states has added numerous new frontiers. Ideological appeals and intellectual arguments cut across frontiers just as new states try to strengthen their boundaries. Propaganda and subversion become widely used techniques of foreign policy, and competing claims for loyalty increase the number of actors in international politics. Groups, organized interests, and classes within states are as much a part of international politics as the national leaders who presumably act for them. In a period during which nationalism has remained dominant, creating the host of new states, and international organizations have multiplied in number if not effectiveness to allow the new states to coexist, new transnational actors have multiplied in number and power: multinational corporations, some of them with far greater financial resources than most states, are only the most noticeable. Some people have argued that such new structures have the potential of the greatest impact in stimulating growth and change in many parts of the world, with consequences as yet difficult to see, and suggest that they will have a greater influence than many national governments and international organizations. In some areas deliberate attempts to transfer loyalties from the nation-state to larger units have tried to capitalize on such transnational linkages. The most successful attempt has been in Western Europe, where a fairly high degree of integration appears to have taken place. But the nation-state retains a strong hold on its citizens, one that is reinforced by contemporary state regulation of the economy, by welfare measures, and by the ability of a society and government to generate "nationalized" versions of the truth.

It is hard for observers and policy-makers alike to assess the impact of all these changes. Against a background of transformation and uncertainty only one conclusion seems clear: all of the developments cited have combined to destroy the old nation-state balance of power system, but nothing very stable has come to replace it. For a brief period in midcentury a tight bipolar system appeared to have come into being, controlled by the two superpowers with a circle of satellite states about them, contesting for influence among the new states as these achieved independence. But bipolarism has changed drastically, and politically and economically the superpowers find themselves challenged on all fronts, even while retaining their physical capacities for destruction on a scale no one else can match. Major wars for conquest of territory—the most familiar kind in the past—appear to have disappeared, to be replaced by localized and internal wars of a variety of types. Whatever may happen, a review of events of these decades indicates that the world is in a state of flux not seen since the feudal world dissolved in the upheavals of 1350–1650.

PART II
1945–1955:
THE ATOMIC AGE

TWO
1945—1947
THE ATTEMPT TO
REBUILD THE OLD WORLD

In the excitement and general chaos marking the end of World War II, many people realized that fundamental changes had taken place in the international system. But few foresaw the nature of the changes; only in 1947 did people come to finally accept that Europe could no longer stand alone, that European countries would find it impossible to reassert control over the rest of the world, and that the Soviet Union and the United States would emerge as the two chief contenders on the world scene in a system that could be characterized as "bipolar." Bipolarism emerged gradually, for from 1945 to 1947 leaders in both countries moved cautiously in testing their positions of power, and in the first year and a half policy-makers devoted much political effort to creating a new world in the image of the old. In the widely prevailing view of this period, Britain appeared to be Russia's chief contender in Europe and the Near East, and the European problems seemed to be drawing up peace treaties and reconstructing shattered economies. Distrustful Americans were ready to withdraw from Europe once the peace was made, and then the United Nations was to become the chief arena of international politics.

THE PEACE TREATIES

Under this prevailing point of view, the United States devoted much of its diplomatic and policy-making manpower to concluding the peace treaties. The Soviet Union followed suit, because peace treaties would remove any last excuse for Western intervention in areas that the Soviets were finding it easier to control. Since Western statesmen both perceived and opposed Soviet aims, and the Soviets used the technique of arguing that they should have influence in the Western-controlled areas in return for Western influence in East Europe, negotiating the treaties proved to be no easy matter.

The Council of Foreign Ministers had been charged with the job of preparing the peace settlements, and its first meetings took place in

September–October and in December 1945, when an earlier optimism should have been dispelled. The first meeting broke up, ostensibly because of procedural differences, but in reality because the Western Allies objected to Soviet activities in Eastern Europe. They demanded that the Soviets implement the terms of the Yalta Declaration on Liberated Areas, and refused recognition to Eastern European governments until these were broadened in composition and legitimated by elections. Soviet Foreign Minister Molotov apparently found these demands outrageous since he had been told by Western powers that they favored governments friendly to the Soviet Union in Eastern Europe. Now Molotov's tactic was to make harsh demands on Italy; he wanted the Italo-Yugoslav boundary to be shifted considerably westward. He repeated the Soviet request for the right to administer Tripolitania (now Libya) as a trustee under the United Nations, and asked for reparations of $600 million, of which a large part would go to Russia and Eastern European countries. As the arguments wore on, Molotov also asked for more control in the occupation of Japan. December brought a measure of compromise. The Russians agreed to modifications in the governments of Bulgaria and Rumania, and Britain and France recognized the Rumanian government on February 5, 1946, although they still objected to the Bulgarian situation. The Western powers also agreed to new arrangements for the Japanese occupation, though final control was still left to General MacArthur.

Subordinates of the foreign ministers then got to work on the text of the peace treaties. But the Council of Foreign Ministers met again on April 25, 1946, partly because the subordinates had made so little progress, partly because tempers had frayed and the conflicts patched over in December had come out in the open. The Russians had delayed their withdrawal from wartime occupation of Persia and Manchuria, guerrilla warfare between Communists and non-Communists had intensified in Greece, and the Russians had attacked Western efforts to reimpose rule in their own spheres, particularly in Indonesia and the Middle East. In Germany the issue of reparations had begun to complicate the occupation.

If these events were part of an emerging conflict, Stalin and Churchill helped intensify the conflict by defining its nature—as they saw it—in a very public fashion. In a speech delivered on February 9, Stalin reminded good Communists everywhere that World War II was not to be seen as an isolated and unique incident, but as a part of a pattern of developing conflict between capitalist-imperialist powers. He thus linked the Western Allies and Germany together in a conflict which would ultimately lead to the downfall of Western capitalism and the triumph of the Communist world.* To this ideological interpretation of the world situation, Churchill, now leader of the Conservative opposition in Britain, responded in a speech given in Fulton, Missouri on March 5. "Nobody," he said, "knows what Soviet Russia and its Communist international organization intends to do in the immediate future, or what are the limits, if any, to their expansive and proselityzing tendencies . . . from Stettin in the Baltic to Trieste in the Adriatic an Iron Curtain has descended across the continent." He went on to say that in the face of the Soviet attempt to expand, the Western democracies must stand together, that the strength of their union would prevent a war that the Soviet Union did not want either.

In the United States, however, opinion remained strongly divided over the meaning of the events to which Churchill had referred. Most people still hoped for a return to normalcy, and to many Americans brought up on older traditions, Churchill's speech was merely another attempt to get the United States to pull British chestnuts out of the fire.

Against this background, the April meeting of the foreign ministers produced so little result that Secretary of State Byrnes concluded that the Soviets had little desire to end their military occupation of Eastern Europe. But in June the stalemate broke, and sufficient agreement was secured to call a peace conference of the twenty-one United Nations members that had been at war with the Axis satellites. The proceedings of the conference (lasting from July 29 to October 15, 1946) were dominated by Russian efforts to impose harsh terms upon Italy (opposed by the United States and Britain) and by Russian attempts to obtain her own terms for the Axis satellites that were now within the Russian sphere. Finally, delegates of the twenty-one nations approved the drafts that were to serve as recommendations for the Council of Foreign Ministers, which met in New York, November 4, 1946, to draw up the final treaties. Here, incredibly, the debate started all over again, and Western delegates registered their incredulity at what they thought was Russian obtuseness. Suddenly, on the threat of American withdrawal, Molotov agreed to most of the terms set at Paris. He had found that he could obtain nothing more from the Western powers. The treaties would also obviate Allied excuses for further intervention through the Control Commissions in Eastern Europe, where Communist consolidation now appeared far more promising

* The implications of the Stalinist position for the international Communist position had been spelled out as early as May 1945, when French Communist leader Jacques Duclos attacked American Communist Earl Browder for his optimistic, reformist, coalition-oriented perspective. Browder was ousted and replaced by William Z. Foster. The incident made clear that there was still a single "line" for all Communist parties.

than before. In spite of the peace treaties, the necessity to maintain Russian communication lines to occupation forces in Germany and Austria meant that Russian troops would remain in the Eastern European countries. Perhaps Molotov agreed also because the peace treaties would remove Western controls in Italy where the Communist party showed great strength. In any event, to American participants and observers the Soviet assent appeared to be a victory brought about by continued firmness in insisting on certain terms. At the same time, Soviet attempts to gain a foothold in the Mediterranean had been blocked.

Peace treaties with Italy, Rumania, Hungary, Bulgaria, and Finland were signed in Paris on February 10, 1947. They denuded Italy of her colonies, provided for reparations payments, mostly to Russia, and made several border rectifications, primarily in Russia's favor and designed to round out the borders as they had existed in Czarist times or to give strategic access to certain areas. Trieste, bone of contention between Italy and Yugoslavia, was to become a free city under United Nations protection. Finally, the Council of Foreign Ministers in New York called a meeting in Moscow for March 1947 to start work on the German and Austrian peace treaties. But events in those two countries since the Nazi defeat dimmed the prospects for any easy success.

GERMANY SPLITS

During the war the allies had considered dismembering Germany; never again would the German people—addicted to militarism and metaphysics —be permitted to rise to disturb the peace. But common sense had prevailed at Potsdam, where the Big Three agreed to treat Germany as an economic unit and to adopt common policies for the restoration of local self-government and democratic political parties. They reckoned without France, however, whose representatives proceeded to block all attempts to implement the Potsdam agreement through the creation of the rudiments of a central German administrative apparatus. By October 1945, the Allies suspended their efforts and began to establish local administrations very much on their own patterns. Necessity impelled them. They might believe in denazification and educational reform, but if production facilities and channels of distribution were to be reopened so that Germans would not starve, order and authority had to be reestablished. Moreover, the Western zones were swollen by millions of eastern Europeans of German descent (the "Volksdeutsch," expelled from their homes), of displaced persons unwilling to return to homes occupied by Soviet Russia and hostile national governments, of Germans expelled from the eastern area occupied by Poland. By the winter of 1945 Western zone authorities began to import food. Deliveries from the Russian-occupied breadbasket were not forthcoming, although the Russians continued to press the Westerners for reparations from their occupation zones. The occupiers had agreed on the level of industry necessary for Germany, beyond which equipment could be considered surplus and available for reparations, and the Soviets asked for delivery. But Western zone authorities answered that the agreed level depended on treating Germany as an economic unit, a policy which was prevented by the French at the level of the Allied Control Commission and also by the Russians, who found a good use themselves for whatever was produced within their zone.

Secretary Byrnes tried a new tack to break the impasse: Would the Russians accept a twenty-five year demilitarization treaty for Germany if the United States would be an active guarantor? Surely this would allay their justifiable fears. But Molotov temporized. What about reparations? Perhaps this really was the crux of the matter; perhaps, on the other hand, the Soviet Foreign Minister had no desire to see the United States pledge itself to such an active role in Europe. In any event discussions returned to the matter of reparations. To Western exasperation, the Russians argued that what they had taken so far need not be accounted for, since it constituted war booty and not reparations. Britain, whose worn economy was particularly burdened by occupation costs, shared fully in the American attitude that finally led American Commandant Lucius B. Clay to suspend all reparations payments on May 3, 1946.

Secretary Byrnes went one step further on July 11 when he offered to merge the American zone with any or all others; on July 30 the British accepted, and lengthy negotiations lead to creation of "Bizonia" on January 1, 1947. The Russians attacked the move as a flagrant violation of Potsdam. In the meantime, however, the whole picture changed as both Russians and Americans gave evidence that they had decided on a different policy than the one followed before. The Soviets announced their intention to help rebuild Germany while denouncing Western attempts to hold the Germans in subjection. Secretary Byrnes, in a speech in Stuttgart on September 6, took up the challenge and announced that the United States, which was in Germany to stay if necessary, would help to rebuild the German economy whose health was so necessary to the well-being of Europe. Germany, he declared, should be given primary responsibility for running its own affairs, and the United States favored early establishment of a provisional German Government for all of Germany.

The meaning was clear: The Russians, who had first thought only of stripping their zone, had decided to stay, to rebuild it under their domination, to appeal to all Germans. The Americans, at first concerned only with how soon they could get out, had arrived at the same decision. Peace treaty discussions were scheduled for 1947, but Germany was split. Still, the attempt by both sides to appeal to all Germans showed that the split was not yet considered irrevocable.

COMMUNIZATION OF EAST EUROPE

The western Allies had shown an early appreciation for Russia's desire to have friendly governments on its borders; at Yalta and later they tried to convince Stalin and his colleagues that broad-based, truly democratic governments might also be friendly. But as the months went by the Soviets clamped more and more rigid controls on the countries they had occupied. Eastern Europe had been notoriously unstable in the interwar period; the political spectrum had ranged from Communism to fascism, and violent nationalist hatreds had been expressed in many ways. Yet agrarian and small-holder parties with liberal or socialist leadership had also emerged. In the postwar period the Russians claimed to be eradicating fascist remnants from political life in the area; in fact, during the two years after the end of the war in Europe, they eliminated by various means all but Communist parties. The process varied from country to country, depending on the conditions the Soviet masters encountered.

For Yugoslavia and Albania there was little problem, since in both countries the Communists had come to dominate the resistance movements, and in the process had destroyed their internal opponents. Both emerged from the war firmly in the Russian camp on the basis of their own efforts.

Rumania had fought first on the side of the Axis, then switched to the Russians. When the Red Army came through, it left in its wake friendly officials, usually Communists, and a tough cadre ready to take to the streets. Non-Communist officials, shaken by Communist-led riots in February 1945, appealed for public support, and the Russians, fearful of the consequences, interfered directly. They forced King Michael—recently decorated by Stalin—to install a government in which Communists held the vital posts of Interior, Justice, and National Economy. Communist control of the first two posts meant that police would arrest and jail non-Communists while giving free rein to their own comrades; the latter meant the resources and power for rewarding good behavior and punishing opposition.

Opponents of the new regime under Premier Groza appealed to the West for help; in the impotent Allied Control Commission, at Potsdam and at meetings of the Council of Foreign Ministers Americans and British protested, refusing to recognize the new regime. The Soviets then broadened the government in January 1946, and Western recognition followed. But in ensuing months—as the split between Russia and the Western powers widened—the opposition parties operated only in a semilegal, semioppressed condition. They were subject to continual harassment; their leaders were arrested, their funds seized, newsprint denied them, and their meetings broken up. By 1948 they were totally destroyed and King Michael was forced to abdicate. Rumania had become a Communist state and a Russian satellite.

Most of Hungary's leaders had sided with the Nazis; as the Russians fought their way through, the country suffered bitterly. The Communists began their political campaign in a popular front coalition, and obtained only one-sixth of the vote in the first, more-or-less free, elections in 1945. But with Russian support they initiated the same tactics used in Rumania. In February 1947, direct Russian intervention took place. Bela Kovaks, Secretary-General of the large Small Farmers' Party was arrested and its leader, Ferenc Nagy, was forced to resign a month later. Under Communist terror a new election took place in August. Non-Communist newspapers were suppressed, the Small Farmers' Party was dissolved. Though Communist "toughs" voted more than once, the Communists secured only 22 per cent of the vote. But the list of allied parties to which the Communists belonged obtained 65 per cent, enough to ensure the formation of a government in which the Communist secured the key posts through which they could destroy first their opponents and then their allies. By the end of 1948 their domination was complete, and the next year Hungary adopted a Soviet-style constitution.

The process was considerably easier in Bulgaria. The country had a tradition of friendship with Russia ever since the Tsar had helped it secure its independence from Turkey, and although it had been at war with the Western allies, its leaders had resisted Nazi efforts to push it into war against the Soviet Union. On September 9, 1944, as Russian armies crossed the border, the Communist-dominated Fatherland Front—a coalition of resistance groups—staged a *coup d'état*, seized control of the police and organs of local government, and purged fascist sympathizers and potential opponents. Elections in November 1945 produced a Communist victory, which Western observers attributed to an atmosphere of terror and falsification of results. At a result of Western prodding, the Soviets instructed the Bulgarian Communists to broaden the base of the new government. But non-Communist leaders balked unless they were given genuine power, and so the Communists continued to consolidate power that was never threatened; they abolished the monarchy, and obtained 78 per cent of the vote in new elections in 1946. By 1948 they crushed all opposition parties and Bulgaria adopted a Soviet-style constitution.

Although Poland benefited from a greater degree of Western interest, the Russians had the advantage of their physical presence and Poland's wartime experiences. The first they could use brutally; the second gave the Communists genuine broad appeal. Nazi plans for depopulating Poland were even worse than the horrors they had actually perpetrated, and while Westerners had been able to do nothing to save Poland, the Russians shared with the Poles a common border. The Communists emphasized Western reluctance to acknowledge the Oder-Neisse border and adroitly used Byrnes' Stuttgart speech to claim that the Americans favored rebuilding Germany. The Warsaw uprising had helped destroy non-Communist leadership within Poland, and the Russians kept refugee leaders from returning except under terms imposed by the Communists. In February 1947 the Polish government adopted a provisional Soviet-style constitution, and by the end of 1948 all other parties had disappeared, leaving only the monolithic Communist party.

Western leaders expressed dismay at the process that unfolded in the Soviet sphere. But since it was gradual, their attention was frequently turned to other pressing problems. Only the occasional dramatic incident made headlines—the resignation of Hungary's Ferenc Nagy or the departure from Poland in October, 1947 of Mikolajczyk, the Peasant party leader and former premier of the Polish government-in-exile. Economic chaos and political weakness in Europe, demobilization of Allied armies, the disturbed situation in China, fighting in Southeast Asia, the American desire to throw off wartime controls and resume normalcy—all competed for attention. Many people could believe that the process of Communization in East Europe was a unique phenomenon and that the Soviets were being just a little overzealous in their standards for "friendly" governments; others could easily be persuaded that much of what was going on involved a domestic process in which "progressive" political movements were sweeping away old "feudal" structures and leaders. Besides, Finland and Czechoslovakia proved that outside of the troubled area just on their European border zone the Communists could get along with other parties.*

Czechoslovakia had welcomed Russian military successes, and the gov-

* In a curious reversion to the naiveté of these views, some more recent interpreters have argued that Westerners had no business intervening in what they assume was the Russian sphere of influence, and that the occasional Western diplomatic protests produced the Cold War, or were actually what brought about the Russian repression. The record of Stalinism hardly bears out the latter interpretation; simply letting the Russians have their brutal way might have made Machiavellian sense, but was politically difficult, given the high hopes at the end of the War. And the shadow of appeasement of Hitler loomed at everyone's shoulder in those years.

ernment formed in March 1945 was a coalition of Communists, Social Democrats, National Socialists, and leaders of the People's Party (Catholic). The Communists held the posts of Interior (with its crucial control of the police) as well as important positions in the Army, Agriculture (responsible for land distribution), and in Information and Education. They held controlling positions in the border areas from which over two million Germans were expelled. But their behavior and that of the Russians was circumspect. Cession of Sub-Carpathian Ruthenia—the eastern tip of the country—to the Soviet Union had caused little ill-feeling, and the Soviets withdrew their troops in December at the same time that a smaller American force withdrew in the west. When genuine elections were held in May 1946, the Communists received 38 per cent of the vote, although they received something of a setback in more heavily Catholic Slovakia, where people objected to Czech centralization.

Communist Clement Gottwald became Premier in the new government, and Dr. Eduard Benes, the prewar democratic leader, retained his wartime exile position as President. Despite the events taking place in neighboring countries, the coalition worked, and, under considerable pressure, the Communists observed the constitution. As 1947 drew to a close many people still hoped that Czechoslovakia might serve as a bridge across the widening gap between Russia and the West.

WINTER OF 1947

If any one thing brought home the realization that the world was going to be very different from what it had been before, it was the bitter winter of 1947.

Before World War II Western Europe had exported industrial goods and bought foodstuffs and raw materials from Eastern Europe, the Far East, British Dominions, and Argentina. The United States, as a massive buyer of colonial products (such as tin and rubber from European colonies) supplied Europe with the dollars needed to purchase its exports. The depression and then World War II changed all this. Destruction in Europe was enormous. Not only were houses, industrial plants, roads and railroads demolished, herds and flocks were killed—and these would take even longer than factories to replace. Moreover, currencies were almost everywhere in disarray, and without a stable unit of exchange a modern complex economy cannot function. In 1945 productivity in Western Europe was perhaps one-third that of 1939. In 1938 western Germany produced 220 million tons of coal and 18 million tons of steel. In 1947— two years after the end of the war—production had painfully climbed back to 143 million tons of coal and only 5 million tons of steel.

Neutrals like Switzerland and Sweden kept their economies intact. Belgium, partly because wartime shipments to the United States of uranium and other metals from the Congo were credited to its account, emerged in fair economic shape and was able to carry through a harsh but effective currency reform in 1946 that restored confidence and encouraged investment. But for the rest, the war was a disaster and Britain—the great prewar creditor nation of the world—although spared the invasions that raged across the continent and through much of Southeast and East Asia, emerged with $15 billion of overseas debts. Everywhere, in the year and a half after the war, hunger and deprivation stalked the land, and all efforts to rebuild were hampered by the very fact of the shortages that rebuilding was designed to correct.

The United States, in contrast, found itself at the end of the war with a revitalized industry able to produce a gross national product of almost twice that of prewar years, and an agricultural plant able to produce an enormous surplus—even though American consumption of meat, for example, had risen from 125 pounds per capita prewar to 163 pounds per capita in 1945. But American citizens—through savings enforced during the war years—also had a large pent-up demand for American production waiting to be released. The question for the rest of the world was whether representatives of the American poeple, clamoring for normalcy, would use part of this productive carpacity to help restore a stable world order, or would insist that it be used for domestic consumption.*

The United Nations Relief and Rehabilitation Administration, established in 1943, helped to sustain Eastern Europe with $2 billion worth of food and clothing. In addition, in the months of transition from war to peace, the American army and navy distributed relief supplies in liberated and occupied areas to the extent of $750 million. Private and voluntary organizations contributed hundreds of millions more. All these showed that Americans were willing to help. But the abrupt termination of lend-lease shipments by President Truman on August 21, 1945, came as a shock. Lend-lease was interallied aid; Britain, for example, was credited with the port services or shipping that it supplied to other Allies, the United States with the munitions and food that it supplied. And the United States had provided the lion's share: $48.5 billion from March 1941 to V-J Day, August 14, 1945.

The British had expected that the United States would negotiate a tapering-off plan, and Secretary of the Treasury Morgenthau had talked of a large-scale reconstruction loan. Both would have helped cushion the

---

* There was no question of needing export markets as some recent writers have argued—and as Stalin thought.

period of transition, but neither was offered.† The American government did, however, offer long-term credits to help pay for lend-lease supplies already negotiated and contracted for, and the liberal terms it gave Britain in the first settlement of wartime lend-lease accounts showed that it was not going to burden the already disastrous postwar world economy with a debt structure like the one that followed World War I. The settlement also represented the view that funds expended against a common wartime enemy should be written off. In 1946 the United States reached settlements with France, India, Turkey, Australia, New Zealand and Belgium, and, in 1947, with South Africa. There was no settlement with the Soviet Union, which had received $11 billion worth and supplied $2 million in reverse, but which had also suffered considerably more casualties and damage.‡

The United States, through these interim measures, as well as a large loan to Britain in 1946 (see below) had responded to a challenging situation. If mass starvation and complete economic breakdown were to be averted, the rest of the world had to look primarily to the United States—the only country with a large exportable surplus beyond what was needed to maintain a high standard of living. Compared to 1939–41 food exports of $350 million, 1946 food exports rose to more than $2200 million.

Yet within the United States the predominant view was that although relief measures might be necessary, there would be a rapid return to normalcy. It was summed up in the lend-lease clauses pledging free trading practices, in the sharp cut-off of lend-lease, in the creation of the International Bank for Reconstruction and Development and the International Monetary Fund and in the rapid elimination of rationing within the United States, where caloric consumption was twice that of Europe. Despite severe drought in 1945 and 1946 in Argentina, Australia, South Africa, French North Africa, India and China, and despite warnings from UNRRA officials that the outlook for 1946–47 gave cause for "profound alarm," the American government abandoned UNRRA.

General Eisenhower and former Mayor LaGuardia of New York, Director-General of UNRRA, pleaded for it. The United States, LaGuardia said, wanted to give aid only to those countries "chosen, picked and acceptable to our government." But, he went on, "We are not giving aid to governments. We are giving aid to the men, women, and children

---

† President Truman later acknowledged that the sudden cancellation was a mistake, based on Congressional specifications that lend-lease was not to be used for reconstruction and on the unforseen rapidity of the Japanese collapse.

‡ Until 1972 (see below, Chapter 8).

throughout the world who suffered so much during the war and who to this very day are still in need." In November 1946, however, Secretary of State Byrnes and Assistant Secretary Acheson, in opposing the continuation of UNRRA, foresaw the position Congress would surely take. International aid *was* going to countries whose governments were unfriendly, and the United States should control its own foreign aid through bilateral agreements. Since the major problems had been solved, the problem was now one of foreign exchange, and this could be attacked through the IMF, the IBRD, and through normal extension of purchase credits by the Export-Import Bank. UNRRA, deprived of its major supporter, ceased to function in December 1946.

American officials were aware of a bad situation. But the first postwar effort to cope with it after the collapse of UNRRA took the form of a bilateral loan to England. The conditions of this kind of loan could be more stringent, and the loan was extended to a more reliable and friendly government than some in Eastern Europe that had received UNRRA money. Nevertheless, the debate over the $3.75 billion long-term, low interest loan negotiated at the end of 1945 revealed confused attitudes in the United States about the state of the world, and Congress took seven months to provide the money.

The loan was designed to set the stage in which the United Nations system already described would work: prewar Britain had been a net importer using interest on its overseas investments to finance the import surplus. But during the war it had sold its assets and piled up debts of $15 billion, held in blocked accounts in London. The countries which now held British notes could cash them in only when the British government allowed them. To resume its position in world trade Britain would have to export more than it imported in order to pay the debts and rebuild investments overseas; yet its industry was worn by war and far less productive than that of its rival, the United States. Moreover, Britian was trying to meet heavy overseas commitments; there was the aid to Greece against Communist guerrillas as well as action in Palestine, the German occupation, and restoration of order in South and Southeast Asia (see below). Unless Britain's position were secured, the world trading system envisaged when the United Nations organs were established could not be attained, and war-time commitments to multilateral trade would never be realized.

The arguments against the proposed loan—mainly from the Republican side—were that the United States should have secured more in return, that British policy in Palestine was all wrong, and—an echo from prewar days—that the United States was supporting British imperialism. But the answer to this came from House Speaker Sam Rayburn:

I do not want Western Europe, England, and all the rest pushed further into and toward an ideology that I despise. I fear if we do not cooperate with this great natural ally of ours, that is what will happen. If we are not allied with the great British democracy, I fear somebody will be and God pity us when we have no ally across the Atlantic Ocean, and God pity them, too.

In the face of increasing tension with Russia, the loan passed the Senate 46 to 34 and the House 219 to 155. The dispute over the loan with Britain put the final seal on another, curiously related issue: reconstruction credits for Russia. The idea had been discussed periodically throughout the last two years of the war; Stalin himself had talked of six to ten billion dollars, and the Soviet attitude had paralleled that of some Americans: the United States economy would need to export in order to keep afloat. In such a simple form it was not true, and Congress' reluctance to allow the Administration any leeway in extending postwar reconstruction credits was reflected in the debate on the loan to Britain. Administration advisers like Harriman and Kennan cautioned that Russia would have a hard time making repayment, that the credits would in no way influence Stalin toward greater cooperation, and that the Administration would therefore have nothing to show the American public for the loan but more taxes. There is still question as to whether the American failure to extend postwar aid to Russia had any influence on Stalin's foreign policy. At most, however, it may have hardened Russian determination to extract all it could from its hapless East European satellites and from Germany in the form of reparations. And in the face of worsening relations no Administration could have faced an economy and normalcy-minded Congress with such a request.*

The various forms of piecemeal aid, the British loan, and the resources of the IMF and IBRD were all insufficient. In Eastern Europe the situation varied from country to country. Hungary and Rumania suffered most; recovery was slow to begin and trade with the rest of Europe lagged. Not until 1946 did Poland and Rumania, the traditional suppliers of coal, grain, and oil to Western Europe, begin to resume exports.

Then throughout Western Europe the winter of 1947 brought a grim situation. German industrial revival slowed; the Western zones were cut off from foodstuffs of the east. In France the shaky political coalition of Communist, Socialist, and Christian Democrat, seeking an acceptable political framework, had made too little economic headway, and inflation and the black market flourished. In the unusually cold winter of 1947 be-

---

* In anticipation of Congressional attitudes the lending capacity of the Export-Import Bank had been increased, so that a one billion dollar credit could be extended without Congressional approval. But this, too, was abandoned.

tween three and four million acres of wheat planted in the fall were lost.
This meant importing two or three million tons of wheat at a hundred
dollars a ton. But there were no dollars. Throughout Western Europe the
situation was repeated. With few consumer goods to buy and with rampant inflation, the incentives to work and to invest were lacking. Hopeless-
ness and frustration helped to weaken governmental authority, reducing
the capacity of governments to take the necessary drastic actions. Imports
were needed; they cost dollars; but there were no exports to earn dollars.
This was the "dollar gap."

Britain's situation, detailed in a series of government White Papers of
early 1947 and Cabinet Surveys was particularly crucial. The British did
not face a sizable internal Communist party ready, like the ones in
France or Italy, to take advantage of a desperate economic, social and
political situation. But Britain's extensive overseas commitments were a
debilitating economic drain. Britain, with its sterling debts to the Empire
and British banking and financial institutions, stood at the center of an
economic complex heavily dependent on these institutions and on British
industrial capacity. Yet in January, the government revealed that instead
of improving its position, each month saw Britain going further into debt
as imports continued to exceed exports; the great dollar loan was being
used up far faster than had been expected. In other words, Britain was
living far beyond her means and would have to retrench. Worse, in January and February, the impossible happened: Britain—the country in
which the industrial revolution started, the island built on coal that had
fueled that revolution—ran out of coal. Industries came to a halt. Those
depending on electricity found their power was shut off several hours a
day; there was not enough coal to generate it. The worst blizzards in
memory halted trains carrying coal and froze barges carrying the desperately needed fuel. Crops of winter wheat froze.

It would take months to recover from this new blow. Exports would be
reduced by hundreds of millions of dollars. Suddenly, to the rest of the
world that had not been watching economic indicators closely, came the
revelation that Europe was close to total disaster; a few blizzards could
cripple the continent that had been the center of the entire world. In February it became clear that Britain, facing a deficit of close to $2 billion
for the year, was on the verge of bankruptcy. The British might have to
give up maintaining order in the Middle East, withdraw from Asia and
the occupation of Germany, forego contributions to relief, default on foreign debts, and—against the rules of the game instituted in the IMF, the
IBRD, and the ITO—impose the most rigid trade restrictions.

By midwinter 1947 the full effect of the war was felt in Europe: not
only had the international system *not* been rebuilt—it seemed about to
collapse entirely.

EUROPE AND THE NON-WESTERN WORLD, 1945–1947

In the four centuries before World War II, Europe, in a series of erratic steps, had exerted its control over the rest of the world. At the end of the eighteenth century and the beginning of the nineteenth, much of the Americas was lost. But the end of the nineteenth century brought the last great surge of empire building: the European powers carved up Africa and began to divide China. Even as they seemed to be consolidating their hold, the export of European administrative and legal systems, the structural changes they wrought in colonial economies, and their exploitation of natural resources stimulated nationalist opposition to European control. The process was inexorable, and World War II greatly speeded it.

France had used the resources and manpower of its vast empire to counterbalance Germany's greater populpation and industry. In World War II, although conservative colonial administrators tended to side with Vichy, the empire nevertheless provided the base—along with England—from which the Free French could work. But everywhere in the empire the weakness of France was seen and understood. Moverover, in Southeast Asia, the Japanese followed the process they used in the British and Dutch territories they overran. First they consolidated their hold and developed a system of economic exploitation, and then put local nationalist leaders into power. In Indochina, in March, 1945, they massacred thousands of resident French garrison soldiers and civil administrators (while Americans in China refused any airborne help to their allies, on direct orders from President Roosevelt, determined that the French should be forced out of the area), and then installed Bao Dai as Emperor of Vietnam. The weak and hapless Bao Dai was unable to control a situation of utter chaos, and when some 1400 British troops moved into the south while 150,000 Nationalist Chinese troops pillaged the north, they found the Democratic Republic of Vietnam in existence, headed by, and under the control of, the founder of the Communist Party of Indochina, Ho Chi Minh. Independent kingdoms existed in Loas and Cambodia. In Burma the Japanese had created an "independent" regime in 1943, and in the former Dutch-controlled East Indies the Japanese Supreme Council for the Direction of the War announced the independence of the area in July 1945. On August 17 Indonesian leaders proclaimed the birth of the Republic of Indonesia.

In the Mediterranean the Axis powers had also appealed to nationalist leaders to resist the control of the Allies. But more important was the extent to which people could see that the Europeans could not maintain their status without American troops and materiel. All through the Mediterranean, the Middle East, South Asia, and Southeast Asia, emergent nationalist leaders made demands for a new postwar status.

The reactions of the various European powers showed considerable continuity with their specific prewar policies.

The French had ruled directly from France through colonial administrators, and had tried to remake the alien cultures they ruled so they reflected French culture. The policy, known as assimilation, included close tying of the economies of the overseas areas with that of France. Postwar French governments recognized the need for reform, and initiated a policy of overseas investment to raise standards of living among the natives, and, in the "French Union," established institutions in which colonial representation seemed significant. But they also tried to reimpose direct rule from Paris.

In North Africa, after exiling nationalist leaders who gained prominence during the war and after quelling Algerian riots in May 1945—riots that gave evidence of widespread Moslem disaffection—French authorities held onto power.

In the Middle East—in Syria and Lebanon, which France had held as mandates under the League of Nations—the Free French, partly because of British pressure, partly to compete for wartime support from the Arabs, had promised independence. But in May 1945, during negotiations for the terms of independence, de Gaulle landed a small contingent of French troops in Lebanon, and tried to insist that the Syrian and Lebanese armies remain under French command. Direct British intervention forced the French to withdraw their demands. The Syrian and Lebanese governments had declared war on the Axis, thus gaining admission to the San Francisco conference; in March 1945 they had helped to create the Arab League. They had been granted recognition as independent states by many other countries without mention of any special status for anyone, and thus they had effectively become independent.

De Gaulle, however, saw the British intervention as a deliberate effort to supplant French influence by British influence in an area where French interests were as important as those of the British. He accused the British of abetting Arab armed action against the French: "It can never be forgotten," he told the British Ambassador. Churchill, on the other hand, saw the matter as a minor misunderstanding in which a mistaken French move had caused unwelcome unrest in the Arab world at a critical moment, and he tried to smooth matters over. Not until the end of 1946 were all French and British troops withdrawn, and the matter came up in the United Nations, where the Soviet Union used the situation to reply to charges about its own conduct in Eastern Europe.

In Indochina the Chinese generals occupying the north withdrew only after extracting political concessions for China from the French. The British in the south facilitated the return of French troops while other French forces were finally released from the inhuman Japanese prison camps into which they had been herded. In the meantime, while doing nothing to bring about the release of the French and, in fact, actually hampering French efforts, the Americans continued aid they had earlier extended to Ho Chi Minh. In March 1946 Ho Chi Minh and a French mission signed what might have been the most historic accord in modern Indochinese history: it created Vietnam as a "free state" within an Indochinese Federation and the French Union, with its own governmental institutions. Unfortunately, in the next few months, the Vietminh delegations sent to Paris found there a chaotic governmental situation and an inability to deal with the issues, while back in Indochina local French commanders undermined the agreement. Further accords were finally negotiated in Paris, but as one author put it

> The French forces sent to Indochina in 1946 were too strong for France to resist the temptation of using them; yet not strong enough to keep the Viet-Minh from trying to solve the whole political problem by throwing the French into the sea.
> The outbreak of the Indochina war can be traced back to that single, tragic erroneous estimate. . . .*

In December, after a series of incidents, the Vietminh launched a concerted attack on French forces, and France was once more at war, a war that would drag on for seven years.

Just as the English had been willing to help reestablish the French in Indochina, they were willing to help restore the Dutch in the vast and important East Indies. There, as in Indochina, an independent state had been proclaimed and a government established, with which, of necessity, the British worked in the first months of their occupation, since they lacked manpower and transport sufficient to govern. Dutch reoccupation was motivated by a reluctance to give up a possession that had been Dutch for 300 years, and by their feeling that the varied peoples in the widespread archipelago in no way constituted a "nation." Moreover, there were 200,000 Japanese troops to repatriate and 200,000 Dutch nationals on the islands who had suffered through the wartime occupation. Underestimating the growth of nationalist sentiment, and returning to the islands in force and by force during 1946, they negotiated an agreement with the self-proclaimed Republic in November 1946. To the Dutch, the

---

* Bernard B. Fall, *Street Without Joy: Insurgency in Indochina, 1946–1963* (3d rev. ed.; Harrisburg, Pa.: The Stackpole Co., 1963) , p. 27.

agreement meant only that the Republic would be one among several states in a loose federation in a union with Holland. But the Indonesian nationalist leaders—Sukarno, Sjharir, and Hatta—wanted more. Within a few months the agreement broke down.

The British, whose overseas interests were as vast and varied as those of the French, responded in a different manner, and demonstrated more flexibility in meeting new situations. There had been less centralized authority in the prewar empire than in the French empire and British administration worked through existing native institutions to a much greater extent. Moreover, the evolution of Dominion status within the empire for advanced overseas territories had provided a way of developing complete self-government while ties to Britain continued. Like the French, the British planned an important increase in overseas investments; they also planned a gradual shift from indirect rule through existing tribal or other native institutions to the development of more modern forms of government.

Africa south of the Sahara posed relatively little political problem since the area had not been subject to the influences of Axis invasion. Egypt, however, had proved indispensable to the Allied war effort and the Suez Canal remained a lifeline; Britain therefore resisted Egyptian demands for withdrawal of all British troops. A December 1946 agreement that the Egyptians maintain British bases while the troops withdrew failed to be implemented because, first, there was no accompanying agreement about the future of the Anglo-Egyptian Sudan which Egypt now claimed, and subsequently because the cold war with Russia developed and the Suez Canal base to which the British had withdrawn their troops gained new importance.

Britain held Transjordan under a League mandate. During the war the British promised Emir Abdullah independence for his little country at the end of hostilities. The British delegate to the United Nations therefore announced that Jordan would not be proposed as a trust territory. On March 22, 1946, Britain signed an alliance with the Emir in which the British undertook to defend his state against external aggression and to subsidize his army, the Arab Legion, in return for certain base rights within Jordan. Britain proceeded to recognize the independence of Jordan, and the other states followed suit, despite Jordan's obvious dependence on British support.

Britain's other Middle East mandate posed far more problems for the Labour Government in London. Zionism—the movement to provide a national home for the dispersed Jews of the world in Palestine—grew rapidly in the first half of the century as Ottoman control over the Middle

East dissolved. During World War I, in order to get Jewish support in the war against the Central Powers, Britain issued the Balfour Declaration, promising the Jews a "national home" in Palestine, a region that then also encompassed what is now Jordan and Syria. British leaders foresaw no conflict with the Arabs, whom they had stimulated to revolt against the Turks by promises of booty and independence, since the area in which the Jews would settle constituted only a sparsely settled one percent of the total area to be wrested from Turkey. But in the interwar years Jewish immigration increased and the well-organized Jewish community bought land and established its own institutions of self-government—and stimulated overall development of the now much smaller area composing the Palestine Mandate. The Arab population of the area increased, and Arab agitation against Jewish immigration arose. Nazi persecution of the Jews intensified Jewish immigration, and riots and incidents multiplied. The British tried to restrict Jewish immigration and institute a local government in which Arabs would predominate.

World War II brought an end of Arab guerrilla warfare in the area, partly because immigration declined, partly because Allied divisions were present. But as the war wore on, illegal immigration increased under pressure of the monstrous Nazi extermination policy, and Jewish terrorism grew. The Jews now found increasing support from the American Jewish community through the American Zionist Organization, which in 1942 had asked for the creation of a Jewish state in Palestine, unlimited immigration, and the formation of a Jewish army. Then, at the end of the war, the camps teeming with displaced Jews from Eastern Europe and the survivors of Hitler's extermination centers intensified the problem. President Roosevelt had told King Ibn Saud of Saudi Arabia that although he thought more Jews should be admitted to Palestine, no step would be taken without consulting both Arabs and Jews. But President Truman addressed an appeal to British Prime Minister Clement Attlee in August 1945, asking for immediate admission of 100,000 Jewish refugees to Palestine. The British, appalled at what they thought was a failure to consider the effect on relations with the Arabs in the area, propose the creation of an Anglo-American Committee of Inquiry to study the matter. Thus the British in Palestine, although still directly administering the area, shifted part of the burden of responsibility to the United States.

State Department and Foreign Office officials emphasized that Soviet influence in the area might increase if the Arabs were alienated, but the Committee of Inquiry nevertheless recommended the admission of the proposed number of Jewish refugees and the transformation of the mandate into a trust territory. However, a higher-level official committee from the two countries charged with working out implementation revived an older British policy of creating a federalized Arab-Jewish state with continued Jewish immigration dependent on Arab consent.

Jews in Europe and the United States were bitter, particularly as news spread of British internment of illegal Jewish immigrants. Immediately before the congressional elections of 1946, President Truman renewed his demand for admission of 100,000 immigrants.

The harsh winter of 1947 was crucial for the Labour government faced with what appeared to be irreconcilable demands. Getting out of Palestine would relieve the British of a costly burden which produced nothing but hatred. On April 2, 1947, they requested a special session of the United Nations General Assembly to consider the whole question. The session met from April 28 to May 15 and created the United Nations Special Committee on Palestine composed of eleven states to prepare and present a report to the regular fall session of the General Assembly. Although Arabs objected that the General Assembly had no jurisdiction in the matter, by mid-1947 Britain was ready to get rid of another outpost of the empire.

Further across the southern perimeter of the Eurasian continent, the British demonstrated their willingness to divest themselves of imperial responsibility in India, Ceylon, and Burma. After the failure to reconcile Hindu and Muslim leaders in India, Prime Minister Attlee, on February 20, 1947, announced a British decision to transfer power into Indian hands by June 1948. It was hoped that agreement would be reached between both parties by then, and that the Labour government could transfer power to some form of central government that would rule the whole area, but power would be transferred then in any case. Lord Mountbatten was to be sent as the last Viceroy, charged with liquidating the British Raj. Said Winston Churchill, speaking for the Conservative opposition, "In handing over the Government of India to these so-called political classes we are handing over to men of straw of whom in a few years no trace will remain."

Lord Mountbatten arrived in India on March 22, 1947. After sounding out Hindu and Muslim leaders, he was determined to speed the transfer of power. The dominant nationalist organization, the Congress Party, strove to maintain unity, and argued for a secular state within which religious minorities would be free, but Muslim leaders balked. Islam has an inherent tendency to dictate the organization of society. When fears of Hindu domination were added to this, it was too much, and the fateful decision for partition resulted. Gandhi, to whom partition was repugnant, said, "The British Government is not responsible for partition. The Viceroy has no hand in it. In fact he is as opposed to division as Congress itself. But if both of us, Hindus and Muslims, cannot agree on anything else, then the Viceroy is left with little choice." On July 4 an Indian Independence Bill was introduced into the British Parliament. By the 18th it had passed and received the royal assent. It provided that "from the fifteenth day of August, nineteen hundred and forty-seven, two independent Dominions shall be set up in India, to be known respectively as India and Pakistan."

Britain and India both faced an enormous administrative task to accomplish within a terribly short time. The armed forces, civil service, and various forms of government property had to be divided. Even more difficult was the drawing of boundary lines and the problem posed by the 562 Indian states with semi-autonomous local rulers through whom the British had acted in the past. Varying enormously in size, they covered some 45 per cent of the land and contained 28 per cent of the population. Through persuasion and pressure, the newly created States Ministry induced the leaders of all but Hyderabad, Kashmir, and Junagadh to sign an Instrument of Accession, thereby guaranteeing unity within the two major states, India and Pakistan. But two of the three that failed to sign proved to be serious problems in the future. And to Indians the presence of a few small enclaves still ruled by France and Portugal after two or three hundred years also remained for some years cause for irritation.

On the night of August 14, when the Constituent Assembly met to hail independence, Nehru declared, "At the stroke of the midnight hour, when the world sleeps, India will awake to life and freedom." Unfortunately, the moment was accompanied by an almost uncontrolled orgy of violence.

No boundary commission could have put all Muslims in one state and all Hindus in the other, nor would all the people have wanted it. But when the boundaries were announced on the day after independence, Hindu attacked Muslim in India, and Muslim attacked Hindu in Pakistan. Millions of refugees left their homes and streamed across borders, under attack all the way. Trains arrived filled with mutilated corpses, and in many areas not only did the constabulary prove ineffective, but in some cases joined in the fanaticism. Neighbor set upon neighbor, burning, looting, killing. The governments cooperated in trying to stem the rioting and in moving and resettling refugees in camps. By the middle of 1948 over 12,000,000 people had crossed the Indian-Pakistani borders. The memories of the dreadful months are still alive. So is the issue of who was responsible for what, and the property claims involved. Relations between the two countries could not help but be bad from the beginning.

These bad relations were also exacerbated by the Junagadh and Kashmir issues. The Muslim ruler of the former, a small state with a predominantly Hindu population, acceded to Pakistan, which accepted it. The population rioted, the ruler was forced to flee, and, on the invitation of a lesser official, the Indian government sent in troops. In February 1948, a plebiscite held at Indian insistence gave an almost unanimous vote for accession to India. In January 1949, the merger took place.

The Kashmir question involved a much larger, richer state. Strategically located near the borders of the Soviet Union and adjacent to Sinkiang province in China, it contained the headwaters of the important Indus river. Here the reverse situation existed; the Maharajah was Hindu, and the population predominantly Muslim. The Maharajah hoped to remain independent, but under pressure from Pakistan, and facing Muslim tribal invaders from the wild northwest frontier area, he appealed to India for military aid. In order to get it, he acceded to India. Indian troops were sent immediately, and pushed back the invaders, who by this time were receiving aid from the Pakistani government. Lord Mountbatten had assured the Maharajah that the accession was provisional, and that a plebiscite would be held. Nehru, too, echoed the view. India brought the matter as a case of Pakistani aggression to the United Nations Security Council in January 1948, and the Security Council maintained representatives in the area to supervise the cease-fire it secured, but no plebiscite was ever held. At first no one could agree on the necessary preliminary steps such as demilitarization. Subsequently India shifted its position, and rejected the idea of a plebiscite. Pakistan claimed that what was right for Janagadh was right for Kashmir. And there the issue rested, but for one thing: in 1957 Kashmir adopted a constitution and India came to regard Kashmir as integrated into India.

Hyderabad, completely surrounded by Indian territory, posed few problems. The Nizam, ruler of this, one of the largest, most autocratic and backward of the native states, was a Muslim; the majority of the populace was Hindu. The Nizam refused to accede to Indian pressures until, in June 1948, India clamped on a complete economic blockade and then three months later sent in troops. Under the circumstances the Nizam finally acceded and withdrew the request for aid he had sent to the United Nations Security Council.

Both Pakistan and India remained members of the British Commonwealth of Nations, the loose grouping of states previously part of the British empire, and still held together by currency arrangements, trading patterns, and similar systems of law and administration. And India was allowed to join as a Republic, accepting the king as the symbol of the free association of the Commonwealth's independent member nations and as such, the head of the Commonwealth.

Further to the east, in Burma and Malaya, Japanese wartime occupation and consequent devastation complicated matters. In Burma, bitter rivalry between political groups and between the dominant Burmese and ethnic minorities led the British to opt for a renewed period of direct British rule while economic reconstruction and preparation for self-government were encouraged. Opposition in the form of strikes and insurrections by Burmese nationalists led the Labour Government in Britain to change course and negotiate an independence agreement in early 1947 with Aung San, leader of the dominant, catchall Anti-Fascist People's Freedom League. In the course of negotiations over continued military ties with Britain, in an ominous portent of things to come, Aung San and six of his colleagues were assassinated by members of a Communist faction he had expelled from the League. His successor, U Nu, negotiated complete independence, to be achieved in January 1948. Fratricidal, factional warfare followed, but U Nu followed a patient course of pacification that brought a measure of peace by the early 1950s.

Malaya posed an entirely different problem from most of the other British controlled areas. Like the Dutch East Indies, it was an important dollar earner through its exports of rubber and tin, and its dollars, paid into the common pool of the sterling area, contributed enormously to British ability to continue to pay for American imports. In addition, there was no Malay nationalism. The area was an ethnic conglomeration— one-third Chinese, one-third Indian, and one-third Malay. At the southern tip of Malaya lay the great strategic port of Singapore, the supposedly impregnable symbol of British imperial might before the war that was, in fact, easily conquered by the Japanese. The returning British, facing a chaotic situation in Malaya, saw the problem not as one of nationalist resistance but rather of creating some semblance of a nation. The first British attempt, in 1946, was to give a separate status to Singapore (whose population is 77 per cent Chinese), and to amalgamate the states of Malaya into a Union in which the local sultans would retain little power. Strong Malayan objections forced the British to withdraw the plan, and they proceeded—at a more leisurely pace than was possible in other areas—to create a more acceptable federation.

One other great imperial power, the United States, faced the problem of emerging nationalism. But the United States, unlike its allies, had entered the war already committed to the eventual independence of its chief Pacific colonial possession, the Philippines. The war left the islands with a shattered economy, enormous physical destruction, and a complete social breakdown. Of 24 Senators in the previous Philippine Congress, seven were dead, seven under arrest as collaborators. Of 98 Representatives, seven were under arrest, 20 others had been in a Japanese-sponsored wartime assembly, 11 others had taken jobs under the Japanese, and many others had been killed or were missing. Yet many Filipinos had strongly resisted the Japanese. Independence came to this broken country on July 4, 1946.

The United States helped; there were large relief operations before the end of the war, and the new government received emergency loans, tax refunds, and more than half a billion dollars to satisfy war damage claims and to underwrite rehabilitation. Unfortunately, in the chaotic situation that prevailed and in the face of immense shortages, corruption in the use of the funds was enormous. Moreover, agrarian unrest was fanned and led by the Hukbalahaps—the anti-Japanese Peoples Liberation Army—a Communist-led organization. For years after independence the country-side suffered from warfare between undisciplined military forces and terrorists who lived off the land. Although greatly reduced in number, the "Huks" continued guerrilla warfare through the 1950s.

By 1947 "decolonization," the process of breaking up prewar empires, was well under way. Those empires had been created by the curiosity, ambition, idealism, or greed of Europeans, coupled with their technological superiority and greater political strength. But their delimitations had usually proceeded from balance-of-power maneuvering within Europe. Unlike the United States, which could expand across an almost empty continent, and at the expense of weak neighbors, European powers had expanded outside of their own continent. An increase in empire by one country was viewed as an increase in power; since none wanted any single power to become too strong, all joined in the race in order to maintain the balance, and often they agreed on rules to follow in dividing up the world.

But the European and American rulers of empires had introduced modern education, transportation, European systems of law, and western forms of trade and finance. Indigenous societies were disrupted, and a new group of leaders adopted the doctrine of their overlords—nationalism. In the postwar period their demands, the revealed weaknesses of their rulers, the prodding of the Soviet Union, China, and the United States, the increased voice given to the small, poorer countries in the United Nations General Assembly and the Trusteeship Council, and the fact that the war was fought in the name of democracy and self-determination, all had an effect in the drive for independence.

It met resistance. The colonial powers had investments to protect: large groups of settlers and descendants of settlers, many of whom had been born and raised in the colonies, felt that all modern developments were due to colonial endeavor. Foreign office and military personnel worried that hasty decolonization would create a power vacuum into which new imperialism might move. Political analysts wondered how an international system including many new powers with abundant reasons for quarreling would function. What would it be like without the sort of safety valve that they had provided for balance-of-power struggles within Europe?

In the early postwar period, no one predicted how far decolonization would go. Africa seemed untouched. But in the Middle East and in Asia, the struggle had begun in earnest.

IRAN AND TURKEY

Iran and Turkey were the first non-European countries where the Soviet Union showed an active interest during the postwar period; the first two years of the period brought Soviet retreat in both.

At the start of World War II Iran had close ties with Nazi Germany. When the Soviet Union came under Nazi attack, Iran appeared to be the most logical supply route from the south, and the Allies asked the Shah to expel German technicians who might sabotage shipments. The Shah refused; on August 25, 1941, the British invaded from the south and the Russians from the north. The Shah abdicated in favor of his son, and Iran was forced to cooperate with the Allies. Soon American services created an enormous supply base in the country, and the Allies signed a treaty with Iran reaffirming its independence and promising withdrawal of troops within six months after the end of the war.

Within Iran various extremist groups became active, and the Russians openly encouraged Communism. They supported separatist agitation of Armenian-, Kurdish-, and Turkish-speaking minorities, and intimidated Iranian officials, while pressing Iran for an oil concession in the north. The British, though obliged to cooperate with their Russian allies, continued traditional British policy towards Iran and helped stiffen Iranian resistance; the Americans, by and large, held themselves aloof, but provided economic assistance and technical aid to the Iranian government. Although Roosevelt was unwilling to actually enter into the political fray, he persuaded the Russians during the Teheran Conference to endorse a section of the final communique reiterating the Big Three's "desire for the maintenance of the independence, sovereignty and territorial integrity of Iran." It was the British, however, who actively opposed the Soviets.

Then, in the last months of 1945, when the war was over, the Soviet Union sponsored the creation of a separatist regime in the Soviet-occupied region of Azerbaijan, and another, less important, Kurdish one in Mahabad. The Soviet Army kept Iranian troops from entering and continued its occupation after the six-months deadline for withdrawal lapsed. It looked as though the pattern in other occupied areas was to be repeat-

ed. Faced with a *fait accompli,* the Iranians, who had embarrassed the
Russians by bringing the matter to the newly created United Nations,
turned to negotiate with their northern neighbor. Britain and the United
States, who had completed their troop removal from Iran, appealed to
the Soviet Union. The Russian price for withdrawal was an oil concession
in the north, the admission of several Communists to the Iranian cabinet,
and withdrawal of the Iranian complaint from the Security Council Agenda. Iran acquiesced and to the surprise of many, the Russians withdrew
their troops. Perhaps Stalin was still hesitant to alienate foreign opinion
which was not yet unalterably hostile to the Soviet Union; perhaps the
main Soviet desire was for the oil concession. In any event, once the Soviet Union had withdrawn, the Iranian army reentered Azerbaijan and the
rebel regime collapsed in December of 1946. The next year the Iranian
parliament—the Majlis—refused to ratify the Iranian-Soviet oil agreement.

The Turkish case was quite different. Following the disastrous World
War I alliance with Germany and Austria-Hungary, Turkey had switched
between the wars to a policy of alliance with France and England. But as
Nazi power advanced toward the Eastern Mediterranean the Turks found
it necessary to be circumspect; Allied leaders understood, and despite
Nazi blandishments (which became easier and easier to resist as the Nazi
tide receded), Turkey remained neutral during most of the war. In the
early period of the war the Soviets, then allied to Nazi Germany, were
annoyed by Turkish alignment with France and Britain. Once the Nazis
had invaded Russia, Russian leaders became annoyed at Turkey's neutrality. But beginning in the spring of 1944, the Turks gradually severed
economic and political relations with Germany, and on February 23,
1945, in order to gain admittance to the United Nations Conference at
San Francisco, they finally declared war on the Nazis.

Although the Turks took pains to dissociate official policy from Pan-
Turanianism—an agitation for union of all Turkish-speaking peoples
which the Nazis had encouraged in an effort to win Turkish support—
they faced increasing hostility from a triumphant Russia. For the first
time the Russians felt themselves in a position to push for a warm-water
entrance to world trade. The way led through the Turkish-controlled
straits between the Black Sea and the Mediterranean, and the Russians
asked for revision of the international convention which controlled the
movement through the straits. They demanded a special position for Russia, with military bases in the Bosphorus and the Dardanelles. The move
—coupled with the demand for a trusteeship over the former Italian territory of Libya—would have made them a Mediterranean power. In addition, they began to push for cession of Turkish border regions—Kars

and Ardahan—and for revision of the Turkish border with Bulgaria in favor of the latter state, now, of course, Communist-dominated.

Through 1946 the propaganda and diplomatic barrage from Moscow increased in intensity and Turkey continued to maintain martial law. (The Russians made much of Turkish wartime relations with the Nazis.) In December 1946, the Turks took vigorous action against Communist groups in Turkey. Relations with Russia had never been more strained, and the Turks faced 1947 with justifiable apprehension. All through the nineteenth century the British had propped up the tottering Turkish Empire against Russian efforts to dismember it. Much of that empire had been lost when the Turks had sided with the Central Powers in World War I, and the Turks had turned again to England. But the winter of 1947 demonstrated the weakness of their supporter, and brought into question their whole policy. They might well be apprehensive about the future.

CHINA

While America tried to make peace, while the lines between Communist-held areas in Europe and the West hardened, while the West faced mounting resistance from areas outside Europe that it had hitherto dominated, the enormous area known as China knew no peace. During the first two years of the post-World War II period the Nationalist government of Chiang Kai-shek attempted to extend its control to all parts of the country, and to reincorporate under the Nationalist regime all Japanese-occupied regions. During this time the United States continued to support the Chinese Nationalists, but, doubting their ability to seize control of the whole area, and faced with pressure within the United States to reduce expenditures, the United States tried to persuade Nationalist and Communist Chinese to enter a coalition.

Throughout the nineteenth century increasing chaos had unsettled the last Chinese dynasty. Revolution within was compounded by pressure from without as the Great Powers maneuvered for spheres of influence in the form of grants of extraterritoriality, exclusive concessions, and outright cession of Chinese territory. Russia, Japan, Germany, France, Great Britain, and the United States vied with one another for influence and control. Early in the twentieth century the United States—drawn in after annexation of the Philippines led to American concern for order in the region—tried to establish the rules under which influence would be exercised: this was known as the Open Door policy in China. But the United States was prepared, if agreement could not be reached, to secure its own exclusive rights. However, not until Japan threatened to overrun all of

China and more of the Far East besides, at a time when American security was also threatened in the Atlantic, was the United States ready to take decisive action to enforce the Open Door.

In 1911 the Manchu Empire, which, unlike the Japanese, had been unable to cope with the strains imposed by contact with modernism, had come to an end. Sun Yat-sen, leader of the Kuomintang (National People's Party), guided the revolt that established a new Republic and attempted the task of modernization. Before his death in 1925, he was unable to establish the Republic's control over the whole area of China. Leadership passed to Chiang Kai-shek, who continued the effort to consolidate internal control and to eliminate great power rights. His break with the friendly Soviet Union also involved a break with the Communist faction within the Kuomintang. The Communists moved into opposition and ultimately established their own territorial base in North China and their own army. Japan, fearing a strong united China, invaded Manchuria in 1931 and easily overcame resistance. In 1937 it attacked China proper. Although an uneasy truce was established for a time between Communists and Nationalists in an attempt to promote a common effort against the Japanese invader, each party conducted hostilities against the invader in a way that would put *it* into the situation of best advantage in case of victory. The Chinese welcomed United States entry into World War II, but (as we have noted in Chapter II) they were disappointed by the United States decision to downgrade China as a main theatre of war. The United States, perplexed by how to deal with a government that could not give orders to its subordinates, had chosen to give priority to its operations in Europe and to MacArthur's island-hopping strategy; all efforts to work with the Chinese seemed to pay off too little. Dismayed, too, at how much Chinese effort went to continue the sporadic civil war, American missions tried to unite all the Chinese against the common enemy. Japanese success in the great offensive of 1944 further weakened the Nationalist government. The United States tried to compensate for its military strategy by building up China diplomatically—by giving it permanent membership and a veto in the United Nations Security Council, obtaining abolition of foreign rights in China, and securing Russian support for Chiang Kai-shek.

At end of the war the Nationalists had elements of both strength and weakness. They had a large army but it was disorganized, poorly trained, and paid only what its generals saw fit to disburse after pocketing what they wanted. (Some generals wanted little, but many wanted a great deal, and the government was virtually helpless.) Although the Japanese were defeated, the Nationalists who had to move into regions that had been occupied by the Japanese lacked the transport and administrative apparatus necessary for the takeover. The United States supplied the Nationalists with transport, but Russian troops in Manchuria hampered their movements and the Russians dismantled Japanese factories and removed machinery from the area. Although the looting supports the belief that Moscow was not very confident of a Communist victory, still Russian withdrawals sometimes facilitated the entry of Chinese Communist rather than Nationalist troops, and thus the Communists obtained a large stock of Japanese weapons.

More weakness was to be seen in the overall economic picture, marked by inflation and shortages. Worn out by war, the Nationalists were unable to cope with the inevitable black marketing and speculation. Disaffection was obvious, and observers were quick to note how much better morale and political and military discipline were among the Communists in the north. Communist propaganda capitalized heavily on these differences. They claimed—with much success—that they, not the Nationalists, were the true heirs of Sun Yat-sen's revolution. As the Nationalists, dependent on the wealthy for support, failed to institute reforms and turned to more and more repression of opposition, the opposition grew—especially among the educated classes.

American observers impressed upon Chiang the need for reforms, but he found it impossible to carry them out. Changing the structure of the army to make it more efficient would undercut the power of local commanders, who would thus resist reform. Land and fiscal reforms would hit many of the people providing the chief support of the Nationalist government.

The Nationalists proceeded in two directions. Strongly encouraged by the United States, they negotiated with the Communists. At the same time they moved into the north. In retrospect it may seem strange that anyone could expect an acceptable coalition to emerge from the talks, but within the context of the times it was not so unrealistic. Relations with the Communists appeared difficult but not impossible; there were coalitions in many countries (and in those never occupied by Russian armies, such as France, the Communists who had entered into the coalition with the hope of capturing more power failed in the end). The Nationalists themselves had long carried on negotiations. Late in 1944, a dispatch from General Hurley, the American ambassador in China, noted that Chiang Kai-shek believed the Soviet Union did not consider the Chinese Communist party to be Communist. Hurley thought Russia was not supporting the Chinese Communists, did not want civil war in China, and wanted better relations with the Nationalist government.

Negotiations for a coalition government failed in 1945. Communist demands proved too much for the Kuomintang leaders, to whom an arrangement preserving their separate Communist military power was unacceptable. The Communists in turn felt sure that any arrangement that did not do this would give the Nationalists the opportunity to destroy the Communist party. They had no reason to think that the Nationalists would provide a genuine democratic choice—any more than did the Nationalists think that the Communists would play according to the rules of any democratic game. Since the United States continued to provide financial and military aid after the end of the war—including the moving of troops into the north—the Communists were able to charge that the Nationalists were using support from outside to improve their strategic position against the Communists. At one point (in August 1945), after the signing of the Sino-Soviet Agreement of August 14 in which the Soviet Union agreed to treat the Nationalists as the sole legal government of China, Mao Tse-tung actually met with Chiang Kai-shek in the Nationalist capital of Chungking, where they did agree on principles. But as the troops of both sides maneuvered for position in the north and in Manchuria, negotiations for implementation broke down.

The United States remained committed to the support of the Nationalists, but many American observers became convinced that the Nationalists might well fail. Therefore, on November 27, 1945, President Truman announced that he had dispatched General George C. Marshall as his representative to try to bring about unification and a cessation of hostilities. Marshall brought with him all the distinction of having been Chief of Staff of one of the two most powerful armies in the world, and an immense personal prestige. But his mission failed: during 1946 the Nationalists continued to move into the North and to clash with Communist troops. Their apparent success strengthened their determination to proceed by force; their troops were three times a numerous as those of the Communists, and they seized city after city. They cleared the rail lines leading from China proper, and with an all-out offensive reached the peak of their success at the beginning of 1947.

It may therefore seem paradoxical that General Marshall, leaving China in January of 1947, announced the termination of his efforts to bring about a peaceful settlement. He apportioned blame to both sides and cited their deep mutual hostility. The statement held out hope for a new democratic constitution and the assumption of leadership by liberal elements, but the tone was one of failure. The reasons were not only the continuation of fighting, but also the growing conviction of many Americans that the Nationalist position was weaker than it appeared to be. The Communists had avoided any major engagements, had maintained their better-disciplined armies intact, while the Nationalists were operating through extended lines of communication that passed through country they could not hold. Their forces in the urban rail centers could not gain control of the countryside.

Thus, at the outset of 1947, when Marshall returned to become the new American Secretary of State, the situation in China was still unsettled. Though the Nationalists seemed to be winning, the base of their victory was precarious.

KOREA AND JAPAN

In Korea and Japan, as in Europe, military occupation was the decisive factor in determining subsequent political alignments.

In Japan, General MacArthur, acting for the American government, resisted the efforts of all other wartime Allies to obtain a real voice in occupation policy.

Unlike Allied commanders in Germany, MacArthur still had an intact Japanese administrative apparatus to work through. It was greatly weakened by the American policy of purging the old, militarist leadership, since few new leaders existed who were dedicated to democratic ideals, but MacArthur proceeded with reforms that eliminated old leaders and created new political forms. Administration—particularly police administration—was decentralized, and on January 3, 1947, after one Japanese draft for a new constitution had been rejected, the Japanese adopted a second draft drawn up by the Americans. This constitution established popular sovereignty and Western-style civil liberties. If the Japanese could not be democratic by themselves, democracy would be imposed on them from above In accordance with ideas about the relationship of social and political forms to aggressive foreign policy, the Americans began to dissolve the large Japanese business cartels, or *zaibatsu,* that had dominated Japanese economic life, and inserted a clause in the new constitution that renounced forever the use of armed force in the conduct of foreign policy. Communist leaders were allowed to resume active political life, and trade union activity was encouraged.

Yet, just as in Germany, reform began to falter almost as soon as it began, principally because of the change in world outlook that was shaped by the events of this period. Both Japan and Germany began to be seen as outposts on the edge of a menacing Soviet bloc, and as outposts whose cooperation might be needed. In both countries the attempt to purge old leadership had provoked resentment—more in Germany, where all democratic political parties disassociated themselves from "denazification" and the punishment of Nazi leadership. But in Japan, too, reform was often seen as revenge, as the imposition of an alien pattern by a victor, as a question not of right, but of might, and the change in foreign policy orientation tended to reinforce cynicism.

For Korea, the story was different. The Allies chose the 38th parallel as the arbitrary demarcation line between Russian occupation in the North and American occupation in the South. Korea had long been the subject of great power rivalry between China and Japan; Japan had decisively defeated and eliminated China in 1895, and then, in 1905, eliminated the new contender, Russia. Outright annexation of Korea followed in 1910, and only with World War II did Korea face the prospect of independence. But the occupying authorities made no progress in setting up joint administrative organs on the spot, so in December 1945 they turned the problem over to the Council of Foreign Ministers meeting in Moscow. The Council established a new joint commission to help form a provisional Korean democratic government. The commission failed to agree, however, on what groups within Korea could be considered democratic enough to be consulted in planning the provisional government. Each power feared the consequence of a hostile united Korea, and soon, as in Eastern Europe, the Russians, who had cultivated native Communist groups, installed a puppet regime in the North.

In the south the United States found that the strongest group was led by Syngman Rhee, a long-time Korean nationalist-in-exile. But Rhee was impatient with the failure to bring about Korean unification and annoyed by continued American occupation. The United States government found itself maintaining a costly operation while under pressure to economize and at a time when demobilization had placed a premium on manpower. In return it received Korean hostility. If the burden could be laid down, the charge that the Korean occupation represented American imperialism would be rebutted. Thus, in 1947, the administration determined to call on the United Nations to handle the problem of Korea. The United Nations, unfortunately, would find it no easy problem.

THE ORGANIZATION OF AMERICAN STATES

The fate of certain areas of the world might have been settled decisively by military occupation as a result of military operations, and that of others might be in doubt. In the Americas, however, the United States—with the concurrence of Latin American leaders—tried to leave no doubt as to what the future should hold, through creation of a genuinely multilateral American security system.

The idea of the "Western Hemisphere" and the vision of a special relationship among the countries in it has long existed in American writing and political discourse, but ideal and reality were very different. In 1823 the United States unilaterally proclaimed the "Monroe Doctrine"—a Presidential declaration to the effect that the United States would not countenance any further European colonization in the Americas, nor permit attempts to reconquer Latin countries that had successfully revolted against European powers. There was little force or genuine will to back it up, little intent on the part of European powers to attempt any further interference in the Americas, and Britain had made clear that its navy would prevent any such attempts for reasons of its own. It became a part of United States mythology, however, and 70 years later, at the turn of the century, when a series of actual and potential European interventions took place (very much spurred by Imperial Germany's naval ambitions vis-à-vis Great Britain), the United States used the Doctrine as a basis for a new interventionist policy, designed to counter European interventions. It would, for example, prevent European states from using the excuse of bond defaults in Latin states to justify their extending a control over the defaulting state by themselves acting as policemen and collecting the debt. In addition, the building of the Panama Canal for trade and strategy reasons then gave the United States an interest in the security of approaches to the Canal—that is, in the security of the Caribbean. Once the German threat had receded after World War I, however, the United States gradually abandoned interventionism, and by the late 1930s accepted defaults and nationalizations in the Latin area with no more than diplomatic representation. It attempted to change the image created by the period of domination and intervention through following the policy of what Franklin D. Roosevelt called "the Good Neighbor."

The attempt to create a Western Hemisphere community, however, was hampered by the difference between strong and weak, rich and poor, and the enormous internal economic and social differences between the Latin American countries and the United States as well. Although the former vary greatly, they have the common heritage of a Hispanic and Catholic colonial past, with its ethos radically different from the Anglo-Saxon society to the north. The contrast is not only between Protestant and Catholic, but also between capitalist and aristocrat, civilian and military control of government, a more-or-less fluid, egalitarian society devoted to technology, and a stratified society characterized by a vast gap between the few rich and the many poor, especially the peasants.

When trade, investment, and travel take place between those that are rich and those that are less rich, although both may benefit, the poorer may only feel exploited. This happened in Latin America. Moreover, the gains from trade too often went to a small group that dominated politically, and part of their continued ability to dominate lay in the wealth amassed from trade with the Colossus of the North.

The depression in the 1930s had a strong impact on Latin American countries since many of them depended on the export of a single raw material or commodity whose price was likely to vary radically on the world market. In spite of the spread of liberal ideas in the nineteenth century, the typical form of Latin American government remained a military dictatorship. Only in Argentina, Chile, Uruguay, and Brazil did a growing middle and professional class appear to create conditions for the growth of somewhat liberal political parties and a free press. The Mexican revolution that began in 1910, and lasted for decades, was a genuine social revolution, which brought the masses into political participation for the first time. It also inspired other groups throughout Latin America. But the depression brought an alliance between radicalism and mass movements with military power all through the area, and a growth of fascism and more or less fascist dictatorships: Italy, Spain, and Germany exemplified how mass politics could be harnessed to dictatorship rather than democracy, and their influence was strong. In response, left wing radicalism also grew. Only Chile, Uruguay, and Colombia maintained liberal forms of government. The Good Neighbor policy of the Colossus of the North had little effect on these developments, although the lowering of American tariffs through the Reciprocal Trade Agreements Act and United States creation of the Export-Import Bank, which helped finance American exports to the area, were of some aid in easing relations.

World War II helped even more by creating a rich market for the export of Latin American commodities. Under pressure from the United States and its allies and—after 1942—in response to the fairly certain defeat of the fascist powers, the left tended to gain power. Only in Argentina, whose exports of beef and wheat had long made it competitive with the United States, did a fascist form of government emerge with Peron's seizure of power in 1945.

With the war's end and the emergence of plans for a postwar United Nations world, the governments of Latin America and the United States shared interest in the creation of a stronger regional grouping. If the United States really intended to participate in a world organization, the votes of the Latin American states would mean something to it. If all the nations in the area voted as a bloc, the smaller states would thus have a louder voice in international politics. At a meeting in Mexico City in February and March 1945, the American states signed the Act of Chapultepec, which promised the creation of an inter-American security system. Thus armed, they proceeded to strengthen the regional provisions of the United Nations Charter at the San Francisco conference where they also joined with smaller states from other areas to broaden the authority of the General Assembly. But difficulties had arisen. The Mexico City conference had been limited to those "cooperating in the war effort," in order to exclude Argentina, which had given and continued to give aid and comfort to the Axis powers. The United States felt that Argentina had to participate in any regional system—otherwise Argentina might expert a strong counterpull for many Latin American states, and might head its own bloc. Still, the United States could hardly support Peron. In subsequent months severe diplomatic pressure was put on Peron by publishing documents proving his complicity with the Axis, and denunciation of him by the American Ambassador, Spruille Braden, who also encouraged opposition to Peron.

But the intervention failed; Peron survived the attempt to overthrow his military regime and, with the aid of the trade unions, he consolidated his power in October 1945. The United States was compelled to accept the situation and in return Peron made some conciliatory gestures. By August 1947, after several postponements, it became possible to convene the Inter-American Conference for the Maintenance of Continental Peace and Security at Rio de Janeiro. Here, after several unsuccessful Argentine attempts to weaken its terms, the American states drafted a security treaty binding themselves to settle their disputes by peaceful means, declaring that an attack on one of them by an outsider would be treated as an attack on all of them and, finally, setting up an inter-American security system in which a meeting of foreign ministers, by a two-thirds vote, could enforce sanctions against any American state committing aggression against another. The next year, at Bogota, Colombia, the same states drew up and signed the Charter of the Organization of the American States (OAS), which created a permanent multilateral political organization for the region. It set up a permanent Council at the Ambassadorial level (in Washington), created organs that would meet periodically (the Inter-American Conference and the Meeting of Consultation of Ministers of Foreign Affairs), made the already existing Pan-American Union a permanent Secretariat for the OAS, and defined the relations of the OAS to various regional specialized and technical agencies. It spelled out the rights and obligations of American states and defined the machinery for the settlement of disputes. Thus, unlike NATO, where political and economic cooperation were aimed at creating military strength against an external enemy, the OAS was far more concerned with establishing a regional collective security system designed to settle quarrels among its members and prevent them from exploding into war.

The Rio Pact (passed pursuant to the Act of Chapultepec of 1945) and the Bogota Charter also represented in part attempts to reconcile the overwhelming economic and military power and influence of the United States with the desires of Latin states to be politically independent and legally sovereign. Nothing more than partial success could be hoped for in the endeavor.

While political and security relations were made multilateral, the United States also continued warborn bilateral military cooperation with Latin American states. Throughout the 1940s it continued to provide military training to their armed forces and military equipment on a modest scale. The action was presumably taken to strengthen the security of the Americas. But military aid appeared to ignore the fact that a well-equipped and trained military group has internal political significance far beyond its numbers in almost any Latin state, and in the years after World War II the military continued to play an active political role.

DISARMAMENT NEGOTIATIONS

The power of the atomic bomb—demonstrated at Hiroshima and Nagasaki—was awesome. The political developments that indicated growing tension between Western powers and the Soviet Union, also evoked a terrible dismay: was it possible that not only had World War II failed to produce a new and better world of harmony, but that it might now be superseded by an infinitely worse World War III? To many, disarmament now seemed more important than ever; it also seemed possible. Fascism, with its doctrine of the right of the strongest, was dead; the Soviet Union, which had suffered extensive damage in the war, would have to devote its resources to reconstruction. Thus Russia would undoubtedly welcome a system that would eliminate the reliance on military force, particularly when force now included atomic weapons. The very existence of the bomb might now force nations to abandon war as a means of foreign policy. The attitude of expectancy has been well summed up in the phrase of James Phinney Baxter: the atomic bomb had "blasted the web of history and, like the discovery of fire, severed the past from the present."

The first major step took place in November 1945 when the United States, the United Kingdom, and Canada, who had all participated in development of the weapon, issued a joint statement offering "to share, on a reciprocal basis with others of the United Nations, detailed information concerning the practical industrial application of atomic energy just as soon as effective enforceable safeguards against its use for destructive purposes can be devised." The offer to share the secret of the bomb led to a widening of the debate over the wisdom of the move. Many Americans asked whether the United States should not keep the secret. President Truman's advisers, however, did not expect the "secret" to be kept for long; the Soviet Union would learn to develop the weapon within several years. In the meantime, if the move were not taken, disarmament and security would be unattainable. Could any nation trust the United States completely? Time, therefore, was short; it had become imperative to establish a system of international control so that the United States could afford to "give up" the bomb. Questioning senators were reassured: the United States would continue to hold it as a "sacred trust" until sufficient controls had *first* been established.

In December, with the Anglo-American-Canadian declaration as the impetus, the Russians agreed to the establishment of an Atomic Energy Commission of the United Nations. It was created on January 26, 1946, and directed to report to the Security Council. On June 14 it received the American proposal, the Baruch Plan, named for the American on the Commission, Bernard Baruch. Five days later the Russians presented their own plan.

The Baruch Plan proposed an International Atomic Development Authority to which would be entrusted "managerial control or ownership of all atomic energy activities potentially dangerous to world security," the "power of control, inspect and license all other atomic activities," and which would itself be "the world's leader in the field of atomic knowledge and development." To this radical proposal to separate atomic matters from national sovereignty, the Russians answered with a suggestion for immediate prohibition of the use, production, and accumulation of atomic weapons and for the destruction of existing stockpiles within three months after the conventions had come into force. Each nation would enact domestic legislation to punish violators of the convention.

All through 1946, attempts to negotiate on these matters proved fruitless. The Russians insisted that there need be no prior provision for inspection and control, and the Americans insisted precisely on the need for a thoroughgoing system of control before any further action. The Baruch Plan, the Russians argued, since it obviated the all-important veto, was a capitalist plot to dominate the Soviet Union through an international monopoly in which capitalist powers would always have a majority voice, and where their agents could spy on all aspects of industrial and military activity. In addition, the United States would retain its weapons while the system was being put into effect, and could refuse to release them to the new agency once its control mechanisms had been set up and had penetrated the Soviet Union. Besides (though they did not say so), the plan would have prevented their own national atomic research and development. On December 31, the Commission submitted to the Security Council its first report, which had been adopted by a vote of 10 to 0, the Soviet Union and Poland abstaining. The report recommended that the Security Council accept substantially the Baruch Plan. The Security Council requested the Commission to undertake further study and make recommendations. In the following years it made no progress, and in 1949 the Soviet Union exploded its first atomic bomb.

CONCLUSION

The first year and a half of the postwar period witnessed the end of the
war-born alliance. As European recovery faltered and the attempt to re-
establish European rule in the rest of the world failed, the United States
and Russia emerged as superpowers. But both moved cautiously. Within
the United States, political pressure to throw off wartime controls, to de-
mobilize, and to cut taxes all combined with the lingering isolationist im-
pulse, distrust of Britain, and some feeling that Russia was being thrust
into the role of the villain. The result was considerable confusion about
what the United States ought to do beyond providing some relief. But
while Europe and the United States attempted to consolidate their hold
on the non-Russian part of the world, they parried the thrusts of Russia
into the Mediterranean, Iran, West Germany, and Japan. The Russians
proceeded to consolidate their hold on their own sphere and block Western intervention into it.

Those who supported an all-out effort to get along with Russia had
strong arguments; the alternative was dreadful to contemplate and no one
could choose it until it was certain that cooperation was impossible. In
the light of history, Russians had good reason to fear the West; even
more, the emergence of two superpowers surrounded by weak states appeared to create a situation in which hostile competition was far more
likely to emerge than in the multipower situation of past centuries. Many
people believed, therefore, that greater efforts were required to avert a
conflict that neither power wanted, a conflict provoked not by Russian
arms, but by the nature of the bipolar situation. Finally, many argued
that Russia was bound to devote most of its efforts to internal reconstruction. The war had devastated the Soviet Union: its resources for reconstruction were limited, and it had expressed a desire for a large American loan. If America were willing to aid Russian reconstruction, would
this not alleviate Soviet fears and provide some cementing ties? Were not
the everyday clashes—of which many Americans and the American press
were making so much—merely the kind of constant political maneuvering that normally takes place on the international scene, but whose importance the United States, emerging from its long period of isolation,
tended to magnify? And were the Russians not justified in fearing a United States armed with the atomic bomb, an enormous industrial capacity,
and bases in Europe and the Far East? Was not their consolidation of the
Soviet bloc merely a rather harsh move for security purposes?

Within Europe many people asked the same questions. But, even
more, most people were more concerned with reconstruction efforts, or
merely with recreating an acceptable private life after the shattering war

years. In France, de Gaulle—who had aspired to great power status for France and had seen an opportunity to become an arbiter between the new giants—resigned in disgust when many of the old political forces that had governed the Third Republic reemerged. In 1946 France had adopted a constitution favored by only one-third of the voting public; it was governed by an uneasy coalition of Christian-Democrats, Socialists, and Communists; it had already begun to fight in Indochina. French leaders found that their capacity to influence the international situation was limited; neither the United States nor the Soviet Union appeared to pay much attention to them, and their foreign policy goal of keeping Germany divided and weak was blocked by growing Russian-American rivalry for the allegiance of the Germans.

In Britain the Labour government, facing an unprecedented economic crisis, had worked out a policy of austerity—keeping consumption down so that Britain could import only what was strictly needed, and export enough to pay for essential imports. At the same time, the British were trying to reequip worn-out industries and to rebuild investments overseas, and also maintain the posture of a great power. By mid-winter 1947 the effort had failed. Many Labour supporters had long thought that capitalism was the main cause of international conflict and that a Socialist government would be able to get along better with everyone. But Ernest Bevin, Labour's Foreign Secretary, was less sanguine than many staunch American capitalists about how well the West could get along with the Russians.

In Russia the war had been the occasion for relaxation of controls on art, literature, religious practice and on contacts with the West, apparently to enlist support of the Russian people against the German invader. Now that the war was over, the restraints were reimposed in even more brutal and rigid form. Dissent was suppressed, reprisals taken against those whose participation in the war effort had been halfhearted, and prisoners of war were joined in labor camps by millions of Russians. Economic reconstruction concentrated on heavy industry rather than on consumer goods. The dread secret police who ran the slave-labor camps emerged as the largest Russian employer. Men under arms were largely demobilized, but the extent of demobilization was concealed, and the Red Army never decreased to less than something over three million men.

Although the Western powers, particularly the United States, were painted in the darkest colors in the Soviet press, Soviet foreign policy was curiously halting. In Iran the Russians retreated. They abandoned some of their goals in other areas. In Eastern Europe consolidation proceeded spasmodically; in the Far East Stalin did not expect a Chinese Communist victory and was ready to work with the Nationalist government while awaiting the outcome. Soviet strength only became clear as the weakness in surrounding territories was felt. Stalin formally annexed only territories to which Russia had some historical claim. Nevertheless, the Soviet Union was not ready to renounce all claims to what it felt were war-born rights in areas outside of the Soviet Union. The winter of 1947 revealed the weakness of former world powers and the extent of world chaos. Stalin faced a situation that gave him unprecedented opportunity for widespread gains, whose achievement, however, depended on two factors: what he *really* wanted, and how Americans would view this situation and decide to act upon their view.

THREE
1947—1950 THE COLD WAR, BIPOLARIZATION, AND CONTAINMENT

Every year is heralded at its outset as a turning point in world affairs—a year during which great decisions must be made, a year that will determine the course of history. Unlike most years, 1947 was actually one of these. In 1947 the Truman administration, in a series of radical new policies, crystallized a view of the world scene, and evolved a new role for the United States. Despite subsequent criticism, the overall policy, summed up in the term "containment," was followed by succeeding administrations.

Containment was based on the assumption that the Soviet Union was bent on a course of limitless expansion, and that this Soviet policy was inspired by the Communist world view of inevitable conflict between capitalist and "socialist" societies.* The containment policy, embodied in many American actions, assumed that the Soviet Union would therefore press outward by every possible means, and that its pressures must be met with positions of strength. In geopolitical terms, containment involved a United States commitment to defend the "rimlands" of the Eurasian continent against pressures from the "heartland." In the period 1947–50, it came to have two aspects: enough military power should be developed to meet Soviet military thrusts or their threat, and the economic, social, and political health of the non-Soviet world would be strengthened to impede Soviet expansion through subversion and revolution by native Communist movements led by Moscow. Proponents of containment hoped that ultimately, the Soviet Union, finding expansion impossible, would relax its efforts as revolutionary dynamism and certainty of world victory faded. As the interpreters of Soviet ideology found that the capitalist world did not behave according to Marxist-Leninist categories, they would be forced to revise their ideology to conform to reality.

* The term "socialist" must be used cautiously. In Communist parlance, only Communist-bloc countries are truly socialist. The Labour government, in England, which considered itself socialist, was therefore by definition not.

Thus, in 1947 the United States launched a program of economic and military aid to Greece and Turkey accompanied by the Truman Doctrine that "it must be the policy of the United States to support free peoples who are resisting attempted subjugation by armed minorities or by outside pressures." Later in the year the Marshall Plan began, a long-range commitment of large-scale economic aid to help rebuild the faltering economies of Europe. In 1948 the impetus of the previous year led to the formation of the North Atlantic Treaty Organization (NATO), and the commitment of American troops to the defense of Europe, along with large-scale programs of military aid. Then, in 1949 President Truman launched the program of technical aid to underdeveloped countries, known as the Point Four Program. The policy of containment, with its commitments, was underway.

The Soviet Union responded by hastening to consolidate Communist control in Eastern European countries, by abetting Communist attempts at take-overs in France and Italy, by bringing about a coup putting Czechoslovakia definitely into the Soviet orbit, and by a squeeze on the Allied outpost in Berlin. But tightened Soviet control led to the break by Tito's Yugoslavia and the subsequent constant threat of "Titoism" within the Soviet bloc, which foreshadowed some of the future complexities of "bipolarism."

The move to unify Europe gathered steam, under the impetus of the Marshall Plan and the growing awareness that a world dominated by several powers had been replaced by one where there were only two superpowers. In the Middle East the continued British withdrawal led to the Palestine War, the emergence of independent Israel, and new bitterness toward the West. In other parts of the world the march toward independence continued complicated by Communist-led insurrections following upon a Russian-sponsored meeting of Asian Communist parties in Calcutta, in February of 1948; in China, it took the form of a Chinese Communist victory over the Nationalists.

AMERICAN INITIATIVES

In January 1947, General George C. Marshall, recently returned from his mission in China, became Secretary of State. His first policy task was to prepare for the forthcoming Council of Foreign Ministers meeting, to be held in Moscow in March, presumably to draft peace treaties for Germany and Austria. In the weeks before Marshall left for Moscow, the seriousness of the European situation became apparent. At the same time the new Republican-controlled Congress was in a mood to cut drastically the administration's budget demands. On Friday, February 21, 1947—

some three weeks before the Moscow Conference—the British government delivered to the State Department a note which, in effect, declared Britain's inability to continue the effort to stabilize the eastern Mediterranean area over which it had gained control during the last century. Greece would need a minimum of $240 to $280 million during 1947 to enable it to cope with the Communist guerrillas and keep its people from starving. It would also need substantial aid in subsequent years. Without this aid, Greece would simply collapse. The British stated flatly that they would be unable to meet Greek needs after March 31. Turkey's army, although kept in a state of readiness, desperately needed modernization. In late 1946 an American naval task force on a courtesy visit to the country had bolstered Turkish resistance to Soviet demands. But if the Russians continued to press them, the Turks could offer little military resistance. Britain could no longer provide the financial resources either to strengthen the Turkish economy or reequip its armies.

Within the administrative branch of the American government there was quick agreement that in some way it must step into the breach, that the loss of Greece and Turkey to the Communists would jeopardize not only the whole of the Middle East but also Europe. The United States would have to give long-range economic and military aid to Greece and Turkey, notwithstanding other troubled areas like Korea and China, and despite the limitations of American military and economic resources and the strong pressure for economy in government. In conversations with Senate and House leaders, the administration determined that strong public appeal was necessary and that unless the wording of the commitment to aid Greece and Turkey were stated within a broader context of aid to free peoples everywhere public support for this particular case would be hard to gain.

Thus, when President Truman made a dramatic appearance before a joint meeting of Congress on March 12 to request funds and announce the new policy, he spoke in terms of an ideological confrontation between the two systems. The debate that followed revealed considerable opposition. From Republican Senators Robert Taft and Everett Dirksen on the right to former Vice-President Henry Wallace on the left—and from many in between—came the attack. This was a proposal to pull more British chestnuts out of the fire. It was nonsense to invoke the slogans, "free people" and sustaining "democracy," neither Greece nor Turkey were democratic countries. The administration was asking for a blank check. The policy was a retrogression to the power politics that had previously characterized Europe. It would divide the world into two armed camps and lead to war, and it bypassed the United Nations. The United States would be intervening in the domestic affairs of Greece, since the plan involved the presence of a large American aid mission to carry out administrative and military reorganization.

It was not easy to answer the criticisms that the policy bypassed the United Nations. The Greek problem had been before the United Nations Security Council several times. Once the Soviet Union had complained of continued presence of British troops, and when the Russians had repeated the complaint, the British replied heatedly that Communist guerrilla attempts to impede elections were responsible for British presence. In December 1946, a Greek complaint that Albania, Bulgaria, and Yugoslavia were harboring the guerrillas resulted in the creation of a Security Council Committee of Inquiry which was actually *in* Greece at the time of the American debate. The administration, however, felt there was no time to work through the United Nations, that the UN Commission would be hamstrung by the Soviet Union, and that the United Nations was not the proper organ for the task that had to be performed. But it did accept modifications of the Congressional aid bill. Provisions were added that the President could be empowered to withdraw American aid if and when the United Nations could assume the necessary tasks and notified the United States to that effect, if the Greek and Turkish Governments asked for an end to the aid, or if the President found that other intergovernmental agencies were accomplishing the purposes of the Act.

Congress approved the program, along with a variety of other appropriations for relief and rehabilitation, for countries like Korea, Austria, Japan, and Germany and for the International Refugee Organization. But it served notice upon the administration that the piecemeal approach was not satisfactory.

In June and July bilateral agreements were signed with Greece and Turkey and the programs of technical, military, and economic aid got under way. The economic aid programs remained independent for only nine months; in 1948 they came within the purview of the new Economic Cooperation Administration of the Marshall Plan (see below). But the military program had economic effects also, since it provided for the modernization of roads and transportation, as well as military reequipment and training. It was a success. By the end of June 1949, Greece had been almost cleared of guerrillas. The program, however, was not completely effective until July 1949, when Yugoslavia's Communist boss, Marshal Tito, successfully defied Stalin, and closed the Yugoslav border to Greek Communist guerrillas.

Success of the Turkish program was harder to measure, but observers reported that the effectiveness of the Turkish armed forces had increased, while the pressure on the Turkish budget of maintaining them was relieved.

THE MOSCOW CONFERENCE

Part of the immediate opposition to the Truman Doctrine arose because it was announced at the very moment when Secretary Marshall was in Moscow for the Conference of the Council of Foreign Ministers. Opponents suggested that a declaration of ideological warfare at this point would surely wreck the conference. But the discussions that took place in Moscow support the view that the positions of both nations were, for the moment at least, irreconcilable.

The conference, lasting from March 10, 1947 to April 24, was supposed to draft peace treaties for Germany and Austria; the United States also proposed a German disarmament treaty, designed to see if alleviation of Russian fears might lead to a relaxation of Russian pressures. But the gap could not be bridged. The United States and Britain wanted a higher level of industry in Germany than the French did. The former felt that European recovery depended on a German contribution. For political reasons the French wanted the level kept low, but they also wanted a higher share of German coal (and more would be left for export if German steel production were greatly restricted). More important, the Russians continued to insist on a high level of reparations from current production while the Western powers argued that that would mean they would be pumping in goods at one end while the Russians went on siphoning them off at the other. The Russians now urged the creation of a strong central authority, where the Communist-dominated East Zone Socialist Unity party would presumably have a leading role. The French, although they had had to abandon their earlier desire for dismemberment of Germany, wanted to begin the reconstruction of political units at the local level, with central units to come later. In between stood the British and Americans, who wanted economic unity and the central political organs this required, but wanted them to be based on a federalism that would leave much power to the states. The West, too, tried to argue about the boundary with Poland, while the Russians wanted it accepted as final. France wavered, since Foreign Minister Georges Bidault wanted the coal-rich Saar excluded from Germany (possibly to be incorporated into France) and also demanded international control of the Ruhr and the Rhineland. The Russians might support France's demands if France accepted the new Polish boundaries, and the French certainly cared little for German feelings in the matter. The Russians tried to bargain: they would work for unity if the British and Americans halted actions to merge their zones, and if they accepted Soviet claims about reparations and the Polish border. But no bargain could be concluded.

There was to be a subsequent meeting of the Foreign Ministers in

November, where procedure would be discussed (should there be a central German government before a peace treaty, or a peace treaty before a central German government?) Here Western demands for economic unity countered Soviet demands for reparations and the ending of joint British and American administration of the West-zone. The Moscow meeting of March and April had really settled the issue of Germany: it would remain divided. Events of the months between the Moscow and London Conferences made sure that the London meeting was only an exercise in futile countercharges.

THE MARSHALL PLAN

While aid to Greece and Turkey and Truman's speech were being mapped out, further long-range studies of the European situation were begun in Washington. The work was hastened by the dismal comedy of the Moscow Conference and by the growing crisis in Hungary. On February 26, Kovaks, the secretary general of the Smallholders' party, was arrested by the Russians after the Hungarian Parliament had refused to bow to pressure to act against him; a general purge of the party followed, and Western protests were to no avail. Open intervention by Russia culminated on August 31 in rigged elections and the subsequent elimination of all further opposition to the Communists.

On May 8, 1947, Under-Secretary of State Dean Acheson, in a speech to a group of business and agricultural leaders, anticipated the thinking of the administration on the question of long-range aid. He noted the imbalance between what other countries needed from the United States and what they could sell to it, and described United States interest in seeing the enormous gap filled. Then, on June 5, General Marshall delivered the Commencement Address at Harvard that initiated the European Recovery Program.

In his speech, Marshall again reviewed the situation. It was logical, he maintained, for the United States to help fill the gap between European requirements and what they could afford to pay—the alternative would be "economic, social, and political deterioration of a very grave character." He added that this policy was "directed not against any country or doctrine but against hunger, poverty, desperation, and chaos," and that European nations should cooperatively work out programs matched to their requirements.

The speech stressed cooperation among European nations. More than that, in deliberate contrast to Truman's speech announcing the program of aid to Greece and Turkey, it concentrated on economic factors. It declared that poverty and chaos—not Russia or Communism—were the enemies. In fact, the speech appeared to allow for Russian and Eastern European cooperation in development of the new venture.

This aspect was quite deliberate. On the one hand, it was designed to counter growing European and American criticism that the Truman Doctrine was "negative"—that it was only anti-something, that it was a declaration of ideological war. Though it was all very well to be anti-Communist, this would not strike at the roots of the problem, which was economic chaos in Europe. It was hoped the Marshall initiative would be looked on as "positive," as indeed it was. Moreover, Western European leaders still saw East Europe as a necessary supplier of grain, coal, and oil for their own countries; the economy of the West was not viable without the East. The Marshall Plan put the burden of choice on the Russians: participation in the Plan would entangle their economy with the West and make it more difficult for them to follow the belligerent path they appeared to be taking. It offered them the possibility of peaceful and mutually beneficial cooperation instead of mutual hostility. Despite the clashes we have so far noted, Stalin had continued to give indications that Russia wanted and needed peace and expanded trade. It was still possible to argue that Russia had expected a more or less free hand in the defensive zone it occupied, wanted to prevent a strong coalition forming against it, and expected that the capitalist United States—to avert a depression—would need trade with the Soviet Union. Also, the Soviet Union did not have the atomic bomb while the United States did. If these were the factors uppermost in the minds of some Soviet leaders, they might still be induced to sacrifice long-term Communist goals for short-term economic needs. In the past they had made internal compromises; egalitarianism and the withering of the state had been postponed indefinitely in the interest of building a strong industrial state. On the other hand, if the Russians fought Marshall's initiative, it would put the onus on them.

In Europe, the British and French Foreign Ministers, Bevin and Bidault, took the initiative and invited Foreign Minister Molotov to Paris for a conference at the end of June to consider the American offer. Here it became clear that the Russians would consider the offer only on one condition: that its cooperative aspect assume a very minor role. They proposed that each state take stock of its needs, which would then be reconciled or scaled down in terms of what the United States was prepared to offer. Each would then go ahead with its own plans. The French and British argued that the whole proposal depended on a *European* inventory of needs, resources, and possibilities of mutual aid. The result was a deadlock. Russia dropped out.

What about the rest of Eastern Europe? On July 4, the British and

French invited twenty-two other countries to attend a conference in Paris on July 12; the invitation was also sent to the Soviet Embassy with an expression of hope that Soviet refusal was not final. But when the conference convened eight countries failed to attend: Finland, Poland, Czechoslovakia, Hungary, Yugoslavia, Rumania, Bulgaria, and Albania. Their presence had been forbidden by the Soviet Union.

Though it was hard to accept a division of Europe that they had been trying for two years to avoid, the European representatives gathered at Paris created the Committee of European Economic Cooperation and rapidly drew up a four-year projection of the European economy and its needs. Given the uncertainties of the situation, the projection had to be rough. For a four-year period, it forecast a balance of payments shortage of $29 billion—an enormous sum. In addition there were differences among the participating countries. France was still reluctant to see the German economy revive; others saw German reconstruction as imperative to their own rebuilding. There was American criticism, also. The report was too much of a shopping list and not enough of a survey of how intra-European trade could be increased; it failed to specify the fiscal and financial measures European countries could take, failed to propose specific reductions in their trade barriers. The report was revised and in September of 1947 presented to the United States. It now forecast a gap of $22 billion, 3 billion of which could be filled from the International Bank for Reconstruction and Development, leaving 19 billion to come from the United States.

Congressional and Presidential committees reviewed the European material, surveyed the general world trade picture, and prepared estimates of the impact of the possible program on the American economy. On the basis of these and the European suggestion, the administration prepared a program to present to Congress in January 1948.

Events in Europe hastened action by the administration. In June 1947, Italy was forced to stop all dollar expenditures except for coal, cereals, and petroleum products. France followed suit two months later. Economists expected that both would run out of foreign exchange by December 1947. Consequently, President Truman asked for, and received from Congress, interim aid of close to $600 million as well as extra aid for Germany. The request—which was for relief, not reconstruction—was buttressed by a review of the planning under way for the European Recovery Program, a plan which would presumably obviate the need for relief in the future.

In February 1948 came the coup in Czechoslovakia that installed a Communist government and decisively moved that sorely tried land into the Soviet bloc (see p. 83) . In France, Communist-led strikes and riots gave evidence of the Party's determination that it should be taken back into the government. As a result, Congress' interest in the Marshall Plan was quickened. On April 2 (some two weeks before the Italian general elections in which it was suspected that the Communists would make a strong showing) , Congress passed the Economic Cooperation Act.

There was much battling over the scale of the aid, the way it would be administered, the forms it would take, the countries that would be eligible for it. Congress agreed to authorize expenditures over a four-year period, but insisted on appropriating the money each year. The actual funds made available the first year (including loans) totaled $6220 million, the second year, $4060 million; and the third year, $2254 million.

From the American side, the European Recovery Program (ERP) was carried out by a new agency, the European Cooperation Administration (ECA) headed by industrialist Paul Hoffman. At the insistence of a distrustful Congress, it was separate from the Department of State. The enabling legislation had specified that the aim of the Act was to encourage unification of Europe. Hoffman spelled this out:

> The long-range goal I put before the OEEC was the effective integration of the economy of Western Europe—the building of a single market of 270 million consumers, in which quantitative restrictions on the movement of goods, monetary barriers to the flow of payments and eventually all tariffs should be permanently swept away.

It did not happen.

But out of the Marshall Plan—once called the greatest creative act of statesmanship of modern times—grew the Organization for European Economic Cooperation and the European Payments Union, both made up of participating members. The former undertook studies, suggested legislation and treaties, and supervised the various forms of cooperation devised under the spur of the Marshall Plan. The latter helped the shaky European currencies to achieve stability and permitted multilateral clearing of payments, thus arresting the long-term trend toward bilateral clearing of payments and trade; the restoration of multilateral rather than bilateral trade in Europe was one of the great achievements of the postwar era. By helping to strengthen European economies, it subsequently helped them to participate fully in the wider-spread United Nations agencies—the International Monetary Fund and General Agreement on Tariffs and Trade. Until the success of the Marshall Plan, the inability of Europe to export and its desperate need for imports had kept the multilateral features of the two organizations in abeyance. Once Europe, revitalized by the Marshall Plan, had recovered and even begun to exceed prewar production levels, European countries could take full part, and at least some of the hopes for the world envisaged during World War II began to materialize. Europe was now free of many inhibiting trade restrictions that had been resorted to in the 1920s and 1930s during periods of inflation and depression.

The OEEC and the EPU were substantial steps in the right direction. Europeans took a further step when German production resumed after the currency reform of 1948 and it became clear that despite French objections German economic expansion would take place. As a consequence, the French proposed a revolutionary scheme, the European Coal and Steel Community—the so-called Schuman Plan.

Most people found it difficult to understand what the Schuman Plan called for, but they were ready to applaud any initiative toward European unity; the time was ripe for the many groups to work for unification in some form. The Schuman Plan (which took eighteen months to negotiate) eventually removed substantially from national sovereignty the coal and steel industries of six continental European countries: France, Italy, Germany, Belgium, the Netherlands, and Luxembourg. It created a complex of supranational institutions to effect the common market in coal and iron and steel. Ultimately, the success of the European Coal and Steel Community inspired another and more important venture—a European customs union that developed in the late 1950s.

The Marshall Plan did much more than give the impetus to integrate the economies of European countries: it gave Europeans some measure of confidence in their own future. Once this confidence was established, governments and industries began to plan and invest. The results were impressive. By 1950 total industrial production had increased by one-half over 1947, exceeding the 1938 level by a quarter. Agricultural production outstripped the prewar average. Marshall Plan officials predicted that if nothing intervened the overall goals of the program would be attained by 1952, and Europe would be self-supporting. Unfortunately the Korean War, with its necessity for an expensive rearmament, did intervene. Hard choices had to be made; American aid tended to shift to military help. But the ECA had laid a real foundation which was not to be shaken by the events of the 1950s.

NATO AND THE BERLIN BLOCKADE

The year 1947 gave rise to the Marshall Plan; 1948 gave birth to the North Atlantic Treaty Organization. Both were part of the new United States commitment to the support of Western Europe, but NATO was a result of British Labour government initiative.

Failure of the Moscow and London foreign ministers' conferences stimulated Britain, France, and the Benelux countries to sign the Brussels Treaty, a fifty-year defensive alliance with permanent peacetime coordinating and planning committees. Foreign Minister Ernest Bevin presented it to Parliament in January 1948, and on March 17—hastened by the Czech coup—the six countries signed it. But from the beginning they knew that European military power, even if pooled, would be inadequate if the Russians decided to use the large peacetime army that they maintained.* They hoped that if the Europeans took a joint initiative in the military as they had in the economic realm, the United States might respond in the same fashion. There had been diplomatic hints to that effect, and in March Bevin proposed American participation to Secretary of State Marshall. In April the Canadian government publicly endorsed the idea. But to the United States the idea meant a drastic reversal of a century and a half of foreign policy, summed up in the phrase "no entangling alliances."

The impetus of the Truman Doctrine and the Marshall Plan was still there, however. Moreover, events in Germany now added urgency to the pressure provided by the Czech coup. In response to the Western creation of common governmental organs for the Western zones of Germany and the extension of the new West German currency to the Western zones of Berlin (and perhaps also because of trouble in the bloc, where Yugoslav resistance to Russian domination was bringing a general tightening of control), the Russians instituted a blockade of Berlin. They began by restricting military traffic in and out of the city in March, then to harass and finally completely stop all land communications on June 24. It seemed inevitable that the Western powers would be starved out of the city of two and one-half million, and would be compelled to agree to Soviet terms.

Instead, under the prodding and direction of the American commandant, General Lucius D. Clay, the Western powers organized an extraordinary airlift to the city. The British were reluctant; fears of war spread; nerves were on edge. But Clay told a worried administration that the action would not mean war:

> We have lost Czechoslovakia. Norway is threatened. We retreat from Berlin. When Berlin falls, western Germany will be next. If we mean . . . to hold

---

* The United States had demobilized from a wartime peak of thirteen million men to a level of 670,000. The Russians had, in fact, demobilized from 11 million to close to three million, but deliberately gave the impression they had maintained a far larger force under arms, and Western estimates at the time reflected this. The purpose may have been to maintain pressure on the West, but it was counterproductive.

Europe against Communism, we must not budge. We can take humiliation and pressure short of war in Berlin without losing face. If we withdraw, our position in Europe is threatened.*

Occupation authorities had calculated that 4500 tons of supplies per day would maintain Berlin at a subsistence level (without any private home heating). In anticipation of the blockade food stocks sufficient for 36 days and coal for 45 had been built up. It took until December before the airlift, begun on June 25, could handle the necessary 4500 tons. But after this the tonnage climbed steadily, and by the spring of 1949 an average of 8000 tons per day were being flown into the city. On May 4 an announcement from the United Nations indicated that the Soviet Union had capitulated. Negotiations there had led to agreement that ground communications would resume, and on May 11 the first trucks and trains crossed the border for Berlin.

In the meantime, the Berlin crisis had had its effect within the United States. To make sure that a proposed security treaty would pass the Senate hurdle of the necessary two-thirds majority (which required Democratic and Republican support), Republican Senator Vandenberg had been prevailed upon to introduce a resolution in favor of American participation in regional alliances "in accordance with the purposes, principles, and provisions of the Charter" of the United Nations. On June 11, 1948, the Vandenberg resolution passed the Senate by a vote of 64 to 6. With Senate support secure, conversations began in July in Washington, while American officers began to participate in the work of the Brussels Treaty committees in Europe. Although the first draft of the treaty was completed in November, negotiations continued into 1949. The question of membership was thorny: could an ex-enemy like Italy be asked to join? Its strategic location in the Mediterranean appeared to answer the question, but the Italian legislature, with its heavy Communist representation, balked. After months of debate the Christian Democratic government obtained support for the pact. Portugal, Iceland, Norway, and Denmark also joined. Sweden and Switzerland maintained their traditional neutrality. Spain was still outside the pale. On April 4, 1949, eleven countries signed the North Atlantic Pact and on October 22, 1951, Greece and Turkey were admitted to membership.

The main purpose of the pact was clear—to keep the United States in Western Europe to help counterbalance Soviet power. Many United States Senators made explicit their objections before the pact was ratified, for it committed the United States to action in circumstances that would negate Congress' power to declare war. In fact, the pact made the obliga-

---

* Lucius D. Clay, *Decision in Germany*, Doubleday (New York, 1950) , p. 361.

tion to act in case of an attack on one of the signatories contingent on the constitutional processes of each country. But the deterrent power of the pact rested on convincing the Soviet Union that an attack on one would really be an attack on all, and that the United States would not wait while Congress leisurely declared war. Thus the United States would have to keep troops in Europe in the line of Soviet fire. An attack upon Western Europe would then inevitably involve the United States. Senate critics therefore concentrated their attack on this commitment and also challenged the constitutional authority of the President, in his capacity as Commander in Chief, to move troops abroad. But they were beaten back, and the Senate received an education on reconciling the Constitution with the necessities of foreign policy once isolation was no longer possible. It approved the pact by a vote of 82 to 13. Republican Senator Taft, voting in the opposition, still claimed that there was no Russian military threat to the United States.

In subsequent months the Congress also approved the first military aid to the countries of Western Europe to strengthen their own armed forces, with an initial appropriation of $1.3 billion in aid. Finally, the pact led to the creation of an elaborate North Atlantic Treaty Organization, with a Supreme Headquarters, Allied Powers in Europe (SHAPE) outside of Paris, a series of joint regional commands, and periodic meetings at the ministerial level for coordination of foreign and military policies and for determining and apportioning the financial burdens.

POINT FOUR

The last chapter in the wholesale reversal of American attitudes toward its role in world politics came in January 1949. President Truman, in his inaugural address, proposed several policies, the fourth of which set off a whole series of programs in subsequent years.

> We must embark on a bold new program for making the benefits of our scientific advances and industrial progress available for the improvement and growth of underdeveloped areas. . . . For the first time in history, humanity possesses the knowledge and the skill to relieve the suffering of these people. The United States is preeminent among nations in the development of industrial and scientific techniques. The material resources which we can afford to use for the assistance of other peoples are limited. But our imponderable resources in technical knowledge are constantly growing and are inexhaustible.

Here was an acknowledgement that the nineteenth-century era of empire was over, a recognition of the desire for independence for new states and of the social revolutions within them as people began to ask, not merely for independence, but for something more than subsistence and subservience. Britain and France—especially France—had initiated large-scale postwar development programs in their overseas dependencies. The United Nations, in strengthening the powers of the General Assembly to discuss almost any matter and in the enhanced status of the Economic and Social Council, had recognized these developments. The increased international interest in Trust Territories and non-self-governing areas had been written into the Charter. One month before President Truman's inaugural address the General Assembly had in fact passed a resolution providing for a long-range program of technical assistance to under developed areas, but it would have been ineffective without the support of the United States.

President Truman's speech began a debate that still continues. In the subsequent battle for legislative support, the program—like the Marshall Plan before it—took anti-Communist overtones; unless technical aid was provided the new countries would lapse into chaos and the Communists would take over. But despite this ideological slant, and despite the various forms of opposition to Point Four aid, the various programs came to represent a new phase in international politics. The wealthier nations of what was coming to be an international community found it necessary to help the poorer members. The flow of private capital was insufficient for, with the exception of a few attractive investment opportunities in such resources as oil, private investors found more profitable fields in the wealthier countries.

In the early years of implementation, when large-scale funds were still flowing to Europe under the Marshall Plan and in military aid, there was little direct capital aid as a result of the Point Four speech. Moreover, not until Septembar 1950 was Congress willing to appropriate $34.5 million for technical aid. In that same year the United Nations began its own modest program of multilateral aid, with the United States paying up to 60 per cent of the total. In the years before the Korean War, the International Bank for Reconstruction and Development also began to find a few worthwhile projects in the underdeveloped countries, and to aid in their financing.

THE COMMUNIST BLOC

Communization of Eastern Europe began well before President Truman's speech to Congress on March 12 calling for aid to Greece and Turkey. It was completed in the ensuing months, during which Russia also forbade the Eastern European countries to take part in the Marshall Plan. Czechoslovakia, whose coalition government still maintained a precarious balance of power, at first accepted the invitation to come to Paris, only to be informed by Stalin that such an act would be deemed unfriendly to the Soviet Union and a breach of the Pact of Friendship and Mutual Aid between the two as well.

From July to February 1948, the Communists maintained a constant political crisis in the hapless country. They discovered Fascist conspiracies, packed the leadership of trade unions and the police, and interfered with the activities of other parties and branches of the government that were not yet under Communist control. On February 12 non-Communist members of the government instructed the Communist Minister of the Interior to reinstate eight non-Communist Prague police chiefs whom he had planned to replace with Communists. When he refused, they resigned in protest, thus precipitating a governmental crisis. Russian interest in the affair was made clear with the arrival in Prague of former Soviet Ambassador Valerian Zorin, now a Deputy Foreign Minister. The parties that had brought the crisis to a head hoped to force an election—one the Communists would lose. Unfortunately, President Benes, aware of the power of the Soviet Union, hesitated; so did leaders of the Social Democrats, one of the major parties. Detachments of Communist-led factory workers paraded through the streets of Prague while gangs of toughs occupied the ministries whose heads had resigned and the headquarters of the parties to which they belonged. Communist "action committees" sprang up all over the country; the police arrested prominent anti-Communists and accused them of conspiracy against the state; a Communist-armed workers' militia revealed itself; finally, the pro-Communist Minister of Defense made sure that the army remained neutral. The only other possible source of opposition—the Western Allies—were unwilling to act. They were caught by surprise, unable to fully foresee the outcome, and hesitant about what they could do. They knew they had little armed strength at hand, while the Red Army could easily intervene. Communist control of the press and radio ensured that the Communist party leaders' demands would be met: they insisted on the formation of a new government without the participation of the other parties and without any elections. President Benes gave in on February 23. All the key posts in the new government were held by the Communists; a few representatives of the other parties chosen by the Communists were admitted.

On March 10, Foreign Minister Jan Masaryk, who with President Benes had carefully worked out the policy of cooperation with the Soviet Union in order to keep Czechoslovakia a democratic bridge between East and West, was found dead in the courtyard of the Foreign Ministry. The death of Masaryk, son of the first great President-Liberator of Czechoslovakia, brought home the tragedy of Czechoslovakia as nothing else could have.*

At the same time that Czechoslovakia was drawn into the Soviet camp, Finland, to the north, came under pressure. Like Czechoslovakia, Finland had been dominated by the Red Army in the course of military operations of World War II. Unlike Czechoslovakia (a "liberated" state), Finland had fought against Russia on the side of Germany. On September 19, 1944, it signed an armistice confirming the 1940 borders (whose establishment after the Winter War of 1940 had involved cession of certain Finnish territories to Russia). A Russian-dominated Allied Control Commission was established, with nominal British participation. Reparations were fixed at $300 million, and Finland ceded several military bases to Russia.

The peace treaty between Finland, Russia and Britain was signed at the Peace Conference at Paris on February 10, 1947, and the Russian Control Commission departed, leaving behind a coalition government in which the Communists played an important part. In this case the coalition government lasted and Finland implemented the terms of the peace treaty. In late 1947 and early 1948 Stalin pressed for a defensive alliance that would allow Soviet troops to move into Finland, if, in Soviet judgment, they might be needed to forestall a German or other attack that also threatened Russia. Under pressure, the Finnish government sent a delegation to Moscow. It agreed to a treaty of mutual friendship and assistance, some of whose terms were ambiguous, but which clearly prohibited Finland from entering into any alliance or coalition aimed at the other signatory. Russia subsequently decided that the Marshall Plan fell within the scope of his clause, and thus Finland did not participate. In this, as in other matters, the Finns moved carefully to avoid any provocation of the Russians; the Communist party continued to operate within the framework of Finnish democracy.

The year 1947 also saw the birth of the Communist Information Bureau (or Cominform), with headquarters in Belgrade. The organization was part of a Soviet effort to tighten its control over the Communist parties of Europe; apparently the Red Army, the presence of Soviet secret police, and the constant journeying to and from Moscow of leading functionaries of the Communist parties, were insufficient. In 1947 there had been dissension among the party leaders on the question of participation

* Twenty years later, during the brief "spring thaw" of 1968, the first genuinely free inquiry into the death of Masaryk began; the Communist regime always insisted he had committed suicide, but many were sure he had been murdered. Evidence piled up to prove murder, but Russian invasion of Czechoslovakia brought an end to the inquiry.

in the Marshall Plan; Yugoslavia's Tito had resisted Soviet efforts to bring his regime under closer control. Unlike the old Communist International (Comintern) of the twenties and thirties the new Cominform was not merely an assembly of revolutionary and conspiratorial parties to be molded to Stalin's will; it was an organization many of whose participants were well on their way to becoming the absolute rulers of their countries, and control of whom was therefore all the more necessary. Among the first tasks of the Cominform was a self-criticism of all parties—Western European ones were taken to task for having disbanded their warborn military formations, which could have come in useful for seizing power*—and instructions to the Western ones to undertake all possible activities to sabotage success of the Marshall Plan and to disrupt Western economies.

In the months after rejection of the Marshall Plan, the Communist countries began to adopt long-range development plans based on the Soviet model, and also oriented their trade more toward the Soviet Union. This was particularly true of countries like Czechoslovakia and Poland, and to a lesser extent, Hungary, all of whom had been trading more with the West in the years 1946 and 1947. In 1948 the Soviet Union sponsored the Council for Mutual Economic Aid (Comecon), presumably to coordinate the economic development of the Eastern European countries. But in fact it also had another purpose: to help organize the boycott by Cominform countries of Communist Yugoslavia, which, in 1948, was forced to break with the Soviet Union. The consequences of this break were to be momentous in the years ahead.

Tito—the most ardent of Communists—appeared also to have the strongest base of independent power among non-Russian Communist leaders. He had emerged as the preeminent politician in the Balkans, and he had envisaged a Balkan federation in which Yugoslavia would have absorbed Albania. He had disputed Russian criticisms of his economic policies and of his too open support for Greek Communist guerrillas, and he resisted infiltration of his administrative apparatus by Soviet agents who were being sent throughout the bloc to foster its consolidation.

The break came when letters sent to all Cominform members detailed a series of charges by Moscow against the behavior of the Yugoslav comrades and a demand that the Cominform investigate them. Yugoslav replies denied the validity of the charges—which involved such matters as mistreatment of and spying on Russian soldiers—and told the Russians they had been misinformed. Moreover, the Yugoslavs, justly fearing ar-

---

* Ironically, Tito was among the most rabid critics of the French and Italian parties for their failures.

rest, were unwilling to send a delegation of their top officials to discuss the matter. Such argument and arrogance could not be tolerated. At a June 1948 meeting of the Cominform in Bucharest, Yugoslavia was read out of the Communist bloc, and an appeal was launched to good Communists within Yugoslavia to take whatever action might be necessary to rectify the situation.

Stalin certainly expected Tito either to give way or be overthrown from within. Khrushchev later reported him as having said "I will shake my little finger—and there will be no more Tito." Neither happened. Arguing strenuously that he wanted to maintain good relations with the Communist party of the Soviet Union, Tito secured the support of his own party and people. A nationalist wave of support swept through Yugoslavia, particularly as other Communist bloc countries under Soviet direction brought pressures to bear on Tito in the months that followed. They initiated an economic boycott, carried out a worldwide campaign of anti-Tito propaganda, abrogated various treaties of assistance, and concentrated troops on Yugoslav borders. Late in 1949 the Soviet Union expelled the Yugoslav ambassador and the *chargé d'affaires*. Purges of other leaders suspected by Stalin of recalcitrance now proceeded apace, and the accusation of "Titoism" became common. But the Yugoslav regime remained firm. Tito at first hoped for reconciliation, and found it difficult to reorient his own world view. Once a steadfast member of the Communist bloc, he had now become an outcast, yet one who remained the firmest of Marxist-Leninist-Stalinists. Under the circumstances, however, he began to look to the West. At first he met only suspicion. Many observers felt that the break was a fraud, and that aid to Tito would only be a help to one Communist government among others. But in 1949, the Truman administration decided that aid to the Tito regime, which represented a real schism within the Soviet bloc, was worthwhile. In 1949, the Export-Import Bank extended loans to Yugoslavia totaling $55 million. Tito also received financial assistance from the International Bank and International Monetary Fund. Although Congress lodged certain objections, the United States extended more aid in subsequent years, both for capital investment, relief in time of drought, and, beginning in 1951, direct military aid.

One immediate consequence of the Yugoslav break was the collapse of the Communist guerrilla movement in Greece. A secondary consequence was the attraction that the continued existence of Tito's Yugoslavia exerted for Soviet-bloc members who wanted Communism without Russian domination and dictation. Tito seemed to prove that such a thing was possible and, therefore was always a threat to the idea of a monolithic bloc.

DEVELOPMENTS IN WEST EUROPE

The achievement of some measure of European cooperation, of economic recovery, and of the creation of NATO has already been recounted, since American initiatives to "contain" Russia within Eurasian rimlands concentrated first on Europe. But this was only one stage in a more complex development.

The growing split in Europe and the hardening of the Soviet sphere changed the position of Communist parties in Western European countries and affected their politics accordingly. There was no Communist problem in England, where, under the relatively stable two-party system now headed by the Labour government, the American initiative was looked on as fundamentally sound (if at times erratic) . In Catholic, continental France and Italy, however, large Communist parties existed, and shared in governmental power. They had gained prestige and respectability during the war after the Nazi attack on the Soviet Union enabled them to combine Communism with patriotism and resistance to the Fascist and Nazi oppressors.* They still hoped to triumph, and controlled several ministries. But on May 4, 1947, two months after the proclamation of the Truman Doctrine, the French Communists were ousted from the governing coalition of MRP (Catholic) , Socialist, and Communist. Although the Communists were later to claim that the United States had forced them out, they had, in fact, begun to clash with the others in the coalition on several issues. In parliament they refused to vote credits for the Government's action in far-off Indochina; domestically they had been in the position of supporting a program of price and wage controls just when workers were striking in virtually every area, and they were afraid of being outdistanced on the left. They therefore moved to oppose the Government's stabilization program. Once out, they were able to take an extreme stand on wage claims and regain control of the trade unions. In November, apparently at Russian direction, they staged a series of strikes designed to bring them back into the Government on their own terms. The police, however, reorganized by a Socialist Minister of the Interior, Jules Moch, maintained order and the strikes were broken. The labor unions split, and never again in the life of the Fourth Republic were there Communist ministers. In subsequent years, however, the Communist party was always able to obtain between a fifth and a quarter of votes in French elections; to have an equivalent part of the French Assembly

---

* Before the attack all the Communist parties were in the uncomfortable position of having to cease opposition to Nazi Germany, since Russia and Germany had signed the nonaggression pact that enabled Hitler to occupy Europe. The reversal brought on by Hitler's attack on Russia brought them the welcome order to reverse themselves again.

permanently opposed to the government meant that right and center opponents of any subsequent French government could always count on
Communist votes to help bring it down; but to reconstruct a new one was
a different matter. Thus the position of the Communist party was a decisive factor in the continued weakness of governments in the Fourth Republic, and in its final demise.

In Italy, too, Communists had shared power with Socialists and Christian Democrats. June 1946 brought the end of the monarchy; December
22, 1947, brought the adoption of a new constitution. But in May 1947,
as in France, the Communists were pushed into opposition, and as in
France, November witnessed a wide series of Communist-led strikes and
riots.

Although the strikes failed to topple the government and to force it to
accept Communist participation, elections in April 1948 (the first under
the new constitution) gave the Party one more chance: as the largest outside the Soviet Union, its leaders felt there was a real opportunity to win
sufficient electoral support to make sure that no government could be
formed without Communist ministers. The Catholic Church brought all
its influence to bear in opposition; Italians in the United States barraged
families in the "old country" with letters; the United States announced
open support for various Italian demands for revision in the peace treaties. And the Christian Democrats won a decisive victory, gaining 307
seats to the Communist 182, with 80 seats going to other parties.

In Western Germany the Communist party always remained a negligi-
ble factor, and as political life renewed under the occupation, two parties
came to dominate the political scene: the Christian Democrats and the
Socialists. In the first general elections in 1949, these two parties polled
60 per cent of the vote and gained 67 per cent of the seats in the new
German Parliament; in 1953, 74 per cent of the vote and 83 per cent of
the seats; in 1957 and 1961, 82 per cent of the votes and 88 per cent of
the seats. From the beginning the Christian Democratic party, under the
leadership of Konrad Adenauer, dominated the government established
in 1949, and the foreign policy of West Germany was Adenauer's foreign
policy. He wanted to rebuild Germany economically, to tie it to some
form of Western European unity, to receive American military protection, and to reunify Germany under conditions of free elections. In all
but the last he was to have gratifying success.

The Berlin blockade had been a Soviet effort to stem the formation of
a West German state; it only hastened the actions of the occupying
powers. In September, 1948 a German parliamentary council met to
draft a new constitution, and the military governors of the occupying
powers met to draft a new occupation statute defining the limits within

which the new constitution of "Basic Law" would operate. On May 5, 1949, the Basic Law was promulgated, and West Germany came into being, though still under certain limitations, chiefly concerning continued disarmament. Faced with this and the failure of the blockade, the Russians persuaded the Western powers to meet with them in Paris in return for lifting the blockade. But the May-June Foreign Ministers meeting did little more than rehearse familiar charges, and West Germany became a reality.

Within Western Europe, the American initiative of 1947 was greeted with mixed feelings. Still suffering from the ravages of the war, the people and many of their leaders were unwilling to accept that the world was in fact divided, even that another war threatened. It was easy to accept the view that *both* sides were responsible, and the Truman Doctrine, seen as a declaration of ideological warfare, was received with distaste. It was easy, many felt, for a prosperous United States, spared the destruction of the war and now armed with atomic weapons, to put forth this point of view. But to most Europeans, it was too much to take. The Marshall plan, however, which first suggested breaching rather than widening the gap, was received with enthusiasm, though after Russian refusal the Communist parties of Western Europe did their effective best to bring it into disrepute.

In England there was somewhat less dissension, primarily because a Labour party was in power. Many of its supporters had long felt that it would be able to get along with the Soviets better than any Conservative government. But Foreign Minister Ernest Bevin came to accept very much the views of Churchill and the Americans on the Russian threat, and carried some of Labour's support with him; Conservative supporters by and large needed little convincing. In France, however, where de Gaulle's early efforts had been to patch up the pre-1914 alliance with Russia, where the chief preoccupation of foreign policy was to keep Germany divided and weak, where leadership in foreign policy was divided, opinion also remained divided. The Hungarian coup in early 1947 and the Czech coup of 1948 did shock the French, but many could still rationalize them as responses to American aggressiveness. Ways must be found, it was argued, to reassure and get along with the Russians. In Italy there was much the same feeling among non-Communists, so that Italy was slow to join the North Atlantic Treaty Organization, which the Parliament did not ratify for several months.

Italy continued to be preoccupied with the fate of Trieste and its former colonies. The peace treaty had made Trieste a free territory whose governor was to be chosen by the United Nations Sceurity Council in consultation with Italy and Yugoslavia. But months of irritated wrangling, proposals, and counterproposals produced no agreement on a governor, Yugoslavia charged that the West was attempting to turn Trieste into an imperialist base; the Western powers countered by proposing its return to Italy (only a few people failed to notice that this was done in March 1948, immediately before the first Italian elections). As a result, Trieste continued to be governed in two zones by the British and the Yugoslavs. With the break between Marshal Tito and the Soviet Union, the Western powers softened their support for Italian claims to the territory. There the matter rested until the mid-1950s, when the two countries reached an acceptable compromise.

The former Italian colonies of Libya, Eritrea, and Somaliland also remained a matter of dispute throughout this period. These last remnants of Italian ambitions to rival the empires of England and France, of Mussolini's tragi-comic attempt to rebuild the Roman Empire, were placed under temporary British administration after the war. By the 1947 peace treaty they were to be subject to Four-Power decision; if the Four could not agree within a year, the matter would be referred to the United Nations General Assembly. Of course, they could not agree, and the General Assembly placed Libya under United Nations administration to await independence in 1952; it united Eritrea with Ethiopia on a federated basis; in 1950 Somaliland was made a United Nations trust territory with Italy as the trustee. But Somaliland was given a 10 year deadline, during which time it should be prepared for independence. Another indication of the prevailing view that Western control of non-Western areas should be continued *only* with a view to their development toward "self-government" and that the international community had an interest in their welfare, Italy's administration was supervised by an Advisory Council composed of Colombia, Egypt, and the Philippines.

The reluctance to accept the division of the world into two blocs—a widely evident view among groups not in power, but shared by those in power—gave impetus to the move for European unity. The movement for some kind of unification had a long history and took various forms. The combination of individual weakness, Russian pressures, American inducements, and the desire to be more than merely part of the American bloc brought it to fruition.

American initiatives, largely inspired by the idea of containment, led to the creation of the Organization for European Economic Cooperation and the European Payments Union—both fruit of the Marshall Plan. The Americans supported Labour Foreign Minister Bevin's view of the Russian military threat, and out of the Brussels Treaty Organization and Western European Union they formed NATO. But there were purely European moves that reflected different aims.

Earliest of these was the Benelux Customs Union of Belgium, the Netherlands, and Luxemburg. Their governments-in-exile in England negotiated and signed the convention establishing the Union in September, 1944. Liberation of the countries raised enormous difficulties in implementation, largely because Belgium emerged in better economic shape than the Netherlands or Luxemburg. A series of negotiations finally led on January 1, 1948 to the institution of a common tariff. Continued differences, however, in internal taxation policies, economic controls, and levels of economic activity necessitated further arduous negoitations during the next few years. Eventually, in the late 1950s, the creation of a broader economic unit in Europe largely superseded Benelux.

On the political front, Winston Churchill's call for a "kind of United States of Europe," delivered at Zurich University on September 19, 1946, helped to inspire the work of a host of new organizations devoted to the idea. Their own activities, Cold War developments, and popular response led to the signing, on May 5, 1949, of the Statute of the Council of Europe. It received sufficient ratifications to come into force in August.

The Council of Europe and the accompanying Committee of Ministers were essentially cooperative rather than supranational organs, reflecting the reluctance of all the governments concerned to surrender any of their powers. They all feared the consequence: the English distrusted the instability of continental countries, the French were fearful of a Europe which contained Germany but neither England nor the Scandinavian countries, and the Germans were afraid a united Europe would be meant to keep them subjugated. Socialist parties all over, traditionally anticlerical, distrusted the fact that the European movement was being supported by Christian Democratic, that is, Catholic parties. Yet some Socialist leaders, notably Paul-Henri Spaak of Belgium, were in the forefront of the movement.

The Council, composed eventually of some 180 delegates, was weighted roughly in terms of population: France, Britain and Italy held 18 seats, as did West Germany when it was admitted in 1951; countries like Belgium, Greece, Sweden, and the Netherlands had 6; Luxemburg 3, Norway, Ireland, and Denmark 4, and Turkey 8. Delegates were elected by their parliaments, and roughly represented the apportionment of parties within them except for the Communist parties, which were excluded by virtue of the Statute. Article I stated that all members must accept the rule of law and fundamental human rights and freedoms. Delegates sat neither by country nor party, but alphabetically, thus stressing their independence and responsibility only to the European idea. In contrast, the Council of Ministers was made up of the foreign ministers of the participating states; there was no question whom they represented.

The Council's basic purpose was to suggest ways of effecting European integration. Since it could only recommend, while governments disposed, a split rapidly developed between the Council and the Committee of Ministers: the Council charged that the Committee kept it from doing any useful work. Within the Council itself another split occurred between "federalists" and "functionalists"—those who wanted to develop a set of viable political institutions first, and those who wanted to build "from the bottom" and thus create forms of economic cooperation, common institutions with limited functions, all of which would eventually serve as the foundations for political organs.

Further developments hinged on Franco-German relations. The earliest French view had been of a postwar world in which Germany would be kept permanently weak and divided and in which the war time coalition would be maintained and strengthened for that purpose. It was in pursuit of this aim that de Gaulle had signed his military alliance with the Soviet Union in 1944. But the world developed in a different way. Germany became a prize, and one that the United States and several European countries felt had to be rebuilt. As a result, the French were forced to revise their tactics. They were forced to accept the creation of West Germany, but they obtained the safeguard of an International Ruhr Authority, consisting of the United States, the United Kingdom, France, and the Benelux countries. Created in December 1948, it would allocate German coal through a system of consumption and export quotas, so that German industry would be under international controls during its reconstruction. The French went even further. In 1946 they had unilaterally included the coal-rich Saar region of Germany in a customs union with France. (The Saar, adjacent to the French border, was within the French zone of occupation of Germany.) Within the Saar they sponsored pro-French political movements, and on March 3, 1950, the Prime Minister of the Saar and the French Foreign Minister signed an agreement which virtually meant its economic annexation by France. It seemed none too soon to the French: in 1949 German steel production had exceeded that of France.

Yet German reconstruction proceeded so fast that to accommodate it French Foreign Minister Schuman had to do even more. He devised a scheme—the Schuman Plan—that would allow for German reconstruction and yet guarantee that it would pose no threat to France. The German and French coal and iron and steel industries would be pooled under the control of a high authority. Removed from the sovereignty of existing governments, the steel industry would no longer provide the foundation for military aggression of one against the other. The story of the negotiation and establishment of the European Coal and Steel Community comes later. As a French adaptation to the new unforeseen pattern of world politics, it was a stroke of genius. But on June 13, 1950, before the actual negotiations got under way, it produced an event that would have long-lasting repercussions: the British Labour Party stated it could not participate: "European peoples do not want a supranational authority to impose agreements." The European movement was now split. On the security level it comprised an Atlantic Community; on the political level it included Western Europe as a whole. But on the economic level, although cooperation among all the Western countries was guaranteed through the OEEC and EPU, the little Europe of the Six began to emerge.

The matter of *what* countries would constitute *what* Europe was complicated by the Scandinavian situation. There were, in the postwar years, discussions of some form of Scandinavian federation. But their outcome was bound to be limited. Finland, which in 1948 got rid of its Communist Minister of the Interior, had to tread warily to avoid provoking the Soviet Union. Norway and Denmark, however, were interested in Atlantic security, whereas Sweden, geographically in between and with a history of successful neutrality, preferred to follow traditional policy, especially since if Sweden remained neutral the Soviet Union would have no pretext to come to Finland's "aid." The Swedish government calculated that 70 divisions would be needed to overcome its army and air force and, since Sweden was not on the main Soviet route toward the West, it might be able to avoid hostilities if war broke out. Moreover, Sweden was one of the first of the small powers to calculate that the United States might well come to its aid even if it did *not* join an American-sponsored alliance. The United States tried persuasion, for American military men were unhappy about the fact that Swedish neutrality would release Soviet armed forces for use elsewhere. But the Swedes were adamant, and there was little opposition to the government's course. To maintain neutrality, Swedish armed forces were kept as well-equipped and trained as possible; by 1950 the Swedish air force was the fourth largest in the world, and Sweden was well on its way to equipping itself with air-raid shelters and underground production and storage facilities. Although weapons developments in the atomic age might render these obsolete and make it possible for the Soviet Union to simply deliver an ultimatum with which Sweden would have to comply, the government took its chances.

Finland was forbidden by the Soviet Union from taking part in the Marshall Plan. Sweden, however, became a party to it, and a member of the Council of Europe. But the Swedish government always maintained reservations about involvement in activities the Soviet Union would consider hostile. Norway and Denmark were fully involved, Swedish diplomatic efforts to keep them neutral having failed. But they were not privy to the new, smaller grouping of the Six.

Monetary stability is necessary to the successful functioning of a modern economy. The International Monetary Fund was designed to help stabilize international rates of exchange so that the international economy could function as it had failed to do during the 1930s. But it could not cope with the pent-up purchasing power and lack of goods in postwar countries. Inflation, with its concomitant effects—speculation, discouragement of investment, and encouragement of barter and black marketing—plagued Western Europe during the postwar years. Belgium, with a relatively strong economic position, was able to stabilize its currency through a drastic monetary reform in 1946. Not for another two years were France and Italy, with Marsall Plan help, able to devalue and stabilize their currencies. The most dramatic reform took place in West Germany in June 1948 when occupation authorities replaced the old currency with a new one. Confidence in it so revived trade that within weeks goods began to reappear in store windows, and within a year and a half industrial production doubled. The reform was a major step in West German recovery in the face of Soviet pressures.

Devaluation of the English pound on September 18, 1949, made the biggest headlines. Nothing could better have symbolized the political and economic change in the world since the beginning of the twentieth century. In the nineteenth century, the pound sterling, solidly based on gold, was *the* international standard of value, and Britain the heart of the world trading system. Now Britain's exports could no longer finance her imports; foreigners would—if they could—trade pounds for dollars, and in the winter of 1947 Britain was on the verge of bankruptcy. American interim aid and the Marshall Plan helped tide it over, while American assumption of British responsibilities in the Middle East lessened overseas expenditures. But the British economy, despite the austerity program of the Labour government, was still in trouble. To reduce imports and increase the exports which could pay for them, the value of the pound was changed from $4.03 to $2.80.

It was no simple matter; the basic situation was complicated by the British decision that it must repay in full its wartime debts to Commonwealth countries, as well as a host of internal factors. The final pressure for devaluation came as people began to speculate that the British *would* devalue the pound. Once such speculation occurred, people deferred purchases of British goods, since devaluation would mean they would get them cheaper. At the same time they tried to divest themselves of holdings of pounds sterling, which might be worth less in the immediate future. But Britain had to continue importing, and pay for its imports with holdings of foreign currencies, while suddenly earning less. The government could have either tried to convince people it would not devalue, thereby encouraging them to resume purchases and to hold British pounds, or it could devalue. It chose the latter course, and thus dramatized the end of an era in world politics.

WAR IN THE MIDDLE EAST

During the period 1947–50, European reconstruction began in earnest, colored by an anti-Soviet tinge and made possible by American support. In the Middle East, however, the central fact of political life had nothing to do with either Communism, the Russians, or the rebuilding of a previous existing structure. Rather it was the creation of a new state, Israel. All the Arab states were involved; to their leaders, whether by conviction or reluctant expendience, Israel became the focus of political life, and the exacerbated national resentments against the West were directed against its existence.

The United Nations Special Committee on Palestine (see p. 48), reporting to the regular session of the Second General Assembly in September 1947, delivered a majority and a minority report. The majority recommended a partition of Palestine into an Arab and a Jewish state linked in a United Nations-supervised economic union with Jerusalem as a separate entity. The minority, composed of India, Iran, and Yugoslavia, warned that the Arab states would not accept an independent Jewish state, and proposed instead a single federated state, into which immigration would be limited. By a vote of 33 to 13, with 10 abstentions, the Assembly adopted the partition plan. It recommended that a United Nations Commission assume administrative authority from the British to effect partition, that the Security Council meet any threat to the peace represented by atempts to alter the partition plan by force, that the Economic and Social Council assume responsibility for bringing about the economic union, and that the Trusteeship Council be assigned the administration of Jerusalem.

But the plans were never carried out. Britain, fearful of further encouraging the anti-Western bias of Arab nationalism, failed to turn over administration of Palestine before surrendering the mandate. In the meantime terrorism—by both Arab and Jew—increased, and Palestine became a battleground. On May 14, with the withdrawal of the last British garrisons, the state of Israel was proclaimed; it was immediately recognized by President Truman. Just as promptly, Egyptian columns began to enter from the south, Transjordanian and Iraqi armies from the east, and Lebanese and Syrian forces began to move in the north. But because the more cautious American State Department shared British apprehensions about Arab hostility—fears prompted partly by the growing American interest in oil—the Security Council faltered. It decided that it lacked the constitutional authority to enforce a political settlement recommended by the Assembly. At one point the United States even tried to get the United Nations to abandon partition—which the United States had supported—and work out a trusteeship arrangement.

Consequently, when the Arab invasion of Palestine took place, the United Nations resorted to *ad hoc* measures and established a United Nations mediator whose task was to bring about a cease-fire and political settlement. The thankless task was delegated to Count Folke Bernadotte, President of the Swedish Red Cross. The first truce went into effect on June 11, 1948. Both sides received some respite, but the Jews took more advantage of it to consolidate their governmental and military administrative apparatus. Fighting broke out again within four weeks; neither side had been willing to make the necessary concessions—the Jews because Palestine had been invaded and they felt themselves gathering strength, the Arabs because they would now lose face if exaggerated early reports of their victories were revealed to be false. The renewed fighting, which lasted 10 days, resulted in a series of Israeli victories that left their armies in control of much more territory than had been allotted to them under the partition plan. A second truce gave rise to a series of secret meetings between Arab technicians and Jewish leaders. They reached armistice agreements marking out lines based roughly on the location of each side's troops at the time of the truce, with demilitarized zones on either side and a Mixed Armistice Commission of representatives of both sides and of the United Nations to supervise the carrying out of the armistice provisions.

Both sides were forced by outside pressures to accede to the armistice. On the part of the Jews, facing Arab leaders who had made grandiose statements about driving the Jews into the sea, there was a strong sentiment for renewal of the war to convince the Arabs there was a need for real peace. But Israel was warned of possible sanctions; in September 1948, shortly after he had recommended an alteration of the demarcation lines in favor of the Arabs, Count Bernadotte was assassinated by men presumed to be Jewish extremists. After the shock, more moderate voices prevailed. An American, Ralph Bunche, took over the task of mediator. In 1949, when the armistice agreements were completed, Israel was admitted to the United Nations.

The short war left a bitter legacy. Six hundred thousand Arab refugees crowded camps around the borders of Israel, and in future years hundreds of thousands of Jews whose homes had been in Arab states left to enter Israel. The Arab states, claiming a right of repatriation for these refugees did nothing to relieve their misery, since such action might give weight to the argument that they would and could be resettled in Arab lands. Henceforth they and other Arabs were continually taught that it was their duty to help destroy Israel; no peace was possible, and the burden of refugee relief was assumed by the United Nations.

The war also revealed the weakness of the Arab states and the divisions among Arab leaders, and did much to discredit them at home and abroad. None would commit his armies wholly to the fight: each was afraid the others would then take advantage of him. Only the British-trained and equipped Arab Legion, which belonged to King Abdullah of Transjordan, really fought well.

Moreover King Abdullah then proceeded to alienate other League members by unilateral annexation of the Arab remnants of Palestine at a time other League members were promoting a new all-Palestine Arab government. Thus he doubled the population of his kingdom, which he renamed the Hashemite Kingdom of Jordan. Heavily dependent on British aid, Abdullah nevertheless emerged as a new leader in the Arab world, devoted to the creation of a unified Fertile Crescent through union with Iraq and Syria. But Abdullah was the only Arab leader who dared consider the idea of peace with Israel and the only one who remained friendly to Britain. Consequently he was assassinated in a mosque in Jerusalem in 1951, and rule passed first to his son, Talal, then to the young Hussein. Both vied with other Arab leaders in proclamations of fidelity to the idea of destruction of Israel.

Although Arab reactions to the Palestine War stimulated ideas of real Arab unity, it also discredited the Arab League, which had been formed in 1945. It increased Arab distrust of the West, particularly the United States. Without the West, Arabs argued, Israel could never have come into being: it represented the new—but last outpost of—imperialism. In subsequent years the Soviet Union—which had supported partition—by simply switching to an anti-Israeli position became the natural friend of any Arab who saw the necessity of destroying Israel.

Finally, the war did much to help weaken leaders of Arab governments whose bungling and corruption had helped bring about the loss of Palestine. In Egypt it strengthened the determination of groups of officers already set to cleanse the Egyptian body politic. In Syria it produced a succession of unstable governments, each of which deposed the previous one in a military coup, each having a different foreign policy orientation —some toward Egypt, some toward Iraq, and Jordan—but all violently anti-American as a result of American support of Israel. Disarray of the Arab lands was complete.

INDEPENDENCE IN ASIA

The weakness of postwar Europe that impelled new American commitments in 1947 also forced European states to hasten their surrender of control in Asia.

The story of Burmese and Indian independence has already been told (pp. 48–51). Ceylon, an island off the tip of India, achieved dominion status in February 1948, at which time it also signed a defense agreement with Britain. Although beset with minority problems that would embitter its relations with India, in October it was host to a conference convened to discuss economic and political problems of Southeast Asia. From this conference came the important mutual-aid program known as the Colombo Plan, to which both the British and Americans subsequently contributed.

Further to the east the period brought continued struggle to Indochina and independence to Indonesia.

In Indochina the French underestimated their political task and their ruthless enemy. Viewing the matter as a relatively simple one of pacification, handicapped by an unstable government and weak economy at home, they never sent sufficient forces nor forged a coherent political-military strategy. Control of the Vietminh by the Communists meant that many Vietnanmese opposed it, but the French government was unable to make the political concessions necessary to obtain Vietnamese support. Abroad—and particularly in the United States—the war was therefore viewed as a colonial one; only after the outbreak of the Korean War in 1950 were the French able to convince American leaders that in Indochina, too, they were making a part of the common effort to contain Communism. But by 1949, Mao Tse-tung's victory in China meant an increased flow of Chinese aid to the Vietminh in the form of both bases in South China for training and recuperation as well as American arms captured from the Nationalist Chinese. By the end of 1950 the war was lost, although it was to drag on for four more bitter years.

In Indonesia one crucial factor was different: the nationalist leaders were not Communist. Nevertheless Dutch belief that their colony was too primitive for self-government was reinforced by anger at reports of atrocities committed against Dutch civilians and resentment against a revolt by an "ungrateful" people. These attitudes clashed with the facts of power, however: the Dutch Government lacked the resources completely to subdue the islands, and, in 1946 it agreed to a federal union of Holland and the Republic of Indonesia. Presumably the Republic would be only one of several states in the islands that had been the Dutch East Indies, but the Indonesians wanted more—a treaty between two sovereign powers, with the Republic having jurisdiction over all the islands. The federal union, they were sure, would merely perpetuate Dutch rule.

In March 1947, at Linggadjati, the two parties signed an agreement defining the terms of federal union. Both made some concessions and both expressed considerable optimism. But all through 1947 and 1948 the two parties tried merely to improve their relative power positions in order to change the consequences of the agreement. The Dutch moved in more troops and blockaded the Indonesian nationalists, while the Indonesians tried to build wider political support both at home and abroad. In mid-1947, Dutch troops went into action to carry out what were described officially as "police measures of a strictly limited character," but were actually designed to narrow the area in which the Republic had real jurisdiction. During a cease-fire they tightened their hold on newly gained areas and created new states within them, and then, in December 1948, struck again. This time the attack was based on an estimate that all organized resistance could be crushed and the Republic would crumble.

Two factors determined the subsequent Dutch failure. First, within Indonesia, support had grown for the Republic, and political groups that had favored federation on the basis of the diversity of the islands now switched to the Republican cause. Thus passive and active resistance proved to be a severe financial and military drain on the Dutch.

But in the second place, the outside world manifested too much opposition to the Dutch venture. The first cease-fire had resulted from a combined Indian-Australian appeal to the Security Council. Here the whole matter became too public for Dutch taste. The United Nations rejected their claim that the whole problem was merely one of domestic jurisdiction —a claim supported only by England, France, and Belguim, also colonial powers—and the United Nations-sponsored cease-fire was buttressed by a United Nations Consular Commission, while a Committee of Good Offices sought to bring the parties to terms. When the truce it arranged aboard the USS *Renville* broke down with the second Dutch attack, events moved apace. The Committee of Good Offices was reestablished as the United Nations Commission on Indonesia, with a broader mandate to make recommendations for "the establishment of a federal, independent and sovereign United States of Indonesia." In the meantime in New Delhi Prime Minister Nehru of India had sponsored a conference of Asian and Middle Eastern states to recommend Indonesian independence, and had threatened to bring the matter before the United Nations General Assembly. These pressures, combined with the continued cost of the military action, brought a change of government in the Netherlands, one more prone to a change in policy. The last straw was American withdrawal of Marshall Plan aid destined for use in Indonesia.

The Dutch bowed to circumstances and agreed at a Round Table Conference in The Hague, August 23 to November 2, 1949, to a transfer of authority from the Netherlands to the Republic of the United States of Indonesia, the two to be joined in a union under the Dutch Crown, in emulation of the British Commanweath of Nations. The outlook for the future was not particularly bright: the United States of Indonesia was beset with difficulties from the beginning. The provisions it had accepted for special treatment of Dutch economic interests in Indonesia were likely to cause intense irritation, and the fate of Western New Guinea (west Irian, as the Indonesians called it) was unsettled. The Indonesians claimed it as a "natural" part of the Republic; the Dutch argued that it had no ethnic, cultural, or national relationship. But at least independence had been achieved.

Western attitudes toward the Indonesian affair differed from those toward Indochina for two reasons. Geography played a part—Indochina was directly on the Eurasian rimland, while Indonesia was not. Second, Indonesian leadership remained non-Communist. In fact, there, as in Europe and other parts of Asia, the Russian reaction to America's worldwide initiatives had resulted in direct Communist action against popular nationalist leadership. From mid-September to mid-November 1949, bitter fighting occurred between Communist-led units and troops loyal to the Republican leaders, Sukarno and Mohammad Hatta. In the end, loyal army forces suppressed the insurrection.*

In China, the 1947–50 period revealed that early Nationalist successes in their campaigns to retake the north were based only on an illusion of strength. July 4, 1947 marked the end of an era of attempts to negotiate, to establish temporary truces, and to reach accommodations: the Nationalist government proclaimed the Communists outlaws. In the meantime, however, the military initiative passed from the government to the Communists, who began a series of successful military offensives early in the year. Bad morale among Nationalist troops, supply failures, the hostility of the local populace in the north whom Nationalist garrisons had treated like conquered people, all contributed to the debacle. Continued economic deterioration and government weakness in dealing with it led to increased inflation, speculation, corruption, and the alienation of most groups that might have supported the government. Intellectuals whose at-

---

* Insurrection in Indonesia occurred at the same time as that of the Communists in India and Malaya. Since Communist parties were also in arms in Burma and Indochina while Mao's armies were triumphant in north China, and the armed action followed upon the Russian-organized Calcutta meeting of Asian parties, Western observers could easily conclude that with the failure in Western Europe, the world Communist movement had switched to a new, Asian insurrectionary strategy.

tempts to form rival parties to the Kuomintang had been frustrated turned to support the Communists. American military missions, surveying the situation, were unanimous in their insistence that military aid could accomplish little without drastic administrative and economic reforms; but the Nationalist government appeared unable to carry them out.

The Nationalist government entered the civil war with a three-to-one ratio in its favor of troops, territory, and population, and an even greater preponderance of industrial potential. It received American economic and military aid and diplomatic support. But continued knowledge that such support could have at best a limited effect led the United States to try to use the aid as a lever for prying reforms from the Kuomintang. The effort failed. Larger measures, such as a massive military intervention, were never contemplated in the face of Congressional unwillingness to spend more, in the light of heavy commitments to Europe, and in view of the very real possibilities that such an intervention might fail, might further alienate the Kuomintang from the people, and could well provoke large-scale Soviet intervention. Russia never did much to help the Communists beyond maneuvering in Manchuria, and its actions there and Stalin's private utterances to high-ranking Communists reveal that under the circumstances Soviet leaders did not expect much from the Chinese Communists. But the United States had to face the problem that this attitude might change; the possibility that it would seemed very real.

In 1948, reorganized Communist troops cleared Manchuria of Nationalists, depriving them of much of their materiel and destroying some of the best troops. In the early months of 1949 the Nationalist retreat became a rout, the capital was moved from one city to another as each in turn fell to the Communist "People's Liberation Army." In 1949, Chiang retired from the government. Elements in the Kuomintang felt that without him it might still be possible to negotiate with the advancing Communists. The effort failed; the will to fight was gone, and in the autumn of 1949, having resumed the presidency, Chiang ferried as much as he could of his army to Formosa, ninety miles from the mainland. In the face of the extraordinary collapse before the Communist onslaught, most people expected that within a year the 600,000-man demoralized and poorly equipped army on Formosa would also suffer defeat.

But there was a pause. In October the new Communist regime proclaimed itself the People's Republic of China and established its capital at Peking, imperial capital of the Manchu Dynasty. In this way it established its link with the old China broken by the Kuomintang, who had tried to turn Nanking into a new capital. Mao Tse-tung outlined the position of the new regime: it would be essentially Stalinist. Agriculture would be collectivized, heavy industry developed, and counter-revolutionaries ruthlessly suppressed. For an indefinite period the regime would be a multiclass dictatorship, led by the Chinese Communist party and composed of a coalition of representatives of workers, peasants, the national bourgeoisie, and petty bourgeoisie. Minor democratic parties would be allowed to exist within the framework of the united front. But on the international scene there would be no doubt of the Chinese stance: China would belong to the Socialist camp led by the Soviet Union. Late in 1949 the regime began its preparations to complete the liberation of Formosa, now called Taiwan, and began also to aid Ho Chi Minh in Indochina. In December Mao Tse-tung and his Premier and Foreign Minister Chou En-lai went to Moscow to negotiate the formal ties that would bind them to the Soviet Union.

They went to Moscow in different circumstances than most other Communist leaders. Although Russian participation had helped defeat Japan, the Chinese Communists had obtained power by their own efforts, not through the Soviet Red Army. But they desperately needed aid, and the Soviet Union was already established in Manchuria by the terms of the Yalta agreements. The result was hard bargaining and compromise on both sides. The Soviet Union extended credits of $300 million; it would turn back the port of Dairen to China immediately and return its share of the Manchurian railways and Port Arthur by 1952; it signed the Sino-Soviet Treaty of Friendship, Alliance, and Mutual Assistance, and agreed to provide military and economic advisers. But the loan was strictly a loan, and repayment would have to start in 1954. Moreover, the Chinese accepted a series of joint stock companies in the fields of civil aviation, mineral and petroleum extraction, and ship-building and repair, similar to those through which the Soviet Union dominated the economies of the Eastern European countries.

The Chinese Communists were thus partially dependent on Russia; if they were to make any progress in reconstructing and modernizing China's society and economy, they would need massive amounts of capital that would not be forthcoming from Western powers and would be hard to generate internally. But their victory in China brought a dramatic change to all of Asia: now the Communist bloc bordered troubled areas like Indochina and Burma, and extended to the undefined frontier area between China and India. The victory put the future of Formosa in doubt and brought fear to Japan. Only time would tell whether Communist China would act strictly in concord with the Russians, and whether the new Chinese rulers would be able to consolidate their position: both issues posed puzzling problems for the policy-makers of other states.

THE UNITED NATIONS IN A DIVIDED WORLD

In the years before 1950 the United Nations system never operated as its planners had orginally hoped. The peace treaties that were to have delineated the world map, to be preserved by the United Nations security system, had not changed the situation. The agreements that would have placed military contingents at the disposal of the Security Council for purposes of collective security were not forthcoming, and the necessary unanimity of the great powers on the Security Council had vanished in the Cold War. Economic dislocations were so much greater than had at first been realized that the escape clauses in the International Monetary Fund were the ones most resorted to. Negotiations for the International Trade Organization, the third of the great international economic organizations, dragged on; but the same factors that restricted the use of the I.M.F. and made the International Bank for Reconstruction and Development inadequate, delayed signature of the I.T.O. treaty. The basic treaty, reflecting the experience of the interwar years, embodied Anglo-American economists' ideas of freeing trade as much as possible through reciprocal elimination of trade barriers. But at Havana the difficult attempt was also made to provide for relations between market economies and socialist, state-trading countries, as well as to embody a series of escape clauses demanded by "underdeveloped" countries— clauses that would have enabled them to protect so-called infant industries or to receive tariff advantages without reciprocally granting any, or would have provided international marketing agreements to raise and stabilize the prices of the raw materials and commodities they exported. As a result, the treaty was not ratified by the American Congress and, although it had been designed as the keystone of the international economic system, it died a quiet death, leaving behind only the General Agreement on Tariffs and Trade. Few governments realized that over the next two decades enormous negotiating energies would be expended on trying to fill the gaps left by the failure of the I.T.O.

Moreover, the protracted disarmament negotiations had bogged down; indeed, they had turned into an effort to achieve stabilization through rearmament. The Baruch Plan seemed out of the question; the Soviet Union had conducted a propaganda campaign to ban the bomb and then shifted policy to support international control through the Security Council after all weapons had been destroyed. Overwhelming General Assembly support for the Baruch Plan brought no further modification in the Soviet position, and it became doubtful that given the current international situation, the American Congress would have accepted the international ownership and management set forth in the Baruch Plan. The great powers had come to act outside the channels of international diplomacy provided by the United Nations: the programs of American aid to Europe and the creation of NATO to provide for Western security against the Soviet Union, indicated how little the powers relied on the United Nations.

Still, the United Nations organization had played an important role in a number of the developments so far detailed—though not the role envisioned for it by many of its supporters, nor one always popular with its member nations. In the Palestine situation, on the Greek borders, in Indonesia, in the secret negotiations that ended the Berlin blockade, the United Nations had provided mediation, fact-finding, and face-saving formulas for ending the wars. In the fields of technical cooperation and of supervision of the trust territories, work immensely useful to UN members and the trust terrotiries had begun. As the breach between the great powers enhanced the inherent weakness of the Security Council system, the energetic Norwegian Secretary-General, Trygve Lie, used all the resources of his office to try to ease conflicts between the powers. Rather than remain a quiet international civil servant, heading a staff that provided secretarial and translating services for international conferences, he had seized upon the diplomatic potentials of his office. When the Communist Chinese came into power, he took the initiative in drafting a memorandum suggesting that a country that refused to recognize the new regime could nevertheless vote for its membership in international bodies. This was part of an overall effort on Lie's part to break the diplomatic stalemate that had developed in the five years since the end of the war, and had brought the world to the brink of another war. In the course of this effort he visited world capitals, urged a new course of action on world leaders, and sketched a "Twenty-Year Program for Achieving Peace through the United Nations." But 1950 brought his endeavor to nought.

In one area the United States had given the United Nations General Assembly a task with which it could not cope. American authorities decided to cast off the burden of occupying South Korea in 1947 and the General Assembly created a United Nations Temporary Commission to oversee elections to be held throughout Korea. But the Soviet bloc refused to cooperate, the Commission was denied access to North Korea, and eventually, under American prodding, the Commission supervised elections in South Korea alone. Other states were reluctant to accept them as valid. It seemed that in still another area of the world the warborn borders were being reinforced rather than eliminated. Nevertheless, by a vote of 4 to 2 the Commission declared that the elections in the south met standards set by the General Assembly, and on December 12, 1948, the Assembly held that the new regime was the lawful government of South Korea. It then appointed a new United Nations Commission on Korea to report on the transition to independence and also to try to unite Korea. The efforts at unification were again in vain. The Soviet Union, however, announced withdrawal of its occupation forces in the north (leaving behind it a Soviet-equipped and Soviet-trained North Korean army and joint Soviet-Korean companies to control main centers of the economy), and the United States then felt constrained to withdraw its own unpopular and relatively weak occupation forces in the south. In speaking of unification, both sides took a threatening tone, and during 1948 and 1949 the United Nations Commission kept an uneasy watch on border forays.

THE ATOMIC BOMB, MILITARY STRATEGY, AND THE BALANCE OF POWER

In the early years of containment, American military policy was based primarily on the atomic bomb. Although the NATO commitment of the Truman administration called for an increase in the number of American troops in Europe, the pressures to keep the military budget low and traditional American views of warfare forced the administration to rely primarily on the Air Force and its limited capacity to deliver an atomic strike against Russia to deter the Soviets from military expansion. The bomb was to compensate for the Russian superiority in manpower and material: Russian armed forces were variously estimated at between three and five and a half million well-equipped men. (Geographical considerations meant that dependence on massive retaliation involved building or expanding air bases around the Russian perimeter, a policy that gave the Soviet Union handy and most useful ammunition for the charge of American imperialism.)

This overall policy rested on one basic assumption: that the Russians would need a long time to make an atomic bomb. But, on September 23, 1949, both the White House and Downing Street issued announcements confirming rumors that an atomic explosion had been detected in Siberia. The estimates concerning the time required for the Russian development had been wrong. One reaction was the opinion, widespread and persistent, that the barbaric and unfree Russian Communists could not have done the job themselves, but must have stolen "the secret." (Discovery of an extensive Communist atomic spy network in England and Canada that reached into the United States bolstered the idea.) More responsible opinion, however, was concerned with another question: How long would

it take the Russians to turn one atomic explosion into the actual manu-
facture of bombs and to have the means of delivering them? And what
were the implications for Western strategy of containment and of reliance
on American atomic bombs? Would the United States really attack the
Soviet Union in response to a Russian drive on some perimeter region if
this involved the possibility of direct Russian retaliation on the United
States? Would not Russian possession of the bomb mean that war would
no longer be limited to a retaliatory attack upon Russia? Could the "in-
between" countries of Europe afford such a war?

One answer came in the growth of "neutralism" in smaller countries—
the view that it was better to try to remain outside the military blocs
sponsored by both major powers. In the United States, newspaper col-
umnist Walter Lippmann devoted an article to the "Breakup of the Two
Power World." The new Russian weapon would make smaller countries
realize that the atomic bomb no longer promised protection as it had during the period of the American monopoly; instead it promised destruction. The desire to rely less on American protection was bound to be
strengthened. Smaller countries would try to escape the conflict between
the two superpowers, and let them fight things out for themselves. Neutralists in other countries echoed Lippmann's words, adding only that the
new course might enable them to act as mediators between the United
States and the Soviet Union, as some had hoped to be able to do five
years earlier.

The year 1950 would have to bring some reevaluation of the course so far
followed.

CONCLUSION

Two opposing trends dominated the years 1947–50: development of a
bipolar world, and continued breakup of old European empires. The first
trend seemed the crucial one; in the United States as well as the Soviet
Union bipolarism came to be accepted as the correct world view. For the
Soviet leaders there was the "Socialist camp" and the "imperialist camp."
To Americans there was the Soviet bloc and the "free world." People in
other countries held more varied views. Yet for the moment, as the superpowers faced each other, other voices were barely heard.

The United States, after a faltering start, had decisively entered the
world arena on the basis of this world view and had reversed a century
and a half of policy to take the lead in building a military coalition
against Russia and assuming large-scale commitments for economic reconstruction and development outside the Soviet bloc. Its intervention
had helped to save a bankrupt Europe, now beginning to show signs of

vitality. Yet every step had provoked discussion: What would successful containment lead to? Was it to be an end in itself; if so, how long must it last and at what expense? Was it supposed to lead to the freeing of people under Communist domination? If so, what would be the response to a situation like Yugoslavia's? The commitments of containment had brought major constitutional changes to the American government, and each of these had occasioned further argument. The discussions had even led people to wonder if the American form of government was suited to the needs of consistent, unsentimental foreign policy. Had de Tocqueville been right in the nineteenth century? "Foreign politics," he wrote, "demand scarcely any of those qualities which a democracy possesses; and they require, on the contrary, the perfect use of almost all those faculties in which it is deficient . . . a democracy is unable to regulate the details of an important undertaking, to persevere in a design, and to work out its execution in the presence of serious obstacles. It cannot combine its measures with secrecy and it will not await their consequences with patience." He was frequently cited in the years under review. The English writer J. B. Priestly wrote that being in the company of the United States was "like being locked in a house with a whimsical, drunken giant." *

There was no question that European governments wanted and welcomed American commitments. But the recipients of aid had lost what had been a high status, and as older, more experienced, but improverished relatives, they could hardly be expected to welcome charity without resentment or criticism. Americans who expected gratitude were sadly misled. Other Americans, more sophisticated and understanding, nevertheless failed to realize how hard it was for Europeans to accept the break with Eastern Europe. Many Europeans rejected the idea that so long as Communist governments existed, the breach would persist, and looked instead to an eventual reestablishment of useful relations with Soviet-bloc countries.

Yet developments within the Soviet sphere—the hardening of the bloc and the Czech coup—hardly augured well for this view. Yugoslavia had escaped Soviet domination, but people had yet to understand what this might mean for bipolarism. Some, failing to see different situations within the Communist countries, hoped that it might serve as a spur to others. Unfortunately, one effect of the Yugoslav break with Russia was to hasten Russia's extension of control over the other members. China appeared to have joined the bloc; yet its leaders had fought their own way

* "You Worry the World," *Magazine of the Year*, October 1947, cited in Harold and Margaret Sprout, *Foundations of National Power* (2nd revi. ed.-New York: Van Nostrand, 1951), p. 415.

to power with little Soviet help, and from the outset some analysts hoped that China might follow the way of Tito. A widely held view in the United States, however, was that Tito was still a Communist and a dictator, and therefore his defection was no victory for the free world. In this view, too, the Chinese Communist success signified Russian enslavement of the Chinese people whom the United States had long befriended and fought for. How bipolar was the world? The disagreements persisted. Official United States view had hardened into bipolarism; yet the Truman administration acted to help Marshal Tito defy Stalin.

In the five years after the end of the war Russia had tried to intervene in areas outside its control: Iran, Turkey, Libya, Greece, the Ruhr in Germany, Japan, Berlin, and less directly, through Communist parties, in Italy, France, India, Indonesia, Burma, India, Malaya, Indochina, and elsewhere. These attempts had met with failure and provoked the hardened Western position. Stalin had therefore sought some settlement. But so long as each major power persisted in proclaiming as its ideal the ultimate destruction of the other's form of government and society, any settlement was difficult to reach.

Implications of the second major trend, decolonization, were just as hard to discern. In the official Communist view, the new states had not left the "imperialist camp," since they were led by "bourgeois nationalists." American leaders did not give too much thought to areas outside the main spheres of conflict with the Soviet Union; they accepted the liberal view that empires and colonies must come to an end and therefore supported independence for Indonesia, Burma, India, and others. They tended to see colonial conflicts in terms of the benefit that might redound to the Communists if colonial countries tried to suppress nationalist revolts.

But American policy-makers had had to begin to face a major dilemma: with great difficulty they had conceived an alliance with a Europe they were helping to regenerate. At the same time they were supporting colonial revolts against European countries. They could hardly expect cheers from their allies. The French, fighting in Indochina, tried to convince their American allies that this, too, was part of the overall battle to contain the Communist bloc on the Eurasian rimlands; the Americans, although seeing merit in the French argument, tried to persuade them to make greater concessions to non-Communist nationalism in Indochina.

The Soviet Union, having blocked all western attempts to maintain some leavening influence within its own, brutally imposed bloc, having abandoned many of its efforts to expand directly into areas outside the bloc, and having failed in its main attempts to use large-scale Communist party subversion, turned primarily to propaganda. Its chief target, naturally, was the United States, which was painted as a war-mongering imperialist state, brandishing its atomic weapons and bent on resurrecting a vengeful Nazi Germany. Its propaganda was often successful. It spoke to a world in revolutionary upheaval, and it was easy for Russia to support revolution with little thought to the consequences, while the Western countries, trying to maintain order or bring about orderly change, were in an inherently conservative position. In France Communist propaganda did much to discredit the Marshall Plan among the mass of the population by asserting that the benefits of the Plan went only to the rich. Since the Plan did, in fact, channel its funds into capital reequipment and renovation, its immediate effects were not apparent to the farmer, worker, or consumer, and the Communist arguments appeared valid.

Development of bipolarity hampered the United Nations even more than did the basic, inherent weakness in the United Nations system. The main political developments of these years took place outside the United Nations framework, where the Security Council, in particular, found its work paralyzed by the bipolar confrontation.

By 1950 the world was in a precarious state. Polls showed that, only five years after World War II, most people expected another war soon. This time it might well be an atomic war, for Russia, too, now had the Bomb.

FOUR
1950—1955 HOT WAR
AND COLD WAR

If the years before 1950 were marked by deepening conflict between the Soviet bloc and the Western powers, the years that followed were dominated by the eruption of the conflict into war in Korea. Although fighting remained confined to that unhappy land, the war had ramifications and consequences throughout the world, hastening rearmament, bringing new alliances, imposing strains on the economies of countries only just beginning to recover from World War II, and speeding the development of new weapons. Explosion of the first hydrogen bombs during these years foreshadowed a new era in international politics, one whose outlines could hardly be forecast. The war and the bomb, however, combined with the inability of European powers to maintain their hold on their empires, gave new impetus to another development that had accompanied the Cold War: the attempt of more and more countries to avoid aligning themselves with one side or the other, despite pressures and inducements from the United States and Britain to join new alliances prompted by the Korean War. To new non-Western nationalism was joined new neutralism.

If war dominated the early years of the period, a groping toward a series of political settlements dominated the latter part of it. The war had led to a hardening of positions and greater hostility; it had brought Communist China into a direct conflict with the United States that might otherwise not have occurred. But the cost and exhaustion of an indecisive war led to explorations of possible settlement. The death of Stalin in 1953 prompted Western statesmen to explore the intentions of his successors. To an uneasy peace in Korea was added an even more uneasy peace in Southeast Asia. In Europe, on the other hand, ways were finally devised for rearming Germany, and the Soviet response was creation of the Warsaw Pact alliance. Finally, in the mid-1950s, a new trend in world politics began to become apparent: Europe—apparently shattered by World War II—showed amazing signs of new life following the disruptions of the Korean War. Americans and Russians had become accustomed to seeing the world in bipolar terms, and the development of hydrogen weapons by the two superpowers appeared to confirm this view.

111

But in Europe as in non-Western areas, the view began to look quite different.

KOREA AND ITS IMPACT

Victory of the Chinese Communists in China led to a broad reassessment of overall American foreign policy. Europe came first; the Marshall Plan's scope and NATO commitments indicated this. Military commitment in Asia would therefore remain limited, and the containment effort would primarily be directed at helping Asian peoples develop healthy and popular governments and economies. The lesson of China—summed up in the State Department's *China White Paper,* published in 1949—was that internal conditions had led to Communist success. The lesson would have to be applied elsewhere. In line with this thinking, most people in the administration were prepared to abandon the remnant of the Chinese Nationalist regime on Formosa, and try to reach some *modus vivendi* with the victorious Communists, who were proving prickly. Some students of Far Eastern affairs already spoke of possible "Titoism" on the part of Chinese comrades: like the Yugoslav leader, the Chinese had come to power largely on the basis of their own efforts, and might be expected to operate somewhat independently of Russia. Conditions were different within the country, and some of its fundamental long-range national interests might prevail over the ties of Communist ideology in the minds of Chinese leaders, particularly since Tito's case proved that Stalin would tolerate no show of independence on the part of other Communist bloc leaders.

There were many differences of opinion within the administration. But the view prevailed that the heavy weight of American responsibilities in Europe dictated a course of limited commitment in the Far East. Given the nature and limitations of American power, this was the only answer that could be consistent with the containment policy, the only answer possible since its inception. Secretary Marshall once recalled:

> I remember, when I was Secretary of State I was being pressed constantly, particularly when in Moscow, by radio message after radio message to give the Russians hell. . . . When I got back, I was getting the same appeal in relation to the Far East and China. At that time, my facilities for giving them hell—and I am a soldier and know something about the ability to give hell—was $1\frac{1}{3}$ divisions over the entire United States. That is quite a proposition when you deal with somebody with over 260 and you have $1\frac{1}{3}$rd.*

---

* John C. Sparrow, *History of Personnel Demobilization in the United States Army* (Washington, 1951), p. 380.

Twice, in 1947 and again in 1948, President Truman had vetoed tax cuts passed by a Republican Congress. In 1949 a Democratic Congress had refused him a $4 billion increase. Without the money, little force to sustain commitments was possible. The new Secretary of State, Dean Acheson, made clear that the United States would fight to defend Japan and the Philippines. But he argued that the other rimland countries would first have to be able to defend themselves and that the United Nations would then have to be called in to aid them. Lurking in the background was the case of Indochina, where the French attempt to suppress an insurrection was hopelessly bogged down. French use of unpopular local elements had allowed the Communists to capture the Nationalist movement. The administration obviously wanted to avoid such a course. In the meantime, since other countries were ready to recognize the new Chinese regime, the United States was reluctant to isolate itself by pursuing a different policy.†

Nevertheless, among the rimland countries of the Far East, Korea presented a special case. It had a United Nations-legitimated government over an area that bordered directly on a Communist state. While the Truman administration had largely turned the problem over to the United Nations, and—to the dismay of Korean President Syngman Rhee—had withdrawn all forces but a 500-man training mission, it also signed a military assistance agreement with Korea in January 1950, and persuaded a reluctant Congress to approve substantial economic aid.

Border incidents between the two halves of the country occurred with increasing frequency in the first half of 1950, and, although both sides professed a desire for reunification by negotiation, the North laid down impossible conditions. Both obviously felt that if negotiation was impossible force would be necessary. Intelligence reports revealed that the military forces in the North were being strengthened. (North Korean forces were about the same size as the army in the Pepublic of Korea in the South, but, with Soviet-provided materiel, were better equipped.) John Foster Dulles, a Republican leader in foreign affairs entrusted by the Truman administration with negotiating a peace treaty with Japan, visited Korea, and in a speech to the National Assembly, promised that the United States would stand by the country.

Then, on June 25, war broke out. North Korean troops crossed the 38th parallel at several places and made numerous amphibious landings. At the same time the North Korean radio claimed that South Korean

† The People's Republic of China received recognition by the USSR in October 1949, by Burma and India in December, by Great Britain in January 1950, and by the Netherlands in March.

troops, which they said had begun the hostilities by crossing into the north, had been repulsed.

In Western Europe, among the newly independent countries of Asia, and in the Communist bloc, there were people prepared to believe that not only had a belligerent South Korea started the fight, but had done so with American assistance. To most historians studying these events, sufficient evidence exists to prove the opposite. Far more important for developments at the time was the fact that the United Nations Commission on Korea was in South Korea and reported immediately that "the invasion . . . was an act of aggression initiated without warning and without provocation in execution of a carefully prepared plan." On the basis of this report from a neutral commission, national leaders throughout the world accepted the fact of North Korean aggression.

They therefore supported action taken by the United States, and gave it United Nations sanction in the form of Security Council resolutions. The first, on June 25, by a vote of 9 to 0 with Yugoslavia abstaining, found that an armed attack by North Korea had taken place in violation of the United Nations Charter. It called for immediate withdrawal of troops, a cease-fire, and asked United Nations members to help execute the resolution and refrain from giving assistance to North Korean authorities. The Soviet Union, which was then boycotting the Security Council because of continued Chinese Nationalist presence when, it argued, the Communist should have taken their seat, was not there to veto the resolution.

On June 27, President Truman announced that he had ordered American air and sea forces to give air cover and support to troops of the Republic of Korea. Later that same day, the Security Council, by a vote of 8 to 1, recommended that United Nations members furnish such assistance as was necessary to repel the attack and restore peace in the area. Yugoslavia opposed sanctions, calling for mediation. India, at first abstaining, voted in favor after receiving instructions from home. The Egyptian government, still opposed to previous United Nations action in Palestine, refused to support the United Nations resolution.

Three days later President Truman authorized General MacArthur in Japan to use American ground forces in Korea, to institute a naval blockade of the entire Korean coast, and to bomb targets in North Korea. On July 7 the Security Council recommended that all military units be placed under a unified command, that the United Nations flag be used, and that the United States name a Supreme Commander. On July 8, Truman appointed MacArthur to the post.

Meanwhile, and through July and August, North Korean forces continued to drive south. American occupation troops from Japan, peacetime enlistees, ill-trained and ill-equipped for fighting an unforeseen kind of war, were hurried into the breach. In short order the North Korean attack pushed them, along with the small British units rushed from Hong-Kong, into an 80 by 60 mile pocket on the southeast tip of the Korean peninsula. But there they were able to gather strength while more American personnel moved into the Far East. On September 15 General MacArthur effected a successful amphibious landing 150 miles to the north, at Inchon on the west coast of the peninsula, while simultaneously launching an attack from the southeast perimeter. Within a matter of days, the whole situation had changed radically; enormous numbers of North Korean prisoners were taken, and the rest pushed pell-mell back toward the north. The war had entered a new phase.

The entire action so far was highly improvised, and hardly an example of what had been expected under the United Nations Charter. Absence of the Soviet Union from the Security Council, the presence of the United Nations Commission on Korea and the presence of American troops in Japan were the factors that made possible United Nations action under a recommendation—not a binding decision—from the United Nations Security Council. The Soviet Union was always to argue that the action was illegal since the Soviet Union had not concurred in the votes, and since the affair was a civil war rather than an international matter in which the United Nations could interfere. The American-named commander in the field had extraordinary leeway. The only link between him and the United Nations was a periodic meeting, held at the State Department in Washington, of representatives of the 16 nations that had contributed troops. Here they were informed of United States actions and could give their thoughts on matters at hand.

In all, 45 countries contributed troops, or supplies or transport. But the United States contributed the lion's share: nine-tenths of the non-Korean troops in action were American.

The American decision to face the attack in Korea was itself no simple one. The basic decision to restrict military commitments in the Far East to areas more easily defended had already been taken. Once the Korean attack came, there were military advisers who felt all the more strongly that this policy should be continued; they argued that the Soviet Union was not directly involved, that this might well be a diversionary attack while the Soviets prepared to use their strength in a still-weak Europe or a weaker Middle East, and that the United States should be ready to face these eventualities. There were those, too, who feared that presidential use of troops in the area would incur the wrath of Congress, some of whose leaders were already upset that the presence of American troops in a potential front line European situation had virtually pre-empted Congressional power to declare war. On the other hand, even though there was no knowledge of the extent to which the Russians or Chinese were involved, American leaders assumed close Soviet bloc coordination. They also felt that if the United States did not back the Korean government against invasion, other governments would feel uncertain about United States backing in other areas. In this particular case the presence of the United Nations Commission on Korea and its report made it far more difficult for people to accept the Soviet position, and ensured general United Nations support of the American move.

Finally, and no less important, the domestic political situation exerted tremendous pressure on the administration. Its overseas commitments to stop the Communists were expensive; it therefore faced the charge of spending too much. On the other hand, the containment policy seemed negative to too many people, and the administration therefore faced the counter-charge of not doing enough, and of only reacting to Communist moves. Since the requirements of foreign policy had led to strengthening the military branch and the executive in general, the administration was also charged with too much centralization in government. But most important, many Americans, since the announcement of the Open Door Policy in China in 1899, had felt some sentimental attachment for China (though this did not extend to allowing many Chinese to immigrate into the United States). American opposition to Japanese incursions into China had finally brought the United States into World War II. Now China had been absorbed by a far more formidable enemy—the Communist bloc. Charges were made that treason was involved, and that the State Department was directly responsible for losing China. An obscure, ineffective, and somewhat disreputable Senator from Wisconsin, Joseph R. McCarthy, had vaulted into national prominence through demagogic and unprovable charges of heavy Communist infiltration into the Department of State. In an extemporaneous section of a speech delivered at Wheeling, West Virginia, he held aloft a paper saying, "I have here in my hand a list of 205—a list of names that were known to the Secretary of State as being members of the Communist Party and who nevertheless are still working and shaping policy in the State Department." The paper was in fact a letter written in 1946 by the then Secretary of State, James F. Byrnes, that said nothing about Communists, and the figure McCarthy had used was whittled down to 81, and then to 57. Eventually the charges came to nothing. He was to use successfully the misrepresentation of documents for similar purposes in the future.

It was true, however, that there had been limited Communist infiltration into the government. A long-drawn out dramatic case that skyrocketed into prominence the young California Congressman Richard Nixon, who had uncovered it, resulted in the conviction of Agler Hiss for perjury. Hiss had held a high rank in the State Department, had traveled to Yalta, and was, at the time of his trial, head of a private scholarly foundation, the Carnegie Endowment for Intrnational Peace. Now he was convicted for having lied in denying that he had passed secret government documents to a confessed former Communist, Whittaker Chambers. Other Communists, too, were discovered in theTreasury, Commerce, and Justice Departments; still others had served on legislative committee staffs. President Truman had set in motion a harsh loyalty program as early as 1947. The number and influence of Communists in government was never strong, and some—having joined out of the most patriotic motives—left the Party fairly soon. But denials by persons high in the government that *any* Communist infiltration had taken place seemed misplaced. Demagogues like McCarthy—and many who should have known better—charged that American policy was virtually directed by Communists; that those who were not actually Communists—such as General Marshall, Dean Acheson, President Truman—were dupes of the Communists, and by implication, guilty of treason.

The historian finds it ironic that members of an administration who had set the United States upon the unprecedented course of containment, and who had accepted its underlying assumptions about Soviet policy, should have found themselves charged with being "soft on Communism." Political discourse reached an extraordinarily low level and assumed an unreality that would have important consequences in the next few years.

It is hard to tell whether and how much the political atmosphere in America influenced the course of decisions on Korea. Europeans, looking at what they considred to be anti-Communist hysteria in a country where the Party was small, weak, and ineffectual (in their own countries it commanded a large and faithful following) were sure that it did. Those involved in the decisions are equally sure that they acted in what they felt were the best American interests, regardless of public denunciations. To those who argued that the administration had abandoned the Far East to the Communists, the Korean decision appeared to be a successful change in policy forced by militant public opinion. But to the Truman administration it was a continuation of previous policy in a set of new circumstances.

In one way, however, Korea did force an immediate change. President Truman ordered the American Seventh Fleet into the Formosa straits, primarily to protect the Chiang regime on Formosa from Communist China.

To Americans, the decision to link defense of South Korea with defense of the Nationalist remnant on an island that properly belonged to

China seemed natural: Communist aggression was one and the same thing. To most people in the rest of the world the action was a mistake; the former was legitimate defense against aggression, the latter interference in a civil war in a country not directly involved in Korea. They argued, further, that the move would prevent any possible accommodation with the new Chinese regime, would force it into closer cooperation with Russia, and, as it could be represented as another example of Western imperialism, would discredit the West in the eyes of Asian nationalists. Certainly it can only have served to confirm Chinese Communists in the view that the United States was *the* enemy, the one power halting reunification of the country and preserving a regime that challenged Communist authority. In the face of the American action, the Chinese halted their build-up of troops in the area opposite Formosa and began to move them to the North, near Korea. For the moment the Chiang regime was safe, but the implications of the action were unclear.

The Korean War served to harden Western assumptions about Soviet foreign policy: leaders throughout Europe and in the United States now accepted the view that because early Soviet efforts to expand in Western Europe had been blocked by the American initiatives of 1947–48, Soviet policy had now entered a new, hard phase characterized by reliance on military force. The Korean venture was one example of new Soviet policy, warfare in Indochina another. In a third area, Malaya, the Communists—as in other areas of the world—had gone over to the offensive in 1948, in the form of riots and strikes. Their failure prompted a shift to guerrilla warfare. Communist guerrillas never numbered more than five thousand and Malaya had no common border with any Communist power that could have given them supplies. But the large Chinese minority in Malaya was sympathetic to the guerrillas, and by 1950 a British army of 35,000 men was tied down in the fight, while hundreds of thousands of constabulary assumed police duties.

The new view of Soviet policy—correct or incorrect—could only lead to a strengthening of Western efforts to counter the Soviet military threat. But the pace of the war in Korea did so much to mold this response and its consequences that we must turn first to the course of that war.

Within two weeks of MacArthur's successful Inchon landing in September, his United Nations troops had reached the 38th parallel, where the war had started. From Washington came a directive that the General's objective should be "destruction of the North Korean Armed Forces," and he was authorized to cross the 38th parallel if there were no indication that Soviet or Chinese forces planned to enter the campaign. In China, Chou En-lai warned that the Chinese People's Republic would not "supinely tolerate seeing their neighbors being savagely invaded by imperialists" and that "if US or UN forces crossed the 38th parallel, China would send troops to the Korean frontier to defend North Korea."

To the commander in the field pursuing retreating troops, a pause that would allow them to regroup would be foolish in the absence of other overriding reasons. In Korea MacArthur had received permission to advance, and did so. The administration then went to the United Nations General Assembly—the Security Council being deadlocked after Soviet return to it—and secured a somewhat ambiguous resolution reaffirming the Assembly's desire for a "unified, independent, democratic Korea," and recommending that steps be taken to "insure conditions of stability throughout Korea." United Nations forces were to remain in Korea only long enough to achieve these objectives. To transform the anticipated military success into political reality, the Assembly created the United Nations Commission for Unification and Rehabilitation of Korea. In the meantime MacArthur's forces continued to pursue the enemy. From India's ambassador in Peking came warning that the Chinese were, indeed, likely to intervene if the move into North Korea continued. So that the Chinese Communists might present their side of the issue directly, India suggested that they be represented in the Assembly. But this move failed.

On October 15 President Truman flew to Wake Island in the central Pacific to meet with MacArthur, his Far Eastern commander, and receive from him an on-the-spot report. McArthur predicted an early victory and reunification, and told the President there was little danger of Chinese intervention—the Chinese had too few troops and materiel. When Truman told him that the administration was particularly concerned with strengthening the defenses of Western Europe and wanted to avoid a war with China at all cost, MacArthur replied that one division could surely be spared from Korea to be transferred to Europe by the end of January 1951.

A NEW WAR

In November, however, as MacArthur extended his lines, he began to run into substantial numbers of Chinese units and notified the United Nations to that effect. At first, contact was sporadic and estimates of the numbers of Chinese troops remained low. Then on November 24 MacArthur launched an offensive with the announced intention of bringing the war to an end and withdrawing the Eighth Army to Japan by Christmas. Two days later an enormous Chinese force—subsequently estimated at 850,000 men—counterattacked, splitting MacArthur's forces, and sending them in a headlong, though orderly, retreat.

MacArthur now insisted that the new war required greatly expanded measures—bombing of Chinese bases in Manchuria, blockade of the Chinese coast, the use of Chiang Kai-shek's forces on Formosa to attack the mainland. But the Truman administration, with full approval of the Joint Chiefs of Staff, preferred to keep the war limited. Full commitment in the Far East might leave the West vulnerable in other parts of the world and might lead to an all-out war for which it was ill-prepared, particularly since Russia by then had the atomic bomb. America's allies, far more vulnerable, were particularly concerned that the war not spread. When a press corps eager for news pushed President Truman into saying that, since any nation in a fight always had to consider what weapons might be used, the administration was considering the use of atomic bombs in Korea, Prime Minister Attlee immediately flew to Washington to argue against such a course, and the newspapers of the world were filled with scare headlines. While groups within the United States pushed for more strenuous action against China, allies and neutrals pleaded for restraint.

Charges and countercharges flew. A Communist Chinese delegation came to the United Nations to argue that the United States was the aggressor in Formosa, Korea, and Manchuria, whose air-space it consistently violated. Meanwhile American troops recovered and regrouped and began again to move northward from their positions in South Korea. Faced with possible alternatives, including the ones suggested by General MacArthur, administration leaders had decided to keep the war a limited one of pressure and attrition which would eventually force the Chinese into negotiations. In the meantime General MacArthur sought to build up public support for his position and build a backfire to force the administration to adopt his ideas. Unable to accept what was clearly insubordination, Truman removed him from his command in April, 1951. "MacArthur left me no choice—I could no longer tolerate his insubordination," he wrote. "And the Joint Chiefs of Staff unanimously recommended that he be relieved."* He appointed General Matthew B. Ridgway in MacArthur's place.

MacArthur's recall led to an extraordinary emotional public display in the United States. The General moved through city after city in a series of tremendous parades, and addressed a joint session of Congress that was televised to 60 million viewers.

Republican opposition, hot on the trail of a winning election issue and sensing the extent of public frustration with the administration's inability to "win the Cold War," fanned emotions. Some asserted that treason had

* Harry S. Truman, *Memoirs* (Garden City N.Y.: Doubleday 1956), Vol. II, p. 561.

caused the hobbling of MacArthur, just as it had been behind the loss of China, and Senators called for impeachment of President Truman. Secretary of State Dean Acheson, General Marshall and others who had formulated the containment policy, were subjected to an extraordinary campaign of vilification; *Time* magazine called Acheson the leader of a State Department group that was "the last to identify the real enemy as Soviet Russia."

The campaign only began to die down when a lengthy Congressional investigation revealed the bases of administration action, and when it became evident that Congressmen and Senators who talked belligerently were totally unwilling to take the responsibility of declaring war. Extending the hostilities would risk involving the whole of the American economy and American society in another war with all its controls and costs— but this time with the presence of atomic weapons.

While people in Europe and Asia looked on in bewilderment, having applauded the President's action, the war went on in Korea, where enormous casualties were inflicted upon Communist Chinese troops. The United States, although using military pressure to force the Chinese to negotiate, had also succeeded in having the United Nations General Assembly brand Communist China an aggressor in Korea. Many members were reluctant, arguing that this would make negotiations harder, and the Indian delegation opposed the action on the basis that the West had been given ample warning of what would happen if the military move were made into North Korea—the Communist sphere. It argued, furthermore, that the Communist Chinese were right in insisting that the United States had intervened in Chinese affairs by supporting the Nationalist remnant on Formosa. On the other hand, the United States effort to obtain the resolution was made easier by the Chinese refusal to meet with a cease-fire group of India, Iran, and Canada in December unless the United States withdrew from Formosa and Korea and unless they were given representation in the United Nations.

Military pressures succeeded in forcing the Communists to discuss an armistice, beginning in June 1951. But for the next two years the Communist Chinese, partly perhaps because of their century of humiliation by the West and partly because events seemed to have confirmed their ideological preconceptions, used every propaganda device possible to discredit the Western negotiators in the eyes of the Chnese and other Asian people. They portrayed the United Nations forces as defeated and begging for peace. They parlayed charges of germ warfare into a worldwide propaganda victory. They succeeded in having agents planted among prisoners of war in American-guarded camps where they organized riots and the capture, in one case, of the American camp commander. To secure his safe release, the second in command agreed to terms that implied the United States had been mistreating prisoners, and the Chinese lost no time in making good use of this. They also gave extensive publicity to the decisions of eleven American prisoners of war to remain in China, while the United States retaliated by publicizing the far larger number of Chinese who declined repatriation to Communist China.

Eventually, military pressure and the economic impact of the war, as well as Indian efforts at securing compromise, brought an armistice agreement in July 1953. Nominally, it was to be the prelude to negotiations for reunification. In fact, few believed it, and Syngman Rhee, President of South Korea, tried to disrupt the armistice negotiations and force the United States to continue the war. He was unsuccessful; but the United States promised economic and military aid and a mutual security pact to protect South Korea against a future attack, and he had to be satisfied with this.

INTERNATIONAL CONSEQUENCES OF THE KOREAN WAR

The savage battle on the Korean peninsula gave a new shape to international politics throughout the rest of the world: in Europe, where the movement for unity was warped by the new haste for rearmament; in New York, where the United Nation's assumed a new posture; in China, where the new leadership altered its plans and came into abrupt and direct conflict with the United States; and in the United States, where the long period of Democratic rule came to an end.

In January 1950 the Trunan administration had adopted a new policy paper on overall strategy that reflected State Depatment dissatisfaction with the adequacy of American response to Soviet pressures. It had rejected preventive war—advocated by some who felt that the United States should strike at the Soviet Union before it turned its new capacity to carry out an atomic explosion into nuclear weapons and added them to its overwhelming strength on the ground. It rejected a turn to a "Fortress America" isolationist policy, publicly advocated by some of the old-guard Republicans, notably former President Herbert Hoover. Instead, it argued for a rapid and large-scale build-up of both atmoic striking capacity in the air and of ground and naval power to deter expansion on the ground by more conventional means, along with a strengthening of American allies. The State Department estimated that the cost would amount to $35 billion annually, at a time when the actual ceiling on military spending was around $13 billion. Curiously enough, a number of military men argued strongly that the American economy would be unable to stand the strain.

The Korean War resolved the issue. Within the United States, military expenditures rose rapidly, not only to prosecute the war, but to build up existing armed strength and mobilization potential in general. In the January 1950 policy paper, 1954 had been named as the danger year in terms of increases in Soviet armed strength. The date was now advanced to 1952 on the basis that the Korean War and Chinese intervention were evidence of a new hard, aggressive Soviet policy, inspired by Russian possession of the atomic bomb.

In September 1950, even before the Chinese attack, the North Atlantic Council had met in New York. Until this time, NATO represented little more than a paper agreement backed by America's atomic striking force. The United States, under the Mutual Defense Assistance Program, had appropriated over one billion, three hundred million dollars in military aid for NATO allies in December 1949, and bilateral agreements on administration of the aid had been signed in January. In July 1950, the second year's appropriation, for a similar sum, was passed. But in August the President asked for, and was granted, another $4 billion. Until this time, however, the governments concerned had only begun to transform appropriations into armed force. Now Secretary of State Acheson proposed concerted action along two lines. He agrued that an integrated force with a centralized command should be built up, and he further argued that an effective force could never be built up unless West Germany contributed to it, to the extent of twelve divisions.

The subject of possible German rearmament had been bruited about for at least a year, and at least some English and French political leaders had spoken in favor of it. But French acceptance meant an even longer and harder step than the ones it had already taken since 1947 in turning to association with the United States and Britain and to a rapprochement with Germany. Nevertheless, in the light of the Korean War, European defenses were found wanting. On October 24, 1950, French Foreign Minister Schuman therefore presented the so-called Pleven Plan, which presumably would make German rearmament acceptable. In brief, it envisaged the creation of a European army with units contributed from national armies merged at the lowest level. For this army there would be a European defense budget and a European defense minister responsible to some European Assembly, perhaps that of the Council of Europe. All European countries except Germany would contribute the units from their existing armies; Germany would contribute only to the European army, and would still have no national force of its own. About the time that the French presented the Pleven Plan, Western negotiators also decided upon modifications in the German Occupation Statute. It would be impossible to obtain German participation in European defense unless

Germany were also allowed some greater measure of sovereignty. Therefore, Germany would be allowed a Ministry of Foreign Affairs and a regular diplomatic establishment, and Allied controls and restirctions over industry and review of German legislation would be reduced.

The growing importance of Germany in the new structure of world politics became far more apparent in the ensuing weeks of negotiation, and one of the strongest cards in the German hand was that of internal opposition to rearmament. Part of the opposition was moral; part of it was simply of an "oh, not again!" sort; part of it, particularly from certain Social Democratic leaders, reflected a feeling that German rearmament posed real security dangers for Germany. It might provoke Russian retaliation before the defense of Western Europe were restored. Even worse, Germans might become cannon fodder because of a strategy that provided for neither liberation of East Germany and its reunification with West Germany, nor real protection of West Germany itself. Given the relative ground strength of the Russians and the West, in the event of war West Germany would serve only as a battleground over which the West would retreat to defensive positions. Therefore, argued some Social Democrats, only if other Western powers planned a militant strategy that would carry them *forward* in the event of hostilities could Germany afford to contribute to armed strength.

The internal opposition enabled the Adenauer government to press the other Western powers for more concessions, particularly since many people found merit in the German arguments. The opposition gave force to the German government's requests: unless they were met, Germany would *not* participate in Western rearmament and in its own defense, now so urgently desired by the Truman administration and approved by the British and French.

And so, in the laborious negotiations that followed, Germany was given more than it had originally requested. But although negotiators performed the difficult task of transforming proposal into policy during the next two years, and signed the treaty setting up the European Defense Community in 1952, it now appeared that French reluctance to allow German rearmament might doom it even in this guise. Added to this reluctance was a conviction that the European army would be unworkable, the fact that the British—with responsibilities throughout the rest of the world—refused to join it, and the opposition of many French political leaders to do anything that would diminish the possibility of independent use of a *national* army. Some observers became convinced that French leaders had in fact devised the unwieldy plan merely to postpone the day when they would have to yield to American pleas for German rearmament. If this could be delayed for a matter of months, or better yet, years, who could tell what might happen? Since no French government anticipated a life of more than a few months, delay might mean that at least it would not fall over the German issue; some future government would face it. And in the meantime the French used the matter to obtain acceptance of the Schuman Plan for a Coal and Steel Community; without this, they would not consent to German rearmament in *any* form.

The EDC issue was not actually settled until 1954, after the death of Stalin and the peace settlements in Korea and Indochina. Under the impact of these, the French Assembly rejected EDC. But German rearmament took place in a different form (see p. 162).

The diversion of EDC slowed the process of German contribution to Western armed strength, but NATO planning began to produce results on other fronts. Besides establishing a unified command structure for NATO in the form of Supreme Headquarters, Allied Powers Europe (SHAPE), and appointing Eisenhower to Supreme Allied Commander, Europe (SACEUR), work was begun to create a network of supply, communication, and airfield facilities behind the lines in Germany. (Before the Korean War, the British and American supply lines in Germany, instead of running vertically to the front, had paralleled it, to Bremerhaven and Hamburg. In places they had been within a few miles of the Russian lines.) Equally important were the complicated diplomatic maneuvers of military planners trying to convince their governments that in the face of Russian millitary power NATO would need one hundred divisions for a holding operation instead of the twelve divisions they had possessed before the Korean War. Each government tried to tell others in NATO what share they should contribute to the buildup. Each argued that what was asked of it was too large and politically impossible.

Nevertheless, although the force levels of almost 100 divisions agreed on at the Lisbon meeting of 1952 were never to be achieved, by 1953 the impetus of the Korean War had transformed the situation in Europe. Weak divisions had been turned into a larger number of heavily armed divisions with appropriate supporting forces—tanks, artillery, and tactical air forces. There were 15 ready on the central front, Denmark and Norway could supply two more, and Italy from seven to nine. If time permitted, even more could be mobilized. Korea also led, in 1952, to NATO membership for Greece and Turkey—scarcely North Atlantic countries. The negotiations were arduous, since some northern and western members were dubious about extending NATO guarantees to the eastern Mediterranean, a region particularly difficult to defend. At any rate, the United States was already committed to the defense of Greece and Turkey. On the other hand, since Greece and Turkey would add another 20 divisions to NATO, and the possibility that in case of war the Soviets would have to divert substantial forces to the area, the two countries were desirable allies.

The Korean War and the urgency it gave to American efforts to build an alliance system affected two other countries: Spain and Japan.

Spain, racked in the 1930s by a civil war that brought Franco to power with the help of Nazis and Fascists, maintained neutrality throughout World War II. Franco resisted Hilter's efforts to bring him in on the Axis side, and Britain and the United States—despite strong domestic protests —helped him to sustain the precarious Spanish economy. To liberals who saw World War II as a crusade against fascism of all forms, Franco Spain remained a detestable anachronism; it was excluded from the San Francisco conference and France closed its Pyrenees frontier in February 1946. America published a White Book detailing Spanish assistance to the Axis, and soon demands were made in the United Nations for action against Franco.

Presumably the very fact that Franco espoused fascism made him a threat to the peace. But since the loudest demands for action came from the Soviet Union, other powers began to question the wisdom of an effort to overthrow the Spanish dictator: What would follow? Thus, they resisted attempts to impose economic sanctions, and the General Assembly recommended instead that states withdraw their heads of mission in Madrid, without severing diplomatic relations.

By 1948, in view of conspicuous lack of result, the French reopened their borders and a number of states returned their ministers and ambassadors. In the fall of 1950, after the start of the Korean War, the General Assembly revoked the recommendation passed in 1946, and Spain was allowed to join United Nations Specialized Agencies. Only a few European countries held out against the revocation; Arab and Latin American states spearheaded the battle for a change and were warmly thanked by the Franco regime for having stood by it during four years. The same year the American Congress, having previously refused to appropriate any money for loans to Spain, reversed itself and provided money in the Mutual Security Aid bill; President Truman declared himself not obligated to spend it.

In 1951, however, the Truman administration found itself in the position of seeking a formula by which Spain could be associated with NATO. American military planners stressed the desirability of bases in Spain, and though the Spanish army was ill-trained and poorly equipped, it was large; with the disparity in manpower under arms between the Soviet bloc and the NATO powers, the Spanish army of between two and four hundred thousand men began to look like an attractive force.

But European governments, faced with emphatic anti-Franco opinion at home, refused to counternance a move whose expediency they felt would lose them more support than any possible military gain would be worth —and many questioned any military gain. Thus negotiations through 1952 and 1953 continued on a bilateral basis. In September 1953, under the Eisenhower administration, the discussions brought agreement that gave to the United States the right to build and use military bases in Spain in return for large-scale American economic and military assistance. Although conclusion of the treaty—after the extended negotiations —brought little stir in Europe, it contributed to distrust of the United States by left-wing groups. They were well aware that much of the impetus had come from Americans—Senators and others—who felt that a Fascist anti-Communist was a sturdier and better one than a Socialist anti-Communist.

On the other side of the world, the Korean War led to the conclusion of a peace treaty with Japan, thus ending the occupied status of that country. Though a treaty had posed delicate and difficult problems, the United States was determined to have one. The administration wanted to bind Japan by another defense treaty by which Japan would allow American troops and bases to remain within its borders in exchange for a guarantee of American protection. Moreover, the United States was determined that the treaty would not give legal sanction to return Japanese lands to Russia or imply that Formosa (whose return to China had been promised in World War II) should go to Communist China. Under the circumstances, a number of countries that had fought the Japanese in World War II were bound to oppose the treaties—not just the Soviet Union, but also countries like India, Burma, and Yugoslavia. All of these refused to atend the final peace conference at San Francisco in September 1951, or to sign the treaty. The settlement imposed no reparations on the erstwhile enemy, but left individuals agreements to be negotiated between Japan and its former victims.

At the same time that the United States secured the Japanese bases that proved so vital in the Korean War, it signed two other mutual defense treaties with Asian countries, one with the Philippines, the other with Australia and New Zealand, creating the so-called ANZUS grouping. An attempt to enlist Arab states in a Middle East Command failed in the face of Arab hostility.

Finally, the Korean War had considerable impact on the United Nations organization. While some viewed action under United Nations auspices as a first proof that collective security could be made to work against an aggressor, others felt that Korea mainly indicated how weak and ineffectual any collective security attempt would be unless the first prerequisite, written into the Charter, could be effected: great power unanimity on whatever action was to be taken. In the Korean situation the Charter provisions for collective security had never really been implemented; it resembled far more an old-fashioned war, but one fought under the threat of nuclear weapons.

Events seem to bear out the second contention, though it, too, was not entirely accurate. The Korean action was improvised, since the agreements that would have provided the Security Council with national contingents for collective security action were never made. It could only be taken under United Nations auspices because the Soviet Union was absent from the Security Council at the time of the invasion.* It could only be done because of the proximity of American forces in Japan. And finally—of supreme importance—the presence of the neutral United Nations Commission on Korea provided definite and reliable information identifying the aggressor. Subsequently, under other circumstances, countries that wanted to avoid being drawn into conflicts between the great powers were to use the excuse that precise knowledge of who was culpable in a conflict could not be obtained. In the Korean War, although the Formosa issue clouded the matter and the subsequent march north of the 38th parallel went beyond the meaning of collective security, at least it was clear that North Korea had been the initial aggressor.

The fact that these particular circumstances—absence of the Soviet Union, presence of American troops, and presence of the United Nations Commission on Korea—had made possible the Korean action led to changes in the structure of the United Nations, in hopes that in future crises the organization would not have to rely on chance. Early paralysis of the Security Council had already made countries use the General Assembly more freely in matters of international peace and security. Now the move was made more formal in the Acheson Plan, or the "Uniting for Peace" proposal. Adopted by the General Assembly in November 1950 with only the Soviet bloc opposed and Argentina and India abstaining, it provided that if the Security Council were deadlocked, the General Assembly could meet on twenty-four hour notice and recommend collective measures including the use of armed force against an aggressor. This would solve the problem that would have arisen at the time of Korea had the Soviet Union stayed in the Security Council. Moreover, to avoid the

---

* This fact led some to conclude that the Soviet Union had actually wanted the United States to be drawn into Korea in the way it had, thereby leaving other areas open to aggression or putting a heavy financial and military burden on the United States. There are many reasons to doubt this interpretation and support another, that the Soviet Union made a mistake so far as the United Nations was concerned. Had it blocked the United Nations action it seems likely that the United States would have acted alone, and thus lost some of the moral prestige of United Nations support.

difficulties that would have occurred had American troops not been available, the plan recommended to members that they keep within their armed forces contingents ear-marked and organized for possible service as United Nations units. To eliminate the element of chance in the decisive presence of the United Nations Commission on Korea, the Assembly created a permanent Peace Observation Commission of fourteen member states that could observe and report on trouble spots anywhere in the world. Finally, the Assembly established a Collective Measures Committee to make recommendations to strengthen the peace machinery.

Of the four innovations, only the first became an important part of the United Nations machinery. The others were doomed, mainly because Korea had really demonstrated how many countries of the world would *not* support collective security measures in distant parts of the world where their immediate interests were only remotely involved. The burden of the Korean War was largely carried by the United States, and many Americans felt that conduct of the war was unduly hampered by restraints exercised by countries whose contributions were minimal. But in other contributing countries in many cases people took the opposite view: they found themselves committed to courses of action about which they were unhappy, precisely because the United States carried the largest share of the burden and could thus act without deferring to their opinions. Many United Nations observers concluded that the Korean experiment would probably not be repeated, that Korea had demonstrated the inadequacy of the concept of collective security almost as effectively as the Ethiopian experience had done in 1936. But the increased role of the General Assembly in diplomacy involving matters of security became an established fact.

Finally, Korea had a direct impact on the leaders of Communist China. They had not been involved in preparations for the North Korean invasion and had weakened their military strength in the north in preparation for the final takeover of the island of Formosa, whose return to China had been promised during World War II. The sudden American interposition of the Seventh Fleet blocked this move. To the Chinese, it was seen only as a direct intervention in their civil war. Then, when American and other United Nations troops crossed the 38th parallel despite Chinese warnings that this was an area of direct interest to them and that the Chinese would act to protect their interests, their hostility was reinforced. The Chinese Communist world view had already set in a hard ideological mold; but events had merely served to confirm it: Imperialist America, everywhere in direct conflict with legitimate Communist Chinese interests, was obviously the main enemy. The regime—drawn into an expensive and unforeseen military venture in Korea—hastened the pace of the internal development necessary to produce the power to cope with American enmity. Sooner rather than later it would exert all possible power on the world scene in opposition to the "western imperialists."

AMERICAN REACTIONS TO FRUSTRATION: INITIAL EFFECT OF THE 1952 POLITICAL CAMPAIGN

The United States was the leader in securing general acceptance of the assumptions upon which containment was based and of the policies involved in building the grand coalition against the Soviet Union. Yet the strains and frustrations of a policy whose success led only to its own continuation instead of to final victory also had political consequences within the United States, and these political consequences, in turn, had widespread repercussions on international politics in the next few years. There were other factors behind the political upheavals of 1950 to 1952; but the containment frustration pervaded them.

One has already been mentioned, the growth of McCarthyism. Though it could not have been successful unless there actually were some spies and subversives, it led to the kind of wholesale vilification of scapegoats that had not been seen for many years in America. If there was no victory, someone must be responsible: the Communists in the Federal government, Harry S. Truman, Dean Acheson, American allies, the United Nations. Men whose only claim to fame lay in their ability to concoct wild charges vaulted into political prominence.

The acclaim given to General MacArthur, who, it was believed, could have "won" the Korean War was another result. Once given a serious hearing by those who would have to take the responsibility of action, he faded away. But more irresponsible men continued to echo his memorable if somewhat meaningless phrase: "There is no substitute for victory."

More complex but equally serious was the strong move to amend the Constitution to curb the foreign policy power of the executive. At a time when many were calling for *stronger* foreign policy action, the suggestion seemed odd; the origin of the so-called "Bricker Amendment" lay in the conviction that executive action was what had strengthened the Soviet Union and weakened the United States. In a sense, like the constitutional amendment limiting any president to two terms in office, it was retaliation against a dead president, Franklin D. Roosevelt. The "Bricker Amendment" failed—but the margin was surprisingly slim.

Herbert Hoover, Robert A. Taft, and others espoused a "fortress America" concept, and condemned the Truman administration for assuming its commitments in Europe. A more influential school of foreign policy thinkers declared that the moribund policy of containment must give place to a dynamic one of "liberation" or "rollback" of Communist power. The most prominent exponent of the idea was John Foster Dulles, Republican foreign policy spokesman who would have been Secretary of State had the Republican candidate, Thomas Dewey, won in 1948, and who did become Secretary of State under President Eisenhower in 1953. Dulles—who espoused the "Bricker Amendment" only until he became Secretary of State, at which point he reversed his stand—spelled out his views in a May 1952 issue of *Life* magazine. Here he wrote that, in contrast to the "static, passive" policy of containment, which promised at heavy cost only that the United States could "live with" peril, not live *without* it, the nation must develop a "dynamic" policy using "ideas as weapons . . . conform[ing] to moral principles." Such a policy could lead, in two, five, or ten years, to the freeing of substantial parts of the captive world. This would be accomplished through "freedom programs" whose precise content, however, defied definition. He declared that the United States did not want "a series of bloody uprisings and reprisals," but pointed to Tito's defection from the bloc as the form of change to which policy should be directed. In January 1953, testifying before a Senate Committee, he said, "Those who do not believe that [liberation] can be accomplished by moral pressures, by the weight of propaganda, just do not know what they are talking about. . . ."

At the same time that the whole basic containment policy was under fire for being insufficient, the administration faced widespread charges of irresponsible spending. Opponents of the Truman administration promised that a change would bring a reduction in the federal budget of 25, 40, or 50 per cent. Since the only area in which such a cut could occur was in defense spending, with perhaps a smaller cut in the field of foreign aid (which was now primarily military), it was rather hard to reconcile the two arguments.

Nevertheless, in the 1952 presidential campaign, foreign policy frustrations played a large part. Charges were made of Communism in government, the weakness of containment, too much spending, and one other —corruption in high places. The sweeping Republican victory rested on these and on the personality of the Republican candidate, General Eisenhower, who had returned from his position as Supreme Allied Commander in Europe to wrest the nomination from Senator Taft of Ohio, leader of the Republican old guard.

There were several immediate consequences for American foreign policy and world politics.

Although Americans were accustomed to campaign oratory that has little relevance to what the victorious party will do once in office, the effect of such oratory was now international. In Eastern Europe, talk of "liberation" rather than "containment" raised high hopes among many people. There might be little chance to revolt against totalitarian power (regardless of Dulles' views, the Yugoslav case was unique, and hardly a model for what might happen in other Soviet satellites) . But the thought that outside aid might be forthcoming added an element of hope. The extent to which American politicians had believed their awn campaign oratory was revealed in early 1953 when a "Captive Peoples" resolution came before Congress. It repudiated past secret agreements made by the United States that permitted enslavement of other peoples. But as debate began, it became clear that in fact the agreements under attack—the Yalta and Potsdam Declarations—were the only documents signed by the Soviet Union that constituted clear engagements *not* to do what it had done in Eastern Europe. Eisenhower therefore worked to prevent passage of the resolution. He was supported by the Democrats in Congress, while his own Republican supporters, who had blamed the Democratic administration for allowing the Russian takeover, finally and reluctantly shelved the resolution.

But the debate had convinced people further that liberation was not an empty phrase. Then the administration took another step that served to bolster this conviction: on February 2, 1953, in a message delivered to Congress in person, President Eisenhower told the world that he had rescinded Truman's order forbidding Chiang Kai-shek to attack the mainland from Formosa. In popular parlance, the President had "unleashed" Chiang. In fact, the original Truman order interposing the Seventh Fleet between Formosa and the mainland had been designed to prevent the capture of Formosa by the Chinese Communists, while minimizing the extent to which the Administration could be charged with interfering directly in the Chinese civil war. Moreover it was subsequently revealed that Chiang's forces had been engaged in hit-and-run raids ever since Chinese intervention in the Korean War. And despite grandiose campaign utterances, the Nationalist Chinese forces had insufficient strength to do anything more. The order therefore appeared to be designed primarily for domestic consumption, but it, too, had its effects abroad. Allied statesmen, who could see no hope of liberation without the force of arms, were beset by the real worry that the United States might now be willing to risk war. Since Dulles, however, continued to disclaim any intention to use force, they expressed puzzlement at exactly what American policy was to be. More European leaders began to ask themselves whether some form of neutralism might not disengage them from a struggle in which the United States now appeared to be becoming more irrational.

Then, on June 16 and 17, 1953, workers in Berlin and other towns throughout East Germany revolted. The East German regime, unable to handle the situation, maintained power only because the Russian army quelled the revolt. The immediate causes were economic hardship, purges, and increased work norms, as well as ferment in Communist leadership brought by the death of Stalin three months earlier. From the point of view of international politics, several things were made clear: the East European regimes had failed dismally to create mass support, and the Soviet Union would probably have to be wary of depending on their armies. More than this, however, the United States, faced with a revolt within the Soviet sphere, did nothing despite appeals for help, and it and the other occupation powers disclaimed any part in the uprising. The talk of liberation had apparently meant nothing. Not until 1956, when a revolt in Hungary assumed even more widespread proportions, was this certain. But again the American administration did nothing. Liberation had not replaced containment, though it had raised high the hopes of many in the captive nations.

A second outcome of the political campaign put further strains on alliance policies and further clouded the international picture. In an effort to reconcile campaign pledges to cut expenditures drastically and also to pursue a more vigorous anti-Communist foreign policy, the new administration in Washington chose a new formula for military strategy: "massive retaliation." First described by Dulles in his *Life* magazine article, the doctrine became official when the administration took office, and in January 1954, Secretary Dulles spelled it out in an address to the Council on Foreign Relations. In essence, the doctrine would abandon the attempt to contain the kind of Soviet probe on the periphery of the Communist bloc that had occurred in Korea. Instead of meeting limited force with limited force, the United States, Dulles declared, would "retaliate, instantly, and by means of our own choosing. We can now," he declared, "shape our military establishment to fit what is *our* policy, instead of having to try to be ready to meet the enemy's many choices." In line with this policy came the "New Look" in the American military establishment. It involved a reduction in overall manpower, as well as in American manpower overseas, and placed more emphasis on nuclear air power.

The key in the attempt to shift military strategy was development of the hydrogen bomb. The potential power of the H-bomb was a thousand times greater than that of the first atomic bombs that devastated whole cities in Japan. The first American hydrogen explosions took place in November 1952, at Eniwetok atoll in the Pacific, a month after Britain tested its first atomic bomb. In August 1953 Stalin's successor, Malenkov, announced that the United States no longer had a monopoly of hydrogen bomb production.

Many Westerners first reacted with the feeling that the Soviet premier must be exaggerating or lying. Dulles commented that Malenkov's statement could only be accepted "with some skepticism." Within hours, however, the Atomic Energy Commission of the United States received confirming evidence. Moreover, it revealed later that the Soviet Union had proceeded with somewhat more advanced techniques than had the United States—thus refuting claims that the Communists had "stolen" the secret of the bomb.

The new era had not yet really begun. The United States still had a far larger stockpile of nuclear materials and claimed to possess means of delivery that the Soviet Union lacked. But the Russians had not failed to see the importance of the latter point, and while speeding nuclear development, also pushed forward rapidly with construction of long-range bomber striking forces and a rocket force. The 1954 May Day parade, which featured a fly-over by the new four-jet Tupolev intercontinental bombers, gave dramatic evidence that their progress had been surprisingly rapid. In the West, the developments caused an extraordinary moment of confusion.

Upon reports that the Soviets had exploded their bomb, the director of the American Office of Defense Mobilization declared that "Soviet Russia is capable of delivering the most destructive weapon ever devised by man on chosen targets in the United States." But the Secretary of Defense said it would be "three years before they have a reasonable number of bombs and airplanes that could deliver them." On the other hand, the recently resigned chairman of the Atomic Energy Commission argued that within one or two years the Russians could destroy the United States.

One thing clear amid the babel of different views was the awesome power of the new weapon. When coupled with the emphasis on the American "new look" and "massive retaliation," it gave statesmen a new source of confusion and doubt. Would the United States actually use massive retaliation against a local attack in the future if the Russians had the capacity to strike directly at the United States? Would other countries depend on an alliance with the United States that counted on deterrence rather than upon local defense? If deterrence failed and the Soviets attacked, the result might be a holocaust. Given the reduction of American ground forces and hints of possible further withdrawals, would the United States, unable to defend on the ground, rely on a deterrence it would then find either impossible or suicidal to use? Adlai Stevenson, the defeated Democratic candidate in the 1952 presidential campaign asked, "Will we turn brush fires and local hostilities into major conflicts? Are we, indeed, inviting Moscow and Peiping to nibble us to death?"

These questions arose not only in the United States, but in Europe and

Japan—where they contributed to growing neutralist sentiment. As a result, administration spokesmen qualified their position: massive retaliation would not be used under all circumstances; American units would be kept in Europe. But the planned troop reductions continued and the confusion persisted. In an attempt to offset the reduction, the administration argued that other countries should provide more of the manpower requirements of the "free world"—a suggestion most of them found politically unpalatable.

In the end the new administration continued to follow the basic policy lines laid down by the previous administration, but with the shift in military emphasis dictated by budgetary considerations. To compensate for the lack of available means for implementing the more "dynamic" aspects of proposed policy, Administration spokesmen, including Secretary Dulles, continued to indulge in the blustering rhetoric of the campaign. Thus the realities of foreign policy were obscured for the American people, and fear continued to be aroused in other countries that the United States would do something rash. Dulles' tendency to see the whole Cold War—and the position of any country in relation to it—in terms of a gigantic struggle between good and evil, between which there was no possible compromise (when in fact compromise was being made every day), made this brilliant but limited man the most mistrusted American statesman in a long time. In some cases, as in French Indochina in 1954 (see p. 141), it appeared that he and those around him had been carried away by their own words. In other cases, as at the time of the Geneva Conference of 1955, it appeared that the other side of this blindness had come to the fore (see pp. 177–180).

THE DEATH OF STALIN AND SOVIET FOREIGN POLICY

Since the late 1920s Stalin had been the virtually unchallenged dictator of a Soviet Russia that had grown enormously in industrial strength and world power. In later years the almost oriental potentate ruled in an atmosphere of mystery, terror and seclusion, the object of sycophantic adulation that was fostered by an enormous propaganda machine. At times supple in policy, he could also be enormously rigid; although the Soviet state had grown, his mistakes had been great, and only the devices of historical rewriting and repetitious propaganda kept them from becoming evident. The Nazi-Soviet pact had almost cost the Soviet Union its independence; the obtuse insistence on the imminent failure of American capitalism after the war had led to a bold policy that had brought the American reorientation to containment with its concomitant commitments abroad—a policy that had effectively blocked further Soviet expansion in

spite of an enormous and costly Soviet rearmament effort. The prolonged
Korean War stimulated a further stiffening of the Western effort and
meant the decisive defeat of Stalin's efforts to keep West Germany from
rebuilding and rearming within the Western European orbit. The attempt
to penetrate Western Europe, Turkey, Greece, and North Africa had
failed, and Yugoslavia had slipped out of Soviet grasp. He had underestimated the new Chinese leaders and his relations with them were not satisfactory; Mao was independent and demanding, and Stalin was penurious.

The balance, however, was far from negative. Despite unparalleled
American power and prestige at the end of the War, Stalin had successfully consolidated the Soviet system throughout Eastern Europe (supervising in the last years a ruthless purge in which hundreds of thousands of
Communists perished or were imprisoned so that there could be no new
Tito). By making Russia a nuclear power, he could congratulate himself
that he had weathered a dangerous period in which the United States
could have coerced Russia but did not do so. After 1948, spurred by the
effect the Marshall Plan would have on rebuilding the European perimeter, by a realization that the United States had switched to a policy of
overseas commitment, he had gone on the offensive in Berlin and Korea.
One bad effect was the Western decision to rearm Germany. But by
1951 it seemed that this no longer was a major worry: in September
1950 a Prague meeting of Eastern European governments resulted in a
request for a Big Four conference to discuss a German peace treaty—
that is, to delay proposed German rearmament. But when the meeting
was actually held, in June 1951, the agenda proposed by the Russians,
over which the meeting collapsed, revealed little interest in the issue. It
appeared that Stalin, now armed with nuclear weapons, had seen something of how long and hard the road toward a German armed NATO
contribution would be, and no longer feared it.

In his last years, Stalin displayed more foreign policy flexibility. He
opened the way to negotiations in Korea, and at the long-delayed Nineteenth Party Congress, where little else was done, an opening was made
toward nationalist leaders of new states. Heretofore they had been stig-
matized as bourgeois lackeys of imperialism. Now they began, in Soviet
parlance, to become a part of a worldwide progressive movement with
which Communists could cooperate, and thus opened new opportunities
for Soviet diplomacy.

Even more, the old dictator gave signs of looking for a wider accommodation in Europe. In March 1952, came a new proposal that made it
look as though he might be willing to give up the Communization of East
Germany in return for a halt to West German rearming. The suggestion
held out the prospect of neutralized, armed, reunified Germany, and all-
German elections to be prepared by a joint commission of East and West

Germans. There were enough potential loopholes that Western countries failed to explore the proposal. They were afraid that negotiations would stall the interallied work on German rearmement and might, by raising false hopes, bring them to a full stop while NATO was still weak on the ground (and Russia was rebuilding her own conventional armed forces). No one was ever to find out whether Stalin was really interested in the suggested bargain. And a year later, during the maneuvering that followed Stalin's death, it appears that his former secret police chief Beria's genuine move to "dump" East German leader Walter Ulbricht in preparation for more flexibility on the issue of unification helped coalesce the opposition to Beria that led to the police chief's rapid downfall.

Above all, however, it was hard in those last months before Stalin's death to make much of a pattern of Soviet policy generally, for internally the regime was enmeshed in a bizarre and labyrinthine plot that foreshadowed a new, large-scale purge similar to those of the late thirties. A group of primarily Jewish doctors were charged with plans to eliminate Kremlin leadership. No one knew who might be implicated in the plot, and a vague dread seems to have gripped Moscow. In the midst of this came the news of Stalin's death and reprieve for all those who might have been attacked. It hardly seemed possible in this situation that foreign policy was being made in a cool and rational manner, and the ensuing struggle for power continued to be enmeshed with considerations of foreign policy.

The struggle was not resolved until Khrushchev emerged victorious in 1957. In July 1953, when Beria attempted to seize power, he failed and was executed. In 1955 Malenkov fell by the wayside. In 1956 came Khrushchev's supreme gamble: a long, secret, bitter denunciation of Stalin and his rule to the Party Congress. His position was shaky, but adroit and wily, he defeated the old adherents of Stalin—Molotov and Kaganovich—who had allied themselves to Malenkov and others. Khrushchev then dumped the World War II hereo, Marshal Zhukov, whose popularity had led Stalin to downgrade him, but who had returned to support Khrushchev. As an ally, he had become too powerful. Finally, in early 1958, Khrushchev demoted Bulganin, who had been his partner in the new diplomacy that began in 1955.

In the meantime, as the new leaders sought to consolidate their power by dismissing or discrediting the older generation of Stalinists who could be made scapegoats for the hardships of earlier times, they put their own claims to legitimacy to a severe test. In East Germany the test came in June 1953, accompanied by rioting in Czechoslovakia. It was successfully weathered, although it revealed weaknesses in the Soviet structure of power as well as weaknesses in Western ability to capitalize on them.

The new Soviet leaders made many concessions outside their own

sphere. They pressured the Chinese Communists to accept the neutral nations' plans for exchange of prisoners of war in Korea. As a consequence,
the Korean armistice was signed on July 27, 1953. It was supposed to be
followed by a general peace conference within three months, and President Syngman Rhee of South Korea, who had unsuccessfully tried to sabotage the peace discussions in order to keep the United States in the war,
declared that if unification did not result from the conference, he would
not feel bound by the armistice. There was no conference, however. Attempts to bring it about finally failed in mid-1954 over the issues of its
composition and agenda, but the real reasons lay in the basic conflict itself and in continued American and Chinese opposition over Formosa
and a seat for the Chinese in the United Nations. Rhee had to content
himself with continued American military support for the independence
of South Korea, a new military security treaty, and large-scale economic
aid.

Russian fence-mending took place elsewhere, too. At the United Nations, Secretary General Trygve Lie had long been opposed by the Soviets for his support of the Korean effort. He had previously come under
American attack for his support of Communist Chinese membership, and
was now under fire for his personnel policies. In November 1952 he resigned; Russian intransigence made choice of a successor difficult. But in
March the Soviets agreed to the appointment of the Swedish diplomat,
Dag Hammarskjold.

Other conciliatory moves included resumption of diplomatic relations
with Yugoslavia, Greece, and Israel, (with whom relations had been broken over charges about the bizarre doctor's plot) renunciation of postwar
claims to certain parts of Turkey and abandonment of Russian demands
for joint Soviet-Turkish control of sea and air bases around the Turkish
Black Sea straits. Late in 1953 Malenkov evinced an interest in settling
certain outstanding financial and border questions with Iran, and the Soviet government began to negotiate a series of trade treaties with other
countries without trying to use the bait of Soviet trade to obtain renunciation of the controls over shipment of strategic goods to the Soviet bloc.
And again, the bait of a peace treaty and cancellation of all war-born
claims was held out to West Germany in order to prevent it from moving
further in the direction of European economic and military integration.

To Winston Churchill, once more Prime Minister of England after the
Conservative electoral victory in October of 1951, the new fluid elements
in the Soviet position seemed to offer a field for diplomatic activity. On
May 11, 1953 he called for a Summit Conference similar to those great
conferences that had helped shape the world scene in war time, suggesting as he did so that it might be possible to reconcile Russian security in-

terests with European unity. But he ran head on into President Eisenhower's view that the Soviets should first show good faith by preparing "to allow other nations, including those of Eastern Europe, the free choice of their own forms of government," and "to act in concert with others upon serious disarmament proposals to be made firmly effective by stringent UN control and inspection." The Soviets retorted that to expect them to accept a series of conditions while the United States accepted none was asking too much. This argument struck a responsive chord in many Western Europeans. But the effort to explore further the possibility of a more explicit détente was thwarted not only by the American position, but also by the failure, in the middle of the year, to reach any agreement on the long-delayed Austrian peace treaty.

THE FAR EAST AND SOUTHEAST ASIA

The years after Stalin's death brought other Far Eastern developments, and the appearance of a general Russian relaxation after the end of the Korean War. The picture was complicated by the American determination to strengthen its position in the Far East and continued Chinese Communist efforts to press for solutions to conflicts through almost any means, regardless of Russian softness.

In Malaya, despite the steady move toward self-government and intensified efforts to stamp out the Communist rebels in the jungles, the rebellion—outgrowth of the concerted decision in 1948 of Southeast Asian Communist parties to resort to violence—continued. In French Indochina, on the other hand, the war finally came to a conclusion, marking another defeat for France in its attempt to restore its prewar empire. It left extraordinary problems in its wake and eventually brought the substitution of American influence for that of the French.

France's attempt to restore its empire had taken the form of the French Union, a device that would permit various forms of dependency, all leaving France in a position of superiority, and still able to carry out its "civilizing work."* The loss of the long, bitter seven years' war in Indochina, like the much earlier loss of Syria and Lebanon, came as a result of French commitments to an aim that was beyond the strength of postwar France. The commitment was a matter of principle to some conservative groups within France, but was also a response to pressures from

---

* The phrase was used at the Brazzaville Conference of 1944 when basic colonial policy was drafted. According to the Charter, "the purpose of the civilizing work accomplished by France in the colonies excluded any idea of autonomy, any possibility of an evolution outside of the French Empire."

the French colonials within Indochina, who wanted to lose neither their special status nor their investments. In an effort to counter popular support of the Communist-led Vietminh, the French made concession after concession to other nationalist groups whom they tried to set up in opposition to Ho Chi Minh and his Vietminh. There was no purpose in setting up other groups, however, unless they continued to recognize the special status of the French. Yet those who did so, like the chosen French instrument, the Emperor Bao Dai, received no popular support. After years of negotiation, the French and various Indo-Chinese groups reached an agreement, ratified early in 1950, creating the three states of Vietnam, Laos, and Cambodia, within the French Union; in a few days most Western states recognized them. (The Communist states countered by recognizing the Vietminh.) But Emperor Bao Dai had difficulty forming a cabinet and setting up a national army. Any French concessions to him were popularly viewed as having been extracted as a result of pressures of the Communist Vietminh. These increased greatly after the victory of the Chinese Communists established a common border through which supplies could flow, and across which the Vietminh could seek sanctuary, rest, and training. The efforts put forward by the French were enormous yet insufficient to accomplish the job. The war cost France a billion dollars a year, drained her of resources that could have been used for internal investments or for reconstruction in North Africa, and, in a circular process, contributed to the weakening of French governments which in turn could therefore do little to increase the vigor of their efforts. The weakness also aided the nationalist movements in other parts of the French Union, particularly in North Africa.

American aid, supplied after Chinese intervention in Korea, and the use of new and different tactics, proved insufficient. Not until 1953 and early 1954 did France take the final, drastic political step of negotiating and accepting full independence—first of Laos and Cambodia and then Vietnam. The French could argue quite cogently that such a step had been impossible while the fighting continued, and that the fight in Indochina was part of the worldwide policy of containment in which they were doing their unrecognized and unappreciated share. But it was also true that the delay had persisted because French *colons* had not wanted to give Bao Dai what they had refused to hand over to Ho Chi Minh. In Asian eyes, therefore, it was a war of nationalists against colonialists, in which Bao Dai was only a puppet.

In the meantime the battle for Indochina reached a psychological climax in the Communist siege of a French-established strong point, the isolated fortress of Dien Bien Phu. For weeks the bitter attack continued against heroic resistance, while the French airlifted supplies and men.

The Communists were determined to capture it: a victory at Dien Bien Phu would immensely bolster their position at the forthcoming Geneva conference, which was to consider the entire Far East situation and which both representatives of the United States and Communist China would attend.

American officials recognized the psychological importance of Dien Bien Phu and nearly committed the United States to the Indochinese war. Already, though the French supplied the manpower, America was paying two-thirds to three-quarters of the cost of the war; the administration had accepted the French contention that a build-up of Vietnamese troops would lead to defeat of the Vietminh within a year if modern arms were available. (Contrary to widely held views, the Vietminh forces were in many cases larger and better-armed than the French.) But since the beginning of 1954 the French position had greatly deteriorated, and all attention was turned to Dien Bien Phu; in April the French government asked for an American air strike against the besieging forces.

Although the administration had previously denied any intent to be involved in the war in Indochina, President Eisenhower now talked of the "domino" theory of Southeast Asia; like a row of dominoes, if one of the weak states went down, the others would certainly go too. Vice-President Nixon launched an off-the-record trial balloon when he mentioned the possibility of using American troops in the area. But Congress registered dismay at the idea, and more sober counsel prevailed, both within the administration and without. After a somewhat belated consultation of European and Asian allies, it withdrew from its extended position. When Prime Minister Churchill told the House of Commons on April 27 that he had made no new military or political commitments and that Britain was not prepared to give any undertakings about military action in Indochina before the Geneva Conference, he was cheered. (One by-product of the consultations was considerable bad feeling between British Foreign Secretary Anthony Eden and Secretary Dulles. Eden thought that Dulles, in an effort to pressure him into supporting intervention, had returned to the United States and publicized as Eden's views the idea that Britain would accept an intervention which in fact Eden opposed.)

GENEVA, 1954: THE FAR EASTERN SETTLEMENT

The Geneva Conference of 1954 grew out of the sequence of events described in the foregoing narrative. As a result of diplomatic exchanges about the future of Germany and Austria during 1953, and as a result of Churchill's estimate that the changed world situation of 1953 was one in which a "Summit Conference" might produce useful results, the three

Western powers had agreed to a four-power meeting of Foreign Ministers with the Soviet Union at Berlin in January 1954.

The chief interest of the United States in the meeting was to demonstrate to its allies and to the growing number of neutrals led by India that the United States was always ready and willing to negotiate, especially when this would reveal the bad faith of the adversary. The European allies hoped for something more, while the Soviet Union used the conference to pursue its aim of securing a broader conference that would consider the Far East and would introduce Communist China to international society. In this the Soviets were aided by the failure, since mid-1953, of all attempts to hold a Korean peace conference. The matter had gone to the United Nations General Assembly in the fall of 1953, where a majority supported the Communist position that the conference should be in the form of a round table rather than a face-to-face confrontation, but had been unable to muster the necessary two-thirds vote in the Assembly.

Three weeks of meetings in Berlin produced continued deadlock over Germany and Austria, as well as a Soviet suggestion for a European security treaty open to all European—not Atlantic—states, and superseding all military pacts. When Dulles returned to the United States his report on the meeting was to the effect that it again indicated that the Russians were completely intransigent and that they still desired to extend their gains while relinquishing none. But to Europeans the absence of propaganda at the meeting led them to hold out hopes that a new conference might, in fact, reach some accommodation. And there would be a new meeting at Geneva in April. Communist China and other Asian states would participate, and the Far East as well as European security would come under discussion. How was it that Secretary Dulles agreed to meet with the Chinese Communists?

The answer lay not only in the necessity to explore further the question of a Korean peace settlement before abandoning all hopes for one, but also the pressures emanating from European states, especially France. Dulles hoped that France would now, after Berlin, proceed to ratify the treaty establishing the European Defense Community, especially if he made some concession to rising sentiment within France for a general negotiated settlement in the Far East. As for Britain, Churchill wanted continued negotiation with the Communists, and the British had begun to be sensitive to the opinion and suggestions of new Commonwealth members —India, Ceylon, and Pakistan—as well as other neutrals like Burma and Indonesia. So Dulles, reassuring Congress that meeting and talking to Chinese Communist leaders did not imply American recognition, prepared to go to Geneva. On February 22 Prime Minister Nehru had appealed for an immediate cease-fire in Indochina, and had subsequently denounced the possibility of American intervention and American plans for a new security organization for Southeast Asia. The Geneva Conference was planned for April 26; on April 28 a number of Asian leaders met in Colombo, Ceylon, where they supported the Indian position on Indochina.

With the military situation deteriorating rapidly in Indochina, the possibility of American military intervention dim, pressures for some settlement growing, and the West in disarray on numerous other issues, the Geneva Conference opened with every prospect that it would lead to deadlock on Korea and either formal ratification of division of Indochina or a breakup over the issue. This, in turn, might lead to more open American intervention or further French disengagement, with possible domestic upheaval in France and disruption of NATO.

The expected deadlock on Korea occurred, and negotiations were broken off. But in the meantime two events precipitated a new, temporary and shaky resolution of the situation in Indochina.

The first was the fall of Dien Bien Phu on May 7, with the capture of its beleaguered garrison. The second, following the fall of the Laniel government over policy in Indochina, was the accession to power of Pierre Mendès-France.

Instability of previous French governments and the unresolved problems of the European Defense Community and the Saar brought the new Premier to prominence. Mendès-France was a new and untainted political figure, ironically, a leader of the moribund Radical Socialist Party. He used the very weakness of the French executive as a source of power: give him, he asked the French National Assembly, a certain period of time within which to reach solutions to the outstanding problems. They would be painful solutions, but there was no other way to end any of the problems that needed resolution. On June 17 he asked for four weeks to achieve a truce in Vietnam. If the Assembly refused to let him do this, unhindered, and did not accept the unpleasant solution he would devise, chaos and revolution would certainly result. In each case the Gordian knot must be cut, and as far as Indochina was concerned too much good money had already been thrown after bad.

At Geneva, nine nations had taken part in the Indochina discussions: the Big Four, Communist China, the three Associated States of Indochina, and representatives of the Vietminh (or the "Democratic Republic of Vietnam"). The French opened with proposals for a truce and a regrouping of forces—a plan unacceptable to the Communists, who wanted to be able to operate freely throughout Indochina. As a consequence of the French proposals, the Indochinese and especially the Vietnamese representatives began to move away from the French. They wanted no partition, while the Laotian and Cambodian representatives maintained that Communists within *their* borders must be considered invaders from Vietnam, and therefore the conference should see to their being expelled. The stiffer Vietnamese line matched that of the United States; both called for a cease-fire, United Nations supervised elections throughout the area, separate treatment for Laos and Cambodia, and some form of international guarantee for the area. On the last point the Vietnamese looked to the United Nations, while the American representatives were busy lining up support for a new organization for Southeast Asia, more or less modeled on NATO.

A sign of increased flexibility in the Communist position coincided with the coming to power of Mendès-France. The conference took a long breathing spell by creating a commission to study the details of how to stop hostilities. Dulles—old proponent of liberation—now decided not to return to a conference whose inevitable outcome appeared to be partition of Vietnam, with the northern half going to the Communists. Chou Enlai, Communist China's Foreign Minister, spent his time mending fences in conferences with Nehru of India and Burma's Prime Minister U Nu, in which all agreed to noninterference in one another's affairs. In the meantime, the British and Americans, long at odds over the crisis, came to a general agreement on the creation of a new security organization for the area regardless of the nature of the settlement in Indochina. Mendès-France, facing further military pressures by the Vietminh, told his Assembly that if an "honorable" ceasefire could not be secured—one that would allow the evacuation from Communist areas of those who wanted to go—he would seek authorization to send French conscript troops to Indochina, a move every government had so far avoided. Finally, under the impact of all these developments, the armistice agreements were signed on July 21. Vietnam, which had a new regime under the leadership of the devoutly Catholic political unknown, Ngo Dinh Diem, registered a solemn protest. Neither he nor American representatives signed the truce.

Neutralization and demilitarization were arranged for Laos and Cambodia, though within Laos a French military training mission would remain and the dissident Pathet Lao Communist forces of a few thousand would be regrouped but allowed some special relationship. Vietnam was divided along the 17th parallel, and the extensive French positions in the north surrendered in return for Vietminh withdrawal in the south. The agreements forbade the introduction of any new troops or equipment or the building of new bases, provided for free transfer of that part of the population that chose one part of the country over the other, and provided for free, general, secret elections throughout the area within two years. International Commissions composed of Canada, India and Poland would supervise the agreements and elections.

There was little doubt that the Communists accepted the arrangements partly because they were confident that within the two-year period the shaky government in the south would fall, thus allowing them to take over the entire area. But they were also influenced by the threat of stiffened resistance on the part of the West to any further direct military attack, by the tardy French grant of complete independence to the Indochinese states, and by the desire to gain the good will of the new grouping of Asian states.

In subsequent months the agreements were implemented by withdrawal of large numbers of Vietminh units from the south and the southward flow of both military and civilian personnel. Ho Chi Minh's regime in the north behaved in a friendly manner toward French civilians and businessmen; invitations to remain and guarantees of good treatment were extended. In the south, matters changed rapidly. Ngo Dinh Diem's regime began to receive the unqualified American support that made it able to disarm varied opposition sects, some of which controlled police forces and could field substantial armies of their own. American support also enabled Diem to operate more and more independently of the French, who found themselves replaced by American influence, to the dismay of French colonial elements. The United States budgeted $500 million for aid to the Republic in 1955, a year that also saw the end of the French-backed Emperor Bao Dai's attempt to continue to retain influence from his comfortable quarters on the French Riviera. A flow of 850,000 refugees southward revealed the extent of opposition to Communist takeover in the north, and with American aid the Diem regime proved equal to the enormous task of resettling them. In mid-1955 Ho Chi Minh traveled to Moscow and Peking and signed trade and aid agreements that effectively coordinated the north half of Vietnam with the other Communist states. July also saw the breakdown of attempts to prepare for the forthcoming elections: Diem declared that he could see no conditions under which the Communists in the north would allow them to be truly free. But the 98 per cent of the vote cast for him in the referendum between him and Bao Dai cast some doubt on the freedom of his own electoral processes. By the end of the year Diem was President, Premier, and Defense Minister of the Republic of South Vietnam.

TAIWAN AND SEATO: THE UNITED STATES EXTENDS ITS ALLIANCES

Settlement of the war in Korea and of the struggle in Indochina—however precarious and unstable the agreements might be—nevertheless stopped people from shooting at one another. Soon after the Geneva conference, however, Chou En-lai reaffirmed a basic Chinese Communist aim:

> In order that international tension may be further eased, in order that the peace secured through the armistice in Indochina may be consolidated and extended, and that the five principles of peaceful coexistence may be carried through, it is imperative that the People's Republic of China liberate Taiwan and liquidate the traitorous Chiang Kai-shek group.

Nevertheless, during the next year the stalemate in the area continued, as did the arrangements made by the United States and Chiang designed to stabilize the situation and produce a *de facto* and tacit agreement. There were abortive attempts by Britain and other states to promote a two-China policy that would lead to the creation *de facto* and *de jure* of two successor states, both, presumably, to be seated in the United Nations. The two states concerned were unswervingly opposed. Each claimed to be the *only* China (tiny Nationalist China, with a population of ten million, continued to pay the United Nations dues assessed upon it when it was a country of four hundred million, in order to buttress its claim). The Eisenhower administration therefore did two things. Having signed a mutual security treaty with Chiang, it secured, in January 1955, a resolution from Congress authorizing it to act in the event of an attack on Formosa or the nearby Pescadore islands. Although the President could presumably go to Chiang's defense anyway, this would serve notice to the Communists of American determination, as well as forestall the kind of criticism that Truman met for executive action in meeting the Korean attack without support of Congress. On the other hand the resolution limited American commitment; to all intents and purposes it "releashed" Chiang since it was accompanied by publication of correspondence about the mutual security treaty that indicated the United States would not aid him if he attempted to attack the mainland. At the same time the administration forced him to withdraw from the Tachen islands, a small group far to the north of Formosa and close to the mainland.

The administration left one thing ambiguous: what it would do if the Communists attacked the Nationalist-held islands of Quemoy (a hundred miles from Formosa and blocking the mouth of the Chinese port of Amoy) and of Matsu (equally far and commanding the approaches to the port of Foochow). Spokesmen declared that if the President felt an attack upon them was a part of and prelude to an attack upon Formosa, the United States would help defend them.

Despite the ambiguity of the last move—one opposed by the British,

who would have liked a withdrawal to Formosa proper and the Pesca-
dores—the clear American determination coupled with the retrenching
moves eased matters in the area temporarily. Another temporary and
unstable Asian "settlement" appeared to have been reached.

The American project designed to buttress the new situation in Southeast Asia—the Southeast Asia Treaty Organization—was brought into
being at Manila in September 1954. Ceylon, Burma, Indonesia, and India believed that the pact would do more harm than good; the Indochinese states were excluded by the terms of the Geneva settlement. As a
result only Pakistan, Thailand, and the Philippines joined with Great
Britain, France, Australia, New Zealand, and the United States in the
pact. It was not an organization in any way similar to NATO. Although
it foresaw some coordination of military strategies for the area, it did not
provide for the stationing of the troops of one member state in the territory of the others, and it did not provide for the almost automatic reaction to threat which NATO did.

The United States was in fact the member that stood out against either
the creation of a unified command or a unified force or the transformation of SEATO into a large-scale organization for economic development
—all of which were proposed by other members. Against the argument
that it could not deal with subversion—the kind of threat to security most
likely to develop in the area—its proponents contended that once the
overt military threat could be removed, action against subversion was easier. The treaty also provided for consultation in case of threats of serious
subversion, and was accompanied by a declaration that its guarantees extended to the territories of the Indochinese states, even though they could
not be parties to it.

MORE STIRRINGS IN THE NON-WESTERN WORLD: IRAN, EGYPT, AFRICA

Developments in Asia between 1950 and 1955 showed the importance of
China on the world scene and the attention Western states had begun to
pay to the views of leaders of such states as India, Indonesia and Burma.
In the same period other areas of the world began—sometimes violently
—to mark the change in their status vis-à-vis Europe and the United
States. In most cases these changes demonstrated a lessening of European
influence; in some they represented replacement of European by American influence. In no case did the Soviets actually bring about the developments, nor did they profit directly from them. But in the latter years of
the period they began to work to use them for their own purposes.

For Iran the period was dominated by Premier Mohammed Mossadegh and his attempt to nationalize the British-owned oil industry. Economic crises, internal instability and corruption, the conservatism of the landed oligarchy, Soviet intrigue—all contributed to a chaotic situation. The Shah of Iran, devoted to the idea of reform, attempted to get economic and military aid from the United States in 1949, but on the basis of reports from the scene, the Truman administration was reluctant to do much for fear that it would pour out money for nothing, as it had done in Nationalist China. Since large sums were being spent in Europe, where things *were* being done, the administration transmitted its view to the Shah: if he could put his governmental house in order so that the aid might be of some effect, he could expect a warmer reception for his requests. All through 1950, with the aid of the energetic Premier Razmara, the Shah proceeded with reform measures. But the expected aid did not materialize and within the Majlis—the Iranian Parliament—there was agitation to find alternative development funds, by speeding negotiations with the giant Anglo-Iranian Oil Company to increase Iran's share of its profits. Anglo-Iranian had long been the sole concessionaire in Iran, and negotiations for a change in the division of profits had dragged on for a lengthy period. Early in 1951 Mossadegh's parliamentary group began to clamor for nationalization of the oil property and on March 20, following the assassination of Razmara by a Moslem fanatic, a nationalization law passed the Majlis and Senate. Mossadegh became Premier, riots and disturbances erupted all over Iran, and the oil operations shut down.

The Mossadegh regime lasted until the end of August 1953. During that time it rested on an unstable coalition of religious fanatics who resisted the modernization of society, on nationalists of every stripe, student groups, and the large left-wing Tudeh party, which was Communist-led. All were united in only one matter: continued national ownership of the oil properties and defiance of Britian.

Mossadegh counted on Europe's need for the oil and on his ability to sell it on the world market. The British counted on Iran's needs for the oil revenues. Both were mistaken: Europe found its oil in the rapidly expanding facilities in Saudi Arabia and especially the tiny Sheikdom of Kuwait. The Anglo-Iranian Oil Company announced that it would take to court any other purchaser of oil from Iran on the basis that the property had been stolen from the company. Since the major oil fleets of the world were owned by sympathetic companies who were also interested in seeing that nationalization fail, Iran was able to sell very little oil. But lack of foreign revenues was not as quickly disastrous as the British had calculated it would be, even though Iran was unable to get foreign aid from anywhere. Past revenues had largely gone to an upper class that was hurt when it no longer had the income to import the luxuries it was accustomed to—but the government no longer rested on this class.

All attempts failed at negotiation, arbitration, action through the United Nations Security Council, and proceedings at the International Court of Justice. The Iranians steadfastly maintained that nationalization was a purely domestic matter, and they would tolerate no modification of the principle.

Eventually, as economic woes grew and policy had to be devised, the shaky unity of the disparate groups supporting Mossadegh collapsed. He began to rule by decree, resisted deposition by the Shah (who was forced to flee the country), and was finally overthrown on August 19 by units of the army who had remained loyal to the Shah.* The Shah returned, and a new regime, receiving emergency American economic aid, negotiated a new oil agreement enabling the Iranian oil industry to resume output. The settlement reflected the fact that no regime could simply have brought back the British: a consortium of eight companies—five American, one French, one Dutch plus Anglo-Iranian—took over the operation of the National Iranian Oil Company.

Although the Iranian episode had future reverberations—it had raised the spectre of nationalization, one never to be allayed—the July 1952 revolt in Egypt had far wider repercussions.

The revolt was the culmination of years of frustration and chaos. The postwar period in Egyptian politics had been devoted to substitution of one political clique by another, while popular dissatisfaction mounted and revealed itself in riots and disorder. The sybaritic King, far removed from popular feeling, had actually tried to rule through the cliques that represented themselves as democratic parties.

Three major issues dominated Egyptian foreign policy: removal of British troops and evacuation of their great Suez base; the future of the condominium with Britain over the Sudan; and relations with Israel. On the first count the political parties had vied with one another in calling for withdrawal. But though the British began negotiations in 1946, they stiffened their stand as Russian pressures mounted. It would be foolish, they felt, to abandon the bases just when they were again needed: World War II had once more proved their strategic importance. No other spot in the Middle East lay athwart such a vital lifeline or possessed such facilities. And as the British stand stiffened, anti-British feeling mounted in Egypt. It culminated in a fight between British and Egypitan troops in Ismaila in January 1952, and was followed by a great day of rioting in Cairo on January 26, during which numerous landmarks symbolizing British influence were burned and sacked.

---

* It has become a commonplace that Cold War and business interests united in producing a CIA overthrow of Mossadegh. In fact, CIA agents seem to have played little part but to have done too much boasting.

Contributing to anti-British feeling was the British attitude on the future of the Sudan. The British argued that the Sudanese should be allowed to choose their own future. Against this, the Egyptians argued for the unity of the Nile Valley: a hostile country athwart the upper Nile could strangle Egypt's livelihood.

Finally, the defeat of the poorly led and miserably equipped Egyptian armies in the Palestine war turned hostile public attention against the regime itself. It was all very well for the politicians to proclaim their nationalism, but if this was the best they could do in defending Egyptian honor, it was far too little. Moreover, the creation of Israel engendered a permanent conflict of interest between Egypt and those Western powers that Egyptian leaders thought had set up and now helped maintain Israel. All through the Korean War Egypt and the other Arab countries abstained from giving any aid to the United Nations effort on the basis that conflict between the United States and the Soviet Union was none of their business and that Russia was no threat to them. The real threat was Zionism, the outpost of Western imperialism.

The Revolutionary Command Council took power with little fuss on July 23, 1952. It represented a "Committee of Free Officers" created back in 1947, and it moved swiftly, first to force King Farouk's abdication, then to destroy the corrupt political parties as well as the powerful Moslem Brotherhood that wanted a return to a theocratic state. A struggle for power within the RCC developed between the man first chosen as a figurehead for the new government, Colonel Naguib, and Colonel Gamal Abdul Nasser, who was the victor. The RCC launched a program of internal reform, concentrating on land reform, labor laws, new irrigation and industrial projects, and studies for even more extensive industrialization. Moving cautiously in the realm of political forms, Nasser eventually established a new authoritarian pattern for Egypt.

In the realm of foreign policy, the Nasser regime liquidated two persistent problems, the Sudan and Suez. Nasser agreed with the British that the Sudanese would be given a transitional period of three years to develop institutions of self-government, after which they would have a free choice of union or independence. Although the Egyptians at first thought the Sudanese would choose union, the possibility became remote and relations deteriorated as the Egyptians redoubled their efforts to create pro-union sentiment in the Sudan. On December 19, 1955 the Sudanese Chamber announced Sudanese independence, and Egypt accepted it.

In 1954, after lengthy negotiations, a new treaty replaced the old 1936 treaty between Egypt and Britain on the Suez Canal. The new one provided for the withdrawal of British troops within twenty months, maintenance of the base by civilian technicians, the right of British re-entry in case of an attack on Egypt, an Arab League state or Turkey, and reaffirmed the Treaty of 1888 that guaranteed freedom of navigation on the Suez Canal. It also recognized that the Canal was "an integral part of Egypt."

In the Middle East people hailed Nasser's diplomatic triumph, and in the West, governments hoped for better relations with the new regime as a consequence of the removal of an old irritant. But because of the Baghdad Pact and Israel—which faced continued Arab blockade and border raids, and retaliated in heavy force—good relations were impossible, and in 1955 the Middle East situation became further complicated and inflamed. International efforts to mediate between Arab and Jew failed one after the other. Arab leaders consistently expressed their determination to destroy Israel, and Israel continued the firm policy of allowing unlimited immigration. On these shoals foundered the effort to work out the "Johnston Plan," for a technical agreement on water-sharing and hydroelectric and irrigation development between Israel and neighboring states. It was an attempt to attack political conflict at the technical level of economic cooperation; its effects would, it was hoped, eventually mitigate the political conflict. Functional cooperation was impossible, however, given the extent and intensity of the political differences. And in Arab eyes the West became further identified with Israel, simply because Western diplomacy, however much it sided with the Arabs on particular matters, nevertheless presupposed the continued existence of Israel within the boundaries set by the Palestine war.

Developments in Iran and Egypt, the role played by India and other Asian states in the Korean and Indochinese affairs and in limiting SEATO, all represent the swiftly changing relationships between Western powers and non-Western areas in the years 1950–55. In North Africa and areas south of the Sahara such changes also began to be evident.

Already in 1949 General Assembly adoption of a resolution on the former Italian colonies had foreshadowed what was to come. It had made Libya independent, federated Eritrea with Ethiopia—restored to independence after the war—and although it had made Somaliland a trust territory, a ten-year timetable had been set for independence. In Kenya in East Africa, the Mau-Mau revolt erupted in 1952, a complicated response to land tenure problems, tribal politics and racism, but which also represented national discontent. The movement was finally crushed by native cooperation with the British authorities; in substance and form it was too backward-looking. But during its course, in 1954, British authorities in Kenya took the step of introducing a new constitution with a large measure of African representation. It was not and could not be completely satisfactory, striving as it did to balance white and nonwhite representation; but it indicated that changes were in the wind.

In the Gold Coast, in Nigeria, in French Africa, Rhodesia, South Africa, as well as in Kenya, African political parties had formed, their nationalism fanned by native wartime service in European armed forces, by the attention paid to them by the United Nations, by the European weakness revealed by the war, and by the facts of new urbanization, education, and industrialization and trade. In the Gold Coast in West Africa, rioting and demonstrations in early 1948 sparked a vast upheaval. They marked the rise of a new African political leader, Kwame Nkrumah (educated in the United States and England) and the end of any attempt to carry out the 1946 Constitution, which had left non-African appointive members in a clear majority in the Executive Council. An All-African Commission presided over by an African judge drew up a new constitution which took effect in 1951. It came close to providing independence, and promised what was virtually Dominion status in the near future. Nkrumah's nationalist Convention People's Party won a surprisingly large electoral victory, and Nkrumah, jailed for organizing a large-scale illegal strike, was released to become the first Prime Minister.

Change in the direction of self-government and independence came easily in direct relationship to the lack of numbers of white settlers. In the Gold Coast there were few; Kenya was exceeded in its proportion of white settlers only by South Africa, the Portugese colonies, Algeria, and the Rhodesias. In an effort in 1953 to reconcile the demands of the Rhodesian whites with those of the blacks, Britain formed a new political unit, the Central African Federation. Landlocked, it was bordered on the south by South Africa, whose dominant white minority had begun to take its own peculiar pathway of segregation, known as apartheid, and on either side by the Portuguese colonies, where rigid suppression of black nationalism would continue to be the rule. On the north were the more African states of Tanganyika and the Belgian Congo. The two Rhodesias and Nyasaland, brought together into the Federation by an uneasy British Parliament, represented an attempt to find a compromise between the dominant white minorities who wanted to maintain their special status, and the new African leaders who unequivocally demanded one man— one vote. For the Africans the Federation was an unacceptable compromise because, although it increased native political participation, it still provided for a special political status for the whites. The whole matter was complicated by the presence of Asian minorities, tribal feuds, splits among white workers, white businessmen, and white missionaries, and by the varying degree of white domination in the three component units. Black opposition made its beginning inauspicious, even though it appeared to be a realistic compromise. The Federation was meant to be a bulwark against the harshness of apartheid to the south as well as a bulwark against the advance of radical black nationalism to the north that would inevitably come into open conflict with apartheid and perhaps shatter the continent. In addition, the Federation made economic sense, but the opposition of black leadership dimmed its promise.

Far to the north, along the Mediterranean coast, events took a different turn. The area was affected by its geographical proximity to European and Middle Eastern political developments and, in Algeria, by the presence of the greatest ratio of white settlers to natives anywhere outside South Africa. Morocco, ostensibly a protectorate, was in fact ruled almost directly through a French-created administrative apparatus and through local tribal chieftains. Moroccan nationalist agitation in this period centered around the person of Sultan Mohammed V whom the French had installed in 1927. The urban groups that formed the core of the movement found in the Sultan an ally with a strong card to play. So long as the French pretended Morocco was merely a protectorate, they had to abide by the rule that the Sultan had to countersign all decrees. He had begun to reject French decrees as early as 1944, and in the early 1950s virtually went on strike, while refusing to disavow and nationalist organizations proscribed by the French. The French responded in 1953 by organizing a rural revolt against the Sultan, then deposed and exiled him on the pretext that he had lost the support of his subjects. As the 'fifties advanced, nationalist agitation using the symbol of the deposed king increased in scope and in aims. In 1955 the new government of Premier Guy Mollet returned the Sultan to his throne, and the next year Morocco was granted full independence.

In Tunisia—another French protectorate since the nineteenth century —nationalist agitation centered in the person of Habib Bourguiba, who had been a leader of the Neo-Destour, or Constitution party, since the 1930s. For the first five years after World War II he had toured the world seeking support for Tunisian independence. He was allowed to reenter Tunisia in 1949, with the prospect of internal autonomy held out bs the French. But Bourguiba demanded more and was subsequently arrested and deported. As in Morocco, the result was an increase in nationalist agitation, supported now by the new revolutionary regime in Cairo, ready to give aid to any North African nationalist movement. In July 1954, Mendès-France, as part of his effort to cut French losses, flew to Tunis and recognized the right of Tunisia to complete autonomy subject to conventions that were to be negotiated. Bourguiba was released and allowed to return to Tunisia, and within two years Tunisia, too, achieved independence.

In Algeria, flanked by Morocco and Tunisia, the years 1950–55 saw far more ominous developments. Algeria was different; one tenth of the population was of European descent, and the French government had incorporated Algeria into France, creating out of it three departments that were represented in the French Parliament and subject to French law. Native residents, however, were second-class citizens. As in the cases of Morocco, Tunisia, and other areas of Africa, the impact of modernization and education began to make itself felt quite early in the twentieth century. And again, World War II gave nationalism impetus, as France went down to defeat, other foreign troops entered, the Atlantic Charter and Declaration of the United Nations began to be taken at face value, and native inhabitants found that European states would compete for their allegiance. An outbreak of nationalist violence in 1945 was quickly quelled and followed by French reforms that gave to the mixed Moslem population a greater degree of political participation. The reforms were not far-reaching, nor were they fully implemented. But the French, fully cognizant of the extent to which the Algerian economy was tied to France, were quite confident about the situation in Algeria; it remained relatively stable after the growth of nationalist dissidence in neighboring Tunisia and Morocco. It was immensely disquieting, therefore, when on the night of November 1, 1954—soon after disengagement in Indochina —the French were confronted with a wave of concerted terrorist violence. The first attempts to quell it, based on accurate estimates that a small band were the perpetrators, failed as young Algerians flocked to the movement. By 1955—although the French had not yet realized it—the beginning of the end had come for the French Empire in Africa.

LATIN AMERICA ENTERS THE WORLD STAGE

In the postwar decade the twenty-one American states established the formal inter-American system (see pp. 60–64). In some ways the system gave the impression that all was well with the Americas, that things would take care of themselves under a multilateralized Monroe Doctrine, that Peron of Argentina with his uniforms, his rallies, and his oversized armies was just a fly in the ointment. In fact, clearly visible beneath his facade were some of the same stirrings beginning to animate parts of the non-Western world. Although the similarities were great, there were differences, too, arising from a different historical experience, culture, geography, and economic situation.

During World War II the countries of Central and South America had amassed large dollar credits through shipments of raw materials to feed the enormous American war machine. The second half of the 1940s had seen those balances dissipated, as well as inflation, balance of payment difficulties, and radical shifts in the prices of the single crops or raw materials that many of the countries exported. The result, as usual, was political upheaval, and constitutional regimes were threatened. The American response was unsatisfactory: at Bogota, in 1948, when the formal institutions of the OAS were created, there were Latin demands for an Inter-American Marshall Plan, even on a smaller scale. The United States, with its heavy commitments in the rest of the world, and the State Department worries about the inadequacy of the American military establishment, was prepared only to ease the terms on which the Export-Import Bank would make loans, and to launch a modest program of technical aid. Americans could point to the many programs financed by foundations and missions, and to continued American private investment. But this did not allay a growing feeling that the United States was neglecting its "Good Neighbors" to the south. The Korean War brought another favorable rise in the price of raw materials. But with the end of the war the boom slackened, bringing another drop in the price of many Latin American exports.

Although production increased in most Latin American countries in the years after World War II, it became evident in the early 1950s that Latin American economies were radically unbalanced, and that population increases were swallowing up production increases. The imbalance could be seen in the contrast between the lavish new apartment buildings, hotels, and offices, and their surrounding slums, impoverished countryside, and somnolent villages. Considering these contrasts, radical politics, using the new techniques of mass communication, were bound to flourish.

Moreover, the United States had enjoyed good relations with the ruling classes in the urban areas, creating a situation in which radicals and reformers could charge successfully that the wealth produced by trade with the United States buttressed the political power of the ruling groups. American investments might raise the general level of the economies of the countries in which they were made; but the gains, many charged, went only to the wealthy few. American efforts in the early 1950s to conclude mutual security agreements with Latin American countries and provide military aid and training were viewed with disfavor by many political leaders: armies in Latin America were too potent a political force, and a policy presumably designed to counter the Soviet threat would have primarily domestic political effects. Also, under the Congressional mandate, the mutual security agreements committed recipient countries to facilitate United States access to strategic materials, to cooperate in limiting trade with the Communist bloc, and to help build up the defensive strength of the "free world." In the more democratically governed countries—Mexico, Brazil, Chile and Uruguay—the debates were bitter and vociferous, and anti-American utterances became general.

The gathering of all these threads into widespread anti-Americanism, based partly on certain deep-rooted antipathies, enabled Dictator Peron of Argentina to aspire to a considerable role on the world scene. Peron had successfully resisted American pressures early in his career. He held power in the one country that had long been officially in conflict with American foreign policy and had excluded itself from the American-sponsored inter-American system during World War II. Now he could fish in these troubled waters. In Argentina itself, he attacked the older oligarchies in the name of social justice and based his political power on the new urban masses, whose status he improved. In so doing, and by encouraging a "hothouse" industrialization, he cut into Argentina's export trade and created a need for new imported raw materials and parts as well as creating a new privileged class of workers. The foundations of a difficult future situation were laid: Argentina began to live beyond its means, yet any effort to cut back the unrealistic standard of living would run afoul of the newly strengthened labor organizations; they would resist any cutbacks and would demand that other groups pay for it. Nevertheless, Peron's brand of social justice, partly because it gave to the new masses a measure of political participation (whether manipulated or not), was immensely attractive to groups all over the Americas, whose new nationalism and anti-Americanism incorporated a strong demand for precisely this kind of social change. In the decade after the war Peronism flourished hand in hand with other nationalist and social-reform movements, and it became hard to distinguish and label political movements as democratic, reform, revolutionary, communist, socialist, or fascist. Complex social and economic situations fostered a demand for change. The demand was articulated by intellectuals, college students, professional agitators, labor leaders—sometimes joined by progressive-minded business leaders, churchmen and officers, and sometimes opposed by them. The only constant became the desire for change. Sometimes, as in the Dominican Republic, it was brutally suppressed, sometimes it found, as in Mexico, some measure of peaceful expression after years of revolution.

At the United Nations the Latin American countries voted frequently as a bloc. Their leaders found common policies in an atmosphere in which the Western nations used the General Assembly to pile up massive majorities against the Soviet Union. But the explosive situation in the Americas was certain to break up Latin American unity. The incident that did it took place in Guatemala.

Overthrow of one regime by another was a common occurrence in American states, but this one had special features. Since the war, the regime in Guatemala had moved steadily to the left. Communists had infiltrated several departments of the government, so that they could claim its radical reforms as their own. Agrarian reform—long viewed as necessary in Guatemala—was carried out mainly by expropriating lands owned by the American United Fruit Company, and compensation proposed by the regime was ridiculously small. Then the regime moved against the company-controlled railway and electric power company. To many leaders in Latin America the moves were merely welcome steps in the direction of progress, and that they involved reducing the influence of a Yankee company was not disturbing: only in this direction lay true independence and sovereignty.

But within the United States, where the Eisenhower regime—having promised to rectify Truman's error of ignoring the Americas—confined itself to diplomatic protests, some people called for stronger action. Former Assistant Secretary of State Spruille Braden called Guatemala a "beachhead of international Communism," and censured the administration for its inaction.

Matters came to a head in 1954. A meeting of the Inter-American Conference of the Organization of American States was scheduled for March. Against the resistance of many Latin states, whose representatives wanted to discuss economic affairs, the United States used the meeting to obtain a resolution that "domination or control of the political institutions of any American State by the international Communist movemen would constitute a threat to the sovereignty and political independence of the American States, endangering the peace of America." The resolution was weakened in passage and it did not specify what action would be taken. Countries with military dictatorships of various kinds were less opposed than the more democratic ones, although Argentina joined Mexico in abstaining. A Uruguayan delegate was quoted as saying, "We contributed our approval without enthusiams, without optimism, without joy and without the feeling that we were contributing to the adoption of a constructive measure." Opposition centered on the notion that this was an unwelcome move toward collective intervention, to which the United States answered that collective intervention was needed to counter *Communist* intervention. Opponents of the American policy also felt there was little reason to single out the Guatemalan dictatorship as against other Latin American ones, particularly since it favored the kind of progressive measures needed in the area.

To protect itself, the regime headed by Arbenz in Guatemala began to step up repressive measures against its internal opponents, and looked for aid from the Soviet bloc. Opponents in neighboring states claimed that the Guatemalan regime was fostering subversion and sabotage within their borders. Then came the revelation on May 18 that Guatemala had received a shipment of arms from Czechoslovakia by way of Poland, and the United States increased its efforts against the government. It called for measures to halt such shipments, it called a meeting of the foreign ministers of the American States, and it authorized increased arms shipments to Guatemala's neighbors, Honduras and Nicaragua, on grounds that these countries were now threatened by the Communist arms. On June 18 a small force crossed the border from Honduras under the command of Colonel Carlos Castillo-Armas, and the Arbenz regime, facing the opposition of the armed forces within Guatemala, quickly fell. Arbenz was later allowed to go to Mexico, and from there he went to Czechoslovakia.

When the revolt—or invasion—took place, Guatemala immediately asked for action in both the Security Council and the OAS, against what it termed "open aggression" by neighboring governments urged on by foreign monopolies. The United States strove to keep the matter out of the United Nations on the basis that it was strictly a regional, and even more, a domestic matter. Thus the importance of the whole matter in the pattern of world politics was revealed: the United States, in trying to block United Nations Security Council action, was concerned with keeping the Soviet Union from becoming openly involved in American affairs. Communist parties had long operated, sometimes effectively, in Latin America. But for the first time since the turn of the century, when the United States had chosen unilaterally to "strengthen" the Monroe Doctrine, a European power—one hostile to the United States—presumed to participate in matters within the Americas. Moreover, the United Nations—and the Communist bloc—had been called upon by a Latin American government which, though it could be criticized for undemocratic practices, was still more legitimate and democratic than many other countries on the continent. When, after Nazi Germany's defeat, Peron's Argentina had tried to make itself a counter pole of attraction to the influence of the United States, Peron had grown weaker; he had even begun to court the Eisenhower administration. Now, for the first time, a Latin American country could and did call on a strong and willing alternative source for support, in the context of the United Nations.

Within the Security Council, a Soviet veto prevented the Council from removing the item from consideration, but the United States was able to defer the issue until the Inter-American Peace Committee of the OAS could investigate the matter and report. It never had to complete its work. With mediation by the American Ambassador, John Peurifoy, matters were quickly settled in Guatemala, a new regime established, and in subsequent months the United States rushed it various forms of emergency economic aid.

Although most Americans at the time were not aware of it, the United States had had a direct part in overthrowing the Arbenz government. The

Central Intelligence Agency had financed, supplied, and helped train the Castillo-Armas forces, and the American ambassador had informed the contending parties what kind of regime would be acceptable to the United States. The new regime was hardly satisfactory to Guatemalans; but it was non-Communist.

The action was followed by a wave of more overt anti-Americanism throughout Latin-American urban centers, where the whole issue was seen in a different light, and where Communist propaganda stressed how Yankee intervention had again overthrown a regime whose only failing was a lack of subservience to American investors.

While in the north the realities of the unstable Latin-American situation had broken through to the surface, at the southern tip of South America another effort to ride and guide the new waves of discontent came to an end; in Argentina the Peron regime was toppled in a four-day revolution in September 1955. Since the end of 1954, Peron's regime was doomed. His economic policies had disrupted the Argentine economy, inflation had taken on disastrous proportions, members of the armed services were disaffected, and Peron, in an effort to capitalize on anticlerical sentiment, had mistakenly attacked the Church. In the summer of 1955 the Vatican excommunicated him. The end came soon after with a revolt by elements of the army and navy, and a new junta took over. Few could look forward to much stability in Argentina.

EUROPE, 1950–55

Several issues dominated the five-year period in Europe: German rearmament, political and economic integration of West Europe, the return of West Germany and Italy to the ranks of world powers, accession of a Conservative government in Britain and of Mendès-France in France, continued liquidation of European empires, a new Korean War-born round of inflation followed by the beginning of an economic boom, continued growth of neutralist sentiment, settlement of the difficult Saar and Trieste issues, and—hovering over all in the latter part of the period—a new hope of an accommodation with Russia's new masters. The account of the impact of Korea, the Indochinese settlement and events in North Africa has already treated some of these events, but some parts of the narrative must now be filled in.

The resolution of the question of German rearmament rested in part on events in Britain and France. The Korean War had hastened consideration of the matter and led, in late 1950, to the desperate French expedient of the Pleven Plan, which subsequent French governments were reluctant to endorse. Korea also hastened general rearmanment plans in

Europe, and these produced a new round of inflation starting in late 1951, for which Europeans tended in large part to blame the United States. By reckless buying of raw materials, they argued, the United States had bid up their prices and produced a scarcity in Europe, whose full share in carrying the burden in Malaya and Indochina Americans did not appreciate. In Britain the long experience of austerity after victory in World War II, coupled with a growing view that nationalization of industry solved little, and with Conservative acceptance of the welfare state, led to a Conservative election victory in 1951. Winston Churchill again took up the reins of government. Since he was a leader in the European movement and had frequently spoken in its support, continental Europeans hoped for greater British participation. They were disappointed. Churchill and his government preferred to continue the close relationship with the United States (cemented during the war years) and the ties of the Commonwealth—sentimental as well as financial. There was, therefore, no question of their joining the proposed European army, although as the situation became thornier, Churchill did pledge (in May 1952) that British armies would not be withdrawn from Germany. This was intended to allay French fears that once Germany was rearmed the British and Americans might withdraw their troops. The United States also joined in this declaration.

But within France opposition to the proposed Eurepean Defense Community continued to grow. The Communists were unalterably opposed, and at the other end of the political spectrum de Gaulle also denounced it, declaring that France must regain its independence from both the United States and the Soviet Union and mediate between the two. All other parties (except the Christian Democrats, who had originated the concept and had controlled the Foreign Ministry since 1945) were split on the issue. Distinguished military men pronounced the European army unworkable; others condemned it as a final, fatal surrender of precious French sovereignty. And even many Frenchmen who had worked for some surrender of sovereignty in the form of European integration nevertheless balked at this particular aspect of it.

The Germans had ratified the agreement; everyone waited for the French, and the Anglo-Americans tried both the carrot and the stick. In April 1954 the British signed a far-reaching, binding agreement with the six European Defense Community governments defining various forms of close cooperation with them and the European army within the framework of NATO. The United States, although not going as far, also pledged close cooperation far beyond the expiration date of NATO (1970) if the Europeans wanted it, promising to share weapons and techniques and to coordinate planning, training, and logistics.

On the other hand Secretary Dulles had spoken at one point of the necessity for the United States to indulge in an "agonizing reappraisal" of its policy toward Europe if the European Defense Community were not established. And in mid-1954 he renewed the warning: if Western Europe were to remain divided there might have to be a "basic shift in United States policy." Talk began of rearming Germany with or without the European Defense Community.

Matters came to a head with the Geneva Conference, the coming to power of Mendès-France, and the Indochinese settlement. Mendès-France had pledged himself to dispose of several matters. One was the German settlement, which was complicated by the insistence of previous governments that the dispute with Germany over the future of the coal-rich Saar must be settled prior to ratification of the European Defense Community. In the meantime Russian diplomacy and propaganda increased in variety and scope. The Russians offered to continue the abortive 1954 Berlin conversations to discuss the future of Germany, the Austrian peace treaties, and a proposed European security treaty. Their offer was an appeal to the many elements within France who believed that German rearmament was provocative and who argued that a great part of Russian foreign policy was in fact motivated by fear of a resurgent Germany.

Mendès-France made an effort to change the treaty so it would be more acceptable to his own Assembly, yet still make it palatable to the other countries who had already signed and had been waiting so long for the French. The changes he proposed, however, proved completely unacceptable, and he returned to Paris in August from Brussels, where the negotiations had been futile. Then, on August 30, in the Assembly, he stood by during a debate, not on the merits of the European Defense Community, but on removing the item from the agenda and passing to other business. Emotionalism dominated, although the European Defense Community had been intellectually taken apart in a series of negative committee reports. The motion to move to other business passed; the European Defense Community was dead. Four years of planning a means of German rearmament within the framework of European integration had come to nothing. Dead, too, was the projected European Political Union which was to have given political guidance to the subordinate European army and would have capped the structure of European economic intergration.

What next?

Dulles, despite his prior warnings and the pinning of his hopes to the European Defense Community, displayed caution. It fell to Anthony Eden, the British Foreign Minister, to devise a way out of the wreckage.

All agreed with Chancellor Adenauer that in some way West Germany must be included in the defense of Western Europe, and on a basis of equality, not subordination. Mendès-France, however, still wanted controls over German rearmament, as did a substantial segment of opinion in other European countries. Eden's solution was to reactivate the Western European Union set up by the Brussels Treaty Organization of 1948 (predecessor of NATO), giving its Council the power to set maximum force levels for *all* members; they could go beyond these only by unanimous consent of the Council members. In addition, when the powers met in London, September 28 to October 3, and then at Paris, October 19–23, they agreed to restore full sovereignity to Germany, while Germany, for its part, renounced the right to build atomic, chemical, or biological weapons and such strategic weapons as missiles and long-range bombers. Britain wrote into the treaty its commitment to keep certain forces on the Continent, and as accompanying protocol admitted Germany to NATO. Mendès-France still made acceptance conditional on prior agreement on the Saar issue, and after hectic negoitations he and Chancellor Adenauer agreed to a form of internationalization: the Saar would become the seat of the European Coal and Steel Community, but France would still retain special economic privileges in the area. But there would be a popular referendum among Saarlanders to approve—or disapprove—the arrangement.

Under a barrage of Soviet suggestions for all-European security conferences and free elections in Germany, the countries proceeded to ratification of the new agreements. Western leaders argued that once the arrangements were made it might be the right moment to test the sincerity of Russian demands for negotiations. The Russians, however, warned that ratification would unduly complicate the picture and make a reduction of tensions far more difficult.

Again France was the center of attention. And again, although willing to admit Germany to NATO and ratify the Saar settlement, the Assembly voted down the whole Brussels Treaty revision. This time Mendè-France told the Assembly that German rearmament without controls would be certain, and made the matter a vote of confidence. On December 30, by a vote of 287 to 260, the Assembly accepted the treaty. The change came primarily because Popular Republican supporters of European Defense Community, who had previously voted against Mendè-France because he had allowed their earlier project to fail, now switched their votes. German rearmament was finally assured.

It took until May 1955 to complete ratification of the agreements. In the meantime the Soviet Union threatened retaliation: it announced that it would create an equivalent organization in Eastern Europe and that it would denounce the treaties of friendship and alliance it had signed with Britain in 1942 and France in 1944. In Britain, France, and Germany, prominent voices were asking that ratification be delayed until the long-called-for summit conference be held. But Churchill, though a proponent of such a meeting, dissented. On May 5 the fifteen member nations of NATO completed the process involved in ratification of the several documents; the occupation of Germany ended, occupation troops became security troops, Allied High Commissioners were transformed into ambassadors, and the German Federal Republic came into existence. On May 14, in Poland, the eight states of Eastern Europe signed the Warsaw Treaty, similar to the North Atlantic Treaty, establishing a joint command for their armed forces with headquarters in Moscow. Communist spokesmen stressed its defensive purposes, and claimed it was necessitated because "West Germany is being turned into a bridgehead for deployment of large aggressive forces."

The urgency with which the whole matter of German rearmament was treated contrasted strangely with a prevalent feeling of international relaxation, compounded of both an internal loosening up in the Soviet Union, the numerous international settlements Russia had reached with Iran, Turkey, Greece, and Yugoslavia, the offers of new trade agreements, and the general new style of diplomacy. In the face of this, and the growing realization that it might take five years to provide a politically screened and reliable German NATO contribution, even Dulles shared in the feeling of relaxation. "There is less fear than there was, I am glad to say, of open military activities," he reported late in the year. Yet if the attitude on German rearmament contrasted strangely with the general good feeling, it did not contrast with one underlying factor: In the years since Stalin was blocked in Berlin and Korea, Russia had quietly doubled its armed forces, while developing its nuclear and thermonuclear capabilities.

German rearmament was only one aspect of the NATO situation in the 1950–55 period. The Korean War had led to creation of an elaborate alliance structure. (p. 125), and General Eisenhower had become Supreme Allied Commander in Europe. When he withdrew to enter the presidential race in 1952, the American General Matthew Ridgway replaced him. Peace in Korea and the advent of the Eisenhower administration, although it did not forestall German rearmament, brought a new emphasis to NATO strategy and a concomitant renewal of neutralist agitation.

The new strategy was prompted mainly by a reluctance to incur heavy expenditures necessary for the integrated force suggested at Lisbon in 1952. In the United States, this reluctance led to the emphasis on "massive retaliation," in Europe, to a shift back to the idea that the land forces facing the Russians should constitute a "trip-wire" or "plate-glass," designed to trigger retaliation, rather than a really defensive hold-ing force. But it was necessary to assure at least some Europeans that *defense* was possible in case *deterrence* failed to keep the Russians from at-tacking, and NATO resorted, in 1954, to arming itself with what were called "tactical" nuclear weapons—small weapons that could be used by troops in the field against attacking units, their bases and supply lines. Presumably these would compensate for Atlantic manpower deficiencies vis-à-vis the Soviet bloc.

The North Atlantic Council meeting of foreign and defense ministers in December 1954 approved the policy; the finger on the atomic trigger would be American; European troop units would receive training in han-dling the weapons that could deliver atomic warheads; the atomic weap-ons would be used even in case of a Russian conventional attack on Western Europe.

The "solution" to the manpower problem—NATO's own "new look" —left many questions unanswered and sparked a long-lasting debate on basic strategy. Some argued that tactical atomic weapons shared the dis-advantages of both conventional defense strategy and of the strategy of atomic deterrence. A build-up of tactical atomic strength—like an in-crease in conventional defense strength—might lessen Russian certainty that the United States would really use its massive retaliatory capacity, and thereby weaken the deterrent effect of the latter. But the tactical atomic weapons shared with the strategic weapons of massive retaliation the unimaginable disadvantage that if used, they would subject Europe to atomic devastation. Could "tactical" atomic weapons be used without leading into a general conflagration? Was not the very term "tactical" a misnomer? Would not the Russians answer by giving their own troops tactical atomic capability, thereby eliminating the advantage the weapons would supposedly give the West? And if the Russians were to "nibble" at some area like Greece or Turkey, or renew their blockade of Berlin, would the West really be prepared to turn to atomic war?

Finally, more and more voices criticized the whole idea of NATO: why equip it with atomic weapons just when a change in Russian leader-ship appeared to offer a real chance to diminish world tension? The new leaders were different from the suspicious, paranoid, power-mad Stalin. In order to consolidate their power they had begun to offer concessions to Soviet citizens and to relax the police-state methods of Stalin's time. This, some people argued, showed that the ideological erosion of Com-munism had begun: face to face with new developments— the persist-ence and spread of nationalism, the development of new and devastating weapons, the strength of Western economic and political institutions—Communist leaders had to revise their dogma and abandon any ideas they might have actually had of conquering the world. (Many people in Western Europe continued to argue that the Soviet leaders had never had such ideas, and others maintained that while the Soviets might really want to spread Communism, this did not necessarily involve an intent to use Russian military power.)

Finally, and perhaps most important, revelations about the awesome power of the new hydrogen weapons affected the discussions. Hydrogen bombs were fundamental to the strategy of massive retaliation. But the general public was shocked by the results of a March 1954 test of one of the new American weapons. Its explosive power—250 times greater than the atomic bomb that had devastated Hiroshima—had apparently not been predicted by scientists, nor had they expected the enormous amount of lethal "fallout" that followed the explosion. Fallout, the radioactive debris that remains long after detonation, can cause painful death, horrible disfigurement to those exposed to it, and threatens subsequent generations with dreadful mutations and malignant diseases like leukemia. Some of this data had come to light because of the exposure to radioactive fallout of the crew of a Japanese fishing vessel, the "Lucky Dragon," which had strayed into a zone from which vessels had been warned away. This zone was in what was traditionally thought of as the high seas, always open to navigation. To the horror of the unknown was added the question of the United States' right to conduct tests in the area.

The Soviet Union had tested its own hydrogen weapons in the fall of 1953, adding to the atmosphere considerable amounts of fallout, the long-term effects of which were equally uncertain. Churchill, in reviewing the available data on hydrogen bombs in the House of Commons on March 1, 1955, said, "The atomic bomb, with all its terror, did not carry us outside the scope of human control and manageable events in thought or action, peace or war . . ." but added that with the hydrogen bomb, "The entire foundation of human affairs was revolutionized and mankind placed in a situation both measureless and laden with doom." He then went on to say, "It may well be that we shall, by a process of sublime irony, have reached a stage in history where safety will be the sturdy child of terror, and survival the twin brother of annihilation." But unlike Churchill, who then justified Britain's decision to build its own nuclear striking force while cutting back on conventional forces, many other people used the information about hydrogen weapons to oppose *all* military strategies, and to argue for renewed efforts at disarmament or neutralism on the part of European countries.

Despite the questioning and argument, NATO governments accepted the new strategy based on tactical atomic weapons in conjunction with massive retaliation.

The debate on Western military strategy attracted considerable public attention. Less dramatic but equally important were developments in the economy of Western Europe. A perilous balance had been regained by the time of the Korean War. The war had upset it again, partly because of the cost of the rearmament effort, partly because of a sharp upward movement in raw material and commodity prices. Nevertheless, with the end of the Korean War, a period of economic growth began in Europe that seemed to mark a fundamental change. In the late 1940s, the Marshall Plan boosted morale, the German "economic miracle" was under way, and the Monnet Plan had started France on reequipment of its industry. Yet Europe was pervaded by a lingering pessimism based on the bitter experience of two generations who had lived through the 1920s and 1930s, when capitalism seemed dying. It had fed on the destruction of the war years. Almost unaccountably, however, the indices of production and employment began to climb in the middle 1950s, and indications were that these were no longer a result of American economic and military aid. A slight recession in the United States in 1954 failed to damp the upward spurt in Europe, although before this it had been assumed that such a recession would cause a sharp drop in European exports to the United States, with serious domestic repercussions. Each year authorities warned that the year ahead might not be so rosy, but 1953, 1954, and 1955 set records far above prewar levels for output, productivity, and employment. Despite the setback to European unity of the defeat of the European Defense Community, Europe appeared to have taken a new lease on life, and even laggard countries like Italy began to show the results of the boom. The index of industrial production for Western Europe published by the United Nations increased from its 1948 base of 100 to 179 by mid-1955. There were soft spots and anachronistic economic practices. Yet governments were tackling them with vigor. In France, Premier Mendés-France set structural readjustments in the French economy as one of the major goals of his government, along with liquidation of the Indochinese war and settlement of the issue of German rearmament; in part readjustments had already begun under the Monnet Plan and the developing Coal and Steel Community. The British, too, began to see some light. Their economic situation had remained precarious. In order to meet their far-flung commitments abroad—including the maintenance of an army in Germany, repayment of World War II debts, and aid to develop overseas territories—the British had to export more than they imported. Yet given the nature of the British economy, many exports contained a large proportion of imported raw materials. A favorable balance of trade came in the first year of the Korean War but gave way, the next year, to an enormous deficit as raw material prices increased and, although World War II rationing was slowly abandoned, a new round of "belt-tightening" took place. All through the 1950s the dilemma apparently inherent in the notion of "belt-tightening" plagued the Conservative government that had come to power because of dissatisfaction with Labour's economic policies: such policies, whose high interest rates and restrictions on consumption were designed to reduce inflationary pressures and decrease imports, also seemed to reduce incentives to increase production and to replace older, worn, capital equipment. Moreover, as the 1950s progressed, the British faced increased competition from resurgent Japanese and German production. The two countries, the British noted, were not hampered by the heavy defense expenditures which in Britain took 10 per cent of the gross national product. In 1952 and 1953 the Conservative government tried to persuade the United States to further ease its import restrictions, so that British goods could more easily be sold on the American market. In this they were somewhat more successful than in another policy designed to ease their situation—the opening of trade with Communist bloc countries. Conversations with Soviet and Communist Chinese officials led primarily to irritation in the United States instead of more exports. Congressional leaders threatened to cut off aid if Britain succeeded, whereas the conversations themselves brought no substantial results.

Despite all the problems and the impact of the Anglo-Iranian oil crisis, the years 1953 and 1954 were the best years for the British economy since World War II, and both showed a substantial favorable trade balance. Rationing and many other direct controls were abandoned, inflation was apparently contained, and full employment and prosperity were achieved. Like the other countries of Europe, Britain began to share in the mid-century boom. The "post-war" years were apparently over; the coronation of Elizabeth in June 1953 seemed really to have inaugurated a new Elizabethan age.

In the Far East, Japan—the only Asian country sufficiently industrialized to be compared to Europe—also shared in the boom. Although exports and imports were still substantially below prewar levels, although Japanese traders complained about unfair restrictions against them (the British, in return, accusing the Japanese of unfair trading practices, tried unsuccessfully to bar them from membership in the General Agreement on Tariffs and Trade) and although Japan, like Britain, sought unsuccessfully to penetrate the tempting yet evasive and ambiguous Chinese market, by 1954 Japan's level of manufacturing stood at 75 per cent over the 1934–36 level, and real income per capita had risen 5 per cent. The figure was not high, especially since the comparison is made to depression years. Yet considering the restriction of the Japanese Empire to the home islands, the ingathering of people to those islands, and the enormous destruction by American bombardment in the last years of the war, the achievement was enormous. It had been greatly helped by American aid —to the extent of $5 billion—and by American purchases and use of Japanese services during the Korean War. Yet it proved to be a solid achievement: the base had been laid for a growth that continued at an increasing rate in subsequent years. No small part of this lay in Japan's successful tackling of the frightening population problem. Still only dimly seen in other parts of the world, it was clearly perceived within the confines of the Japanese islands, and governmental action had been forthcoming: in 1949 the Japanese legalized abortion for economic as well as medical reasons. Now that it was cheaply available through regular doctors, widespread abortion and increased use of contraceptive practices cut the inflated postwar birth rate almost in half by the mid 1950s.

DEVELOPMENTS IN THE UNITED NATIONS

The years 1950–55 were bleak for the United Nations. The organization moved into its handsome new quarters in New York. But the Korean War moved out of its control and as efforts to invigorate the concept of collective security failed, regional alliances such as NATO became far more important to many states. Although United Nations agencies continued and even expanded their varied and useful services to the international community in the economic and social fields, on political matters the organization frequently found itself stymied. Final settlements of such matters as the Arab-Israeli dispute, lingering Indonesian-Dutch problems, the status of Southwest Africa (formerly held by South Africa as a League Mandate, now simply held) all proved impossible. The Soviet Union used its veto not only on questions of membership but also on political recommendations, and refused to recognize Secretary General Trygve Lie upon extension of his term of office. To everyone's relief, it agreed to the appointment of Hammarskjold in 1953. But the dismal charade of disarmament talks continued. In 1952 the separate atomic and conventional weapons discussions were combined and a single Disarmament Commission established. But against the background of rearmament efforts occasioned by the Korean War, the American efforts to expand its alliance and foreign base system, the development of the hydrogen bomb, and estensive Russian peace propaganda, the discussions were fruitless. There was some hope that development of the new and more horrible weapons and changes within the Soviet Union might lead to more serious efforts to find a way out of the impasse, particularly since a number of political settlements had taken place. Attention shifted from comprehensive schemes which had many pitfalls, to less ambitious proposals that might lessen the chances of war; both sides acknowledged that existing supplies of nuclear warheads could not be discovered by inspection, and the discussions began to take on a more realistic tone. President Eisenhower's "Atoms for Peace" proposal delivered to the General Assembly in December, 1953 reflected some of the new thinking: transfer of nuclear material—denatured to prevent its use for military purposes —to an international agency for use for development purposes under international control, would convince both sides of the other's willingness to diminish its stockpile, while circumventing the inspection problem. Perhaps such measures might reduce tension without decreasing military security. Yet few could miss the irony of raising new hopes about disarmament at the very moment the West had successfully found a way of rearming Germany. And the deadlock of the issue of admission of new members to the United Nations continued through the 1954–55 General Assembly.

CONCLUSION

In 1950 people the world over feared the worst—that Korea would be the spark to explode the Cold War into World War III. Yet as the major powers continued to display caution, people began to breathe more easily. Nevertheless, the Korean War and the continued fighting in Indochina had shaped a Western attitude that would prove to be of great significance. The United States led in interpreting the new situation as one in which a well-coordinated Communist bloc, dominated by Russia, had begun to take the offensive. This attitude inspired a major shift in American aid from economic to military categories. It led to a new emphasis on force-in-being for European defense and to wholesale rearming of the West, to a desperate effort to incorporate Germany into the defense system without worrying its neighbors, and to the extension of NATO to the eastern Mediterranean. It allowed the resurrection of Western Germany and Japan, those recently defeated countries whose conquerors had been determined never to let them rise again. They had now become the recipients of extensive American aid and the objects of American blandishment. Whether the thinking behind these shifts was sound remains open to question. American interpretations were colored by the events of the preceding winter: the end of bipartisanship and bitter recrimination over the "fall" of China; the discovery of Russian atomic spy rings and the Alger Hiss case; the beginning of McCarthyite pressures on the Administra-

tion. There were misconceptions aplenty behind the containment policy
—over Russia's role in Greece and the extent of Russian influence over
the Chinese Communists. There is still disagreement about the relative
roles of the Russians and the Chinese in the Korean attack and the
long, drawn-out war that fololwed. But in the United States at the time assumptions about the aims of Soviet foreign policy never came into question; rather, it was the validity of the response to Soviet policy, and the
period was marked by an acrimonious and fruitless debate about containment and liberation that did not help in formulating a coherent foreign
policy. It did, however, inspire greater distrust of American leadership
among America's allies.

The uneasiness was even more intense because, with the threat of general war hanging over the world, both sides now possessed nuclear weapons. Europeans were always ready to argue that Americans did not know
what war was really like, since their country had not been a battleground
in recent times. Yet as the threat of war receded and a series of precarious settlements were reached in Asia, some people asked whether it was
not, indeed, the threat of use of the weapons that had produced the settlements, since no one could benefit from enlargement or continuation of
expensive wars.

In any event, the settlements in Asia, the development of thermonuclear weapons, and the changes in Russian leadership occurred just when
the enormous reconstruction efforts in Europe were proving to be successful. And as European nations started to enjoy unforeseen economic
prosperity, they began to examine their relationship with the United
States. Europe had desperately needed America at the end of the war and
in the late forties, America had responded. But was America still needed
in the same way if more reasonable men were Russia's leaders? The uneasiness about America's posture toward the Soviet Union and about
America's apparent inability to understand different interpretations of
the world situation, when combined with a desire to be independent,
helped to speed the move toward European unity. The Americans themselves had prodded Europe to unite, but the process had faltered with the
fiasco of the European Defense Community—itself a product of the Korean War. Still, with the process of recovery virtually completed, Europeans found unity attractive not only in terms of strength vis-à-vis the Soviet
Union, but also in relation to the friendly but dominating United
States.

Thermonuclear weapons sparked a new debate during these years:
What did they mean for strategy and international politics? Did they, as
Churchill suggested, bring a new and perhaps more stable balance of ter-
ror? Or should they call forth a new effort at disarmament? Given their

existence, was massive retaliation the correct military doctrine? Past experience hardly provided answers, and the debate was certain to continue.

Weapons, economic developments, internal political changes, and mass attitudes underlay the day-to-day details of international politics, shaping them and giving them patterns, though the patterns were frequently hard to discern at the time. Changes in leadership played a part too. When Churchill had come back to power in 1951, European leaders hoped that the Labour-imposed isolation from European unity would be reversed. It was not. Churchill put ties to the Commonwealth and trans-Atlantic unity ahead of ties to the Continent. When Eisenhower assumed power many people in Eastern Europe expected to be liberated. They were not. Eisenhower preferred containment. With the death of Stalin, no one knew what to expect. Would his heirs seek to decrease tension in order to consolidate their position at home, or would they increase it to prove that they were the legitimate heirs of Marxism-Leninism-Stalinism? Stalin himself seemed to have sought limited settlements; in the early years, his successors did the same, all the while promising the people of Russia an easier time than before. The latter policy gave promise, too, of a softening of Russian foreign policy. Yet Stalin's heirs had the hydrogen bomb and, as of 1954, the means to deliver it.

Developments in the West, in Russia, in Korea, and in Indochina overshadowed those in the rest of the world. No one yet saw a pattern in the revolt in Egypt, the nationalization crisis in Iran, the new wave of terrorism in Algeria, the revolt and its suppression in Guatemala. Yet these foreshadowed vast changes to come, in which the move for political independence was to be coupled with the idea of social revolution and a desire for some sort of economic independence. They indicated that rejection of Western political domination was likely to include rejection of Western political and economic institutions. Yet if the people in new countries were going to modernize their economic and social structures in order to improve their miserably low standards of living, they could not return to old forms. What alternatives would be open to them?

Conditions in all of the vast belt of "underdeveloped" countries that extended from Southeast Asia across to Africa and South America were such that economic development would be enormously difficult: climate, resources, social structure, population pressure, all would make development a politically difficult task. Those who had begun to call for narrowing the income gap between the poor countries and the wealthier countries of Europe, North America, and Australia-New Zealand hardly realized what they were asking for, and what upheaveal was involved; as yet, they ignored the portents of Egypt, Iran, Algeria, and Guatemala. So far the question of *how* to deal with demands of the new states was discussed primarily on the level that unless they received economic aid they might "go Communist," with the tacit assumption that this meant joining the Soviet bloc as a Russian satellite. Most people thought in terms of a successful Communist revolt or a *coup détat*. Few saw the alternative suggested by the Gutemalan affair: Russia might reverse its position on the question of cooperation with non-Communist governments whose desire for social and economic change brought them into conflict with the Western powers. If this were to happen, Western leaders might have to search for more new policies. Already some observers had begun to speculate whether the major powers' inability to really threaten the use of thermonuclear weapons might not open opportunities for venturesome new policies that could not be countered by force. The fluid situation in the new states, with their promise of new conflicts wtih the West, might invite such Communist initiatives. There was one hope—that the major powers would discern a common interest in avoiding mutual annihilation by thermonuclear weapons and find ways to reduce tension. As yet, no one really knew what changes the thermonuclear age would bring.

PART III
1956: THE ONSET OF
THE HYDROGEN AGE

FIVE
1955 AND 1956
COEXISTENCE AND
CONFLICT—A NEW
WORLD BALANCE

Stalin's successors employed more flexible tactics than the old dictator had in his last days. But the elements of continuity in Soviet foreign policy were striking. After the Communist parties' failure in their use of violence in Europe and Asia in 1947–48, after the failure of the Berlin blockade and the split with Tito, Stalin himself seemed to become more cautious. The invasion of Korea was the last new Communist probe; with the stalemate reached there in 1951, much of the dynamism went out of Russian foreign policy, and there are those who believe that Stalin was genuinely in search of a wide-ranging detente, that the West failed to understand, and that American insistence on a military build-up in the Eurasian rimlands combined with talk of "liberation" of captive nations forestalled such an understanding or settlement. Whether or not this is true, the last year of Stalin's life saw the beginning of a new Soviet approach to foreign affairs in which—as his successors took over—vituperation lessened, settlements were agreed to in several areas, and people began to hope. Some argued that this change was the consequence of internal developments in the Soviet Union, that as new men came to power they sought to gain the approval of the masses by increasing consumer goods production, by diminishing the arbitrary use of terror and police methods, and that to do this, they had to reduce the international tension which had been the excuse for those methods. Others argued that the change was due mainly to the resolute effort made by the West to rearm and to put its own house in order, combined with the awareness on each side of the deadly nature of the new weapons each wielded.

Whichever was true—and the problem for policy-makers was that each explanation implied a different policy for the future—the trend culminated in 1955–56. In 1955—despite the Western agreement on German rearmament and the Soviet response of the Warsaw Alliance—the Russians finally signed a peace treaty ending the occupation of Aus-

175

tria, and Malenkov's successors, Khrushchev and Bulganin, agreed to meet with President Eisenhower, Prime Minister Eden, and Premier Faure at Geneva. The meeting produced the term "the spirit of Geneva" —presumably one of more willingness to discuss and to compromise— and was followed by a meeting of the foreign ministers. At Geneva each assured the other that he wanted no nuclear war, and the conclusion seems to have been reached that indeed neither of the two superpowers could afford to use thermonuclear weapons.

In contrast, however, to the sunny smiles and the handshakes of Geneva and the Austrian peace treaty, there were also the beginnings of what some believed to be a huge new Soviet offensive conceived in nonmilitary terms and conducted under the umbrella of mutual nuclear deterrence. By 1955 the Soviet Union completely abandoned the old Stalinist line that nationalist leaders of new nations were merely bourgeois tools of the imperialists, and replaced it with the view that these same leaders represented a new and progressive force. With this matter safely settled, it became possible to approach them on new terms. The result was a whole set of aid programs, propaganda appeals, wholesale admissions to the United Nations, and visits by Khrushchev and Bulganin to countries all over the world in an effort to win new friends. A rapprochement with Tito followed, and the gains for the Soviet Union seemed startling. Meanwhile, in 1955, the new states of Asia and Africa made known their own views of their importance on the world scene at a conference at Bandung, Indonesia.

But the period of easing of relations and of peaceful competition ended in 1956 when the Soviet Union's rapprochement with Tito and the attempt to relax Stalinist controls brought an unforeseen response—revolt within the Soviet bloc. At the same time the West was in disarray; serious differences of opinion over how to respond to the new Soviet flexibility led to the Suez war and an American-Soviet alignment against France, Britain, and Israel. What had seemed clear in 1955 became increasingly blurred in the following years, and the Cold War assumed new dimensions.

"DEEDS NOT WORDS"

For years, whenever non-Soviet people of any political persuasion suggested that talks with Russian leaders would be a worthwhile effort that might lessen international tension, the standard reply of many Western political leaders was that such talks would be meaningless unless the Russians first proved their willingness to compromise by deeds, not words. But the Soviets could point to many "deeds" since 1952 and in May

1955, came the most striking one of all: Russian signing of the Austrian peace treaty and the subsequent withdrawal of Soviet forces from Austria. Negotiations over Austria had dragged on ever since the end of the war, but conclusion of a treaty had always been prevented by Russian insistence on using it as a bargain counter for other matters—successful resolution of the Trieste crisis, prevention of German rearmament, or some other matter. Moreover, the Soviet government had always insisted on clauses that would have subjected the Austrian economy to Soviet domination.

Suddenly, in the midst of a speech to the Supreme Soviet in February, Foreign Minister Molotov (not yet demoted as a scapegoat for Stalinism) suggested that these conditions might be modified, and the Austrian treaty negotiated on its own terms. Exploratory talks followed and the Russians gave up all their economic demands in return for certain cash payments and a guarantee of delivery of Austrian oil for ten years. The proposed treaty stipulated that Austria would never unite with Grmany, and was accompanied by an Austrian declaration that it would remain permanently neutral and never join any military alliance. In short order the wartime allies signed the treaty restoring Austria to sovereign independence; by September 15 all Soviet and other foreign troops were withdrawn from Austrian soil.

The payments to Russia were onerous, and the status of permanent neutrality—although modeled on Switzerland's successful neutrality—might prove difficult to interpret. But the Austrians were jubilant, the West had proof of Soviet willingness to cooperate in "deed," and when the four foreign ministers met to sign the treaty, they agreed to begin preparations for a summit meeting.

GENEVA IN JULY

Numerous changes on the diplomatic scene preceded the meeting at Geneva. In the Soviet Union, Malenkov had demoted himself and although Field Marshal Bulganin replaced him as Premier, it became obvious that Party Secretary Nikita Khrushchev was now the leading member in the "collective leadership" that presumably had deplaced Stalin's one-man rule. In England, the man who had originally called for a summit meeting in 1953, Winston Churchill, had had to retire, to be replaced by his long-time heir-apparent, Anthony Eden. The new Soviet leaders had begun to effect a rapprochement with Yugoslavia (see p. 182) and had indicated their desire to initiate diplomatic relations with Adenauer's newly sovereign West German Republic.

Technical arrangements for the summit conference were made under

United Nations auspices, and the sessions took place at the old League of Nations building now used as European headquarters for the United Nations. The conference proved to be far different from the initimate top-level conversations Churchill had originally envisioned: it took place in a blaze of publicity. In effect, the leaders of the four powers did little more than stake out positions and reassure each other of their peaceful intensions. Not much more could be expected; the agenda covered such topics as Grman unification, European security, disarmament, and development of contacts between East and West—all highly technical and complicated matters. But more important, the leaders' statements—though laced with expressions of good will—indicated fundamental disagreement on all the agenda topics: the Soviets would not agree to free all-German elections; their idea of a general European security treaty, which would include the two Germanies and lead to an abandonment of all military alliances, was clearly foredoomed since the Western powers were far from ready to abandon NATO. Approaches to the issue of increased contacts between East and West also differed: the Russians were interested in more exchanges of official delegations (presumably because these could be more adequately controlled for national and propaganda purposes) and in a relaxation of Western controls of strategic materials shipments to the Soviet bloc; Western leaders were interested in freer movement of individuals and publications.

In the field of disarmament, President Eisenhower made a dramatic move that immediately caught world attention. Old approaches to disarmament had already been rehearsed. But in a speech in which he turned to the Soviet leaders and, in front of all the apparatus of the world's mass media, vowed that the "United States will never take part in an aggressive war," Eisenhower also advanced a startling proposal: each major power should supply the other with complete blueprints of its military establishment and permit it to make aerial photo-reconnaissance missions over its national territory.

The suggestion was electrifying, even though political leaders—including Americans—soon began to ask exactly what it meant. Like the earlier Atoms-for-Peace plan, presented to the United Nations in 1953, the Open Skies proposal was presented with too little thought about its implementation and perhaps too much thought about the propaganda advantage to be gained. Once sober second thoughts took over, the first propaganda advantage enjoyed by the United States was soon dissipated; people felt they had been taken advantage of. Nevertheless, President Eisenhower impressed many world leaders with his sincerity, and there was evident desire to explore the proposal. Among other things, it reflected a hope that the old pattern of sterile disarmament negotiations might be broken now that the thermonuclear age had arrived. Perhaps one way to avoid the difficulties inherent in any proposal for the actual reduction of weapons might be in schemes to reduce the possibility of surprise attack. Such measures might restore mutual trust and lead to further measures of actual *dis*armament. In subsequent months, however, Soviet leaders entered many objections to the Open Skies idea, and American congressmen questioned the wisdom of allowing Soviet planes to fly over the United States taking photographs while we supplied the Soviet Union with "blueprints"—whatever these might be—of the American military establishment. Nevertheless, the United States worked on the details of implementation, and negotiated on the plan. Various suggestions and countersuggestions for opening different zones for pilot-project aerial inspection were presented. In the end, the proposal came to nothing.*

The Geneva conference led to no hard and fast agreements, except to hold further conversations among the foreign ministers in the fall which, in turn, were inconclusive. But it appeared to have two effects. It created an atmosphere of relaxation, an atmosphere the Russians exploited unsparingly in their propaganda during succeeding years when Khrushchev, in fact, initiated bold new Russian foreign policy probes far beyond the continental limits to which Stalin had, more or less, limited himself: as the Western powers continued moves to maintain their chosen security posture, the Soviets charged them with violating the "Spirit of Geneva," a public charge designed to be heard especially in the newer countries of the world, whose leaders had been so eager to see in the Geneva Conference the beginnings of a real détente. The second effect appeared to be the mutual recognition that nuclear war would be disastrous for all parties.

Behind this apparent tacit agreement lay some complex factors. Within the Soviet Union, it had been forbidden for many years to suggest that nuclear weapons could be decisive in war. The argument had been that since the inevitable course of history would result in the triumph of "socialism," success in war was therefore determined by permanent underlying social and economic factors. Since a capitalist country—the United States—had first developed atomic weapons, unless the laws of Marxist history were wrong, the weapons could not be considered decisive. And under Stalin, the latter became dogma. It did not prevent the Russians from starting a crash program to develop nuclear weapons of their own,

---

* But within a short time the United States did in fact begin aerial surveillance overflights of the Soviet Union by the secret, high-altitude U-2 "spy-plane." They led to much embarrassment in 1960 (see below, p. 306), but were also to prove of vital importance in the Cuban missile crisis of 1962. Finally, both the Soviet Union and the United States ended up in the 1970s with intensive satellite surveillance of one another; once more, unbelievably rapid technological developments outmoded complicated and long drawn-out diplomatic negotiations.

however, or from conducting a worldwide propaganda campaign to mark the weapons as significantly different from other weapons, and therefore to inhibit the United States from using them under any circumstances.

But once Stalin was dead and the Soviet stockpile of weapons began to grow and once thermonuclear weapons became a reality, a new debate arose in the Soviet Union. Now it became possible to revise the Stalinist formulations and to discuss the weapons as something new in history that might, indeed, *change* the laws of history. It became possible to argue—as Malenkov did at one point—that both capitalist *and* socialist states might lose disastrously in a thermonuclear war, regardless of the fact that the laws of history *ought* to leave the socialist state triumphant. Malenkov retracted and, after his fall, Khrushchev and Bulganin were more circumspect in their rejection of the old Stalinist line. Khrushchev proceeded to take measures to enable the Soviet Union to fight and, hopefully, survive and even win a thermonuclear war. The whole matter of the importance of surprise attack became open to discussion in the Soviet armed forces press. Previously, for the same reasons of Stalinist dogma, surprise attack could not be viewed as decisive, since this would theoretically give an advantage to a capitalist power that used it. Now the reasoning could be more realistic. Despite Khrushchev's more "circumspect" position—that war might still be possible and therefore that the Soviet Union would have to continue to prepare for it—it became the generally accepted line that for the first time in history the capitalist powers were put into a position that made it sucicidal for them to initiate war; for the first time it seemed possible that history might move forward without that last dying convulsion of bitter war so long expected by most good Marxist Communists. Not only had a new period in history dawned with the advent of thermonuclear weapons and their possession by the Soviet Union, but Eisenhower had shown at Geneva that he, too, realized this. While leaders throughout the world believed that Geneva signified tacit agreement by the major powers that nuclear war had become impossible, that a nuclear stalemate existed, to the Soviet leaders, within their framework of thought, it meant something more: the opportunity to pursue foreign policy by other means and to push forward with little or no danger that the capitalist powers would retaliate with nuclear war. Thus, all through 1955 and 1956, they proceeded to take advantage of the stalemate.

NEW SOVIET INITIATIVES

To the north Soviet leaders demonstrated their good will and removed an irritant by returning Porkkala Naval Base to Finland. Troops began to leave in 1955 and the formal surrender of the base—whose lease, extracted as part of the World War II peace settlement, was to last until 1997—took place on January 27, 1956. Soviet leaders made much of the fact that this, along with the return of Port Arthur to Communist China, liquidated all Soviet bases abroad apart from those required for communications to Germany and those held under the Warsaw Pact; they invited the Western powers to do likewise, since it was well known that foreign bases were a chief cause of international tension. Their moves, they pointed out, gave evidence of their own sincere desire to reduce tension, and the moment the West abandoned NATO and its bases, the Soviet Union would abandon the Warsaw Pact.

Since the Porkkala Naval Base had been held in order to protect the avenue of approach to Leningrad from the kind of attack and the city from a siege such as the one the Germans had carried out in World War II, and since the Soviet leaders now assumed diminished likelihood of any major war (and certainly of any that repeated the pattern of World War II), some observers felt that the move had cost the Soviet Union little.

At the same time, the Soviet leaders initiated a dramatic new peripatetic diplomacy; Bulganin and Khrushchev formed a traveling team that became almost affectionately known in the British press as "Bulge and Krusch." Their first and perhaps most important visit was to the old enemy, Tito of Yugoslavia. It represented part of an overall effort to win Tito back into the Communist fold.

Tito had himself been busy making friends with the leaders of new states—exchanging visits with Premier U Nu of Burma, and receiving Prime Minister Nehru of India. All were receptive to the new Soviet point of view that peaceful coexistence was now not only possible—it was also imperative. All were receptive to the idea that continued American military expenditures and bases abroad threatened coexistence. They reacted more unfavorably to American Secretary of Defense Wilson's statement that nothing at Geneva justified reducing defense expenditures, than to Khrushchev's statement on September 17, 1955.

> We are in favor of a détente, but if anybody thinks that for this reason we shall forget about Marx, Engels, and Lenin, he is mistaken. This will happen when shrimps learn to whistle . . . we shall always adhere to the building of socialism. . . . We don't believe that war is necessary to that end. Peaceful competition will be sufficient.

Marshal Tito now received aid from the West; at the same time he appeared to be building some sort of third, neutral force consisting of countries not bound by any military alliances, and in May 1955, he entertained Bulganin and Khrushchev. The earlier attempt to tie Tito more closely to the West through the Balkan Pact had ended quietly. Negotiated in 1952 and signed in March 1953 when Stalin's hostility was still evident, the pact constituted an alliance between Yugoslavia, Greece and Turkey. Since the last two were also in NATO, the pact was, in effect, an indirect way of bringing Yugoslavia into NATO, without exposing Tito to the charge that he had completely abandoned Communism by aligning himself with the most capitalist of nations. But the softer Soviet line led to a quiet death for the pact. How much would Tito now respond to Khrushchev's blandishments? How far could the Kremlin leaders go to repudiate the whole Soviet bloc campaign against Tito?

The answer was that they would go far. The method was simple but rather crude: when Khrushchev arrived at the airport in Yugoslavia, he made the late Lavrenti Beria (executed head of the Soviet secret police) the scapegoat for the whole program of vilification, subversion, and economic and diplomatic pressures against Yugoslavia, for all of which he apologized abjectly. The accusations against Tito "were fabricated by the enemies of the people, detestable agents of imperialism who by deceptive methods pushed their way into the ranks of our party."

The meeting ended with a communique in which Tito supported many Soviet positions on international affairs, and endorsed peace, brotherhood, sovereignty, independence, noninterference, coexistence, and so on. Although much of this was meaningless rhetoric, some at least was an explicit repudiation of Stalin's attempt to dictate to Yugoslavia. Certain more concrete items followed: agreements for expanded trade, cancellation of debts, and provisions for improved communications. In a further move to conciliate Tito, Khrushchev abolished the Cominform. It had originally been created to coordinate Communist regimes, but one of its main tasks had been to organize the campaign against the Yugoslav leader. Yet Tito also moved to reassure the West: he told the United States that he would abide by restrictions on strategic trade with the rest of the Communist bloc (this was necessary for the continuation of American aid) and he received Secretary Dulles cordially when he visited Belgrade in November 1955.

A rapprochement, nevertheless, had been effected. Tito had been restored to a respectable place in the eyes of the Soviet hierarchy, while the West continued to woo him. But if Tito was now respectable and the whole campaign against him had been a plot of "imperialist" spies, what about all the leaders in other satellite countries who had been purged, sometimes executed, for Titoism? And what about the current leaders who had done the purging? If Tito, who had chosen his own path to socialism, were readmitted to the Communist camp, would other countries be allowed to choose their own paths? No choice had been possible during Stalin's life when the Stalinist model for society *had* to be accepted. Khrushchev's initiative toward Tito had opened a Pandora's box for the Communist bloc: already these questions were being asked in various quarters. The concept of peaceful coexistence had been designed, many thought, to lull the West and bring to the fore the differences among the Western powers that had been eliminated as a result of Stalin's hard policy. But now the policy posed some dangerous dilemmas for the Soviet bloc. (See below, pp. 193–198).

Khrushchev and Bulganin found other fields for the new diplomacy in those new states with which Tito, too, had been seeking solidarity. India's Prime Minister Nehru visited Moscow in June, and later in the year, during November and December, the two Soviet leaders made an unprecedented return visit to India with side trips to Burma and Afghanistan.

There they made full use of existing conflicts with the West. Both India and Afghanistan had quarrels with Pakistan. India's, growing out of partition, concerned mainly the status of Kashmir. Afghanistan's dispute was over its sponsorship of self-determination for the Pathan tribesmen living in the north of Pakistan. The Indian quarrel with Pakistan had been intensified by Pakistan's military aid agreements with the United States signed in 1954, Pakistani accession to the Southeast Asia Treaty Organization, and its signature of the new Baghdad Pact late in 1955. By these moves, Pakistan had aligned itself solidly with the West; so far as India was concerned, this meant an extension of the Cold War to Asia. But, more important, India felt that the increment in Pakistani military power was directed primarily against India: Pakistan was directly involved in conflicts with India, not with Soviet Russia. Only India would feel the weight of the new power, and Indian leaders made their severe displeasure known to the United States.

When Khrushchev and Bulganin arrived, they proceeded to condemn all pacts, and to support the Indian position on Kashmir as well as the Afghanistani position on an independent state for the Pushtu-speaking Pathan tribesmen. Then, with a fanfare of publicity, the Soviet leaders unveiled their own new foreign policy weapon—economic and technical aid. Such aid had long been used by Western powers; the Soviet Union, after abandoning the rigid Stalinist position toward newly independent states, would now also proceed to influence them by helping them. At first the Western press ridiculed the offers of aid as purely rhetorical but aid, trade, and credit agreements were soon forthcoming, and economic ties of the countries to the Soviet bloc began to become a small but important reality. The new Soviet line was not adopted without some strain:

domestic Communist parties had long opposed the regimes in these new countries as reactionary, bourgeois, handmaidens of the imperialists. Now that the Soviet line changed, and many of the regimes were welcomed as progressive forces on the world scene, the native Communists also had to change their line. The process was painful and led to serious divisions within several of the parties.

In India, where the Party now announced its support for Nehru, Nehru promptly repudiated it: good relations with the Soviet Union did not necessitate coming to terms with antidemocratic parties *within* India.

The Arab world offered another field for new Soviet initiatives, and again, Soviet leaders were able to capitalize on divisions between countries in the area and on their conflicts with Western powers. In this case, the Arab-Israeli conflict and attempts to extend the Western alliance system to the area gave Russia its opportunity. Although the British had agreed in 1954 to withdrawal of the great base at Suez, they maintained continued influence in Jordan and Iraq (where they trained local armies and maintained base rights), in the smaller sheikdoms of the Persian Gulf (whose oil had proved so important during the Iranian crisis), and in Aden, at the southern tip of the Arabian peninsula. In 1955 they buttressed this remaining influence by the Baghdad Pact—an alliance of the states composing what had been called the "Northern Tier" in the Middle East—Turkey, Iraq, Iran, and Pakistan. Attempts to enlist other Middle Eastern states—Lebanon, Syria, Jordan and Egypt—failed: all saw the pact as a means of continuing imperialist influence in the area just when it should be ending. Egypt's President Nasser was particularly incensed. The alliance potentially strengthened Iraq, and Iraq—though it had less than half the population of Egypt—was Egypt's rival for Arab leadership in an area where Arab nationalism conflicted more and more with the local nationalism in states that had been created only thirty years before. The United States did not join the Baghdad Pact, although presumably giving it full support. In thus trying to have the best of both worlds, the United States only got the worst; the leaders of the Baghdad Pact states who felt the prime purpose of the Pact was to commit the United States to the area were annoyed at it for abstaining, while leaders of the other states that the United States had tried to appease by staying out of the Pact were hostile because they felt that the Pact would not have existed without the United States. Their view focused on American support rather than on American nonmembership.

In addition, the Israeli-Arab issue continued to exacerbate relations with the West. In 1950, England, France, and the United States had issued the "Tripartite Declaration" guaranteeing boundaries in the area and imposing something of an arms blockade for the region in an effort to stabilize it. So far as Arab leaders were concerned—especially in the face of massive aid to Israel from private Jewish sources in the United States—this meant that the West backed the existence of Israel. Western powers were also reluctant to force Israel to take back the growing numbers of Arab refugees, or force it to return to the 1947 partition plan boundaries. Therefore they seemed to support Israel in all important matters. It meant little that, in the hope of averting even more Arab hostility, Western powers did nothing to implement Security Council resolutions calling on Egypt to open the Suez Canal to Israeli shipping or Israeli-bound cargoes. And the Eisenhower administration's efforts to improve relations had little effect, even though Dulles visited Naguib in 1953 (leaving him the rather inappropriate gift of a pair of handsome pistols). When Israel adopted a policy of inflicting heavy retaliatory raids on neighboring Arab posts in response to continued Arab sniping and infiltration, the Western powers strongly condemned Israel in the Security Council. Dulles tried to assuage Arab fears that the United States would back Isreli aggression or expansion, and, at the same time, Israel was told by an American Assistant Secretary of State to recognize that it was a Middle Eastern state rather than the "headquarters, or nucleus so to speak, of worldwide groupings of peoples of a particular religious faith who must have special rights within and obligations to the Israeli state." Although Dulles belonged to an administration that had adopted the policy of "massive retaliation," he called on Israel to renounce "the conviction that force and a policy of retaliatory killings is the only policy that your neighbors will understand." He also asked Israel to adopt a policy of restricted immigration; the policy of unlimited immigration fed Arab fears of Israeli expansion in order to accommodate a growing population. (Israel protested strongly that this advice was an interference in Israeli internal affairs.)

At the same time, however, the United States tried to work for some measure of accommodation by promoting the Jordan River Valley development scheme (through which Arab states and Israel would share power and irrigation benefits) and asked the Arab states to "accept the state of Israel as an accomplished fact." In 1955, Dulles offered financial assistance to resettle the Arab refugees, and a guarantee of Israel's borders after "adjustments . . . needed to convert them to boundary lines of safety." In November, Prime Minister Eden went further and suggested—to Israeli horror—a "compromise" territorial settlement.

But, as one Arab spokesman put it, all American offers and all Dulles' initiatives contained "one fundamental flaw." Dulles, he said, "assumes the continued existence of Israel. We don't."

Under these circumstances, Khrushchev could not ignore the oppor-

tunities that were present. The Soviet Union had at first supported the
Partition Plan and recognized Israel. But gradually, in the 1950s it
veered to stronger and stronger condemnation of Israel, and in late 1955
Khrushchev took a position that strongly backed the Arabs:

> . . . from the first day of its existence, the State of Israel has been taking a
> hostile, threatening position toward its neighbors. Imperialists are behind
> Israel, trying to exploit it against the Arabs for their own benefit.

More important, the Soviet Union—for the first time since the British
began their nineteenth century policy of blocking Russian influence in the
Middle East—burst into the area by a simple and spectacular move. The
Soviet leaders agreed, in late 1955, to trade Egypt a large quantity of
modern arms in return for a heavy proportion of the Egyptain export cot-
ton crop. By this stroke, the Russians leap-frogged the northern tier to establish an undeniable influence in the area, backed the strongest state in
the Middle East, took advantage of the Arab-Israeli dispute, and, by upsetting the balance Western powers had tried to maintain, made themselves a force that would have to be reckoned with in all future policy toward the Arab states. Moreover, the move symbolized the manner in
which their new initiatives had changed the whole world scene: new
states, aggressively nationalist and bent on developing a policy of nonalignment, could now—if they failed to find satisfaction from Western
powers—seek support from the Soviet Union. Guatemala, in 1954, had
been both a little too early and too close to the United States. But other
countries would now certainly follow the example set by Egypt in the
military area, and by India, Burma, and Afghanistan in the economic
sphere. In short order, Syria and Lebanon began to expand their economic and cultural relations with the Soviet bloc.

The Egyptian move was in fact one of a whole series: Egyptian pilots
began to train in Communist-bloc countries and Nasser increased trade
contacts with both East Europe and Communist China (to which he extended diplomatic recognition). Meanwhile Nasser spelled out the concept of a "neutralist" foreign policy: the new balance of power allowed a
smaller state like Egypt to exist in relative safety without aligning itself
militarily with either of the two superpowers. An alliance involved subordination to and domination by the larger state, and alliance was not even
necessary, since if either of the large states did, in fact, threaten to attack
a country like Egypt, the other would probably come to its aid. But even
excessive economic and diplomatic links with one bloc might well be the
equivalent of domination. For Egypt, Nasser felt, ties of trade and investment in the past had meant exploitation and domination by the West.
The new contacts with friendly Communist countries did not bring the

dangers that Westerners warned him they would. They were, rather, a way of overcoming excessive reliance on the West, and of establishing real independence.

And, as Nasser proceeded with his program, there were rumors that the Soviet Union had offered to help Egypt with its cherished Aswan Dam.

The projected High Dam at Aswan, on the Nile River was the sort of grandiose project bound to appeal to a government seeking a dramatic move to appeal to its people. One of several different projects for increasing power and irrigation from the Nile River, its cost was estimated at over $1.3 billion and the time required to build it fifteen years. Nasser's deals with the Soviet bloc prompted the Western powers to attempt to recoup by proffering aid for the dam. In December 1955 Britain, the United States, Egypt, and the International Bank reached a tentative agreement: Egypt would supply $900 million, the International Bank would lend $200 million, and Britain and the United States would supply the rest. The International Bank loan, like all its loans, necessitated an Egyptain commitment to some measure of economic self-discipline. Nevertheless, for Egypt the first fruits of the deal with the Soviet Union had begun to ripen.

The most spectacular of Khrushchev's initiatives involved the new non-Western countries, but the energetic and jovial Russian leader also found time to try his luck with lesser countries in the West. Chancellor Adenauer traveled to Moscow to receive assurance that some of the still-detained German prisoners of war—from more than a decade ago—would be returned. In exchange, Moscow and Bonn traded ambassadors; Adenauer had previously refused an exchange because of Soviet support for the East German government. Neither accepted the others' position about German boundaries in the east nor could they agree on whether West Germany represented all of Germany. But the exchange represented another understanding arising out of Geneva: only Russia could produce German reunification. It would, therefore, have to be on terms acceptable to Russia—a bitter pill for the West German Government to swallow. Adenauer had built his policy on close economic and military ties with the West *partly* as a means toward reunification, and it now became clear that only abandonment of those ties could lead to reunification, and even then only on Russian terms. Domestically, the German Social Democratic opposition made much of this and of the need to test further Russian intentions and the new Communist diplomatic flexibility. Abenauer tried to put the best light on the exchange by countering that Russia had finally been forced to recognize that there was a viable West Germany—one the Soviet leaders would have to do business with.

Although the Soviet leaders held out the bait of reunification within a

European security system that would supersede NATO, they also assured
the East German Communist leaders that they would not abandon them:
by a unilateral Soviet act on September 20, 1955, all Allied (this meant Soviet) controls over the area were ended. East Germany became the German Democratic Republic; it was given complete control over its internal
and external affairs, and became a full-fledged member of the Warsaw
Pact. The Soviets announced that any questions concerning relations between East and West Germany could now be taken up directly between
them. West Germany responded by announcing it would break diplomatic relations with any country recognizing East Germany. Nevertheless, in
many areas of the world, countries are forced by circumstances to accept
de facto situations that they feel are unjust or illegal, and West Germany
accepted the fact that many of the newer countries would be involved in
trade and cultural negotiations with East Germany. As long as they
avoided the formal step of exchanging permanent diplomatic representatives with East Germany, West Germany would not break off relations
with them.

Khrushchev and Bulganin made a further effort to test the strength of
Western ties. They accepted Eden's invitation to visit Britain in early
1956. Here their appeal was twofold: they stressed Britain's military vulnerability to the Soviet Union's growing strength of new, long-range missiles tipped with thermonuclear weapons, and they played on the enticing
possibilities of increased trade. In so doing, they touched a fundamental
point of difference between many Europeans and Americans. Most
Americans were still suspicious of increased contacts and cooperation
with Russia, and judged them solely in terms of whether or how they
would help the Soviet Union in the overall strategic balance. Most European leaders, however—while usually not denying the strategic problem
—viewed increased contacts as ways of bridging the gap between East
and West, ways of reducing tension, and perhaps, in the long run, a
means of reducing the strategic problem. The British visit had few concrete results. But it exposed some of the differences among Western
powers.

THE BANDUNG CONFERENCE

Khrushchev's initiatives arose out of a combination of circumstances: the
new and growing economic strength of the Soviet Union, the nuclear balance that appeared to lessen the possibilities of war, and the independence of a host of new states, all of which had previously been under the
subjection of Western powers in some measure.

Nothing better symbolized the emergence of the new states and the role they aspired to play on the world scene than the conference held at Bandung, Indonesia, April 18–24, 1955. Sponsored by the Colombo Powers—Burma, Ceylon, India, Indonesia, and Pakistan—it assembled representatives of twenty-four other countries from Asia and Africa,* with a population totaling 1.5 billion. Although the main consideration in issuing invitations had been the desire that "all countries in Asia and Africa which have independent Governments should be invited," there were "minor variations and modifications": since all invitations had to be unanimously issued by the sponsoring powers, Israel was not included, nor were North and South Korea, Nationalist China (all of the five sponsoring states recognized Communist China) , South Africa, Australia, and New Zealand.

All the countries participating sent high-level representatives—prime ministers, foreign ministers, or both. Perhaps most significant was the simple fact that those who attended came with little idea of what the substantive matters before the conference would be. It was not intended to settle any outstanding political or economic problems, and it did not. Their willingness to attend revealed, instead, the importance they themselves attached to a meeting that symbolized their emergence to independence. Moreover, it gave them an opportunity to meet one another. (In the past most of the countries represented had relations primarily with the particular controlling colonial power.) Most of them felt that the heritage of colonial domination and the problem of state-building gave them common interests: Bandung let them establish ties through which in the future they would be able to work out these interests cooperatively. Finally, the conference gave them an opportunity to define a set of general attitudes toward the current international political scene. On this count, despite the expressions of cordiality and common feeling, the conference also revealed that contact might mean not only cooperation and common viewpoints, but also conflict.

Thus the closing communique consisted of promises of cooperation in economic development, technical aid, and cultural exchange, expressions of concern over the status of Dutch New Guinea (which the Indonesians claimed as West Irian) and events in North Africa, and a plea for world disarmament, nonintervention in the domestic affairs of states, and increased membership in the United Nations. It also expressed concern over colonialism, "an evil which should speedily be brought to an end." This phrase represented a compromise reached to a dispute during which

* Afghanistan, Cambodia, People's Republic of China, Egypt, Ethiopia, Gold Coast, Iran, Iraq, Japan, Jordan, Laos, Lebanon, Liberia, Libya, Nepal, the Phillippines, Saudi Arabia, Sudan, Syria, Thailand, Turkey, Democratic Republic of (North) Vietnam, State of Vietnam, and Yemen.

the representatives of many states insisted that this must also mean Communist colonialism. The phrase calling for "abstention from alliances serving only the interests of big powers" indicated the split between neutralists and others. Indian's Nehru had wanted a condemnation of all military pacts, but half the members of the conference belonged to military alliances of one sort or another, and the resulting description of the kind of alliance to be avoided was thoroughly innocuous.

Bandung served a useful purpose for Communist China. Foreign Minister Chou En-lai proved himself a thoroughly skilled diplomat. He exuded a spirit of conciliation and friendliness and declared himself willing to negotiate any question with anyone, including the United States, whose representatives he invited to sit down with him in an effort to resolve the Formosa dispute. Secretary Dulles was not in Washington when word came of the Chinese offer, and Under-Secretary Herbert Hoover, Jr.—appointed to administer the department efficiently, and not expected to be well versed in policy matters—answered instead, rejecting the suggestion out of hand. The dismay expressed in other countries was echoed in the United States: again, in a day when the Soviets and the Chinese demonstrated flexibility in the face of new circumstances, the United States appeared to adopt a rigid posture. It was the supposedly inflexible Dulles who hastened to correct the position, and to declare that direct talks might indeed be acceptable and useful. This led, in following years, to a series of protracted but unrewarding conversations in Poland.

Chou En-lai came away from Bandung with an aura of respectability that served Communist China well. So far as most of the Afro-Asian states were concerned, China was and ought to be accepted as a full-fledged member of the international community. Here and in other places Chou flourished the *Panche Shila*, a statement of five principles which he declared ought to govern the relations between states. Originally stated in a 1954 treaty between China and India in which India acknowledged Chinese sovereignty over Tibet, they were: (1) Mutual respect for each other's territorial integrity and sovereignty; (2) mutual nonagression; (3) mutual noninterference in each other's internal affairs; (4) equality and mutual benefit; (5) peaceful coexistence. Many states proceeded to pledge adherence to the statement.

Bandung did not represent a complete victory for the neutralists, and Chou En-lai, who had started in a strident manner, tailored his approach accordingly. But it was significant that Sir John Kotelewala of Ceylon, the most strenuous Asian anti-Communist at the Conference, was roundly defeated in an April 1956 election. Although the campaign was fought largely on local issues, it put into power Bandanaraikel, head of the heterogeneous but Marxist-oriented United Freedom Party. A thorough neutralist, he quickly established relations with Moscow and Peking, began a program of nationalization, and negotiated withdrawal of the British from the important base they had held at Trincomalee.

Bandung was not the cause, but its spirit was certainly represented in changes that subsequently took place in French-controlled territories. In September 1955, Cambodia, a participant at Bandung as a more-or-less neutralist country, elected a government headed by Prince Norodom Sihanouk, whose first act was to withdraw Cambodia completely from the French Union in which it had remained after the Indochinese settlement of 1954. In early 1956, both Morocco and Tunisia attained full independence from the government of Socialist Guy Mollet. Although Tunisia's Prime Minister Habib Bourguiba rejected neutralism and Communism, he nevertheless proceeded to argue that Algeria, which the French still considered an integral part of France, would also have to attain independence. Finally, in May 1956, France turned over to India a series of small enclaves which it had held for two centuries.

In the same years, Indonesia—seat of the Bandung Conference—acted to increase its own independence through abrogation of the Netherlands-Indonesian Union of 1949 and its accompanying financial agreements. And President Sukarno symbolized his international position by visiting first the United States, then China, and the Soviet Union (which extended technical aid and long-term low interest loans to Indonesia).

December 1955 marked a development in another aspect of the whole decolonization process: end of the membership stalemate in the United Nations with admission of sixteen new members. The Soviet Union had previously vetoed membership for Western-sponsored states because the West had found majorities to block entrance of Soviet-sponsored countries. In this case the veto seems ultimately to have served its purpose: to persuade the great powers to come to a negotiated agreement rather than simply vote against one another. But it could occur only in the spirit of rapprochement that United Nations members seemed determined to salvage from Geneva: Western countries agreed to admit Albania, Hungary, Rumania, and Bulgaria, and the Soviets agreed to the other 12.* There was the possibility of a last minute breakdown of the package deal when Nationalist China added the Republics of (South) Korea and Vietnam and expressed its determination to block the Mongolian People's Republic, originally included. Pressure on China resulted in abandonment of the proposal of membership for the divided countries, and in return for the exclusion of Outer Mongolia, the Western powers agreed to drop Japan.

---

* Jordan, Ireland, Portugal, Italy, Austria, Finland, Ceylon, Nepal, Libya, Cambodia, Laos, Spain.

Informally, all agreed that membership for Japan would be considered at the next Assembly. It was now certain that as new countries became independent, none of the permanent members would take the onus of vetoing their admission. The question of whether United Nations membership should be universal, or whether it should be restricted in terms of vaguely stated qualifications in the Charter, had been resolved for all but the divided countries. The march to independence and full international status symbolized by Bandung continued.

But not without pain. The French denied that Algeria had any desire to be or right to be independent. In the face of continued terrorism, France had removed three of its five NATO divisions to Algeria (thus enabling the Soviets and neutralists to claim that NATO aided French colonial suppression). According to the French, Algerian terrorism was supported by only a minority; the majority of Muslims were terrified into passivity. The matter, they said, was strictly domestic, and called merely for pacification; the only thing that made it a matter of international concern was direct interference by Egypt and other countries; they were the ones that should be censured by the United Nations. When in late 1955 the United Nations General Assembly voted to consider the matter of Algeria, the French underlined their point of view by walking out, to return only when the item was removed from the agenda.

In another spot, Cyprus, the British echoed the French argument. Terrorism had broken out in the tiny island, on which was one of Britain's remaining eastern Mediterranean bases, close to the Suez Canal and the oil fields of the Middle East. The terrorist National Organization for Cyprus Struggle (EOKA) claimed to embody the widespread desire for the Greek Cypriot community for unity with Greece. The British maintained that so long as terrorism existed, there was no way to measure popular feeling, since the people were cowed by the terrorists. To justify continued control, they involved the Turks in the situation. Since almost one-fifth of the population of Cyprus was Turkish and the island lay close to the Turkish coast, the British insisted that Turkey should be consulted. The result was a deterioration in Greco-Turkish relations and bad feeling between the two communities in Cyprus. Britain again imitated the technique used by the French when they had deported the Sultan of Morocco: the British exiled Archbishop Makarios, leader of the Greek Cypriots, charging him with having aided and abetted the terrorists. Attempts to draw up a new constitutional document for internal self-government failed, and Greek agitation for Cypriot self-determination began to undermine Greek relations with NATO. Given the problems of the Turkish minority and British determination to hold Cyprus as a base, the whole issue seemed destined to remain a festering, insoluble matter on which Communist and nationalist could make common cause.

THE SOVIET TWENTIETH PARTY CONGRESS

The year 1955 had seemed an auspicious one in many ways: Bandung had marked the coming to maturity of a group of new countries, and Geneva had demonstrated that, in the face of new weapons, both super powers saw the need to reassure one another that they would try to avoid war, thereby reducing tension. Although Geneva produced no tangible political accords, it was preceded by a series of settlements of outstanding issues on the world scene, and seemed to presage a new era in world politics. Many leaders of new states were especially optimistic, finding as they did on their doorsteps a smiling pair of Soviet leaders who praised their cultures and their efforts at state-building, and who were willing to help them with long-term credits and barter agreements that would avoid the fluctuations of world market prices, plus gifts of new factories or paved roads and technical aid. To Western leaders, the Soviet salesmen seemed much more ominous—precursors, perhaps, of Soviet economic penetration for purposes of political control, and purveyors of the weapons that had upset and disturbed the balance in the Middle East. Nevertheless, the optimists reproached the alarmists. When Secretary Dulles called neutralism "immoral," neutralist leaders like Nehru attacked him bitterly. Dulles' attitude, Nehru said, "left no room for any country to sit on the fence . . . [it divides the world] into two hostile camps, each of which is ready to spring at the throat of the other." Many people felt that Russian internal changes since the death of Stalin involved a genuine liberalization and even democratization. They were even willing to overlook the harshness of the Stalinist period, for Russia, like many of their own countries, had had to industrialize far faster than Western countries, and tough measures had been necessary. Insofar as foreign policy was concerned, Western powers, they thought, had not only been imperialist in the past, but had been reluctant to relinquish their empires, and had done so only under pressure and as a result of weakness. There were things about the new Soviet Union and its surrounding states that one would not wish to emulate, but conditions had vastly improved.

However, the situation within the Soviet Union and the relations between it and its satellite states had been greatly strained by events since Stalin's death and by the very fact of relaxation of international tension. In the first years the main change had been Malenkov's New Course; this involved diminishing the power of the secret police, and increasing light industry and the production of consumer goods at the expense of continued emphasis on heavy industry. The New Course was welcomed in most of the satellites. In some of them it relieved almost intolerable strains imposed by the Stalinist pattern. Although its initiation had been followed by the riots of 1953 in Germany, these had been quelled, and there was no repetition there. Moreover, though Malenkov's foreign policy followed closely upon the course Stalin had begun, involving a search for settlements in various areas, the ties of the Soviet Union to the satellite countries also began to change. Stalin had dictated to them as much as he had to his associates at home. The New Course let them adapt somewhat to local conditions, and to work out problems more on their own. The trend intensified after Khrushchev replaced Malenkov, primarily because the "reduction in tension" symbolized by Geneva appeared to eliminate the whole issue of "liberation" of Eastern Europe from the international scene. This meant to Communist leaders of East Europe that their existence and the stability of their regimes now depended less on the Soviet Union's protection, and they could concentrate on policies that would build domestic support. Finally, the Soviet rapprochement with Yugoslavia appeared to indicate that a country that followed its own policy in both domestic and foreign affairs could be welcome in the Soviet bloc, despite Khrushchev's domestic reversal of Malenkov's emphasis on light industry and consumer goods and his renewed emphasis on heavy industry in the Stalinist pattern.

On the other hand, Yugoslav respectability posed some immediate difficulties for leaders in the other satellite states. Normalization of relations with Tito after years of bloody purges of "Titoists" was ideologically difficult: How could they continue to justify leadership when their particular claim to legitimacy was that they had unmasked Titoists? Poland was in the throes of an intellectual ferment as a result of the de-Stalinization process (as it was already called), and "rightwing deviationists" who had been purged in the past for Titoism—notably Poland's Wladyslaw Gomulka—stood to benefit from Tito's rehabilitation, and endanger the position of existing leaders. Tito pressed home the point, making barbed remarks about Communist heads of state who had followed Stalin's lead which Soviet leaders now condemned. He charged them with lacking "the Communist courage to admit their errors." "These men," he said, "have their hands soaked in blood, have staged trials, given false information, sentenced innocent people to death." Satellite leaders responded to the whole development hesitantly. They established correct but not cordial relations with Tito, found scapegoats for past excesses, and praised Stalin's accomplishments while admitting that he had committed errors.

The Twentieth Party Congress in February 1956, however, made their course far more difficult. Khrushchev had been busy consolidating his domestic position by popular reforms. He granted amnesty to some political offenders, laid a greater stress on legal procedures through the courts instead of arbitrary executive action by the police and other administrative branches, allowed greater freedom in the arts, and attacked unpopular bureaucrats. He also proceeded to fill local party positions with his own men. Then, at the Congress—which endorsed Khrushchev's views that parliaments might also serve as organs of "genuine democracy for the working people" and that there were acceptable "separate paths to socialism"—Khrushchev attacked Stalin in the most violent terms, outdoing Western critics in Stalin's time. He spoke of Stalin's dictatorship by terror, of injustice on an unbelievable scale involving the executions of thousands of innocent people. He described how Stalin's closest associates lived in fear of him and his whims: this was what had kept them from protesting or stopping the dictator. Of necessity, Khrushchev did not suggest that the system that permitted such a thing to happen was wrong. The fault, he said, lay in the "cult of the individual," which was now replaced by "collective leadership."

Khrushchev had gone out dangerously on a limb and, in fact, there were many repercussions. Khrushchev had tried to make Stalin the scapegoat for all that had been bad in former years and to identify the new leadership with opposition to the repressive features of the previous regime and absolve it of complicity. But the attempt at absolution was bound to raise further questions about degrees of guilt, as well as about the many leaders who had been deposed for anti-Stalinist activities by Stalinists still in power. (Khrushchev spoke of the many within the Soviet Union who had been rehabilitated since 1953.) Together with the rapprochement with Tito, relaxation of tension with the West and the wooing of bourgeois nationalist leaders, the Twentieth Party Congress speech further jeopardized the position of satellite political bosses and party leaders outside the Soviet bloc.

THE STALEMATE SHAKEN: HUNGARY AND SUEZ

The events of 1955 and early 1956—the détente, de-Stalinization, the new Soviet initiatives in foreign policy, and the rise of new states to a position where they were wooed by both sides—culminated late in the year in two events that shook the world and challenged the whole concept of a nuclear stalemate. They were the revolt in the Soviet bloc and the abortive Suez war.

Within the bloc, Stalin-style industrialization had created an extremely unstable situation in two countries, Poland and Hungary. Czechoslovakia and East Germany were already industrialized to some degree, and in the latter, memories of the failure of the 1953 uprising lingered. Rumania, Bulgaria, and Albania had not suffered such difficult experiences; Bulgaria had a much longer tradition of Russian friendship and was, like Albania, still essentially an agricultural country with a peasant society.

In Hungary and Poland, however, the postwar period of rapid, forced industrialization had created great strain, and Malenkov's New Course was strongly welcomed. In Hungary it brought to power Imre Nagy in 1953, who adopted its tenets. The fall of Malenkov in 1955 had its parallel in Hungary, where Nagy not only had to give up the premiership but was expelled from the party. The Stalinist Rakosi replaced him, but found a dangerous situation: Nagy's reforms had unloosed all the intellectuals' and workers' objections to Stalinism, and had again called forth Hungarian nationalism. Some Hungarian party leaders began to talk of an alternative to Stalinist emulation of Soviet Communism: *national Communism* with national variations determined by local conditions. Moreover, Rakosi assumed power when the Soviet rapprochement with Tito was well under way and when the anti-Stalin campaign was launched in earnest by Khrushchev's Twentieth Party Congress speech. Faced with mounting popular pressure within the country, Rakosi was forced to resign. His replacement by Erno Gero, a leader less tainted with the Stalinist hue, failed to satisfy popular demands for reforms, and agitation grew in Budapest for the recall to power of Nagy and even of non-Communist leaders.

In the meantime, events in Poland had their effect on Hungary. The tension in Poland led in June to workers' riots in the industrial center of Poznan. Although the riots were condemned by the Soviets as engineered by foreign agents, the Polish Communist Party's Central Committee admitted that they were the result of clumsy handling of justifiable complaints about working conditions. Then, on August, 4, Wladyslaw Gomulka, ousted in 1949 and imprisoned for Titoism, was readmitted to the party, and by October 16 the situation had so changed that he attended a Politbureau meeting where he was restored to the Central Committee. Since he appeared to stand for radical reform in Poland, he seemed a threat to the delicate new balance Khrushchev had been trying to establish between Soviet leadership and recognition of national differences within the Soviet bloc—a balance made even more precarious by Yugoslav insistence upon its pound of flesh. Alarmed, Khrushchev and three other Politbureau members flew to Warsaw to restrain the course being taken by Polish nationalism. The attempt to intervene, accompanied by undisguised intimidation in the form of troop movements, failed; Gomulka was elected First Secretary of the Polish Communist party on October 21.

These events, including Poland's successful defiance of the Soviet leaders, were watched in Hungary. On October 23, a demonstration began in Budapest demanding Nagy's appointment as Premier, punishment of Rakosi, and the withdrawal of Soviet troops from Hungary. When Hungarian security police fired on the crowd, demonstration turned into outright rebellion. The army, instead of siding with the government, either stood by or, in many cases, sided with the demonstrators. Nagy came to power and made concessions to popular demands, but Soviet troops entered the fighting. The next week was one of extraordinary confusion; church dignitaries and others were freed, a general strike spread through the country while young Hungarians, who fought against the Soviet forces, called for aid from the West. The Communist apparatus in Hungary completely collapsed as Nagy took non-Communists into the government, and it became quite clear that under mass pressures Hungary would actually move out of the Communist camp. Soviet troops became inactive, and on October 30 Khrushchev issued a declaration to the effect that the status of Soviet troops stationed in East Europe was always subject to reexamination; their withdrawal could be negotiated, but only with the concurrence of all signatories. Relations between members of the bloc were governed by the principle of equality and non-interference in one another's affairs. Mikoyan and Suslov, the Praesidium members most concerned with Hungarian affairs, flew to Hungary to discuss the situation. Here they learned of the demand for complete evacuation of all Soviet forces, and found that the Communist party would have a minimal future role if events continued on their course.

Poland and Yugoslavia extended messages of friendship to the new Nagy regime, and the Soviet press declared that a counterrevolutionary *putsch* had been suppressed by joint action of the new Nagy government and Soviet forces. Mikoyan apparently promised the withdrawal of Soviet forces, and in New York, a meeting of the United Nations Security Council, called to consider the situation, adjourned with no action, hoping for the best.

But the situation deteriorated. Under continued internal pressure and on receipt of reports that Soviet armored units had begun to roll across the Soviet-Hungarian border, Nagy and his cabinet withdrew from the Warsaw Pact, announced Hungarian neutrality, and sent a message to the United Nations to this effect, declaring their hope that the United Nations would undertake to guarantee and protect it. During the next two days Soviet units moved to seal off Hungary's border with Austria and to encircle Budapest. In the meantime, the Soviets, having decided on the move, had recruited two members of Nagy's government who would assume power once he was overthrown. On November 2, the Soviets formally agreed to open negotiations for withdrawal of their troops. But the agreement was a ruse. The discussions began in Budapest on November 3, and in the evening shifted to Soviet military headquarters 20 miles away. Here the Hungarian negotiators were arrested and the orders issued for the Soviet forces to crush the Hungarian regime.

They met with extraordinary but futile resistance. Nagy took refuge in the Yugoslav embassy, which he later left on issuance of a safe conduct by the Soviet leaders, who immediately arrested him and subsequently tried and executed him. Desperate Hungarians appealed to the West for help that never came, and eventually two hundred thousand fled the country. Janos Kadar took over the job of making the best of a bad situation as Premier.

The Soviet decision to intervene had tremendous significance. Soviet leaders knew that intervention would cost them heavily among supporters abroad and would greatly damage the image they had been creating during the last few years.* But overwhelming factors seemed to favor intervention: the Hungarian revolution might spread to other satellites, not only to Poland where Gomulka was displaying far more caution and might be swept aside, but perhaps also to Rumania, and even to Germany or Czechoslovakia. Moreover, Khrushchev had faced severe internal opposition to his new foreign policy; it was tremendously important for him personally to keep it from ending in disaster.

Then, too, there was the question of what the West might do, and luckily for Khrushchev the answer came quickly. Eisenhower and Dulles, despite earlier talk of liberation, were not prepared to take any action in Eastern Europe that might lead to open and armed conflict with the Soviet Union. On October 27, Dulles welcomed the developments taking place within the Soviet bloc and advised the satellites that they could draw American aid even if they did not abandon Communism completely (that is, if they assumed a Titoist or even a Gomulka-like position). He tried to forestall Soviet intervention by assuring the Soviets that the United States did not seek military allies in the area. But earlier he had also declared that the United States could not intervene directly to aid the Polish people because this could precipitate a world war. And Eisenhower declared that America would "do all within [its] peaceful power. . . . We ourselves," he said, "have abstained from the use of force—knowing it to be contrary both to the interests of these peoples and the spirit and methods of the United Nations."

If American reluctance to take direct action was one factor Khrushchev could weigh in favor of intervention, a second aspect of the Western position must have been equally important in his decision. The Western powers were deeply embroiled in the disastrous Suez War, a result of an earlier Soviet venture into the area.

At the very time that the Soviets moved into Hungary, Israeli, French, and British troops were attacking Egypt. World attention, divided, could

---

* To minimize the extent of the damage, Khrushchev claimed that Kadar, on November 1, had constituted a new and legitimate Hungarian government that had asked Soviet aid against a foreign and fascist-inspired revolution headed by Nagy.

more easily be diverted to focus on Western imperialism, where, because the United States disapproved of its allies' attack, the Soviet Union could line up *with* the United States and actually secure effective United Nations action impossible to achieve in Hungary.

The attack on Egypt arose out of a series of developments in the Middle East centering on the Aswan Dam project, control over the Suez Canal, and Arab-Israeli hostility. Nasser's prestige in the Arab world had soared since consummation of the Egyptian-Soviet bloc arms-for-cotton deal. Egypt became a center for pan-Arab propaganda and agitation that reached throughout the Middle East and across North Africa. But then the Aswan Dam project (see p. 187), the American counter to Soviet arms, ran into trouble—first with the American Congress, then with the Administration. Secretary Dulles, furious with Egyptian attempts to play off the Soviets against the West by spreading rumors that the USSR would perhaps give Egypt a better bargain, decided to administer a public and stinging rebuff to Nasser by withdrawing the offer to help build the dam. In addition to curbing Nasser, the move would serve notice to other new countries that they could not play the same game. A note delivered to Nasser on July 19, 1956, gave several reasons why the United States had to withdraw from the tentative agreement of the year before: Egypt had not reached agreement with other states on the Nile River about the question of dividing of its waters, and Egypt, in the light of its commitment of future foreign exchange resources for purchase of arms, would not be able to contribute its share to build the dam. The United States would, however, continue to help Egypt in other, more feasible development plans. Withdrawal by the United States automatically made void the British and International Bank aid offers.

The timing was not calculated to ease the blow. When the note was delivered, Nasser was conferring in Yugoslavia with the other chief exponents of neutralism, Nehru and Tito. The Egyptian President remained quiet for a week, and then, in an impassioned speech delivered at Alexandria told the roaring crowd that he was nationalizing the Suez Canal. The Canal, he said, had been built by unpaid Egyptian labor (a hundred thousand had died in the process) and Egyptian shares and Egyptian profits had been stolen by the Canal Company. He was retaking stolen property. What did he care about American aid? The company returned profits of a $100 million a year, and he could dispens with the American $70 million a year spread over a five-year period. Americans might complain about the nationalization, but,

. . . whenever I hear talk from Washington, I shall say, "Choke to death on your own fury." . . . I never saw any American aid directed towards industrialization as this would cause us to compete with them. American aid is everywhere directed towards exploitation. . . . Today, when we build the edifice of our dignity, freedom and pride, we feel that it will not be completely sound until we eradicate domination, humiliation and submission. The Suez Canal constituted an edifice of humiliation.

Nasser also linked the seizure directly with the Aswan Dam and declared that Egypt, now able to collect the annual income of the Canal—the $100 million—would "build the High Dam as we want it."

The action and seizure set off a frenzied wave of diplomatic and military activity, of argument and recrimination. In fact, the dam could not be built with the profits of the company—the figure cited by President Nasser was gross profit, from which operating expenses had to be deducted. The United States formally protested the allegations in the speech which, it said, were entirely inconsistent with the friendly relations that existed between Egypt and the United States.

After Nasser's initial outburst Egypt played the diplomatic game skillfully. Egyptian studies had already been prepared on nationalization of the Canal, the concession for which would expire in 1968. Only the occasion was needed. When the American action over the High Dam provided it, the Egyptian Government was therefore ready. It claimed the sovereign right to nationalize a property lying within its borders even if the shareholders were foreign, since it would compensate the shareholders according to fair market value of the shares and would respect the various international treaties that guaranteed freedom of passage to all countries. To those who asked how anyone could expect Egypt to fulfill these commitments, Egyptians had a simple answer: a single country, England, had undertaken them before. Was England more trustworthy than Egypt?

To this, political leaders in France and England retorted that Egypt was certainly not trustworthy. In 1951 the Security Council had declared that Arab armistice agreements with Israel—although not constituting a final peace settlement—gave Egypt no legal right of belligerency, no right of self-defense to block Israeli ships and cargoes from passage through the Canal. Yet Egypt had continued to do so.

Nasser knew that the Western case was weak. Since 1951, although the British had guarded the Canal, Western powers had done nothing beyond the Security Council resolution to ensure Israeli freedom of passage. Therefore it ill-became them to accuse Egypt on this score. Moreover, any further attempt to repeat the Security Council declaration would now be blocked by a Soviet veto.

In his *Philosophy of the Revolution,* Nasser had told the world that he proposed to use Egypt's vital geographical position to build up Egypt.

The vital element in that geographical position was Egypt's control of the Canal, through which was shipped almost two-thirds of the oil that had become essential to Europe's economy. Every maritime nation in the world depended upon smooth working of the Canal.

Because of this, as well as Nasser's aid to Algerian rebels, French and British reactions were particularly sharp; Prime Minister Eden took a position from which it would be hard to retreat:

> No arrangements for the future of this great international waterway could be acceptable to Her Majesty's Government which would leave it in the unfettered control of a single power, which could, as recent events have shown, exploit it purely for purposes of national policy.

Both he and Premier Mollet of France referred to Nasser as a new Hitler: appeasement would only whet his appetite, and the Canal seizure must not result in another Munich. Both countries immediately considered a military expedition against Egypt.

But both tried diplomacy first, spiked with the threat of economic or military pressures. Here, however, they met confusion sown by the United States; American leaders admitted that a nation might ultimately have to use military pressures to assure its vital interests, but then backed away from the implications of the point. The Administration did support one form of economic pressure: like Britain, it froze Egyptian assets. Then Dulles persuaded the British and French to call a conference of Canal users to prepare a project of international control for the Canal. Nasser, denouncing the idea, refused to attend. Support for his nationalization move was widespread—it was applauded not only in Moscow, but in most of the new countries. Among Arab peoples his prestige had soared; Dulles' move had seriously backfired.

The conference that met in London during August produced a majority and a minority plan. The minority plan—supported by India, Indonesia, Ceylon, and the Soviet Union—would have left the Canal in Egyptian hands and associated some kind of representative body of Canal users with Egyptian management. The majority plan would have taken the Canal from Egypt and given it to an internationally responsible Suez Canal Board. Presentation of the plan to Nasser by a delegation headed by Prime Minister Menzies of Australia produced no result. The United States—now standing by its position that it would not allow the use of force—came up with the idea of a "Suez Canal User's Association" that would employ its own pilots, collect tolls, and coordinate traffic. It would pay Egypt for use of the Canal.

The British and French immediately asked whether, if Egypt refused to cooperate, "SCUA" would run ships through the Canal under threat of force. What did Dulles intend? Statements emanating from Washington gave rise to further confusion; both British and French appeared to think the plan had been meant to exert serious pressure on Nasser. But Dulles explicitly disclaimed any attempt at either boycott or "shooting our way through the Canal." In the months of September and October, as plans for setting up SCUA went forward, the organization looked less and less attractive and such users as Japan and Pakistan refused to join. Some who joined made known their views that it could only be used to negotiate terms acceptable to Nasser.

In the meantime an attempt to show that the Egyptians could not run the Canal by themselves failed. Foreign pilots walked off the job, but hastily trained Egyptian, Russian, and Yugoslav pilots successfully replaced them. The Anglo-French effort to bring Nasser to task therefore shifted to the United Nations Security Council.

Here all the differences between the powers were revealed. Dulles had on one occasion in September said, "I don't think you can go on forever asking nations not to resort to force." Later came his insistence that force must not be used. Then, in a press conference, he had called American differences with the British and French a matter of "colonialism" and of a difference of attitudes on "colonial" issues. Nothing could more infuriate the British and French than this terminology, borrowed from Nasser. Would Dulles consider that opposition to nationalization of American property abroad constituted "colonialism"? Finally, at the United Nations, Dulles seemed to say that if only Egypt accepted the principle that operation of the Canal should be insulated from politics of any one nation everything else would be all right—without any mention of international control. The British and French now felt that Dulles had merely been playing for time to keep them from acting. At the United Nations they came to a broad agreement about principles that should govern operation of the Canal, but there was little satisfaction in this, and they now engaged in private conversations that excluded the United States. By the end of October, as the situation in Hungary worsened, the Anglo-French military buildup in the eastern Mediterranean proceeded rapidly.

While public attention focused on the drama being played out in the Soviet bloc and on the Suez issue, deteriorating relations between Israel and its Arab neighbors came to play a part in the spectacle. The previous two years had seen an increase in pin prick attacks on isolated Israeli border settlements and the development of the Israeli technique of large-scale retaliatory raids. The latter caused far more casualties and earned Israel frequent condemnation by the Mixed Armistice Commissions. In October 1956, Israel was censured by members of the Security Council.

Secretary General Dag Hammarskjold had visited the area in an attempt to bring some measure of calm. But Israel's fears for its security—already heightened by growing shipments of Communist arms to Egypt— were increased by October elections in Jordan that returned a large pro-Nasser faction to the Parliament, and by reports that Egypt, Jordan, and Syria were establishing a joint army command for time of war. The Jordanian Chief of Staff was quoted as having announced: "The time has come for the Arabs to choose the appropriate time to launch the assault for Israel's destruction."

The only factor in Israel's favor at the moment seemed to be France's growing enmity for Nasser, whose Canal seizure threatened her economy and who also openly gave arms and supplies to the Algerian rebels. The French (with approval of the United States, which would not accept the onus of taking the action) had sold modern weapons, including Mystère fighter planes and tanks, to Israel. French technicians were in Israel, and Franco-Israeli diplomatic contacts increased. With one eye on the immediate situation and the other on Soviet embroilment in Eastern Europe, the Israelis mobilized on October 29 and struck rapidly—not at Jordan, as expected, but across Egypt's Sinai peninsula.

Events of the next few days were completely unexpected. As Israeli forces occupied the Gaza strip and cut across and down the Sinai peninsula, Britain and France, instead of acting with the United States on the basis of the Tripartite Declaration of 1950, vetoed an American Security Council resolution calling for a cease-fire, withdrawal of Israeli forces, and denial of aid to Israel. Instead, Britain and France delivered a 24 hour ultimatum: Egyptians and Israelis should withdraw 10 miles on either side of the Canal—which is deep within Egyptian territory. Upon expiration of the 24 hour period they proceeded with their plans to intervene to secure compliance: their armed forces moved to occupy the Canal Zone.

On October 31 they began aerial bombardment of Egyptian targets and five days later paratroopers and other contingents landed and began to move toward the Canal, occasionally meeting heavy resistance. In the meantime, Egypt had fully blocked the vital waterway with scuttled ships.

The Anglo-French move—one of various alternatives earlier discussed but decided on only at the last moment—proved a monument of miscalculation. Aimed at securing the Canal and toppling Nasser, it did neither. Instead, the two countries found the United States ranged with the Soviet Union and much of the world against them. Under extreme pressure they were forced to withdraw with no objectives achieved, but leaving the Canal blocked. In addition, oil pipelines running from Iraq across Syria to Mediterranean ports (bypassing the Canal) were destroyed by Egyp-

tian sympathizers in Syria. Britain and France thus faced financial difficulties and a potentially large-scale fuel crisis with winter coming, and
other European countries that also depended on Canal shipments felt little sympathy for them.

Had it not been for a marvelous piece of improvisation at the United
Nations, the threat of Soviet intervention might have become real; Khrushchev first suggested joint military action with the United States, then
threatened to send volunteers as well as to attack Briain and France directly by missile. A hasty invention of Lester Pearson of Canada—
worked out in detail by Secretary-General Dag Hammarskjold—provided
a face-saving formula for the British-French-Israeli withdrawal: the United Nations Emergency Force.

UNEF was far from the original concept of an international armed
force to be set up under the collective security provisions of the United
Nations Charter. Its precise makeup, characteristics, tasks, and limitations arose out of an immediate situation: it was a force of some 6000
men, designed only to be interposed between the hostile parties, to fight
only in self-defense, to go only where permitted. Moreover, it was composed of men from many nations but from none of the great powers nor
the belligerents. Its function was essentially to ease withdrawal of the invaders. As time went on it came to constitute a permanent border patrol
along the Israeli Egyptian border and at Sharm-el-Sheikh, which controls
the Gulf of Aqaba and the Straits of Tiran, entrances to Israel's southern
port of Elat, hitherto blockaded by Egypt.

England and France tried to delay their withdrawal from Egypt until
they had salvaged something from the operation. But President Eisenhower insisted that there must be no rewards for aggression (the collective security argument in purity) and that issues and problems in the area
must be negotiated *after* their withdrawal. The two faced many pressures: a run on British currency, Russian threats, and suspension of action by an American government-supervised committee of oil companies
previously organized to rechannel oil shipments in case of any emergency.
In creating the committee no one had envisaged an emergency caused
by Western powers instead of by Nasser or others of his kind.
Even oil men had difficulty calculating how bad a European oil shortage
might become since the answer depended on many political as well as
technical variables. (Not the least of the political problems revolved
around state regulation of production within the United States. If state
boards, charged with equating supply to demand refused to increase supply, the effect on Europe might be serious. And the Federal government
in the United States was loath to appeal to the state boards.)

Under the circumstances, Britain and France played for time, agreeing to withdrawal if UNEF could keep peace. Hammarskjold obtained Egyptian consent to UNEF entrance, granted because Egypt could then be sure of Anglo-French withdrawal. All excuse for remaining gone, British and French troops began to pull out in early December. They had gained nothing by their actions but blockade of the Canal, further distrust by the new nations, internal political difficulties, and an oil shortage. Israel, however, held out for more and gained something: from the Egyptian army it had seized large quantities of Russian delivered supplies; by proving the Israeli army's effectiveness in action, it had enhanced its value as a deterrent; Israel also obtained guarantees before withdrawing from Gaza and Sharm el-Sheikh that both would remain under United Nations control. In fact, Egypt later did reoccupy Gaza, but the border, patrolled by UNEF, remained quiet. The important port of Elat remained open.

On one importamt matter, Israel was unable to obtain satisfaction: transit through the Suez Canal. When the Canal was reopened to navigation, Israeli shipping was still excluded.

Nasser emerged greatly strengthened. His propaganda pictured the Egytian army as having roundly defeated the invader (though the fact that UNEF presence hastened the Anglo-French-Israeli withdrawal made this possible). Most countries of the world had supported him, including those that had orginally looked with disfavor on his propaganda activities and seizure of the Canal. He also had unquestioned control of the Canal, now being cleared of wreckage under United Nations auspices.

The Soviet Union gained. It sucessfully posed as the champion of the Arabs, ready to come to their help whenever they beckoned. Moreover, the whole Suez affair helped to deflect attention from what was going on in Hungary. Some observers reproached the United Nations and its members governments with doing too much in the Suez case and too little in Hungary. But the political alignment in each case made effective action in one possible that was impossible in the other. Nations responded with alacrity to the situation in which something could be done. In the Hungarian case, however, they had to content themselves with helping the thousands of refugees.

A curious aftermath to the Suez War typified American attitudes toward the Cold War and the role of the new states in it, and the quite different views maintained by most leaders of these states. The Eisenhower administration believed that British influence in the Middle East was decisively ended. This was the culmination of a process that began in 1947 when Britain informed the United States it could no longer support Greece and Turkey. The new sucessor states were independent but weak —there was much talk of a Middle Eastern "power vacuum." Moreover, under Khrushchev's new diplomacy the Soviet Union had gained considerable influence and in the process had vaulted over the Baghdad Pact, now even weaker because its members had broken with England over the Suez affair. The administration, therefore, decided that it must step into the breach, just as it had done in Europe in 1947–48 and, more recently, in the Far East and Southeast Asia.

President Eisenhower had just been reelected by a sweeping majority. In January 1957 he went before Congress to ask for passage of a joint resolution that would do several things. It would authorize the President to use the armed forces of the United States to protect any nation or group of nations in the general region of the Middle East requesting such protection against overt armed aggression from any nation controlled by international Communism. In addition, the resolution would authorize military and economic assistance to countries of the area.

It seems doubtful that the Eisenhower Doctrine, as it came to be called, had any of the desired effect. Rather, it revealed the profound gulf between the American administration's world view and that of most Arab leaders, who saw no threat arising from Russia or Communist bloc countries. They had, in fact, just seen one Arab country come under military attack from non-Communists: Israel, England and France. There was little doubt that the Eisenhower administration's position in the Suez War had won it much goodwill throughout the Middle East; Nasser himself emphasized the differences between the United States on the one hand and Britain and France on the other. But the Eisenhower Doctrine was immediately interpreted as an attempt to replace faded French and British domination with American domination, on the basis of a fraudulent issue, and it dissipated all good feeling. A few states whose leaders had already aligned them with the West welcomed it—Iraq (the only truly Arab state) and Iran, Turkey and Pakistan. Nasser spearheaded opposition to it, however; there was no "vacuum" in the area and the Arabs would never again allow their countries to become a sphere of influence for any foreign power. "Arab nationalism was the sole basis on which Arab policy could be formulated." * The threat was not communism but "imperialism, Zionism, and colonialism." The Soviet Union immediately capitalized on these views by expressing its willingness to prevent aggression and interference in the internal affairs of Middle East states. It suggested the withdrawal of all foreign bases and troops and an embargo on shipment of arms into the region, while stepping up its arms shipments and technical aid. By these maneuvers it underlined the contention that its own moves in the Middle East had been a response to the Baghdad Pact and concomitant shipments of Western arms.

---

* Declaration issued January 19, 1957, by leaders of Egypt, Syria, Saudi Arabia, and Jordan, in Cairo.

In Jordan, a country whose imminent disappearance had been predicted periodically by experts ever since its original formation at the end of World War I, young King Hussein barely escaped deposition. His unstable country had long depended on British subsidy, and the famed Arab Legion—the best-trained force in the Middle East—had been led by British officers. In March 1956, after months of Egyptian agitation, Hussein had courted popularity among his own people by removing long-time British commander John Bagot Glubb, along with lesser British officers. The October elections that returned a pro-Nasser majority to the Parliament were a contributing cause to the Israeli attack on Egypt, although the first indications were that Israel, fearing that Hussein was about to invite Iraqi troops in, might attack Jordan.

Hussein disagreed with the course set by his new pro-Nasser Parliament, particularly when the government of Premier Nabulsi, under the impact of the Eisenhower Doctrine, announced its intention of establishing diplomatic relations with the Soviet Union, of accepting Soviet aid, and of rejecting not only the Eisenhower Doctrine but *any* American aid. When army leaders sided with the government against the King, the very existence of Jordan seemed in doubt. The King, however, was able to rally to his side the Bedouins that composed the mass of the Arab Legion, and an announcement of United States support for the "independence and integrity of Jordan" along with dispatch of the Sixth Fleet to the eastern Mediterranean, enabled him to weather the storm and consolidate his position. Egypt and Syria had earlier promised to substitute their own financial support for British subsidy, but deterioration of relations with Hussein put an end to this possibility. Through the aid of King Saud of Saudi Arabia—ruler of the most anachronistic and backward of the Arab states, assiduously courted by the United States—American financial aid was dispatched to Hussein. In future years his independence was to depend on the United States rather than on Britain.

CONCLUSION

Although many people failed to see it, 1955 and 1956 marked the emergence of a new, more complicated and complex world balance, one that no longer could be characterized as "bipolar." Churchill had declared in 1953 that hydrogen weapons ushered in a new age, one in which, ironically, the balance of terror might offer more security than had ever been known before; the 1955 Geneva summit conference seemed to prove to many people that he had been right. And if leaders of the two superpowers now felt less fear that the one might attack the other with hydrogen weapons, the leaders of smaller countries found in the situation new opportunities to exercise independence. With less necessity to rely on protection by major powers, they felt freer to act without their approval. Yet the years also showed there were limits to the possibilities open to them: within the Soviet bloc Poland and Hungary tried to go their way, while in the Western bloc Britain and France tried to use force to defend their interests in full knowledge that the United States would disapprove. Within the Soviet bloc the Russians crushed Hungary, while the United States acted to force British and French withdrawal from Egypt. Greater possibilities for action had led men to go too far, and the limits of independence were learned.

Outside the blocs, the years seemed to show that the opportunities for independent action were greater, and neutralism gained more and more adherents. Neutralism expicitly rejected the view that the world was bipolar. It was a view that security would be greater *outside* military alliances with the great powers: alliances brought the greater danger of being in the line of fire if war did come, they provoked counter action by the other side and restricted the freedom of action the neutralists desired. For neutralism also involved the view tht economic, diplmatic and cultural links with both sides reduced dependence on either and brought concrete benefits through bids for favor. At the same time, the new neutralism tended to equate both sides in the Cold War and thus gave a moral sanction to the neutralist proposition that the Cold War was not to be viewed as the American response to a Russian Communist threat, but rather as a quarrel between the two superpowers in which neither was better than the other.

The events of these two years marked the breakup of the bipolar world under the impact of the new weapons, of relaxation in the Soviet bloc, of the independence of many countries, and of emerging economic strength in Europe. But the years also marked its limits: the Soviet Union would not allow a real breakup of the Communist world, and the United States would not allow its allies to take strong action toward the newly independent countries that might jeopardize American relations with them. The new situation, then, produced its own new crisis, and it also produced a new series of dilemmas. For the United States, the first one was summed up in the ill-fated Eisenhower Doctrine. In traditional balance-of-power style, the American administration had decided that where weakness existed—as a result of the inevitable withdrawal of British power—it must step in to protect the area against encroachments by the only other power strong enough to step in. The United States would act not only for the sake of the inhabitants of the area, but also to prevent the Soviet Union from the inevitable increase in power that would follow Russian domination of the area. In that case, according to this point of view, the "balance of power" would be upset. But the fate of the Eisen-

hower Doctrine showed that balance-of-power politics could be successful only where the people in the area concerned saw the Soviet Union as
a dangerous opponent. In the era of mass politics and thermonuclear
weapons, mass views could no longer be ignored, and in the Middle East,
few people shared the American view of the danger.

The second dilemma engendered by the breakup of the bipolar world
was intimately linked to the first: the United States found itself, in the
Suez case, lined up with the Soviet Union against its own most important
allies. This was simply the extreme case of a situation building up since
World War II in which the United States consistently advocated independence for the possessions of its allies and argued that the repression of
nationalist demands would only create worse situations. Its allies had
countered that too rapid independence would lead to chaos, that nationalist demands increased precisely because nationalist leaders found support from the United States, that in many cases so-called nationalist leaders had little real popular base and would merely become local tyrants,
and finally, that the United States was indulging in competition with the
Soviet Union in supporting nationalist demands—an unfair competition,
since the Soviet Union, which stood to benefit from chaos, did not care if
chaos followed independence. Moreover, as the Suez case and the Eisenhower Doctrine indicated, once the United States had helped push its
allies out of an area, it suddenly saw the necesity for a Western presence in
the area and moved clumsily to replace them. Although there might be
poetic justice in American difficulties in assuming the role it had helped
force its allies to abicate, this hardly solved the strategic problem that all
faced jointly. All through the postwar years the United States struggled
with the problem. Its policy-makers were genuinely convinced of the ultimate need to meet new nationalistic demands, both on the grounds of justice and of political necessity, yet their stand often brought them into conflict with their allies, and, at times, with what appeared to be strategic
necessity. Worse yet, they were sometimes accused of forcing the withdrawal of Western states precisely so that American interests could move
in.

Finally, the new balance and the Hungarian case raised another issue
for the Western powers: Hungary had shown that the Soviet Union
would, despite the high political cost, be quite willing to use force to hold
its satellites within its bloc, while the United States would not be able to
use force to help those within the Soviet bloc who might want to escape.
But Krushchev seemed to believe that the new hydrogen weapons made
possible and even required peaceful coexistence—a stage in history in
which the socialist camp could now be expected to extend itself by peaceful means. Some Westerners therefore concluded that peaceful coexist-

ence and the various new Russian trade and aid programs meant that the Communist bloc would do everything short of force to draw in new members, but would never relinquish any. In short, as one writer put it, the Russian stand was "what's mine is mine and what's yours is negotiable." But the issue was not so simple; this kind of analysis rested on a bipolar view of the world that what was outside the Soviet bloc was a part of the "free world." A more realistic view had to take into account that there was a Communist bloc, a Western bloc, and a growing number of states uncommitted to either bloc. Despite adherence to dogma that declared that ultimately all states must become Communist, it was primarily toward the latter group that Khrushchev was directing his efforts, which were in the form, as he put it, of peaceful competition. There was little guarantee that the new Soviet activities would, in fact, bring new adherents to the Communist bloc. Although Westerners were quick to warn the new recipients of Communist aid, the recipients were equally quick to respond that they had no fear of Russian domination. Rather, they welcomed it as an alternative to Western domination.

In these two years that revealed the difficulties and problems of the new balance, one development gave hope to many people: the new role assumed by the United Nations and its Secretary-General, whose prestige rose immensely. It seemed quite possible that, given the nuclear stalemate and the possibility for focusing publicity on dangerous spots, intervention by the Secretary-General and the use of such devices as UNEF might keep major powers from the temptation to intervene in them. Many of the 21 new states admitted since the 1955 bargain pressed this view strongly: it gave promise of a way to stop the old balance-of-power vicious circle where one major power intervened in the affairs of weak states simply to keep other major powers from so doing, and therefore only provoked the other major powers to try to get there first. It might, in other words, provide a solution to some of the dilemmas the years had revealed. At the same time, however, the new states gave indication of their view that, under modern conditions, collective security was dead and ought to be buried. In expressing hope that Soviet forces would withdraw from Hungary, they expressed the view that under *no* circumstances should force be used. The United Nations, they argued, should concentrate on peaceful settlement of disputes; one of its prime functions should be to hasten and help the process of liquidating nineteenth-century empires and "neo-colonialism," and particular care should be taken not to widen and spread conflicts but rather to localize them. Their admission to the United Nations tended, therefore, to give it a new orientation; but it was one that involved an active role in international politics.

PART IV
EUORPE, THE UNITED STATES, JAPAN, AND THE SOCIALIST BLOC: THE ESTABLISHED POWERS IN THE HYDROGEN AGE

SIX
THE BREAKUP OF
THE ATLANTIC
ALLIANCE

From 1945 to 1956 no Western state could contest American supremacy. In these years a smaller but viable Europe re-emerged from the ashes of World War II; yet American opposition to the 1956 Suez adventure appeared to define the limits of European independence. Europeans no longer depended upon American economic aid, but a major part of their trade was with the United States. They had rebuilt and reequipped their own armies, but the presence of 350,000 American troops and American control of atomic weapons demonstrated that NATO, under United States leadership, was still the guardian of European security. Despite anger over Suez, mistrust of Dulles, misgivings about American foreign policy generally, and years of often effective Communist propaganda, America retained an unassailable position and role; young people in Europe still named it as the country in which they would most like to live. American leaders and the American people thought of themselves as the leaders in the fight against both colonialism and totalitarian tyranny.

The next 15 years brought a startling change. Stimulated rather than dejected by the defeat of the proposed European Defense and Political Communities in 1954 and by the Suez disaster of 1956, European leaders gave the idea of unity a new lease on life, and produced the European Economic Community (EEC) or Common Market. Booming success of this international venture soon made the English reappraise their own international position and apply repeatedly for a membership that would, ultimately, mean the end of both British leadership of the Commonwealth and of the fading special relationship with the United States. Success of the Common Market also brought an abortive attempt by the United States to create a new pattern of "Atlantic Partnership" in which the United States and Europe would now cooperate as equals.

Both countries had rough going. England—erstwhile leader of the British Empire on which the sun never set—was reduced to the status of frequently rejected suitor, and was finally admitted to the Common Market only in 1973, on stiff terms that generated heavy domestic opposition. As

213

for the United States, its prestige was battered on all fronts—at home, where the issues of race, poverty in the midst of unprecedented riches, and the unforseen ecological and social consequences of affluence had all come to plague "the American way of life"; abroad, where prolonged use of its tremendous power to batter the tiny nation of Vietnam overshadowed all its official protestations that it was trying to stop "Communist aggression." Its financial and trade relations—distinguished in the 1960s by the degree to which American businessmen were investigating in Europe—had come to be looked upon widely as hegemony, and a persistent imbalance in its international payments had seriously weakened the dollar. Its preeminent role as military leader of the "free world" too often appeared to people to result in unwarranted and dangerous military interventionism, primarily on the side of undemocratic regimes. Despite limited moves in the direction of stabilizing the arms race, one administration after the other continued to spend enormous sums for armanents—while gradually cutting back on foreign economic aid. Only in 1972, when it effected a rapproachement with China and the Soviet Union while winding down the Vietnam War, did the United States appear to have reconciled itself to the changing structure of the international political system.

Numerous international crises engaged the West between 1956 and 1973. Events in Berlin, Cuba, Indochina, and the Middle East may have overshadowed all the rest, but wars in the Congo and South Asia, among others, had important effects.

In the early 1960s Berlin and Cuba brought the last great confrontations between the United States and the Soviet Union, terrifying because both now possessed thermonuclear weapons and means of delivering them. One result was greater caution and moves to prevent repetition of any such crises. Perhaps even more important was what the Cuban missile crisis revealed about Khrushchev's foreign policy, and the subsequent changes by his successors: by placing missiles ninety miles off American shores and deep within what had been deemed to be the American sphere in the bipolar Cold War, Krushchev displayed that he had been gambling from a position of weakness; his policy had been dangerous "adventurism," as the Chinese called it. The United States might be a "paper tiger," but it possessed immense nuclear superiority. In succeeding years the Soviet Union's leaders therefore mightily increased their weapons arsenal, and by early 1970s had reached a parity with the United States.

But Cuba also dramatized another change: the growth of nationalist, populist desires in "third world" countries to change their relationship with the wealthy United States in ways that it would resist. Bipolarism, or "free world unity"— of the American-defined, Cold War security zone —had really come to an end.

War in Indochina in the 1960s underscored the point. The 1954 settlement came unstuck and the United States was drawn into a bitter battle that appeared to contribute little to American security or world freedom, but mightily to Vietnamese suffering and to the shattering of the American image. The Middle East war of 1967 did not involve the United States directly, but in the minds of Arabs the United States was indelibly associated with the victorious Israelis, and Khrushchev's successors profited. They profited, too, when in the second of two India-Pakistani wars of the 1960s, the United States and Communist China found themselves supporting the losing Pakistanis. British withdrawal from the subcontinent and the Middle East had indeed, in the long run, led to Russian influence where it had never been before. But Russian influence was no longer necessarily in competition with the United States: in India, Russia seemed far more concerned with an even more important conflict of the sixties—between itself and Communist China. The supposed Cold War balance between the United States and the Communist world, in which ANZUS, SEATO, the Japanese security treaty, and the alliance with Nationalist China offset Communist expansionism into the Asian rimlands had been replaced by a far more complicated equation: Russia, China, and Japan now all entered into a situation in which, pretty clearly, there was no longer any element of old-fashioned expansionism through conquest of territory. The so-called "Nixon Doctrine" of a lower posture in Asia, announced in 1969, merely reflected this.

In the first decade after World War II the sheer necessity for reconstruction and a fear of brutal Russian Communist power had produced a new sense of purpose in the West. In the next 15 years, paradoxically, the very attainment of the aims embodied in this sense of purpose brought its dissolution, and the Western world was set adrift. Its wealth increased spectacularly, yet seemed to create increasing unease and alienation—particularly as the wealth seemed to set it further and further apart from the rest of the poverty-stricken and overpopulous world, and as the realization developed that Western countries consumed an inordinate share of the world's nonrenewable resources. Atlantic unity foundered on European distrust of America and on growing American suspicion that European unity was aimed primarily at America. By 1970 it was common to voice a fear that the United States and Russia, having achieved a standoff, would engage in a dialogue that would lead to a joint world hegemony. Such a dialogue did indeed grow as the bipolar Cold War waned; but it was a multiple one with many participants. It faltered with the Berlin and Cuba crises of the early sixties; it faltered again when Russia invaded Czechoslovakia in 1968. But it produced arms control and stabilization agreements, dialogue and resumption of relations between the Germanies on one end of the continent, the Koreas on the other, and cooperation in numerous technical spheres. Clearly, the Atlantic nations that had provided the cockpit of war for three centuries now constituted what some analysts called a "security community"—an area in which contending organized groups no longer contemplated using armed force to resolve their differences. Even more important, it appeared that the chances of war between the superpowers was also drastically diminished, whether by calculation, escalation, or accident. Armed conflict occurred far too frequently in and among third world states (and incipient armed conflict still threatened between the two Communist giants). But in the northern hemisphere the conflicts appeared to have become technical, complicated, economic ones. The world had moved on to a new era.

In reviewing development of the growing complexities of a no-longer bipolar world, Chapters 7 and 8 will first recount the story of events in Europe and then account for the changing role of the United States in world politics. The two subsequent chapters will review Communist bloc politics and then the international politics of the emerging third world. In a world continually growing smaller, any such division is arbitrary—but so is any other.

THE COURSE OF WESTERN UNITY

If Bandung, 1955, symbolizes the emergence of new, independent, non-European states on the world scene, and Hungary, 1956, the failure of the Russians to weld together a popularly supported Communist empire, the signature in Rome on March 25, 1957 of the treaties creating the European Economic Community and Euratom may be used to mark another major development of the postwar period: the emergence of a prosperous and self-confident Europe after 40 years of wars, depression, and social and political chaos. The new European prosperity was more widely shared than in the past; Western European countries had by and large divested themselves of empire, and the eastern boundaries of the new Europe were far to the west of where they once had been. German division continued to plague the continent, and the nuclear threat shadowed everything. But for the first time in over half a century—and in spite of much questioning of the established order—Europeans again believed in a future.

The European Economic Community included only six nations: France, Germany, Italy, Belgium, Luxemburg, and the Netherlands. Prosperity, with all its attendant difficulties began in the early 1950s, long before the formation of the EEC. Nevertheless, the establishment of the

EEC so soon after the collapse of the European Defense Community and the proposed Political Community in 1954 was an extraordinary political step, testifying to the ingenuity and energy of all those men who rallied from the earlier defeat to bring to fruition the new proposals.

What they planned, in short, was a broad customs union—an association of states in which trade barriers among them would be eliminated and a common tariff to the outside world established around them. Britain declined to participate in the negotiations, pleading its Commonwealth and Atlantic commitments. The French, in early 1957, still attempting to integrate Algeria into France and trying to forge a new set of relationships with their other African territories, almost halted the negotiations with their demand that some kind of associated status be arranged for overseas territories. In the end, the other countries paid the French price to get the Common Market: overseas territories would have access to the Common Market without having to pay the common tariff. They could, however, maintain their own external tariffs against the rest of the world, and their developing industries could retain some protection against European products that would not be allowed to regular Common Market members. The price also included establishment of a Common Market development fund to be channeled to the associated territories (including the Belgian Congo and Ruanda-Urundi). But other states also received concessions: the Common Market included a bank to channel funds to low-income areas within the Market—which meant, in practice, southern Italy.

The planners of the Common Market hoped for one thing: that the stages of growth through which it was to pass would lead to eventual political unity. They reasoned that establishment of a common customs boundary around a free-trade area would mean that the countries involved would eventually have to bring into harmony their social security laws, tax systems and fiscal policies, and policies on investment. The planners hoped that as each stage was reached, with the concomitant necessity for further harmonization of domestic policies, the countries' governments would find that the easiest way to bring policies into line was through handing them over to the central organs of the Common Market.

But people who were not particularly interested in such political integration supported the Comon Market on the basis of economics alone. They could believe its aim—the creation of a huge internal market— could be achieved through cooperation rather then unity. Full achievement of the Market would take 12 to 15 years, so that events might well modify some of the later stages and escape clauses could be invoked. In other words, people with a variety of views were able to support the proposed Common Market, and ratification proceeded with relatively few difficulties. The treaty and the companion one establishing a European Atomic Energy Community took effect on January 1, 1958. The Market members soon began cutting their internal tariffs and modifying other internal restrictions—quotas, subsidies, discriminatory transport charges, and so on.

Ten years later, and despite various crises, internal tariffs disappeared completely and the common external ones came into effect. In the meantime the various Councils of Ministers and Commissions of the Common Market and Euratom and of the earlier Coal and Steel Community merged, while all came to share a Parliament, Court of Justice, and legal, statistical, and information services.

In 1965, the French, resisting the gradual transition to effective supranational power for the Community, began a six-month boycott of the Market, ostensibly over the complex agricultural policy, where different forms of national subsidies, different levels of efficiency and different patterns of imports required a complicated solution. Although France was, in fact, interested in farm prices lower than those wanted by German farmers so that the more efficient French farmers would expand their production to fill German needs, they also wanted barriers to lower-cost foreign imports. Nevertheless, the real aim was to reduce the independence of the Common Market Commission, which had taken to making too many proposals under the leadership of President Walter Hallstein, and to resist the forthcoming transition to the third stage of Conmon Market development, in which the Council of Ministers could make decisions on certain policies by a qualified majority vote. It was President de Gaulle of France, in power since 1958 (see below, p. 220) who was the most articulate opponent of supranationality, claiming that only the nation-state had organic roots in the people, while international organizations were mere mechanisms that would never command respect and loyalty, and thus should only operate on the basis of cooperation. What the EEC planners had forseen, however, came to pass: there were now too many interest groups committed to, and planning for, the Common Market. Too many French farmers, for example, needed the German market. As a result, and despite a tense six months, the EEC survived.

In January 1966, the six agreed to a compromise: the system of qualified majority voting would come into effect, but in cases of vital national interest states could reserve their positions. It appeared that the drive toward unification had, at the very least, slowed down. The popular enthusiasm for European unity of the early 1950s had faded before the mass of technical economic details; many early supporters had worked for the idea of a new "Europe" as against the narrow and exaggerated nationalisms of the immediate past. Now they found that "Europe" seemed to mean faceless bureaucrats working in conjunction with representatives of powerful organized interest groups. Moreover, by providing a framework for businesses organized on a Europe-wide rather than a nationwide basis, "Europe" seemed to be giving birth to a new moloch, the multinational business, capable of escaping from the public controls organized on a nationwide basis—but much too strong for the weak institutions existing on the level of European unity. De Gaulle thus touched on a deep chord of feeling.

Nevertheless, in the next four years the six agreed on common internal forms of taxation; following a first monetary crisis in 1968, they agreed to coordinate monetary policies more closely, and provide a common reserve fund to prevent a run on one anothers' currencies. In late 1969, they decided to provide the Communities with direct tax monies, by stages, and by 1975 to allow the parliament to have the power to alter budget proposals that came to it from the Council of Ministers. Three years later a sumit meeting of EEC ministers agreed to complete economic and monetary unity to be achieved by 1980 and to harmonization of commercial and financial law, social welfare programs, foreign aid, and even a measure of political unity. Once again it was France, however, that resisted a Dutch move in favor of having the European parliament directly, popularly elected.

"Europe"—enlarged by British, Irish, and Danish membership in 1973—had come far. France, as always, remained the key element in the fluctuations. In the early years, around 1950, leaders of the Fourth Republic had made far-reaching proposals for unification because their weakness in the face of a resurgent Germany led them to look to means of limiting the independence of their potentially far stronger neighbor. Yet it was the French who killed the European Defense Community in 1954. They had then accepted the European Economic Community with the supranationalism it eventually entailed—yet in the mid-sixties proceeded to slow its progress and, then, at the end of the decade, to accept the new spurt of unification measures. In good part, these fluctuations were a consequence of the views and the rise and decline of one towering figure, General Charles de Gaulle.

De Gaulle came to power in 1958 when military insurrection threatened the weak and vacillating government of the Fourth Republic. France had never been more prosperous. But the officers of an army that had fought long and bitterly in Indochina only to withdraw in 1955 felt they had been sabotaged by governmental weakness at home. The army had gone into Suez in 1956, and a weak government had capitulated to foreign pressure and withdrawn from it. In 1958 four to five hundred thousand French troops were in Algeria, attempting to quell a nationalist insurrection. A million French Algerians insisted that Algeria remain French, and discovery of oil deposits that might lessen French dependence upon the unstable Middle East led to increased pressures to hold onto Algeria. Yet the rebellion persisted; guerrillas faded indistinguishably into villages and used sanctuaries in Tunisia and Morocco, and popular pressures for withdrawal began to build, particularly among students and intellectuals. Increasing reports of army use of torture to extract information, of wholesale destruction of villages, mounting costs of the war, all stimulated the demand. Once more, behind a determined Army, the government wavered. De Gaulle and his supporters had long held that the only solution to France's perennial governmental instability lay in elimination of Parliamentary supremacy and the party system; in May 1958 they and Algerian settlers found the army ready to act. Officers seized power in the North African territory, and other officers in France refused the government's demand to order them to relinquish it. Under threat of paratroop attack upon the mainland, the Parliament and President bowed, and de Gaulle, the army's choice, was invested as Prime Minister.

In short order, and with Parliamentary sanction, a Gaullist Constitution was produced, submitted to public referendum where it won acceptance by a 4 to 1 vote, and de Gaulle became President of the new Fifth Republic. The Constitution drastically curtailed the powers of Parliament while increasing those of the President. Subsequent changes approved by referenda further strengthened the office.

De Gaulle's successes and failures colored much of the development of the Common Market. In his first years in office he succeeded in disengaging France from Algeria. The effort involved the ultimate transfer of the vast majority of the million French Algerians to mainland France, and suppression of an army coup in which the officers tried to repeat their success in putting de Gaulle into power—this time to overthrow him. Liberated from the agony of Algeria, French energies could be turned to other tasks, and de Gaulle took more and more command in the international field. The French economy entered a boom period, and a favorable balance of payments led to substantial gold and dollar reserves. The end of the Algerian affair enabled France to reknit its ties with third world countries.

The General appeared, therefore, to be in an almost unassailable positio o of strength when he diluted the supranational features of the Common Market in 1965. A majority of Frenchmen undoubtedly agreed with his aim of transforming the Common Market into a looser arrangement of sovereign states (although there was probably less support for his use of France's new-found prestige in other international areas—see below).

The stability was misleading. A young French magazine publisher, Jean-Jacques Servan-Schreiber, argued in an important book, *The American Challenge*,* that European industry in general and French in particular had little of the dynamism of American industry, allocated far less of its funds to research and, in fact, faced its fastest-growing competition not abroad, but in American-owned industry in Europe. Moreover, the almost unbelievable growth of Japanese industry in the 1960s was producing a new competitor, just when French industry found itself being opened up to more and more competition from its EEC partners, as the Common Market internal tariffs crumbled. Unnoticed by all but financiers, speculators, and some few government officials, another development posed a further threat: the growing American balance-of-payments deficit. The United States could correct the excess outflow of American dollars in several ways; almost any one of them would involve reduced sales or exports to the United States. This alone, was bound to hurt European economies. But even more, it would lead the Japanese, limited in terms of what they could sell to America, to further penetration of the European market.

So it was, in May 1968, when French students joined in a worldwide movement of student protest, and triggered a general strike by laborers whose expectations and dissatisfactions increased as the affluence of the surrounding society increased, the whole Gaullist edifice toppled. In short order the inflationary effects of the 1968 wage settlements made themselves felt; a run began on French currency culminating in a serious payments crisis in November 1968. His prestige gravely diminished, vulnerable on other fronts as well, de Gaulle weathered the 1968 crisis but resigned on April 28, 1969 over subsequent defeat in a referendum on a relatively minor matter of governmental reform. It became apparent to de Gaulle's successors, despite proclamations of fidelity to his principles, that the Common Market could serve their interests in the matter of American, Japanese, and other European competition better than could attempts at independent action. The result was that they agreed to the already described new lease on life for the EEC.

If the fortunes of de Gaulle and France were a prime factor in developments within the Common Market, they were also of the highest importance in affecting Common Market relations with the rest of the world.

From the beginning, other countries were fearful that the Common Market would be protectionist, restricting external trade as much or more than it freed its internal trade. The United States had supported the drive for European unity from the days of the Marshall Plan, partly to hasten

* New York: Atheneum, 1968.

European recovery, partly to erect an efficient bulwark to the spread of Communism. Now, however, Americans joined the British and other Europeans in expressing concern. African countries that were not a part of the French Community raised the issue of protectionism. So did spokesmen for Latin American states, afraid the special privileges of associated states would enable them to supplant Latin America in supplying tropical products to Europe. Even Socialist bloc countries protested. In sum, formation of the EEC led to years of tangled and complex diplomacy.

The British began by attempting to form a greater European Free Trade Area. Such an area would eliminate trade barriers between its members, but each member would keep its own external tariff toward the rest of the world. There would be less cooperation in other economic fields, and a country like Britain would be able to maintain special Commonwealth ties. The EEC, the British argued, could participate as one of the members of the Area.

All through 1958 an intergovernmental committee wrestled with the difficult problems involved. EEC members, especially the French, felt that the proposal would give a country like England the benefits of Common Market membership while retaining for it those of Commonwealth preferential tariffs. Thus England would import cheap Commonwealth food rather than buy food from the Common Market, but would now be able to sell its manufactured goods in the Common Market area. Among EEC proponents there was a fear that such an association would dilute the supranational aspects of the EEC.

De Gaulle's accession to power resolved the issue. On November 14, 1958, he killed the proposal for making the EEC a part of a larger free trade area.

In July 1959 representatives of Austria, Denmark, Norway, Portugal, Sweden, Switzerland, and Britain nevertheless agreed to form a European Free Trade Association along the lines of the earlier proposal, but without the EEC as a member. While some thought of it as a useful organization in itself, others saw it as a means of generating greater bargaining strength for purposes of resuming negotiations with the Common Market.

By 1960 American diplomats had become thoroughly alarmed at these developments. Not only could Common Market discrimination harm American agricultural exports and hurt the United States balance-of-payments, an irrevocable split between EEC Six and EFTA Seven also seemed to have disastrous political potentialities, and the effect of EEC association of the former French territories on Latin American and other underdeveloped countries' exports might be extremely serious. In January 1960, therefore, the United States proposed a series of committees to examine relations between the EEC and EFTA, the question of aid to underveloped countries, and suggested reorganizing the old Organization for European Economic Cooperation, originally set up to help carry out the Marshall Plan.

Results were mixed: the OEEC was indeed transformed into a new agency in which the United States and Canada were full members—the Organization for Economic Cooperation and Development (OECD). The new organization would try to see that the various economic communities would operate within an overall framework of Atlantic cooperation, and at the same time coordinate aid and trade policies toward underdeveloped countries. This would serve two purposes. It would help convince a more prosperous Europe to share further the burden of foreign aid with the United States (American foreign aid helped to create the balance of payments problem). At the same time it would bring pressure on the EEC not to discriminate against underdeveloped countries outside the associated states.

But the negotiations between the EEC and EFTA were futile, and as a result Britain made a momentous decision. Despite formation of EFTA, and after years of deliberately staying out of Europe, it applied for membership in the Common Market.

Several factors prompted the decision. Britain's overall trade with the Commonwealth countries had declined as a percentage of her total trade, and Europe had become a more important trading partner (trade with the United States had increased even more). Since de Gaulle had indicated that the new Europe would be a looser knit political union than previously proposed, it became easier for Britain to conceive of joining it. More than this, however, other economic facts stood out: growth rate within Common Market was at a far higher level than in the comparatively stagnant British economy (Italy, for example—so long a laggard country—had the highest rate of industrial expansion in the world next to Japan in 1960); Common Market area exports had increased 115 per cent since 1951 while British exports—a matter of life and death to Britain—had increased by only 30 per cent; trade among the Common Market countries was increasing enormously. In the years 1959–60 French imports from the other five members had increased by 50 percent, exports to them by 79 per cent. The Macmillan Government in Britian hoped membership in the Market might provide the stimulus of competition to British industry that it appeared to need so badly.

The British application created severe problems for other EFTA countries and members of the Commonwealth. In the former group, Denmark and Norway reacted by also applying for EEC membership. The other EFTA members sought some form of association that would minimize economic discrimination against them.

Although total British exports to *all* Commonwealth countries amounted to only 42 per cent of all British exports, many of these countries' exchanges with Britain represented the major part of their trade; 90 per cent of New Zealand's meat and dairy products went to the United Kingdom. If Britain succeeded in joining the Common Market, the Market's external tariff wall would tend to exclude such products while encouraging Britain to buy from other EEC members. Prime Minister Macmillan assured them that the British Government would bargain for an overall low external EEC tariff, so that Commonwealth countries, too, would have access to the growing European market. In this, he argued, lay the best course. They remained skeptical.

There was plenty of opposition within Britain too. Old Tories deplored the idea that Britain should join with continental foreigners. Britain was the oldest nation-state; her Parliament, upon which so many others had been modeled, was the oldest functioning one, and Britain had been politically stable for centuries, fortunately isolated from continental conflicts by the Channel and British control of the seas. Labour party leaders argued that Britain's economy suffered from policies followed by the Conservative government, and that joining the Common Market as a way of dealing with Britain's ills was really a Tory way to evade the problem of internal reform. Nevertheless, Macmillan staked his prestige on the application.

Then, at a press conference on January 14, 1963, with superbly contemptuous disregard for the views of other EEC members, de Gaulle vetoed British entry into the Common Market.

The veto stunned a great many people who should, perhaps, have known better. De Gaulle had long distrusted the English and Americans. At the time of the Liberation in 1944 they had always been willing to disregard French interests as he defined them, both within France, and further afield, in Indochina and the Middle East. In 1954 the United States had been unwilling to come to the rescue of the French in Indochina unless the action took on an international character, and Britain had been unwilling to lend it such a character. At the time of the Suez War in 1956, the United States had acted forcefully against its French and British allies. In the defense of Western Europe, the United States had always refused to share control over atomic weapons, and de Gaulle, like many others, was far from sure that the United States would use the threat of them simply to protect Europe. In September 1958 de Gaulle had suggested to Eisenhower that France, Britain, and the United States form a tripartite leadership group within NATO, to coordinate foreign policies throughout the entire world. He had been rebuffed. Finally, only a month earlier at Nassau (see below p. 238) the United States had told

Macmillan that for budgetary reasons it would not supply the British government with the Skybolt missiles upon which its defense plans depended, and had worked out another arrangement. To de Gaulle, it was simple evidence that the British were willing to accept a subordination to the United States that the United States imposed on them.

The British and Americans were insular countries, not continental. In his view, this gave them a different culture and a different outlook. Britain in the Common Market would be the American stalking horse and give the EEC a different character. He envisaged, ultimately, a Europe independent of the United States, made up of cooperating sovereign states stretching from the North Sea to the Urals. The ultimate aim of his diplomacy was, as he put it, to eliminate the "hegemony" of the two superpowers, end an outmoded bipolarism, and restore the independence of Europe. Britain and the United States would hinder such a grand design; the processes of de-Stalinization in Russia, however, were beginning to render it possible.

And in pursuit of this aim, within a few days after his veto of British admission to the EEC, de Gaulle persuaded a somewhat reluctant German government to sign a treaty of friendship and cooperation (although Germany would have preferred British membership in the Common Market). His purpose was to set the pattern of how European matters should be settled: not by technocrats, bureaucrats, and interest group representatives within the confines of EEC offices, but by the political heads of sovereign states who would consult with each other at the political level.

Over the next several years EFTA became a going concern; Finland, careful never to alienate the Soviet Union by too close a relationship with Western countries, nevertheless became an associate member of EFTA. Yugoslavia initiated a loose cooperation in 1967 and Iceland was admitted as a member in December 1969. EFTA countries prospered; their trade with one another almost trebled while their trade with the rest of the world doubled. *Total* world trade doubled during the same period, while EEC trade to the rest of the world also doubled. This put to rest to a certain extent fears about its protectionism. But EEC countries' trade with one another *quadrupled* over the same years. Moreover, while EFTA countries imported 33 per cent more from the EEC than from each other, they exported *less* to the EEC than to each other.

Consequently, Harold Wilson's Labour Party Government, returned to power in 1964, decided to reapply. Britain, many of its members felt, had misjudged its possible postwar role for almost a quarter of a century, trying to remain a worldwide power with far-flung responsibilities, exaggerating the importance of the Commonwealth and of Britain's leadership within it, and placing too much emphasis on Britain's supposed special ties with the United States. In the late forties it discouraged any idea of a Europe-wide free trade area, and restricted any possible powers for the Council of Europe. It refused to join European Coal and Steel Community, the proposed European Defense Community, and withdrew from negotiations for the Common Market. When these proved successful, it tried to dilute the Common Market within a broader, looser Free Trade Area. When, in 1961, Macmillan finally reversed British policy, he did so halfheartedly: the negotiations must respect Britain's particular Commonwealth relations, British agriculture, and British ties with other EFTA countries. Wilson's application in May 1967 was supposedly more wholehearted (although there were indications that public opinion within Britain had turned against joining the EEC). It made no difference. Six months after Wilson reopened the matter, de Gaulle again blocked British entry.

The events of May 1968, the subsequent franc crisis, and de Gaulle's withdrawal in April 1969, presented Britain with a new opportunity. Prime Minister Heath's recently elected Conservative Government seized it, and this time de Gaulle's successor, President Pompidou, accepted genuine negotiations. They lasted one year and were successfully concluded in the summer of 1971. Wilson's Labour Party, sensing the shift in public opinion, now opposed the tough terms of the agreement. Enough Labour Party members dissented, however, to endorse entry by a 112-vote majority. On January 1, 1973, after complicated further negotiations and legislation, including an agreement to phase out the pound sterling as an international reserve currency, Britain became a member of the Common Market.

So did Ireland and Denmark, both of which had approved entry by a public referendum. Norway, whose negotiators had a difficult time over fishing rights in Norwegian waters, finally signed an agreement with the EEC, but did not join. In September 1972 the Norwegian people rejected the entry terms.

Norway and the other remaining EFTA members did get what EFTA had been unable to obtain back in the old de Gaulle days: a free trade agreement with the EEC in manufactured goods, signed on December 21. Commonwealth countries, in turn, were given the option of signing association agreements or free trade agreements with the EEC, while by early 1973 more than 100 less-developed countries were given preferential tariff access to the Comon Market.

It took, then, 15 years for Britain and the other to join the Common Market, and for the Common Market to arrange and stabilize its relations with the remaining EFTA countries. "Europe" appeared to have become a stronger political entity. This prospect prompted the United

States to spend these years trying to find a new relationship with the emerging Europe that it had helped create. It failed to arrange a satisfactory one. In July 1961 John Kenneth Galbraith, US Ambassador to India, wrote to President Kennedy that United States policy had been one of " . . .building up Europe, which is already economically powerful, against the United States." In fairly short order the Kennedy Administration devised the strategy of initiating a whole new round of tariff talks on the basis of a much wider Congressional grant of tariff-cutting authority than had existed before. By persuading the Common Market of the advantages EEC countries would have of greater market penetration in the United States, the EEC could be persuaded to cut its overall exterior tariffs to a very low level. For three years, from 1964 to 1967, representatives of over 40 countries met in Geneva, pursuing extraordinarily complicated negotiations. The result was, as the *Economist* put it, to "demolish the follies of the thirties" when, in response to the world depression, countries had raised their tariff walls to unprecedented heights.

The Kennedy Round, as the negotiation came to be called, was politically notable for three things: the EEC negotiated as a single participant (but with cumbersome and time-consuming reference back to representatives of all six countries, and with a temporary breakdown in 1965, when France boycotted the EEC) ; the less-developed countries who participated with much promised to them in terms of access for their products to more developed countries emerged greatly disappointed, their view reinforced that new organizations such as the new United Nations Conference on Trade and Development, under less Western domination, were necessary (see p. 423) . Finally, in the course of the bargaining, the Kennedy Round became simply a highly technical matter of tariff negotiations, losing all the overtones with which the Kennedy Administration had imbued it at the outset. Along with negotiations in other fields it was to create "Atlantic Partnership." By 1967 no one talked about this any more.

American involvement in far-off Vietnam had helped kill it. So did the emergence of three more complex, interrelated areas of economic conflict that developed during the sixties: the problem of the United States balance of payments, of American investment in Europe, and of international liquidity.

When the United States originally initiated its European rescue operation in the mid-forties, money was no object. Other countries had little to sell to the United States, but wanted to buy all they could: the "dollar gap" measured the difference between the two, and for a long time American foreign aid filled it. In the fifties, however, as European economies continued to expand, United States foreign expenditures became heavier. American troops remained abroad in large numbers, the flood of American tourists swelled, and American businessmen began to invest heavily in the booming European market. European and Japanese sales to the United States rose. In 1959, for the first time, the United States balance of payments showed a deficit.

Americans still sold more abroad than they bought from the rest of the world and would continue to until the late 1960s. But the troops, tourists, investments, and aid programs played their part in producing the new dollar surplus, and by 1969 the trade imbalance began to contribute to it, too.

The dollar surplus did one thing: it provided other countries with the major part of the reserves they used in their international trade—that is, instead of holding onto gold and small amounts of varied foreign currencies, they held onto dollars, which in turn were presumably based on the extensive American gold holdings proverbially buried in Fort Knox. Two aspects of the situation emerged in the decade of the sixties: one was simply that American investment abroad could continue *because* foreign countries were willing to hold onto American currency as a reserve. The other was that countries like France began to resent the extent of what they considered to be domination of their economies by American capital —and that they might fight back by bringing the value of the dollar into question, through the simple expedient of immediately asking the United States to give them gold for the dollars they held. If the American gold reserve were drawn down appreciably, banks in other countries would feel the United States might eventually have to suspend payment, and might therefore rush to cash in their dollars before this happened. Such a rush on the dollar would develop its own momentum.

The matter of American investment in Europe came to public attention in the mid-1960s at the same time as that of the balance of payments, when Jean-Jacques Servan-Schreiber's *The American Challenge* received wide circulation. Projecting current trends for 15 years, he argued that the third industrial power in the world after the United States and Russia would be American industry in Europe. In 1961 European investment in America still exceeded that of America in Europe by four billion dollars. In 1966 American investments had drawn even. What was more important was that the rise, in which Europe received a larger and larger share of American foreign investments, was marked by several distinctive features: European capital in America was largely in the form of indirect, portfolio investment, while American companies tended to simply take over European companies, turning them into directly controlled subsidiaries. Thus when General Electric bought controlling interest in the French computer company, Bull, there was no independent French computer company left. What this could mean from the point of view of someone concerned with French sovereignty was soon illustrated: the French Government asked the United States to license export of an American-built computer to use in its atomic industry and was refused. The case, which stirred a storm in France, illustrated another aspect of the problem: American investments tended to be concentrated in certain modern industries, such as electronics; American-controlled companies manufactured 50 per cent of European-made semiconductors, 80 per cent of computers, and 95 per cent of integrated circuits. In part, the American takeovers were a result of American tax laws; in part they were an American adaptation to opportunities offered by the enlarged European market and a way of overcoming its tariff barriers. Servan-Scheiber argued that they demonstrated the greater dynamism of American industry, its interest in research and development, and the lack of a European capital market. European companies seeking to expand were forced to look to the United States for funds. His own prescription was for European companies to emulate American ones. But what struck the broader public was the fact of the takeovers, the seeming extent of American penetration, and the argument that it was made possible by continued foreign acceptance of the imbalance in American payments.

President de Gaulle again precipitated the latent crisis. In February 1965, at one of his perennial press conferences in which he referred grandly to "Europe, the mother of modern civilization" and "America, her daughter," he attacked the "privileged" positions of the dollar and pound, suggesting that it was time for the international system to return to the gold standard, abandoned shortly after World War I. With this, the drain began on American gold. The United States proposed reforms of the international monetary system that would give to the International Monetary Fund greater right to create new reserves, thus removing some of the sources of nervousness and instability. French diplomats, however, argued that it was up to the United States to put its own house in order, eliminate internal inflationary pressures, limit the flow of investment abroad, and disengage itself from Vietnam. The gold standard, they said, would enforce discipline upon the monetary systems of participating states.

In the 1960s American gold reserves diminished steadily declining to a mere fraction of American foreign indebtedness. There was a temporary respite in 1968–69, when the French internal crisis halted the French attack on the dollar and the Germans revalued the mark, while the so-called Group of Ten—the 10 leading trading states of the world—negotiated an international monetary reform that created Special Drawing Rights, that is, "paper gold," reserves administered by the International

Monetary Fund that would actually create new international reserves to supplement the gold, dollars, and pounds being held by states.

The relief provided by these three developments was only temporary, as the American imbalance in payments continued and even worsened. Central banks, companies with dollar holdings, speculators, all afraid that the dollar might be devalued and the holdings therefore become less valuable, proceeded to divest themselves of their dollars and buy German marks, Swiss francs, Japanese yen—and gold. American gold holdings dropped further, and something had to give. In August 1971, it did, and another era came to a close. President Nixon announced that the United States would no longer pay out gold at the previous fixed price to central banks holding American dollars. In addition, he announced a willingness to negotiate new international monetary and trade arrangements, froze domestic wages and prices, and imposed a temporary import surcharge (which would give him negotiating leverage in trying to persuade other countries to help in the new negotiations) .

By refusing to exchange gold for dollars at the existing fixed rate, the United States government effectively changed the entire basis of the postwar international monetary arrangements—arrangements that had supported an unprecedented increase in international trade and economic growth and development. The move, probably a necessity, nevertheless brought surprise, confusion, and some bitterness. For the Japanese, this was the second "Nixon shock," the other being his equally surprise announced visit to China in 1972 (see below, p. 336) . The Japanese had long followed the American lead on relations with China, and depended heavily on their trade with the United States, and the Japanese government lost face as a result of having been consulted on neither move. The world as a whole was greeted with the almost unthinkable spectacle of stranded American tourists unable to turn their dollars into local currency. Suddenly, no one seemed to want the "almighty dollar." And diplomats and trade ministers launched into a flurry of diplomatic activity in half a dozen locales, while President Nixon and his special negotiator, Democrat John Connally of Texas, explained their point of view to world leaders. The result was a general agreement signed in Washington, December 18, leading to a wholesale realignment of some 120 world currencies, a devaluation of the dollar (the first since Roosevelt's devaluation in the depths of the depression, 1932) , a host of other lesser measures, and an engagement to launch new, general trade talks in 1973.

The agreement, hailed by President Nixon as "the most significant monetary agreement in the history of the world . . ." that would bring "a more stable world . . . more true prosperity . . .," was deceptive. Within six months Britain faced another payments crisis, and in February

1973, despite all the measures taken to improve the American balance of payents, another run developed on the dollar, and the United States devalued its battered currency a second time, by another 10 per cent, while other currencies floated to new levels. The reign of the dollar had come to an end; disorder and uncertainty came to plague international monetary relations among Western states.

The startling money crisis of these years reflected fundamental economic changes: the rise of Japan and Europe to challenge the economic pre-eminence of the United States, and the overextension of the United States as a result of earlier Cold War policies. They required new policy shifts, and these were complicated by ties to other areas of the world—the socialist states, less-developed countries, the oil-rich states of the Middle East. It was relatively simple for the United States to press Germany to increase its share of the burden of Western defense in order to help the United States' balance of payments. It was harder to do this in the Far East, where a reluctant Japan had constitutional limitations on its military power, and where the Nixon administration moved toward a general Asian withdrawal based on a calculation that Russian and Chinese power would check each others' possible ambitions and that each would therefore curry some favor with the United States (a remarkable shift from the early sixties, when the US Department of State still issued statements about Sino-Soviet bloc expansionism in Asia).

Other political realms also reflected the economic changes. Prompted by balance of payments difficulties, the United States found it easy to reduce its foreign economic aid, particularly at a time that such aid had come under attack as failing to produce the progress it was supposed to promote. In addition, most of the remaining aid was "tied"—had to be spent in the United States for American goods. Less-developed countries objected that it reduced the purchasing power of the aid, but had to be content with the explanation that it was either tied aid or even less aid (although they could continue to argue cogently that some other aspect of the balance of payments could perhaps be changed with less harm to the poorer states).

By 1970 the Soviet leaders had had to forget Khrushchev's boasts about outstripping the capitalist countries in consumer production, and were in fact hunting for markets for Soviet goods so that they could finance desperately needed imports. In mid–1972 they arranged enormous feedgrain purchases from the United States, where the Nixon administration was happy to increase American exports. But less than a year earlier, in order to get the Common Market to admit more American fruit, the United States had agreed to curb production of feedgrains. When harvests were poor and drought took its toll in Asia and Africa, a world shortage of feedgrains resulted, sending prices skyhigh, and drastically increasing meat prices in the United States. The result, in 1973, was domestic discontent, a partial curb on exports, and cries of anguish from Japanese officials, for Japan depended heavily on American exports. It appeared that the foreign policies of countries like the United States, the Soviet Union, and Japan and economic units like the Common Market were dictated primarily by the price of soybeans!

Of equal importance, however, was the price of oil, and there were many political ramifications. The Middle East, where Russian power seemed now ubiquitous, was the main source for Europe and Japan. But as the seventies got underway it appeared that the United States would also come to depend heavily on the same area, if not upon the same particular states. In the face of hostility on the part of Iraq, Syria, and Libya, the United States sought its oil in Saudi Arabia, Iran, and the tiny Persian Gulf sheikdoms. To help cement its relations with these countries it sold them modern arms, to the dismay of the Israelis, who foresaw a possible revolt in Saudi Arabia such as the one that had occurred earlier in Iraq and then Libya, bringing to power a hostile government. For the first time in history, the early seventies witnessed a measure of unity among the diverse oil-exporting states, through the means of the Organization of Petroleum Exporting Countries, with its central offices in Vienna. As the oil-producing states began to demand and receive a greater share of oil revenues (most of which had been going to oil companies and into the tax coffers of governments of consuming states) American officials began to fear that a new deficit element would develop in the American balance of payments. Americans were treated to the unusual spectacle of being exhorted to use less gasoline by oil companies, and again it was brought home to Americans as it had been to Englishmen before them that domestic affairs might well be contingent upon the previously ignored balance of payments, and upon political developments in a volatile area.

From the international point of view matters such as these raised the well-founded fear that European, Japanese, and American trading practices and problems might lead to the formation of rival and competing trade blocs, with potential runious economic and political consequences. Their economies, plagued by inflation, continued to flourish, linked by a volume of trade no one would have foreseen 25 years earlier, supported by a series of continuing consultative institutions. Yet a generalized unease had spread in the last years, compounded of intellectual questioning of the goals of the wealthy societies that existed, as they did, in the midst of prevailing world squalor, and of a series of specific crises reflecting the shifts in economic power that had taken place in the quarter of a century. The crises cast doubt on the adequacy of the international institutions created at the end of World War II and in ensuing years—the IMF, the GATT, the OECD, Group of Ten, and others. As of the time of this writing, negotiations for a new international monetary system and for new trading relationships had only just begun. European unity had taken great steps forward; Western unity no longer existed.

WESTERN SECURITY

Before 1956 Western leaders were relatively certain of what military policy for security should be. In the next 15 years the world military pattern lost all clarity, and so did military policy. Two decades after the first hydrogen bomb explosions the United States and the Soviet Union still stood in a class by themselves, each able to virtually destroy the modern world. England, France, and China had joined the nuclear club, but their stock and means of delivery were limited, and the implications of their nuclear establishments unclear. The Russian-American standoff was characterized by spurts of new weapons development, policies to compensate for the other side's possible new advantage, and the pervasive fear on the part of each that the other might make some new breakthrough that would, somehow, put it ahead and give it a strategic superiority. The decade of the sixties brought limited, stabilizing arms agreements that nevertheless failed to halt new weapons developments. It brought increased production on the part of the Russians, who caught up in sheer brute power with the Americans. The 1970s, with the strategic arms limitation talks, brought the promise of further stabilization, but continued weapons development.

The continued armament programs of the superpowers produced an enormous financial burden. For years, too, they were commonly seen as part of a race that threatened world peace, despite government disclaimers that they were necessary to maintain a balance that supported peace. By the 1970s popular fears about the arms race seemed to have eroded. The two giants were evidently hobbled giants; their power served only to keep one another in check. And one result of this view was a persistent but unrealized pressure from within the alliances to dissolve them. Another was that the temptation to turn to other forms of military force under the shelter of the nuclear umbrella proved irresistible both for nations ideologically committed to world revolution as well as those attempting to maintain or to merely revise the status quo. Thus, there was a period in the 1960s when Communist leaders trumpeted their aim to resort to guerrilla wars of national liberation to bring about the world revolution, while Western powers answered by examining the requirements for successful counterguerrilla warfare. It was obviously a dangerous game. In 1961 Khrushchev declared that nuclear was between the superpowers was impossible, that conventional war between them too dangerous (for it might escalate into nuclear war), but that the Soviet Union must continue to support wars of national liberation. History, after all, had to progress, but it simply could no longer do so through the first two forms of warfare. The speech may have been prompted by internal troubles. Khrushchev had reneged on his pledges of nuclear arms aid to China in an effort to trade a non-nuclear Asia to the West for a non-nuclear Germany, and the Chinese were vituperatively accusing him of the worst sins of revisionism. He had to prove he was still the leader of world revolution. But Western observers took him seriously (as they had on occasions that he had threatened a rain of rockets), and many felt that he had provided a new canonical view of the present stage in world history: it would be one in which he would try to defeat the West by new means. Peaceful coexistence would mean no nuclear or conventional war, but support for local Communist-sponsored guerrilla wars—with a view to the ultimate balance between capitalism and Communism. For, as he once said, "we shall remain Communists until shrimps learn to whistle."

Western strategic analysts had long discussed the meaning and implication of nuclear weapons. Khrushchev's speech confirmed what many had felt. Revolutions and guerrilla wars would be directed and supported from Russia and China and the West must be prepared to counter them. A whole new literature on guerrilla and counterguerrilla warfare sprang into being, and in the United States the new Kennedy administration hastened the creation and training of Special Forces for counterinsurgency warfare.

One result was that revolutionaries throughout the "third world" reached the conclusion that Communist powers would help them, while the West would be bound to oppose them. The West appeared to have set itself up as irrevocably counterrevolutionary. As a corollary, regimes that feared insurgency looked to the United States for training, aid, and equipment.

In fact, the situation was far more complicated, as the split between Russia and China indicated. There was question of whether the talk of aiding "wars of national liberation" was primarily rhetoric designed to prove Communist purity. Even more, there was question of whether the coming to power of new, revolutionary regimes—whether aided by Russia or not—would represent an accretion of power to the Communist bloc. For despite all Khrushchev's desperate efforts since the Hungarian revolt of 1956, that bloc appeared to be fracturing into several disparate groups.

(There was a third aspect to the Russia-United States nuclear standoff that might have even longer-run implications for the international political system. In the nineteenth century the Great Powers had acted to police and limit minor conflicts, more or less successfully. The Charter of the United Nations, with its assignment of primary responsibility for peace and security to the Security Council where the five supposed great powers had permanent membership and the veto, suggested that this was still the case. Yet if the Great Powers were in fact tied down by the nuclear stalemate—and by the new factor of mass politics—could they carry out such a police function? The answer already seemed clear that they could not. But what, then, would replace this, given the lack of any central international authority? Would the third world lapse into an anarchy in which only local balances would operate to check it?)

Finally, it should be mentioned that in the sixties the entire rationale of the arms race came under a questioning that has not ceased. A decade earlier it was possible to accept that American armed strength guaranteed peace in the bipolar Cold War. Winston Churchill had said as much in 1955. But by the end of the sixties many people were convinced that insofar as major weapons were concerned, the race had its own momentum. Before, arms races had sometimes been the result of the aggressive designs of one country and the defensive response of others. Rather than being the cause of wars, therefore, they had been the result of underlying conflicts. In other cases, they had revealed the Hobbesian security dilemma: each nation's desire for security had led to the armament and insecurity of all. Now, however, people wondered if a new factor hadn't been added—that is, if the military and the huge, complex and ingenious industry behind the extraordinarily complex weapons systems had not developed a momentum independent both of underlying conflicts *and* of the actions of potential opponents. In other words, some people suggested that the men employed in making arms and the legislators who supported them, those in the complex research and development industry, and the military men who always wanted to have the newest and best weapons, might all be convinced of the necessity of what they were doing. They could explain that if *they* were doing it, surely those on the other side were too and, therefore, it must be necessary.

And they might in fact be able to point to continued development on the other side. Those who argued that the installation of an antiballistic missile system, for example, would not affect the actions of the other side in causing a new cycle in the arms race, might be correct; the actions of each might well have become independent of the other. More and more, in the United States, at least, people had begun to raise this issue by 1970 and conclude that the arms "race" was being run without looking at where other runners were going or whether there were other runners at all. *If* this were true, then what was needed was internal political action to stop it, rather than either settlement of political issues *or* international agreement on arms limitation.

There were many others, however, who disagreed, arguing that even if these were the dynamics of the arms race, the fact that the Russians might have gotten caught up in the same internal processes would not mean that if the United States stopped, the Russians would, too. Nevertheless, by 1970, within the United States, pressure had led to a reduction in the size of the military budget relative to gross national product (to the accompaniment of charges that the United States was "falling behind"). And on the international front, talks started on strategic arms limitation. A complex series of events lay behind these developments.

On October 4, 1957, the Soviet Union boosted into orbit the first man-made satellite. Khrushchev was hardly a man to slight any degree of prestige he could obtain from the feat, nor ignore the power such prestige might mean. American chagrin intensified when the first highly publicized American attempt failed dismally. In subsequent months there were American successes; but the Russians lifted larger satellites.

The Eisenhower administration had been involved in a budget-cutting operation that weighed heavily on weapons research and development. It started out by denigrating the Russian achievement: "we are not," said one official spokesman, "engaged in a game of celestial basketball." But the Russian feat did, in fact, have important military implications: it showed a Russian superiority in missiles; Khrushchev had not been boasting idly a few months earlier when he had told the United States that the USSR could strike at it directly with intercontinental missiles.

At the time of the Suez war he had threatened Western Europe with a rain of missiles if Britain and France did not withdraw their forces from Egypt. One result of the Russian development was that America's European allies questioned their reliance on American deterrence more than ever before. After all, Secretary of State Dulles' successor, Christian Herter, told a Congressional committee:

> I can't conceive of the President involving us in an all-out nuclear war unless the facts showed clearly that we are in danger of devastation ourselves, or that actual moves have been made toward devastating ourselves.

Did this mean that the United States would not respond to an attack in Europe if an attack did not threaten the United States? Could the Russians coerce Western Europe with the threat of nuclear power warning the Americans to stay out if they did not want their cities destroyed?

The British answer was clear. They exploded their own, first thermo-nuclear device on May 15, 1957, and Duncan Sandys, the Defense Minister, put the position to Parliament:

> We think it is just as well to make certain that an appreciable element of nuclear power shall, in all circumstances, remain on this side of the Atlantic, so that no one shall be tempted to think that a major attack could be made against Western Europe without the risk of nuclear retaliation.

Overall, the British adopted a new strategy of increased reliance on nuclear striking power and a reduction of British conventional forces overseas. Economic factors and difficulty in holding overseas bases in the face of nationalist agitation played a part; the new strategy was in this sense merely a continuation and extention of a process that had begun at the end of World War II. It raised the same questions that were raised in the United States at the time of the "New Look": what now about non-nuclear attacks or guerrilla war? Was not the government cutting off any possibility of response? And what about the expense of a national nuclear deterrent force?

The Macmillan government and its successors tried to handle this primarily through cooperation with the Unied States. In 1957 they accepted an American offer to station "Thor" and "Jupiter" Intermediate Range Ballistic Missiles in England, even though the warheads would remain under American control. It was this particular provision, combined with the nature of the missiles, that made all other NATO countries but Turkey and Italy decide against similar agreements. The problem was that these liquid-fueled, above-ground missiles would take too much time to get off the ground to serve for retaliation and therefore deterrence; they could be destroyed on the ground if the Soviet Union struck first. What was worse was that this implied that their only use was in a first strike. They might, therefore, constitute a provocation, a statement to the Soviet Union that the west might, in spite of President Eisenhower's declarations to the contary, actually *start* a thermonuclear war. And possession of the missiles might bring a country into a line of fire that it might otherwise escape.

Despite these objections, the weapons stayed in place until 1963, when they were finally replaced in the American armory with weapons that apparently overcame these objections: Polaris missiles fired from submarines while still underwater, that therefore would be able to survive a first attack.

Since the warheads of the weapons were still under American control, this particular form of cooperation still failed to resolve the doubts raised about American determination. The British therefore continued to work at producing their own delivery system; the decision to do so proved to be a costly error. The force of bombers built to carry nuclear weapons rapidly became obsolete. Construction of the Blue Streak missile to replace the bombers became too expensive and the British came to rely on an American-supplied missile, the Skybolt, to be fired from bombers in flight while still a thousand miles away from a target, and presumably from the target's defenses. The Skybolt would prolong the useful life of the heretofore obsolescent bombers. In 1962, however, the Kennedy administration decided to abandon development of the Skybolt. It was too expensive and unreliable, given the alternatives of the new "family" of intercontinental ballistic missiles and the unforeseen rapidity of development of the submarine-based Polaris. To compensate the British, whose dependence on the United States was thus emphasized, President Kennedy met with Prime Minister Macmillan at Nassau, in the Bahamas, and suggested establishment of a multinationally manned and controlled seaborne force that the United States would equip with Polaris missiles. (The effect of all this upon de Gaulle and Britain's application to the Common Market has already been described.)

For three years the planning, negotiating, and experimenting for what came to be known as the MLF—multilateral force—dragged on. In addition to being a formal compensation to the British, the fleet was supposed to keep the Germans from demanding greater access to control of nuclear weapons and from the crisis that would undoubtedly be precipitated if they did. For years European doubts about the United States had produced proposals for some kind of multilateral force—NATO Commander General Norstad had proposed one in 1959 and Secretary of State Herter had endorsed the idea. Now the United States had to convince its allies of the merit of the idea. while attempting to convince the Russians that it was not actually giving nuclear weapons to anyone who didn't already have them—which in practice meant that the United States would still have a final veto on the use of the weapons, however mixed the nationalities of the crews might be on the MLF ships. The result was that in 1965 the proposal died a quietly diplomatic death.

For the British, the episode meant, eventually, an overall contraction of the size of their military establishment. At the end of the sixties the bombers were being phased out. By this time, and again with American help, they would have four Polaris-type submarines. In 1966 they announced an overall cutback in military forces; in 1967 they increased it, and the Labour government that replaced the Conservatives in 1964 decided to abandon what was left of British commitments east of Suez— that is, the small forces maintained to help protect Singapore and Malaysia, sheikdoms in the Persian Gulf, and the Eastern Mediterranean. It cancelled an order for 50 United States-built F-111 multipurpose fighter-bombers, and decided to cut back the British Army of the Rhine, stationed in Germany. By 1971 the last of its aircraft carriers would be gone, and British defense efforts were virtually limited to commitment to NATO. Even the Polaris force was assigned to NATO command. If the British succeeded in their new bid to join the Common Market, their deterrent force might very probably end up being merged with that of the French. The withdrawal from Singapore and the Persian Gulf opened up a whole new situation in light of political instability and increased Russian activity all through the Indian Ocean area in the late 1960s. While the Soviet Union suggested a joint security arrangement with the United States, the United States instead flirted with China, and Iran, which had long played off the British against the Russians, tried to establish itself as the strongest Persian Gulf military power. (See below, chapter 11.)

The French, despite the series of British problems, had gone ahead on their own, too—but, under the influence of de Gaulle and the French military, they had done so without the entanglement with the Americans. They would have been willing to have the United States help them develop their own weapons, to have the United States give them some, or to have NATO forces, including the American deterrent, come under a genuine joint directorate of France, Great Britain, and the United States. Such moves were either legally impossible or politically unpalatable to the United States government. Fortified in their distrust, especially after the Skybolt incident, the French first built their own fleet of low-level Mirage IV bombers, designed to fly at levels at which radar and missiles would be ineffective. They designed their own underground, silo-based missiles, and by the mid-sixties had begun the installation of a planned eighteen of these in the south of France, in Haute-Provence. On their own, they proceeded also toward creation of a fleet of four missile-launching submarines. By the mid-seventies, not only would all of these become operational, but five of their eight armored divisions would be equipped with French-built tactical nuclear weapons. At the same time they proceeded to modernize their conventional force.

All of this was done in a manner that stressed French sovereignty and independence. French troops that had been withdrawn from NATO to fight in Algeria were never replaced under NATO command. In 1964 the last French naval units were withdrawn from NATO, while de Gaulle, having told the British what he thought of their entanglement with the Americans, warned the Germans they would have to choose between cooperation with the French in a "Europe of nations" and in the Common Market or with the United States. Then, to the consternation of the

Americans, in early 1966 de Gaulle announced that all French armed forces were to be withdrawn from NATO commands by July 1, and—what was more shocking—all NATO units and commands would have to leave French soil by April 1, 1967. This meant not only the immense communications, staff, and command complexes around Paris, the logistic network with its great supply bases, but also 26,000 United States troops and dependents, along with air defense and attack units.

The Americans and other NATO members protested violently; France could not force them to leave. France would have to pay for the bases and communications networks left behind. The Germans, with American support, told the French the French troops not a part of NATO forces could not, of course, stay in Garmany. When the French asked them politely whether they wanted them withdrawn, the Germans backed down. So did everyone else, and in 1967 NATO headquarters were transferred to Brussels, to Brunssum in the Netherlands, and to Stuttgart. The de Gaulle government insisted that it was still a party to the North Atlantic Treaty, which called for mutual assistance in case of attack, but was no longer going to participate in the elaborate organization devised at the time of the Korean War.

In 1962 the United States and the Soviet Union had agreed on a pact to ban nuclear tests in the atmosphere (see below, p. 262). France refused to sign, and continued nuclear tests. On September 24, 1968, the French exploded their first thermonuclear device.

1969 marked the 20th anniversary of the signing of the North Atlantic Treaty. Given the French attitude, the determination of the British to diminish the size of the British Army of the Rhine, pressures within the United States to withdraw some of the expensively maintained American troops, general dissatisfaction with the organization, and increased distrust of the United States under the impact of the Vietnam war, many people thought that at least the French would withdraw. The one attempt to satisfy Europeans about the American deterrent had been creation of closer cooperation at the level of nuclear planning.

If any one event revitalized the organization, however, it was the sudden and brutal invasion of Czechoslovakia by the USSR and other Warsaw Pact nations on 21 August, 1968 just 20 years after the Communist seizure of power in Prague. (See below, p. 321.) While the most probable interpretations of the action never included an estimate that the Russians had renewed their threat to Western Europe, the fact that they would use armed forces under these circumstances created a new climate. Moreover, permanent stationing of Russian troops in Czechoslovakia meant that the Russians had taken up a more advanced position than they had had before. And there developed, too, a realization that the large number of Russian divisions stationed in Europe had, as military analysts had known all along, been well re-equipped with the most modern conventional arms. The NATO anniversary passed in April with a declaration reaffirming the need for alliance, both for purposes of the security that it had helped enhance and for purposes of pursuing a genuine detente with the Soviet Union on the basis of equality. The declaration reaffirmed the "forward strategy" developed in the early 1950s to satisfy the Germans, the maintenance of a credible conventional and nuclear deterrent, and the need for "sufficient and substantial North American and European conventional forces and ready reinforcements." A month later the Defense Planning Committee went ahead with its projections for 1971–75 force levels. A call from the Warsaw Treaty Organization's Political Consultative Committee for a general European security conference was treated gingerly, although not rejected; Prime Minister Pierre Trudeau's declaration that Canada would cut the forces it had committed to NATO was received coldly. NATO was still in business.

But the differences from the past were apparent, both in NATO and the Warsaw Pact. The latter's Political Consultative Committee was slow in meeting, because the Rumanians refused a Russian demand that Warsaw Pact countries put their forces under a unified command that could move them anywhere and hold maneuvers wherever it wanted. Just as Secretary of State Rusk's plea in 1966 to associate NATO with what he called the southern flank in Vietnam had fallen on deaf ears, so Russia's aim of having the Warsaw Pact countries endorse its quarrel with China and its invasion of Czechoslovakia had failed.

Moreover the country most centrally located in terms of any potential military clash—West Germany—itself adopted a more flexible foreign policy attitude. In October 1966, the Christian Democrats who so long dominated foreign policy fell from power when one of the small parties allied to them in the parliament withdrew support. The Christian Democrats succeeded in persuading the Socialist Party to join them in what was called the "Grand Coalition" and Willie Brandt, former Mayor of Berlin, became Foreign Minister under Chancellor Kurt George Kiesinger. They continued to favor British entry in the EEC, told France "we refuse to be talked into making a false and dangerous choice"—that is, between France and the United States, and perhaps, most important of all, moved to improve their own relations with the countries of Eastern Europe, including the Soviet Union. In January 1967, Germany established diplomatic relations with Rumania, the first Socialist bloc country with which it had done so since Adenauer had gone to Russia in 1955. It re-established relations with Yugoslavia, broken off in 1957 when Yugoslavia recognized East Germany. With this came the final end to the "Hallstein Doctrine," under which, in an effort to keep East Germany from being considered a respectable member of the world community, the West Germans had threatened to break off or refused to establish diplomatic relations with any country that recognized the East German regime. In the meantime, while explicitly denying that they were recognizing the sovereignty of East Germany—for if East and West Germany were two states, they were not foreign to each other—they initiated negotiation at the government level, with the declared intention that these should lead to contractual cooperation.

Again, the invasion of Czechoslovakia interfered: since the Russians argued that German revanchism had played a part in the rise of reaction in Czechoslovakia, it was hard for them to continue to negotiate with the Germans. And there seems little question but that the Russians had feared that German "penetration" was playing a part in further shaking up Eastern Europe; the East German regime, now playing a leading role within the bloc, appears to have warned against close relations with West Germany unless the latter eventually accorded it diplomatic recognition and recognized the Oder-Neisse eastern boundaries. But the move to better relations could not be denied. Within two years the Social Democrats gained power in Germany, and Brandt, now Chancellor, reopened the dialogue with the east. West German diplomats again engaged in conversations with the East Germans and with other Eastern European governments. On August 12, 1970, West Germany signed a nonaggression treaty with the Soviet Union, renouncing the use of force and affirming the inviolability of present borders. For the first time West Germany had accepted the Russian-imposed Oder–Neisse line between Germany and Poland. Five months later, with a public display of contrition over Nazi policy in Poland, Brandt signed a West German-Polish border treaty that included a mutual renunciation of force.

In return, the Russians agreed to hold four-power talks on the status of West Berlin. From the point of view of geography, nothing would ever make Berlin free of possible pressure, but legal commitments from the Soviet Union and East Germany seemed eminently worthwhile. A year later, in early September 1971, the four World War II victors—France, Britain, the United States, and the Soviet Union—did in fact reach an agreement, defining the city's relationship to West Germany and renouncing East German claims over both Berlin and control of access routes to it. The Russians insisted that West Germany ratify the Polish and Russian nonaggression treaties with their border provisions before they would ratify the Berlin agreement. Brandt faced heavy internal opposition: what was he gaining by actions that virtually accepted the eastern border dictated by the Soviet Union, and gave international status and virtual recognition to East Germany? His arguments sufficed to overcome the opposition: the agreements would bring stability for Berlin, recognition of the facts of life that could not be changed—whatever Adenauer had hoped in earlier years—and a detente that in the long run would be preferable to continued uncertainty. The agreements were ratified on May 17, 1972, marking a very large turnabout in postwar German foreign policy. Five months later Brandt initialed a treaty with East Germany committing the two states to consultation and future exchanges. His hand strengthened by elections that indicated general approval of his Ostpolitik, he obtained Parliamentary ratification of the East German agreement. East Germany was granted observer status at the United Nations on November 24, a status which West Germany had enjoyed since 1955, and in September 1973, both were admitted as full members.

And in the meantime, on May 31, the NATO Foreign Minister reached agreement to attend a European Security Conference in 1973 and to participate in East-West talks on troop reduction in Europe. Leonid Brezhnev, in a speech delivered in Moscow in March 1973, indicated for the first time that Russia now accepted the Common Market as a going concern, and sought long-term agreements with it; he negotiated a trade pact with Franco Spain in September (and Spain for the first time signed numerous consular agreements with East European countries); he signed an agreement to help build a power plant for the military regime of Greece (a government so horrendous to liberal and progressive groups in the West that they had long asked all governments to stop supporting it. It had been expelled from the Council of Europe—but the People's Republic of China established diplomatic relations with it on June 5!) In July 1972, North and South Korea initiated talks that led to an agreement in November for a measure of normalized relations. Most important of all, following a precedent-breaking, historic visit to China in early February 1972, President Nixon went to Moscow in late May, where, among a series of other agreements on technical and cultural cooperation and exchanges, he signed the first Strategic Arms Limitation treaty, which restricted the antiballistic missile systems both countries could deploy and included an interim agreement curbing expansion of existing intercontinental ballistic missile systems, as well as a commitment to continuation of the SALT talks.

Symbolically, nothing could have been more important. The two countries had taken a major step toward curbing the long-standing arms race, in spite of all the criticisms to which the agreements were put.* They

---

* In the United States Presidential aspirant Henry M. Jackson was particularly critical and argued that they permitted the USSR to surge ahead technically while the United States gradually lapsed into genuine inferiority. The result, he claimed, was inevitable, since the United States military budget included large sums for the high pay designed to attract volunteers, while the Soviet Union paid its draftees very little and spent a much greater percentage on technical development and arms production—a view echoed by the United States military establishment.

were the first to genuinely limit arms deployment; they were the culmination of 25 years of usually fruitless and acrimonious discussion, whose main positive results were the consequence of the scare everyone got during the 1962 missile crisis: the above-ground nuclear test-ban agreement, the Moscow-Washington hot-line installation, and the outer space agreement. Most people hoped that SALT I indicated a general recognition of the desirability to halt the arms race and, therefore, that it presaged further treaties. Taken together with all the other developments cited, there was good reason for people to feel that the Cold War had definitively come to an end. It would take only peace in Vietnam to put the final seal on it—and in January 1973, it appeared that this, too, would occur. (See below, p. 284.) What was more remarkable was that at the time the Moscow agreements were signed, the American President was engaged in an all-out air offensive in Vietnam, a result both of a major Communist offensive launched in March and of the virtual end to an American troop presence in the battered country. The Communist offensive may have been timed to precede the President's visit to Moscow, to put pressure upon him or upon Brezhnev or both; it led Nixon to intensive bombing and to mining the port of Haiphong on May 9—a move long suggested by military men who saw supplies pouring in by sea, and resisted by an administration that realized it was an action contrary to all international law. The remarkable thing was that the situation in Southeast Asia, while provoking limited Sino-Russian cooperation on land transportation to Vietnam, did not stop Brezhnev from seeing Nixon and from signing the spate of agreements. Detente was far more important than Vietnam.

CONCLUSION

Three major conclusions could be drawn from the record of these years. The first was that, despite a series of crises, despite the level of nuclear arms—which included the huge Soviet buildup after 1963—the detente was real, compounded of a fear of the ever-present nuclear weapons, of a turning inward of political attention, of a decline of influence of ideology in holding the blocs together. The Sino-Russian conflict, traced in detail later, was of prime importance: it made both countries' leaders turn to the United States to keep it from favoring their antagonists. For the first time in centuries, the North Atlantic area was one in which peace seemed to be the rule, rather than the exception, both among the Western countries whose moves toward unity had been by fits and starts, and between East Europe and the West. In the Atlantic area, an enlarged Europe had emerged, but time had eroded the concept of Atlantic unity. In the Russian sphere, the Czech invasion of 1968 showed that the Russians would use force to hold their empire together; it showed that they would resist attempts to turn detente in the direction of freer personal relations, but conceived of it in government-to-government terms.

It also gave an insight into the unstable underpinnings of the more relaxed and peaceful world. At the time of Czechoslovakia the West made no move, just as none had been made in 1956 and 1953. Would this always be true? If there were a Yugoslav crisis after Tito, would the Russians stand by? If not, would the West?

Perhaps more important, the balance of terror buttressing the detente and now so widely accepted was itself based on shaky foundations: it assumed that the main danger was one of rational decision, and rational leaders had shown they understood it would be fatal to decide to use the weapons. But in so doing they had glossed over the continued possibility of accident or irrationality. Both were guarded against, but still possible, and SALT had left the arsenals intact. Furthermore, by limiting the deployment of antimissile systems, and by abandoning the thought of elaborate shelter programs of the sort bruited about in the early 1960s, the two countries had essentially come to depend upon what was called "Mutual Assured Destruction" for deterrence: the capacity to retaliate in ways that would mean the destruction of a sufficient proportion of the others' population if either country started nuclear war. Mass population was the hostage and guarantee, which might work in the case of rationality or to prevent escalation. But what of accident or irrationality? Was detente really possible as long as the Russian and American *people* constituted hostages to one another's government?

Nevertheless, it was peace of a sort. At the same time, however, another major aspect of international politics of the time emerged: complicated economic problems became the major political preoccupation of governments and the main theater of international struggle—and not only among the developed countries. The facts of economic and ecological interdependence had almost exploded into public attention; even a China whose government stressed self-reliance after the end of the abortive aid relationship to Russia in the 1950s, was now searching for markets in order to be able to import needed foodstuffs. So was Russia, where Stalin, Malenkov, Krushchev, and Brezhnev had all failed to solve the Soviet Union's "farm problem." With a measure of military security and a large dose of economic development, had come a host of new problems needing most delicate and complex resolutions, and all of which would have important domestic consequences for all states. They involved three interrelated areas, and it was hard to negotiate on each of them while keeping in mind the implications for the other of the three areas: overall East-West relations, Europe-United States relations, and inter-European relations within the framework of the enlarged Common Market. Overall East-West relations, with their emphasis on the security sphere, might vitally affect Europe-United States relations if Russia, playing on American desires for stability and decreased foreign expenditures, could persuade the Americans to diminish their presence in Europe. In the face of a Europe whose efforts at unity have been primarily economic and who show little sign of military or political unity, such a move might exacerbate general Europe-United States relations, already marred by American feeling that Europe was building a broad and exclusive trading bloc. Russia would be freer to turn its attention to China and to its flanking moves to Asia. A renewed effort at political unity in Europe might prove more fruitful. But could anyone foresee it? (In the meantime the Chinese gave every indication that they were in favor of both NATO and a continued American presence in Europe—as checks upon Russia!)

It was a moot question whether governments and the international organizations they had formed a quarter of a contury earlier were up to taking care of these problems, especially since the world leaders of that earlier time had lost so much influence. The Nixon administration's recognition of the facts of political life, reflected in the President's trips to Peking and Moscow, showed that it could make dramatic moves. But they were moves that showed an American acceptance of a diminished world role and lowered sights. They reflected the political strength of Russia and China, the economic independence of Japan and Europe, and the diminished prestige of the United States, affected by its interventionist policies of the 1960s. To these the next chapter will briefly turn.

SEVEN
THE UNITED STATES
IN LATIN AMERICA
AND VIETNAM

In the decade of the 1960s the United States embroiled itself in a series of situations that brought into question the entire conduct of its foreign policy and helped create the image of a superpower out of touch with reality, blunderingly using its brute strength on the basis of outmoded concepts, or, worse, to maintain an empire it had been building since the turn of the century, an empire now challenged by rising nationalisms throughout the world. The United States was charged with still seeing the world in bipolar terms, or trying to preserve its internal economic system by external expansion, or hiding actions designed to serve its ruling economic interests under the cloak of national security action necessitated by the Cold War. Not all people accepted one of these explanations. But they became widespread enough to force politicians and analysts alike to examine once again the bases of American foreign policy, and they became widely enough accepted abroad to greatly diminish American influence.

The United States was not the only country that intervened directly by force in the affairs of other countries during this period. At the time that it sent 13,000 men into Lebanon in 1958 at the request of the Lebanese government, the United Kingdom sent armed forces into Jordan and Libya (see below, p. 396). In subsequent years Britain used troops to protect Malaysia during the "confrontation" provoked by Indonesia's Sukarno; Sukarno's confrontation was itself an unwarranted intervention in Malaysian affairs. The United Kingdom sent troops into the tiny British West Indian island of Anguilla in the Carribbean in March 1969, when a dispute occurred over its secession from the Associated States of St. Kitts, Nevis, and Anguilla. It was in pursuit of orderly withdrawal that Britain used its troops in Cyprus in the late 1950s and in the South Arabia Protectorates before it left in November 1967. The Soviet Union entered Czechoslovakia in 1968 and installed its troops there permanently, and Russian pilots ind crews manned Russian planes and anti-aircraft missiles in Egypt in 1970. Egypt itself intervened with over 50,000 troops in a long, bitter, and costly civil war in Yemen as well as in civil strife in the Congo. During the calamitous civil war in Nigeria, 1967 to 1970, there were charges that the Soviet Union supplied Nigeria with more than just military equipment; certainly the United Kingdom, France, and Portugal all helped one side or the other with arms. France sent its troops into Gabon in 1964 to restore the deposed President and into Chad in 1968–69 to help put down rebellious Touareg tribesmen in the North. African states justified their interventions against white-minority-ruled states in the south, and India felt no need to give justification for its massive intervention that helped divide Pakistan in two and create the new state of Bangla Desh in 1971.

Armed interventions of various types were therefore common practice. But interventions by the United States in the cases of Cuba, the Dominican Republic, and Indochina evoked wider condemnation on the world scene and within the United States than those by other countries. Somehow, in the 1960s, the United States seemed to be intervening where it shouldn't and—in the case of Indochina—with force out of all proportion to any conceivable view of the situation.

Advent of the Nixon administration in the United States brought into the open certain lines of development obscured by the continuing agony of Vietnam. The new President accepted that the United States should play a less vigorous role in many parts of the world, would accept without question Russian hegemony in Eastern Europe while welcoming relations with the countries of the region, would accept the fact of the People's Republic of China and its Far Eastern interests (dropping all pretense of support for Chiang Kai-shek's continued aim of reconquest of the mainland) and would welcome all moves toward a detente, regardless of the Kremlin's reiterated ideological aims. If there were ambiguities to President Nixon's position it was because there were ambiguities in a world situation in which Russia asked for a settlement, but Brezhnev could make a speech at a dinner in honor of Fidel Castro in 1973 saying "we must be prepared for the ideological struggle to be intensified and to become an even sharper forum of the confrontation between systems . . ." while the Chinese delegate to the United Nations could, shortly after the Nixon-Mao-Chou en Lai toasts, reiterate Chinese support for "just" wars on the basis that wars were inevitable so long as mankind was divided into classes. The Charter of the United Nations in which China had been seated might pledge its members to renounce force but, the delegate said, it was a betrayal to advocate the nonuse of force indiscriminately—a position in which he was supported by a majority of

United Nation members who wanted force to be used to liberate the southern parts of Africa.*

In short, there was no general objection to the use of force in international affairs. The old theory of the just war existed in a new guise. British and French actions received little approval. But in the case of the United States critics felt that it had singularly abused what was, after all, the greatest degree of physical power ever concentrated in the hands of one nation, intervening for misconceived purposes on the side of reaction. The story, perhaps, called for more complex conclusions.

THE CUBAN CONFRONTATION

Fidel Castro came to power in Cuba in January 1959. The bearded, cigar-smoking revolutionary had had created for him an aura of Robin Hood romanticism; his tiny band of rebels in the mountains vanquished an army and sent an unsavory dictator into exile; he conquered all odds and swaggered into Havana to the delighted shouts of the masses, and with the open support of the educated and professional classes and the more respectable business groups. Millions of Americans had seen him on television; a popular and staunchly Irish-Catholic television personality had gone into the mountains to interview him, and Castro had agreed with one of his observations: since most of Castro's men wore crucifixes, they couldn't be Communist.

From the beginning, however, Castro made it clear that this was not to be a revolution like so many other revolutions in Latin America, a mere change in the ruling clique, from one comfortably corrupt group to another. The revolution, he said, had just begun. What most Americans and most Cubans did not realize (and many could not understand) was that Castro was determined to make a genuinely social revolution, one that involved radically changing the entire social, economic, as well as political, structure of the tiny country. It is quite doubtful that at the time Castro had any definite picture of how he would do it. He was no Communist, although there were some Communists and fellow-travelers around him; he had received no support from the Cuban Communist party as such during the campaign that put him into power. But the radical-nationalist viewpoint he espoused brought him their support and he came to rely upon them more and more.

The radical-nationalism and Cuba's proximity to the United States

* In the 1972 General Assembly members voted 99–5 to recognize the "legitimacy" of the anticolonial armed struggle. The United Kingdom, France, South Africa, Portugal—and the United States—were in the minority.

were what made the Cuban revolution so important on the international scene. Chapters 4 and 5 have already pointed out how underlying social tensions, exacerbated by population increases, contrasted with the facade of inter-American relations. Peronism in Argentina and the abortive Guatemala revolution were reactions to a set of like factors that combined differently in each Latin American country. All of them had extremes of wealth and poverty, a facade of modernisation against a background of peasant society, an entrenched landlord class and an Indian peasantry. Everywhere the military was a factor in politics; intellectuals chafed against the form of society while defending their culture against the materialistic barbarism of Yankee culture imported by the moneyed classes, and a Catholic priesthood existed that was too often identified with reaction. In many of these countries American investment in mineral extraction and plantations fostered resentment against absentee ownership: in Cuba people believed widely that American sugar plantation owners conspired with a well-bribed government to avoid paying of taxes and to ensure that land would not be used for other purposes.

In these circumstances, ideas for radical change abounded. Political legitimacy was hard to come by as one revolutionary regime succeeded another and, in fear of the next, tried to crush opposition, thereby forcing it to adopt revolutionary means of repression. The cycle was and is self-perpetuating. And only in a few cases had revolution produced any real social change. Castro set out to do this, and attracted the attention and support of radical elements all through Latin America. He also set out on a direct collision course with the United States. Unlike Arbenz in Guatemala five years earlier, he obtained support for his revolution from the Soviet Union and ended up declaring himself to all intents and purposes a member of the Communist bloc.

Castro did not need anti-Americanism to mobilize popular support. There was some fear of Castro in the United States, but also much goodwill and a desire to rectify the errors of the past. Inside the government and out, many Americans felt that past policy of maintaining good relations with any regime, so long as it kept order and protected American investments, had been wrong. True, a different policy might involve the United States in intervention on the side of those whom it saw as "the good boys"; nonrecognition of governments had hardly produced good results in the much earlier cases of the Soviet Union, Mexico, of Japanese conquests in the Pacific, of Communist China. Yet the Caracas declaration of 1954 made a Communist government incompatible with the inter-American system: didn't this imply a kind of collective intervention to regulate the internal form of government?

In the Cuban situation, at first, the dilemma did not have to be faced.

The administration by and large looked upon Castro with cautious favor, and Castro received a ringing welcome when he visited the United States. But Castro saw himself as the leader of a revolution that would spread throughout Latin America, one that was bound ultimately to be blocked by a United States whose foreign policy—so he argued—was dictated by its business interests. On the one hand, he set in motion a program of domestic reform; on the other, he began to replace the non-Communist elements that had brought him to power by more radical elements. Right-wingers who accused *all* reform elements of Communism seemed to be crying "wolf," and only confused an already complicated situation. Castro seized on the emotion of pride in the revolution and encouraged Cubans to believe that American imperialism meant to crush it; it was easy to cry "he who is not with us is against us," and to eliminate as opponents of the revolution those who at first welcomed and supported it. Castro had only to wait until they began to object to growing Communist influence and totalitarian methods.

In the meantime a program of wholesome nationalization and expropriation, mass execution of Batista men, and demands that the United States return Batistianos as criminals rather than political refugees strained the worsened relations between the two countries. The American press and Congressmen criticized the Cuban leader, and he cried out that the United States opposed the revolution. As they talked of growing Communist influence, Castro was enabled to equate anti-Communism with counter-revolution; in a series of moves in late 1959 he dismissed or arrested some of his most important supporters because they objected to Communist infiltration of the most important branches of government.

The United States played into Castro's hands. It was slow in preventing anti-Castro groups from using small airfields in Florida to launch hit-and-run air raids on Cuba; its reaction to land reform was to demand compensation; the outcry about public executions sounded hypocritical coming from a country that had not objected to Batista's brutality and had maintained correct relations with the regime until the end (though many chose to forget the United States embargo on arms to Batista after March 1958). There was in the United States a kind of patronizing and mocking attitude taken toward the young revolutionary that betrayed a terrible failure to understand the appeal of his radical idealism throughout Latin America.

In early 1960, Major Ernesto Guevara, head of the powerful Agrarian Institute, made it clear that more expropriation of American business was in order; the Cubans blamed the United States for explosion of a munitions ship in Havana harbor, and Castro and other Cuban spokesmen began to talk of the necessity to "defeat" the United States. An extensive new trade agreement, accompanied by Soviet credits of $100 million, resulted from the visit of Soviet Deputy Premier Anastas Miuoyan in February. About this time Guevara argued that the American quota for imports of Cuban sugar constituted economic enslavement, but the Cuban government also—paradoxically—cried "economic aggression" at the hint that the United States might reduce the Cuban quota.

The quota was a result of United States protection of its own sugar producers. It allowed only certain unilaterally determined amounts to enter the United States and, under the circumstances, the United States paid a higher price than the world price. Guevara's argument that Cuba thus had to buy United States goods above world prices had little merit; the dollars could have been spent elsewhere. The quota, however, was set by the United States alone, and it was true that low Cuban tariffs to American goods tended to direct trade with the United States. Once the idea was implanted that the quota might be reduced, however, American critics of Castro began to agitate for it, giving the Castro regime full opportunity for its propaganda. "Cuba Si, Yankee No!" became a popular war-cry, and Cuba a magnet to discontented revolutionaries all over Latin America who applauded defiance of Goliath by David. Cuban broadcasts and shipments of propaganda materials to the rest of Latin America increased; at home Castro moved to establish totalitarian controls as opposition increased. The stream of refugees flowing into Miami swelled, and opposition began to organize inside and outside Cuba. There was validity to Castro's charge that the United States was helping refugees who wanted to overthrow him; subversion on the part of the American Central Intelligence Agency had already begun.

The mood of the summer of 1960 conspired to make the situation worse. A scheduled Eisenhower-Khrushchev summit in Paris had blown up (see below, p. 306) and the United States was involved in an election campaign in which Cuba was to become a central issue. Kennedy hammered hard at the theme that American prestige had suffered grievous blows during the later years of the Eisenhower Administration, while that of the Soviet Union, particularly with its successful sputniks, had soared. But he wanted to leave open the possibility for pursuing a détente with the Soviet Union. Khrushchev, whose policies before the U-2 affair appeared aimed in that direction, had suggested another summit meeting with whoever succeeded Eisenhower. One result was a deliberate decision not to attack the Soviet Union but rather Communism in Cuba. In this way, Democrats could avoid the "soft-on-Communism" issue that the Republicans were always eager to pin on them, but at the same time avoid attacking the Soviet Union directly. Kennedy quoted rabid right-wingers on how the Eisenhower administration had been misled by pro-Communists about Cuba. Democrats and Republicans in Congress were entangled in the battle, and Eisenhower did his campaign stint for Nixon: he asked Congress for stand-by power to lower the sugar quota. The Democrats disliked giving it to him; each party accused the other of being "soft on Cuba"; but the law passed.

In the meantime Castro had won another victory by importing Soviet crude oil (at a lower price than oil from the United States). The American oil companies operating refineries in Cuba refused to refine it (it was one of their grievances that Castro imported the oil to avoid paying debts due to the oil companies). In retaliation Castro nationalized the refineries, a move popular throughout Latin America, where American oil companies are always a target for nationalist resentment about American theft of natural resources.

The fall of 1960 brought the heads-of-state meeting of the General Assembly in New York, and Castro emulated other world leaders in seeking the spotlight. He and Khrushchev embraced each other before newsmen, and the Cuban leader took the opportunity to call both the United States presidential candidates "beardless, brainless youths." Khrushchev had warned the United States that an attack on Cuba would bring a rain of rockets in retaliation, though when Castro repeated this to cheering crowds in Cuba, Khrushchev told him that it had been only figuratively speaking, and Castro proceeded to recognize Red China and North Korea. In January, before inauguration of the new American president, Castro ordered all but eleven members of the United States embassy staff to leave Havana within 48 hours. Eisenhower retaliated by breaking off diplomatic relations.

In more serious moments, Cuban delegates to the United Nations complained of American training of would-be guerrillas preparing to invade Cuba, a charge that was palpably absurd and easily turned aside. But it was also true.

Under the Eisenhower administration plans had gone forward to help Cuban refugees on the grounds that Castro's totalitarian methods made it impossible to overthrow him from within. The job was handled primarily by the American Central Intelligence Agency, which appears to have botched it badly. Unable to tell left from right, it relied on unpopular former Batista men, could not patch up quarrels among factions, failed to inform the underground in Cuba of what it was doing, and drastically underestimated Castro's ability to meet the small force that it finally helped land on Cuban soil on April 17, 1961. Ill-concealed training bases sprang up, not only in Florida and Louisiana, but also in Guatemala, and the anti-Castro forces were equipped with American weapons.

When Kennedy became President, this policy and many others came under review. The new President agreed to go on with the training and equipping of the forces. He would allow them to carry out the operation against Cuba *if* his advisers assured him of success even if the United States itself carried out no overt military operations. Both the Central Intelligence Agency and the military gave him this assurance, as well as several of his personal advisers. Pressures in favor of the operation included what had been said during the political campaign, as well as a genuine conviction that Castro's growing alignment with the Communist bloc posed a severe danger to the Americas in the light of his popularity among left-wing groups. Moreover, what was to be done with the trained forces already in existence and the organized Cuban political groups that were supposed to take over after the overthrow of Castro? Finally, it became known that Soviet jet fighters were on their way to Cuba and Cuban pilots were training in Czechoslovakia. It might soon be too late, and the President of Guatemala told American authorities that the camps in his country would have to be closed by summer.

In the circumstances, the President authorized an invasion that turned out to be a perfect failure. Fifteen hundred men landed and were attacked by Castro's air force, which also kept them from being resupplied. Castro was able to mobilize his army and militia of over 250,000 men, and bring his forces rapidly to bear on the small beachhead at the Bay of Pigs. Within three days it was all over. There were no multiple landings to force him to divert his forces; because the Central Intelligence Agency was unable to establish reliable contact with any of the underground within Cuba, there was no internal uprising. When President Kennedy was asked to authorize an American air strike at a time the invasion attempt was palpably failing, he reminded those appealing to him that he had authorized the operation only on the basis that no American forces need be directly involved: the United States was not to be charged with its own Hungary. Moreover, no one could now assure him that more would not be required. The United States had already jeopardized its good name by backing the invasion; it would not go further.

And it seriously jeopardized its reputation and prestige. There were many previous Castro supporters among the ranks of the invaders, but Castro was also able to parade Batista murderers from among them. The American Ambassador at the United Nations, Adlai Stevenson, had told an emergency meeting that two B-26 bombers that landed in Florida on April 15 were Cuban air force planes flown by defecting pilots. He was wrong, They were American-supplied planes flown from bases in Nicaragua to destroy Castro's air force on the ground—a job at which they failed. (There was to have been a second air strike, but as the press began to unravel the story of the first one, President Kennedy cancelled it.) Stevenson at least had not lied in the United Nations: he had been misled by his own administration, and the United States had put itself—to say the least—in an awkward position. Reaction against the American-sponsored invasion mounted throughout the rest of the world and especially Latin America, where the Cuban revolution had touched wellsprings of emotion never tapped during the Guatemala affair.

The Bay of Pigs invasion came close to wrecking at the outset the new administration's plan to deal with the tensions and frustrations throughout Latin America that had led to Castro in Cuba and would probably lead to more radicals in power in other countries. A suggestion by Castro himself, in mid-1959, that the United States embark on a long-range multilateral aid program amounting to $30 billion, had received scant consideration. A year earlier Vice President Richard Nixon had set out on a goodwill tour of Latin America which had been a total failure. Nixon was pelted with eggs, physically attacked, and his wife endangered by radical hoodlums. President Eisenhower alerted a force of a thousand marines in the Caribbean to protect him. The move was scarcely likely to endear the United States further to Nixon's host countries, but they had hardly provided hospitality. The tour might have served to give the administration some indication of how badly relations with countries to the south had deteriorated. But for years they had been seen as Latin playgrounds, the source of new dances, the province of Pan American Airways and Grace tour liners, picturesque neighbors who could be counted on to vote the American way in the United Nations, united by a tradition of revolution against foreign domination and devotion to ideals of individual freedom. All of these attitudes were hard to drop. Revolutions, Americans knew, took place; but they generally meant that one military junta replaced another. Only Peron in Argentina and Cardenas in Mexico had tried to do more, and Roosevelt in pursuit of his good neighbor policy in the 1930s had tolerated the nationalist eccentricities of Mexico. Many American citizens found it was nice to work for an American company in Latin America; they could live well very cheaply and find so many servants. And many saw no further than this pleasant life.

Nixon's unpleasant treatment made headlines in the American press and raised some puzzled cries of "Why?" But when a group of Latin American leaders suggested a long-range multilateral aid program, the administration gave them a cold shoulder: traditional policies were sufficient. These included extension of credit by the Import-Export Bank for the purchase of American exports, loans from the International Bank, Point Four technical aid programs, military aid to help increase the strength of Latin American armies so that they might resist Russian invasions, and suggestions to follow conservative fiscal policies that would avoid foreign exchange deficits and consequent import controls.

In 1960, when Democrat and Republican vied with one another to attack Castro verbally, the administration belatedly changed its mind: it suggested a $500 million aid program for the rest of Latin America, for which people throughout Latin America ironically thanked Castro; it agreed that American aid could go to state-controlled enterprises or nationalized industries; and it joined in setting up an Inter-American Development Bank.

The new Kennedy administration was staffed with thinkers from the universities who, caught up in the academic concern for the problems of emerging countries, had worked out elaborate schemes of the economic, social, and political requisities for economic development. They conceived the Alliance for Progress. The Alliance would be the answer to Fidelismo, to Communism, to the whole tense situation throughout Latin America that produced the need and demand for radical solutions.

Therefore, while Kennedy did battle with Castro over captured Cuban refugees (whose ransom by private groups he later felt impelled to sanction), he also presented a new broad-scale program that would attack the underlying causes. At a conference of finance ministers at Punta del Este, Uruguay, in August 1961, the American states signed a series of multilateral agreements that provided for three aspects of the Alliance: a promise of $20 billion for development aid from the United States over a 10-year period; commitment to fundamental social change on the part of participating governments, in the form of land reform and changes in the frequently regressive and inequitable tax structures; and a plan to make a group of Latin American economists working under the Economic and Social Council of the Organization of American States a clearing house for coordination of long-range development plans presented by participating states. In this way development funds could be equitably apportioned and perhaps some measure of economic integration be achieved. Cuba was specifically excluded from the Alliance.

(The Alliance failed, ultimately. Its aims were perhaps too grandiose given the obstacles to and complexities of development in Latin America. Some countries showed rapid growth, but it was often unbalanced in a politically unpalatable way, and other areas made no progress relative to continued rapid population growth. Many Latin American analysts charged that it was too much to hope that societies would reform themselves: revolution was therefore necessary, yet revolution was the one thing the United States hoped to forestall by its reformist policies. While one school of economists placed their hope in reform through international institutions that would redistribute the gains from trade between poor and rich countries, another came to develop the idea that the chief obstacle to development lay in the very trade and investment relations with the rich countries that the others relied on. In the face of such divergent analyses it was hard to develop coherent policies.)

While the Kennedy administration expanded Eisenhower's programs to deal with what it considered to be fundamental problems of Latin America, the Organization of American States became the scene of an American attempt to obtain multilateral action against a Cuba more and more closely tied to the Communist bloc. Castro, in December 1961, announced that he was and always had been a Marxist-Leninist (not, as some immediately translated it, a Communist Party member). Krushchev still hedged his bets on Castro in 1961, seeing him as a too romantic rebel; economic support was still tentative, and Soviet technical aid personnel vied with many from China. But Castro's personal blend of Marxism-Leninism had wide appeal in Latin America, his subversive activities became more intense and, in the United Nations, Cuba became to all intents and purposes a member of he Communist bloc. The process was a strange one. It was not one of Russian and Communist subversion; rather Castro, influenced by Communists and radicals around him, handed Cuba to Khrushchev as a satellite state. There was much evidence to support the view that Khrushchev was unsure what to do with the gift, particularly one as provocative to the United States.

But the United States *was* determined—in a more respectable manner —to do something; there was evidence that as Castro continued his activities even left-wing forces in the Americas were becoming fearful of having their thunder stolen by someone too closely tied to Russia. On the basis of this growing disenchantment with Castro, he United States suggested that the Organization of American States undertake collective sanctions against his regime, now that it had come under extrahemispheric domination.

Under considerable pressure from the United States fourteen of the OAS Foreign Ministers, meeting at Punta del Este in January 1962 voted to exclude Cuba from participation in the inter-American system. Brazil, Argentina, Chile, Ecuador, Bolivia, and Mexico—the most populous and in most cases the most democratic of Latin American states—abstained. There were internal repercussions from the voting, too. In Argentina, the military forced President Frondizi to reverse his position and assume a harder line against Castro. The issue then figured in an election which saw heavy returns for Peronists, and brought a confusing military coup to annul the returns. In April 1962 the Brazilian government, following a more "independent" line in foreign policy, reestablished diplomatic relations with the Soviet Union. (But this government, too, was later overthrown by a military coup in which there were charges of CIA intervention.) Collective intervention appeared to achieve few results in Cuba.

THE MISSILE CRISIS

Quiet reigned in Cuban-United States relations for a few months; the Caribbean was more concerned with a coup that ended the long and hated Trujillo regime in the Dominican Republic, with the effort to replace it by a more democratic regime and an attempt by the Trujillos to regain power—foiled partly by a show of force on the part of United States naval forces. Then in mid-year, it appeared that the Soviet Union had decided to provide massive support for Cuba. The economic situation in the island appeared grave; Krushchev apparently decided that he could not allow the first Soviet bloc member in the Americas to collapse. Increased shipments from the Soviet Union, however, included a large number of modern weapons, accompanied by military technicians. In September American Congressmen charged that the Soviet Union was shipping nuclear rockets to Cuba.

Military analysts, with little corroborating evidence, were skeptical. Many had long thought that American liquid-fueled rockets around the Soviet Union were obsolete and ought to be withdrawn: such rockets, which could easily be destroyed in a first strike, had no retaliatory value. This would also be true of Soviet weapons in Cuba and, given the superiority in American nuclear weapons under the increased procurement program of the Kennedy administration, the Russians would know that they could not afford a first strike.

In August, in response to stepped-up Soviet shipments and intelligence information, the administration increased aerial surveillance of Cuba; in September flights were hampered by bad weather and by publicity over Chinese destruction of a U-2 plane sold to the Nationalist Chinese. Then, in early October, and unmistakably by October 14, photographs showed emplacements for Soviet intermediate range ballistic missiles plus assembled Soviet jet bombers. What Khrushchev had never done for China he had now done for Cuba, ninety miles away from the American coast.

The Kennedy administration reacted promptly. Discarding the alternatives of protesting to the Soviet Union, or of bringing the matter up before the United Nations or the OAS, it considered three others: a direct attack upon Cuba, mounted swiftly and preceded by an air strike to destroy missiles and planes before they could be launched; an air strike alone; or a naval blockade of the island until Khrushchev would withdraw the weapons.*

---

* Secretary of Defense McNamara first suggested that the weapons in Cuba did not change the strategic balance and therefore did not call for action that might bring hostilities. But others in Kennedy's entourage rejected the view. The political consequences were too great.

The first two might provoke nuclear war, and would certainly cause a tremendous reaction and revulsion against the United States throughout the world. They would cause not only Cuban deaths, but also Russian deaths. If Cubans resisted, banded behind Fidel Castro, there might be a nasty prolonged situation in Cuba after the initial conquest. Although it was unlikely that Khrushchev would immediately retaliate against the United States, given American power to strike back, he might respond in Berlin, in Turkey, in Iran, or in Iraq, and escalation would be a possibility.

The third choice had its own special dangers. If the Russian ships tried to run the blockade (which would extend only to weapons), this would force further, more painful decisions. It was also possible that the weapons build-up had been completed and that the Soviet Union would now only be shipping the kind of conventional supplies to which the blockade did not extend. In this case, the policy would be insufficient, and further steps would have to follow.

Nevertheless, the administration decided on the naval blockade, calling it a "quarantine" in order to conform in some way to traditional international law (whose legal categories, however, hardly appeared to cover the kind of new situation that involved an internal build-up of rapid-fire nuclear weapons). It kept in reserve a contingency invasion plan.

Preparations for the quarantine were carried out in utmost secrecy, using the cover of previously scheduled naval maneuvers in the Caribbean. Florida was heavily reinforced, and the administration took what precautions it could against the outbreak of a large-scale conflagration. On Monday evening, October 22, President Kennedy, having previously informed the Soviet Union of his intention, broadcast to the nation his decision to institute the quarantine on October 24. Having first taken the action, he then called the Security Council and the OAS Council into session. The latter voted 10 to 0 to authorize the use of armed force to prevent further Soviet arms shipments into Cuba. In the UN Security Council the Soviet Union found itself caught in a falsehood when it denied the presence of weapons which the United States was able to prove were there. It then argued that there were no *offensive* weapons in Cuba: the Soviet Union had supplied missiles to Cuba so that the Caribbean country could deter the United States from attacking it, and the Bay of Pigs incident and subsequent American actions gave ample evidence to suspect that an invasion was imminent.

Secretary General U Thant of the United Nations asked both sides to suspend action for a two- or three-week period so that the crisis could be resolved by peaceful negotiation. Khrushchev agreed, and Kennedy agreed to negotiate—on condition that the blockade would continue until negotiations for withdrawal of the bases.

Never before had world tension been so high. Modern communications made the confrontation a public matter everywhere. Throughout the world, people waited anxiously to see what course would be taken by the twenty-five Soviet vessels heading for Cuba. Would they turn back? Would they submit peacefully to American search? Or would the first encounter lead to nuclear war?

A number of the vessels, presumably carrying arms to Cuba, turned back. Others, carrying only petroleum and similar products, were allowed to proceed after search. Khrushchev had drawn back. The orders to the Russian ships were accompanied by an offer to Kennedy for mutual withdrawal of bases from Cuba and bases in Turkey, but Kennedy refused the offer, and Khrushchev agreed to stop work on bases, dismantle the weapons under United Nations supervision and ship them back to Russia. Kennedy, in return, pledged that he would not invade Cuba and that the quarantine would be lifted when the United Nations had taken the necessary measures.

But what of Castro? It appeared that he had been a pawn in a great power play, and that Khrushchev was now abandoning him without consultation. The Cuban Premier, after inviting U Thant to Havana, refused to allow United Nations or Red Cross inspection, and asked for American withdrawal from the Guantanamo naval base, which was on Cuban territory.

At this point, Kennedy made his concession; despite knowledge that domestic criticism would rise, satisfied that the Soviet Union was beginning a withdrawal, he determined to rely on naval and aerial surveillance. The United States did not insist on further inspection. In short order the weapons were withdrawn.

It was an extraordinary episode. Khrushchev, criticized bitterly by the Chinese for his cautious revisionist attitudes, had gambled heavily. Two men made it clear again to the world that in spite of the appearance of new centers of power, they and they alone had the awesome power to destroy much of the world. Khrushchev apparently wanted to bolster his position within the Communist world by one bold stroke, to solidify the shaky position of the Cuban regime in the face of growing American concern and in the same move increase its subversive possibilities. But he was also trying to restore a nuclear balance that his military experts must have told him was shifting numerically to the side of the United States. He withdrew with two gains: an enhanced reputation in the non-Communist world for acting cautiously at a dangerous moment, and a promise that the United States would not invade Cuba to overthrow Castro. But within the Communist block the effect was much worse for him. The Russian-Chinese break was still not fully in the open. The Chinese nevertheless accused Khrushchev of dangerous "adventurism" in putting the missiles into Cuba, and cowardice in withdrawing them in the face of the United States—a "paper tiger." The incident contributed not only to a rapid worsening of Russian-Chinese relations, but also to internal opposition to Khrushchev. It was hard for outside observers to analyze, but Khrushchev, in using de-Stalinization to get rid of opponents, had alienated many old Party men; he had risked all in 1956 and the result was Hungary, from which he recouped. Then, with Sputnik, he had shifted to a forward foreign policy, yet cut back on military expenditures, thus alienating the Armed Forces; in an attempt to recoup, he had placed the missiles in Cuba while his diplomats had denied before the whole world that he was doing it—and in a move to compensate for weakness had risked destruction of the whole world. There is no question that his overthrow two years later was linked to the missile episode as well as to gathering internal enmity for his eternal meddling in all spheres of administration.

Kennedy found much support for his firm stand and the restraint that he, too, displayed. Still, outside of the United States he was criticized for having instituted the dangerous blockade instead of having chosen a less risky alternative, and many thought he should have bargained away the obsolete American bases in Turkey (which, in fact, the administration had already decided to abandon). Some thought that this was the sole motive for Khrushchev's action: it would make the United States realize what it meant to have such bases so close to its border. Yet while many people drew a comparison between the two sets of bases, others pointed out that in fact the many Soviet bases were on the borders of the Western bloc, and that only a United States move to establish such bases in a country previously friendly to the Soviet Union—Poland, for example— would have been comparable. They also knew that Kennedy, by limiting himself to the action taken, would come under further attack at home for not having liquidated the whole Cuban problem—and he did.

Several events followed immediately upon the Cuban confrontation. The Kennedy administation, while denying domestic criticism that a deal was involved, announced withdrawal of its Thor and Jupiter IRBM's from their European bases. Their functions would now be carried out by Polaris submarine-based missiles, and the new solid-fueled Minuteman intercontinental rockets. In early 1963 Khruschev agreed to a "hot line" between Moscow and Washington. This direct teletype link had long been under consideration; it would allow rapid communication between the two capitals in case of a nuclear accident, a small outbreak of violence that threatened to escalate, or a confrontation such as had occurred in Cuba. In a time when almost instantaneous response was possible, it might give the two major power a chance to avert a response neither wanted. Finally, the crisis appears to have influenced the Soviet Union and the United States to adopt the partial nuclear test ban agreement of mid-1963. From that time forward, neither country has produced an airborne nuclear explosion, although both have continued underground tests.

There is also little doubt that the United States, by informing but not consulting its allies on steps that could have led to nuclear war, strengthened de Gaulle's determination to build France's own independent nuclear deterrent force.

More important, perhaps, were the effects of the crisis on strategic policy on both sides.

Some American argued that the showdown demonstrated how well deterrence worked. Others went further, reasoning that the confrontation showed a necessity of having an overwhelming superiority in missiles in order to be able to prevent the threat of nuclear blackmail. But some analysts drew an opposite conclusion: it was the American preponderance that had stimulated Khrushchev to put the missiles in Cuba; the preponderance might have enabled Kennedy to get out all right, but it had gotten him into trouble in the first place. The answer, therefore, was not in continuing to maintain the lead, with all the dangers this implied and the unmeasurable social costs, nor in simple arms control measures, but in genuine disarmament.

There may have been debate in the Soviet Union, but the Russians gave their own simple answer. Khrushchev and his successors, determined never again to be faced with the superiority and the opportunities for pressure it gave to the Americans, vastly increased their expenditures for nuclear weapons. The buildup took time; it increased in 1964 and accelerated again in 1967. At this point the United States had 1054 intercontinental ballistic missiles and the Soviet Union 400. The United States maintained the same number in subsequent years while working on research and development or replacing older missiles with newer types. But the Soviet Union increased their number to 1618 by the time of the SALT agreement in 1972, while matching the United States in the number of seaborne missiles. The rough parity achieved by the early seventies explains much: willingness of the Soviet leaders to come to the SALT agreements; willingness, too, to carry out an active and advanced foreign policy in the Middle East, South Asia, and the Indian Ocean and to confront China in the Far East, secure in the knowledge that they had nothing to fear from the United States. Khrushchev had gambled on the illusion of greatly superior power and had made far-flung commitments; he had actually bluffed with nuclear weapons; he had had to succumb to American pressure. His successors would never feel the need to do so.

Although economically weak and preoccupied with China, they could negotiate with Europe and the United States, give little, and obtain, finally, recognition of the bloc in Europe as well as excite the Americans into giving them extended credits and advanced technology. Since the United States had been tarnished by its interventionism and living beyond it means, the Russians would be able to get Nixon to accept nuclear parity and perhaps induce the Americans to withdraw from Europe which would then be easier to deal with. It was all, in part at least, the legacy of Cuba and of the episodes now to be discussed.

DOMINICAN INTERLUDE: 1965

Earlier American intervention in the post-World War II period had been equipped with the ideological conviction that such action prevented a drift into totalitarianism, a political system from which, whether Communist or Fascist, there was then no recourse. It had taken outside intervention to help Europe throw off the totalitarianism of the Nazis; now, as Hungary had shown in 1956, only outside intervention could have allowed a people to throw off the totalitarianism of the Communists. Communism could be imposed by a small minority, masquerading perhaps in some other guise, as had been true in Cuba. Once established, it would destroy all opposition, as it did in Cuba, in North Vietnam in the late 1950s, in China all through the period since it had come to power in 1949. In democratic, constitutional systems the individual had rights that could be protected and he could participate in changing a government that was inefficient or corrupt or disliked. To these comforting precepts Americans clung in the early 1960s. They did not mean that the United States would try to impose its own system. But the memory of Nazi totalitarianism was still strong; the Russians had themselves revealed the continued evils a Communist totalitarianism would produce—however noble the ends to which it was supposed to aspire; and the United States, to help the "free world" remain strong enough against the growth of the Communist system, must continue to resist the encroachments of the Communists. It was for these reasons that it had begun to abandon the 1930s doctrine of nonintervention, had persuaded reluctant Latin American states to sign the Caracas Declaration in 1954, which stated that a Communist government was itself incompatible with the Inter-American system, and had sought a way to obtain multilaterally sanctioned interventions to prevent what it called "Communist intervention." The development of popular Castroism in Cuba was not enough to shake either the faith that lay behind the new interventionism, nor to forfeit all support by other states, because Castro had lost much support both by allowing the

Russian missiles to be placed in Cuba and by his sponsorship of the idea of guerrilla warfare and subversion as a means of spreading his revolution. But the Dominican episode of 1965 did much more.

Six months earlier Lyndon B. Johnson had won a sweeping victory against Senator Barry Goldwater. The radicalism of the Senator's views seemed matched only by his lack of knowledge of the world. On national television, he suggested bringing pressure to bear on the Soviet Union by withdrawing diplomatic recognition, and went on to say that this, of course, would have to be done by Congress, not the President. What frightened more people were the Senator's views of the world: he rejected the notion that there were different kinds of Communists; he branded Communism as the principal disturber of peace, the enemy of all who want to be free and, therefore, an enemy that must be defeated. "Victory," not accommodation, must be the goal; the way to cement NATO, he suggested, was to give the NATO commander final authority over a stock of nuclear weapons; the United States must stop all trade with Communists. These views were what made officially neutral governments abroad give a collective sigh of relief when Johnson won overwhelmingly.

Then, in short order, Johnson began the large-scale escalation of the war in Vietnam, based on secret contingency planning done while Goldwater was attacked as trigger happy. And in April came the Dominican affair.

In 1961 the corrupt and oppressive Trujillo regime was overthrown in that island. Twenty months after the dictator's assassination, free elections put into power the mildly left-wing Dr. Juan Bosch, much favored by the Kennedy administration. But Bosch, in turn, was overthrown by a military coup in September 1963, under the pretext that his inefficient administration was unable to cope with the legacy of thirty years of Trujillo's mismanagement—and that it was too favorable to local Communists.

United States officials were generally unhappy with the development. The tendency of the Kennedy administration was to use the power of recognition or nonrecognition to foster what it considered to be democracy. There had recently been military coups in Guatemala, Ecuador, and Honduras, and to attempt to stem the tide, the Kennedy administration withheld recognition from the right-wing civilian junta that succeeded Bosch, and suspended all economic aid.

But Lyndon B. Johnson, succeeding Kennedy, apparently felt the attempt to boycott or punish military regimes—itself a form of intervention —would in the long run either fail or hurt the United States. He therefore resumed relations with the Dominican government (as well as with Honduras and the unsavory regime of Dr. Duvalier in Haiti, where for a while Kennedy had actually brought pressure to overthrow the dictator).

The junta was unsuccessful in dealing with the problems of the country. On April 24, 1964, a military revolt by young, pro-Bosch officers gained some initial successes. A counteraction by other officers produced bloody strife in the streets of Santo Domingo. Both sides appealed to the United States, and President Johnson decided to help the counter-revolution. Presumably the most important factor was that the CIA, the State Department people on the spot, and the United States military attaché were afraid that Bosch and the group around him were too inclined to allow Communist or pro-Castro activity, although they had little solid information. President Johnson, himself, seems to have feared being charged with allowing another Castro to come into power, and the American administration never made any attempt to discuss affairs with Bosch, the legally elected president and the man they had formerly favored. Instead, under a number of pretexts, American troops were sent in to prevent a rebel victory. At first, the official reason was to protect American lives. Then it became to prevent a Communist takeover—after the previously democratic forces (which the Administration had not helped) had, it was said, been taken over by Communist leadership. By May 6, 21,000 American troops were ashore, with 9000 more on ships nearby. By this time President Johnson insisted that the United States had intervened to prevent other, outside Communist-led guerrilla forces from taking power.

Yet within three weeks the United States was pressing the very junta it had supported to compromise with the rebels and arrived at a coalition government under someone who would be more widely acceptable. By this time United States officials asserted in public that the Communist elements had retreated and gone underground, seeing that they could not win.

What had happened in the meantime was a reassessment within the administration that resulted both from the enromous public outcry, almost universal condemnation from Latin America and Europe—a condemnation that echoed in the halls of the United Nations in New York—and from a realization that perhaps United States action had been precipitate. There had been no OAS sanction of the action; this was sought afterward, and was purchased only by withdrawal of support for the junta leaders, some of whom were forced into exile. The United States attempted to legitimize its action by getting the OAS to declare that American troops, bolstered by Latin American soldiers, constituted an international force. By a slim majority and with much reluctance, this was done and OAS mediators were sent to help organize a new government. In the meantime, at the United Nations, countries like Russia that were always ready to use an incident such as this one to embarrass the United States were now joined by many of the latter's allies. Consequently, the United States was not able to plead that this was a regional matter, better left to the OAS: many Latin American opponents of the United States wanted to see the United Nations involved also, believing that the OAS was too much under the influence of the United States. As a result, in addition to OAS mediators, representatives of the UN Secretary General participated in the peacemaking.

By the end of August a provisional regime had been patched together that would have to disarm the various factions, restore order, and produce a new and more permanent regime. The provisional government of Hector Godoy, Foreign Minister under Bosch, was able to do so, although it faced months of riots and continued clashes between political factions and between leftists and members of the "Inter-American Peace Force," (nine-tenths from the United States). Juan Bosch reappeared as presidential candidate, but was defeated on June 1, 1966 by more conservative Joaquin Balaguer. President Balaguer's desire for continued presence of the Inter-American Peace Force meant that the last American soldiers did not leave until September 19, 1966. In the meantime, both the provisional govxernment and the new Balaguer regime received substantial emergency economic aid from the United States.

The official view was put forward at various times by various members of the Johnson administration. Veteran diplomat Averell Harriman spelled it out in a speech at Columbus, Ohio on May 12, 1966: "Cuban-trained Communist activists infiltrated and exploited a democratically-motivated rebellion" reflecting Russian-Chinese competition. "Moscow seemingly wants to outdo in Latin America what Peiping is trying to achieve in the Far East. . . ." To prevent similar disorders, the United States pressed the OAS strongly for a permanent Inter-American Peace Force available to act in any similar situation. The suggestion fell on deaf ears. There might exist widespread fears of subversion among Latin American governments, but the wide popular dislike of intervention under any pretext outweighed them.

VIETNAM AND INDOCHINA

The Cuban and Dominican interventions, however, pale before the scope of the second Indochina war. It came to stand for all that was most wrong about American foreign policy and perhaps, too, with the United States. For many people it put the final seal on the new image of the United States.

The 1954 settlement in Indochina came on the crest of a wave of

Communist victory. Yet Ho Chi Minh accepted half a loaf—the north of the country—and promises of elections two years later. He probably did so because of Russian and Chinese prodding. But it was also true that there was little organized non-Communist nationalist opposition before him, and therefore little reason to think that the military-psychological victory of 1954 could not be transformed into political victory. If there was one uncomfortable aspect of the situation, it must have been that the Soviet Union and the People's Republic of China acquiesced as easily as they did in accepting mere partition; but the provision for elections in two years seemed to guarantee early reunion.

There were three problems. One was that the two year waiting period might see a consolidation of the many non-Communist political groups: Catholic, Buddhist, nationalist, and other. But the two years would allow for Communist consolidation in the North and penetration of the groups in the South.

The second problem was that the Vietnamese government in the South had not signed the accords, and proceeded to denounce them bitterly. But the new Prime Minister, Ngo Dinh Diem, appeared to have little base of political power, and Emperor Bao Dai, in France, had even less.

The Americans constituted the third problem. They had not signed the accords either; but they had promised not to use force to disturb them. They had also declared that they would continue to seek unity for divided nations through free elections under United Nations supervision, while viewing with grave concern "any renewal of the aggression in violation of the aforesaid agreement." To what did "aggression" refer? How much support would they provide for the Diem regime?

The 1956 elections were to be preceded by consultative conferences concerning the conditions of the elections. The Diem regime in the South argued that under no circumstances could free elections be held in the Communist North and refused even to participate in the conferences. Diem's ability to defy the call for discussions was based on the withdrawal of the French—committed to the agreements—and their replacement by a growing American presence. France still had a large and effective armed force in Vietnam at the time of the armistice, and could have exerted pressures for observation of the Geneva agreements. But, embroiled in problems in its remaining North African possessions (see above, p. 153), it withdrew the last of these forces three months before the scheduled elections, choosing rather to allow the Americans to have their own way. When Ho's government presisted over the next four years in asking Diem for conferences to work out procedures for "free general elections by secret ballot," it met only a rebuff. There are people who cite this as evidence that here was an opportunity that an oppressive Diem regime simply could not afford to explore; others point out that while Diem's government was itself repressive, Diem was correct in seeing that no opportunity for free elections could ever exist in the Communist-dominated North. It is probable that "elections" would have little meaning in the social confusion of the South or the Communist authoritarianism in the North: no organized structures needed for free elections existed in either place. What was more important was that neither Russia nor China did anything more than give the issue a measure of verbal support.

The result was that the Eisenhower administration, having decided to salvage what it could from a bad situation, saw in South Vietnam a good place to "draw the line" in Southeast Asia, and in Ngo Dinh Diem the untainted, nationalist alternative to tyrannical Communism who could build the viable political system necessary for achieving this aim. "Communism" could be contained in Vietnam. President Eisenhower returned to the image of the falling dominoes coined during the Truman administration when the decision was made to aid the French: if the somewhat artificial state of South Vietnam fell to the Communists, then one after another the other countries of Southeast Asia would too. The commitment was not unconditional: the President's offer of support asked for "assurances as to the standards of performance it (the Government of Vietnam) would be able to maintain in the event . . . aid were supplied," and expressed an expectation that aid would be met by "performance on the part of the Government of Vietnam in undertaking needed reforms." But the offer was reinforced by negotiation of the Southeast Asia Collective Defense Treaty and its accompanying Protocol. The signatories were Thailand, Pakistan, the Philippines, the United States, Britain, France, Australia, and New Zealand, and the protocol extended coverage to Laos, Cambodia, and South Vietnam. Together they pledged each of the signatory states to recognize the danger to one in an aggression upon any other, and to consult on measures to be taken under their constitutional processes. To this it added the provision that if the sovereignty or political integrity of any state signatory to the treaty or named in the protocol was "threatened in any way other than by armed attack," or if it was "affected by any fact or any situation which might endanger the peace of the area" the parties could consult on measures to be taken for the common defense.

In this manner the United States signaled its opposition not only to armed aggression across a national frontier, but to what Secretary of State Dulles called "indirect aggression."

In the north, predictably, the Communists spent the next years consolidating their hold in a manner reminiscent of Communists everywhere. This involved purges, the dissolution of opposition groups, the liquidation of arbitrarily designated classes through expropriation of all private property and confiscatory taxation, and the execution of large numbers of both dissident or potentially dissident individuals. It was done within a framework of village denunciations of individuals, "thought rectification" campaigns, and a fairly bloody collectivization of the land. The leaders of North Vietnam themselves acknowledged "errors" in their program after they had had to repress a revolt in Nghe An province.

But the story in the south was one of progressive alienation of all of the groups and individuals who might have been persuaded to support Diem, and with whom he might have come to terms. It was one of harsh repression, nepotism, and corruption, and reform measures halfheartedly applied, of a government based on the traditional mandarinate model, apparently no longer suited to the conditions of contemporary times.

Diem received sufficient American aid to keep his government alive. A large part of the population was indifferent, but there were many who were receptive to non-Communist nationalism. Among these were the over 800,000 Catholics who had fled from the north; unfortunately, it was from among these rather than from varied southern groupings that Diem staffed his government. There were curious semireligious, semipolitical sects in Vietnam that in various ways derived income from the police, prostitution, or gambling, and that controlled whole areas and fielded their own armies: the Binh Xuyen, the Cao Dai, and the Hoa Hao. These Diem had to crush as systems of organized power, and to the surprise of many, he was able to, despite their support by the French; but he did nothing to reconcile their members to the government, more and more to be dominated by his own family.

Ridding himself of the Emperor Bao Dai by plebiscite, Diem alienated the monarchists. Soon the urban intellectuals opposed the closed regime, and a peasant opposition developed when lands seized by the Vietminh earlier were taken from the peasants to which the Vietminh had given them and returned to the original landlords. Any organized political opposition became a target for imprisonment with the result that few potential political leaders would support Diem. By 1960 even his army was in revolt, and the attempt to keep it under wraps by a constant shifting around of commanders and of setting unit against unit simply created inefficiency and disaffection. In the last stages, urgently needed units were kept from fighting the Vietcong to protect the regime. Once the Vietcong revolt broke out in the late 1950s, the attempt to deal with its rural terrorism and to deprive it of a rural economic base by creating strongholds into which the peasants could be herded backfired, creating mainly a peasantry as resentful of government protection as it was of Vietcong exactions and terrorism. In 1963 militant Buddhist factions clashed with the police and army over repression, and Buddhist monks publicly burned themselves to death to protest the regime. Rather than compromise, as his American advisors wished, Diem sent troops to raid the Buddhist pagodas; students joined the revolt; finally Diem's entire general staff moved against him. As one friendly American observer put it,

> Saigon, those last days of Diem, was an incredible place. One felt that one was witnessing an entire social structure coming apart at the seams. In horror, Americans helplessly watched Diem tear apart the fabric of Vietnamese society more effectively than the Communists had ever been able to do. It was the most efficient act of his entire career.

After years of publicly unconditional support the United States tried to put pressure on Diem to reach some kind of compromise with opposition groups or to step down. It was too late; on November 1, 1963, after intricate plotting, and with American foreknowledge, Diem's generals overthrew him and killed him and his brother.

True to its original conception of the situation, the United States had continued to aid Diem throughout this period. The views of Dulles, former Vice President Nixon, and others were on record: extension of Vietminh power to South Vietnam would mean an increase in Sino-Soviet bloc power, an extension of Soviet Russian imperialism. Moreover, Mr. Nixon pointed out, "the main target of the Communists in Indochina, as it was in Korea, is Japan. Conquest of areas so vital to Japan's economy would reduce Japan to an economic satellite of the Soviet Union . . ." [!]

Thus, the United States aided Diem in consolidating power, both by seeing that funds were cut off to his opponents and by varied programs of direct aid to him. At one point in 1955, when President Eisenhower's emissary in Vietnam, General Lawton Collins, flew to Washington to recommend "dumping" Diem, Diem forced the United States' hand by taking decisive military action against opponents, using the army that United States policy had already put into his hands. The administration then backed him in his refusal to hold the elections provided for in the 1954 agreements and, on the pretext that China was aiding North Vietnam's army, helped him reorganize his own. Between 1956 and 1961, when John F. Kennedy became President of the United States, three-fifths of United States aid to Diem was military in nature; by 1961 the United States had about 600 men in its Military Assistance Advisory Group. There were, in addition, various technical and administrative aid programs underway. And in the United States, a highly favorable climate had been created for Diem by a variety of publicists and writers, including the influential Cardinal Spellman. He was presented as incorruptible, ascetic, and nationalist—the very model of the man who could create a free alternative to Communist tyranny. Diem visited the United States in March 1957 and addressed a joint session of Congress.

But by 1959, the insurrection had begun in the south.

The official United States view was that the insurrection was instigated, maintained, and enlarged by the government in Hanoi, directed by Ho Chi Minh, and ultimately a creature of the international Communist conspiracy.

The weight of evidence supports another view: that the insurrection was local, begun by groups resisting Diem, some of whom had been in the Vietminh resistance against the French, and some of whom were obviously Communist. Many Vietminh *were* non-Communist; in the earlier war the enemy was clearly foreign. In the second war, after 1958, and until the massive American intervention of 1965, the situation was far less clear for a Vietnamese patriot. Opposition and ultimate aims were varied; there were ethnic minority groups, members of the religious sects destroyed by Diem, intellectuals and students, and party leaders denied a role in government. At first their one common aim was to bring Diem down. In December 1960, five weeks after an attempted army coup against Diem, which showed he might be vulnerable, this coalesced in the National Liberation Front (NLF). The Front's fighters came to be known popularly as the Vietcong. The front came out for ultimate unification of Vietnam after the ouster of Diem and the Americans.

There seems to be little doubt that at the outset the Vietcong had scant aid from Hanoi. Even the American State Department White Paper of 1965 justifying American intervention could list few arms captured from the Vietcong other than ones the Vietcong had seized from the South Vietnamese Army or had retained after partition in 1954. On the other hand, Hanoi, Moscow, and Peking all gave ideological support to the Front and the Vietcong. There is much evidence to sustain the view that the North had its hand forced by resistance fighters in the South, who began to fight back against Diem's repression even though Hanoi had done nothing. Within Hanoi there seems to have been a "Russian" faction, who regarded the resistance fighters as adventurists, and a "Chinese" faction, who wanted them not only to be helped, but saw such help as a blow in the developing breach between "revisionist" Russian Khrushchevism, with its line of "peaceful coexistence" and the more militant line being taken by the Chinese (see below, Chapter eight).

Eventually the Hanoi government, having given up on political pressure for reunification, came to support the Front fully. In mid-1959 it accepted the resort to armed force; in September 1960, it called for violent overthrow of Diem and removal of American imperialist rule. It gave little concrete help in the immediate years to come, but substantial northern-trained cadres infiltrated the South. The basic tactic of the Communists in South Vietnam was to mobilize the rural populace through the NLF and Vietcong activity, to destroy the administrative apparatus of the central government through assassination and terrorism, and ultimately to unify Vietnam.

The South Vietnamese government fought back, even though the military who toppled Diem did so in part because they felt he used too much military strength simply to keep himself and his family in power rather than to defeat the Vietcong. And in the process of fighting back they turned to the United States and the Kennedy administration for more aid.

Walt W. Rostow, Deputy Special Assistant to the President for National Security Affairs, gave a typical official view of what the struggle in Vietnam was all about: the crises in Cuba, the Congo, Laos and Vietnam —all current—were the result of "a successful Communist breaching . . . of the cold-war truce lines which had emerged from the Second World War and its aftermath. In different ways each had arisen from the efforts of the International Communist movement to exploit inherent instabilities of the underdeveloped areas of the non-Communist world, and each had a guerrilla-warfare component."*

This was the view presented to Kennedy in April 1961 by a special interdepartmental task force, a report by the Joint Chiefs of Staff at about the same time, and by a special mission in October headed by Rostow and General Maxwell D. Taylor, later US Ambassador to Vietnam, and a long-time critic of the Eisenhower administration's military policy, which he felt had concentrated too long on nuclear deterrence, and not enough on the possibility of small conventional wars such as the one now being fought in Southeast Asia. *All* of these reports to Kennedy recommended that United States combat troops be sent to Vietnam in pursuit of the United States commitment to hold the area against the advance of world Communism.

The Task Force Report and the other reports emphasized the importance of forcing Diem to make reforms and broaden his political base. But this recommendation—repeated so many times—was constantly lost in the shuffle. All also urged support for an increase in Diem's army, and this was forthcoming.

---

* Quoted in Gruening, *Vietnam Folly*, p. 199. It is important to understand this statement, for the ideas underlying it were widely accepted by American leaders and were fostered by Khrushchev in speech after speech, as well as by Marxist proponents of guerrilla warfare.

Kennedy rejected the troop advice but chose an unsatisfactory alternative: he greatly expanded the military effort, sending in combat support units, air combat and helicopter teams, more military advisers and instructors, and Green Berets—the special forces—to train South Vietnamese in antiguerrilla warfare. None of these were combat troops. Kennedy, in 1954, had warned that no one could hold Vietnam unless its government had support of the people, but had called it "the cornerstone of the Free World in Southeast Asia, the keystone to the arch, the finger in the dike."* Now he was quoted as having said that "if it were ever converted into a white man's war, we would lose as the French had lost a decade earlier." But the support units soon came into the line of fire. By the end of 1963 there were 15,000 Americans in Vietnam.

The American press kept the people informed of the growing commitment, and supported it. *Time* magazine for August 4, 1961, citing the "impressive achievements" of the Diem regime, declared " . . . if the United States cannot or will not save South Vietnam from the Communist assault, no Asian nation can ever again feel safe in putting its faith in the United States." And two years later, having consistently supported American commitment, the *New York Times* wrote on September 6, 1963 "their war (is) our war . . . a war from which we cannot retreat and which we dare not lose." Two weeks later it wrote that "the stakes in Southeast Asia are too high for us to see the war lost."

There is some evidence that Kennedy's growing disenchantment with Diem in the months before the latter's death was matched by a disenchantment with the whole operation in Vietnam, and a determination to pull out after the 1964 elections,* but Kennedy died in Dallas and Lyndon B. Johnson became President. And Johnson, at first far more concerned with domestic reform within the United States, reluctantly opted to win the war by military means.

In 1964 the new President, determined not to make the Vietnam war an American war, was subject to conflicting advice. Within the Congress a Republican group advocated that the United States take over the fighting from the ineffective and demoralized troops of the Republic of Vietnam. Leaders within the administration urged a greater effort. In May, Johnson discussed with his cabinet the possibility of a Congressional resolution that would buttress his authority to use American forces in Vietnam. On the other side, distinguished political commentators began to publicly oppose the extent of American involvement—people like George

---

* Quoted in Chester L. Cooper, *The Lost Crusade* (Dodd, Mead & Co., New York, 1970) , p. 168.

* Kenneth O'Donnell and David Powers, *Johnny, We Hardly Knew Ye* (Boston-Toronto: Little, Brown & Co., 1970) , pp. 13–18.

Kennan, the architect of containment, who had asked whether anyone had really considered how strategically valuable Vietnam was to the United States, and Hans J. Morgenthau, whose writings always stressed the role that power played in politics, but who suggested that American policy was based on the outmoded view that the Communist countries constituted a single bloc, failing to take into account the divergent trends within the bloc. American involvement against the Vietcong coupled with threats of attack against the north forced North Vietnam to rely on China. Yet the Vietnamese had always feared Chinese power, Morgenthau argued, and whether Communist or not were inclined to independence of the sort Eastern European Communist countries had with respect to Russia. He supported some form of neutralization for the entire area of Indochina, including Laos, where earlier the Eisenhower administration had tried to support a right-wing government against the Communist Pathet Lao. The situation had been more-or-less stabilized by an international conference, but the Pathet Lao had again stepped up their attack against government and neutralist troops (see below, pp. 284–287).

On January 31, 1964, President de Gaulle reasserted French interest in the area: he disassociated himself from the American effort, suggested neutralization, and proceeded to recognize the government of Communist China. Few moves could have been more irritating to the American administration, whose members feared that the suggestion would undermine whatever Vietnamese will to fight still existed, as well as encourage the neutralist tendencies of Prince Sihanouk of Cambodia, who like others, had come to believe that the best course was to come to terms with China.

In the meantime, in Vietnam, one coup succeeded another as the officers who had deposed Diem battled among themselves.

In the 1964 Presidential campaign in the United States, Johnson painted his opponent, Senator Barry Goldwater, as a trigger-happy and reckless man, who might well plunge us into nuclear war. Goldwater had, indeed, advocated the use of nuclear weapons to "defoliate" hidden jungle trails through which North Vietnam was supporting the Vietcong. Johnson reiterated his theme:

> There are those who say you ought to go north and drop bombs, to try to wipe out the supply lines, and they think that we should escalate the war. We don't want our American boys to do the fighting for Asian boys. We don't want to get involved in a nation with 700 million people and get tied down in a land war in Asia.

Yet within the next year, this was precisely what he was to do. The action never had all the consequences his antiwar critics were to forecast: it did not bring Russia and China together again after they split with one another in the late fifties. Nor did it make China intervene directly in the war. But the consequences it did have were hardly those foreseen by the advocates of escalation.

In August, before the really tough Presidential campaigning, Johnson obtained from the Congress the so-called Tonkin Gulf Resolution, by a vote of 416 to 0 in the House and 88 to 2 in the Senate. In it the Congress gave virtual approval to the administration's version of what had happened in the area, and authorized its taking all steps necessary to halt further aggression, assist by military means all countries in the SEATO system, and restore international peace and security.

The occasion for the resolution, designed to ensure Johnson of backing for any action he chose to take in the area, was a double attack upon United States naval vessels in the Gulf of Tonkin, in international waters, by North Vietnamese torpedo boats. There was little debate or question as the Congress heard about the incidents and rushed through the resolution. Later on, its members were to find that the details of the attack as reported to them were dubious, indeed, and that it appeared that the American vessels, the USS *Maddox* and USS *C. Turner Joy,* had been gathering intelligence in part for South Vietnamese hit-and-run attacks on the North Vietnamese coastline, carried out as one of an intensified set of pressures under direct American command. In any event, Johnson ordered retaliatory attacks upon North Vietnamese shore establishments and proceeded to order large numbers of naval and air units into the area. Quite obviously, since the retaliation was far greater than what was warranted by the attacks, the President had seized upon the occasion to attack North Vietnam so as to discourage it from increasing support to the Vietcong.

In the next five months, despite repeated attempts by third parties to arrange negotiations, the administration made the fateful decision for larger-scale escalation: bombing of the North and combat operations by American forces in the South. The reason seems to have been that the situation in South Vietnam was simply crumbling: coup succeeded coup. "A parade of meaningless names marched across headlines, mixed with reports of new Vietcong gains."* Riots, demoralization, and opposition to the war spread through the South. Johnson and those around him were determined not to withdraw; Hanoi, obviously sensing a winning situation, was determined not to compromise.

It was easy for the administration to find new occasions for escalation: a Vietcong attack against a base at Pleiku on February 7, 1965, led to a

---

* A US Public Affairs Officer in Saigon, quoted in Gruening, *Vietnam Folly,* p. 257.

retaliatory strike. A second attack on another base brought further retaliation. Only now, with no recourse to Congress or public announcement, the air strikes against the North became continuous. (The Pleiku retaliation took place at the moment that Soviet Premier Kosygin was visiting North Vietnam, having just received an appeal for mediation from President Shastri of India.) On March 6, two Marine battalions landed at Danang for "limited duty" related to perimeter defense of airfields. The nation was assured that although these were combat units, their role was to be strictly defensive. Soon United States casualties served as the excuse for reinforcements, and by June the White House admitted that troops were authorized to enter into combat under carefully defined and limited conditions—"nothing new." By the end of the summer the United States was at war. The State Department White Paper of February 27, 1965 issued to prove North Vietnamese aggression became famous for one thing: its lack of evidence.

The next three years witnessed a continuous growth in the American effort, an increased involvement of North Vietnam in the actual fighting, continual efforts by third parties to get negotiations started, and growing and bitter opposition to the war within and without the United States. There was horror in the sheer immensity of the United States effort directed against guerrillas and the tiny country of North Vietnam, in the "search and destroy" methods used, in the constant "body counts" reported by the United States military, and dubiously legal and dreadful weapons employed. There was a terrible irony in the fact that most intelligence reports through the years denied the utility of the widespread bombing. Yet enormous B–52 intercontinental bombers dropped more tons of bombs on the tiny hamlets and jungle trails of Vietnam than were dropped in all of World War II. The fact that the United States tried to carry out a limited war (but not one very "limited" for the Vietnamese) while maintaining relative normality at home meant that one segment of the population—young men of draft age—faced combat duty, while the rest of the populace went about its business as usual: there was no sense of common necessity and effort. And so the divisions deepened. In 1967 black leader Martin Luther King, long in the forefront in the struggle for civil rights, linked the struggle to the war in Vietnam: the antiwar movement and the civil rights battle were one and the same, a movement directed against the institutions that had led the United States down a pathway to disaster. From this point on the antiwar movement assumed a more radical character.

What especially dismayed observers was the inability of the United States administration to accept one point. It continually justified the battle as one against an extension of Communist power. But certainly the

Vietnamese Communists viewed it as a civil war between Vietnamese factions in which the United States had intervened, and where for years the United States had propped up clearly unpopular governments that could not have existed without United States support. The Chinese and other Marxists insisted that Vietnam was the test case for wars of national liberation against the oppressive political systems in underdeveloped countries that were maintained only by world capitalism—that is, by the benefits their ruling classes obtained through international trade—and the United States administration used the Chinese position to justify its intervention since it seemed to show that China *was* behind such wars. But to the people of Vietnam the war was their own affair in which the United States had intervened at the request of a particular faction. One consequence was that while there were many attempts by the American administration and by various intermediaries to get negotiations started, they foundered upon the American desire for compromise, which was interpreted to mean that if America stopped the bombing, the North Vietnamese should stop infiltration into the South or stop Vietcong attacks on towns in the South. But the North Vietnamese refused. The Americans in their view, were the aggressor, and it was up to them to stop their aggression. Why, in justice, should the victim do something in return for having the attacker stop attacking him? (The same was true of China, where the United States had interposed the Seventh Fleet between Taiwan and the mainland in 1950 to prevent "Communist expansion"; to the Chinese it meant that the United States had intervened in a civil war to keep a rival's claim to power alive. All moves by the United States in the 1960s to better relations with the People's Republic of China came up against this impasse. To the Chinese, the United States was *still* intervening in their unfinished civil war.)

The United States had acted on old balance of power principles—act to prevent an increase of power of your potential opponents—but at a time and place and in a way that made them seem irrelevant and that destroyed any utility they might have had. In the nineteenth century it was still possible to trade off areas on such principles with little thought as to what their populace wanted. In the middle of the twentieth century, the era of mass politics, it was no longer possible to do so. Hanson Baldwin might write in the *New York Times* that it was better to fight and block the Chinese in Vietnam than later in Hawaii. But critics replied that a Communist Vietnam need not have meant an increment in Chinese power, and asked what analysis of Chinese power could lead one to think that they would have a capacity—or any interest—in fighting in Hawaii? A more careful involvement than the mere backing of Diem might have even meant that all of Vietnam would not be Communist; yet even if it had become Communist, the United States, in the mid-sixties, got along better with some Communist powers, such as the Rumania visited by President Nixon in 1969, than it did with some of its own allies. On May 6, 1965, a week after United States marines landed in the Dominican Republic and on the occasion of a Senate vote of 88 to 3 for supplemental funds for the war in Vietnam, the *New York Times,* changing, editorialized: " . . . the Johnson doctrine means that emphasis is now going to be on resisting the advance of Communism anywhere in the world with military force rather than on differentiations between various kinds of Communism or trying to coexist with any of them. The United States gives the appearance of heading toward the unenviable self-righteous and self-defeating position of world policeman." Time and again administration spokesmen talked of Vietnam as the testing ground for "wars of national liberation," where it must be shown to "the Communists" that such wars could not succeed. What they ignored was that the Vietnamese were not fighting to prove a theory to be applied elsewhere. They were now fighting a foreign foe for national independence. They were, in the face of American escalation, ready to fight on to the end—which meant death.

There were many states on the Asian perimeter that hoped for some continued United States presence to balance the potential of Chinese power. This was especially true of "neutralist" India after the open warfare between India and China in 1962 (see below, p. 329), when Indian officials asked for vast amounts of American military aid (and when the United States, so often accused of unwarranted interventionism, backed away from suggestions for a military alliance—leading India to turn instead to Russia, whose leaders were willing to give treaty guarantees and military aid). But the very tactics and nature of the Vietnamese intervention, with its divisive influence in the United States, seemed to guarantee a lessened United States involvement in the future. (The United States, in an effort to capitalize upon this desire, worked hard to associate other states with its effort in Vietnam. Its success was limited and expensive. It had to pay the full cost of South Korean, Thai, and Philippine units. The small Australian and New Zealand units came at their own governments' expense, but ultimately contributed to domestic unrest in those countries just as American participation brought dissent in the United States. In all, 65,000 non-United States men helped in Vietnam, with South Korea the largest participant.)

In the years 1965, 1966, and 1967, American forces in Vietnam rose from 23,00 to 510,000 men. Casualties by mid-1967 had risen to over 11,000 dead and 80,000 wounded. On several occasions there had been bombing halts and peace feelers, some well-publicized and others not. The period was replete with optimistic statements by United States military and political leaders that the war was virtually won; a little more effort in the field and a little less opposition at home would see it through. The opposition at home, they warned (probably correctly), strengthened the North Vitnamese and Vietcong's will, for these would interpret them as a flagging of the United States will and therefore be encouraged to continue to resist. Far more important, however, was the fact that full-scale American intervention brought greatly increased Russian and Chinese material aid to the North Vietnamese, and that the bombing of the relatively primitive economy did less material damage than it gave the North Vietnamese moral stature and a cementing of morale.

After three years of United States action enemy casualties were great—but so were those of the Americans and South Vietnamese. And the North, now fully in the war, was if anything in better shape, thanks to aid totaling several times the damage caused by bombing. Johnson and his small circle of trusted advisers could think of nothing to do but increase the action—and action that had cost 9000 American dead and 60,000 wounded in 1967 alone. And there seemed no timetable for when to taper off; Johnson appeared to depend upon an admission by the North Vietnamese and by the Vietcong that they were defeated and would stop fighting. But they were not defeated. In December President Johnson flew to Vietnam to visit troops, stopped off at airbases in Thailand, from which bombing of the North took place, flew to Rome to assure the Pope of his desire for peace—and lashed out at the growing dissenters and doubters at home, who by now constituted a majority of an uneasy Congress—but a Congress that could not undercut American soldiers while they were still fighting.

Then, in January and February 1968 came what seemed inexplicable in the light of what military spokesmen had been saying. In a three-pronged attack upon Saigon, provincial cities and all through supposedly secure areas of the countryside, the Vietcong and North Vietnamese went on what came to be known as the "Tet offensive," from the name of the Vietnamese new year. In Saigon they penetrated to within the United States Embassy compound. There and in other cities three days of enormous effort were required to root them out. The physical destruction of the American counterattacks was extraordinary; casualties on both sides were heavy, and civilian casualties were estimated at 25,000 in just a few days of fighting. The administration issued statements that implied this was the dying gasp of the Vietcong. Not only were their losses heavy, but they did not provoke the sympathetic uprising of the South Vietnamese that they had called for. But the Americans could not hide the capabilities demonstrated by the enemy, nor conceal the setback to programs of rural pacification. Moreover, the Vietnam Communists proved hard to dislodge; in one area after another they held on against heavy United States counterattacks. Then, in the midst of the optimistic statements, news leaked out that the American commander in Vietnam was asking for 206,000 more men—a figure that would call for an overall manpower increase in the Armed Forces of a half a million men.

The American President had eased out Secretary of Defense McNamara, whose optimism had vanished over the years, and replaced him with Clark Clifford, a wealthy Washington lawyer who was known to be favorable to a continued effort of the type the administration was making. When, on assuming office, he assembled a task force to examine the new request, there was only one conclusion he could reach, and the majority of the group shared it with him: the United States must find another way. After the previous repeated statements of overblown optimism, the United States would be torn apart by a new escalation, with its new costs.

On March 12, running on a peace ticket in the New Hampshire Democratic Primary, a relative unknown, Senator Eugene McCarthy of Minnesota, came within a few percentage points of defeating the incumbent President Johnson; on March 13, Senator Robert F. Kennedy, brother of the late President Kennedy, asked President Johnson whether he would accept the creation of a new commission to explore the whole course of events in Vietnam. Johnson immediately rejected the proposal, since it would be a virtual admission of error, and Kennedy proceeded to enter the Presidential race. In the middle of war and a national crisis, the Democratic party was about to tear itself apart.

From his United Nations ambassador, Arthur Goldberg, Johnson received a plead for a bombing halt to get negotiations started. Johnson rejected it coldly. Deputy Secretary of Defense, Paul Nitze, proposed to resign rather than testify before Congress on the new troop request, since he could only oppose it. President Johnson consulted his old hardline, anti-Communist friend, former Secretary of State Dean Acheson, who told him the same thing: "victory" in Vietnam was a mirage.

While domestic pressures on the American President mounted, the Vietnamese put on their own pressure, trying to create out of the isolated American base at Khesanh a new Dien Bien Phu. The fact they could mount the attack so soon after the Tet offensive was in itself startling; they failed in their aim, but only because the Americans threw in virtually all the airpower they had in order to pulverize the five-mile square area around the base. Twenty-five hundred sorties by intercontinental B–52's dropped 100,000 tons of high explosives, more explosive power than was dropped on any single target in World War II, including Hiroshima.

On Sunday, March 31, 1968, President Johnson startled the world by announcing a partial bombing halt in the hope of starting negotiations, and by withdrawing from the Presidential race. The wholesale conversion of all but a handful of his closest advisors had had the effect of making him aware of the depth of public and Congressional opposition to the course of escalation; the prospect of electoral defeat was all too real.

To the surprise of many, Hanoi replied promptly, and after incredible hassling first over the site of the talks, then over the shape of the table and the seating of delegates, the talks got underway.

The problem was relatively simple: the two sides still clung to irreconcilable demands and each hoped to hold on to a sufficient position of strength to make its aims prevail. Although Johnson had curtailed the area to be bombed and agreed to talks, he wanted to salvage a non-Communist Vietnam. (The actual rate of bombing increased in the next months and years.) Strategy therefore remained basically the same: to support the Thieu-Ky regime in Saigon with American forces while strengthening the South Vietnamese army. This meant no representation for the National Liberation Front, since the South Vietnamese government opposed it; hence the battle over the peace-talks table. If the NLF were seated it would assume stature as a legitimate party to the talks, and compromise would have to include its views. But, by the same token, the North Vietnamese who argued that the Thieu-Ky regime had no legitimacy, being only a puppet supported by American arms, opposed any representation—and therefore a seat at the table—for that regime. Since April 1965, Hanoi had insisted that the only basis for peace lay in its own four-point proposal: complete withdrawal of American forces, elimination of the South Vietnamese regime, unity of the North and South, and neutralization of the entire area. The two positions seemed irreconcilable; neither side seemed able to "win." What now?

An Arab assassin removed Robert Kennedy from the American political scene, and the lukewarm peace candidate Eugene McCarthy failed to gather enough professional support. Hubert Humphrey, earlier an opponent of escalation but later a tireless public advocate of Johnson's course, became the Democratic candidate after a horrifyingly divisive demonstration at the Chicago Democratic Convention. Richard M. Nixon returned to the American political scene as the Republican candidate. Indicative of the disruption in the American body politic, racist third-party candidate George Wallace became a serious contender, at times appearing to be ahead of Humphrey himself. (His candidacy lost steam when he chose General Curtis Lemay as his running mate. Lemay, former head of the Strategic Air Command and Air Force Chief of Staff, was an advocate of using anything, including nuclear weapons, in war, and talked of "bombing North Vietnam back into the stone age.")

The campaign, deprived of a clear antiwar candidate, inevitably became embroiled in the actual negotiations. To give a belated lift to Humphrey, whose cautious foray in a Salt Lake City speech on the possibility of a complete bombing halt had irritated Johnson, the President nevertheless tried to negotiate such a bombing halt. Yet his own posture dictated that Hanoi must do something in return. In October the Northerners indicated that they would finally accept Saigon at the negotiating table. Now it was Thieu's turn to balk—in part at least, war considerations aside, because the move might help Humphrey's chances, while Nixon appeared to be more of a hardliner, who might be inclined to continue the war. But coerced by the administration, Saigon tentatively agreed, and on October 31, a total halt to the bombing of the North was announced. The announcement might have put Humphrey over the top— Nixon won by only one-quarter of a percentage point and had the smallest plurality in more than 50 years—except for the fact that at the last moment Saigon backed out of participation. Only later did Thieu and Ky accept the inevitable, and only then to continue the lengthy charade in Paris.

But in this puzzling election, where great issues were at stake and were avoided, where did Richard M. Nixon stand on the war? Here was a man who made his career out of being a tough and unscrupulous anti-Communist, who had been used in the Eisenhower administration to test out public reaction to strong action that Eisenhower was uncertain about (such as intervention at Dien Bien Phu in 1954), the man who first suggested the Bay of Pigs invasion—yet also a man who knew that President Lyndon B. Johnson had been destroyed by the war in Vietnam while American society was ripped apart at the seams. Many antiwar Democrats had simply not voted, since their two candidates, Kennedy and McCarthy, had left the scene. Others had voted for Richard Nixon, believing him more capable than any Democrat would be of withdrawing from the war in Vietnam while avoiding the charge of selling out the world and the United States or both to the Communists.

The next four years provided the answer: Nixon continued the gradual process of diminishing the American effort in Vietnam, even though at times military action was heavy. But rather than cut his losses and withdraw rapidly, the new President chose a middle way: he would try to salvage the position by a slow withdrawal during which time the Thieu-Ky regime could build a position of strength. Since 1965, when Johnson had begun the massive escalation, South Vietnam had hardly participated in the fighting, and many administration critics felt that no effective pressure could be put on the Saigon regime so long as the United States was willing to assume the burden of the fighting. With a rough timetable for stages of American withdrawal, however, the regime would have to take the internal measures essential to its own continuation.

In April 1969, four months after Nixon had assumed the Presidency, there were 543,000 Americans in Vietnam. Over the next three years he withdrew more than four-fifths of them, effectively muting most antiwar protest in the United States. He visited China in February of 1972 and planned to visit Russia in May; the latter trip was preceded by a new North Vietnamese offensive to which the President responded by stepping up bombing of the North and taking the unprecedented step of mining the vital North Vietnamese port of Haiphong. There were domestic and international protests, but in the meantime the withdrawals had brought American manpower to a new low of 66,000 (although there was an increase in Thailand and in naval manpower off the coasts of Vietnam). During all this time the Paris peace talks dragged on; Nixon offered reconstruction aid to both North and South Vietnam; the mining was accompanied by a new United States offer to pull out all of its troops within four months of the signing of an internationally supervised ceasefire if the North Vietnamese would release all American prisoners of war at the same time. It was an election year in the United States, and the Democratic Party platform demanded an immediate and complete withdrawal with a cutoff of military aid to South Vietnam. The Republican platform merely repeated the offer made at the time of the mining of Haiphong. Then, just two weeks before the election, administration spokesmen announced that agreement had been reached in Paris to bring the hostilities to an end.

There could hardly be joy. The ghastly mess had dragged on too long, and too many people thought the same terms now announced might have been reached three years earlier. Nevertheless, the Nixon administration had achieved peace of a sort, the last men would be brought home, the 595 American POW's released, and there would still be some sort of non-Communist regime in Saigon, although only the administration and a few supporters seemed to care any more.

The settlement, however, came unstuck. Administration opponents immediately criticized Nixon for an election trick, but it appeared that the North Vietnamese had pushed for rapid announcement and conclusion of the agreement feeling that Nixon would want to be able to proclaim peace before the election and, therefore, would make concessions to get it. The strategy failed, and to everyone's dismay negotiations dragged on through the election and after. In December President Nixon unleashed a new wave of massive bombing of the North. The North had by now installed what may have been the most modern, concentrated antiaircraft system in effect anywhere, and the United States lost fifteen of its big

B–52 bombers and numerous other planes in two weeks of bombing. Nevertheless, perhaps because of the pressure, on January 23—a day after the death of the man who had so deeply involved the United States in Vietnam, Lyndon B. Johnson—the four participants signed an agreement ending the Vietnam War.

A battlefield truce was to take effect on January 28, final withdrawal of American troops would be carried out within sixty days, American prosioners would be released by the same date, and a four-nation International Commission for Control and Supervision—composed of Hungary, Poland, Indonesia, and Canada—would police the truce, the withdrawals, and the elections. The dividing line between north and south would remain, but the three Vietnamese factions involved would establish a framework for reconciliation, and the Thieu government would stay in power until elections were held. North Vietnamese troops were allowed to stay in place in the South, and the United States would remove the mines it had laid in the North.

The war had cost the United States 46,000 combat deaths and over 303,000 wounded; South Vietnam losses were listed as 184,500 dead and 496,000 wounded. No one really knew what North Vietnamese and Vietcong casualties were. A United States Senate Subcommittee on refugees estimated that 415,000 civilians had been killed, almost one million wounded. The United States had spent 110 billion dollars on the war. On March 29, 1973 the last American soldiers left Vietnam and the last American POW's were released; 8500 civilian advisers remained, attached to the South Vietnamese government.

The main problem with the peace settlement was that there was very little to make it stick, and within a few months the Canadians pulled out of the International Control and Supervision Commission, charging that they were prevented from fulfilling their mission. Fighting between Vietnamese continued sporadically. What was worse in 1973 was that the peace settlement that was supposed to extend to Laos and Cambodia failed to do so, and the United States continued heavy bombing of Communist-dominated areas in Cambodia in defiance of a United States Congress that had voted heavily in favor of stopping it. Public attention was thus turned to the two smaller neighbors, where the situation had been much different, but where, in the end, North Vietnamese and American involvement was both as questionable and, perhaps, as destructive.

LAOS AND CAMBODIA

The 1954 Geneva settlement for Indochina left a very different situation in each of the three countries. In Cambodia there was no effective Communist force, and Prince Norodom Sihanouk managed to cling to a precarious neutrality until he was overthrown in 1970. In Laos the Communist-led Pathet Lao movement was regrouped into an area in the northeast of the country, adjoining North Vietnam. Despite the differences, both countries came to be vital to North Vietnam as it supplied insurgents and then its own troops along the supply lines running through them.

In Laos, North Vietnam operated primarily in territory still held by the Pathet Lao after 1954. In 1959 the Eisenhower administration tried to help royalist Laotian forces come to grips with and defeat the Pathet Lao, but Khrushchev came to their aid and began to airlift supplies and military equipment. The United States-backed royalists had little stomach for the battle, and a large number defected to form a third, neutralist force. When Kennedy came into office, he tried to salvage what he could from the situation. Laos was a rugged, landlocked country with ill-defined borders. Would the Soviet Union agree to a truce there? Khrushchev appeared willing, perhaps in the interest of a general detente or because Laos meant little to him, perhaps because he wanted to secure the situation in an area where conflict with China might otherwise ensue. In negotiations that dragged on in Geneva from the summer of 1961 through 1962 representatives of fourteen Western, Communist, and neutralist states worked out an agreement for a coalition government of three factions—royalists, neutralist, and Pathet Lao—under a neutralist premier, Prince Souvanna Phouma. The right-wing royalists had to be coerced by the Kennedy administration into joining the coalition—a curious spectacle, since it took place at the very time that Kennedy was under pressure to intervene more forcefully in Vietnam.

The situation never fully stabilized in Laos. The Communists, led by Souvanna Phouma's half-brother Prince Souphanouvong, withdrew from the coalition in April 1963, declaring that all decisions by the neutralist and right-wing forces were "null and void." When Pathet Lao military successes produced a right-wing coup in the capital, the United States, with cooperation from Britain and France, forced the right-wing military junta to take Souvanna Phouma back as head of a new coalition regime. Prince Souphanouvong and the Pathet Lao rejected all efforts to bring them back in, however. Souvanna Phouma merged the right-wing and neutralist armies and factions, and the United States began a program of limited military aid to his regime, on the basis that the Geneva agreements had broken down: the North Vietnamese, the Americans charged, had never left Pathet Lao territory, which now served as a primary supply route to South Vietnam.

The Soviet Union supported recalling the fourteen-nation Geneva

Conference; the Western states and the Laotian government demurred, on the basis that the Pathet Lao would not participate in a coalition nor give up the territory they had gained in recent offensives. Meetings of leaders from the various factions broke down. By 1965, when the United States began its all-out escalation in Vietnam, it had also, with the approval of the heretofore neutralist Souvanna Phouma, begun aerial bombardment of the "Ho Chi Minh" trail that ran through the area controlled by the Pathet Lao.

For the next five years, despite occasional minor offensives in one direction or the other, the situation remained relatively quiet. In 1969 Prince Souvanna Phouma visited the United States, where he asked for more aid, declaring that there were at least 40,000 North Vietnamese in the Pathet Lao area. Both sides exchanged frequent charges; Souvanna agreed that bombing would stop if foreign troops were withdrawn. Both he and President Nixon appealed to the cochairmen of the 1962 conference, the United Kingdom and the Soviet Union for aid on the withdrawal of troops. As opposition to the Vietnam war mounted in the United States, the Laotian situation came into question, and on March 6, 1970, President Nixon felt compelled to make a report to the nation to quell speculation. He told Americans that there were no United States ground combat troops in Laos, but that there were about 1000 Americans involved: some three hundred odd American military advisers, another three hundred involved in logistics, and the balance in various aid capacities. It later developed that Americans *had* been sent into the North to act as ground observers to guide bombing by Royal Laotian and American planes; there had been some three hundred American casualties since 1962, half of which were military; four hundred planes had been lost over Laos, half of them coming from bases in Thailand to bomb either in Laos or North Vietnam. Finally, to the discomfiture of American foreign aid personnel, the administration revealed that the Laotian aid operation had been used as a cover for Central Intelligence Agency operations. A declaration to the effect that Laos was the only country in which this was the case did little to relieve suspicions that would now arise about other aid ventures.

Over the years of increasing American involvement in Vietnam, then, there had been a concomitant but surreptitious rise in both Vietnamese and United States activity in supposedly neutral Laos. Early in 1971 a new, brief chapter in Laotian history was written when South Vietnamese forces struck into southern Laos in an effort to cut the complex of North Vietnamese supply line that ran through the beleaguered country. Although given intense aerial support by Americans, they were badly mauled by the Northerners and forced to withdraw.

Ultimately, Laos benefitted from the successful United States-Vietnamese negotiations. The Pathet Lao and the Royal Laotian government finally reopened talks in late 1972, and in February 1973 agreed to a standstill cease-fire, in which the government made numerous concessions to the Pathet Lao. Among other provisions the agreement called for a cessation of American bombing, the establishment of a provisional government equally composed of Pathet Lao and Royalist representatives (instead of one-third of each of these and of neutralists, as the government had insisted upon), and with the withdrawal of foreign—that is, Vietnamese—troops sixty days after the establishment of the provisional government. The United States, which had intensified bombing after the January 15 cessation of military activity in Vietnam, ceased all bombing in Laos on February 22. But negotiation for the formation of a coalition government dragged on. As of mid-1973 little progress had been made —and Vietnamese troops therefore still formed the mainstay of Pathet Lao power, while some 15,000 Thai troops remained on the other side of the line. Geneva, in 1954 and 1962, and Paris a decade later, had yet to provide peace in the divided country.

In Cambodia, however, where there was no separate Communist enclave in 1954 as there was in Laos, Prince Nordom Sihanouk did everything possible to keep his tiny country free of conflict. He withdrew from the French Union in 1955, the year of the Bandung Conference (see above, p. 189), and abdicated as King to become Chief of State and virtual one-man government of Cambodia. His main problem was that he faced increasing pressure from traditional enemies on either side—Thailand and Vietnam—and that both of these became embroiled in Communist–non-Communist conflict. France had stabilized the Indochina area during its tenure, but the swift withdrawal of French influence after 1954 meant a possible renewal of old pressures with added elements of Great Power involvement.*

By 1960, when insurgency was well underway in South Vietnam, Sihanouk found himself under attack for allowing the Vietcong to use Cambodian territory both for refuge and supply routes. Observing the growing warfare and increased American involvement, he opted for neutralism as the only way to keep his own country free. He received economic and military aid from both the United States and from China, and chose to follow "socialist" policies at home. In 1960 and 1961, having recognized Communist China, he broke relations with both Thailand and South Vietnam, and became increasingly critical of their protector: the

---

* Thailand had seized Cambodian territories during World War II, while French influence was absent. It had been forced to disgorge them after the war.

United States was furnishing arms to the countries that had always threatened Cambodia, and border incursions by the Vietnamese had become frequent. He claimed that the CIA was financing the so-called Free Khmer movement directed at overthrowing him, and sought in vain to have the United States find and destroy rebel radio transmitters situated outside of his borders.

By 1963, witnessing the devastating effect of the American-supported war effort in South Vietnam, certain that the United States would have to withdraw, that the Communists would control Vietnam, and that China would have a predominant interest in Southeast Asia, Sihanouk decided that his only hope for a continued independent neutralist stance was to effect a further rapprochement with the Communists and to terminate any American presence. He therefore negotiated an end to American aid programs (but was disappointed at a lack of French and Chinese response when he approached them for aid in replacement.) The deaths of Diem in Vietnam and Premier Sarit of Thailand were soon followed by the assassination of President Kennedy; the Cambodia radio rejoiced and Sihanouk was quoted as saying "the three enemies of Cambodia are now in Hell to pursue their SEATO meetings." The result was a withdrawal of American diplomatic personnel. Yet the Prince then decreed a three-day mourning period for the dead American President. Eighteen months later he broke diplomatic relations completely upon the occasion of American bombing of a border village and publication of an article in an American newsmagazine declaring that Sihanouk's mother derived her income from running a string of bordellos.

The 1954 Geneva Conference had created an International Control Commission of Poland, India, and Canada to verify compliance with the Geneva agreements. In 1966 the Americans and Vietnamese complained to it that the port of Sihanoukville and border areas were being used by and for the Vietcong, but the ICC denied the charge. By 1967, after numerous United States incursions across the border, and alarmed at the increasing Vietcong activity as well as the American reaction it could bring, Sihanouk agreed to an enlargement of the ICC and its use of American helicopters. The Poles, however, refused to go along, and the Russians pointed out that the agreements allowed only for diminishing the size of the Commission, not enlarging it. "We are," said the unhappy Prince, " a country caught between the hammer and the anvil, a country that would very much like to remain the last haven of peace in Southeast Asia." In June 1967 he crushed a "Red Khmer" revolt in the countryside; it broke out again the next year, and Sihanouk warned the Communists—both local and Vietnamese—that if they persisted there would undoubtedly be a military coup, Cambodian neutrality would evaporate, the United States would intervene, and then there would be no chance for Cambodia. In 1969, still trying to balance both sides, he renewed diplomatic relations with the United States and openly charged the Vietcong and North Vietnamese with having used Cambodian sanctuaries; at the same time he recognized the Provisional Government of the Vietnamese National Liberation Front. His requests that China and North Vietnam scale down their use of Cambodian territory went unanswered. In December his Defense Minister General Lon Nol estimated that there were 35,000 to 40,000 Communist troops operating in Cambodia.

On January 4, 1970, the Prince flew to France for medical treatment. At home, egged on by anti-Communist factions in his government, mobs assaulted the North Vietnamese and South Vietnamese Provisional Governments' Embassies, while all over the country the homes and businesses of the large resident Vietnamese minority were attacked and looted. Desperate, Sihanouk flew to Moscow to ask Russian help in obtaining withdrawal of the Vietcong. He did not obtain it; the Russians told him that attacks on the Vietnamese would bring Cambodia only trouble. On March 18, by unanimous vote in the National Assembly, Sihanouk was deposed. The Assembly declared a national emergency, voted full powers to a government headed by General Lon Nol, and declared that Sihanouk would be arrested for treason if he returned. Twelve hours later, with what some people thought was suspicious haste, the United States declared that there was no problem in recognizing the new government; all Cambodian missions abroad accepted the new government but those at the United Nations, Cairo, and Dakar.

General Lon Nol told the world that Cambodia remained strictly neutral, asked for return of the International Control Commission, which had left at Sihanouk's request a year earlier when the cost of supporting it had apparently become onerous, and declared that he was prepared to discuss the withdrawal of Vietcong and North Vietnamese troops with the North Vietnamese government. He then closed the port of Sihanoukville to shipments to the Vietcong.

Sihanouk chose not to return home. Instead he threw in his lot with those whom, on occasion, he had previously declared he feared the most: the Chinese. He flew from Moscow to Peking, where he declared that his deposition was illegal, but that he would submit to a national referendum. On March 23, however, he announced organization of a National Liberation Front and formation of a National Liberation Army. On May 5, under the impetus of events in Cambodia he organized a government in exile, whose members included radicals he had ousted from the government earlier, and which was recognized by China, North Korea, Vietnam, Cuba, Syria, Iraq, Albania, Rumania, and Yugoslavia. The Soviet Union sent him greetings, but continued to maintain relations with the new regime in Cambodia. Since under the circumstances Sihanouk had opted to work with the Chinese, the Russians were not eager to encourage his return. On May 18 the Russian newspaper *Pravda* accused China of trying to rule "at least Asia if not the whole world. . . ."

In the meantime, between April 29 and May 1 the United States and Vietnam opened offensive operations of a limited nature within Cambodia. The purpose, said President Nixon, was to help end the war in Vietnam by destroying the Communist bases and supply lines in Cambodia. There was no intention of spreading the war to Cambodia, and the act could not be considered an invasion since the area attacked, close to the Vietnamese border, was completely Communist-occupied. (In fact, as it much later turned out, the United States had heavily bombed the area with giant B–52's for many months, while denying to the American Congress that it had been doing so.) True to its word, the administration withdrew the American troops within two months, claiming success for a mission that had uncovered and disposed of large caches of Communist arms; it thus gained time for Vietnamization and the securing of a just peace. It now played down its earlier statements that the whole command structure for the North Vietnamese operations in South Vietnam would be destroyed in the course of the raid. In addition, it made no mention of a basic underlying reason for the action: the attempt to aid the Lon Nol regime in resisting the rising tide of opposition in Cambodia, headed by Prince Sihanouk's Royal Cambodian Government. This government was allied with the Khmer Rouge who had rebelled against Sihanouk in 1967 but who rallied to him in 1970, and with the Cambodian Communist Party, and was backed by North Vietnam and China. For despite the American incursion, Sihanouk's coalition apparently controlled two-thirds of the countryside, and in the next two years tightened the ring inexorably around the capital, Phnom Penh. The January 1973 Vietnam settlement provided a lull in which political maneuvering led to an offer by Sihanouk that he would negotiate with Lon Nol if the United States would end its support for the Republicans. The United States refused, and resumed intensified bombing. As Sihanouk's forces advanced—despite a withdrawal of most Vietnamese support since the cease-fire—only the American bombing maintained Lon Nol, whose turn it now was to offer negotiations to Sihanouk.

But it was the Prince's turn to refuse. He knew that American actions both at the time of the incursion two years earlier and now in continuing bombing had provoked a constitutional crisis in the United States. The Congress, more and more effectively, had begun to challenge the administration's right to carry out armed action without Congressional sanction and, in the case of the massive 1973 bombing, with specific Congressional direction to stop and its refusal to provide funds. Now that there were no longer American men fighting on the ground, waverers who had felt they had to support American soldiers could shift to a new position and vote to deny money for what they considered an illegal and unconstitutional action. (In the longer run, the Cambodian affair also sparked Congressional attempts to draft a measure that would severely limit the President's power to use armed action overseas within a short, specified period without Congressional assent.)

It appeared that Sihanouk might be one of the first deposed heads of state to return, in modern times. He had tried, and failed, to keep his tiny state neutral in the Southeast Asian conflict. He would return with the backing of the People's Republic of China, whose hegemonial tendencies he had once professed to fear. The state of the situation in South East Asia was dramatically highlighted by the fact that Russia continued to maintain an embassy in Phnom Penh, accredited to the American-supported Lon Nol regime, and that Sihanouk had angrily charged the Russians with trying to subvert the Red Khmer into abandoning him and rallying to the Republic!

CONCLUSION

The history of international affairs among the Western states since Suez and Hungary has few clear themes running through it. Perhaps one stands out: the ending of the American era.

In 1970 the United States was the richest nation on earth. It produced one-third of the world's income and could virtually blow the rest of the world out of existence. From the vague liberal internationalism with which it had emerged from World War II devoted to collective security, decolonization, democratization, a free multilateral trading system—and reservations about all of these—it had embarked upon a new form of balance-of-power politics in the new setting of bipolarism, called "containment." Partly out of internationalism, partly for the sake of containment, it had helped to rebuild Europe, forged the Western alliance, rearmed the West, and begun to aid the lower-income countries. In the 1950s—the era of Eisenhower—the rhetoric and the paper policies of containment had become more strident and, unfortunately, contributed to a public mood equating proper foreign policy with "anti-Communism." Yet a cautious President was far more moderate in action, and in a last speech warned against the "military-industrial complex" which, he said, had been built up to meet the needs of the Cold War but now threatened to have a momentum of its own.

The feeling that underlying changes had left the Eisenhower administration far behind led a vigorous young President Kennedy to resume a
more active policy, both in the fields of aid and military intervention, and
to increase the military options open to the United States to meet what he
felt were the challenges of a new military era. The result of this, and of
the determination, pride, and stubborness of his successor, led to interventionism in Cuba, the Dominican Republic, Indochina, and to a lesser
extent, the Congo (see below, p. 352).

Yet critics of what was seen as a growing interventionism failed to note
Kennedy's settlement in 1962 in Laos and his caution in India as well as
in the Congo, and the many opportunities to intervene in other parts of
the world that he passed over. In addition, the complicated nature of the
problem of intervention was emphasized by the effort of the Kennedy administration to act in favor of what could be called progressive regimes in
Latin America while penalizing reactionary and oppressive ones. This
policy failed and was abandoned by his successors.

The basic liberal drive behind these policies derived from a reading of
history: democratic regimes were thought less likely to start wars and
more likely to satisfy human aspirations for freedom. The same theoriz-
ing lay behind the abandonment of the older protectionism in favor of the
postwar attempt to build a relatively free, multilateral trading and payments system, and also behind the anticolonialist pressures on other
Western states. Yet by 1970 many people had come to view the multilateral trading system as an ideological mask for American economic hegemony and despoliation, much as the English free-trade movement had
been, while the demise of the old empires was seen by critics as masking
a new "neocolonialism" in which ruling classes were sustained in their
privilege by the benefits they derived from their economic relations with
the United States and the other Western states. The very country whose
leaders had considered it the epitome of freedom, anticolonialism, and
anti-imperialism, the nation whose statesmen felt it could set the world an
example of how to combine order, law, and individual freedom, now
found itself challenged from both within and without as the antithesis of
all of these. A bitter book by a professor of linguistics, Noam Chomsky,
said: "By any objective standard, the United States has become the most
aggressive power in the world, the greatest threat to peace, to national
self-determination and to international cooperation."* The same view
was being repeated all over the world. In a speech at the United Nations
Marxist President Allende of Chile, elected in 1970 and deposed in a

---

* Noam Chomsky, *American Power and the New Mandarins*. (New York: Random
House, 1969).

military coup in 1973, accused the United States of an economic imperialism "subtle . . . cunning . . . terrifyingly effective in preventing us from exercising our rights as a sovereign state." The Central Intelligence Agency was orginally created in 1947 out of recollections of the failure of intelligence that brought about Pearl Harbor, a realization of the extent of the Russian espionage and subversion establishment, and the new role the United States was necessarily preparing to play. It had now become the international bogeyman. It helped overthrow the Arbenz regime in Guatemala in 1954; in its bumbling way, it had masterminded the Bay of Pigs invasion of Cuba in 1961; it had played a role, however slight, in Iran in 1953 and in Indonesia, Burma, Laos, Cambodia, and elsewhere. How much was boasting, how much was reliable accusation, how much was true was now hard to fathom, but it had come to the point that Prime Minister Indira Ghandi of India even accused the CIA of being behind food riots in India in 1972. When her accusation was rejected and the United States asked for evidence she declared "It is not for us to prove that this agency is working in our country. It is for the CIA to prove that it is *not* active in India." The logic might escape some people, but not all. When the giant International Telephone and Telegraph company faced the possibility of expropriation in Chile in the early 1970s its executives were ready to contribute one million dollars if the CIA would help prevent the coming to power of the Allende government. While the State Department gave the corporation short shrift, the CIA apparently chose to act, and with the highest approval.

The United States participated in United Nations-sponsored nonviolent embargoes on arms to the southern part of Africa, where various white-minority regimes faced growing African resistance movements. The United States informed American investors that there would be no United States government guarantees if they put funds into Namibia, the territory still held illegally by South Africa, if there should be a change in regime. For a time in the late sixties and early seventies the Nixon administration had tried to curb indiscriminate arms sales abroad to countries other than ones like South Korea, Taiwan, South Vietnam, or NATO states. But what was more evident to the public eye was that the United States Congress, out of pique, had voted to break the United Nations-sponsored economic blockade of the white-minority government of Rhodesia, that the Nixon administration had agreed to a new agreement with Portugal in return for continued use of the Azores, despite continued Portugese repression in Africa, had negotiated home port rights for the Sixth Fleet with the Greek military regime, and had reversed itself on the issue of arms sales when it saw countries like France, Canada, or the Soviet Union benefiting from the diminished United States effort. In providing training and weapons for Latin American armies it had—wittingly or unwittingly—supported a particular and potent political force.

Cuba, the Dominican Republic, and Indochina were not aberrations, many people thought, but part of a pattern. A vast majority of Americans must have still felt that it was a land of both opportunity and freedom, and one capable of solving the new problems that success had brought to it; but the critics were louder: the American "system" had enshrined inequality and privilege through the corporate power structure; private affluence existed in the midst of almost unimaginable public ugliness and squalor. At the same time, alongside the affluence existed a massive minority of the poor in rural slums and ungovernable, filthy, traffic-choked cities, characterized by rising crime rates and now, finally, revolutionary pressures—that would bring on a cycle of repression. Some of the critics resided within those proud American universities to which students and scholars from all the rest of the world had flocked. Yet these same universities were now attacked from without for fostering revolution and from within for epitomizing the system.

The revolutionary spirit was not confined to the United States. In Western Europe the same criticisms were raised and fought for: liberalism had brought merely inequality, materialism, and the consumer society, and the mad race for more goods with its despoliation of the entire earth. If this was what the majority wanted, it was because it was being misled by the consumer society in which it existed. If this was what the workers wanted, they were wrong. And if Russia's leaders also wanted to establish a consumer society, then it must be because it, too, was capitalist—state capitalist.

And because the wealthy West existed in a world where the vast majority of the increasing population seemed not to be sharing in the increasing wealth, the revolutionaries and radicals of the West reached out to take the hands of the radicals and revolutionaries of the third world. Liberal President John F. Kennedy had called for a Decade of Development at the United Nations in 1961; the Western countries had failed to make the necessary adjustments in their policies, and the Decade had failed. And so the radicals rejected, *in toto,* the liberal international institutions created by the West.

The radical movement reached its height when it helped mobilize pressure to bring down Lyndon Johnson in 1968, weakened de Gaulle in May of the same year, and claimed an affinity for the Red Guard students rampaging through China during the Great Poletarian Cultural Revolution (see the next chapter). As a movement, it then splintered. Some members turned to a useless and self-indulgent terrorism; much of the movement degenerated into a hedonism of little relevance to its professed aims that, however, could be rationalized as a response to the ability of Western institutions to sustain its assaults. Still its critique lived on.

But the record of the postwar years could be read quite differently. A quarter of a century had passed since World War II, during which 70 new countries had arisen from the ruins of the old system of empire. Western unity had, in fact, progressed; institutions had developed that brought a degree of cooperation unthinkable in earlier days. Conflicts existed between Western states, yet war as a way of resolving them now seemed inconceivable. The United States had led the way. If it no longer did so, it was partly because the success of its policies meant that in the West it now dealt with countries that could afford to act independently, yet in cooperation with it in the myriad technical fields that characterized modern international relations. It had, for a while, occupied a position of real hegemony. It had not always acted wisely, but in spite of all, it had not often used the position brutally, and its policies had contributed to the emergence of a Europe and a Japan that now challenged it.

The American Era had been a short one. President Kennedy, with his conception of Atlantic Partnership embodied in such measures as the Kennedy Round and the Multilateral Force, had tried to maintain it. President Nixon, in a speech at Guam, July 25, 1969, had proclaimed the need for a reduced American presence in Asia, and that presence was slowly reduced. And in the meantime, by trips to Peking and Moscow, he had affected a rapproachement that no Democrat could have made, virtually establishing de facto diplomatic relations with China in 1973. By the first SALT agreement, continuation of the SALT talks, and participation in the Mutual Balanced Force Reduction talks, he gave evidence of further intentions to reduce tension with Russia. He raised fears in Europe that the United States would reduce its forces unilaterally, and the British *Economist* called the results of the Nixon initiatives, not a new era, but "mostly bubbles." It argued that an economically weak Russia facing a hostile China to its rear should be making concessions but, instead, was getting all it wanted. Certainly, much remained at issue: the shaping of better relations with the industrialized world (a difficult task, given a rising tide of American protectionism), a cooperative coping with underlying ecological issues, the unsatisfying state of relations with less developed countries. What the radical critique of the American Empire generally ignored—in both its attribution of the cause of the Cold War to the United States and its view of the American hegemony—was that the state of relations within the Communist bloc, between Communist states and the West, and between all of these and the so-called third world, warranted a more complex conclusion about American policy; the next chapters will turn to these sets of relations.

Whatever one's conclusion, it was tempting to draw a parallel between the sudden decline of England, still dominant throughout the world at the start of World War I, and the decline of the United States in the years since the Truman administration when, with a heady sense of destiny, Americans seized the initiative in forging a worldwide coalition against what was viewed as a Russian-dominated world Communist conspiracy —or, since the flare-up of the Kennedy years, when a young, dynamic, incoming President could say "We shall pay any price, bear any burden, meet any hardship, support any friend, oppose any foe to assure the survival and the success of liberty."

EIGHT
RUSSIA, CHINA, AND
THE SOCIALIST BLOC:
THE END OF UNITY

The dilemmas provoked by attempts to de-Stalinize Russia after 1953 were never fully resolved, and disunity in world Communism following the invasion of Hungary matched the growing disarray in the Western world. The story of Communist foreign policies became one of both co-operation and of open conflicts between bloc members. Since 1956 the superior power of the Soviet Union has been held in check by the resistance of other Communist states, and Communist leaders have had only limited success in creating an integrated socialist system. As late as 1968 Russian leaders had to use massive force to coerce one of their own bloc members, Czechoslovakia; they considered the use of force against another, Rumania, and they fought a limited border with Communist China. Furthermore, when one Communist state, North Vietnam, came under heavy military attack by the United States, the Soviet Union, although constrained to help it militarily, did not even break off the relatively friendly relations it maintained with the United States—and Russia and China found it virtually impossible to cooperate in helping their fellow Communist government. Rumania joined Yugoslavia in pursuing a completely independent foreign policy, and in 1969 Albania left the Warsaw Pact. That same year Russia accused China of trying to dominate at least Asia if not all the world, and appeared to view Chinese foreign policy as more dangerous than American foreign policy—while China insisted that social imperialism (Russian) was worse than imperialism (American); the two vied for influence in the third world countries, where Russia moved rapidly to check Chinese influence.

The cautious, brutal conservatism manifested by Russian leaders at home and in many areas of foreign policy had its effect on revolutionary and radical movements throughout the rest of the world. Many slipped from Russian influence; some looked to China for inspiration and support. But Mao Tse-tung's domestic effort at enshrining permanent revolution against modern bureaucratization, "the Great Proletarian Cultural Revolution" of 1966–69 diminished Chinese attention to foreign policy;

as a result the growing numbers of radical and revolutionary movements, nominally inspired by the injustice and misery they saw all around them, became more and more varied in orientation and aim. There was certainly no "World Communist Conspiracy" of the kind that American leaders had once conceived and fought against. Yet as the 1970s dawned world political leaders could not ignore Russian penetration into the Middle East and the Indian Ocean, where India signed what amounted to an alliance with Russia. Nor could they ignore the continued Russian arms buildup and the modernization and transformation of its short-range defensive fleet into one capable of supporting its interests in distant parts of the globe.

Crucial to these years were themes outlined by Khrushchev, seemingly accepted by his dour successors and long opposed by the Chinese: with the development of the hydrogen bomb, war between capitalist and socialist states was no longer inevitable; peaceful coexistence and even cooperation between East and West had become necessary (although these could not prevent the onward march of Communism) ; there were different pathways to socialism, although only some were acceptable; ultimately, Communist society must be achieved by satisfying the material needs of the people.

For the international system this meant that the Soviet Union and the United States must act to prevent war with each other and to stabilize the existing balance. Slowly, they moved to do this. But in the meantime China came to constitute a potential third great power, posing a challenge to Russia along its Asian frontier and to the United States along the Asian rimlands—and to both in terms of its support to revolutionary movements throughout the world. The result was a more complex relationship: China might accuse the United States and Russia of having agreed to tolerate each one's domination of its own sphere and to have established a joint world hegemony, but Russia began to fear that China and the United States might act jointly to check Russian power. Developments in the 1970s fed the fear, and Russia moved to stabilize the European front and mend fences with the United States, while the Chinese, succeeding in having Taiwan ousted from the United Nations, took their own seats in established international organizations and resumed diplomatic relations with countries throughout the world.

To recount this complex story this chapter will first review the two Krushchev periods, when Russian leader moved from attempting to combine detente politics with restoring unity of the Communist bloc, to a more belligerent stance and ultimate failure; the foreign policies of his at first, more cautious successors; the implications of the Russian-Chinese split and, finally, the course of Chinese foreign policy.

KHRUSHCHEV (I): THE PERIOD OF DETENTE

The internal pressures in the mid-fifties for relaxation of Stalinist controls throughout the Communist bloc and the political need to destroy opponents by branding them as Stalinists led Khrushchev to take the gamble of demythologizing Stalin. It was a question of either making Stalin a scapegoat for all that had been wrong—or admitting criticism of the whole system of which he, Khrushchev, was a part. Since the legitimacy of many Communist governments lay in their Stalinist purity, however, he brought into question the very basis for their existence, and the 1956 revolt in Hungary was one result. There and in Poland, where the Poles balked at Russian attempts to remove the reformist Gomulka, Khrushchev appeared to have failed. In 1957 his old Stalinist foes at home—former Foreign Minister Molotov, Kaganovich, Voroshilov, and Malenkov (whom earlier the first three had helped Khrushchev to depose)—moved in for the kill, seeing their opportunity to get rid of the man they felt was not only a crude opportunist whose policies had almost sacrificed the international gains of Stalin's period, but also a man personally dangerous to them. Khrushchev proved the wilier maneuverer. Branding his opponents the "Anti-Party Group," relying upon men like Marshal Zhukov and Bulganin (both of whom he later sacrificed) he emerged as the paramount leader. But his situation could never be like Stalin's. The Soviet society had changed too much, generating new interest groups, and Khrushchev himself realized it. What he also saw better than his opponents was that new groups gave new political opportunities: when his Politburo opponents voted him out of office he did the unheard of thing of appealing to the much larger Central Committee of the Communist Party, packed with his supporters as a consequence of his having shifted power to outlying districts and away from Moscow. It was here that he won: but the very fact of having to rely upon such an appeal demonstrated the degree to which his power was checked. Much of his erratic and seemingly inconsistent foreign policy resulted from the continued unseen internal political maneuvering that characterized his entire period of dominance.

On the international front Khrushchev faced the grim and angry Stalinism of the Czech and East German leadership, the deviationism of the Polish Gomulka, and the revisionism of a Tito who continued to insist on the logic of Khrushchev's anti-Stalinism. Given this range of positions and the very real underlying social stresses and strains prevalent throughout Eastern Europe, the task Khrushchev faced was one of allowing a measure of diversity but also of setting acceptable limits to it—and bringing the center of decision-making power back to Moscow. He had the support of the Chinese. They had disapproved of both his secret speech attacking Stalin and of the fact that he had used a Congress of the Communist Party of the Soviet Union as his forum for launching a policy that would affect all Communist parties. But their overriding concern was for bloc unity, and they fully sustained Khrushchev's new efforts.

He could tolerate Polish deviationism, since Gomulka agreed to adhere to bloc foreign policies. But to protect the East German and Czech leaders and to disarm the Stalinists at home, he moved to end the rapprochment with Tito. The Yugoslav leader was first attacked in the Chinese press, then throughout the bloc. At the November 1957 celebration of the Russian Revolution he was condemned for having received American aid, for revisionism, for abandoning Marxism, and for refusing to acknowledge the primacy of the Soviet Union.

The November 1957 celebration was, in fact, used by Khrushchev as the scene of an attempt to solve the problem of bloc unity and diversity once and for all. He came to it strengthened by his elimination of the "Anti-Party Group" in June and by his popular triumph when the first earth satellite or "Sputnik" was successfully launched into orbit in October, months before the United States was able to launch its own, much heralded "Vanguard." The Chinese were much sobered by their own, recent attempt at liberalization, when Mao had said "let a hundred flowers bloom, let diverse schools of thought contend"—and the resulting revelation of intellectual opposition to the regime led to a hasty and severe repression. As a result, Mao was now ready to support relatively rigid statements on bloc unity and Soviet primacy, and to insist that a multilateral meeting of Communist parties—such as this one—could determine the line to be followed by each Communist state. Tito's opposition no longer counted, and Gomulka, who had hoped earlier for Chinese support, had to accept the principle that the bloc as such could dictate the common features characterizing any state trying to build socialism.

While Khrushchev used the November meeting to re-establish an ideological line, he also used the year 1957 to restructure the Stalin-imposed economic relations between bloc members—relations that had meant, as Westerners had long charged and Communists denied, an exploitative situation favoring the Soviet Union. With this situation rectified and the people of Eastern Europe convinced by the invasion of Hungary that they might as well try to get along within the system, the bloc regimes were able to begin to better their situations. East Germany, never fully a bloc member so long as some Russian leaders still thought they might bargain it away to prevent integration of West Germany into NATO and the EEC, was now accepted as a full-fledged participant, and within ten years became one of the most important industrial countries in the world. Its leader, Walter Ulbricht, rode out the waves of de-Stalinization and the Berlin crisis (see below, p. 304) and gained a position from which he could exert a strong influence on Soviet leadership. Gomulka, too, first regarded as a dangerous liberal, hewed closer and closer to the Soviet line, gradually clamping down on intellectual freedom and opposition within Poland.

The 1957 settlement, however, never really stuck. For one thing, as Khrushchev became embroiled in a growing split with China in the 1960s, he had to seek allies and curry favor with potential supporters all of which gave them a measure of leverage over the Russians. Rumania became the prime example. It retained a rigid internal system, but pursued a more and more independent foreign policy. Beginning with a gradual reorientation of trade,* the Rumanians went on to resist Russian efforts at greater economic integration of the bloc, promoted under the rubric of a "Socialist division of labor." They preferred to build their own heavy industry, which the Russian plan for national specialization would have denied them, and in effect rejected multilateral bloc economic decision making. They remained neutral in the Russian-Chinese dispute, and maintained friendly relations with Israel when Russia, pursuing its own Middle East policy, directed bloc action against the Jewish state. They abandoned compulsory Russian language training in their schools.

And then, while China split from the bloc, Yugoslavia remained to give the rank and file in other Eastern European countries the example of a socialist state that avoided Russian domination. Its relations with bloc members reached a nadir after its condemnation for revisionism at the 1957 meeting of Communist parties. The Yugoslavs, partly in retaliation, issued their own party program in which they declared themselves to be virtually the only legitimate Marxist standardbearers of socialism. In a further extension of the heresy, they condemned both the Western bloc *and* the Communist bloc as dangerous to the peace—which, again, was tantamount to saying that the socialist bloc states were not really Marxist-Leninist. On the other hand, the Yugoslavs declared, there could be a variety of different paths towards socialism, including *non*-Communist ones. The point was extremely important in terms of relations to less-developed countries, more and more of which called themselves socialist. The standards set at Moscow would deny their claim to socialism and, ideologically, Communists would be committed to their overthrow. The Yugoslav position, of course, made it possible to support them as genu-

* While bloc trade with the Soviet Union remained fairly stable as a percentage of overall external trade between 1950 and 1967, Russia's share of Rumanian trade declined from 52 to 28 per cent.

inely socialist. Ultimately, as the Russo-Chinese split developed, the Russians came to accept virtually the same position. But in 1958 it meant a serious division.

Gomulka's government formulated what was to be the official bloc position on Yugoslavia for two or three years: Tito might profess to be a Communist and did not join the Western bloc, but *objectively* his stand favored imperialism. In the early 1960s, however, with Khrushchev now courting allies against the hostile Chinese, the situation changed again, and Yugoslav-bloc relations improved. Only the Russian disapproval of liberalization in Czechoslovakia in 1968 and subsequent Russian invasion of the country—roundly attacked by Tito—brought this period to an end.

Khrushchev and his successors spent much time and energy on the question of interbloc relations. But Khrushchev was also the man who broke out of Stalin's essentially continental mold in the field of foreign affairs and carried Russian policy into previously uncharted realms. The change strained Russian resources. It also gave rise to policies that seemed at the time strangely inconsistent, and therefore strained the understanding of those having to deal with them. Some of the inconsistencies were explainable in terms of Khrushchev's need to maneuver among hostile groups and incompatible demands at home. But the growing rift with China was even more important. It overshadowed all aspects of Soviet foreign policy, and in terms of the structure of the world political system, was matched only by the Russian-Western detente.

Certain of Mao Tse-tung's aims were particularly relevant to the course of Russo-Chinese relations and to the two countries' relations to the rest of the world. Mao obviously wanted to redress a century of grievances against the West by building in China a modern and powerful state that could deal on equal terms with other nations. For this and other reasons, Chinese society would have to undergo almost total transformation, one that would strain the capacities of the Chinese people to the uttermost. The first international task was that of rounding out Chinese territory by liberating Formosa and rejoining it to the mainland. The Korean War prevented this when the United States shifted its policy to provide protection for Chiang Kai-shek. Then, in late 1950, China came into direct conflict with the United States in Korea itself. The war cost China heavily, but was the occasion for speeding up the process of transforming and mobilizing the society.

Mao came to power independent of Russian help. But Stalin was not slow to help the men who professed to look to him as the leader of Communists everywhere, and in 1950, provided important, but conditional, financial and technical aid. His successors helped again in 1953 and in

1954 when they also rescinded the onerous conditions Stalin had imposed: they sold China the shares in the joint-stock companies created in Stalin's time (companies of a type Stalin had used to maintain an important Russian influence over industrial decision making throughout the bloc).

Again in 1956 a new agreement was negotiated that lay at the heart of the first real Chinese five-year industrial development plan. By the late 1950s Russian relations had become essential to Chinese industry; in 1950 5 per cent of China's trade was with Russia; now the figure was 50 per cent. Three out of four complete industrial plants being sent abroad by Russia either as aid or trade were going to China, where an entire basic modern industry was being developed without the Chinese having to design and create the blueprints for it. The building of a railway link across Sinkiang, and frequently established airline flights, would greatly facilitate the exchanges involved.

In 1954 China became a member of the world community through its participation in the negotiations at Geneva, and in 1955 received the approbation of large numbers of the leaders of new states at Bandung. Some months earlier, in late 1954, relieved of the burden of both aid to North Korea and the Vietminh in Indochina, the Chinese Communist leaders turned their attention once more to liberation of Taiwan, still held by what was generally referred to as "the gangster Chiang Kai-shek clique." Again the United States blocked them. But at Bandung, while charming his neutral friends, Chou En-lai offered to negotiate the matter with the United States, and the United States, after some fumbling, agreed to talk.

The agreement hardly resolved the conflicting claims, but it led to an on-again off-again series of talks in Poland that, until 1971, constituted the one official though tenuous link between the People's Republic of China and the United States. But certainly on the Formosa issue, in Vietnam, and in Korea, the United States was the chief enemy. Moreover, it ringed the Chinese mainland with bases—in Korea, Japan, Okinawa, the Philippines, and Formosa—and with military agreements with these countries as well as Australia and New Zealand to the south. The United States was the country that blocked Chinese entry into the United Nations where it should legitimately take its place as one of the Great Powers; it worked actively against Communist parties everywhere.

Yet the United States was the country with which, in the late 1950s, Khrushchev prepared to come to overall agreement. The lesson he drew from America's failure to intervene in Hungary in 1956 and from the success of Russian missiles in 1957 was not—as Mao would have it— that "the East Wind prevails over the West Wind," but rather that competitive coexistence must be the new strategy. War was no longer inevitable; Russia clearly had shown that it could deter the United States and would be able to in the future. The Americans must be induced to agree that coexistence was the only path, but since Communists could not abandon the path of history, they would win by proving the material superiority of the Communist system. Hence Khrushchev's boast about overtaking and surpassing the United States in production. Success in this would lead other states to follow suit and become Communist too.

So it was that his foreign policy from 1957 to 1960 was by and large conciliatory, even if at times it appeared to Westerners not to be. Disarmament discussions showed signs of progress. In 1958, when the United States and Britain sent troops into Lebanon and Jordan at their governments' request (see below, Chapter 11), Khrushchev engaged in some bombast, but his major move was to suggest a summit conference at which India would represent Asian states. After a hurried visit to Peking he dropped the project—probably at the insistence of the Chinese, who resented his building up India as a power in Asia and also the idea of a United States-Soviet Union summit conference just when Khrushchev should be using the image of Soviet military might for more important purposes.* In 1959 Khrushchev nevertheless visited the United States in a circuslike atmosphere and sat down for heart-to-heart talks with President Dwight Eisenhower. The program of cultural exchanges was expanded, popular acclaim in the Soviet Union for young American pianist Van Cliburn, who won the international Tchaikovsky competition, was matched only by the ovation given to the spectacular Russian Moiseyev dancers in the United States.

One event marred the developing climate engendered by Khrushchev's espousal of peaceful competition—the Berlin crisis. It was of Khrushchev's making, dragged on for three years, and came to be of crucial importance. To the Americans it was the result of an aggressive and provocative action inexplicably taken by Khrushchev at a time that he seemed to be conciliatory on other fronts. But it may be argued that it was Khrushchev who could not understand why the Americans saw it this way, that for the first two years during which the crisis stretched on he considered it merely a diplomatic proposal to eliminate one of the remaining Cold War issues that tended to cloud relations between Moscow and Washington.

On November 10, 1958 and in notes delivered two weeks later Khrushchev suggested that the time had come to end the four-power status of Berlin, left over from Allied occupation of Germany. He proposed that

* G. F. Hudson argues this point in G. F. Hudson, R. Lowenthal, R. MacFarquhar (Eds.), *The Sino-Soviet Dispute* (New York: Praeger, 1961).

the city be united and absorbed into East Germany or, since he did not think that the first proposal would be acceptable, that the three western sectors be established as a separate "free city"—neutralized, disarmed, and barred from carrying on subversive activities against its neighbors.

From the time of the end of the Berlin Blockade of 1948, West Berlin had been integrated more and more into the economy and polity of West Germany, which gave it special subsidies. It had become a thriving, booming, and colorful city—and a thorn in the side of drab East Germany surrounding it. It provided an escape route for the continuing flow of refugees who wanted to leave behind the economic hardships of the East, and its radio and television stations constantly interfered with Communist attempts to isolate their people from the West. All of this would cease under Khrushchev's plan. He gave the West six months to negotiate a solution. At the end of this time he would turn over all Allied rights to East Germany, which would then control the roads, the rail lines, the canals, and airlines leading to the city. One thing was certain: an airlift of the 1948 variety would not keep the city alive. Its total imports and exports were ten times what they had been in that drab era of postwar impoverishment.

But, although the Allies met to discuss the situation and issued statements of unity to cover a typical situation of disagreement, nothing happened. (It was a time when uncertainty about de Gaulle, the Common Market, and the Free Trade Association made agreement about anything difficult.) The Allies rejected the Soviet proposal and talked about reinforcing their military strength. Yet President Eisenhower rejected the possibility of using force to fight through to Berlin if the East Germans imposed a blockade. In early 1959 Soviet Deputy Premier Mikoyan made a goodwill tour of the United States. He denied that the six-month period had been a time limit or ultimatum, and thereby reopened the possibilities of negotiation: the Western powers had said nothing could be done under the shadow of an ultimatum. Instead, the Soviets asked for a summit conference to deal with all major international differences.

Prime Minister MacMillan favored it; de Gaulle and Eisenhower felt it would serve no useful purpose unless a lower-level meeting of ministers indicated the possibility of genuine agreement; and Adenauer feared it at this time, thinking that the British were far too willing to barter away German demands for unity under free elections, and that de Gaulle was too ready to settle for the Oder-Neisse line as the eastern boundary of Germany. As a result, the four agreed with the Soviets to a foreign ministers conference to meet during the summer. It met and accomplished nothing, but recessed in a spirit of optimism at the news that Khrushchev was to visit the United States in September.

While in the United States, the Soviet Premier dispelled any notion of a renewed ultimatum on Berlin, and seemed anxious to avoid any difficulty that might prevent the summit conference he wanted. The spirit of goodwill engendered by the tour and the meeting with the President at Camp David, made the Russians appear ready for genuine negotiation on disarmament. Although Khrushchev then went before the General Assembly to call for general complete disarmament within four years (a demand that many people interpreted as a return to propaganda), some observers noted that the Soviet proposal included references to a comprehensive system of control to be achieved by stages, and to aerial observation and photography—a form of control the Soviets had resisted until now.

Then at the beginning of 1960 the peripatetic Soviet leader took a second trip to South and Southeast Asia, where he visited India and Indonesia, making promises of economic aid. While in Indonesia he also announced the opening of Friendship University in Moscow (subsequently renamed Patrice Lumumba University)—an institute specially designed for the training of personnel from the underdeveloped countries. In part the trip may have been an effort to counter the good impression created by President Eisenhower on his own Asian trip in December 1959, when he drew enormous and enthusiastic crowds. In any event, Khrushchev's visit led to large aid commitments to India and Indonesia: total Soviet credits to help India fulfill its third five-year plan amounted to $500 million in rubles.

The Eisenhower administration, still lukewarm and unable to make much sense of Khrushchev's roving diplomacy, had agreed to a summit conference in Paris, in May, and again before the meeting, Khrushchev returned to the theme that Russia must sign a peace treaty with East Germany, after which the Allies would have to renegotiate their rights to Berlin with the East Germans.

KHRUSHCHEV (II) : HOSTILITY AND FAILURE

The Paris conference was a disaster. It appeared to initiate a new period of renewed hostility that ended in the Cuban missile crisis. The immediate occasion for the blowup at Paris was the shooting down of an American U–2 spy plane on a flight over the Soviet Union, from a base in Pakistan, and the revelation that such planes had been flying across the country since 1956. The United States government proved embarrassingly unable to cope with the revelation, at first denying it, then admitting it. The Soviet premier refused to accept President Eisenhower's statement that the flights would be discontinued. Instead, he arrived in Paris, delivered a

blistering attack, demanded a personal apology, and declared that negotiations with the United States were meaningless until the fall elections
had replaced its moribund leadership. He had staked his position on
growing friendship and good relations with the United States, he had not
taken any decisive action on Berlin, he had come closer to accepting
Western disarmament positions, and how had the West responded? By
placing new intermediate range ballistic missiles in Europe, by introducing new criteria into the disarmament talks, and by flying the U–2 spy
planes over the Soviet Union. A month later, when an American RB–47
reconnaissance bomber was shot down over the Barents Sea, he claimed
that it had violated Soviet airspace. The United States answered that it
had been 30 miles out over the ocean and that Soviet fighter planes, having failed to force it over the Soviet Union, had then shot it down.
Whether or not the American story was true, the worried British warned
that they wanted prior notification of such flights from British bases. In a
time of rapid retaliation it seemed dangerously provocative to send such
planes even within 30 miles of the Russian coastline.*

At this point Khrushchev, who had earlier invited Eisenhower to visit
the Soviet Union, coldly told him he had better "postpone" his visit. In
June, Japanese demonstrations against American treaty ties reached such
proportions that the Japanese government felt constrained to call off Eisenhower's visit to that supposedly reliable ally in the Far East. In January 1961 Cuba, now firmly tied economically to the socialist bloc, forced
a break in diplomatic relations with the United States. Later in the year
Khrushchev informed the United States that in light of American ob-
structionism it would be wise to abandon the separate nuclear test-ban
talks that had been going on. He pointed to the new factor of French nuclear testing: the de Gaulle government exploded its first atomic bomb in
the Sahara on February 13, 1960, during the period of an informal mora-
torium on testing between the Soviet Union and the United States. In the
light of President Eisenhower's declaration that the United States would
feel free to resume testing, since no formal test-ban agreement had been
reached, the Soviet Union, declared Khrushchev, would also feel free to
resume. And in the fall the Russians embarked on a series of forty tests
that included, on October 30, the largest explosion yet, of a weapon
equivalent to 50 or 60 million tons of TNT. In response, the United
States began with small, underground tests that produced no fallout: it
was true that the Atomic Energy Commission, certain military men, and

---

* In later years it became common knowledge that both the Russians and Americans
continually tested one another's defensive reactions and dispositions by sending isolated
flights over vital sectors. And, ironically, 1970s arms control agreements depended upon
the capacity both sides developed to fly spy satellites over each others' territory.

numerous Congressmen had urged resumption. In mid-1962 the United States resumed atmospheric testing.

In the meantime, Khrushchev came to the United Nations General Assembly meeting in the fall of 1960, to which he had encouraged attendance of heads of states. Here he embraced Fidel Castro, suggested that neutral states should now participate in disarmament negotiations (raising the suspicion that he was again using the talks mainly for propaganda purposes) and introduced a plan designed to appeal to new states to replace the single Secretary-General of the United Nations with a three-man committee, or "troika" (named after a Russian sled drawn by three horses). The occasion was the crisis in the Congo, in which many African leaders had lost confidence in UN Secretary-General Dag Hammarskjold; the plan would not only lead to his replacement but give new states a greater voice in the conduct of United Nations affairs.

Finally, during the summer of 1961, he brought to a conclusion the crisis that had been hanging over Berlin.

That year the economic situation in East Germany was bad. At Vienna, in May, Khrushchev had renewed his request to the new American President Kennedy that the Berlin issue be solved, and the President had come away dismayed at what he considered to be the Premier's toughness and unwillingness to compromise. In ensuing weeks the Russian repeated the request, and with this threat in the air, the flow of refugees from East Germany to the West swelled to a torrent. Among the refugees were many of the technicians, doctors, and other professional men most needed by the regime in the East. In July Khrushchev told the Western powers he would have to rescind the proposal he had made a year earlier for a one-third cut in Soviet and Western armed forces. President Kennedy responded by asking for increased military appropriations and draft calls. On August 13 came the long-awaited—but unexpected—Soviet move. The Russians merely closed the border between East and West Berlin to any traffic by erecting a wall across the city and, as the months went by, greatly strengthening "the Wall."

It was a shocking move, dividing families, people from their place of work, friend from friend. But it left West Berlin and the routes to it intact.

Kennedy—under a wave of criticism for not having prevented the building of the Wall—sent Vice-President Lyndon B. Johnson, General Lucius Clay of Berlin airlift fame, and a small extra combat force to Berlin. There were intense protests and solemn resolves that the Wall must come down. But the West was not ready to risk war for freedom of movement between East and West Berlin, and the Wall stood.

And in 1962 came the missile crisis in Cuba.

Westerners—and especially President Kennedy and his advisers—sought to explain the mercurial Khrushchev's moves. After 1957 had come the period of easing relations. Then came the Berlin crisis and the Paris blow-up, the RB–47 incident, the attack on Hammarskjold, intervention in the Congo (see below, Chapter 9), aid to Castro, intervention in Laos, resumption of aerial nuclear tests, threats and harassment, the Berlin Wall, and the missile crisis. What had happened?

The answer seems to be threefold. On the one hand the West had either been unable to understand or else to respond to the view of Berlin and East German independence and sovereignty held by Khrushchev. In a period in which the two superpowers recognized that they must come to an accommodation to avoid the possibility of nuclear war, Berlin was an anachronism, an island far within the eastern sphere, and one that continually served to disrupt relations by upsetting conditions within East Germany, for whose existence and boundaries he wanted to get international recognition. West Berlin constituted a continued denial of East Germany's status. Moreover, Khrushchev must have felt that he had offered the West several ways to resolve the situation; he had not insisted on incorporation of the western zones into the east zone, had set no time limits, had given warnings. Finally, when the Wall was built, it was, in a sense, a "minimal" solution: one that did *not* interfere with the status of West Berlin as the West had come to define it, economically and politically linked to West Germany, and occupied by the Allied Powers. In other words, what the West saw as an aggressive move may well have been seen by Khrushchev as an attempt to stabilize relations. The West may have made a mistake; but so may have Khrushchev.

A second factor certainly lay both in Khrushchev's personality and in the political role he had to play. He was a Communist: "We shall remain Communist until shrimps learn to whistle." In 1961, in a speech in which he declared nuclear war and conventional war too dangerous for mankind, he nevertheless declared that the Soviet Union would have to support "wars of national liberation," those wars in which progressive domestic elements tried to overthrow the imperialist governments that ruled over them. And he told Americans that their grandchildren would live under Communism;" We shall bury you." By which he meant, presumably, that the Communist system's superiority would lead even Americans ultimately to adopt it.

Yet he was also the head of state of a superpower; to advance its interests and his own, he was quite willing to sacrifice Communist parties abroad, as he did in the Middle East—only remonstrating with Nasser over the Egyptian's suppression of the Egyptian Communist Party. When he saw an opportunity to extend Russian power, as in the Middle East, or

when the United States appeared noncooperative or threatening, he acted.

But his political position was even more important. He had faced internal opposition to his assumption of power and had overcome it. Yet in
the complex society that he now attempted to rule, completely arbitrary
power such as Stalin had exercised was impossible; too many organized
interests, too many entrenched and institutionalized practices blocked it.
There were managerial groups, technicians, scientists, party organization
men, people devoted to continued emphasis on heavy industry as against
people who wanted priorities shifted to services and consumption goods,
centralizers, and decentralizers in the planning and administrative fields
—an extraordinary number of now vocal interests. In addition there was
the military, critical of Khrushchev's tendency to cut military spending in
favor of consumer goods—and the Chinese, to whom his "Goulash Communism" meant two things: an emphasis on material incentives foreign to
their conception of what Communism should be, as well as an orientation
toward raising consumption in the Soviet Union at the expense of aid to
the world Communist movement. This, of course, was in addition to their
growing conviction that Khrushchev was far too ready to compromise
with their main enemy—the United States. Consequently, when the U–2
overflight came to public light, laying the Russian premier open to the
charge that he had jeopardized Russian security by trusting Eisenhower,
a variety of groups were ready to attack him—not only for this, but also
for other reasons.

One result was general backtracking on a number of internal reforms;
the other was the rather more general policy of hardness and—as it later
came to be called by opponents—"adventurism" in foreign affairs. In a
very real sense, to preserve his position, Khrushchev had to prove that he
was a tougher Communist than others were. It seems also possible that
Khrushchev resented American failure to make matters easier for him
by acknowledging the sovereignty of East Germany. In so doing the
United States kept open the issue of legitimacy of the entire Eastern bloc,
and did so while placing missiles around its perimeters. In any event, the
1960 to 1962 crises and threats followed, culminating in the Cuban missile
crisis.

Cuba shook and sobered many people, including the ebullient and
blustering Khrushchev. Once more, as at the time of the Twentieth Party
Congress Secret Speech, he had taken an incredible risk. In the face of
the awesome possibility of nuclear war, vast American missile superiority, and President Kennedy's sagacity in not pressing the American advantage too far, the Russian accepted defeat and put the best light possible

upon it. To compensate the military, the Soviet government increased its arms budget by 40 per cent the next year, and the weakened Khrushchev had to agree to the move (even though he had already appeased the military in 1961 by suspending a demobilization he had ordered in 1960). On the international scene, however, his response showed that he had drawn the same conclusion as the Americans: the balance of terror was too dangerous and needed stabilizing. In early 1963 the Russian and American governments agreed to a "hotline" direct teletype link between Washington and Moscow. In the case of a nuclear accident, a small outbreak of violence that threatened to escalate, or the kind of direct confrontation that had occurred in Cuba, and in a time when technological developments had led to the possibility of almost instantaneous response, such a link might give the two major powers a chance to avert a response neither wanted. Later, that same year, and despite a Chinese warning to the Soviet Union against it, the two countries concluded a ban on testing nuclear weapons in the air.

KHRUSHCHEV'S SUCCESSORS

Then, to the surprise of most outside observers, on October 14, 1964, Nikita Khrushchev was removed from office by unanimous vote of his Politburo colleagues. Summoning him back from a sojourn in Georgia, they attacked him for a long list of errors and shortcomings: economic failure, agricultural failure, administrative failure; lack of coordination and sudden switches of policy, lack of consistency, boasting; unrest in satellites and the bitter quarrel with China, division in the Communist world and willingness to sacrifice all to an accommodation with America; cultivation of a personality cult and policy-making without reference to his colleagues. The Soviet Union, they declared, cannot be controlled by the impulses of an old man. And Nikita Khrushchev, who had dominated one of the world's two most powerful states for almost a decade, became an unperson, scarcely mentioned in the Soviet Union, soon to disappear from the history books, buried at his death in 1971 in a grave outside the Kremlin walls, among lesser personages of recent Russian history.

For the next three years after Khrushchev's deposition there were no daring initiatives on the part of the new Soviet leadership. Brezhnev and Kosygin consolidated their administration at home, and while the United States enmired itself so disastrously in Vietnam, the Russian leaders, relatively speaking, hardly reacted. They told President Johnson in 1966 that there was no hope of a detente while the United States continued the war, and they stepped up their shipments to North Vietnam. Yet the supposed leaders of the world proletarian revolutionary forces signed a consular agreement and an air transport agreement with the United States, began negotiation of the nuclear nonproliferation treaty, signed in 1968, and the treaty banning nuclear weapons in outer space. (To indicate displeasure with the course of American policy in Vietnam they postponed ratification of the consular treaty for a year and a half.) In the meantime they concerted with France on the type of color TV system they should adopt, invited the giant Italian Fiat automobile company to build a plant in the Soviet Union, and further expanded trade with the West. In March 1967, when a Russian trade mission arrived in Colombia, Fidel Castro angrily attacked the Soviet Union for helping to support ruling oligarchies and suppress revolutionaries.

On June 23 to 25, 1967, Premier Kosygin, attending a special United Nations meeting on the Middle East war (see below, p. 313), met with President Johnson, in the tiny college town of Glassboro, New Jersey, where they reviewed a host of issues. Clearly, they differed over how to end the war in Vietnam as well as how to resolve the new Middle East crisis. But they agreed that neither conflict should be allowed to become a wider one. China called the meeting a step toward a global American-Soviet deal intended to enhance the anti-China anti-Communist, anti-people, and counterrevolutionary Washington-Moscow alliance and intensify the suppression of the surging revolutionary struggle of the peoples of the world.

On his way home Kosygin stopped off in Cuba, presumably to tell Castro to slow down his revolutionary efforts and to warn him that the USSR could not support wars of liberation in Latin America.

In the meantime, in 1965, when India and Pakistan fought a brief and bitter war that ended with a United Nations-sponsored cease-fire (see below, Chapter 10), it was the Soviet Union that acted as a sponsor of a meeting held in Tashkent, in January 1965, where, using Russian good offices, India and Pakistan agreed to pull back their military forces, resume diplomatic relations, and work toward solving some of the political problems that had brought on the war.

In the light of all these apparently normal relations, was it not wise to assume that the leaders of the Soviet Union had undergone the process suggested by George Kennan in his famous memorandum on containment in 1947—that is, they had come to accept coexistence of different social systems on all levels, and in all its various forms? At the offices of the General Agreement on Tariffs and Trade, in Geneva, Switzerland, the joke went around that the only reason the Soviet Union didn't join this particular western organization was China, and how its leaders would, so to speak, capitalize on it. Which may, perhaps, reveal more about jokes at international organizations than about Soviet international behavior. After all, Russian leaders were under domestic pressure to better their economy, where Khrushchev's boasts had proved to be empty; they occupied a position of strategic inferiority to the United States; they had, however, a secure position buttressed by control of Eastern Europe and a well-recognized world role supported by their large-scale aid program. On the other hand they had certainly found that the newly independent states—the fruits of the shattered western imperialism—had not fallen easily into the "progressive" camp. They had, in short, too much to lose and too little to gain by an adventurous foreign policy.

And yet in 1967 and 1968 two major world events, the Middle East War and its aftermath and the invasion of Czechoslovakia, showed that the Russians aimed at more than a protective detente with the United States. Moreover, their subsequent actions showed that they had spent the years since the Cuban missile crisis in catching up and overtaking the United States in missiles, modernizing their large conventional forces, and even more important, creating a navy that transformed Russia from a landlocked continental power into a world naval power. World War II had ended any possible German or Japanese naval threat; the next quarter century saw the decline of the British Navy to peripheral importance and its withdrawal from virtually all advanced bases. Only the American Navy could block Russian sea communications to the rest of the world and by the end of the sixties Russian leaders revealed that they had decided to meet the challenge. It was hard to know how much of the enormous military buildup and deployment was response to American policy and the defeat in Cuba, how much to difficulty in accepting other commitments to far-flung revolutionary forces, how much to the perceived threat of a hostile China determined to build its own nuclear power, how much to the continuously threatened breakup of the Russian-dominated empire in Eastern Europe. All were linked. In any event, the months after the war in the Middle East and the invasion of Czechoslovakia set the pattern for the gradual deployment of the new and improved forces.

The June 1967 Middle East War was the third war between the new state of Israel and its Arab neighbors, and as in the second one, in 1956, the Soviet Union played an important role. When France moved out of the Middle East in the postwar period and Britain's power declined, the United States had felt it necessary to move in, sponsoring the still-born Middle East Defense organization and the Bagdad Pact, creating the Central Treaty Organization. (There had been justifiable fears of Russian intentions in the area, based on Russian-expressed interest in the area at the time of the Hitler-Stalin pact, on Russia's postwar demands for a trusteeship over Libya and joint control with Turkey of the Dardanelles, its reluctance in moving out of Azerbaijan province in Iran, and its subsequent pressures on Turkey. And, as usual, there had been the ever-present Communist parties, still much under Russian direction.) The Russian response, once it reversed its previously favorable position to Israel, was the arms deal with Egypt in 1955. By this, and subsequent aid to other non-Communist regimes in the area, Russia suddenly became an important factor in the Middle East. It was this new presence that emboldened Egypt in 1956, led to the Suez war, and to the Eisenhower Doctrine of 1957. In the next few years the Soviet Union re-equipped the Egyptian army, helped build the Aswan Dam, and provided economic and military aid to Syria and Iraq. The more radical Arab states had found an ally in their fight against Israel and against Western policy; the oil-poor states, Egypt and Syria, also had an added element of strength in their struggle to obtain a share in the oil riches of the others.

Relations between Syria and Israel became especially bad in 1966 and 1967, when the new radical Syrian government deliberately fostered guerrilla raids into Israel. At the United Nations the Soviet Union vetoed even the mildest of resolutions calling for conciliation, and in Egypt Nasser found himself under attack for not pressing home the war against Israel as his Syrian brothers were doing. In early May, repeating an earlier charge, the USSR told Egypt that Israel was preparing to invade Syria and, as tension mounted in the Middle East, advised Nasser that while it would not intervene in war between the Arabs and Israel it would act to neutralize any American attempt to do so. On May 30 it announced plans to almost double its Mediterranean fleet, already engaged in harassing the U.S. Sixth Fleet.

Armed with this knowledge, all about him a frenzied clamoring to end the long-standing insult to Arab honor, Nasser to bolster his fading prestige, took a fateful step: he ordered withdrawal of the United Nations Emergency Force that had patrolled the Egyptian-Israeli cease-fire line since 1956. Most important, the UN Secretary-General was forced to remove it from Sharm-al-Sheikh, the point guarding the Strait of Tiran that gave Israel access to the Red Sea and Indian Ocean. Israel, deprived of trade through the Suez Canal, had long warned the Egyptians that closure of the strait would be a *casus belli*—an act tantamount to war. Nasser proceeded, on May 22, to close the strait.

Russian spokesmen later denied knowledge that Nasser would take the action; Nasser himself may not have realized that Israel would keep its word, but he promised the Arab world that if it did, Arab forces would deliver a crushing retaliatory blow. On May 30, King Hussein of Jordan, facing intense internal pressure, patched up his long-standing quarrel with Nasser and signed a mutual defense pact. Algeria, Iraq, and others promised to send troops.

Instead, in a series of lightning blows that began on Monday, June 5, the Israeli armed forces crushed the Arab armies facing them on three fronts, and when, under United Nations auspices, a cease-fire was established a week later, found themselves holding the Egyptian territories of Gaza and the entire Sinai peninsula, Jerusalem and the west bank of the Jordan river in Jordan, and the Golan Heights in Syria, a border area from which the Syrian Army and guerrillas had long harassed Israeli farmers and fishermen. Egypt was deprived not only of the Sinai, with its newly developed oil resources, and the Suez canal whose east bank was now held by Israel, but also of a billion dollars worth of Russian-supplied weapons.

Arabs blamed their own military leaders, the United States for active participation on the side of Israel, the Soviet Union for not intervening on their side and then for forcing them to accept a United Nations cease-fire.* The Soviet Union blamed the inept leadership of the Arab armed forces (and suggested that Nasser had acted precipitously, when they had tried to hold him back), and of course, the Israelis for launching the war. For the Israelis, the whole episode demonstrated the weakness of international guarantees and institutions and the necessity for them to rely upon their own armed forces and control of strategic geographic areas. Nasser, they pointed out, had only to speak for the U.N. Emergency Force to melt away. Then, when he proclaimed blockade, no one else was ready to take real action to stop him.

For the past decade the Soviet Union had found it convenient to paint Israel as the outpost of American imperialism fighting against the progressive, socialist forces of Arab national liberation movements. The Middle East conflict—and the Russian position in support of the Arabs —could in this way be assimilated to a view of the world divided between a wavering imperialism and a growing progressive coalition of socialist states proper and states seeking national liberation against the domination of imperialism—rather than, as many analysts would have it, a conflict of nationalisms. But the Soviet Union found itself embarrassed, its client states in a situation of abject defeat. The question was, what should it do now?

To regain and buttress its position among Arabs as their only true friend, the Russians sought, but failed to get, harsh condemnation of Israel at the United Nations and a call for a return to the *status quo ante.*

* King Hussein and Nasser at first asserted that the United States had participated in the air raids that destroyed the Egyptian air force. Nasser later retracted the charge, but the myth was well established, and several Arab governments broke off relations with the United States as a result. Despite Nasser's subsequent disavowal, many never re-established them.

The United States worked hard to get a resolution that would not only bring Israeli withdrawal but would resolve some of the conflicts that had produced the war. It failed, too. Eventually, on November 22, the Security Council passed a British-sponsored resolution that called for withdrawal of Israeli forces, the ending of belligerency, guaranteed territorial inviolability and political independence and security for states within the area, freedom of navigation through international waterways, and a just settlement of the now heightened refugee problem. Syria promptly rejected the resolution and Nasser declared it inadequate: he would never recognize Israel, negotiate with it, make peace with it, or permit it to navigate through the Suez Canal. Israel refused to withdraw until the other parts of the resolution were secured as a result of direct negotiations between Israel and the Arab states involved.

Despite their vociferous support for the Arab cause and a barrage of condemnation of Israel as the spearhead of imperialism, Kosygin and Brezhnev nevertheless assured the United States they wanted a peaceful, political solution, and somewhat more privately warned the vengeful Arabs not to resume the war. Cautiously, they resumed shipments of arms to Egypt to replace the enormous amount of material seized or destroyed by Israel.

Frustrated by military defeat of Arab states, displaced Palestinians took to increased guerrilla warfare and to international terrorism to focus attention upon their cause and try to get other countries to bring pressure on Israel. Israel struck back across the cease-fire lines, deep into Jordan, Lebanon and Syria, while exchanging gunfire across the Suez Canal. In mid-1969 Nasser renounced the cease-fire and declared a war of attrition; Israeli air attacks increased in number and depth of penetration; UN Secretary-General U Thant reported that the cease-fire had virtually come to an end.

In the meantime the Soviet Union reached a major decision to increase the flow of arms into the area. By mid-1970 it had re-equipped the Egyptian forces alone with over $3.5 billion worth of tanks and airplanes, to the point where the armies of Egypt, Syria, and Iraq vastly outnumbered the Israeli forces in modern weapons. Israel, facing a French embargo on arms, turned to a hesitant United States, which in turn continued supplying arms and training to the more conservative Arab states of Jordan and Saudi Arabia.

Israel refused to withdraw its armies until peace talks had produced solid agreements. Arab leaders who were willing to talk peace refused to do so until Israel had withdrawn to all the pre-1967 boundaries. In the face of their growing military strength, the war of attrition and the threatening tone of Arab spokesmen, Israel proceeded to raid further into

Egypt, capturing and demolishing radar stations, destroying factories close to Cairo. Then, in April 1970 the Israeli government announced that the Soviet Union was deploying ground-to-air missiles in Egypt manned by Russian crews, and that Russian pilots were flying the new MIG–21 planes supplied to the Egyptian air force. The danger of a large-scale Russian intervention in the area appeared, and Israel charged that even as the Soviet Union was engaging in big-power peace talks on the area, its open military support for Egypt increased Egyptian intransigence and the chances for war.

In the face of the new Soviet commitment, buttressed now by increased naval forces that had entered the Mediterranean a year earlier, American Secretary of State Rogers launched a new peace initiative, based on the November 22 Security Council resolution. He called for a cease-fire for a limited period while peace talks with UN Mediator Gunnar Jarring resumed, and a standstill on introduction or construction of any military installation within a 30-mile zone each side of the Suez Canal. Syria, Iraq, and the guerrilla forces all rejected the proposal, and in Israel, it caused a serious government crisis. Nevertheless Israel accepted, assured by the United States that the cease-fire provisions would be observed—and so did Egypt and the Soviet Union, which in turn assured the United States it would observe the provisions. The guns and raids stopped on August 7, and August 24 talks began again at the United Nations, in New York. Two weeks later, Israel suspended them: in the first weeks of the cease-fire, the Russians and Egyptians had constructed some fifty new missile batteries with five to six hundred missiles within the prohibited zone—probably, as the Israeli Prime Minister said, "the most advanced missile system in the world." To Israelis, the incident illustrated once again how meaningless international guarantees and promises were, and reinforced their determination to hold fast to the position they held until they could be certain of their own security (yet in a situation of almost ruinous security expenditures). To the Arabs, the incident was a further indication that Russia was their main friend and at the same time, the new missile bases with their Russian crews secured the air over Egypt, previously dominated by the Israeli air force. In the fact of the continuously growing Arab military might, Israel turned again to the United States and received a half-billion dollar military credit; on the basis of this, it returned to the peace talks at the end of the year, even though it had declared it would do so only if the new missiles were withdrawn.

The Soviet presence in Egypt served to highlight a general and growing Russian naval presence not only in the Mediterranean, but since 1968, all through the Indian Ocean. A reopening of the Suez Canal would provide a useful link, cutting thousands of miles from the trip between the

Indian Ocean and Soviet ports on the Black Sea. While the naval presence remained a minor one through these years, it nevertheless came at a time when other navies were withdrawing from the Indian Ocean, and when the Soviet Union had begun to develop a series of substantial interests in the area.

The interests have been various, beginning with Khrushchev's early sallies into South and Southeast Asia in company with Bulganin in 1955 (see above, Chapter 8), reaffirmed in 1960, when the Soviet leader took a second trip, during which he committed the Soviet Union to large-scale aid to India and Indonesia: total Soviet aid to India's third five-year plan was to come to over $500 million in rubles.

In 1961, while relations with the West were bad on all other fronts, the Soviet Union intervened directly in the crisis in Laos, where a truce precariously maintained since the 1954 Geneva settlement had broken down (see above, Chapter 7).

Subsequently, as the war in Indochina increased in intensity, the Soviet Union became the chief supplier to North Vietnam. The main supply routes lay across China, but the split between the two Communist giants made the communications difficult. Although the Chinese charged Russia with failure to aid fraternal Communist North Vietnam, the Russians charged the Chinese with obstructing shipments, and there is evidence that the Chinese did force the Russians to resort to ocean shipping, perhaps because it would bring them into greater conflict with the United States. In any event, the importance of ocean routes and their security was made clear to them, just as it was in the case of the drawn-out Congo crisis of the early sixties when for a variety of reasons, including the difficulty of supplying the groups it supported, the Soviet Union withdrew from an audacious advanced position.

As the split with China developed, Khrushchev and his successors became more and more important supporters of the Indian and Pakistani governments, on the Chinese borders. In 1959, when Chinese forces overran a rebellious Tibet and India opened its borders to thirteen thousand refugees, Khrushchev was openly critical of the Chinese. Three years later, when China and India created a major international crisis over their border war high in the Himalayan mountains, Khrushchev hesitated momentarily, but ended up continuing economic and military aid to India. Walter Ulbricht of East Germany delivered the strong bloc condemnation of the Chinese (see below, p. 329).

In 1965 India and Pakistan fought another brief and bitter war. The result, in terms of Soviet foreign policy, was multifold. Pakistan had long been an ally of the United States. But the United States had conceived of the alliance as directed against the Soviet Union and China, not India.

India had disapproved of the alliance in part because it was convinced the American arms would ultimately be used against India, as they were. When war broke out, Western arms sales were cut off to both countries, with the result that India turned to the Soviet Union, and Pakistan to China. The Indian Navy was now equipped with Russian-made submarines, escorts, torpedo boats, and patrol boats, while Russian-built MIG–21's became the backbone of its air force. Fearful of the Chinese, who not only bested Indian forces in the brief border war of 1962 but had since developed a nuclear capacity, Indian officials felt they could best rely on the Soviet Union. Pakistan, unable to get all the types of weapons it wanted from China, also turned increasingly to the Soviet Union.

The 1965 war and its aftermath resulted not only in an increased military dependence on the Soviet Union. Kosygin and Brezhnev came forward to offer their services as mediator and were accepted by both countries. And so the world was treated to the spectacle of the Soviet Union, at Tashkent, in January 1966 working out a pullback of military forces, resumption of diplomatic relations, and agreement to work on the political problems that had originally brought on the war. The constructive role played by the Soviet Union gave it increased diplomatic leverage with the two countries—and was without question played with an eye to the effect it would have on the position China aspired to in Asia and the world.

One result was that the Soviet Union obtained access to docking facilities throughout the subcontinent. To these must be added the various rights of access to port facilities it has acquired in the Red Sea area (where the USSR helped the Yemeni rebels and has become the chief arms supplier to the government of the Sudan). Further to the south, the Soviet Union has expanded and modernized the port of Mogadishu, in Somalia, to which it also became principal arms supplier. In addition, it has obtained port rights in the Mauritius island grouping, and provided arms aid to such countries as Uganda and Tanzania.

At the eastern end of the Indian Ocean, both Russia and China lost out in Indonesia in 1965, when an army coup forestalled a Communist one abetted by the President, Sukarno (see below, p. 390). Although Sukarno had used Russian-supplied weapons to attack Malaysia and try to establish an Indonesian dominance in the area, the Malaysian government was willing to increase its trade with the Soviet Union, which has become the chief purchaser of its largest export, rubber. In addition, the Soviet Union obtained access to Singapore ship repair and replenishment facilities, on the Straits of Malacca, which connect the Indian and Pacific Oceans and through which, for example, pass 90 per cent of Japan's oil.

The result of quiet diplomacy, economic and military penetration, and aid was that Russia came to constitute the chief—and about the only—large power presence in an area where only a few years earlier Britain dominated, and where Russia had previously never had any political position.

If the Suez Canal is ever to be reopened, Russia, whose trade through the Canal was minimal in the past, will now be one of the most interested parties. In May 1969, Peking denounced the entire Russian effort as an attempt to contain China, and called the Red Navy a tool for establishing the supremacy of a new colonial empire.

For many years the Soviet Union concentrated on an enormous conventional submarine fleet. (In 1970 it still had 320 such submarines in operation, compared to 67 for the United States). In this, like the Germans in the previous 50 years, it had assumed the defensive posture of a continental power. Submarines can be used to cut the sea communications of an insular power such as Britain or the United States when they are trying to exert power on the continental landmass, but cannot well be used to support commitments off the landmass. What the foregoing shows is that Russia has come, in the last decade, to assume such commitments, and begun to create the kind of naval power requisite to them. In the last years of the 1960s it created, for the first time, what it called naval infantry and expanded its amphibious landing capabilities; it launched two helicopter carriers and began construction of an attack carrier; it continued a buildup of a variety of the most modern, missile-equipped, surface vessels and proceeded, in a remarkably old-fashioned manner, to "show the flag" in ports all over the world. By 1970 Russian Navy ships in the North Atlantic outnumbered NATO vessels six to one; its Mediterranean armada was larger than the American Sixth Fleet; it had conducted joint maneuvers with Cuban units in the hitherto inviolable Gulf of Mexico and had built docks and repair facilities in Cuba, whose ports were visited dramatically in mid-1969 by a Russian naval squadron led by a rocket cruiser. Russian missile submarines cruised the American coasts, and Russian naval yards were outbuilding the United States by a ratio of eight to one. The Russian nuclear-powered missile submarine fleet appeared destined to outstrip that of the United States by the early 1970s. And, as already pointed out, another aspect of the military situation became clear in the latter part of the decade: Khrushchev's successors would no longer accept a position of inferiority in numbers of intercontinental missiles. In 1965, to the United States' 934 ICBM's, the USSR had only 224. By the end of 1969 the United States had 1054, and the Soviet Union 1109. A year later, while the United States retained the same number, the Soviet Union had added another 330. And both had begun to put multiple warheads on the missiles.

THE CZECH INVASION

Back in 1956 there was a war in the Middle East when Arab states, having for the first time received support from the Soviet Union, felt they could now rectify injustices imposed upon them from without; there was at the same time a Russian invasion of an Eastern European state—Hungary—that had threatened to leave the fold. In 1967–68 there was a war in the Middle East, again based on Russian support for Arab aims; once more, this time in Czechoslovakia, another Russian invasion of an Eastern European state took place. And in some ways it seemed a repeat of 1956. After apparently friendly talks, Russian tanks and troops occupied a Socialist state, removed an obviously popular leadership, and forced the people to accept a government they opposed. The differences, of course, were great. For one thing Khrushchev was no longer in power; his successors were the far less colorful and seemingly more cautious Leonid Brezhnev and Alexei Kosygin. All states shared in the very much larger measure of bloc independence. Czechoslovakia was one of the members, however, where much of the old-line Stalinist leadership had ridden out the Khrushchev period, and clung to an old-style repressive system. Only in 1967 did the dam begin to burst, and as in Hungary, against a background of economic difficulty, the intellectuals began to question the nature of the regime.

Part of the problem was that the entire Communist bloc was in economic difficulties. In the late 1950s Khrushchev had promised that the Soviet Union would begin to catch up with the United States in per capita production of meat, milk, and other consumer items. In what came to be derisively called "Goulash Communism," he had suggested that in a period in which war was no longer inevitable Communism would win because it would outperform capitalism in supplying consumer goods. But Goulash Communism failed, and by the mid-sixties, while the Soviet Union had to ignomiously import enormous quanities of grain, all the Communist states began to experiment with new economic forms to try to stimulate lagging production. Much of the experimentation involved measures that were the very antithesis of Stalinist economic practices: reliance upon market incentives, factory profits, and in connection with this, considerable decentralization both of planning and production. Such measures and debates about them were bound to stimulate ideological polemics, and this happened in Czechoslovakia and elsewhere. In the meantime, the change in government in West Germany in 1966 and in more flexible German diplomacy stirred misgivings among the hardliners and guardians of the faith. Rumania, the chief apostate, had established diplomatic relations with West Germany in January 1967, and German emissaries were seeking talks throughout Eastern Europe. Czechoslovakia proceeded to negotiate and sign a new trade agreement in midyear.

In January 1968, Antonin Novotny, long-time First Secretary of the Central Committee of the Czechoslovak Communist Party resigned, to be replaced by Alexander Dubcek, for five years First Secretary of the Slovak Communist Party. For the first time in twenty years the breath of liberlization swept through Czechoslovakia—and soon turned into a whirlwind. Press censorship was abandoned in February and formally abolished in June. Oldline Stalinists in the police, the army, and other ministries resigned or were dismissed. Liberals purged almost twenty years earlier reappeared and were rehabilitated through the now rejuvenated courts. Within months a new government appeared, freedoms of assembly, of the press, and of travel abroad were established, and a widespread debate developed on the role of a Communist Party in a truly democratic society. Excitement rose, among warnings to avoid excesses and the fate of Budapest in 1956. A new, humanized socialism would be established —but Dubcek, his name now a symbol of hope throughout Europe, took care not to repeat the Nagy mistake of withdrawing from the Communist system.

The Czech development could not but have an influence in the rest of Europe. In Poland, where over the years Gomulka, the apparent liberalizer of 1956, had presided over an increasingly repressive regime, students rioted, crying for "a Polish Dubcek." They were answered by wholesale arrests and expulsions, and purges of the university staff. Demands for liberalization were linked to Zionism, and the repression—using the old, long-established Polish anti-Semitism—took on vicious overtones. Gomulka invited Jews to leave Poland.

Russia, East Germany, and Bulgaria joined Poland in condemning what was rapidly becoming "revisionism" in Czechoslovakia, and held inconclusive talks with the Czechs. Warsaw pact maneuvers were held in southern Poland and Czechoslovakia in June, and the Czechs complained about how slow the troops were in leaving after completion of the exercises. The Russians indulged in a prolonged war of nerves. Janos Kadar, installed by the Russians in Hungary in 1956, warned the Czechs not to go too far; in July, Tito and Ceausescu of Rumania warmly commended the Czechs, and both were met by cheering crowds when they visited Prague in mid-August to lend further support. Russian leaders apparently came to fear the very real possibility of a little entente that might even look to the West for assistance.

And then, within a week, on August 20 and 21, Warsaw pact troops spearheaded by the Russians but including East German, Polish, and Hungarian contingents crossed the Czech frontier and occupied key points all over the country. A few days later there were 500,000 occupying troops, and five hundred Russian tanks in Prague alone. Dubcek and other members of his government were arrested but soon released, as the Russians met stubborn, generally passive resistance—as well as condemnation not only by the United Nations but by almost every Communist party abroad. The East German government of Walter Ulbricht had urged the move on the Russians, fearful of the spreading rot of liberalization, and the Russians invaded, fully conscious of the repercussions the move would have. In October they imposed a treaty on the Czechs to legalize continued stationing of Russian troops in the hapless and hostile country. They continued a slow and relentless pressure that led, eventually, to a restoration of the old, repressive system, and a thorough purge of all the liberals. In November 1968 at the Fifth Congress of the Polish Communist Party Leonid Brezhnev spelled out official doctrine:

> When internal and external forces that are hostile to socialism try to turn the development of some socialist country towards the restoration of a capitalist regime, when socialism in that country and the socialist community as a whole are threatened, it becomes not only a problem of the people concerned, but a common problem and concern of all socialists.

In other words, he re-emphasized that national independence must be subservient to multilateral bloc decision making. The Russians did not kill Dubcek, as they had killed the Hungarian Nagy. Dubcek remained at his post, trying to moderate the Russian pressures, and was finally ousted and exiled as Ambassador to Turkey, a position from which he finally retired in 1970 for reasons of health.

Rumania and Yugoslavia both protested the invasion, and prepared for the possibility of one themselves. The attack never came, but the Rumanians subsequently defiantly refused Russian demands to place all their forces under a Warsaw Pact joint command and in 1969 welcomed a visit from President Nixon. It is hard to imagine any event better symbolizing the changed world situation.* The Chinese condemned the Brezhnev doctrine. But Czechoslovakia was safe for "socialism."

The massive and smoothly conducted Czech invasion demonstrated to the world that the Soviet Union had thoroughly modernized its conventional land forces. It jolted Westerners who had hoped that detente would

---

* Unless it was that de Gaulle's France, still a party to the North Atlantic Treaty, actually *trained* a small group of Russian paratroopers in Pau, in the south of France, during 1967—or that a tiny dissident, pro-Chinese Polish Communist Party was formed in Albania in the same year!

extend beyond formal government to government relations and, as recounted, gave new life to NATO, whose military leaders noted that the impressive Russian action took place while 60 Russian divisions were immobilized in the Far East, along the Chinese border. Clearly, whatever debates may have taken place between factions within the Russian establishment, Khrushchev's successors had all agreed that when Khrushchev had broken out of Stalin's basically continental orientation, his reach outstretched his grasp. They would not be caught short again. According to the NATO Defense Planning Committee, Russian military outlays rose five to six per cent per year from 1965 to 1969, while that of European NATO members dropped by four per cent per year.

The Czech invasion also revealed that a dozen years after Hungary the Communists had still not been able to build a satisfactory socialist commonwealth. Despite all Russian coverup propaganda, Dubcek's thaw was no capitalist-oriented counterrevolution, but a revolution that aimed at trying, within the limits imposed by Russia, to create a humane, democratic socialism. The system could not stand it. Russian demonstrations of intent to stay in Eastern Europe might force people to accept the system and relapse into passivity; but the incident again demonstrated that there was international danger in the instability of the Communist system. When East-West negotiations resumed on a large scale two years later, culminating in 1973 in the two conferences on mutual force reduction and European security, the Russians made one thing clear: they wanted any detente to guarantee continued control of their security sphere, regardless of the wishes of the people. It was hard to reconcile this with force reductions, and gave a certain air of unreality to the conferences. World arms spending remained at incredible levels (an accepted estimate for 1972 was 200 billion dollars). Many people still looked to arms for rectifying injustice or for defense, but there was certainly a widespread desire to diminish the expenditures, and the one hopeful area seemed to be the North Atlantic one, where desire for detente prevailed. Unfortunately, the implications of Czechoslovakia hung heavily over the negotiations.

Finally, the Czech invasion leads back to the oft-mentioned Russian-Chinese split. In 1968, the Russians demonstrated to the Chinese that they were indeed willing to use force to defend their vital interests as they defined them, and would do so massively and ruthlessly. The Soviet buildup in the years since Khrushchev might serve many purposes; but a review of Russian military-political policies in the Middle East, Africa, Asia, and even South America comes inevitably back to the Russian desire to check the influences of Mao's China and to the need to counter Chinese foreign policies.

THE RUSSIAN SPLIT WITH CHINA AND CHINESE FOREIGN POLICY

The Khrushchev years of detente politics in the late 1950s brought to the surface the series of latent conflicts with China, deriving from the facts of geography, from long years of history, from the different stages of development reached by the two countries, and from personal diplomacy. At the time that the United States was China's chief enemy, Khrushchev sought detente with the United States and met with Eisenhower at Camp David for private discussions. At a time when China was in conflict with India, Khrushchev continued to provide material support to the Indian government. When China sought nuclear weapons, Khrushchev first provided aid, then abruptly withdrew it, engaged in serious discussions with the United States on limits on such weapons and eventually reached general arms control agreements. With China dependent on Soviet economic aid for industrialization, Khrushchev turned to "Goulash Communism" with its emphasis on internal consumption and consequent limitations on any surplus available for aid. While giving verbal support to "wars of national liberation" Khrushchev continued to argue that bourgeois nationalist governments of newly independent states were objectively progressive and should be courted and supported.

In 1960 what had been only a subdued conflict based on these international differences broke into the open. The Chinese made grandiose claims for the "Great Leap Forward" of 1958–59, and Khrushchev disputed them. He found Mao's domestic opponents ready to listen to him, and Mao knew it; but Mao found in the remnants of the Russian "anti-party group" led by Molotov, allies against Khrushchev's brand of detente and revisionist politics—and Khrushchev knew this, too. In the case of China, Mao, by claiming that the Great Leap Forward, in which the mass of the people joined "communes," was a more rapid step toward Communism than those so far taken in the Soviet Union, ran afoul of other Chinese who felt that the communes with their emphasis on self-sufficiency and localized production marked a retrograde step in a country desperately trying to industrialize; in Russia, Molotov and others objected to Khrushchev's attempt to conduct an adventurous foreign policy while downgrading the role of heavy industry and military production at home. The Maoist Chinese ideological claims (and consequent opposition to Khrushchev) gave fuel to the Molotov group; the anti-Maoists in China could find support from Khrushchev. Khrushchev, to protect himself, took a double action: he assumed a tougher foreign policy, producing the Paris conference crisis of 1960, his rough handling of Kennedy at Vienna, the Laotian intervention, the visit to the United Nations and appeal for deposition of Hammarskjold, the Berlin Wall, and, finally, the Cuba missile crisis. But he also struck directly at China: without fanfare, Russian technicians were withdrawn from China in the summer of 1960, and all aid to nuclear development ceased. Dollar value of shipments of Russian goods—mainly machinery necessary to continued Chinese industrial development—fell from $500 million in 1960 to $100 million in 1961.

Despite this, at the November 1960 world conference of Communist parties representatives of the two Communist countries tried to patch up their differences; their agreement was only short-lived. Khrushchev now insisted that the Communist Party of the Soviet Union must be recognized by other, equal parties as their leaders, not because (as in Stalin's time) it was the first to make the revolution, or the only Communist party with a territorial base, but because it was the only one to have entered the state of Communist development—a claim directly counter to the Maoist one for the Chinese system of communes. In addition, he attacked the Chinese for trying to build support among other parties to unseat him, for their incorrect denunciations of his travels in the West and efforts to settle matters peacefully, and for their factionalism, which tended to split the world Communist movement. The Chinese, furious about the aid issue, now added the charge of revisionism, the very issue on which, in 1957, they had supported Khrushchev against Yugoslavia, Poland, and his internal opposition. By late 1961 Mao, involved in his own continual internal struggle to keep the Chinese revolution on the course of mass spontaneity and egalitarianism, held up the postrevolutionary materialism of Soviet society in the sixties as a terrible warning example of what his own opponents' policies would lead to once China had reached a similar level of economic development.

The struggle had begun with differences over international policy toward third world states. The Chinese had urged greater revolutionary daring and haste, while Khrushchev, seeking good relations with established bourgeois or radical non-Communist governments and making much more of Western military might, displayed more caution. Now the conflict was transferred to the domestic scene and, in short order, to the bloc itself; a struggle within Albania led to the triumph of a hardline Stalinist leadership; Albania was isolated from the bloc by Soviet-Yugoslav rapprochement, in which it was unwilling to acquiesce. In the resultant conflict with Russia over policy, Albania looked to China and found support, and after conversations with the recalcitrant Albanian leadership, Khrushchev declared that he could more easily come to an understanding with English Prime Minister MacMillan than with them.

In 1962, the Chinese denounced Khrushchev for his "adventurism" in installing the missiles in Cuba, and for "capitulationism" in removing them. It was the same year that Khrushchev supplied India with arms at the time of the Chinese-Indian border war. By 1963 Chinese and Russian spokesmen vied with one another in denunciations and revelations of the others' earlier treachery. What had once been, to the outsider, a veiled dispute clothed in almost impenetrable ideological guise, was now fully in the open, and the earlier appeals to opposition groups within each others' borders became open calls for overthrow of each others' ruling groups.

There were wide ramifications for the international movement. Communist parties split into Russian or Chinese factions. Some parties sided wholly with one or the other country, and Russia and China courted them as a means of exerting leverage on the other. In a number of Asian parties, Chinese influence appeared to dominate: in Indonesia, perhaps the largest and potentially most powerful one outside of the bloc; in Korea, Vietnam, Japan, Thailand, and Malaya. By mid-1964 Khrushchev decided to call a meeting of Communist parties from throughout the world, with the intent of reading the Chinese Communist Party out of the movement. Only his deposition on October 14 prevented that meeting. His successors reopened talks with the Chinese who had greeted his removal as a triumph, hoping that the disappearance of personal invective might ease relations. Two weeks of talks with Chou En-lai revealed not only that the basic causes for the conflict remained, but had, in fact, increased: within 24 hours after the removal of Khrushchev the Chinese detonated their first nuclear device, demonstrating that despite the economic shortcomings associated with the Great Leap Forward of the late 1950s, they had continued to concentrate resources in the nuclear field. The new Russian leaders looked on the development with dismay. (Earlier in the year Mao had in fact complained about Soviet massing of forces on the Chinese frontiers. It appeared that he feared a Russian preventive strike against Chinese nuclear installations.) In the next nine years the Chinese, like the French, refused to participate in nuclear weapons control agreements, arguing that all those proposed left intact Russian and United States nuclear forces and, thus, their joint world hegemony.

Chinese nuclear policy helped cement Indian-Russian ties, and prompted some Indians to call for Indian nuclear weapons, as well as for rejection of the nuclear nonproliferation treaty of 1963. Indians argued that the Treaty would keep them from acquiring a nuclear arsenal at the very time that China was building its own. For Mao, the lesson was again clear: the people could create by themselves and must never depend upon foreign aid; Russian aid had been proferred and then withdrawn— in the long run, a good thing, since it had made the Chinese self-reliant. And in Chinese comment on the world revolutionary situation in 1965

Lin Piao, Mao's chosen successor, read out the same lesson to revolutionaries the world over: they must depend on their own will and initiative and not look to outside aid. China could offer encouragement, training, and even some material help, but could never lead the revolutions.

In the next five years Chinese-Russian relations grew even worse, especially during the new internal Chinese convulsion called the Great Proletarian Cultural Revolution. In this two-year long upheaval, watched with bewilderment by outsiders, Mao proceeded to break up the Communist Party and destroy most existing forms of authority. With Little Red Books of Mao's thoughts in hand, groups of young radicals known as Red Guards roamed China, attacking all tendencies toward excessive specialization, establishment of any form of hierarchy, whether within factory, government office or school, and assaulted—verbally, physically, and psychologically—hundreds of thousands of old guard party and government leaders and cadres. In the course of this new Revolution, designed to prevent the nation from settling into a bureaucratic mode and to stir up mass participation, China almost severed its diplomatic connections with the rest of the world, virtually abandoned its effort to build a powerful block of anti-Russian Communist parties, and engaged in military skirmishes with Russia along their 4500-mile border.

The issue of the ill-defined Chinese borders actually arose earlier, in other contexts first. For some countries it contributed to the image of an aggressive Chinese foreign policy, to others of a state willing to settle contentious problems by negotiation. In 1961 the Chinese signed a border agreement with Burma, relatively favorable to Burmese claims. Later in the year they signed an equally favorable agreement with the tiny state of Nepal, and in November of 1963, with Afghanistan. The long border with Mongolia was confirmed by Chinese maps in the early 1960s, and China and Pakistan—a state that was, after all, member of a Western-sponsored alliance—began talks that ended in a border agreement in January 1965.* But in the meantime they fought a bitter border war with India that helped bring the latter into intimate relation with the Soviet Union and, as Russian-Chinese relations worsened in the 1960s led eventually to the treaty of friendship signed by India and Russia in 1971.

The border conflict in the south began with Tibet, over which China had long claimed a sovereignty disputed by both India and Tibet. In 1959 the Chinese ruthlessly crushed a Tibetan revolt stimulated by Chinese abrogation of a Chinese-Tibetan agreement allowing local autonomy. The Indian government charged that in addition the Chinese had

---

* India considered the agreement a hostile act, since it covered an area in Kashmir that it considered Indian.

made incursions into Indian territory, and they opened their borders to 13,000 Tibetan refugees including the Dalai Lama, spiritual leader of Tibetan Buddhists. Prime Minister Nehru reacted bitterly to Chinese charges that India had instigated the revolt. For the first time he made public the fact that a dispute existed over some 40,000 square miles of Indian-Chinese border area and that several border incidents had taken place during the previous decade.

In the next three years Chinese border units strengthened their position. In 1962 fighting broke out again; Nehru announced that Indian troops had undertaken an offensive to push Chinese soldiers out of Indian territory. Instead, Chinese troops drove deep into Indian territory, sweeping the Indian forces before them.

A storm broke over the Nehru government, which hastily passed increased appropriations and encouraged emergency enlistments in the armed forces. Nehru, under pressure, dropped his unpopular anti-Western Secretary of Defense Krishna Menon, and asked the Western powers for military aid. It was rapidly forthcoming, but not in the quantities the Indians had asked for. On the other hand, Khrushchev maintained deliveries of planes already ordered by India. India's neutral neighbours offered mediation and conciliation—and the Chinese, facing unprepared Indian troops, proceeded to stop and then, almost contemptuously, withdraw from some of the positions they had occupied.

In the West speculation centered on the Chinese motives for what appeared to be wanton aggression at the very time that China had reached favorable agreements with Indian neighbors. Why had the Chinese attacked the leading neutralist power when it had tried so hard to get along with them? Were they an openly aggressive power, preparing to overrun the Indian subcontinent now before them? Had they seized the border areas in order to be able to pressure India in the future? To discredit it as a leader in Asia? To divert attention from the internal failure of the Great Leap Forward of 1958–59? Or, as later analysts of the war were to claim, did India really bear an equal share of responsibility, having been unwilling to negotiate until the Chinese used force—and this really only to retake what they claimed to be their own?

What ever might be the explanation, the war meant that India turned more and more to the Soviet Union for support and, as the Chinese-Russian conflict worsened, the Soviet Union became more than willing to provide it, since it meant a broadened political influence in the subcontinent—on China's southern flank, for to the north the two powers had come into direct territorial conflict.

The Chinese had long held that Russia occupied immense areas in the northeast of Asia as a result of treaties imposed upon a humiliated China in Czarist times. In 1964 the Russians denounced the Chinese for coveting a half a million square miles of Soviet territory; Mao attacked Khrushchev for bringing Outer Mongolia under Russian domination and intimated he had designs on Sinkiang. Khrushchev replied that China followed "an openly expansionist program with far-reaching pretensions."

In the mid-1960s the situation worsened. Russia massed over sixty divisions to face the 47 Chinese divisions spread over the thousands of miles. Chinese hostility grew, attacks on revisionism became even more intense during the Cultural Revolution, Red Guards manhandled Russian nationals—and in 1967 China exploded its first hydrogen weapon. "Authoritative rumors" abounded to the effect that Russian leaders were considering a military strike against both Chinese border fortifications and the Chinese nuclear establishment.

The Russian invasion of Czechoslovakia and the announcement of the Brezhnev Doctrine in late 1968 fanned the flames. Chinese spokesmen condemned the Czech "revisionist leading clique" but voiced support of the Czech people, as well as of Albania, Rumania, and Yugoslavia, all of which appeared menaced by Russian force. But the willingness of the Soviet Union to use force was not lost on the Chinese. In February 1969 Soviet troops were put in a state of combat readiness and authorized to fire in disputed areas. On March 2 Chinese border troops ambushed an outnumbered Soviet patrol at the disputed island of Chenpao, on the Ussuri River, and inflicted heavy casualties. Two weeks later, on March 15, an even more serious clash took place, apparently initiated by the Russians. In both countries the governments used the clashes to stir up domestic opinion. Mass demonstrations were staged all over China, and in Moscow, the Chinese embassy was attacked by a rock-throwing mob. Russian broadcasts pointedly reminded China of Russia nuclear superiority. The two border clashes were followed by others, but a variety of inducements and changes brought a decrease in tension and, eventually, negotiations. Apparently the government of North Vietnam, shipments to which were hampered by the conflict, urged the two to hold talks; so did other Communist parties. The governments of Eastern European countries failed to rally to the Russian cause, and China, amazingly enough, appeared ready to seek a rapprochement with the United States as a counterweight. On the Chinese side, the threat that Russia might use force, especially in a quick strike against its nuclear plants, probably weighed heavily. Internal developments contributed: the waning of the worst excesses of the Cultural Revolution, the disbanding and dispatching to manual labor in the countryside of the Red Guards, and the attempt to create a new administrative apparatus to replace the shattered Chinese Communist Party and governmental bureaucracy—coinciding with the return to prominence of Chou En-lai and resumption of diplomatic relations with a number of countries—all presaged a return of some sort of "normalcy" in foreign relations. Polemics did not cease. But at least the two countries negotiated.

Certainly, during the period of the Cultural Revolution, Chinese foreign relations had gone through an extraordinary phase. In 1965 the Chinese dilemma, well-known to the Russians 40 years earlier, was that of a revolutionary power in an international system it could not change overnight. At war, then, were the moral inclination to promote revolution throughout the world, and the need to find allies against hostile powers as well as with whom to trade. Chou En-lai, visiting Africa a second time in 1965, repeated that Africa was "ripe for revolution" a view that did not endear him to the governments of host countries. For although he could go on to explain that he meant revolution against imperialism, colonialism, and neocolonialism, too many governments appeared, by definition, to fall into the last category. Moreover, part of his diplomatic efforts were expended in trying to persuade African governments to vote against Russian participation in Asian-African conferences, and they saw no reason to get dragged into this particular quarrel. In the next few years, several countries broke relations with China over the issue of subversive activities of Chinese diplomatic missions. Nevertheless, Chinese activities continued in the east African and Arabian peninsula areas.

The whole picture changed with the onset of the Cultural Revolution. The failures of Khrushchev's policies in the early 1960s made the Chinese reaffirm the need to support radical elements. Khrushchev had been willing to work with and support "progressive" non-Communist governments in the less-developed countries, and fostered the idea that rapid progress would result with Soviet aid (a view akin to the many optimistic liberal Western views of the time). But the downfall of leaders like Nkrumah of Ghana, Sukarno, Keita of Mali, Ben Bella in Algeria (see Chapter 9) and the souring of relations with other progressives who had wasted aid or pressured the Soviet Union for more than it could afford had led Khrushchev's successors to be more circumspect and "realistic" in their aid and general relations. Peking had drawn the opposite lesson: Khrushchev had placed an incorrect, revisionist, emphasis on the wrong factors.

But the Chinese effort to build a Chinese-oriented world Communist front in the same period had also collapsed: as Russia became disenchanted with the Nkrumahs, Sukarnos, and others, and found leaders like Castro intractable, China had tried to use them. The fall of Nkrumah and Sukarno became, then, a Chinese defeat. And in March 1966 Castro was to declare that Cuban-Chinese relations would get better when China rid itself of "senile leaders"—and cut the Chinese mission staff. The Great Cultural Revolution, in particular, had its effect on major parties on whom the Chinese had counted: the Japanese, North Korean, Indian left-Communist, and Vietnamese; the seeming chaos inside China and the intellectual justification for it had little appeal. Russia finally found in propaganda about the convulsion an effective counter to the long-standing Chinese gambits of race, revisionism, cooperation with the imperialists, and stages of development. North Korea's Kim Il-sung, for example, had aligned himself completely with the Chinese before 1964, condemning Khrushchev's revisionism bitterly. He had refused to sign the nuclear test-ban treaty, and to attend the proposed 1964 conference of Communist parties. In retaliation, Russian economic and military aid had declined, and China could not fill the gap. In 1965 Kosygin visited Korea, promised a resumption of aid, and the Korean Communist Party began to resume relations with those of Eastern Europe. When, in 1966, as the upheaval began in China, the Chinese government insisted that all true Marxist-Leninists must take an inflexible stand against the leaders of the CPSU, Kim Il-sung declined, agreeing with the Japanese and Russian party declaration on the need for a united front to oppose imperialism in Vietnam. Imperialism, not revisionism, was the main enemy.

The Cultural Revolution had an extraordinary impact on the conduct of foreign relations, especially during the year-long rampage of the Red Guards, who vilified and attacked the foreign minister, invaded the ministry on several occasions, and tore up diplomatic correspondence, while insisting on a thorough purge of ministry personnel. The internal conflict extended to Chinese missions abroad, some of whose personnel joined the Red Guards, and a few of whom defected. All Chinese ambassadors but one were recalled for consultation, and many of them never returned. Diplomatic correspondence virtually ceased with many countries, while most aid programs faded out. (In fact, the Cultural Revolution probably simply hastened a process already underway. Since 1956 China had pledged Middle East countries some $850 million worth of aid, of which only $300 million was delivered. In contrast, the Soviet Union had poured in $5 billion worth, and took pains to point out the contrast. Only since the end of the Cultural Revolution has the trend reversed; in the 1970s China rapidly resumed a substantial foreign aid program.)

In addition, several violent incidents took place. The Dutch Chargé d'Affaires in Peking was held hostage for the return of a Chinese technical mission to the Netherlands after the latter group came into conflict with the Dutch police. The British mission in Peking was sacked and burned by Red Guards, while its personnel had to flee for their lives. After incidents in Mongolia involving Chinese teachers, riots in Burma against the Chinese, a clash in Paris between Chinese students and French police, an attack on the Chinese embassy in Delhi, India, and an incident concerning a Chinese vessel in an Italian port—all provoked by Chinese attempts to in some way or other spread the Cultural Revolution —the embassies or missions of these countries were attacked by mobs in Peking. Tunisia, Kenya, and Indonesia all indulged in a mutual withdrawal of embassy staffs with the Chinese. The worst incident, predictably, came in February 1967, when the Russian mission was invaded, diplomats manhandled and held incommunicado for hours, and the mission then besieged, so that neither food nor people could enter nor leave. When the Russians evacuated the wives and children of diplomats, mobs struck and spat on them, making one group of women and children crawl on their hands and knees under portraits of Mao and Stalin—while French and British diplomats trying to protect them were also attacked.

The excesses waned when the Red Guards were dispersed. But the effects remained. In the next two years Chinese government attention was focused primarily on the border conflict with Russia. It sought influence in the East Africa-South Arabia area, and continued to maintain good relations with Tanzania, while losing influence in some areas to the Soviet Union. The agreement reached with Tanzania in 1966 to build a railway across to landlocked Zambia, presently forced to trade through white-dominated Rhodesia and South Africa, remained in force, and despite the Cultural Revolution, work got under way in 1968. Relations with the Arab countries remained generally poor; the Arabs depended on the Soviet Union for important material support, and the Chinese charge that the 1967 war was a result of American and Russian plotting against the Arabs found few takers. When the new, organized Palestine guerrilla forces rose to a position of prominence, however, their leaders looked to China. Russia's relations with Arab governments were too close, and their interest in peaceful settlement seemed genuine. The Chinese, on the other hand, agreed with the guerrillas that only war could settle the issue, and that the governments in the area were too prone to make peace with Israel. They offered mainly moral support, however.

The years of the Cultural Revolution hardly helped China cope with its economic problems (although one of its aims was of long-run importance; the creation of a new, individual consciousness that will reject desires for more material goods than are really necessary and see instead the necessity to work for the public good). Food production had declined relative to the ever-increasing population, and China needed to import wheat. It turned to Canada, which had a large export surplus, and one result was that in 1970 Canada extended diplomatic recognition to China. Trade began to pick up with other countries. In 1969 the new Nixon administration in the United States proceeded to relax long-standing restrictions on trade and travel to China. The first responses were cold, since the United States remained, for China, the imperialist aggressor in Vietnam and Taiwan. Yet two years later the world was treated to pictures of Richard M. Nixon visiting Peking and sitting down to chat with Mao Tse-tung. It was, if anything, more remarkable than seeing men walk on the moon, and it came about unexpectedly. It was a result, however, of both Chinese and American perceptions of fundamental changes in the world situation and in each others' potential role in the international system.

THE NEW TRIANGLE

Despite America's consistent opposition to Chinese interests after the Communist victory in 1949, there had been occasional overtures from the Chinese—as at Bandung in 1955—rebuffed by the Americans. The Cultural Revolution eliminated Liu Shao Chi and those around him who appear to have felt that the United States was a more dangerous element than Russia, and the emergence of Chou En-lai restored flexibility to Chinese foreign policy. Chou engineered restoration of normal relations with most countries and reinstituted aid programs that soon outstripped those of Russia. What appeared to count most, however, was the continued Russian threat, a growing worry about Japan, and a view that the realistic Nixon had accepted a fundamental point about America: its period of world supremacy had come to an end; its currency and trade crises were clear indications that it no longer had the economic power to consider all the world its stage; it must retrench and redefine its interests more narrowly. But in so doing, it had allowed the deep Russian penetration of south Asia, and it had alienated the rebuilt Japan, whose power in some as yet undefined form might flow into the vacuum left by American withdrawal from Asia.

While in one direction Chou drove deep into the enemy camp, restoring friendly relations with Yugoslavia and, even more important, with Rumania, in the other direction he proceeded, in April 1971, to initiate what came to be called "ping-pong" diplomacy by inviting table tennis teams from several countries competing in Japan to visit China—including the American team. The team was warmly received, its members met with Chou, who solemnly declared that their visit had turned a "new page" in American-Chinese relations. On its side, the Nixon administration gave Chou solid indications of its own desires, by lifting all travel restrictions to China, relaxing commercial and financial restrictions, and initiating moves to expedite both trade and travel. A Presidential commission recommended on April 26 that the United States work for admission of the People's Republic of China to the United Nations (while retaining Taiwan, whose population, it noted, was greater than two-thirds of the other United Nations members). On July 15, most startling of all, President Nixon announced on television that as a consequence of secret talks between Chou and the President's National Security Assistant, Henry Kissinger, the President had accepted Chou's invitation to visit China, where he would seek a normalization of relations. Obliquely, he told the Chinese Nationalists on Taiwan that his action "was not at the expense of old friends" and the Russians that it was "not directed against any other nation." And in fact, three months later, he announced that he would visit Moscow in 1972.

In the months to come the President, forced by trade and financial circumstances to resort to protectionist measures in August, carried out some rapid fence mending. He met with President Pompidou of France in the Azores, with Prime Minister Heath of Great Britain in Bermuda, Chancellor Willy Brandt of Germany in Florida, and in January, a month before his visit to China, with Prime Minister Sato of Japan. With Pompidou he publicly announced devaluation of the American dollar.* For Heath he announced abandonment of the objectionable import surcharge imposed in August. For Brandt he promised that there would be no reduction of American troop strength in West Germany. For Sato he confirmed that Okinawa would, indeed, be returned to Japan in May of 1972. (This was not much for the hapless Japanese Prime Minister. Against strong internal opposition he had followed the earlier American line on China, and had been caught by surprise when the President announced the projected Peking visit; Japan had been sharply hit by the American financial and trade measures of August. Disenchantment with the United States seemed complete.)

And in the meantime, having fought hard to keep Chiang Kai-shek's Republic of China in the United Nations, the Nixon administration accepted the October 25 vote in New York which, by 76–35, with 17 abstentions, seated the People's Republic of China and expelled Taiwan. (Taiwan was subsequently expelled from most other international organizations. In 1972 the Indian chief Public Information Officer of the United Nations resigned in protest when Taiwanese correspondents were denied accreditation. As of July 30, 1972 there is no mention of Taiwan in United Nations documents—including statistical reports!)

---

* Pompidou made the rather crude gesture of flying to their meeting in a Concorde supersonic transport prototype, thus rubbing in the American abandonment a few months earlier of construction of its own SST and demonstrating to the world that Europe had *not* fallen behind the United States technologically.

For a week, from February 21 to 28, 1972, the Nixons and their entourage visited Communist China. The President was met coolly but correctly; the visit warmed up after his first day talk with Mao and the lengthy talks he held with Chou. In the final communiqué—with no little historical irony—the two countries' leaders agreed to the time-honored *Panch Shila,* or five principles of peaceful coexistence, endorsed normalization of relations, listed differences over policies on Vietnam, and found a suitable formula for the thorny issue of the future of Taiwan: United States forces would be reduced "as tension in the area diminishes," thus leaving the way open to a Chinese settlement of the problem in some indeterminate future.*

The agreements were hailed by Communist countries like Rumania and North Korea, but condemned by Moscow as demonstrating a "dangerous plot . . . intensifying purely military measures to prepare for war." Significantly, the North Vietnamese joined Russia in its condemnation. But more important, the shift in United States-Chinese relations hastened a host of new diplomatic moves. Russia increased its efforts to mend fences in Europe and the Middle East and with the United States; Japan, having lost a clear lead from the United States, whose President was now on his way to Moscow, moved to better its relations with both China and Russia—a move complicated by the desire of each of those two countries to keep Japan from being too friendly with the other.

In Europe, Russia pressed for completion of the agreements on Germany and for the European Security Conference and talks on force reductions; with President Nixon in Moscow, Brezhnev signed the SALT agreement, and finally, after 27 years, settled the Lend-Lease debt so that a broad trade agreement could be negotiated; Japan and Russia finally signed a peace treaty, ending World War II; in the Middle East Russia negotiated the treaties of friendship and mutual assistance with Egypt and Iraq similar to the one signed earlier with India. But it suffered reverses, too, arising from the complexity of the pattern it was attempting to weave. Having earlier assured the United States that it would not support a resumption of war in the Middle East, it finally had to tell a Syrian delegation that such must be the case. A fortnight later, to general surprise, the Egyptian government of President Sadat ordered Russian military advisers and experts to leave, placing Soviet bases and equipment under exclusive Egyptian control. President Sadat explained the move: Russia had hindered him from resolving the Israeli question by the end of 1971,

* Just how indeterminate that time may be is revealed by the fact that despite general diplomatic isolation and Japanese diplomatic recognition of Peking, Japanese-Taiwan trade doubled in the first six months of 1973 in comparison with the same period a year earlier.

as he had publicly and popularly announced he would do, and had put conditions on the use of equipment it had supplied. SAM crews would stay, and Russia could continue to use naval facilities in several ports. But the rest would go.

Japan followed the American example, and proceeded to establish diplomatic relations with China while retaining economic ties to Taiwan. (As of this writing, the People's Republic of China and the United States do not formally have diplomatic relations, but maintain missions equipped to carry out all the functions of an Embassy.) It began lengthy negotiations with Russia over resource development in Siberia, an area that Russia also held out as bait to the United States. Since the Soviet Union had little to offer in the way of exports for needed imports, it offered investment in Siberian energy resources and promises of future exports of gas and petroleum in repayment. Both Japanese and American entrepreneurs appeared interested.

Clearly the American-Chinese detente had released a flood of activity. While many writers referred to the new triangular relationship, President Nixon spoke of the greater opportunities for stability offered by a five-power world, one that included Japan and Europe as well as China, Russia, and the United States.

Analogies to the earlier balance of power period were weak, given the differences in military and economic power of the powers, the kinds of weapons at hand, the differences imposed by mass politics and industrialization. Europe was not yet "one" and the Russians would try to keep it from becoming one. Moreover, internally generated instability would continue to plague the new relationships: at the very time President Nixon was in Moscow the Russians were engaged in putting down nationalist riots and demonstrations in Lithuania. In mid-1972 Mao's proclaimed and acclaimed heir Lin Piao was apparently killed in an airplane crash in Mongolia, attempting to flee China after failing to overthrow Mao, or so the Chinese were later to explain, adding that Lin Piao was supported by Moscow. Was Mao's regime so unstable that treachery extended to his second in command? And the American President, re-elected in 1972 by a large majority, found his negotiating abilities severely weakened in 1973 when investigations revealed that his closest associates had been involved in widespread illegal political activities. The Chinese-Russian conflict appeared to have simmered down, and no more military clashes were reported. Still, at the time that China vetoed the admission of the new state of Bangla Desh to the United Nations in 1972, its spokesman inveighed against "Soviet socialist imperialism . . . [and its] most insidious role in South Asia." "India," he said, "has concluded an aggressive military alliance . . . stripped off its own cloak of non-alliance." The USSR seeks "to further control India and Bangla Desh, to expand its spheres of influence and bully Pakistan at will . . ." while the Soviet representative retorted that the Chinese had adopted the views of the late John Foster Dulles.

The new era had arrived.

CONCLUSION

The fiftieth anniversary of the October Revolution occurred in 1967. Marxism had come a long way: from an approach and a way of thought adhered to by a relatively small group of men, it had become a doctrine —Marxism–Leninism—under the authority of which at least a third of the world's population was now governed. The rhetoric accompanying the occasion was clear: Marxist-Leninist socialism was monolithic and triumphant.

Yet in January 1967, Marxist-Leninist, socialist Rumania established diplomatic relations with West Germany, to the anger of East Germany and Poland; refused to join bloc condemnation of Israel after the June War; had its Foreign Minister Manescu elected President of the UN General Assembly; participated—for the first time in years—in Warsaw Pact maneuvers; yet heard its Premier Ceausescu suggest that both NATO and the Warsaw Pact should be scrapped. And Czechoslovakia had begun to move toward a situation in which, even though it remained Communist and within the Warsaw Pact, the military forces of several Marxist-Leninist countries would invade it, despite the mass opposition of its population.

The Chinese, Albanian, and a number of Asian party leaders did not appear in Moscow to help celebrate the 50th anniversary of the first successful Marxist-Leninist revolution, while the Cubans pointedly snubbed their hosts for their failure to support revolutionary activities.

And 1967 was the year in which Chinese Red Guard mobs inflicted brutal and humiliating treatment upon the diplomatic representatives, wives, and children of *Russia,* the first Marxist-Socialist state.

Socialism, clearly, had failed to bring the international solidarity it had promised, and its leaders no longer simply blamed the continued machinations of the remnants of imperialism. Relations with the nonsocialist countries and among socialist countries assumed a terrible complexity.

Some analysts thought that Russia had simply become more cautious and conservative as its leaders saw that they could not have their way in the postwar years, and as they came to appreciate the dangers posed by thermonuclear war. Yet Khrushchev, whose erratic manner of policy-making brought about his downfall, both demonstrated conservatism and realism in foreign affairs and liberalism at home at one time—only to become bellicose and adventuristic at others. The men who replaced him may have been conservative in their first years, provoking the continued fire of the Castros and Maoists who blamed them for not supporting revolution. Yet in their later years they were involved in the deception that led to invasion of Czechoslovakia, dangerous and deceptive action in the Middle East, border skirmishes in the continued tense conflict with China, and a naval expansion that transformed them into the chief potential power in the Indian Ocean.

Geographically, Russia now faced a hostile China on one side—and used its extension of power into South Asia to aid countries on China's south flank—while facing unrest in its East European empire, where the people appeared not to have lapsed into the political passivity that characterized most Russians. In Europe, it still faced the NATO alliance of West Europe and the United States, an alliance it did much to revive when it invaded Czechoslovakia. At one point its leaders tried to deal with their problems by suggesting some sort of Asian security arrangement to the Americans. But the latter had already embarked on detente with China, the very country that seemed to threaten the Russians, so that Brezhnev instead turned back to security projects in the Atlantic-European area with member states—while wooing the enigmatic Japanese.

Outside of this strategic sphere, Russian leaders have apparently come to accept that world revolution is, in fact, something for the future, and its advice to Communist parties seems to be to cooperate with others—not for purposes of seizing power, but for construction of the social bases for modernization. Its diplomatic, aid and trade policies have been ones that have provoked the ire of revolutionaries: they are geared to working with those governing elites that will cooperate with the Soviet Union and will be able to provide profitable trading opportunities or investments that will produce complementarity with the Soviet Union.

This Chapter's survey shows that the potential for serious conflict with Western countries always remains; leadership in the Soviet Union is now divided and less predictable, and some of its members will push for a harder or more revolutionary line than others; the peacemakers of Tashkent were in the same government that invaded Czechoslovakia and threatened Rumania and Yugoslavia—and sent its men to fly MIGs and man missiles in the supposedly standstill zones along the Suez Canal.

China presented another picture during this period. The rhetoric of revolution and support for wars of national liberation was stronger in the earlier years. After 1960 the rhetoric was turned against Russia for its conservative attitudes. Yet Chinese military manpower in its first decade of existence was used only in Korea, once United Nations forces had gone beyond the line the Chinese government had said it could tolerate, and to attempt the liberation of Formosa, which everyone agreed was Chinese. In the early 1960s, it could be argued, Chinese leaders had become even more cautious, their attention largely turned inward except for purposes of necessary trade and to build support in their conflict with Russia. They continued to encourage revolution abroad, but stressed the necessity for revolution to be indigenous and self-sustaining. And they established diplomatic relations with countries that would recognize the People's Republic of China, support its United Nations membership, and trade with it. In such countries they gave no support to "national liberation movements."

The Cultural Revolution brought change; to buttress the call for revolution at home Mao appeared to feel that it was necessary to reinforce the demand for it abroad, and Chinese personnel provoked innumerable incidents from their foreign missions. As upheaval at home died down, so did disruption in other countries. Even the issue of borders to the north and south became muted and Chinese negotiators sat down with Russians. In 1971 Mao's China even supported Pakistan when the latter carried out a bloody repression in separatist East Pakistan, only to lose to India when the latter came to the aid of the rebels. It was disillusioning to foreign Maoists, but Machiavelli and Hobbes would have understood. They would have understood, too, the startling events that followed, when President Nixon was wined and dined in the very heart of Peking.

China did not constitute a power of the same dimension as the United States or the Soviet Union. In physical terms its productive plant was far smaller, its army equipped with older weapons and organized primarily for home defense, its navy tiny, its air force small and equipped with obsolescent planes. It had, however, created nuclear and thermonuclear weapons, and its launching of a satellite in 1970 demonstrated its missile and guidance capabilities.

Russians feared the development, and a Chinese rapprochement with the United States, against which they warned; the Chinese repeatedly charged that the Soviet Union and the United States operated jointly in world affairs to crush the legitimate aspirations of the people. Both acted to try to keep the United States from too firm an arrangement with their opponent. In both cases, in order to undermine the legitimate revolutionary authority of the other, the rhetoric of revolution remained strong. Nevertheless, when it came to major foreign political activities, the international system, with its tendency to impose balancing policies on its members, appeared to have swallowed up the Communist revolutionaries.

PART V
THE "THIRD WORLD" IN
THE HYDROGEN AGE

INTRODUCTION
THE NEW STATES:
A THIRD WORLD?

By 1956 most Asian, Pacific, and Middle Eastern remnants of Western imperialism were gone, leaving only a scattering of enclaves to arouse nationalist agitation. Africa, however, remained very largely under European domination, and where European countries did not exercise direct control, white European minorities did.

In the next ten years most areas of Africa obtained independence, leaving only the handful of white-dominated ones in the south to envenom international relations on the continent. The older Latin American and Caribbean states now sought to act in conjunction with the new states of Africa and Asia, and in the nineteen sixties some unity of action developed within the confines of the United Nations and in the plethora of regional organizations. But the main purpose of unity was to try to put pressure on the older, developed states, especially the United States, for more aid for development or changes in the distribution of benefits from trade. The new states found the path of development—whatever the term might mean—much more difficult than most of them had anticipated. In many cases the nationalist leaders who had agitated for independence were replaced by new elites. In most countries, including the older states of Latin America, parliamentary institutions disappeared, and military men seized power. Their attitudes varied; many took a "radical" stance in both domestic and international affairs. What soon developed was that the idea of unity—of third world states or Africa or Africa-Asia—was more of an idea than anything else, and in one area after another local confrontation and conflict developed. Some analysts argued that, in fact, the possibility of armed conflict among the developed states of the Atlantic world or between these and the socialist states had become almost impossible; the chief source of instability and war would now be among the less-developed countries.

This was certainly not the point of view espoused by new states' leaders. In the early and heady years of independence, many of them saw themselves as a new fresh and untainted force in international politics and began to define their role in the international system in terms of "neutralism" or "nonalignment"—a point of view that rejected alignment

with one bloc or the other in the Cold War but foresaw an active role of
mediation and peacemaking. But many of the new statesmen found neutralism an insufficient guide to action as the Cold War faded. They needed to be able to cope with local conflicts, which might require support
from one of the major powers. Or they needed to press demands upon
the wealthier countries on the basis of other considerations.

For these reasons neutralist India sought military aid and even the possibility of an alliance against China in 1962 and turned to a virtual alliance with the Soviet Union later; Egypt, whose leader had earlier been a
chief neutralist spokesman, found itself in alliance with the Soviet Union
in the late 1960s. Neutralist countries of Africa sought help where they
could get it in their struggle with the white-dominated south; since Western countries would not subsidize the use of violence, they would find the
subsidies elsewhere. And countries like Somalia looked to military aid to
help them in purely local boundary squabbles with countries like Kenya
and Ethiopia; Indonesia's President Sukarno, before his fall in 1965, had
built up an enormous Soviet-equipped military machine, one of whose
major aims was to "crush Malaysia."

In virtually all the new states, economic development became a key
goal, in terms of both a rise in gross national product and in per capita
income. They lobbied for aid, for better aid terms, for more investment,
for trade advantages from richer states, and for intergovernmental organizations to promote and institutionalize these and other changes. They
nationalized existing investments but asked for more. The problems of
development lent themselves to no easy solutions. There was genuine evidence of progress in many states in terms of these goals. But in the light
of the constantly increasing population throughout the world, such progress seemed both agonizingly slow and too unevenly distributed, and most
third world leaders felt the rich countries were too bound up in their own
concerns and barely responsive to the increasingly evident division between rich and poor. In the early 1950s people spoke of closing the gap
between the haves and have-nots. By the early 1960s a simple fact of
mathematics had become clear: if a state with per capita income of $100
has an annual per capita growth rate of three per cent, at the end of a
year its per capita income would be $103. If a state with a per capita in-
come of $2000 has a somewhat smaller growth rate, of two per cent per
capita, at the end of the year the per capita figure would be $2040. The
first is growing faster, but the second has—in absolute figures, whatever
they may mean—gained 13 times as much. All figures were suspect and
cross-cultural comparisons subject to myriad interpretations. But there
were plenty of people who could reach a simple conclusion: despite lots
of talk, lots of conferences, lots of new international organizations, the

situation was getting worse. The result was the growth of revolutionary, primarily Marxist, movements of one stripe or another in all three continents, most of them calling for an end to present relationships or a violent re-ordering of them. They differed in analysis, but at least one common thread ran through them: the view that in present relations the rich exploited the poor and tended to inhibit the radical domestic structural change necessary in the poorer countries. Leaders of these movements argued that in many cases investment, trade, and aid served only to buttress in power a particular class that exploited others. For this reason some third world leaders were calling for more aid, trade, and investment; others arguing for a shift in the terms of these; still others for abolition of trade relations with almost any nations except particular socialist countries.

Finally, throughout the world, sober analysis seemed to reveal that increases in population were outstripping efforts to provide economic betterment, and underlay world poverty and instability far more than did the structure of existing international relations. The situation was particularly acute for countries that lay in the great arc extending from east Asia, through southeast and south Asia, the Middle East and North Africa, and extending into Latin America. In all, the growth of population threatened organized society's capacities to provide, and the "green revolution" of recent years—the introduction of new, American-developed strains of very high-yield grain—would serve only to provide a breathing spell. Moreover, the experience of the developed countries in the decade of the sixties seemed to show that "development" in the Western sense of providing a continuous high rate of growth might bring as many problems as it solved, either in the form of social malaise, or in the form of an ecological disaster that would outweigh any disaster so far provided by war.

When the United States emerged from World War II in its special power position, its leaders felt generally that they had a special role to play in helping to dismantle the old system of empires and create a new, stable system of independent states. It was, as an attitude, a part of the heritage of Wilsonianism, and in line with the expressed desires of non-Western leaders—an idea whose time had come. But the Cold War intervened and took precedence. As European statesmen predicted they would, the Americans began to feel that the new states would not be able to stand alone in the face of the Communist-Russian menace, and that as European powers withdrew, the Americans would have to step in, dispensing aid and advice on a needed transition to modernity and stability, without which the Communists would profit and the world balance ultimately tip.

But it looked to many people that the United States had merely tried to discourage European influence in order to substitute its own. Thus by the 1960s third world leaders often viewed the United States as the chief imperialist power, and the Soviet Union—or, on occasion, China—as the useful and friendly counterbalance. Their view of the United States was of course buttressed when the new issue of relations of rich and poor nations side-by-side came to the fore as the century wore on, for certainly the United States was the richest of the rich. If the rich were to be blamed for the impoverishment of the poor, then clearly the United States deserved the most blame. In the early 1950s Americans had held their country up as the model of modernity. If America in 1970 represented modernity, many thought, then perhaps modernity had to be reconsidered.

As a result, and after flirtations with the Soviet model, some third world leaders began to look to China, where it seemed possible that Maoism aimed at creating a society in which people would be kept from developing demands for goods and services that the world could not, in the final analysis, provide for all people.

Were there other alternatives? How would their choice affect the workings of the international system?

NINE
AFRICA—INDEPENDENCE
AND ORDEAL

THE MARCH TO INDEPENDENCE

Malaya was the last major Asian state to become independent, as a consequence of the long fight against Communist guerrillas. It achieved sovereignty in 1957, and in 1963 joined with a series of smaller enclaves and states to form the Federation of Malaysia: Sarawak, Brunei, Singapore, and North Borneo. Still later Singapore broke away to become an independent and influential city state.

The late 1950s became the age of African independence.

Few people expected events in Africa to move so fast. In 1956 Tunisia, Morocco, and the Sudan, all former protectorates, joined the ranks of independent Libya, Liberia, Ethiopia, and Egypt. Throughout the African continent that earlier had seemed so settled, nationalist pressures grew. Ghana's turn came in 1957. A year later Guinea chose independence over membership in the new French Community created by de Gaulle. In 1960 Somalia, formerly Italian and then a trust territory, reached the ten-year deadline set for its independence by the United Nations in 1950. Within two months the large state of Nigeria, with a population of 35 million, became free. In the same year, the former French territories that had joined the French Community chose independence. These countries spread all across the great western bulge of Africa, down into the central African jungles, and included the Malagasy Republic off the east coast (formerly known as Madagascar). Some chose to retain a status within the French Community, some opted to leave it. Togo and Cameroun achieved independence, and in the Mediterranean the long, bitter struggle over Cyprus finally concluded with the end of British rule and the establishment of a precarious equilibrium between the Greek Cypriot majority and Turkish Cypriot minority—an equilibrium destined to explode into violence. The same year saw the end of Belgian rule in the Congo, the next year the end of British rule over tiny Sierra Leone and Tanganyika; 1962 brought independence to Uganda, to Rwanda and Burundi—formerly held as trust territories by Belgium and subsequently to be shaken by prolonged tribal violence—and outside of Africa, to

Western Samoa, in the Pacific, to Jamaica and Trinidad-Tobago (both of which seceded from the Federation of the British West Indies and were followed in 1966 by Barbados) to Kuwait in the Middle East, and finally, to Algeria. In 1963, Kenya, rocked by terrorism in the 1950s, finally achieved independence; the tiny island of Zanzibar in December; in 1964, with the breakup of the Central African Federation, Northern Rhodesia and Nyasaland became, respectively, Zambia and Malawi. The fate of Southern Rhodesia provides a more complicated story (see below, p. 363).

The strategic Mediterranean island of Malta reached independence in 1964, although the British maintained their great naval base, on which the island's economy depended. (In 1969 a long drawn out crisis began, during which Malta pressed the British for either far larger payments for use of the base or else to get out. The Maltese Prime Minister used presumed Russian or Libyan interest in the base as his bargaining counter; eventually Britain and its NATO allies accepted larger payments. Their precarious situation in the Mediterranean seemed to necessitate the base's retention.) Britain retained control of three landlocked territories in the south of Africa until 1966, when two of them, Lesotho and Botswana became independent, followed by Swaziland in 1968. The United Kingdom had refused a South African request that the three be ceded to it in 1949 because of South African apartheid, and the fact that they depended largely upon economic relations with South Africa complicated the cause of independence.* In short order several other tiny states achieved a precarious independence: Gambia, the smallest African state; Equatorial Guinea, previously Spanish; the Maldive Islands and the island of Mauritius; the Republic of Southern Yemen; and in South America the racially and politically troubled country of Guyana. In the United Nations the issue of the mini-states was raised. Could such states, some of them with a population of a hundred thousand, really exercise sovereignty and independence? Did they not require some special international status? In the fall of 1973 there were 135 states in the United Nations, both Germanies having joined, along with the tiny state of the Bahamas.

The transition to independence was not easy. Anticolonialists in the United Nations charged that in many cases the colonial power was impeding what could be an easy transition by encouraging communal dif-

---

* Africa contributed thirteen new landlocked states to the international system. Such states—and Afghanistan, Hungary, Czechoslovakia, Austria, Rumania, Switzerland, Bolivia, Paraguay, and Outer Mongolia do not exhaust the old list—have special problems of communication with the rest of the world and can be subjected to pressures by their neighbors. In 1964 a group of them negotiated and submitted an international convention on the rights of landlocked states to the United Nations.

ferences. The fact was that such differences existed and fears of domination by one group or another were often well grounded. So were the fears of domination by a strong neighboring state. Less well grounded were Western fears that weak successor states might succumb to Communist subversion and become prey to a new imperialism; the anticolonialists in international organizations were vociferous in condemnation of this attitude, which they viewed as an excuse for prolonging colonialism. Finally, there were frequently dominant classes or groups desperately defending a privileged position, knowing that independence would destroy it. Such had been the case in Kenya, where the Mau-Mau insurrection was quelled but independence ultimately granted; such was the case in Algeria, where a long, drawn-out bitter war ended, finally, in independence and the flight of a million Algerians of French descent to a France many of them had never known. In areas in the south of Africa, white minorities tried to see to it that there would be no repetition of these events (see below, p. 362).

In other parts of Africa all of these problems of transition played a role. Khrushchev's "adventurism" in the period between 1955 and 1962 helped contribute and so did the clearly stated Chinese interest in Africa as the continent most ripe for revolution. The first occasion came in 1958, when de Gaulle, newly in power and sensing the tide of events, gave to French African states the opportunity to either become independent, or join an association with France, the French Community, which would also give them a privileged position vis-à-vis the new European Economic Community. It marked a radical shift from earlier French policy: far more than the British, the French government had been devoted to a policy of assimilating the overseas territories to the motherland. In the face of a barrage of propaganda on the benefits of the Community, only the state of Guinea, led by Sekou Touré, voted against joining. The French responded swiftly and harshly. They withdrew all their colonial administrators, ended financial aid, and took with them all administrative records. Touré responded by forming a loose union with Ghana and accepting a Ghanaian loan, and also by receiving large-scale aid preferred by Russia. Alarmists in the West began to call Guinea the first Soviet satellite in Africa, and argued that Britain and the United States had missed their chance to forestall the Russians by failing to offer the needed aid.

The judgment was simplistic and premature. Touré was an independent man, and at one juncture, when he felt that the Russian mission was being used as a center for subversion, compelled Russia to recall its ambassador.

Five years later journalists were to make the same judgment about Zanzibar. Within a month after it received independence from Britain in

December 1963, its ruling Arab minority, long favored by the British, was overthrown in a confused coup that brought to power black leaders. On January 18 they proclaimed the country to be the People's Republic of Zanzibar, a one-party state; they expelled Westerners, and proceeded to establish diplomatic relations with other Communist states, including East Germany and China. They received Russian arms, Chinese credits, and technical aid, and replaced British civil servants with Communist bloc personnel. Again, Western newspapers referred to the first "Soviet outpost in Africa" and commented that Zanzibar might serve as a center for subversion for the rest of the continent. But the leadership in Zanzibar was not completely united. On April 23 a new and surprising agreement between Tanganyika and Zanzibar created a close union of the two countries and was ratified within a week. President Karume of Zanzibar, who became the first Vice President, and President Nyerere of Tanganyika sought in the union a way of dealing with extremist pressure in both of their countries.* In this they were successful, and Tanzania's single-party socialist system has come to rely on trade with Western and Asian countries, and aid from both the West and China. President Julius Nyerere has gained much admiration from young people throughout Africa as a radical nationalist devoted both to creation of a political system suited to the particular conditions of Tanzania and to liberation of blacks in the white-dominated areas to his south and west. The latter orientation brought him into conflict with Western countries that continue relations with Portugal, South Africa, and Rhodesia. (From 1965 to 1968 Tanzania had no diplomatic relations with Great Britain because the latter refused to use force against Rhodesia for becoming independent under white-minority domination.) Dar es Salaam, Tanzania's capital city, is host to the Organization of African Unity's Liberation Committee, which gets most of its arms and supplies from the Soviet bloc, China, Cuba, and Yugoslavia. In addition China, over the years, became Tanzania's biggest supplier of technical, capital, and military aid; in the late 1960s thousands of technicians came to build the Tanzania-Zambia railway, designed to free landlocked Zambia from dependence for trade on communication through white-dominated Rhodesia and South Africa (after Western failure to provide financing for the railroad). Yet—and despite the 1965 Sino-Tanzanian Treaty of Friendship—Tanzania retains an independence many Africans would argue is greater than that of other African states.

---

* Nyerere himself had been weakened three months earlier, when an army mutiny for higher pay forced him—and neighboring Kenya and Uganda—to call in British contingents to quell the mutiny. But he survived the crisis.

In October 1963, a labor-led revolt in the former French territory of the Congo (Brazzaville) overthrew the first president, Fulbert Youlou, a defrocked priest accused of corruption. His planning minister, Alphonse Massamba-Débat, became president, established relations with the Soviet Union and China, and imported a Chinese group to plan the Congo economy. In 1966, after a withdrawal of the United States mission, the President imported a contingent of Cubans to serve as his own militia. Resentful young army officers proceeded to overthrow Massamba-Débat in 1968 and expel the Cubans. The new regime continued the leftist course, proclaiming the Congo a People's Republic and establishing a single, Marxist-Leninist political party. It has, on innumerable occasions, proclaimed its ideological affinity with the People's Republic of China. But the economy, despite important selective Chinese aid, continues to be tied to France and the EEC.

A 1969 coup in Somalia, on the horn of Africa, raised the alarm again, when President Shermarke was slain and a Supreme Revolutionary Council installed. The government, armed chiefly by the Soviet Union, nevertheless has essentially a puritanical leftist style; in 1970 it passed nationalization measures against foreign enterprises of a style becoming familiar throughout the third world—for good or bad.

Africans, in the face of these few incidents and their own tendencies to see greater danger in continued economic domination by former colonial powers or in what they consider to be an international trading system badly askew, tend to discount the importance of such events and to explain them in terms of internal needs. Some, however, were angered or discomfited by Chou En-lai's visits of 1963 and 1965, when he called the continent ripe for revolution: too many African leaders felt that in the context of their countries, development the Chinese Foreign Minister's summons could only raise trouble. Denunciations of African leaders like Tshombe in the Congo or Hasting Banda of Malawi by Chinese diplomats in African capitals did not sit well with African leaders, however radical, who found that the Chinese-Russian quarrel seemed to have brought the Cold War into Africa in a new way. And, finally, the extent to which China and Russia pressed their quarrel with reference to the abortive Afro-Asian Conference at Algiers angered many more (see below, p. 424). However, there were groups and leaders within countries who were willing to play off West against Communist in order to obtain benefits from one or both; there were others ready to invoke aid from one or the other—which could, and in some cases did, provoke a counterintervention. Chiang Kai-shek's Republic of China offered aid in order to keep African governments from dealing with the People's Republic, from voting to seat it in the United Nations, or simply to demonstrate Nationalist superiority. And, from another quarter, Israel created a widespread aid program to counter Arab influence.

THE CONGO

Transition to independence of the Congo produced a drama that dominated headlines for three years in the early 1960s. The events and most of the persons involved are long gone, yet the repercussions and implications of the incidents extended far beyond the confines of time and place.

In the 1950s Belgian administrators still planned to take at least thirty years to bring the Congo to independence, during which time they would gradually spread fundamental education and create a stable base for the important and difficult transition period. But the rising tide of African nationalism outside of the Congo—in Ghana, the French Union, in pan-African meetings—brought a heightened consciousness to Congolese leaders, resistance to Belgian rule and, despite reforms instituted in 1959, a rapid breakdown of the Belgians' capacity to maintain order. To everyone's surprise, early in 1960, a roundtable convoked in Brussels recommended that independence be granted in six months, and at the end of June the capital city of Leopoldville celebrated the birth of the Republic of the Congo.

Chaos resulted. Since there were few educated Congolese, the first stages of independence were predicated upon a continued widespread Belgian presence. But within days, Congolese troops mutinied against their Belgian officers, threatened other Belgians, and the Belgian government reacted by flying in paratroopers to protect its nationals. At the same moment Moise Tshombe, a wealthy, Western-educated tribal leader, declared independence of the vital, mineral-rich province of Katanga, in the south. Katanga bordered white-dominated states, and its economy was run by powerful Belgian mining companies, whose exports produced most of the Congo's foreign exchange.

The whole edifice of independence, carefully balanced on a federalist solution that respected tribal differences, threatened to come crashing down. Young Patrice Lumumba, the volatile Prime Minister—perhaps the only leader to emerge with a national following—called upon President Eisenhower for military aid. Eisenhower wanted to avoid becoming embroiled in what would be another American intervention, however well-intentioned, and—with strong urging from Ghanaian President Kwame Nkrumah, who took a personal interest in the fate of the Congo and in Lumumba—suggested referring the matter to the United Nations, where the precedent of the United Nations Emergency Force might provide a pattern for a Congo force. The Security Council concurred (with reluctance on the part of several of its members, who saw it becoming involved in the internal affairs of a state), and it directed Secretary-General Dag Hammarskjold to move the force into the Congo and secure removal of the Belgian troops.

Hammarskjold was at the height of his prestige. He had been able to take advantage of the breakup of the tight bipolarism of the early fifties, and create a whole new role for the United Nations under the concepts of preventive diplomacy and peace-keeping by United Nations forces. Since the superpowers were reluctant to come into conflict in a way that might erupt into major war, and conceded also that smaller states could now remain outside of the blocs, the United Nations could interpose itself in minor conflicts both to help resolve them without allowing a great power to try to take advantage of them and, at the same time, to reduce the calculations by either of the great powers that if it did *not* become involved the other would, in order to gain what might be a crucial advantage. The Secretary-General, by his diplomacy, might be able to keep the old balance of power, contingent necessity, maneuvering from taking place. The Congo offered, once more, the opportunity to exercise this new and growing role. Russians had had minimal contact with Africa in the past and now evinced some interest; but Eisenhower's adherence to anti-interventionism made it possible to get support from the growing non-Western majority for a United Nations operation that would also remove temptation from the Russians. There need be no great power competition in the Congo.

Within days the United Nations force was assembled—primarily from African states but with Swedish and Irish contingents—and Belgian troops began to withdraw. But with Belgian support, Moise Tshombe, in Katanga, produced tragedy. The United Nations force was to stay neutral with regard to internal conflicts; Hammarskjold interpreted his mandate to mean that his force could not be used to reintegrate Katanga, but only to see that Belgian troops withdrew after order was restored. This would create the conditions under which the Congolese could resolve their own problems. Tshombe's resistance to entry of United Nation troops led Prime Minister Lumumba to ask for more vigorous action on Hammarskjold's part, and when the latter, in constant consultation with African states' representatives in New York, refused to put the United Nations force at the Prime Minister's disposal, the whole operation began to unravel: Lumumba decided to ask for outside help and Khrushchev sensed an opportunity to cripple the new United Nations capacities before they became too great. Hammarskjold was caught between two fires, as Khrushchev tried to persuade some of the more radical African states to support him and Lumumba in their attack on the Secretary-General; other

African states continued to support Hammarskjold who patiently tried to persuade Tshombe to accept some form of federated solution. Tshombe, with large funds at his disposal—mining receipts that should have gone to the central government—temporized, agreed, and broke his agreements. At the United Nations, in New York, Khrushchev attended the General Assembly to address it and call for replacement of the Secretary-General by a three-man Secretaryship, with one from the West, one from the socialist bloc, and one from the third world. The move was designed to appeal to the growing body of third world delegates who might feel that the United Nations was too Western-oriented an institution, and it received such attention, although it failed in the end. But in the meantime Lumumba was overthrown, arrested, then transferred to Katanga where he was murdered and quickly became an African nationalist martyr, whose death could be blamed upon the West for not having succeeded in ending the Katanga secession. Hammarskjold, too, died as he flew to Katanga to talk once again to Tshombe. Various ad hoc governments succeeded one another in the capital, but until January 1963 Tshombe succeeded in holding out. Then, with a new Secretary-General in charge, U Thant of Burma, and a strengthened mandate for the United Nations forces from the Security Council, United Nations soldiers moved into Katanga where Tshombe's regime collapsed.

In the meantime, several African states had lined up to support dissident, Russian-armed "governments" pretending to Lumumba's mantle; others opposed the move, and the two groups crystallized into the so-called Casablanca grouping, of Ghana, Mali, Morocco, Guinea, Algeria, Egypt, and Libya, and the more cautious Brazzaville powers. Even more important, the Soviet Union and France declared that the whole operation was illegal, having been recommended by the General Assembly and not directed by the Security Council. They were therefore under no obligation to pay their share of the costs. The United Nations was already virtually financially crippled as a result of the long drawn-out operation, and the purpose of the Russian maneuver was to see that any such future operations be carried out only under Security Council directives, where the veto could be applied. At the United Nations the United States used every ounce of diplomatic muscle it could to oppose the move; but too few countries wanted to oppose the Soviet Union on the issue. It appeared that for the foreseeable future, United Nations peacekeeping, as Hammarskjold had devised it, would be out of the question. The Soviet Union was able to convince many of the Afro-Asian group that the Congo issue was another case of Western colonialism; Tshombe could not have held out without Western complicity. And fire was added to flames in 1964 when, after withdrawal of the last United Nations forces,

Tshombe returned at the head of a government of national reconciliation, a new Lumumbist revolt broke out, spread, and was only quenched when the United States and Belgium came to the aid of Tshombe's government with planes and paratroopers. They did it because the rebels made the mistake of seizing two thousand white hostages whom they threatened to kill if the government attacked. The Belgian rescue of the hostages raised another furor, however, despite Belgian protestations that only a humanitarian operation had taken place. Then Tshombe's subsequent overthrow brought General Mobutu to power; he again had to face a revolt and received American aid. But his subsequent nationalist course confirmed his power, and he set the African style of renaming places with older African names: the Congo became Zaire.

Although the Congo crisis helped radicalize African politics, reaction set in before it ended: the flow of Russian arms to Lumumbist rebels in the east, through Egypt and then the Sudan, ended when the Sudanese government in Khartoum began to fear that arms would find their way to tribesmen in revolt in the south. Burundi, another source of rebel support, broke off relations with China and expelled its ambassador after a confused sequence of events including the assassination of the Prime Minister. Later, when the President of Niger escaped assassination by a Chinese-trained terrorist operating out of Ghana—responsibility for whom was vehemently denied by Kwame Nkrumah—the taste for revolution began to decline even further. Kenya's President Kenyatta arrested his Vice-President Oginga Odinga, denouncing the latter's predilection for Russian aid arrangements and Chinese subversive activities. The Chinese-Russian quarrel had been transferred to Africa as each maneuvered to keep the other from being invited to conferences, and African leaders voiced their annoyance at the attempt to use them. Chinese Premier Chou En-lai's tour of Africa in 1965, when he declared the continent ripe for revolution, disturbed even more leaders. All these events helped lend respectability to the new Congolese government, which has since remained in power.

FURTHER AFRICAN CONFLICTS

There were other African conflicts, in some of which the United Nations participated, in some of which the new Organization of African Unity (OAU) created at Addis Ababa in 1963 took a part, and some of which were allowed to go their way according to whatever help the parties involved could get.

In the first category the main conflict was of course, the Congo; the difficulty of resolving this and the complications afforded by the presence of so many countries in the Congo situation stimulated the African states to repair some of the fissures between them and create their own regional organization to perform policing and mediating functions. Its activities would not keep African states from using United Nations organs, particularly in dealing with territories still governed from outside Africa, like the Portuguese ones, or with countries ruled by a white minority, like South Africa and Rhodesia. But even in these cases, the new OAU was brought into the picture.

Scarcely five months after it had been created, presumably healing the rift between Casablanca and Monrovia powers, the OAU was called upon to intervene in a war that broke out between newly independent Algeria and the more conservative Morocco, which laid claim to a desert area of Algeria even larger than Morocco itself, and probably rich in mineral resources, including oil. A personal intervention by Emperor Haile Selassie of Ethiopia and President Modibo Keita of Mali (a conservative and a radical, respectively) led to an agreement to stop hostilities and negotiate within a purely African framework, using an ad hoc commission created by the OAU Council of Foreign Ministers. The Commission—forerunner of a more permanent Commission of Mediation, Conciliation, and Arbitration—was unable to accomplish much. The conflict merely fell into abeyance until in 1969 King Hassan of Morocco invited Boumedienne for a visit during which they reached a border agreement and signed a treaty of cooperation. (Observers have long thought that the Maghreb—the area of Tunisia, Algeria and Morocco—formed a "natural" unit for cooperative development. But past cultural and historical differences have combined with differing governmental institutions and orientations to prevent this. Morocco remains, as of this writing, a monarchy; Algeria has had a radical Arab orientation; Tunisia has been governed by a self-styled moderate government under the domination of the able but aging Bourguiba. Each has proceeded with its own internal development policy.)

Morocco also claimed the entire country of Mauretania, and an odd little cold war drama was played out over it: the Soviet Union used this claim as the excuse for employing its pre-1955 tactic of vetoing Mauretanian membership in the United Nations until such time as Outer Mongolia were admitted. Within a year the deal was consummated, and both states became United Nations members. This particular Moroccan claim was also abandoned .

The OAU was also called to mediate a conflict between Somalia, and Kenya and Ethiopia. Their roughly delineated boundaries cut across tribal grazing grounds, and Somalia, once it achieved independence in 1960, claimed about one-fifth of the national territory of both countries. Arguing, in the OAU, that there could be no talk of unity until "misdrawn" boundaries were revised, Somalia concluded in 1963 a large-scale arms agreement with Russia. It also used the Russo-Chinese conflict to obtain Chinese aid, particularly when a Russian rapproachement with Ethiopia made it difficult for the Russians to back Somalia. By the late 1960s— more on their own than through international agencies—Somalia and Ethiopia appeared to have reached an unstable modus vivendi. (There remained a Muslim separatist movement in the south of Ethiopia, which Somalia could continue to support, and where occasional military flare-ups took place. But one by-product of the damping down of the conflict was resumption of growth of Russian influence in Somalia, where advisers appeared at virtually every level of government, and where Russia established its main communications base for the Indian Ocean. Quietly, it had become a vital spot in world politics.)

In the meantime, Ethiopia had begun to encounter armed guerrilla resistance in Eritrea, which was joined to it by international agreement in 1952 and which it made into a province in 1962. The Moslem rebels against a primarily Christian Ethiopia received help from the Sudanese government, Somalia, and Arab Middle East governments, especially Syria, whose government has furnished the rebels with officers and Chinese-supplied weapons.

And in the Sudan, to the west, a revolt of the Christian and animist south, split into several independence or autonomy movements, long engaged the capital, Khartoum, where a succession of governments were unable to come to terms with the rebel groups or with the black governments to the south who sheltered or supported them materially. Steady intensification of the armed struggle eventually led to a coup in 1969 by disgruntled young nationalist officers, then a bloody coup and counter-coup in mid-1971, when the Sudanese Communist Party seized power for three days, executing numbers of the radical nationalist officers. They were thwarted by the army, supported from abroad by Libya's President Qaddafi and Egypt's President Sadat, and the most prominent Communist leaders were executed in turn—this even though the Sudanese Communist Party was one of the only strong Communist parties in Africa. In 1971, fortunately, the military government reached a modus vivendi with the rebels in the south and in February 1973 one of Africa's most bitter struggles ended, with a large measure of southern autonomy.

The OAU found it equally difficult to take action when Chad accused the Sudan of harboring an "Islamic government in exile." This rebel group provoked an unsuccessful uprising in 1966 and a subsequent one put down only with the help of French troops. The overlap of Muslim Middle East with Africa in the northeastern part of the continent has

thus both affected and been a cause of incipient local conflicts, and the
support of outside powers—including China and the Soviet Union as well
as France—has been a feature of the confused and unhappy situation.
The Arab-Israeli war of 1967 contributed in no small measure. It exacerbated relations between supporters of an effort against Israel and those
who frankly didn't care much. By cutting off trade through the Suez
Canal it hurt the economies of countries like the Sudan. The Sudan, in
addition, cut off relations with the United States because of the war, and
the United States, which had hitherto been providing it with economic
aid, now stopped. The resultant economic situation contributed to the
military takeover of the government in 1969.

In subsequent years the fiercely puritanical Muslim and anti-Israeli
Colonel Qaddafi in Libya used all the diplomatic instruments he could
command to turn African states against Israel, with which, until the 1967
war, they generally enjoyed good relations. In the case of Chad, for example, Qaddafi first supported the Muslim revolt in the north, then called
it off, in return for which Chad broke relations with Israel and assumed a
pro-Arab stance. In the case of Uganda he supplied financial aid that Israel had been unable or unwilling to. (And President Amin of Uganda
turned over the Israeli aid offices to the Palestine Liberation Organization.) In other cases (Niger, the Congo, Mali, and Ethiopia) other factors—Islam, or real disapproval of the Israeli stance—operated to bring
a break. In 1971 the OAU itself attempted to mediate the Arab-Israeli
dispute to no avail.

There were other conflicts, most of them a result of internal differences in the new states. Worst of all was the long, drawn-out ordeal in
Nigeria—a civil war, according to the government, and therefore of no
interest to the international community except insofar as the legitimate
government sought aid to suppress the revolt; an international war according to the leaders of the secessionist Eastern Region, which they
named Biafra and for which they sought international recognition aid,
and intervention.

Nigeria, at the time of independence, had a British-imposed federal
form of government, with three (later four) states. In each of them a
party controlled by a particular tribe or group came to dominate, to the
detriment of the situation for lesser tribes, and to the detriment, too, of
federal government functioning. The enormous Northern Region, run by
the aristocratic, traditionalist Emirs of the Hausa tribe and the Eastern
Region, controlled by the energetic and adaptable Ibos, struggled for an
alliance with the dominant Yorubas in the Western Region. The prize
was control of the federal government, which functioned increasingly for
the personal benefit and power of those manning it. In 1966 a bloody

military coup brought to power Major-General J.T.U. Aiguiyi-Ironsi, an Ibo. His Ibo-dominated government was pledged to reduce corruption and to install a more efficient unitary state. But northerners and western-ers died in the coup, and Ibos, who had come to dominate much of the Nigerian economy and civil service had now seized the government. The result was widespread anti-Ibo rioting and a second coup in the middle of the year, replacing the Ironsi group by a government drawn largely from minorities, including the new leader, Major-General Yakubu Gowon. Ironsi himself was killed, and a new wave of anti-Ibo riots swept the north. Tens of thousands of Ibos were killed; others fled to the Eastern Region, and Ibo leaders, fearing the possibility of even greater massacres, demanded greater state autonomy. The attempt of the central govern-ment to create a new, 12-state constitutional system that would have both reduced the inflexibility of the old, four state one and the dominance of particular tribes and groups, seems to have made matters worse. So far as the Eastern Region Ibos concerned the new system reduced their control over the rich oil resources of their region. On May 30, 1967, the Eastern Region, calling itself Biafra, announced its independence. Fighting broke out in July. Few people could foresee that it would drag on for three long, bitter years.

Under the leadership of General Odumego Ojukwu the Biafrans took the offensive. But within two months superior Nigerian numbers began to count, and for the next year and a half the Nigerians drove slowly ahead against a foe who contested every foot. In May 1968 Biafra lost Port Harcourt, its point of access to the sea.

For Biafran leaders aid from abroad and popular support at home were the essentials for survival. They focused on the right of self-determi-nation and on what they described as a Nigerian determination to exter-minate the Ibos. In April 1968 they received diplomatic recognition from Tanzania, then from Gabon, the Ivory Coast, Zambia, and Haiti. The Tanzanian statement declared that the Ibos in Nigeria had become like the Jews in Nazi Germany, and had earned their right to a land of their own. Even more, Biafra began to receive desperately needed material support from abroad. Sweden—unofficially—provided planes and pilots. France, whose de Gaulle declared that he shared the Tanzanian senti-ments, provided all-important financial support. Portugal, South Africa, the Ivory Coast, and Haiti contributed, and Catholic relief organizations distributed important food and medical supplies. In the meantime the Ni-gerian government came under diplomatic pressure to negotiate with Biafra. England, its chief former arms supplier, faced internal domestic demands that it halt supplies. Belgium and the Netherlands embargoed military shipments. The United States tried to remain neutral, a stand that still condemned it in Nigerian eyes, particularly since Biafra appeared to have gained widespread sympathy in the United States, from where privately donated relief money flowed in.

But the Soviet Union jumped into the breach, supplying Nigeria with planes and then financial and technical aid on a large scale. It was apparently enough to tip the balance. On January 10, 1970 Ojukwu fled the tiny remnant of what had been Biafra, and two days later his successors surrendered, deprived of the single airstrip that had been their link with the outside world.

Countries had been genuinely torn between sympathy for the Ibos and fear of what a breakup of Nigeria might portend for tribal separatism throughout Africa. Also, many had not wanted to alienate whichever country would win. Nigeria had long refused negotiations unless based on the principle of Nigerian unity; Biafra had refused them unless they were preceded by a cease-fire. Under all these contrary pressures the OAU had proved ineffectual and, of course, was split after Tanzania had hoped to pressure Nigeria into negotiations by recognizing Biafra. The Commonwealth Conference, the United Kingdom, the Pope, and a group of neutral countries—Switzerland, Austria, Sweden, and Yugoslavia—had all tried to mediate or offer good offices, to no avail.

Observers reported that after the victory Nigerian authorities acted promptly to end the mass starvation and disease rampant in the battle areas. But the Nigerian government made it clear that it had no use for anyone who had wanted it to negotiate on any other basis but unity, or for those who had expressed too much sympathy for Biafra.

There were several curious footnotes to the war. Some African analysts feared that Tanzania's recognition of Biafra had come through Chinese prompting, so that Chinese weapons and influence could counter the growing Russian influence in Nigeria. Others pointed out that it was Muslim Egypt who supplied pilots for Nigeria's Russian jets, while organized Catholic influence and aid was thrown into the balance for Biafra. And, indeed, the Nigerian government expressed bitterness at Catholic aid to the enemy. Yet others could see in the war only imperialism: a struggle for control of the rich oil resources located in the Eastern Region, near Port Harcourt. Each side tried to paint the other in the most sinister light: Biafra pointed out not only that Egyptians flew Russian jets for Nigeria, but so also did South African and Rhodesian mercenaries. Nigeria pointedly reminded Africans that Biafra accepted aid from Portugal and South Africa.

Nigeria had once been portrayed as a showcase for how federalism could reconcile local tribalism with the necessity for a modernizing centralization. The task of reconstructing after the war was not an easy one.

In East Africa, in the early 1970s, Idi Amin Dada's seizure of power and ousting of Milton Obote in January 1971 brought sporadic international conflict and much internal upheavel to Uganda. Obote took refuge in Tanzania, from where, Amin declared, he launched attacks against Uganda. The uncertain border situation justified internal security measures that led, Obote charged, to 90,000 Ugandan deaths. (Police were told by Amin that those who held political meetings at night "were to be treated as armed robbers and shot on sight.") Amin earned international condemnation when, in 1972, he brutally ousted eighty thousand Asians from the only country they knew, permitting them to leave with only the meagerest possession. Yet his move was widely approved of in Africa and by African leaders, although his neighbor Nyerere of Tanzania called it "racialism." Somalia acted to mediate the Uganda-Tanzania dispute after Amin charged in September that guerrillas trained and harbored across the border had again invaded Uganda. In the meantime the ubiquitous Qaddafi entered the picture by providing support for Amin when other sources of aid dried up and Amin, breaking with Israel, declared that Hitler had done the only right thing in killing six million Jews—while continuing to wear the Israeli paratrooper wings he had won training in Israel. There were elements of the ridiculous in the situation, but too much that was tragic.* The same was true in nearby Burundi, where the ruling Tutsi tribesmen, repelling one of several bloody Hutu uprisings engaged in what came to be called selective genocide—the killing off of all potential Hutu leaders and their families. By the end of 1972, the UN Secretary-General and others estimated that 200,000 may have been killed. The OAU and most African leaders maintained silence over what they considered an internal affair, and the United States after investigation also remained silent, although privately trying to get the UN and OAU to act. Only Nyerere of Tanzania and Mobutu of Zaire, whose countries harbored thousands of Hutu refugees, tried to prevent the killing, but with no success; Amin and Quaddafi both expressed support after President Micombero announced a diplomatic break with Israel in April 1972, and there were reports in Dar es Salaam that Qaddafi had rewarded the Burundi government with weapons. At the tenth anniversary meeting of the OAU, which Amin addressed, no mention was made of Burundi.

---

* Amin's logic was sometimes interesting. When an Asian refugee living in Kenya won the prestigious East African Safari motor race, Amin sent him a telegram: "I send you my very best wishes for having won the East African Safari of 1973. Although the Safari this year was not a true East African event since it took place only in Kenya and Tanzania because of imperialist sabotage tactics, and although you are now a refugee in Nairobi, after the milking of Uganda's economy for the last seventy years, your success goes on to show the determination of Ugandans. It further shows that Uganda has a good representative refugee who has been able to defeat powerful competitors."

The OAU tried to apply Western principles of sovereignty and independence, classifying some matters as international and others as domestic, just as the UN Charter tried to do; the OAU, concerned with individual human rights, could do it no better and, just like the United Nations, found itself being highly inconsistent, as it organized attack upon white domination in southern Africa. The inconsistency existed in the nature of things.

WHITE-DOMINATED AFRICA

Three areas of Africa faced international condemnation as they resisted the tide of black African nationalism: Portuguese Angola and Mozambique, South Africa, and Rhodesia. In 1960 their position looked merely anachronistic. Independence movements similar to those preceding independence in Ghana and Kenya had arisen in the Portuguese colonies; South Africa was discredited before the world by its policy of apartheid and by the Sharpeville massacre, when over eighty black Africans were shot down by white police; its economy faltered as fear arose of the black revolution, and it withdrew from the Commonwealth to become a Republic. Meanwhile, in the Central African Federation, created by Britain in 1953 out of three units, Northern Rhodesia, Southern Rhodesia and Nyasaland, constitutional development appeared to assure an orderly progression toward majority rule. But even more, as the tide of black nationalism washed over Africa, it swept into the UN General Assembly, where the new African nations could join Asian and socialist bloc allies to focus attention on the remnants of white rule in the south and bring pressure for its destruction.

Prime Minster Harold Macmillan of Great Britain addressed the South African Parliament in February 1960. "The wind of change," he told them, "is blowing through the continent."

A decade later the position of those discredited white minorities looked much stronger. As a result there was bitterness between the black African countries and Western countries they charged with supporting the white minorities, and between African countries who wanted to interfere in what were clearly domestic affairs.

Portugal transformed its colonies by constitutional change into provinces, and claimed to be following a gradual policy of modernization that would eventually move the overseas provinces with all their black population onto a level equivalent to that of the home country. But when guerrilla warfare first broke out, African states at the United Nations succeeded in bringing in a Committee Report to the General Assembly that characterized the situation in Angola as a threat to the peace, if only because people in other countries would not let their governments stand by and do nothing. The Assembly condemned Portuguese practices, called on it to cease repressive measures and demanded that Portugal allow self-determination on the basis of freely conducted elections. The Portuguese carried out reforms, but the Portuguese dictator Salazar maintained a diametrically opposed view: "unity does not allow transfers, cession or abandonment . . . Plebiscite, the referendum, auto-determination do not fit into this structure either." Subsequent UN Committees, the General Assembly, and the Security Council all dealt with both Angola and Mozambique, where armed resistance began on a serious scale in 1964. Ultimately, the General Assembly recommended that all states break off trade and financial relations with the Portuguese-held areas and cease any aid at all to Portugal.

In the meantime, the Organization of African Unity created a National Liberation Commiteee designed to draw together resources from the rest of Africa to aid in the liberation fight. Based in Tanzania it was able to provide some limited help. It was hindered partly by the reluctance of certain African states to contribute, but even more by the divisions that developed within liberation movements for the two Portuguese states. By the end of the decade the Portuguese continued to maintain an army of over 100,000 in the colonies, at heavy cost. Yet economic development of Angola and Mozambique had proceeded rapidly; the regime that succeeded Salazar's upon his death showed little disposition to unload the burden. Only a growing war weariness and the continued economic drain gave any portent of change. International efforts had so far failed.

The independence of Rhodesia on November 11, 1965 threw fuel on the flames. A remnant of the Central African Federation that broke up in 1964—of which Malawi and Zambia were the two other parts—Rhodesia was also governed by a tiny white minority, which resisted all British efforts to make it accept a constitution ultimately leading to universal suffrage. While some African leaders accused Britain of not doing enough, others turned again to the United Nations; in 1962 a General Assembly resolution asked Britain to suspend the 1961 Rhodesian constitution, one which severely limited black suffrage. Britain told the United Nations the issue was a domestic one. In 1965, however, the General Assembly voted a trade blockade. But Britain refused the African demand that it use force, resisting widespread condemnation for its refusal to do so.

The United Nations Security Council then voted mandatory economic sanctions, which have also failed to bring down the regime, although contributing to a restructuring of the Rhodesian economy. Trade through South Africa and Mozambique grew, and ways were found to circumvent the blockade. In 1972 the United States Congress, with Administration acquiescence, violated the sanctions by allowing imports of chrome and nickel; when charged with this at the United Nations, the American spokesman replied that many of the states attacking the United States themselves violated the blockade covertly.

In 1970 Rhodesia left the Commonwealth and became a republic. Several countries that had continued to maintain consulates, including the United States, now closed them. No state had established diplomatic relations with the Ian Smith government.

In early 1972 came failure in one last British attempt to negotiate with the Smith regime. The Conservative Heath government reached an agreement that would provide for limited black participation in the Rhodesian parliament. But it provided that a British Commission would have to survey black opinion in Rhodesia to see whether it would support the compromise. It did not, as the Pearce Commission was forced to report to Parliament in May. And so, ambiguously, the state still stands, excluded from the international system, and now facing increasing guerrilla infiltration from surrounding states.

If these countries to the north of South Africa have found preservation of their systems against international pressure painful and costly, South Africa has been able to withstand its increasing diplomatic isolation more easily.

One aspect of its situation was clearly international. Since World War I it had controlled the former German colony of South West Africa. But it had done so under the mandate system of the League of Nations, in which, rather than being able to simply annex the territory, South Africa governed it under League supervision, with certain commitments to the welfare of its native inhabitants. At the end of World War II the United Nations Trusteeship system replaced the old League mandates system, providing for more direct supervision and contact between inhabitants of trust territories and the Trusteeship Council. It was generally expected that countries supervising mandate territories not yet ready for self-government would transfer them to the trusteeship system. But South Africa, setting out on its course of institutionalized apartheid, refused to do so, and asked the United Nations to approve incorporation of South West Africa into South Africa proper. The General Assembly refused. South African authorities decided to forgo incorporation, but also refused to place South West Africa under the trusteeship system. The International Court of Justice ruled that South Africa continued to have mandatory responsibilities for reporting, but that it could not be forced to transform South West Africa into a trust territory. Throughout the 1950s and early 1960s the General Assembly used unsuccessfully a variety of diplomatic pressures. In 1966, to the anger of African states, the International Court ruled that it could not entertain a suit brought by Ethiopia and Liberia on several issues concerning South Africa's rule in South West Africa, because neither of the two applicants had the legal right or interest to advance their claims against South Africa.

African states reacted strongly in the United Nations. In a series of moves they declared the mandate terminated, Southwest Africa to be the independent state of Namibia, created committees to oversee the transition to independence, and sought to have the Security Council bring sanctions to bear upon South Africa for refusal to comply—all to no avail. Nevertheless, they continued the pressure and changed tactics. In 1970 they succeeded in having the Security Council request the International Court for an advisory opinion on the legality of South Africa's continued administration of Namibia in the light of the 1966 Assembly termination of the mandate. This time the Court could not avoid giving an opinion, and by 13–2 (the French and English judges dissenting) it ruled that South Africa was illegally in control. With this ruling in hand the African states hoped to be able to move through the courts of member states to block normal contacts with South Africa. It would be a slow process, however, and many people advocated violence to bring about the desired change.

The second issue concerned the practice of apartheid itself. For several years before the independence of African states the issue was brought into the international forum by India and Pakistan, on the basis of discrimination practiced against the many Asians inhabiting South Africa. They obtained no satisfaction, but the cudgels were taken up by African states, who eventually—as they increased in number—imposed an unparalleled diplomatic isolation upon South Africa, excluding it from one international organization after another, even from the Olympic Games. In 1963 the General Assembly recommended an arms embargo; in 1964 the Security Council called upon South Africa to hold a convention of representatives of all the people for purposes of instituting constitutional change; in 1965 the General Assembly recommended economic sanctions.

In the face of these and other pressures, however, South Africa has been able to stand firm. Its trade, primarily with non-African areas (apart from Rhodesia), has not suffered. Unable to obtain major arms from Britain or the United States, it has found France an eager supplier. In the year that its limited trade with African countries was cut by boycott, its trade with the People's Republic of China increased by an equal amount. It remains secure in the conviction that the major trading states of the world will fail to break off financial relations with it, and will reject any call for military sanctions against it or Rhodesia to its north, to which it has extended a helping hand.

In the early 1970s it achieved a limited diplomatic breakthrough among black African states. The occasion was the independence of the three landlocked countries—Botswana, Lesotho and Swaziland. Although opposed to South Africa's internal policies, they accepted that they could not end their economic dependence upon it. The South African government thereupon demonstrated its willingness to work with states with different social systems by extending them aid and going out of its way to establish friendly relations. A more important consequence was that the government of Hastings Banda in another landlocked state, Malawi, broke African ranks in the late 1960s, established diplomatic relations, and received important South African economic aid.

This limited diplomatic achievement, combined with the failure of blacks to acheive external support sufficient to make liberation efforts meaningful, led to a second major diplomatic change. On November 4, 1970, President Houphouet-Boigny of the Ivory Coast announced that he planned to call a meeting of African leaders to urge direct negotiations with South Africa. He declared that the problem of apartheid could not be solved by force, that arms embargoes and diplomatic isolation were "tragic" and "ridiculous," and that threats merely forced South Africa into a more militant, armed posture. In ensuing days and months he received both support and condemnation. President Tsiranana of the Malagasy Republic welcomed the initiative, declaring that his country would benefit by trade with South Africa. Prime Minister Kofi Busia of Ghana supported Houphouet-Boigny, declaring that sending "freedom fighters" meant sending a few people to be slaughtered. Gabon, Dahomey, Uganda (after Amin's coup in January 1971), Togo, and the Central African Republic approved. Others expressed reservations, but Nyerere, in Tanzania, opposed it outright. The government of Somalia declared the offer of a dialogue to be a "betrayal of the African cause," and a portent of the breakup of the OAU, at a meeting at which in February, Emperor Haile Selassie of Ethiopia also opposed the move. Meanwhile the government of Zambia issued a bitter denial to the charge that it had maintained secret contacts with the South African government while it opposed dialogue. On the contrary, Kaunda argued, South Africa had approached his government, which had refused discussion.

Whatever the outcome—and there were those who viewed the initiative in the most sinister light—a whole new possibility appeared to exist. In 1970, however, there was a brief, abortive invasion of Guinea by Guineans from Portuguese Guinea. Sekou Touré, who weathered it and brutally purged large numbers of people allegedly involved in the plot, brought both the OAU and the UN into the situation, and African spokesmen now argued that the incident, raising as it did the specter of colonialist influence again, had jeopardized the approach to South Africa. The conclusion seemed premature. But in 1972 President Tsiranana of the Malagasy Republic was driven from office, and the successor government cancelled the South African economic aid agreements he had negotiated. And earlier in the year, in Ghana, the civilian government of Kofi Busia was overturned by a military coup, amid charges of corruption and countercharges that the military had acted to forestall cuts in their privileges. Busia had been perhaps the most important African leader to approve the approaches to South Africa.

All in all, the situation in southern Africa looked more stable in the beginning of the 1970s than most people would have anticipated a decade earlier. The Rhodesian government was under pressure, recognizing now the disaffection of blacks and facing increasing security problems for rural residents near its borders. Yet the state continued to exist. South Africa was made uncomfortable in the world's international councils. But it was safe for the foreseeable future. Its government entered into an inconclusive dialogue with United Nations officials over Southwest Africa, or Namibia as it was now known, in order to point out that there was little internal opposition, and that the social expenditures it made in running the area far outclassed what the international community could do. (The OAU disapproved of the dialogue and pointed to the growth of national spirit among what had been isolated tribes.) South Africa faced a wave of black strikes in 1972–73, but they could be taken as evidence that economic imperatives in what was a booming economy were forcing the government to improve the lot of those blacks not in the separate Bantu areas—and perhaps into a realization that apartheid would have to be modified. Despite the anger of African states, Western countries took the attitude that harsh sanctions would work only harm, and that the best course was to pressure South Africans—many of whose white ancestors had arrived before some of the black tribes had come down from the north—into improving and ameliorating the lot of the blacks. In retaliation, at the UN General Assembly, African states obtained a 99–5 vote recognizing the "legitimacy" of anticolonial armed struggles. Only France, the United Kingdom, United States, Portugal, and South Africa voted against it. The Chinese representative pledged China's support for "just wars." Since imperialism, colonialism, and neocolonialism used force to maintain themselves in power, it would be a betrayal to advocate the nonuse of force indiscriminately—as the UN Charter did.

The Portuguese territories were under more pressure and seemed more vulnerable, even though not distinguished by the clear racism that marked Rhodesia and South Africa. Yet even the threat to them appeared far from immediate, and Portugal received encouragement when the United States, in order to continue its base rights in the mid-Atlantic Azore Islands, extended it further aid.

The picture was thus mixed. China, helping to build the Tanzam Railroad so that Zambia could trade through Tanzania instead of South Africa, gave evidence that some external forces would come to bear upon the situation. Efforts to get the Western powers to do more than observe the most limited restrictions on trade failed; much bitterness resulted, and some analysts predicted that ultimately a murderous race war would break out. Southern Africa looked less dangerous than the Middle East in terms of international conflict. But it also looked as though the level of violence would gradually rise.

REGIONALISM IN AFRICA

When new states emerged in the Middle East or in Asia, they did so individually and with little regard for what happened to their neighbors. The states of Latin America had been independent countries with relatively well-delineated boundaries for a hundred years before World War II. Among these states, regional action or moves toward some form of unification in the postwar period was essentially based on a need for cooperative ventures, and took place as a consequence of negotiation between established governments.

The situation was very different in Africa. The borders were colonial ones, representing European balance of power considerations and the hazards of exploration. Two trends therefore emerged. Whether they were opposed, complementary, or contradictory was hard to discern.

One took place within the framework imposed by colonialism: the development of nationalist movements devoted to producing sovereign independent states within the existing boundaries. If the first task was to throw off colonial authority, the second was to create the authority of the new successor government, which in practice often meant substituting that authority for a tribal or ethnic group or using the old to create a base for the new.

The other trend, and it was a strong one, stressed the need for a broader unity based on something other than past European caprice. As a set of ideas and ideologies it insisted that a series of small successor states would be economically and politically weak, their search for legitimate authority hampered by that very fact. Either larger, regional, more rational units must emerge, or Africa itself must become a unit. But the major theoretical problem was simple: what larger units? What constituted "Africa"? The political problem derived both from the difficulty in defining what should constitute the larger units—and from the concrete situation of emerging nationalist movements defined by past and existing institutions, leading, inevitably, to sovereign, independent states. Would they be merely steps on the way to something else, or become an end in themselves? The well-founded fear of Pan-African leaders was that new ruling elites would develop a vested interest in the existence of their new states, and quickly find that their states had divergent economic and political interests despite the unifying bonds of a colonial past and color. And even the latter were deceptive: until 1958 most African leaders had little contact with one another. Most of the areas that became independent had little trade with each other. East Africa had been subject to far more Arab influence than had West Africa, and religious differences persisted. The different colonial administrations left different legacies of law, education, language, and political parties.

There were few Africans at the Bandung Conference of 1955. More appeared at the January 1958 Cairo Afro-Asian People's Solidarity Conference, attended by the Soviet Union and China, and which devoted itself to the idea of liberation of Africa. It marked the high tide of Egyptian efforts to lead the new Africa; in subsequent years Egypt would be torn between its African and its Middle Eastern interests, in the end opting basically for the latter. In December the African states took over the leadership of the independence movement, when the first Conference of Independent African States took place in Accra, Ghana, a setting that symbolized both the stature that Kwame Nkrumah had rapidly acquired and his own commitment to Pan-Africanism as a movement whose immediate aim should be a rapid transition to genuine African unity.

In ensuing months many other congresses were held, marking the emergence of pressure groups and parties cutting across state boundaries: the first Conference of North African Political Parties in Tangier in April; the first Pan-African Students Conference in Uganda in July; the first Conference of the Confederation of North African Students in Tunis in August; the first meeting of the Pan-African Freedom Movement for East and Central Africa in Tanganyika in September; and most important of all, the first all-African People's Conference in Accra in December. Here 500 delegates of parties and other nonofficial bodies met to plan, as President Nkrumah put it, "a final assault upon imperialism and colonialism." For Tom Mboya, delegate from Kenya, the theme—in deliberate contrast to the "Scramble for Africa" set off by the Berlin Conference of 1888—was "Scram out of Africa."

While these activities marked the emergence of Pan-Africanism, the new United Nations Economic Commission for Africa, modeled on other existing United Nations regional economic commissions, began operation in Addis Ababa, and in New York, Charles Malik of Lebanon, President of the Thirteenth General Assembly, called it the "African Session," because of the prominence of African issues of the agenda.

Yet the very emergence of African independent states complicated the idea of African unity, and the next years saw a proliferation of groupings, with overlapping and conflicting membership. The union of Guinea and Ghana took place soon after Guinea's independence in 1958, but Guinea's separate membership in the United Nations typified the loose nature of union. Talk began at this time, too, of a union of the Maghreb—Morocco, Algeria, and Tunisia and, indeed, Tunisia's President Bourguiba became embroiled with France over Tunisian aid to the Algerian rebels. Once Algeria achieved its independence, however, the Maghreb union failed to materialize. Instead, in 1963, Morocco and Algeria engaged in warfare over Moroccan claims to Algerian territory. In April 1959 Senegal and the Sudan formed the Mali Federation. It broke up in August 1960, and Senegal's President Senghor wrote that Senegal's new role would be to exemplify not a Pan-African but an inter-African policy: the notion of cooperation between independent units began to compete with the idea of an organic unity. The Sudan, which retained the title of Mali, proceeded on the other hand to join the loose Ghana-Guinea union.

In the meantime there were moves to unite the four states that had emerged from French Equatorial Africa—Gabon, the Central African Republic, Chad and the Congo Republic—resulting in a customs union of the four plus the new state of the Cameroons, while the former states of French West Africa, with the exception of Guinea, took a similar step. Then twelve of these—again excepting Guinea, Mali, and Togo—met to form an Afro-Malagasy Union to develop cooperation in defense and diplomacy, at the same time creating an Afro-Malagasy Economic Cooperation Organization (OCAM) that would eventually lead to a full-scale common market.

These so-called "Brazzaville Powers" had one other common interest that tended to set them apart from other African states. In Europe, in 1957, the six members of the European Coal and Steel Community signed and ratified agreements to set up the European Economic Community or Common Market. In a momentous decision, Britain, which had kept apart from the European movement, decided not to join. One price that France extracted from the other powers in return for French ratification was a provision that members of the French Union could become "associated states," along with a provision setting up a common development fund. The form of association gave the African states formerly belonging to France access to the new European Common Market without the common tariff barrier that other states would face, including other nonassociated African states. Ghana took the lead in charging that this constituted a form of "neo-colonialism" since it would subordinate to the Common Market the economies and therefore the politics of the African countries involved.

Association of the former French territories to the Common Market was the only concrete result of the grandiose idea of "Eurafrica." For years, especially in France, men had talked of a Eurafrica that would draw upon the raw materials and manpower on both sides of the Mediterranean—a region in which the Mediterranean would be only a central lake, as it had been under the Roman Empire. Military men pointed to the strategic importance of North Africa, and cited its role in World War II to buttress their arguments. The dream lacked two essentials: equality of status between the people who would presumably participate, and a real desire to take part. Nevertheless, the concrete benefits of the Common Market were not to be cast aside.

From the point of view of international relations, however, association of the former French colonies with the Common Market meant another overlapping regional grouping in Africa, competing with others, and working potential hardship on them: behind Ghana's complaint of neocolonialism lay the fact that it would be harder for African nonmembers to export to the European market. (Latin American countries feared the same thing, and they, along with a few other raw material exporters, tried to pressure the Common Market to keep its outside tariffs low.)

Eventually, as the dream of Pan-African unity faded, other states signed association agreements giving them preferential trading arrangements with the Common Market: Kenya, Tanzania and Uganda, and Morocco and Tunisia. And in 1969, OCAM's original agreement with the Common Market, the Yaoundé Convention, was renewed for another five-year period. But OCAM itself was seriously weakened by withdrawal of several members in the early 1970s. Moreover, once Nigeria began to recover from the civil war that devastated it for three long years, a conflict began to develop between the remaining OCAM members and those leaders who wanted cooperation between French and English speaking states so that they could develop a new association with the EEC, now that Britain had joined. In such as association, Nigeria would play a leading part, but it would mean the end of OCAM as such, and organizations do not easily die.

In East Africa another regional grouping weathered several periods of severe strain. In colonial times Britain had forged a number of ties between Kenya, Uganda, and Tanzania, in the form of common public services, a customs union, and a common currency. The benefits of these outweighed nationalist considerations at the time of independence. But by the mid-sixties it appeared to many that Kenya, more economically developed, benefitted more than the others. Negotiations for a common central bank broke down, and in 1966 the common currency was abandoned. President Nyerere of Tanganyika, charged with being an opponent of continued unity, took the diplomatic initiative. Federation, he argued, was not valid for the present, although there had been much earlier talk in favor of it. But the East African grouping, with its East African Common Services Organization, must not break up as a consequence of the currency dispute. A series of summit conferences ensued, and leaders of the three states negotiated a new agreement, expanding the Services Organization into the East African Economic Community and Common Market. Inaugurated in December 1967, it made an attempt to distribute the benefits of union more equitably, and there was considerable optimism that it would stand the test. By 1969, Zambia, Somalia, Ethiopia, and Burundi had applied for membership. It appeared probable that the union would withstand the temporary political rupture of relations between Tanzania and Uganda in early 1971, when President Obote of Uganda was overthrown by General Idi Amin. General Amin appeared ready to slow what he considered Obote's too hasty moves toward socialization; Obote toured African capitals to try to enlist support, and although most countries eventually recognized Amin's new government, Nyerere—with support from the governments of Somalia, Zambia, and Guinea—stood by Obote. The subsequent strain between Uganda and Tanzania slowed any further progress.

While the fortunes of regional groupings waxed and waned, and national entities hardened, two continent-wide organizations developed steadily. One was the Organization of African Unity, the product of several initiatives in the 1961–63 period, when the Casablanca and Brazzaville groupings had come to represent radical and conservative tendencies in Africa, exacerbated by the conflict in the Congo. The other, the Economic Commission for Africa, was in fact a creation of the Economic and Social Council, like the other United Nations regional economic agencies—the Economic Commission for Europe, for Asia and the Far East, and for Latin America. (There was none for the Middle East, since the Arab states would not agree to one with Israel, nor Israel's friends to one without it. So an Economic Office operated out of Beirut, instead.) Although nominally responsible to ECOSOC, the Economic Commission for Africa (ECA), located in Addis Ababa, seat of the OAU, worked in close cooperation with it and in the main, merely drew its funds from the United Nations. Through technical studies, conferences, and publications, the ECA has helped promote both national and regional development. A related African Development Bank, created in 1966, suffers from lack of capital.

The OAU has not proved to be the nucleus of a greater, unified Africa, as some had hoped it would be. In a very real sense it was not designed as such, but rather as a counter to the potentially subversive idea of unity as it was propounded by men like Nkrumah. Leaders of more conservative states were fearful that the radical unifiers would end up trying to overthrow established governments (and in fact accused Nkrumah of attempting to do so). The OAU has therefore paid careful attention to nonintervention in the domestic affairs of states, and supported governments that have tried to prevent other states from harbouring political refugees who are mounting a subversive effort, and there have been many of these in the tumultuous decade of the sixties. The obvious exception to this rule, of course, has been in the area of relations with white-dominated Africa. Yet here, as the record has shown, the OAU has faltered.*

CONCLUSION

The pattern of relations in Africa is a mixed one. At the outset, with the formation of the Bazzaville and Casablanca groups, it appeared that a sort of regional balance of power system was developing. Yet, while OCAM still represents the older, conservative Brazzaville grouping, the Casablanca group dissolved, and the idea of Africa as a political unit died with it. Internal changes have been too rapid for any stable groups to develop with fixed international political concerns; the concerns have been mainly economic, racial, or tribal. On the political level, therefore, the OAU has served as a center for concerting diplomatic efforts, while various ad hoc groupings with particular interests have formed and reformed. The Nigerian war revealed all the problems inherent in the structure that has developed. The OAU, not being any sort of supranational institution, was unable to stop it; the principle of nonintervention was at war with the desire to end the killing of Africans; when, eventually, the principle of Nigerian unity was endorsed, four countries nevertheless recognized Biafra.

Africa, as a continent of generally independent states, did not represent the unified force in world politics that people like Nkrumah had hoped it would. Like other areas of the world its states shared some interests and cooperated or reached accommodations with respect to them. They also conflicted over others and fought and negotiated to resolve

---

* An almost prophetic development occurred at the time of formation of the OAU, when Nkrumah and Nasser lost in stature, but Ahmed Ben Bella of Algeria gained, primarily because he appeared willing to actually use Algeria's slender resources to help the liberation fight in Southern Africa. Yet he was overthrown in June 1965, and the new government turned back to domestic and Arab concerns.

these conflicts. And as with other areas of the world, the interests resulted from internal considerations, from regional political patterns, and from patterns of relations in, and with, the rest of the world and its problems. It was only to a limited extent that African institutions had isolated African problems from outside influences.

TEN
THE ASIAN SPHERE

Throughout the great arc of South Asia and the Far East the international scene continued to shift at a dizzying pace. Indian-Pakistani hostility failed to abate, culminating in 1971 in a war that led to the breakup of Pakistan and the emergence of India as the sole regional great power in the area. In the process, India continued to move closer to the Soviet Union and away from friendly relations with the United States. The Russian leaders, keeping a wary eye upon China, moved to bolster their aid to a faltering Indian economy just as the United States fell into more and more disrepute—in part because, with the People's Republic of China, it had favored the Pakistanis in the final war.

In Southeast Asia states followed varied paths, some attempting to maintain an unstable nonalignment, others getting caught up in the remnants of the Cold War. The chaotic and belligerent Sukarno regime came to an end in Indonesia, and with it China's chief ally in its third world struggle with Russia. In the course of the more complex rivalries of the time, Japan re-emerged as a major but uncertain influence in the Far East.

SOUTH ASIA

Indian publicists and spokesmen long maintained that their country would have something to teach the rest of the world in the field of international relations. They would build foreign policy out of the legacy of Ghandi, anti-imperialism, and opposition to international relations conducted on balance of power principles by blocs. Nonalignment with military blocs would not mean noninvolvement in international affairs; from the position of nonalignment India would take an active diplomatic role in trying to help resolve conflicts between nations. In particular, it would be in a position to act in a mediating role between the US and USSR, as it was when Indian troops were sent to Korea to supervise the truce there.

In 1954 Prime Minister Nehru, who also held the post of Minister of Foreign Affairs, had to acquiesce in increased Chinese control of the former buffer area of Tibet. The Chinese had built new roads, airfields, and installed new garrisons along the borders; the Indians had not. But the agreement formalizing the new situation was accompanied by mutual congratulations, declarations of esteem and, most important, subscription to the *panch shila,* or "Five Principles of Peaceful Coexistence." Nehru virtually acted as Chou En-lai's sponsor at Bandung in 1955; at the United Nations it was India that pushed most actively for Chinese membership. Delegations were exchanged, friendship societies formed, and trading agencies opened several offices in each country. Indian diplomacy was premised, for a brief period, on a determined effort to overlook Chinese claims to territory held or claimed by India, and an acceptance of Chinese statements that revolution was not for export—for India, after all, was a "bourgeois nationalist state" in the lexicon of Communism.

In the meantime, India condemned its neighbor Pakistan for joining the South East Asia Treaty Organization and the new Central Treaty Organization, created in 1955 under British sponsorship, and for its arms aid agreements with the United States. These had brought it into the line of Russian and Chinese diplomatic fire, thus bringing the Cold War into Asia. And although this had, for the Indians, the advantage that Russia took India's side in the Kashmir dispute and assiduously courted Nehru, it also meant that the Pakistani army now would face India in much better shape.

In 1959 a diplomatic revolution in the entire web of South Asian relations impended. General Ayub Khan had taken over complete power in Pakistan the year before, while in Burma Prime Minister U Nu, unable to rule his strife-torn state, resigned in favor of a military caretaker regime headed by General Ne Win. In previously stable Ceylon, the leftist regime of S.W.R.D. Bandanaraike brought bloody communal rioting and the deportation of Tamils to India. To the north, the situation became more ominous when the Chinese moved to crush the Tibetan revolt of 1959, sending refugees streaming into India. The Nehru government downplayed the event, as well as the unwelcome issue of its own border relations with China. It had ample warning, but publicly failed to heed these and other diplomatic portents: Chinese condemnation of growing Russian aid to India, and Chinese approaches to Pakistan and Burma.

There had long been a border dispute with Burma, and while U Nu was premier, Chinese claims seemed extravagant, and the Chinese People's Liberation Army, esconced in what Burma considered its own territory, impossible to dislodge. But in early 1960 General Ne Win reached a settlement in which China forfeited much of what it had, claimed.

Ayub Kahn, despite cordially worded Chinese offers to negotiate the Kashmir-Chinese border, suggested a rapproachement to India. Together, with Western backing (and Russian backing for India), they could withstand the now apparent Chinese threat to the north. But such a rapproachement would require *some* resolution of the Kashmir question, and this proved impossible. Nehru, once willing to accept the idea of plebiscite for the region, had long ago rejected it when he realized Kashmir would probably opt for Pakistan. The principle of maintaining rule in Kashmir rested on the necessity of showing that a secular state was possible: once the principle was established that Muslims could opt out because they were Muslims, the breakup of India was threatened. Even though Ayub Kahn did not raise the issue of self-determination, but merely resolution of certain economic questions, no satisfactory Indian answer was forthcoming.

With the 1959 revolt in Tibet, India assumed a forward strategy, reinforcing its presence in the buffer states of Nepal, Sikkim, and Bhutan, and moving troops into border areas it had previously left undefended. Late in 1959 there were border clashes. In 1960 the Chinese and Indian governments negotiated on the border issue but failed to reach agreement (but Pakistan held talks with the Chinese to delineate their own frontier, and the talks proceeded smoothly). In the meantime, as though to demonstrate the Indian Army's prowess shortly before the 1962 elections, the Indian Army moved to liberate the tiny Portuguese enclave of Goa, long a subject of acrimonious dispute. The Indian government claimed that it had exhausted all diplomatic means to bring about self-determination and to remove this remnant of colonialism and center for smuggling. The Indian government may have also been influenced by its own lagging position as third world leader in the face of growing numbers of independent African states who were fighting remnants of Portuguese colonialism in Africa. Western powers in the United Nations charged a double standard —non-Western countries approved India's use of force for "good" purposes, despite the fact that the Charter, as India had often pointed out, outlawed force except in self-defense. But the Westerners found little support among the growing anticolonialist majority in the United Nations, now aligned with the Communist countries on such issues. The Indian Army and its Defense Minister, Krishna Menon, faced the future with confidence. In August 1962, shortly after the Goan liberation, there were more border skirmishes with Chinese forces, and Nehru ordered the Army to advance. Instead, the Chinese counterattacked and drove ahead for thirty days, both in Assam, on the eastern tip of India, and in the border area of Ladakh in the west. In India there was panic, dismay, and recrimination.

India, that long-time proponent of nonalignment and *panch shila,* now asked for and received military aid from the United States, Britain, and—ultimately—Russia. The suppliers suggested again that India and Pakistan try to mend their quarrel and so reduce their vulnerability. Again the two countries held prolonged but unsuccessful talks. Agreement foundered on Pakistani insistence on plebiscite and Indian firmness on the status quo with the exception of minor border rectification.

Within Pakistan Ayub Kahn found himself in a difficult situation. Pakistan's previous alliance with the West had brought Russia to the aid of India. Yet now nonaligned India in the face of a presumed Chinese threat, was receiving Western as well as Russian military aid. But, the Pakistani leader declared, there was no significant Chinese menace. Pakistan had just reached a relatively favorable agreement on its frontier with China; the Indians, on the other hand, by refusing conciliatory Chinese offers had forced the Chinese to issue a rebuff to India, whose intention was to humble them. Ayub Kahn argued that, in effect, China had neither the desire nor the capacity to sweep down out of the mountains into the Indian plains. Moreover, the Western powers had strengthened the Indians' position in Kashmir by funnelling them arms against the nonexistent Chinese threat—and this despite their repeated declarations in favor of negotiations over the disputed area (where in 1963 and 1964 there were popular uprisings against Indian rule) .

In the midst of the charged Asian situation, Nehru died in May 1964. He had commanded wide respect and affection; he had held India to a democratic course when all around him democracy had failed. But his dreams of world peace and of an Asian example had proved empty. He had been unable to settle the matters that divided India and Pakistan, unable to respond to Pakistani overtures. History might judge him as an Indian Lincoln, who had held a democratic, secular state together under incredible pressure; many contemporaries judged him as simply too obdurate. His successor, the relatively unknown Lal Bahadur Shastri, inherited the Kashmir dispute, and perhaps to cement domestic political support, made further moves in late 1964 to integrate Kashmir more fully into Indian political life.

Ayub Kahn, angered, turned to China. The Chinese could not offer as much aid as the United States, but they could help; within the next few years they sent Pakistan some 200 T-54 tanks and several squadrons of MIG-19 fighters. The Pakistani President thus demonstrated his independence from the Americans, worried both them and the Russians, and tried to build domestic support. In fact, the Russians quickly moved to counter Chinese influence by normalizing their own relations with Ayub Kahn. In April 1965 he visited Moscow, where a series of exploratory talks paved the way for substantial future arms aid (against which the Indians protested vigorously) .

But Ayub also visited Peking and entertained President Liu Shao Chih, Prime Minister Chou En-lai, and Foreign Minister Chen Yi in Karachi. In retaliation and because of open Pakistani critcism of American involvement in Vietnam, the American government postponed indefinitely visits to Washington by both Ayub Kahn and Shastri. Congress questioned the scope of continued American economic aid, by now a vital part of the economic life of both countries. The action probably heightened the welcome Shastri received when he visited Moscow.

Abandonment by India of any willingness to discuss further autonomy for Kashmir and the tipping of the military balance as arms flowed into India increased tension intolerably. In April fighting broke out over a high, desolate area known as the Rann of Kutch; each charged the other with responsibility; fighting was bitter and casualties high. Both used American-supplied arms, as well as those from other countries. Under diplomatic persuasion from the United States and Commonwealth countries, Shastri and Ayub agreed to a cease-fire and program for settling the dispute. But now, with opinion inflamed in both countries, the other tensions told. In August fighting spread to Kashmir.

Perhaps Pakistanis were emboldened by the Rann of Kutch incident to move to prevent India from cementing its hold on Kashmir while the rest of the world stood by. Pakistan claimed that India initiated the fighting, while India, supported by outside observers, charged that the war was initiated by several thousand Pakistani infiltrators. In response India attacked and seized border posts, while trying to round up potential infiltrators on the Pakistani side of the demarcation line. Pakistan drove armored columns into Indian-occupied Kashmir, and India responded by further thrusts into Pakistani-held territory. In early September Pakistan launched a major offensive; this time the Indians countered with an offensive into Pakistan proper, aimed at the city of Lahore.

Western powers, UN Secretary-General U Thant, and the Soviet Un-Union all begged the two parties to stop the fighting, and at a series of Security Council meetings were able to agree on unanimous appeals for a cease-fire and withdrawal behind the previous demarcation line. But China backed Pakistan, its Foreign Minister supporting the Pakistani position on Kashmir as just, and condemning the United Nations for failing to implement previous calls for a plebiscite. With this backing, the Pakistani government took the position that a cease-fire would, indeed, solve nothing unless preceded by an Indian commitment to a plebiscite. Then, in the middle of September, while the war continued, the Chinese presented India with an ultimatum demanding evacuation of certain disputed border areas and dismantling of their border posts within three days—a time schedule extended to six, at which point the Chinese said that the Indians had complied.

While Chinese support for Pakistan materialized in this fashion, the Western powers, in support of U Thant's repeated personal efforts to obtain a cease-fire, suspended both military and economic aid to both sides. Both the costs and disadvantages of the indeterminate fighting also began to tell, and on September 22 the two countries accepted the third and peremptory United Nations call for a cease-fire. Pakistan, however, declared that it would accept only on the understanding that the United Nations would seek to bring about a fair and honorable solution to the Kashmir problem. Both countries expressed bitterness at the United States position: Pakistan, aligned with the United States, had nevertheless come under American pressure through the withholding of economic and military aid, and had received no guarantee about Kashmir. India also complained about the pressures, including United States prodding to *do* something about Kashmir. Both wanted a resumption of aid—but not to the other. Despite continued violations of the cease-fire, the United States did provide emergency food relief, and Ayub Kahn visited the United States in December. In the meantime the Soviet Union had stepped into the breach as peacemaker.

Prime Minister Kosygin offered his services at the height of the conflict, and suggested the city of Tashkent, capital of Uzbekistan, as a site for a meeting. The role of mediator was a novel one for the Soviet Union; Kosygin met with Ayub Kahn and Shastri for a week in January 1966, and obtained an agreement for withdrawal of military forces, resumption of diplomatic relations, and commitment to further negotiation. Success of the venture was marred by the sudden death of Lal Bahadur Shastri within hours after the agreement was signed. Mrs. Indira Ghandi, Nehru's daughter, succeeded Shastri as Prime Minister and pledged herself to observe the accord. Nevertheless despite much talk of "The spirit of Tashkent," the accord did nothing to resolve the Kashmir issue. On this matter, India stood firm, and Pakistan could gain no satisfaction. Both the United States and the Soviet Union found that their diplomacy had accomplished little, and bitterness persisted in South Asia. The Soviet Union, however, demonstrated its new position of great power influence in the area.

In only a few years, during which relations never improved, the situation suddenly deteriorated further as a result of internal developments in Pakistan.

In the decade of the sixties Pakistan, under Ayub Kahn's leadership, appeared to have done well economically. The benefits of rapid rises in national income, however, were not spread widely and, as usual, led to demands for more. The President had promulgated a Constitution in 1962, when he ended martial law. It retained a fairly authoritarian structure, using indirect representation and a system of locally elected councils. More important for the future of Pakistan than the denial of a parliamentary system, however, was the limited degree of autonomy accorded to East Pakistan. The eastern region was more populous, earned more foreign exchange through its jute exports, but was underrepresented in the Civil Service, the army, the judiciary, and received back in federal funds less than it payed in taxes. Yet officials in East Pakistan claimed that per capita income in their region had declined sharply relative to that of the western part. They spoke bitterly of exploitation by the corrupt rich who ran the government under Ayub Kahn. During the war with India, it was said, the central government had left East Pakistan virtually undefended.

While bitterness increased in East Pakistan, in West Pakistan Zulfiqar Ali Bhutto, formerly Ayub's Foreign Minister, founded the Pakistan People's Party, declaring that the Tashkent agreement was a surrender to India, that Ayub was too pro-Russian, and demanding an alignment with China, which had supported Pakistan during the crisis.

In East Pakistan the leader of the Awami League, Sheik Mujibur Rhaman, published a manifesto of February 12, 1966, demanding a federal form of government in which autonomy for the East would extend to matters of trade, taxation, and even military affairs. Like Bhutto, he demanded a return to parliamentary rule. Other political figures, often with divergent demands, joined Bhutto and Mujibur in dissociating themselves from Ayub, who was now faced with widespread rioting, demonstrations, and unrest to which he responded with a combination of repression and reform. Bhutto, Mujibur, and hundreds of others were arrested for inciting to riot and for plots against the sovereignty of Pakistan. Trade unions took to the streets with red flags, calling for unity with the Chinese people and the end of capitalism; general strikes paralyzed the nation; and, ironically, students attacked family planning centers. In February Ayub withdrew from the forthcoming presidential race. In March, he announced that he had agreed to free elections and parliamentary government; political prisoners were released. But the situation worsened. In East Pakistan anarchy reigned outside of the cities; civil servants and supporters of the regime were massacred and local government disappeared. On March 25, Ayub resigned, declaring that all civil administration and constitutional authority had broken down. Turning the government over to Commander in Chief of the Army, General Yahya Kahn, he declared that only the armed remained to retrieve the situation. His own efforts had failed.

President Yahya Kahn established martial law, and disturbances virtually ceased. He allowed the resumption of political activity, prepared for elections for a National Assembly in October, elections that had to be postponed until December when massive floods and a disastrous cyclone struck East Pakistan. His own foreign policy position was made clear during a November visit to Peking, where, with Chou En-lai, he signed a communique supporting the Chinese position on Taiwan, Vietnam, Israeli withdrawal from Arab territories, and in which Chou supported him on Kashmir. In December the elections loosed the avalanche.

Sheik Mujibur Rhaman's Awami League devoted to Eastern autonomy, won almost all seats in East Pakistan, giving it an absolute majority in the National Assembly, even though Bhutto was victor in West Pakistan. Their positions on autonomy for East Pakistan were irreconcilable; the President postponed opening of the Assembly in hopes that the leaders would come to some basic agreement. It was impossible. On March 26, 1971 a clandestine radio station announced the independence of East Pakistan as "Bangla Desh"—the Bengal Nation. Within three weeks, despite Indian prohibition of overflights from West to East Pakistan, the Pakistani Army seized all key population centers. Hundreds of thousands of East Pakistani refugees streamed across the borders into already densely populated and poverty stricken East Bengal in India. Yahya Kahn accused India of aiding the revolt, told the cautious Russians to tell India to stop meddling, and sought aid from the Chinese, who declared support for the Pakistani central government. By the middle of the year it was estimated that six million refugees were encamped in misery across the border in India, where cholera began to run riot; by the end of the year the number had increased to an inconceivable ten million! In East Pakistan the Pakistani Army indiscriminately hunted down and killed supporters of Bangla Desh.

In the end, Pakistan came under worldwide criticism, retaining open support only from China (whose position in defending a military regime's repression of a liberation movement because of Russian influence in India dismayed many of its ideological supporters). The United States had again cut arms aid early in the year. In September and October Mme. Ghandi visited Moscow and Western capitals to obtain support for her position that India could not simply sit by—nor absorb the ten million refugees. Prime Minister Kosygin agreed with her that it was "impossible to justify the actions of the Pakistani authorities." A Bangla Desh Consultative Committee was created in Calcutta with an overseas mission in London to coordinate foreign support. Numerous Pakistani diplomats throughout the world defected to protest their government's repression in the east. In late November fighting broke out between Indian troops massed on the borders of East Pakistan and Pakistani forces. By December 3 open warfare existed. On December 6 India recognized the independent state of Bangla Desh.

The war did not last long. Pakistani troops were now fighting in what was essentially hostile territory, and they faced numerically superior and better armed Indians. On December 16 they surrendered unconditionally in East Pakistan, and a day later a cease-fire was signed in the West. The Indian subcontinent, divided into two states in 1947, was now three. Pakistan, greatly reduced in size, faced internal upheaval; General Yayah Kahn resigned and was replaced by the volatile Ali Bhutto who would have to chart a whole new course. Sheik Mujibur Rahman, imprisoned and facing a possible death sentence for treason, was released and returned to a wild hero's welcome in Bangla Desh. The United States, which had found itself on the same side as the Chinese, condemning Indian action and actually making threatening moves with its fleet in the Indian Ocean, faced general opprobrium.

In the meantime, shortly before the war, Indira Ghandi's government had taken an important symbolic step. On August 9 it signed a Twenty-Year Treaty of Peace, Friendship and Cooperation with the Soviet Union, thus sealing the growing bonds between the two countries. The Treaty provided for immediate consultation between the two in the event of an attack or threat of an attack by a third country and prohibited either country from entering an alliance directed against the other. It was not, said Mme. Ghandi, a reversal of the Indian policy of nonalliance. But India and Russia had come a long way since the end of the British Raj in 1947.

The end of the war unfortunately brought little respite to the subcontinent. India, Pakistan, and Bangla Desh continued to quarrel over prisoners of war and war criminals; Kashmir remained at issue, and Pakistan faced a renewal of Pathan separatism in the north. In fact, some feared that the loss of East Pakistan might lead to complete breakup of the Moslem state. And Bangla Desh, devastated by cyclone, repression, war, and almost insuperable economic problems to begin with, faced a hard future. But India, for the first time since independence—and despite continued economic hardship—had emerged as the sole great power in South Asia.

While India and Pakistan underwent their agonies, Ceylon, their neighbor to the south, equally linked to the outside world, reflected all the tensions that beset third world nations.

Its internal politics, and the alternation between the Western-oriented United National Party, which was ready to look to institutions like the World Bank for help, and the "leftist" Sri Lanka Freedom Party, were based largely on ethnic and language differences and outlooks. The Sri Lanka Freedom Party was led by Mme. Bandanaraike after her husband's assassination in 1959. In power from 1956 to 1965, it regained power in 1970. In 1964, after bitter riots and much wrangling, Mme. Bandanaraike had negotiated with India the transfer of 500,000 Tamils from Ceylon while agreeing to integrate into Ceylonese society 300,000 of this minority, descendants of Tamils from the South of India who had come to Ceylon during British rule. Her own party was based in the Buddhist traditionalist Sinhalese majority, whose language was made official for the country as a whole, thereby alienating the English-speaking technical elites, many of whom left Ceylon. Her new 1970 government, oriented toward national socialism, was a coalition that included Trotskyist and Communist party representatives; it recognized East Germany, North Vietnam, North Korea, the Communist insurgents of South Vietnam, and suspended relations with Israel. And then, in March 1971, it faced an organized insurrection of young people in the People's Liberation Front, a self-styled "Che Guevarist" movement. The Front drew mainly upon students who found themselves in the same position that students in much of the continent did: without jobs commensurate with the status that a liberal arts university degree gave them. Ideologically, they were simply radical. But so was the government, and Mrs. Bandaranaike attacked them harshly as misguided youth. She received help from the United Kingdom, the USSR, India, Pakistan, Yugoslavia and helicopters from the United States. The insurrection was put down with bitter fighting. On April 13, the North Korean Mission was ordered out of the country. Presumably its personnel had helped the rebels, some of whom she claimed had trained at Patrice Lumumba University in Moscow.

What happened in Ceylon was not an isolated event: it was related to developments in the rest of Asia, in Europe, and in Latin America, to the problems of governments coping with modernism or modernization, heightened mass expectations, mass alienation, and the rise of new millenary movements that purported to have the answers for dealing with these problems. International revolutionary movements were now more genuinely international than before. Ironically, they were also always linked to local dissatisfactions and peculiarities and their very attempt at universalism caused them to fracture irrevocably. Russia was not the only country to find this to be true.

SOUTHEAST ASIA

In that great arc of countries on the rim of Asia extending from India on the west to Japan on the northeast, attention centered in the decade of the sixties on Indochina, where war engulfed Vietnam, Laos, and Cambodia. The history of this war had already been briefly recounted (Chapter seven). But international relations in the area involved much more.

Before World War II Britain, France, and Holland dominated the area, with a lesser United States presence in the Philippines. Japan challenged them, and was defeated largely by the Americans. The European powers had tried to return. However, the British, who quit Burma fairly rapidly, had reservations. They were ready to leave Malaya but stayed on primarily because of the Communist guerrilla insurrection that they fought and defeated. The Netherlands withdrew from Indonesia under pressure, and the French from Indochina after a terrible seven years war. At the end of the War the Americans had little expectation that they would remain; the Philippines were to be given independence in short order, and the only American presence would be in the form of strategic trusteeship over scattered islands in the Pacific. At the insistence of the American Navy, this trusteeship would give advanced bases that would preclude another Pearl Harbor and still give leverage over events in the Far East, including protection of lines of communication to Japan, a country whose occupation would surely be short.

Establishment of the People's Republic of China in 1949 and the outbreak of the Korean War six months later, changed all this. They brought the United States to the help of the French in Indochina and to Chiang Kai-shek on Taiwan. With Japan permanently demilitarized by its own American-imposed Constitution, the Americans affirmed their intent to remain in Japan and in the string of bases to the south. Once the French had left Vietnam, Chinese Communist presence to the north made the Americans decide to draw the line and prevent what they feared: a takeover, under Communist bloc direction, of all of southeast Asia. And so they created the Southeast Asia Treaty Organization and enmeshed themselves in the toils of the Vietnam War. As Under-Secretary of State George Ball wrote in the Department of State Bulletin in 1964, the United States "felt it necessary to extend its protective military shield to embrace large areas of the world left undefended by the disappearance of colonial power."

In general, the people of the area viewed the situation differently. On Taiwan, the Chiang regime knew that it must depend on the United States. The Philippine government, remembering the Japanese occupation, stuck by its long-time alignment, although it caused internal strain. To the southeast, Australians debated the issue, but mindful of how close they had come to being invaded by the Japanese in 1942 and of how only an American naval victory at the Coral Sea and Midway saved them, they accepted a United States alliance. Other nations had varied attitudes.

Burma espoused neutralism, and was one of the first beneficiaries of Khrushchev's ventures beyond the old Stalinist bloc limits. Its first experiences with Russian foreign aid were not happy ones. Moreover, it faced internal difficulties that made operation of its democratic system almost impossible. In the circumstances Prime Minister U Nu turned the government over to his Commander-in-Chief, General Ne Win, in September 1958. During a period of military rule the various political parties were to purge themselves of corruption and attempt reorganization, while General Ne Win carried forward the fight against Communist guerrillas in the north. The General reviewed relations with the United States, and accepted offers of aid previously rejected as incompatible with Burma's sovereignty. But he had also observed the border difficulties that embittered Indian relations with Communist China, and he managed successfully to conclude a border agreement with the Chinese, thus resolving a potential dispute of long standing.

Return to civilian rule in 1960 under U Nu proved to be brief: in March 1961 General Ne Win seized power, claiming that the political parties had again demonstrated their incapacity to rule and that they had opened the door to Communist subversion. This time the military junta took more severe steps, even blowing up the student center at Rangoon University, which it claimed was a center of Communist subversive activity. But at the same time the junta also ended the aid and research activities of all foreign private groups like the Ford and Rockefeller Foundations. A general curtailment of Western influence followed.

Burma's answer to its new strategic situation was thus one of increasing isolation from both regional or broader concerns. The attempt was not entirely successful during the 1960s (and may be less so in the future). The Burmese economy deteriorated; domestic strife and insurgency continued, and in the erratic period of the Great Cultural Revolution, China evinced some interest in again supporting at least one of the many ongoing insurgent movements. Safety of the Burmese government appeared to lie in continued division among its opponents. But Burma borders India, China, Laos, and Thailand. Developments in these countries would have much to do with the future of Burma.

In fact, it was within the borders of Thailand that a new challenge to the Ne Win regime arose in the late 1960s. Former Premier U Nu, who had first settled in India, moved to Thailand, where, quietly supported by the Thai government, he began a propaganda campaign to oust Ne Win.

Thailand itself took a completely different course. The Thais continued the uneasy Western alignment chosen by Field Marshal Pibul Songgram and largely followed by his successors, Field Marshals Sarit Thanarat, who seized power in 1957, and Thanom Kittikachorn, appointed after Sarit Thanarat's death in 1963. The alignment has brought American largesse, much of which went into deserving pockets, and the Thai economy prospered. But Thailand became enmeshed in the Indochinese war in the 1960s: paid by the United States, it sent ground combat units to Vietnam and Laos, allowed the Americans to bomb Communist targets in both countries from bases in Thailand, and continued to play host to SEATO headquarters in Bangkok. But while the Thai government appeared relatively secure, on all of its borders there lay trouble. The unstable Burmese situation hinged partly upon Chinese-sponsored rebellions to the northwest of Thailand. In Laos, to the northeast, the Chinese were building a road down to the Mekong River near Nan Province in the north of Thailand, where they supported the insurgency of mountain tribes. The North Vietnamese-supported Pathet Lao increased their control over southern Laos. And in Cambodia, to the southwest, two-thirds of the countryside appeared to be under the control of Communist forces by the end of 1972.

In April 1970 a "Summit Conference of Indochinese Peoples" took place in China, attended by the Communist leaders of Laos, North Vietnam, South Vietnam, and Cambodia, along with the ousted Prince Sihanouk of Cambodia. While confirming the diversity of the countries involved, it created, as Sihanouk later wrote, an "Axis" of the "revolutionary peoples" of Cambodia, Vietnam, Laos, China and North Korea to face the "pro-United States Pnompenh, Saigon, Bangkok, Vientiane Axis." The prospect was for a "Federation of Indochinese Peoples" under Hanoi's sponsorship.

In the face of this, Thailand attempted to rally Asian-Pacific support at an eleven-nation conference in Jakarta in May 1970, and to further develop cooperation with the governments of Laos, Cambodia, and South Vietnam. The conference, however, went no further than to recommend neutralization for Cambodia, and Thailand was, in the end, dubious about how much it could commit itself to Indochinese governments whose existence would be in doubt after American withdrawal. In mid-1973 Thailand remained solidly aligned with the United States, harboring bases and American manpower that had been withdrawn from Vietnam; a student-led revolt in October, however, ousted the military and presaged a gradual shift in relations.

It was not only the Indochina war, the shadow of China, and the enormous but wavering United States presence that was crucial to these maneuverings. Developments in the archipelago constituting Malaya and its neighboring islands and Indonesia were of equal importance.

In 1955 President Sukarno of Indonesia had gained immense international prestige as host of the Bandung conference. In the years that followed, by playing upon international issues and focusing attention upon irridentist claims, he performed the political miracle of keeping himself in power and then, introducing the concept of "guided democracy" in 1959, consolidating his position, despite the steady deterioration of the Indonesian economy under his regime. He used the army to suppress insurrection on the outer islands, areas that had long resisted domination from the center.* He procured army loyalty by making the army the largest and best-equipped force in southeast Asia: enormous supplies of military equipment came from the Soviet Union, which also supported wholeheartedly his aim of liberating "West Irian" or Western New Guinea. The area was one still under Dutch control, and with no real ethnic or particular geographical affinity to Indonesia. Nevertheless, other governments were not about to fight Indonesia over the large jungle territory with its few stone-age inhabitants, and under threats from Sukarno a face-saving arrangement was made in 1962 by which the United Nations would supervise the territory for one year, then turn over administration to Indonesia until 1969 at which time the inhabitants would be consulted as to their wishes. Sukarno, by the time of the agreement, already began to speak of only "internal" self-determination.

In the meantime Sukarno banned the political activities of parties other than the Communists and came to rely more and more on Communist leaders—and on his growing ties to Peking, to which the Indonesian Communist Party was oriented. The Party had recovered fully from its disastrous insurrection against the Republic in 1948 and became the largest and most tightknit party outside of the Communist bloc. The fact that Sukarno was willing to work with it rather than oppose it, as Nehru opposed the Communist Party in India, meant that it profited from Soviet and Chinese support in a way the Indian Party could not.

Once the issue of West Irian was resolved to his liking, the Indonesian leader found another issue in the creation of Malaysia, an issue arising once more out of the gradual withdrawal of British power and the arrangements to be made in its stead. Early in 1961 Malay Prime Minister Tunku Abdul Rhaman suggested creation of a federation of Malaya, Singapore, the British colonies of Sarawak and North Borneo, and the British-protected Sultanate of Brunei. Conversations among the four proceeded so well that the British government approved formation of Malaysia in November, and formed a commission to make recommendations for implementation. At this point the Foreign Minister of Indonesia welcomed the proposal. In June 1962, after consultations with groups and individuals throughout the area, the Commission made its report, based on findings of widespread support for the Federation and general agreement on most of the problems involved. Only one problem, division of

---

* Although the United States denied all charges, there was some evidence that the United States Central Intelligence Agency provided support for the rebellions.

the oil revenues of oil-rich Brunei, was insoluble, and failure to agree kept the Sultanate out of the Federation. The other territories and Great Britain set August 31, 1963 as the day for formation of Malaysia.

But in December 1962, Indonesia began a campaign against the new state and found an ally in the Philippines, whose President Macapagal had earlier laid claim to North Borneo. At a meeting in Japan between the Tunku (the title of the Malay Prime Minister) and President Sukarno, the two agreed to "take every possible measure to refrain from making acrimonious attacks on and disparaging references to each other," and in June, in Manila, representatives of the three countries agreed to set up machinery for regular consultation and to examine a Philippine proposal for a loose confederation of the three. But in July Sukarno claimed that the Tunku had broken his pledge that he would allow a plebiscite in Sarawak and North Borneo. The Malayan retorted that he had never given any such pledge, and Sukarno responded in turn by threatening to "crush Malaysia . . . a British project . . . aimed at destroying the Indonesian revolution."

In an effort to satisfy all parties, the Tunku agreed to allow a United Nations investigation of sentiment in the disputed areas, and to postpone the formation of Malaysia until September 16, 1963. Britain also accepted, while making it clear that it nevertheless retained sovereignty in the areas and could therefore dispose of them as it wished. Secretary General U Thant of the United Nations provided a team to conduct the investigation, with observers from all the interested parties, and the Philippine and Indonesian governments stated they would "welcome the formation of Malaysia provided the support of the Borneo territories is ascertained by an independent and impartial authority, the Secretary General of the United Nations or his representatives."

On September 14 the mission reported that all elections in the area appeared to have been free, and that having reached a wide cross-section of the population, it was convinced that a majority showed a desire to join Malaysia. On September 16, as scheduled, the new state came into being, and Indonesia promptly broke off relations, while encouring mobs to sack the British and Malay embassies and British homes. All British business properties were taken into protective custody, while Britain tried in vain to find out if this meant confiscation. Indonesia then seized all Malaysian properties, set out on an economic boycott of Malaysia (one that cost its own economy heavily and produced a new round of inflation in Indonesia), and sponsored guerrilla movements within the new Federation.

Sukarno based his "confrontation" on the view that Malaysia represented British neocolonialism: Britain retained its great base at Singapore and was pledged to give both economic and military aid to Malaysia. He also argued that Malaysian weakness would lure the Chinese Communists into the area. Finally, he claimed that Malaysia, with a population of 10 million, threatened Indonesia, whose population is 100 million. Few foreign observers found the arguments convincing, but in Indonesia Sukarno was unchallenged. Attempts at negotiation failed, and in 1964 the confrontation continued. Malaysia was admitted to the United Nations and Sukarno was able to block its designation to a seat on the UN Security Council during the 1964 General Assembly session.

The flamboyant Indonesian President had vowed to "crush Malaysia" before the cock crowed on January 1, 1965. In this, he failed. But he proceeded to withdraw Indonesia from the United Nations.

The move startled the world's diplomats. Sukarno calculated that the time had come to bring about a realignment of revolutionary governments in a new organization to replace the United Nations. He spoke of "NEFO," the New Emerging Forces, aligned against "OLDEFO," the Old Established Forces, and presumably viewed this as an organization of Asian-African radical states along with Communist China and Cuba and others that would undoubtedly join soon. The forthcoming Algiers conference, which never materialized (see below p. 424) would be a further occasion to promote the concept. In the face of United States involvement in Vietnam his relations with the United States worsened. Then, on August 9, 1965, came news that Singapore had seceded from Malaysia. The reasons lay in issues of balance between Chinese and Malay in the Federation, issues that would continue to plague it in the future; the Singapore-based People's Action Party of Lee Yuan Kew had sought to become federationwide, and Malays foresaw domination by the economically stronger Chinese who composed it.

Sukarno, of course, delightedly declared that it showed the artificial nature of the Federation, and invited Singapore to join him in "confronting" the remnants of Malaysia. Lee Yuan Kew, however, refused, and instead continued to support the Federation.

But time had run out for the aging, sick Sukarno. On September 30 began a coup-countercoup series that ultimately curbed his power, destroyed the powerful Communist Party of Indonesia, and reoriented Indonesian foreign policy. Pro-Communist Army officers tried to assassinate a group of leading army generals, apparently hoping then to cooperate with the Communist Party and to neutralize any possible army opposition to a Communist takeover. Sukarno had foreknowledge of the coup, and was prepared to stand aside.

But the young officers mismanaged the killing and failed in their larger purpose, and the generals rallied the army against the young officers' movement. They neutralized Sukarno, who plaintively called for reconciliation, and in short order destroyed the Communist party apparatus. In the meantime, throughout the country, there raged a popular revulsion against the Party and Communist China, based in part on long standing resentment of economically dominant Chinese minorities. Chinese establishments were attacked with an enthusiasm even greater than American ones had been attacked in the past; there were even cries of "Long live America!" The numbers of people assassinated in the bloodbath, however, grew; estimates ranged from one to five hundred thousand.

Once the convulsion had run its course, the new regime led by General Suharto soberly reassessed the Indonesian course. Gradually, fearing that Sukarno could still assert some of his old magic, they eased him out; step by step they ended the confrontation with Malaysia, giving that country a new lease on life and permitting Britain to withdraw the large force it had maintained to aid Malaysia. They arranged for consolidation and deferment of the enormous debt incurred by Sukarno (except with the Russians, who were loath to accept the change that had taken place). They sought to curb the rampant inflation, meet conditions for aid and a resumption of investment, and develop again the export markets that had once existed for Indonesia. In 1966 Indonesia resumed its place in the United Nations. In 1970, Sukarno—once a towering figure on the world scene—died quietly.

The events had wide significance. They marked the end of what had been an important Chinese Communist effort to build a coalition of third world Communist parties against the Soviet Union, allied to other radical movements and states. The disasters in Indonesia came at a time that their African effort faltered, too, and shortly before the Cultural Revolution with its own effect on Chinese foreign policy. Within a short time after the collapse in Indonesia, parties that had wavered between Moscow and Peking once more sought good relations with Moscow.

On the regional level, the results were equally important. Although there was still room for much conflict between states in the area, there was also now the possibility for regional cooperation, and the states of the area sought it. In 1966 the Asian Development Bank was established, with substantial contributions from the United States and Japan; a revived three-country Association of Southeast Asia (Thailand, Malaysia, and the Philippines) was replaced by a broader Association of Southeast Asian Nations, which included Singapore and Indonesia; there were also, significantly, meetings of the Asian and Pacific Council, created under Japanese auspices. In 1970, at the time of the Cambodian invasion by the United States, Indonesia organized an Asian Foreign Minister's Conference in Jakarta to develop an attitude on Cambodia—and on Asian security generally—notable for being the first occasion on which a Japanese Foreign Minister had met to discuss security matters with other Asian Foreign Ministers since World War II—and for the fact that the Australians and New Zealanders participated also. In the face of the United States setback in the previous five years, and the probable withdrawal of its large-scale military presence, the possibilities inherent in a Communist Indochina, and the uncertainties about the role of a nuclear-armed China after the Cultural Revolution, the ministers of the non-Communist states sought some measure of unity. From the non-Communist gateway to China, Hong Kong, the *Far Eastern Economic Review* called for a neutralized Southeast Asia; there was a growing discussion as to what role Japan could play and whether it would replace the United States in maintaining a balance in the Far East and Southeast Asia. Suddenly, in the space of a few years, Japan again loomed large in Asia.

JAPAN AGAIN

In 1968 Japan—defeated and prostrate at the end of World War II— passed West Germany to achieve a gross national product second only to those of Russia and the United States. Japanese industries now had assembly plants in Taiwan and Singapore to take advantage of low wage rates. In the early 1970s they began to invest in the United States. At home, where the leftist student associations had succeeded in blocking an Eisenhower visit in 1960, they caused only relatively small disturbances at the time of renewal of the Japanese-American security treaty in 1970. In the face of divided opposition the ruling conservative Liberal Democratic party, despite a decline in voter support, increased its representation in the lower house of parliament in the 1969 elections, with 300 of its 486 seats. Wages improved continuously, and there was little labor unrest.

There was a negative side to the ledger, compounded of alienation on the part of the young and student unrest that presaged something more to come in the future, of unease about the compatibility of the new materialist orientation with old traditions—and in very concrete form this was represented by an unprecedented degree of environmental pollution, to which the government would have to devote far more resources than it had in the recent past. Moreover, the Japanese economy remained highly vulnerable to changes in world prices or commodity and raw material supplies—especially oil, of which 95 per cent of its needs came from abroad.

All through the sixties Japanese had questioned their relationship with the United States. Many were especially concerned by United States re-

tention of administration over Okinawa, where the United States stored
nuclear weapons and poison gas, and from which its giant B–52 intercontinental bombers flew sorties in Vietnam. In 1969 the Nixon administration sought to remove the irritant by negotiating return of a nuclear-free
Okinawa to Japan by 1972. American bases on the island would then be
subject to the same restrictions as bases on Japan proper: they could be
used only after consultation with Japan. The next year the administration
moved further: it planned a reduction of American armed forces in Japan, as well as in Okinawa, the withdrawal of virtually all its combat
planes from Japan, and the closing of several of the more than one
hundred bases that it still retained. On trade issues, however, the two
countries found themselves at loggerheads. The Japanese piled up a huge
balance in their trade with the United States, and the Americans accused
them of practicing import and investment restrictions no longer justified
by their postwar economic situation. In turn, the Japanese objected to
American attempts to impose restrictions on imports of Japanese textiles,
as well as to American charges of "dumping"—selling goods such as television sets in the American market at lower prices than prevailed in Japan.

What had become clear by the end of the decade of the sixties was that
Japan was again a power in Asia. What was unclear was what this meant.

Japan's relations with China and Russia were colored both by the Jap-
nese alignment with the United States and by the relations of the Communist powers to each other. The Sato government, like its predecessors,
resisted enormous internal pressure to recognize Communist China, following the United States lead. Besides, except for three years preceding
the Cultural Revolution, its trade with Taiwan remained larger than its
trade with mainland China, although the latter kept holding out the bait
of far larger trade in the future if Japan would only change its policy.
Insofar as military security was concerned, the Japanese government relied largely on the American nuclear umbrella, while building up its own
relatively small self-defense forces. Neutralists within Japan insisted that
the nuclear protection was unnecessary and its abandonment—and the
ousting of the Americans—would produce better relations in the Far
East. The Chinese nuclear explosions confirmed the government in its
course; the opponents argued that China would not have put so much
into its nuclear effort if Japan had not continued to harbor the Americans. In spite of the argument and despite Chinese and Russian blandishments and threats, the Japanese government chose to renew the treaty,
arguing that Japanese prosperity and peace had been well-served by
alignment with the United States.

To the south, however, the question became more urgent. Was Japan to become some sort of counterweight to China in Southeast Asia as American power was withdrawn? Should it act as a stabilizing force in the area?

There was still much suspicion of Japan for her wartime incursion into the area. Moreover, while Japanese trade and investment had become an important contributing factor to economic development, and the Japanese government had evinced a desire to exert economic leadership, this very development had again raised the issue of undue Japanese influence. Nevertheless, even though Japan could make no military contribution, the presence of the Foreign Minister at the 1970 Jakarta conference had seemed to many an important step forward in making some new, orderly arrangement for the area.

What some few people feared was that if the United States did, in fact, withdraw its forces from Southeast Asia, the Japanese would be under pressure to abandon their disarmed status and create a far larger military establishment than was represented by the self-defense forces. For although sentiment was strong against rearmament in Japan (particularly because of Chinese nuclear armament), Japanese interests in an orderly Southeast Asia had become perhaps strong enough to carry Japan beyond polite diplomacy or even economic aid and support: much of its trade and virtually all of the oil vitally necessary to the existence of an independent Japan passed through the area. Much depended on how people assessed the role China aspired to in Asia.

Events in the early 1970s increased the self-searching within Japan. America's pressure on its trading partners in the fall of 1971 to revalue their currencies hit the Japanese particularly hard, as did the temporary import surcharge. President Nixon's gradual rapprochement with China, climaxed by his visit—announced to Japan's Sato only minutes before news of the projected visit was made public—brought further irritation; for years, Japan had faithfully followed the American lead. Now the Americans, without consulting Japan, had taken a radically different course, bringing to the Japanese leaders an intense loss of face. Meanwhile Russia alternately wooed the Japanese, offering large, joint Siberian development ventures, and blew cold upon them, as if to let them realize how uncomfortable Russia could make them if they chose a rapprochement with China. Japan faced difficult days of decision. It had great means at its disposal, but it depended heavily on world markets, both for its raw material purchases, and for sales to sustain its industry. As though to underline the complex nature of today's politics, its trade with Taiwan—Nationalist China—increased enormously again in the year after it switched to diplomatic recognition of the People's Republic of China.

ELEVEN
THE UNSTABLE
MIDDLE EAST

No group of new states displayed more instability and hostility than those composing what is roughly known as the Middle East. Although their leaders might trumpet that Zionism and Imperialism were the cause (the former the result of the latter) it was hard to ignore other factors. The June War of 1967 and—finally, after many decades—the increased Russian presence in the area were certainly two major developments in the years after the Suez War (see Chapter five). But the history of the area was much too rich: in failure to find unity, in splits between radical states and between radical and conservative states, in smaller wars, successions of military coups, irredentist claims and civil strife.

THE FERMENT OF ARAB POLITICS

Unity at the time of the Suez War of 1956 was superficial. Syrian sympathizers did destroy the pipelines that ran across Syria from Iraq to the Mediterranean; Iraq denounced Britain, though allied to it in the Bagdad Pact; Jordan moved to purge itself of British influence. Yet Iraq was unhappy about the loss of oil revenues resulting from Syria's show of solidarity, and Hussein in Jordan had to defend himself against Nasserites in his own state. In 1957 a new and more radical government in Syria brought trouble with its neighbors late in the year when it turned to the Soviet Union for extensive economic and military aid. Dulles retaliated by expediting delivery of arms to neighboring Jordan, Iraq, Lebanon, and Saudi Arabia, and Khrushchev charged him with inciting Turkey to make war on Syria, warning Turkey that aggression would bring retaliation by rocket. Egypt responded by sending troops to Syria, and the crisis was brought to the General Assembly, where it appeared to evaporate. Khrushchev told the Arab states that intervention by the Soviet Union had again preserved peace in the Middle East.

The incident did lead directly to what appeared, for a time, as the precursor of a more widespread move for unity, under the leadership of the man rapidly becoming the symbol of unity in the Arab world, Gamel Abdel Nasser. In February 1958, Egypt and Syria joined to form the United

Arab Republic. One reason had certainly been to curb some of the more radical elements in Syria. But the countries' leaders obviously hoped that it would provide a base for a greater Arab union.

In answer to Nasser's initiative, however, King Faisal of Iraq and King Hussein of Jordan announced a merger of their own two kingdoms—a merger designed to check the spread of Nasser's influence. Nasser predicted that it would be "scattered like dry leaves before the wind." And in short order, it was.

In May a crisis developed in Lebanon, whose government charged that a rebellion was being incited by the UAR radio and supported by arms flowing across the border from Nasser's northern province of Syria. After an appeal to the United Nations with a formal charge against the UAR and after an attempt to work through the Arab League, Lebanon obtained the services of another hastily improvised United Nations body, the UN Observer Group in Lebanon, which would try to survey the frontiers. It had only begun to operate when, in what would be the forerunner of a series of coups, the young King of Iraq, his uncle the Crown Prince, and the long-time pro-Western strong man of Iraqi politics, Nuri es-Said, were assassinated. An army clique took over, led by Abdul Karim Kassim; the Jordan-Iraqi union had, indeed, been short-lived.

Seeing this as part of the threatening Nasserite wave unfurling over the Middle East, government leaders in strife-torn Lebanon and unstable Jordan reacted similarly: Lebanon cabled the United States for armed help while King Hussein asked for British aid. Within days American Marines had landed on the beaches in Lebanon under the gaze of bikini-clad girls, and a British airborne unit arrived in Jordan (as well as one in Libya, to which the Westerners hadn't been invited).

The action may have saved the regimes from internal overthrow, but it soon developed that the Iraqi regime of Premier Kassim, although welcomed by Nasser and Pan-Arabists all over the Middle East, was not about to submit to Nasser's leadership and was not for export. Kassim had directed a coup against what the military viewed as a corrupt, oligarchic regime, and against its alignment with the West: he withdrew Iraq from the Bagdad Pact a year later, in 1959. (It was later reconstituted as the Central Treaty Organization, without Iraqi membership.)

In the meantime, of course, the United States had endured a stream of disapproval for its intervention. Nasser flew to discuss the crisis with Khrushchev, who called for a summit meeting to end "the present military conflict" while Eisenhower denied that there was any. At the United Nations the USSR prevented a graceful Western withdrawal by vetoing Security Council resolutions that would have put a new and expanded United Nations presence in the area. But with reassurances about

the Kassim regime's intentions and the patching together of a new compromise government in Lebanon, Western powers now accepted simply
the continued presence of the UN Observer Group in Lebanon and the
presence of a special representative of the UN Secretary General in Jordan. The American and British troops withdrew. The new Lebanese government assumed a somewhat more neutralist pose, explicitly rejecting
the Eisenhower Doctrine, to which the previous government had adhered.
King Hussein, whose flight abroad for a brief vacation was turned back
over Syria, told excited crowds of supporters that UAR fighter planes had
tried to shoot him down. For a while, at least, he was a popular hero.

Kassim's independence seemed to set back Nasser's Arab ambitions,
and the latter busied himself with African conferences, meetings with
neutralist leaders, and with domestic problems. He had begun to establish
the framework for what he called Arab socialism, and with Soviet help
started construction of the giant Aswan Dam. He also unwittingly laid the
groundwork for future trouble for Khrushchev by suppressing domestic
Communists, and Khrushchev, incensed, told him not to aspire to too
great a role. In addition, the Egyptian continued to lead the undeclared
war against Israel, attempting to tighten the economic boycott and develop his own arms production with the help of German technicians.

Then, in September 1961, what was to have been the nucleus for true
Arab unity suddenly broke up. Conservative elements in Syria resisting
Nasser's brand of Arab Socialism and Army officers opposed to Egyptian
domination of the armed forces seized power. Nasser threatened force,
but failed, and Syria resumed an unstable independent course. In the next
five years coup succeeded coup; the Baath Socialist Party eliminated other political parties, including the Communist Party, swung the country
into alignment with the Soviet Union, and proceeded on a staunchly
anti-Israeli course. The latter policy brought it into cooperation with
Egypt, but never again into the organic unity contemplated by Nasser
earlier. In Iraq Kassim, who seemed for a while to bear a charmed life,
finally fell in 1963 and was executed. As in Syria, succeeding coups installed the Baath Socialist Party in power.

By the mid-1960s there had developed a new pattern in the Middle
East. Ranged on one side, but with no organic ties, were Egypt, and the
more "radical" Syria and Iraq, all with military-led regimes, seeking support from the Soviet Union, devoted to one form or another style of
"Arab Socialism," and professing irrevocable hostility to Israel and imperialism. They constituted the self-styled "liberated," revolutionary, Arab
states. (For a brief period in 1963 they worked at negotiating a new union, and excited crowds in Jordan agitated for overthrow of the monarchy and union with the other three states. It all came to nothing, ending

in recrimination.) On the other side were states like Saudi Arabia, an oil-wealthy but almost medieval kingdom that abolished slavery in 1962; Jordan, a poor and heterogeneous monarchy, whose king's political power rested on the support of bedouin tribes, but whose people included the much more modernized Palestine Arabs, opposed to the king and pro-Nasser; the absolutist Persian gulf sheikdoms, some of them fabulously wealthy (Kuwait and Abu Dhabi have a higher per capita income than the United States), and the sheikdoms and imamates surrounding the southern edge of the Arabian peninsula, of which Yemen was the largest. Most of these sheikdoms were still under the protection of Britain in the early 1960s.

To the west of Egypt King Idris of Libya had found immense oil wealth in his land—exports began in 1961, to the delight of Europeans, since they did not pass through the Suez Canal—and the King tried hard to spread the wealth. In the early sixties, the United States still maintained the giant Wheelus Air Force base in Libya. Tunisia was the epitome of "moderation" under a government that bore the imprint of President Habib Bourguiba, who styled himself a "pragmatic idealist." Algeria, however, aligned itself with the "liberated" states, both under Ahmed Ben Bella and his successor, Houari Boumedienne. Finally, Morocco, under King Hassan, remained largely aloof from the concerns of the Middle East.

Significantly, the only Arab socialist state that had large oil revenues was Iraq. Other oil-rich states were ranked, in the pantheon of modern Arab thought, among the conservatives. Conservative, too, was the non-Arab but Muslim state of Iran, which bordered Iraq and the Persian Gulf. Since the Mossadeq incident of 1952 (see above, Chapter four) the Shah had presided over his own political system, trying to bring about a modernizing revolution from above. As in the past, he counted on the west to counterbalance Russia to the north; he had no quarrel with Israel, and remained aloof from the concerns of the volatile Arab states. His regime also remained the target of leftist attacks throughout the decade, although to some observers his social revolution appeared to achieve far more than those of some of the "progressive" states. It was, like the progressive states, politically repressive. But it was bitterly attacked as reactionary because it maintained relations with Israel.

In this conglomerate of radical and conservative states, Nasser tried to make the radicals appear the wave of the future. Blocked in terms of political unity through the failure of the UAR—whose name Egypt symbolically retained—he nevertheless had a name and an influence throughout the Arab world. In 1962 he tried to make a flanking move that would capitalize upon Nasserism.

In September 1962, a coup overthrew the Imam of Yemen, at the southern end of the Arabian peninsula. The new republican government announced the death of the Iman and plans for modernization of the semifeudal country; several Asian states, Communist countries, and the liberated Arab states recognized it. But Jordan and Saudi Arabia saw the move as one that could effectively lead to more radical moves around the rest of the peninsula and eventually one aimed directly at them. In fact the new Yemeni government soon announced its intention to unite the entire peninsula and liberate it from the "Saudi shame." Although the United States and several European states proceeded to recognize the government, Britain did not. Like Jordan and Saudi Arabia, it saw the development as a threat to its influence in East Africa, its oil interests in the Persian Gulf, and to its base at Aden, in South Arabia, from which it acted to protect its interests.

The new government, however, failed to gain effective control of the country. The Imam reappeared in Saudi Arabia, created a government-in-exile, and found support among Yemeni tribesmen, as well as from Saudi Arabia, which signed a defense pact with Jordan. In short order Egyptian troops began pouring into Yemen, where they encountered unexpected resistance. For the next five years up to seventy thousand Egyptian troops were bogged down in the bitter war; they were not withdrawn until the defeat of Egypt in the 1967 Six Days' War with Israel. In 1964, at an abortive Arab heads of state conference in Cairo where diplomatic relations between Egypt and Jordan and Saudi Arabia were re-established, there seemed evidence that the latter two would accept the republican regime in Yemen in return for Egyptian moderation toward their own governments, and Algeria and Iraq announced a willingness to mediate the dispute. But it proved intractable, in part because the British announced in 1966 their withdrawal from Aden and their cutting of commitments in the Persian Gulf.* This encouraged Nasser to hang on. The fighting continued; Egypt was charged with using poison gas; upon Egyptian withdrawal republican and royalist continued their own battle, while republican pro-Nasserites and anti-Nasserites also fought. Finally, in 1970, the royalists, who had deprived the Iman of much of his power, came to an agreement for a coalition regime with the republicans.

Prospective British withdrawal from South Arabia, adjacent to Yemen, kept Nasser in Yemen until his defeat by Israel in 1967. But in the situation that developed there, Nasser's grand strategy of encirclement of Saudi Arabia in a move toward the Persian Gulf oil riches received only a limited success.

---

* The end of Indonesian-Malaysian confrontation enabled them to do so.

Yemen had long claimed the collection of emirates to the south that the British proceeded to bring together into what they called the Federation of South Arabia, and the Iman of Yemen, against Saudi Arabian opposition, had received Arab League backing. More important, Yemen became affiliated to the United Arab Republic when it was formed in 1958. The affiliation never had much meaning in any administrative sense, but it did permit Nasser to lend his direct influence to Yemeni claims on Southern Arabia and, thus, merge Egyptian and Yemeni interests. (The Imam was to regret the move later, when Egyptian influence was used to overthrow him and establish the republic.) Britain, supporting the conservative rulers of the Federation, found itself under fire from several sides. Terrorists within were aided by the Yemeni exile groups from without who attacked the British and the Federation's Arab rulers indiscriminately. Each exile group claimed to be the sole proper representative, and refused to negotiate with the British for a transfer of power unless Britain recognized it as the sole successor. The unexpected resistance of the Iman of Yemen to republican and Egyptian forces brought Saudi Arabia into the picture. When British withdrawal was assured after events in Indonesia (and necessitated by Britain's financial inabilty to maintain old overseas commitments), Saudi Arabia agreed to help the Federation of South Arabia. However, despite the Egyptian setback in the area as a consequence of the Israeli war, the Federation could not stand. In September 1967 one of the revolutionary groups, the National Liberation Front (NFL) suddenly seized power throughout the Federation. The British responded by now dealing with this new, de facto authority, withdrawing its large force and handing over power to the NLF leaders. The Federation of South Arabia was transformed into the People's Republic of South Yemen, dedicated to the "liberation" of all Arab lands.

For Egypt it was only a very partial victory, since it had primarily backed the other main contending liberation group, and had tried hard to get the two together. Nevertheless, another "liberated" revolutionary state had been established on the flank of Saudi Arabia. And in 1969 matters took a further turn for the better: in May in the Sudan and June in South Yemen the governments were overthrown by even more radical ones. In South Yemen, since victory, there had been several internal upheavals, and a "Maoist" revolt had been crushed. Some of its leaders appeared in the new groups that took power in 1969. They declared that their guiding principle would be relations with socialist countries, especially the Soviet Union, closer relations with other Arab countries and the Palestine liberation movement, as well as support for the "Liberation Front of the Arabian Gulf"—a group dedicated to further breaking the power of such rulers as the Sultan of Oman and Mascat on the southeast tip of the Arabian Peninsula and then the Persian Gulf sheikdoms (the Persian Gulf, significantly, being called the "Arabian Gulf"). It immediately proceeded to recognize East Germany.

The first foreign policy action of the new Sudanese regime was also to recognize East Germany. The Sudan, still wracked by civil war in the south, was renamed the Democratic Republic of the Sudan by Colonel Jaafar Mohammed al Numeiri, who formed a government that banned political parties and suspended all parliamentary institutions. Its foreign relations, it declared, would depend on countries' attitudes toward the Arab-Israeli conflict; it would support liberation groups; and it would not re-establish diplomatic relations with the United States, broken by the former government at the time of the 1967 war. The government of the South Yemen was the first to recognize it, but it was given an equal welcome by Egypt, Syria, Iraq, and Algeria.

Strategically, the Sudanese coup meant that revolutionary Arab states now controlled the eastern side of the southern exit of the Red Sea (and Somalia the other), while extending their control further down the Western side. And politically, it meant an increase in numbers of the revolutionary group opposed to Saudi Arabia, Jordan, the oil states of the Persian Gulf, and to Libya, Tunisia, and Morocco. (Tunisia was, for a while, the archenemy, when its President, Habib Bourguiba suggested in the mid-sixties that a political settlement with Israel might be possible. In 1966, diplomatic relations between it and Egypt were actually broken off, and in 1968 with Syria, which it accused of subversion. Despite anti-British and American mob rampages at the time of the 1967 war, Tunisia continued to stand aloof from efforts to involve the resources of all Arab states in the cause of Palestine.)

Revolution in Libya, in September 1969, further increased the ranks of "liberated" states and soon gave promise of another attempt at greater organic political unity among at least some of them. The aging King Idris had proved unable to reconcile the interests of traditionalists and of the new forces released by oil wealth in his kingdom, and toleration of two British and one American bases despite the 1967 war was a final straw. His overthrow by army officers, led by a 27-year-old captain, was followed by the creation of a "Republic" like other republics in the Middle East, where power is lodged in a military clique. Here it was called the Revolutionary Command Council, the Captain—now Colonel Qaddafi —became its Chairman, Prime Minister, and Minister of Defense, and the Council quickly reoriented Libyan foreign policy. It negotiated immediate withdrawal of American and British personnel from the bases, nationalized most foreign businesses and confiscated the property of resident Italians, left over from colonial days. The new regime received immediate recognition from the United Arab Republic, Syria, Iraq, and the Sudan, and soon was accepted by other states. France proceeded to sell it 100 Mirage fighter-bombers although the French Foreign Minister, defending the sales against strong criticism in Parliament, admitted Libya had only two pilots qualified to fly them. Still, Libya had promised not to transfer them to a third power.

Late in 1970 came a joint Libyan-Sudanese-Egyptian decision to agree to an eventual federation of the three countries, the way to be carefully prepared by committee work. Leaders of the three countries envisioned it as the nucleus of genuine Arab unity, and Syria asked to be associated in the move. It would not be easy; the Sudanese government revealed that it had expressed reservations about the speed of unification and even about the word "federation," and a smooth transition was hardly promised by an upheaval in that country. Pro-Communist officers were ousted, partly because they opposed the unity move (the Communist Party not being tolerated in Egypt). They then failed themselves in an attempted counter-coup in mid-1971. Nevertheless, the groundwork was laid for another attempt at Arab unity.

Colonel Qaddafi surged to prominence in the Arab world in the early 1970s, after the death of Nasser, mainly because his burning zeal was united to almost unlimited oil funds. Internally, he established a puritanical Muslim society (puritanical enough to repel the Egyptians, who hoped for access to Libyan oil money, but were bent upon a much more lenient modernism). Externally, it was Qaddafi who was willing to use oil as a weapon against the United States, even to the point of forgoing oil profits; it was Qaddafi who boasted of trying to overthrow Hussein in Jordan and King Hassan of Morocco. (The latter coup failed in early 1972. It was one of several, but the only one to be openly supported from outside.) Qaddafi also boasted of helping the outlawed Irish Republican Army in troubled Northern Ireland, and used his oil money to help persuade African leaders like Amin of Uganda to break relations with Israel. Following the Chinese, he launched what he called his own "Cultural Revolution." It was anticapitalist and antibourgeois; but it was Muslim, and not Marxist. It appeared, however, that his zeal for reform jeopardized his zeal for unity.

THE SIX-DAY WAR

Arab unity never seemed so important as in the confrontation with Israel, still the center focus of all that went on in the Middle East. The story of the Six-day War has already been recounted in connection with increased

Russian interest and presence in the Mediterranean and in the countries surrounding Israel, but the Arab context and consequences must be reviewed here.

There were close ties between the events that have just been recounted and onset of the 1967 war. The growing number of resolutionary regimes overthrew an old order that was associated with past Western domination and borrowed Western institutions. These—parties, parliaments, capitalism—were linked with foreign control, domestic oligarchy, corruption, and the debasing of native institutions. All of this had to be changed and, in general, the army seemed to be the vehicle for controlling and promoting that change. Russia offered the model of a unified party and a strong army; more, it offered the arms, trade, and hostility to Western policy that were part and parcel of the whole deal. It had no qualms about "upsetting the balance" in the Middle East. And there was Israel, a Western state that had humiliated Arabs and seized what was theirs, with whom the Westerners kept asking them to make peace. Every part of the pattern came together, and radicalism meant increased opposition to Israel.

Jordan did not fit. But its own hostility to Israel came from the large Palestine population that it harbored. Its failure to do enough and join the growing ranks of radicals brought opprobrium and efforts to unseat Hussein, who alternately looked to Western support or to accommodation with his volatile neighbors—whom, in the end, he could never satisfy.

In 1964 Arab leaders met at a Cairo summit conference, and Hussein and Nasser patched up their quarrels, embracing as brothers. The occasion was Israeli tapping of Jordan River waters in accordance with a division proposal made way back in 1955 by an American envoy, Eric Johnston, who had hoped to bridge Israeli-Arab hostility on the functional level. Although Lebanon, Jordan, and Syria would have shared in the benefits of the plan, opposition to Israel had kept them from participation. Now there was determination to keep Israel from taking its own allotted share. But despite Syrian prodding for military action, Nasser and Hussein agreed that Arab military might was insufficient. They would divert Jordan River waters, organize a new command structure for Arab armies that would give them better future capabilities, and establish a new Palestine Liberation Organization (PLO) as the basis for Palestinian resistance to Israel. Hussein insisted that activities of the PLO be coordinated by the new United Arab Command, knowing very well that Palestinian commandos could embroil Jordan in unwanted hostilities with Israel. His insistence was insufficient. The PLO under Ahmed Shukairy and the more radical Palestine Liberation Movement based in Syria, un-

der the leadership of Yasir Arafat, began to harrass Israel from within
Jordan, where Hussein came into conflict with them in attempting to control them. (The United Arab Command never really functioned.)

In 1965, when West Germany negotiated arms sales to Israel, Arab
states were ready to cut relations with it and turn to East Germany.
(Again, it was prerevolutionary Libya, Tunisia, and Morocco that failed
to do so, and Tunisia earned hostility for its suggestion that negotiations
with Israel might be in order.) In 1966 the radical faction of the Baath
Socialists gained power in Syria, unleashed the commandos (in Jordan as
well as in Syria) and Nasser saw his leadership in the Middle East begin
to slip, while Hussein came under more and more pressure. Eventually
Nasser moved to recoup his position by joining Syria in a new military
pact, and resuming, along with the commandos and the Syrians, his attacks upon Hussein. The explosion of raids and counterraids led, in November 1966, to Israeli destruction of the Jordanian village of Samu, base
for the PLO: Israeli troops clashed with Jordanians, and Hussein found
himself under increasing attack at home. Hysteria mounted throughout
the Arab world, and Nasser, in May 1967, moved by the Soviet reports
that Israel was about to attack Syria, made his fateful decision to call for
removal of the UNEF and closure of the straits of Tiran. The actions
made war ineviable. Hussein, whether out of honor or sure knowledge
that he would be overthrown if he did not participate, flew to Cairo for a
reconciliation with Nasser, who only a week earlier had called him the
"Whoremonger" of Jordan. They both knew that they were not ready for
war, but—under pressure from the Palestinians and their Syrian supporters—they brought it on themselves.

Defeat of the Arab armies in Egypt, Jordan, and Syria revealed again
how little proclamations of unity meant, and when military humiliation
was coupled to inability of the United Nations and of diplomatic pressure
to force an Israeli withdrawal, with unwillingness of Western states to exert really strong economic pressure, and with willingness of the Soviet
Union to return to the area in force, all together helped provoke the further moves toward radicalism in the Arab world. De Gaulle, incensed by
Israel and trying to build relations with a third world that seemed increasingly hostile to the West, embargoed arms for Israel, including fifty
Mystere fighter bombers for which it had paid. France had been Israel's
chief source of arms, and its willingness to give up this market made
Arab leaders appreciative. Arab attempts at economic pressures on the
West to force them to bring pressure on Israel failed when they were unable to maintain an oil boycott. The United States' position was made
completely untenable when Arab masses believed Nasser's false charge
that America had actually participated in the air war on the side of Is-

rael. As Russia poured arms into Syria, Iraq, Egypt and finally manned some of them, the United States reluctantly moved to balance the situation by limited arms aid to Israel (as well to the "conservative" Arab states). In so doing it jeopardized its capacities to serve as an arbiter of the conflict.

Apart from cease-fire resolutions pressed during the actual course of the June War, United Nations bodies were unable to reach agreement on any resolution until November 22, six months after the fighting. In this they reflected the opposed views of member states: the Soviet Union and all bloc states but Rumania sided with Arab demands that Israel—labeled as the aggressor—withdraw immediately. The United States supported resolutions that looked to something more than the unsatisfactory status quo ante, calling for arrangements that would maintain international rights and provide for establishment of international peace in the area. These were equally unacceptable to the Soviet Union, to Arab states, and to the many African and Asian states that supported them. Israel's incorporation of Jerusalem at the very time of the United Nations debates and its defiance of United Nations resolutions were of no help in attempts to achieve compromise. The Soviet Union, rearming the Arab states, assured the United States on several occasions, including Kosygin's visit to Glassboro, that it opposed a resumption of the fighting, and it agreed to increases in United Nations truce observers along the embattled cease-fire lines. As usual, when the Arab states tried to concert their own policies at meetings in Khartoum and Baghdad, they were unable to do so; among other things, the effort to use an oil embargo to pressure the West failed before the oil rich states' insistence they must sell oil if they were to give financial support to the Arab states that had been hurt by the war—Egypt and Jordan. The best they could do at Khartoum was agree on the principle of "no peace with Israel, no negotiation with Israel, no recognition of Israel and maintenance of the rights of Palestinian people in their nation." But Algeria and Syria rejected the corollary principle that withdrawal of Israeli forces must be effected by diplomatic means. Nasser's freedom of action was circumscribed. Upon military defeat he had resigned; paradoxically, there had been an outpouring of popular support for him, and he had retained office. But within his administration there was military dissatisfaction with his course, and he had to deal with it—as well as agree to withdrawal of his troops from Yemen for financial reasons.

Finally, in November, Britain devised a Security Council resolution that was vague enough to secure acceptance, to divide the Arab states, and to obtain unwilling Soviet acquiescence. While it called for Israel's withdrawal from the occupied areas, it linked this to an enumeration of

principles for a lasting peace and provided for designation of a Special
Representative of the Secretary General to assist the parties to effect it.
The Arab states, in the light of the Khartoum principles, might be viewed
as having compromised themselves by accepting it. But since the timing
of effectuation of the peace principles was left open, and withdrawal of
Israeli forces specified, while *direct* negotiations were avoided—and since
clearly, for the time being, military possibilites were minimal—all but
Syria and Iraq stilled their objections. Signs of flexiblity on the part of
both Egypt and Jordan in terms of demilitarized areas and rights of passage coincided with Israeli proposals to help integrate Arab refugees into
the overall economy of the area (but in the context of an overall peace
settlement). So Gunnar Jarring, Special Representative of the UN Secretary-General began his round of what proved to be fruitless talks.

For the whole next year he moved from capital to capital in a series of
secret discussions. His efforts were supplemented in 1969 by Big Four
talks—the Soviet Union, France, Britain, and the United States. All parties remained firm; on the Jordan-Israel border, raid and counter-raid
proliferated; along the Suez Canal 1968 was marked by only an occasional artillery duel and raid; Israeli seizure of the Golan Heights in Syria
meant that the border there remained quiet. But with political failure and
the inflow of Russian arms, 1969 brought an increase in military action
on the Egyptian front, so that by July Secretary-General U Thant had to
report that the cease-fire had broken down completely and the ninety-two
United Nations observers were mere sitting ducks.

In the meantime, as diplomacy solved nothing, the organized Palestine
guerrilla movement, based in Jordan, Syria and now, also, Lebanon, received a new lease on life and became an even more important element in
the conflict. New guerrilla leaders arose to replace those discredited by
the June War, and the guerrilla numbers increased. Some were more radical than others, professing to draw their inspiration—and receiving verbal support from—China. All were committed to return of all Palestinians, and some developed the idea of creation of a binational Palestine to
replace Israel, encompassing the part of Jordan annexed at the end of the
1947 war. With Hussein involved mainly in trying to keep his throne,
Syrian leaders divided, and Lebanon willing to give only lip service to the
Palestine cause, the guerrillas acted on their own, and found themselves
in conflict not only with Israel but also with Jordan and even Egypt and
Russia. The latter, after all, accepted the existence of the Jewish state,
and since the guerrillas did not, they did their best to see that no peace
settlement was effected. Hussein, unquestionably, would have to go.
World sympathy had begun to turn against Israel for its hardline attitude,
and the rising "new left" in Europe and the United States had come to

support the view that Israel was, indeed, the product of American imperialism and the opponent of revolution in the Arab states. The guerrillas therefore had a fertile ground to cultivate, particularly since they could also pose as part of the whole rising world liberation movement. To dramatize their cause they began attacks on Israel airliners and offices outside of the Middle East. Their most dramatic early move consisted of hijacking several airliners in 1970, blowing one up at the Cairo airport to protest Egyptian acquiescence in exploring an American peace plan for the Middle East, and blowing three others up—one American, one British, and one Swiss—in the desert outside of Amman. The action eventually backfired and resulted in a loss of world support, when the commandos used the several hundred passengers as hostages. In August 1970 a new American peace initiative at the United Nations gave some promise and was accepted by Jordan, Egypt, and the Soviet Union (see below) but the guerrilla leaders (and Syria and Iraq) rejected it completely: "We will not lay down our arms until all Palestine is liberated," said one; "we reject peace with Israel, and reject any leaders who talk peace—and that includes Nasser." In September 1970 Hussein acted decisively to break the power of the guerrilla movement in Jordan. The bitter fighting even involved Syrian units who came to the support of the guerrillas. But in subsequent months and at great cost, their strength was severely reduced.

Israel, faced with the constant probing guerrilla attacks, retaliated in ways not always designed to help its position in world opinion. In response to an attack on an Israeli airliner in the Athens airport, where Lebanese-based Palestinians sprayed a loaded plane with machine-gun fire, Israeli commandos raided the Beirut airport. Landing in French-built helicopters, they destroyed thirteen Lebanese airliners, after removing all personnel. Shocked governments condemned the raid; so did the UN Security Council. France banned shipment of even spare parts that Israel had paid for. Israel's defense was that its airliners and those of countries flying to Israel were under constant threat of attack from commandos based in Arab countries that refused to curb them; the raid was to show that Arab airlines could be attacked, too, unless the governments restrained the guerrillas.

Ultimately, after further outbreaks, the Lebanese government did act to curb commando attacks on Israel. Defeated by both the Jordanian and Lebanese governments, lacking support from Egypt, some of the Palesinians turned to outright random terrorism, murdering the American Ambassador to the Sudan, sending hundreds of letter bombs throughout the world, killing 11 members of the Israeli team at the 1972 Olympic Games in Munich, Germany, and—through the use of three Japanese thugs traveling by air—killing 25 unwary travelers and wounding 75 more during disembarkation from an airliner at the Tel Aviv airport. Their action was acclaimed in the Arab world, and the Popular Front for the Liberation of Palestine took credit for the airport massacre at its headquarters in Lebanon, whose government denied responsibility. The Israeli government's response was to make governments who harbored the terrorists suffer the consequences; the terrorists, whose actions resulted simply in random deaths, felt that they dramatized their just cause. An American attempt to have the UN General Assembly condemn international terrorism at its 1972 session failed when the resolution was sidetracked for study—including study of the causes of terrorism.

When Soviet armed forces were introduced in mid-1970, the United States was spurred to a new peace initiative in August 1970. Secretary of State Rogers suggested a three-months cease-fire, resumption of negotiations with UN Mediator Gunnar Jarring under the November 22, 1967 Resolution—that is, with a view to withdrawal of Israeli forces from occupied Arab territories and Arab recognition of Israel's right to exist with secure boundaries. Approved of by the permanent members of the Security Council, it was accepted by Israel, Egypt, and Jordan. The United States informed Israel that it had received assurances from Egypt and the Soviet Union they would not increase arms in the Suez Canal zone delimited by the plan. Syria refused the plan, yet accepted Egyptian explanations; Iraq attacked Nasser for accepting, and the guerrilla forces, adamant in their opposition, finally provoked the desperate Hussein into the attack that ultimately led to their destruction as an organized force. Algeria, too, firmly rejected the project.

Despite the deception involved and already recounted (see above, Chapter 8), in which the Russians and Egyptians immediately used the cease-fire to move advanced missile forces into the supposedly demilitarized zone—and Israel's withdrawal from and then resumption of the talks —the cease-fire lasted. But no real progress could be made in the talks. Israel adamantly refused withdrawal until border rectifications were agreed to that would give it geographically secure frontiers; it refused any longer to accept big power guarantees; if anything, the cease-fire experience strengthened this position: despite guarantees, Egypt and the Soviet Union had again acted unilaterally, and nothing had been done. But the Arab states could and would do nothing until Israel had withdrawn completely behind the pre-1967 frontiers. All negotiations must lead to this. On September 28, 1970 Gamal Abdel Nasser succumbed to heart attack, shortly after arranging for mediation between the Palestine guerrillas and the vengeful King Hussein. He was only 52, but seemed to have dominated the Middle East forever. Five million people witnessed his funeral cortege, and many wept.

His successor, Anwar Sadat, vowed to continue Nasser's policies: Arab unity, support for Palestinians, opposition to Zionism and imperialism, nonalignment but strengthened relations with the good friend, the Soviet Union, and support for Afro-Asian peoples and for liberation movements.

But Sadat, without Nasser's prestige, followed a cautious course. He resisted Libyan President Qaddafi's efforts to prod him into an early war with Israel, as well as Qaddafi's attempt to hasten the proposed Libyan-Egyptian union (the Sudan appeared to have opted out). At one point in 1971 he declared that he would settle the Israeli question by the end of the year. When he did not he explained that the Indian-Pakistani war had upset his calculations and that he actually *had* been ready to reopen the war with Israel. Later he blamed the delay on the Russians who, he said, restricted free use of their weapons. And so it was Sadat who, on July 18, 1972, ordered Soviet advisers and experts to leave Egypt, turning over Russian bases and material to exclusive Egyptian control. They could leave crews to man the advanced SAM anti-aircraft missiles, and would retain access to naval facilities in such ports as Alexandria, Mersa Matruh, Port Said, and Sollum.

At once, the Middle East situation was again changed. Prime Minister Golda Meir of Israel suggested immediate negotiations, declaring that Israel set *no* prior conditions, had *no* fixed borders, *no* intention to perpetuate the cease-fire lines.* It appeared that she, at least, interpreted Sadat's move as one that might open the way to more peaceful relations. But Sadat refused the offer, and other leaders interpreted the move differently: it came shortly after the Russians had told Syrian Communists that they were opposed to a new round of war (which, they declared, the Arabs could not win), were opposed to a confrontation with the United States, and were for a peaceful solution on the basis of the November 22, 1967 resolution. They wanted reopening of the Suez Canal and disapproved of Arab slogans calling for the destruction of Israel. In addition, Sadat now agreed to union with Qaddafi's Libya; it was Qaddafi who in June had complained that the Soviet Union had not given the Arab states enough material to resume the war with Israel. Taken together, these events might mean that Sadat felt the Russians restrained him too much, and now that Egypt was rearmed, it could act.

Subsequent events seem to show that Sadat was playing a waiting game, trying to disarm domestic opposition (there were student strikes at

---

* The Arabs knew, however, that the offer did not encompass Jerusalem, The Golan Heights along the Syrian border, nor the Egyptian town of Sharm-el-Sheikh, overlooking the straits of Tiran. The Israeli government had already declared that these were vital to Israeli security.

Cairo University, with the students crying for war). He must look militant, but was not sure if he could be. The political unity with Libya was set for September 1, 1973, and Sadat dragged his feet. In late November 1972 the Arab People's Conference for the support of the Palestine Revolution met in Beirut to form a new organization with a new secretariat in which, in addition to Palestinians, there would be Communist Party representatives from Lebanon, Algeria, Syria, and Iraq. Representatives from Russia and Eastern European states attended as observers, along with others from the Vietcong, Uruguay's terrorist Tupamaros, and representatives of the ruling parties of Syria, Iraq, and the Southern Yemen. A month later chiefs-of-staff of 18 Arab armies met to concert military planning against Israel and the Egyptian Minister of War was put into nominal command of the Egyptian, Syrian, Libyan, and Jordanian armed forces. The Suez Canal remained closed and Israel continued to occupy Arab territories—while Israelis, instead of discussing the future of the territories with the states from which they had been seized, debated their future with other Israelis.

Even more than southern Africa, the Middle East was a powder keg with a short fuse. There were Middle East experts who felt they had witnessed the first 20 years of another hundred years' war.

TWELVE
LATIN AMERICAN
FERMENT

From the end of the nineteenth century, when the United States imposed a hemispheric Pax Americana, until 1954, Latin America remained essentially a peripheral area to world politics. Briefly, during World War II, German influence increased and resulted in American postwar efforts to institutionalize a regional collective security system. Until the mid-fifties the effort looked plausible: there was little friction between Latin American states, and they had emerged from the war relatively prosperous. The prosperity evaporated quickly; at Havana, in the late 1940s, when the International Trade Organization was under negotiation, they made known a series of demands to be incorporated in the Charter of the proposed Organization, all of which would have created special trading arrangements for underdeveloped countries. The ITO Charter was never adopted (partly because of US Congressional opposition to the special considerations for the underdeveloped countries), and they shifted their pressures to other United Nations organs and to the United States. (The Korean War, with the high raw material and commodity prices it fostered, temporarily lessened the underlying urgency.) But the Peron period in Argentina—widely misinterpreted—and then the 1954 Guatemala incident, revealed the ferment beneath the surface of good relations, and in the Cold War context these colored all further developments. United States' policy-makers became likely to look upon radical movements as potential threats, representing increased Soviet Russian influence; Latin reformers *and* radicals looked upon the United States as the power likely to try to block radical change; and many, such as Castro only a few years later, decided that to check the United States they would, indeed, have to look to outside powers such as the Soviet Union. And the Soviet Union, now freed from Stalin's provinciality, had become willing to entertain ventures abroad, thereby confirming American policy-makers in their own view. Cuba and Castro, of course, completed the circle, helping to produce Johnson's ill-fated return to military interventionism in the Dominican Republic in 1965, with its concomitant rienforcement of Latin views of the United States.

411

THE ALLIANCE APPROACH

In the late 1950s the Eisenhower government in the United States was subject to both internal and external pressures to do more about Latin America and its developing discontent. From men such as Brazil's President Kubitschek came warnings that revolution threatened the hemisphere unless intense reforms were undertaken; the United States must help reformers in a Latin American development program—"Operation Pan America." Within the administration the President's brother, Milton Eisenhower, had presented two reports (the last one shortly after Vice-President Nixon's disastrous 1958 tour revealed the extent of widespread hostility). He had called for a wide review of all American policies, and supported Latin governments' requests for commodity agreements to stabilize and even raise the prices of their exports, plus a new inter-American public loan agency. Both of these and other demands were articulated at inter-American meetings during the 1950s, but resisted by the administration. In 1958 the United States reversed itself, and helped create the Inter-American Development Bank, which began operations in 1960. Subsequently it also dropped its opposition to international commodity agreements. At the Inter-American Economic Conference held in Bogota, Colombia, in October 1960, it signed the Act of Bogota. This series of recommendations, resulting from Kubitschek's earlier initiative, committed the United States to the proposition that normal trade, technical assistance, private investment, and funds from existing international banking institutions were not enough for Latin America. National development planning would involve social development that could not be financed through these channels. A Special Inter-American Social Development Fund would be created to supplement national efforts, to which the United States pledged $500 million. In 1960 the administration also acquiesced in the strong stand the Organization of American States took against the Trujillo dictatorship in the Dominican Republic, which was accused of trying to promote assassination of the President of Venezuela.

The event highlighted another development: in the period from 1957 to 1960 constitutional government appeared to be gaining throughout Latin America, and the time appeared ripe for a concerted effort to rid the hemisphere of the remaining unsavory dictatorships in the Dominican Republic, Nicaragua, and Paraguay. The United States, therefore, supported Latin governments' determination to sever diplomatic and most economic relations with the Trujillo regime.

Two events hastened the overall change in American policy: the advent of the Kennedy administration in the United States and the course taken by Cuba's Premier Castro in forcing a break with the United States while turning to the Soviet Union for support. Kennedy and his advisers accepted and made explicit a series of assumptions that constituted a unified new view of what should take place in the Inter-American system, and proceeded to turn them into policy; they were greatly influenced by their view that Castro had, indeed, betrayed the Cuban revolution by rejecting democracy and taking Cuba directly into the Communist bloc— and by serving as an outpost from which to spread subversion throughout the volatile Americas. The Cold War, Kennedy felt, had come to the Western Hemisphere. American power must check Russian power.

Two basic policies were to be followed. One involved diplomatic isolation of Cuba. The other, symbolized by the Alliance for Progress, involved the commitment of American resources to help produce rapid but evolutionary development throughout the hemisphere. Such development involved a combination of economic growth with agrarian and tax reform to spread the wealth, the bolstering of democratic socialist forces that would provide reform, international infusions of aid as leverage for the reforms, and United States aid to Latin American armed forces so that they could block the guerrilla warfare presumably being championed by the Soviet Union and China and applied in Cuba and now Indochina. In addition, aid to the armed forces would modernize them so that they would no longer be the reactionary forces in politics they too often had been. The United States would support multilateral trading arrangements, commodity agreements, and public funding of needed public ventures. The United States would come to stand as a bright alternative to authoritarianism.

The Alliance for Progress was built upon the foundations of the Act of Bogota. At Punta del Este, in August 1961, the American republics pledged themselves to a cooperative development venture, to which the United States would contribute the major part of the $20 billion in public loan funds needed from external sources in the next decade (and $1 billion in the next year). They agreed to work toward an explicit series of social and economic reforms, and they created the international institutional framework through which to work, drawing heavily on the existing machinery of the Organization of American States, the new Inter-American Development Bank, and the UN Economic Commission for Latin America.

The 1962 missile crisis and even more, the 1963 OAS investigation of Cuban attempts at subversion in Venezuela and discovery of supplies of arms shipped from Cuba helped in the program of isolating Cuba. Prior to these events the United States had, by considerable pressure, suceeded in obtaining suspension of Cuban participation in the Inter-American system so long as Cuba maintained its Communist ties. But major states like

Argentina, Bolivia, Brazil, Chile, Ecuador, and Mexico abstained on this and on the recommendation for an arms embargo. In mid-1964, however, at the Ninth Consultative Meeting of Foreign Ministers, they agreed by a 15–4 vote to break off diplomatic and consular relations as well as trade in all but supplies necessary for humanitarian reasons. (Mexico refused, charging that the action was illegal.) The result was that Cuban trade shifted to Japan, Canada and Western Europe as well as the Communist countries. Castro's course was made more difficult, but he used the events to build domestic support, while leftists in other Latin American countries pointed out again how the United States would try to stifle any *genuine* revolution. Reform under the Alliance for Progress was merely an attempt to buy off the countries that most needed genuine revolution.

In the meantime, in line with the whole Kennedy reorientation toward promoting reform, the United States supported the coup that finally overthrew the Dominican Trujillo regime in 1961, and helped the democratic-socialist Juan Bosch who came into power. A display of American naval power off the island a few months later was intended to forestall a Trujillo countercoup and, when a military coup replaced Bosch after only seven months, Kennedy retaliated by cutting off foreign aid. The move was not effective, and President Johnson soon reverted to normal relations. In 1963 the United States made an ineffectual attempt to help indigenous forces overthrow the unsavory dictatorship of "Papa Doc" Duvalier in Haiti.

The anti-Bosch coup might have looked like an isolated military interference in politics at the time, but throughout Latin America the supposed trend to constitutional government that Kennedy had hoped he could help along came to an end. Between 1962 and 1964 democratically elected presidents were overthrown in Argentina, Peru, Guatemala, Brazil, and Bolivia. In the face of this development, the Johnson administration abandoned the effort to distinguish between constitutional and military governments, and to work with whatever government was in power —so long as it was not, in the words of an administration spokesman, under the control of "forces dictated from beyond the shores of the continent." It was this point of view that produced the Dominican intervention. Fidel Castro saw in the overthrow of Goulart in Brazil by a military coup, in the Dominican intervention, the OAS sanctions, and perhaps the far-off Vietnam intervention, a worldwide attack against the revolutionary force he represented. His own declared aim became to create "two, three, one hundred Vietnams." But he failed in exporting revolution to Venezuela, Peru, Colombia, Guatemala and, most publicly, Bolivia, where his comrade-in-arms Ché Guevara died after an inept and ill-starred attempt (and where the orthodox Communist Party may well have helped bring about his defeat).

Angered, he attacked the Soviet Union for its failure of nerve, its lapsed militancy, its cooperation with the very bourgeois governments it should be trying to overthrow. Despite his trade dependency upon Russia (now about 50 per cent) he snubbed the 1967 Moscow celebrations of the 50th anniversary of the Revolution, and even accused Russian leaders of trying to overthrow him.

The dependency had become too great. There were hints of Russian economic pressures. In August 1968 Castro voiced support of the Russian invasion of Czechoslovakia; by 1970 Cuba began to be more fully integrated into the socialist economic bloc. In 1972 it joined the Council for Mutual Economic Assistance and granted Soviet naval vessels base rights in Cuba.

In the meantime, events had moved apace in the rest of Latin America where, if Castroism had failed, a wide variety of populist nationalisms—military, socialist, or otherwise—had come to power. The Inter-American System hardly existed any more, and Castro found it easy to breach the diplomatic blockade, reestablishing diplomatic relations with some, negotiating trade agreements with others—and signing compensation accords with France and Switzerland for earlier nationalizations. In 1972 there was even some hope that the United States, where the Nixon administration had orchestrated its detente with China and the Soviet Union, might find some means of decreasing tension with Cuba. The two countries entered into conversations that led to an agreement on aircraft hijacking. But there were no signs of any further developments.

Throughout the hemisphere, political upheaval became the rule. New military regimes in Peru and Bolivia adopted populist, nationalist stances, expropriating selected American enterprises. In Peru the military clique, headed by General Velasco, that seized power from President Belaunde in October 1968 took over the assets of the International Petroleum Company, a Standard Oil of New Jersey subsidiary and, claiming that the company owed Peru immense back payments, refused any compensation. The United States soft-pedaled the issue, finding ways to avoid Congressionally imposed sanctions. Peru's seizure of American fishing vessels in a zone extending 200 miles into the Pacific further exacerbated relations, while General Velasco established diplomatic relations with Russia and all the Eastern European countries. In Bolivia, where unsteady administration had prevailed since the revolution of 1950 and where Ché Guevara had hoped to lead a guerrilla movement that would turn all the Andes into a new "Sierra Maestra," military governments took power in September 1969, and then again one year later, and like Peru, courted popularity by nationalizing the Bolivia Gulf Company. In both cases, leaders took the risk of cutting off future foreign investment from the United States in return for national control over their own resources (a course Bolivia first followed when it nationalized its tin mines in the early 1950s. It led neither to great improvement in the tin-miner's situation nor in eliminating future United States investment in other areas) . Ironically, Torres, the new head of the left-oriented Bolivian regime, was the man who had been in charge of the anti-Guevara operations. Meanwhile, in Chile, the reformist Christian-Democratic regime of Eduardo Frei Montalva, regarded by many constitutional democrats as one of the last hopes for peaceful development in Latin America, came to an end in 1970 with the election of Salvador Allende y Gossens by a slim plurality in a three way election between a conservative, a Christian Democrat, and the Marxist-Socialist Allende. Frei had worked hard to cope with the endemic problems of Chile—a land rich in mineral resources, sophisticated, with a high degree of administrative centralization, and a large public sector, but with a standard of living unequally shared and really beyond its means. He had tried to satisfy public opinion by a process of gradual nationalization of the American-owned copper mines, with compensation, and by a program of gradual land reform. He established diplomatic relations with a number of Communist countries. Allende was to go much further: his government began large-scale nationalization and a re-orientation in foreign policy that would lead to re-establishment of relations with Cuba and increased trade with Communist states. He headed a minority government and faced strong political opposition. But it was he who led the attack upon the United States in Latin America. At the UN, the OAS, meetings of the International Monetary Fund and the World Bank, at the third UN Conference on Trade and Development, he charged the United States with blocking development loans to his and to other nationalist regimes; Peru echoed his attacks. Industrial nations, Allende said at UNCTAD, have created a world where "the toil and resources of the poor nations pay for the prosperity of the affluent peoples." He attacked multinational corporations for the influence they wielded over the economies they operated in; the International Telephone and Telegraph Corporation, which his government was going to nationalize, had secretly tried to enlist United States government support against him. The United States government displayed its displeasure at uncompensated nationalization by blocking further credits, arguing that in the light of Chile's huge external debt and internal practices it was not creditworthy, while it was not poor enough to qualify for IDA loans. Moreover, the United States pointed out that it had recently extended credits to Bolivia and Guyana, despite their nationalizations—because they were genuinely negotiating compensation agreements.

In September 1973, after the onset of disastrous inflation, outbreaks of uncontrolled property seizures, and a resultant alienation of virtually the entire middle classes, Allende was overthrown in a military coup that brought in its wake a dreadful repression and widespread international condemnation. The causes were essentially internal but the United States had helped and was widely blamed.

It all indicated the increasingly troubled relations between Latin American states and the United States, and the desire of the former to try to establish relations outside of the "Western hemisphere" to balance relations with the United States. As Europe rebuilt and emerged, as Japan became an economic giant, and as the socialist states painfully developed world trading relationships, the alternatives presented themselves. The United States, with its Alliance for Progress, became a state whose twentieth century hegemony could be resisted without danger.

In the years between 1961, when the Alliance was launched, and the end of the decade, the Alliance as an economic development effort and reform-mover faltered and died. It began with too much rhetoric and raised too many hopes. Ridiculed as Fidel Castro's gift to the rest of Latin America—for it seemed that the heightened United States effort would not have taken place unless Kennedy and his advisers had seen Castroism as a threat—the Alliance was perhaps too sanguine in its expectations that native oligarchies would reform themselves out of power and domination. In some countries the effort produced a high rate of growth. But that growth was swallowed up by continued population increases.* What was also not foreseen was that growth and change would produce upheaval rather than political stability.

In 1964 an effort was made to change the Alliance from what had become a series of bilateral aid programs into a more multilateral effort. This was done through the creation of the Inter-American Committee for the Alliance for Progress, which would recommend distribution of Alliance funds. In 1967 further efforts were made to amend the OAS Charter in order to give the organization both wider representation as well as more tasks, and at Punta del Este, in April 1967, President Johnson finally committed the United States to accepting the idea of preferential tariffs for goods from underdeveloped countries—something they had long been asking for, even though these might benefit the exports of only a few countries. (The United States' position remained that these tariff preferences should be granted by all developed countries to all underdeveloped countries. This would depart from the policy set by the Com-

---

* The AID estimated in 1969 that overall Latin American GNP had grown by 4.9% per year since the start of the program. But population growth meant that per capita income had only grown 1.5% per year.

monwealth and the European Economic Community, with their preferential arrangements for only their own members and associates. If this failed—and African states were loath to give up their assured preferences in the EEC for general preferences, a move that would open the EEC to goods from other less-developed countries—the United States might then grant preferences to Latin American states alone. The prospect of such trading blocs was not reassuring to all economists. For years the UN Conference on Trade and Development worked on general preference schemes. As of this writing there were none in effect.) At the time, the OAS member states pledged themselves to work for a Latin American Common Market akin to the European Common Market in a period of no more than 15 years.

REGIONALISM AND NATIONALISM

The idea of a regional common market had long had a hold on the imagination of Latin policy-makers, but such a market was hard to put together, given the dissimilarities and lack of complementarity of Latin economies and political systems. Two embryo structures already existed and gave some indication of the difficulties: the Central American Common Market (CACM), established in 1960 by Guatemala, Nicaragua, El Salvador, Costa Rica, and Honduras, and the Latin American Free Trade Association (LAFTA) created by the Montevideo Treaty in 1960, whose members were Argentina, Bolivia, Brazil, Chile, Mexico, Peru, and Uruguay. The former was to create a customs union with common external tariffs within five years, while promoting new industry that would serve the whole region rather than just one country. And in a few years, trade between the five countries did in fact burgeon. But within those few years, as the customs union necessarily led to increased mobility, several hundred thousand workers migrated from overcrowded El Salvador to Honduras, which, because of increasing social costs, began to evict immigrants. The resulting tension broke into the open in July 1969, when riots over a soccer game escalated into a full-scale four-day border war. Negotiation within the CACM and the new Organization of Central American States finally brought agreement to create a demilitarized border zone, but the prospects for further intergovernmental cooperation were dim, and Honduras virtually withdrew from the customs union.

LAFTA, proceeding more slowly through arrangements for specific commodities and new industries that would serve the whole zone, showed less progress. Dissatisfaction with its slow pace led to creation of the Andean Common Market by Bolivia, Chile, Colombia, Ecuador, Peru, and Venezuela, all of which also wanted to offset the dominating influence in LAFTA of Argentina, Brazil, and Mexico. The new grouping insisted it was compatible with LAFTA: it had, in fact, little in the way of objective material factors in its favor. Only three percent of the countries' trade was with one another, they had territorial disputes, and were unequally developed. Nevertheless they displayed more political will than might have been expected, and the cementing factor proved to be nationalism. By the early 1970s they had arrived at a common policy of stringent controls on foreign capital, and appeared to be making progress on other common policies. Once more regionalism was aimed at reduction of external influence.

By the end of the 1960s the Alliance was dead insofar as the American Congress was concerned, too. It sharply cut appropriations. In addition, the new Nixon administration in the United States took a far cooler position vis-à-vis Latin America, obviously rejecting many of the earlier Kennedy-era assumptions about the nature of the area and its problems. The worsening United States balance of payments situation meant that during the 1960s the United States had imposed a host of minor irritating trade and aid restrictions; Nixon promised to review some of these, and to work for preferential tariffs—but faced a strong labor bloc in Congress on this issue. At Viña del Mar, Chile, in 1969, representatives of Latin members of the OAS produced a document known as the Concensus of Viña del Mar. Prepared in connection with demands being made within the UN Conference on Trade and Development, it cataloged the ills of United States trade policy as Latin states saw them. Perhaps unfortunately, President Nixon had sent his special representative Governor Nelson Rockefeller of New York to make a whirlwind tour of Latin America. The move was ill-received by many Latins, to whom the name Rockefeller was synonymous with Standard Oil and American imperialism, and because at Viña del Mar they had just produced their own set of findings. Nevertheless, the Concensus of Viña del Mar served as a basis for future negotiations, and President Nixon indicated that he would pay attention to it and the problems it enumerated: the heavy debt-burden, excessive profit repatriation, trade restrictions, "tied" aid (aid that could only be spent in the high-priced United States market), and "additionality"—a Congressional requirement that countries receiving aid continue to spend as much in the United States as they had spent before the aid, and others. In addition, presentation of the Concensus served as a warning to the United States by *all* Latin governments not to react harshly to the nationalization measures taken by the new Peruvian government.

In one area, the Kennedy initiative lasted until 1971. He had restricted arms aid and sales of weapons to Latin America; Congress, in agreement, buttressed the move by limiting aid to countries that bought specified sophisticated weapons elsewhere.

Latin American countries had traditionally purchased most of their

arms from European suppliers, and these were now only too happy to
oblige. Countries like Argentina, Brazil, Peru, and Chile greatly increased their purchases, especially from France. Venezuela, for example,
engaged in a border dispute with Colombia over potentially oil-rich territory, bought 130 French medium tanks, 15 supersonic fighters, and another 29 from Canada. In the face of these sales, the Nixon administration relaxed the restrictions somewhat in 1972, arguing that Latin states
were spending more for the more expensive foreign-built equipment.
Congress, where there had been a move afoot to end all military aid and
sales and to do away with all United States military missions, went along.

If any overall trend could be discerned at the start of the 1970s, it was
the growth of various forms of nationalist socialist regimes bent on some
form of regionalism or seeking extrahemispheric ties. From a declared
Communist-bloc state like Cuba, to the embattled Marxist government of
Chile, through the military-led but generally socialist states of Peru and
Bolivia, to the repressive regime in Brazil with its booming economy, and
the paralyzed military regime of Ongania in Argentina, which, attempting to come to terms with the large, populist Peronist element, finaly allowed the aging former dictator to return—all these governments shared
both a strong nationalism aimed at reducing United States influence, and
to further this goal a professed desire for regional arrangements. Earlier,
many people had either hoped or feared that Castro's Cuba would become a model for the rest of Latin America, and Ché Guevara appeared
to have embodied the hope; later, people began to look to Frei's Christian Democracy in Chile as a model; and for a while Allende's Marxist
democratic socialist regime was hailed as providing a pattern that other
governments must follow. However, there seems no reason to think that
any one pattern would be applicable anywhere else; the conditions of
Latin American countries are too dissimilar. Castro himself warned the
Chilean Allende and the Peruvian and Bolivian regimes not to follow the
Cuban course and provoke a break with the United States. The Cuban
experiment appeared to have exchanged excessive United States influence
for excessive Russian influence. The Marxist Allende was the subject of
praise by the neofascist Peron of Argentina and Ongania of Argentina,
until he left office, sought a link with Allende and the Spanish-speaking
countries to the northwest rather than to Brazil. Brazil experienced an
economic boom under its military regime and, like the leftist Peruvians,
proceeded to extend its claim to territorial waters to 200 miles. (It also
refused to sign the nuclear nonproliferation treaty while building up its
naval forces, aspiring, apparently, to a role as a regional if not a world
power.)

And, as if to confound all attempts at finding an order in Latin American relations with the United States, in October 1970, ten Peruvian naval units participated in joint Latin American-United States naval maneuvers.

Ernesto "Ché" Guevara gained world fame and a romantic image as the instigator of guerrilla warfare in Bolivia; his failure and death only added to his luster, and for revolutionaries and would-be revolutionaries everywhere he symbolized a new tide. Yet his defeat marked a significant change. Rural guerrilla movements faded and were replaced by urban guerrillas and terrorists, who, in 1969 shifted their tactics from mere bank robbery and attacks on government buildings to kidnapping of foreign diplomats. They operated in Argentina, Brazil, the Dominican Republic, Guatemala, and Uruguay. Between September 1969, when US Ambassador C. Burke Elbrick was ransomed for 15 political prisoners and December 1970, when the Swedish Ambassador was kidnapped, Brazil witnessed the ransoming of the Japanese Consul-General for five prisoners and the German Ambassador for 40. The Uruguayan guerrillas, called Tupamaros, gained the most notoriety, but Argentine guerrillas gained the distinction of trying to kidnap a Russian diplomat.

Yet the guerrillas themselves were composed of warring groups. In Argentina the non-Marxist Peronist groups were the strongest. And Castro himself condemned them all sarcastically in 1970, on Lenin's birthday, as "superrevolutionary theoreticians, superleftists, supermen!" Communist parties throughout Latin America had long been at odds with Guevara-style guerrilla movements, and belonged firmly in the Russian group of parties; as such, they had also come under attack from the independent-minded Castro. In Bolivia it appeared that the Communist Party had helped bring about the capture of Guevara. Now, in the face of nationalist and socialist regimes, some military and others not, Marxists of various stripes were hard put to find their own ordering principles to apply to Latin American affairs. Allende, in Chile, was apparently an enthusiastic supporter of the Andean Pact, to which states like Colombia and Equador belonged.

Invariably, the search for new political forms involved international politics, for countries like Venezuela, one-quarter of whose gross national product was generated by its oil exports, or Bolivia, whose economy depended heavily on tin exports and American aid, could not divorce themselves from their international economic relations. They could attempt to diversify their economies, their exports, and their trading partners, and press for changes in the terms of trade and for more aid. But there were limits to how much could be done.

THIRTEEN
THIRD WORLD UNITY

At Bandung, in 1955, the first Afro-Asian Conference gave rise to high hopes, even though it revealed that a number of African and Asian states sought alignment with one or the other of the major powers and rejected the idea of nonalignment. In years to come the concept of some form of organized unity among third world states never died; neither did it come to fruition.

There were several forums—Afro-Asian, nonaligned, and United Nations. In the United Nations, the General Assembly, with its annual gatherings of representatives of all states, crystallized a growing conviction among third world states in the late 1950s and early 1960s that new world trading arrangements should be made that would be more favorable to the less-developed countries. With the support of the socialist states and leadership by Yugoslavia, 75 states (later more than 80) formed a sponsoring group for the resolution that produced the United Nations Conference on Trade and Development, a new organization that they conceived of as potentially more important than other principal United Nations organs. The experience of consulting, working together, and voting as a bloc led them to formalize their procedures; representation on governing boards and committees was allocated by "Group"—Western, Socialist, and Group of Seventy-seven as it came to be called—and the Group tried to enforce voting discipline. Over the years its accomplishments fell short of earlier hopes, and divisions developed over specific issues. But the Group of Seventy-seven continued to exist.

Outside of the United Nations attempts at organization were marred by competition between the Afro-Asian approach and the nonaligned approach, complicated by the Russian-Chinese rift and attempts made by these two powers to manipulate third world relations in terms of their own conflict. China supported Afro-Asianism; Russia consequently supported the nonaligned group.

President Sukarno of Indonesia, eager to maintain revolutionary elan, and finding more of it in China than Russia, derided nonalignment in the early 1960s. It was, he argued, impossible not to take sides against imperialism. And he found the leaders of many countries ready to take the same position (even though they failed to follow him out of the United Nations in 1964). President Tito of Yugoslavia—who could not participate in the Afro-Asian approach—took the nonaligned lead, finding fellows among leaders like Nehru (particularly after the 1962 war with China) and Nasser. And since China could take part in Afro-Asian activities but not nonaligned activities, it tried to have Russia excluded as a non-Asian power. The result was that during the 1960s Russia (the leader of a bloc) tried hard to look like a member of the nonaligned camp!

The first official conference of 25 nonaligned countries took place at Belgrade in 1961. Nehru acquiesced in the Tito-Nasser initiative in part because he was already anxious about relations with China in the Tibetan and border areas. It was a moment of considerable international tension, following upon Soviet resumption of nuclear testing, the chilling Vienna meeting between Khrushchev and Kennedy, and antagonism over Cuba and Berlin. It was at Belgrade that the differences in approach made their first real appearance: Sukarno concentrated on the eradication of colonialism, while Nehru, Nasser, and Tito stressed the overriding importance of lessening international tension. Nehru, in fact, compared discussion of the anticolonial struggle to debates at the League of Nations about the opium trade which, he said, he had heard at Geneva in 1938! Most important, the conference reaffirmed that decolonization and co-existence were *not* incompatible.

In April 1964 a preparatory meeting at Djakarta laid the ground-work for a second Afro-Asian Conference, 10 years after the first, at Bandung. By now the Chinese-Russian conflict was in full swing, and China backed the Indonesian initiative: Chou En-lai had toured Asian and African countries in recent months seeking support for the new meeting, and arguing that it should be held before the next nonaligned meeting, now scheduled for late 1964. (Pakistan, too, held out for the Afro-Asian meeting since, as a member of CENTO and SEATO, it could not attend a nonaligned conference.) India, attacked for suggesting that the Soviet Union should attend, was nevertheless able to get the Afro-Asian Conference postponed until 1965, and in the interim the second conference of 42 nonaligned states met in Cairo in October 1964. It denounced colonialism in all its forms and gave specific support to the demands of particular states but, most important, it reaffirmed the concept of nonalignment itself. For Nehru, Tito, and Nasser, concerned over Chinese activities in Africa, it was a triumph, and Nasser emerged as an African leader.

The Afro-Asian Conference, scheduled for June, was preceded by a series of running battles over who should be invited. Indonesia opposed Malaysia as an example of neocolonialism; India, supporting Malaysia, also continued to support an invitation for Russia. Ten days before the Conference was to convene in Algiers Ahmed Ben Bella, President of Algeria, was deposed and Houari Boumedienne assumed leadership. Confusion in Algiers led states to postpone dispatch of their delegations; China insisted that any postponement would be to the advantage of the imperialists; African states held back, and Arab states worried over the deposition of a prominent Arab leader. It soon became clear that without African participation the Conference could hardly be called Afro-Asian, and the Conference was postponed until later in the year. Preparatory exploration revealed that China would not come if Russia was invited and if the United Nations Secretary-General was asked to address the meeting; other states refused to bow, and Afro-Asian meetings came to an end with the curbing of Sukarno and as China turned inward to the Great Proletarian Cultural Revolution. In the end, African states seemed to find that the annual summit meetings of heads of African states at the new Organization of African Unity were sufficient when combined with joint action at the United Nations, and avoided the complications of the tiresome Russian-Chinese quarrel.

Nonalignment, however, was not dead. In 1970 a summit conference of 54 nonaligned states met at Lusaka, capital of Zambia, with 16 chiefs of state in attendance. (Pakistan decided not to persist in its demands for admission, and several states declined invitations.) The assembled states condemned colonialism, racism, military power blocs, Portugal in Africa, South Africa in Namibia, the United States in Southeast Asia, and Israel in the occupied Arab lands. They agreed to continue summit meetings every four years but rejected creation of a permanent secretariat. They still saw nonalignment as a limited but vial approach.

There were numerous other international forums for third world countries, but these had been the main ones. The failure of the second Afro-Asian Conference led to one abortive attempt at creating something else, at the time of convening of the Afro-Asian-Latin American People's Solidarity Conference at Havana, Cuba in January 1966. Its purpose was to "oppose the world-wide enterprises of imperialism with a global revolutionary strategy," and Yugoslavia, leader of the nonaligned camp and champion of co-existence, was not invited. Five hundred delegates came from Communist and other leftist parties, liberation movements, and from a few African governments. It could not achieve unity; China was viewed as divisive for its attacks on the Soviet Union. The conference endorsed peaceful co-existence despite Cuban President Dorticos' opening declaration concerning the right to oppose the violence of imperialism with revolutionary violence. Co-existence was simply declared to be compatible with violent anticolonialism. Plans were made for future conferences and a Secretariat established in Havana. But no further conferences have taken place.

The "third world" did not exist, except as a figure of speech and a propaganda concept.

Seventy-five years ago, outside of the Americas, the international system was composed of a handful of competing European states several of which had empires that encompassed the rest of the world. Twenty-five years ago, with internal erosion hastened by the impact of Japanese and German conquests, those empires began to disintegrate rapidly. The world became "bipolar" and the two superpowers, surrounded by their satellites and lesser followers, moved to fill the "vacuum" left by disintegration of the empires. But leaders arose within the weak successor states to proclaim that new conditions in the world had created a new international politics, in which balance-of-power considerations no longer warranted compensatory and pre-emptive moves by great powers to gain influence in weak states. These weak states could stand on their own and, by banding together and refusing alignment, both gain their own ends and mediate the conflict between the superpowers. Moreover, by banding together they could exert pressure upon the older states who had previously dominated them—and who still sought to do so—to repay all that they had taken during the centuries of imperialist exploitation, an exploitation that continued through the newer means of neocolonialism. Ultimately, if the old, rich countries did not give satisfaction to the new, poor ones, the later might well have to rise up in wrath and take what was rightfully theirs. In the meantime they would give the Western world one last peaceful chance.

If the above was a dominating point of view among the leading elites of the new states, another one dominated in the West: the enlightened Western states had given freedom to peoples whom they had tried to lead to modern nationhood. Now they had some sense of responsibility to keep them from falling into chaos and prey to Communism, but they were obviously limited as to what they could do materially.

For Communist states the view was rather different. Once Stalin was dead, the way was open for Khrushchev to repudiate the old "two-camps" thesis. Communist countries could align themselves with the newly independent states in their anticolonial stand and find not only new allies, but potential new converts. The decay of empires was a double step in the march of history: it helped ensure the security of socialist states by weakening the imperialist camp, and was a move toward the spread of international socialism under the leadership of the USSR. Russia was handicapped in its wooing of the third world mainly because it headed one of the two blocs and, as nonalignment developed, blocs themselves were condemned.

Then when the Russian-Chinese conflict developed, China—with the support of Sukarno after 1961—upheld Afro-Asian activities, primarily because it could work to exclude Russian participation in these; consequently, if somewhat awkwardly, Russia came to support Yugoslavia's efforts to promote nonalignment. Both Russia and China, nevertheless, shared a view about the third world.

But all the views—those of the third world, of the Western states, and of the Communist states—were falsified by events.

The countries of the third world vary enormously, often having far more significant differences than similarities. They conflict among themselves—with often tragic results—and they cooperate in a variety of overlapping groupings. Their capacities to bring pressure upon the richer states have proved limited except in the case of those already rich in one vital resource: oil.* And the limits of their capacities have emerged as two matters have become clear: the Western states' leaders do *not* share underdeveloped countries' assumption that the latter's poverty is a consequence of the formers' exploitation of them, and are in fact much more concerned with internal domestic pressures than with those that come from the underdeveloped countries. The second factor is that both superpowers no longer assume that each must "win over" the third world states to prevent the other from doing so. Certainly both try to gain influence for a variety of purposes—trade and investment opportunities, prestige, even political power, as in the case of Russia versus China. But certainly both have stopped assuming that if a previously Western-oriented state, for example, becomes a one-party "people's republic," it means an accretion of Russian power that has importance in terms of what used to be called "tipping the balance of power." The result is that has become harder for poor states to play off one superpower against the other. In some areas countries like France have regained an old influence (which, however, can never mean that they can count upon African manpower, for example, as they used to in order to compensate for their own falling birth rate). In other areas, such as Asia, old-fashioned balance-of-power principles have had meaning in terms of Russian-Chinese competition for influence—but again, in different terms than before. One consequence of this very much more confused and unanticipated situation has been the rise of radical nationalism in a variety of guises; another has been the for-

---

* In 1973, having achieved a unity impossible earlier, and facing a favorable high demand situation in which alternatives did not seem feasible, the oil-exporting states of the Middle East not only worked to double prices, but also to take control of refining, shipping, and distribution—and also to use oil pressures for political purposes: reduction of foreign support for Israel.

mation of regional groupings designed to bring some strength to the international political efforts of the third world states. But these consequences, in many cases, have had limited and shifting value and results.

Bitterness and anger has become endemic, forecasting of the future difficult. Earlier views that the poor might eventually force the rich to disgorge their ill-gotten gains dimmed as power realities became apparent. In frustration, the third world states found unity in turning the United Nations away from the original Western-devised Charter purposes of keeping the peace and promoting peaceful change to promoting change either peacefully *or* by force. Legitimation of anticolonial armed struggle in 1972 was by vote of 99–5. At the 1972 session of the United Nations Educational, Scientific, and Cultural Organization the budget was passed by a vote of 94–19, in which the 19 comprised Western Europe, the United States, and the socialist bloc—which together contribute 75 per cent of the total budget. By an overwhelming majority, third world states voted curbs on free exchange of information and broadcasts using satellites. They had no military power, but they had numbers. Did they have economic power?

Was it true that the industrialized states would become more and more dependent upon the raw materials of the poor as population and economic growth continued, thereby enabling the poor to extract higher prices? Or did the poor need the markets of the rich more than the latter needed the goods of the poor? On issues of this kind, dependent upon the future of industrialization in the Western countries and the desirability and possibility of industrialization in the non-Western countries, hinged the shape of future international relations. Debates raged on the answers to all of these questions. In some cases experience provided answers that were politically unpalatable: Cuba, for example, had wanted to avoid dependence on its main export, sugar, and to force through an industrialization that, in Marxist theory, it had been denied by its colonial relationship to the United States. But it failed, despite a wholesale shift in its trade to other states and large-scale Russian aid and guidance, both of which served to curb Castro's independence. Population increased at a continued impossibly high rate. Would it only be curbed by widespread natural disaster?

The issue of what form "development" might take was intimately linked to international relations. The Qaddafi regime of Libya, courting union with Arab states, had opted for a rigorous and ascetic traditional Moslem form of society at home, while trying to begin an industrialization that would protect it once its huge oil resources were exhausted. The more cosmopolitan Egyptians showed no desire to share in the social forms imposed by Qaddafi's "cultural revolution," and many people felt these were incompatible with modernization. But some observers felt that Qaddafi's youthfulness showed him to be one of the first of the postindependence generation; other third world leaders had been brought up under colonialism and Western influence; other developmental models had failed to measure up. Perhaps Qaddafi did indeed represent a new future, consonant with dedication to hard work, incorruptibility, and compatible with world conditions that demanded better living standards but that could not support the mass of the world's people in a way of life remotely similar to the one that had developed in the West. Perhaps a younger generation of Egyptians would take a different view. And, of course, similar questions were asked about China, particularly when compared to the less egalitarian, more pluralistic, and democratic India, where by 1973 progress was hard to discern.

FOURTEEN
CONCLUSION

Twenty-one years after World War I—the "War to end Wars," the "War to Make the World Safe for Democracy"—an even more devastating World War II swept across the globe. Almost 30 years have passed since World War II. The world has hardly developed as statesmen of those times thought it would; it has been characterized by vicious, destructive, intermittent, scattered warfare. But the prospect of major war originating in the Atlantic area, source of most of the major wars of the past 400 years, has grown less and less likely.

Such high hopes had been raised by the end of World War II. Many who fought in it thought that this time the war was truly a crusade, a war against an identifiable evil: fascism in all its forms, a philosophy that denied individual dignity and freedom. (General Dwight D. Eisenhower captioned his memoirs *Crusade in Europe.*) Once the evil was crushed, a new and better world would emerge; there were high hopes that under the auspices of the new United Nations, international relations would take a radically different turn.

When America dropped the atomic bombs upon Hiroshima and Nagasaki, the hope was turned to certainty: in the face of this ultimate horror, something *must* be done to eliminate the old tendencies of balance-of-power politics, now thoroughly out of date. Wendell Willkie, the Republican Presidential candidate in 1940, had already written his plea for *One World;* state legislatures in the United States began to pass resolutions in favor of world government; former Secretary of Agriculture and Vice-President of the United States, Henry A. Wallace, began to advocate help from the wealthier nations of the world for the poorer ones.

What emerged in the chaotic, postwar years was very different from "one world." Statesmen like Churchill and professional diplomats were not caught by surprise. National sovereignty could not be abrogated by any single state or group of states: all would have to do it, all would fear that some might not, and therefore none would do it. Individual differences of sovereign states were too deeply rooted for them to adopt any single form of overriding government. Thus all the tendencies of a political system with no central political authority continued to bring states face to face with the security dilemma, despite all the changes in communications, weapons, and ideologies. These made the situation highly unstable, yet the old system survived the predictions of those who argued that advent of the atomic age had made world government imperative.

But it survived with many changes: changes in the number of states involved, in the structure and hierarchy of power within the system, in the kinds of relations that came to characterize international affairs, in the role of ideology, and in the types of violence employed. It was bound to be an era in which national self-determination would play an important role, if only because of the weakening of the old empires. But few people foresaw the advent of some 80 new states, each claiming all of the attributes of sovereignty and all participating in the elaborate dance of diplomacy. And few foresaw that the accompanying nationalism would remain so strong in the face of a supposedly growing interdependence, far outstripping the efforts made within newborn international organizations to deal with some of the resulting problems. At the end of the war some analysts like E. H. Carr, in *Nationalism and After,* foresaw the substitution of continent-size states like the Soviet Union and the United States for the older, smaller, European states. The latter had been able to provide protection for three centuries, but could no longer be counted on. A whole literature grew up on the integration of larger political communities out of smaller ones. But, in fact, the years saw a breakup of larger ones into smaller ones, and the only concession to integration lay in the growth of areas where the independent states no longer threatened force against each other—in the Atlantic area, for example.

The fifties and sixties was the era of gestation and birth of new states; it has come to an end. In the sixties the new states attempted to re-invigorate international organizations and bend them to new purposes. The effort produced UNCTAD in Geneva, UNIDO in Vienna, located the new environmental agency in Nairobi, brought an end to any idea of collective security as the key concept underlying international security efforts, and tried to make the United Nations into a grand coalition against the remnants of colonialism and its offspring. It was all a far cry from what Western nations had envisaged at San Francisco and earlier, and just as the Western effort to create a collective security system failed, and just as the West had tried to turn the United Nations into a grand coalition against the Soviet Union, so the less-developed countries' efforts failed to produce the desired results. United Nations' technical agencies were essential to communication between states, to trade, and even to the functioning of domestic economies, but they hardly served to build the base of support for its more political tasks. Its corridors served as an essential locale for what was actually a vast amount of traditional bilateral diplomacy; but it limped along, with none of the underlying concensus necessary to its efficient functioning in the security sphere, and little chance to build it.

The numbers of states and their variety marked one major change (along with their persistence in the face of interdependence). The new structure of political power within the international system constituted another. From a Europe-dominated system in which a half-dozen more-or-less major states and 20 minor ones were the main actors, it had become for a brief historical period a bipolar one in which the United States and the Soviet Union established—each in its own fashion—a hegemony within its own sphere, challenged the hegemony of the other, and sought to ensure the allegiance of new states as they appeared on the world scene. By 1956 the picture had changed again; the two blocs began to fracture, and both major powers began to admit that neutralism was an acceptable stance. The Soviet Union used force to keep its own bloc intact, but could not overcome the resistance of Yugoslavia, Albania, and China and the more limited independence shown by states like Rumania. The iron control Stalin had tried to exercise over Communist parties throughout the world—in the interest of Russian foreign policy—was broken. A De Gaulle in France effectively challenged United States leadership of the Western bloc; Castro took Cuba from the Western sphere into the Communist camp, and the United States, ineffectively, tried to prevent a repetition of this in countries as far apart as the Dominican Republic, where it won a Phyrric victory, and Vietnam, where it lost what remnant of moral leadership it had kept. China, having broken from Russia, became a minor nuclear power on its own and a political rival to Russia, wooing Communist and non-Communist states alike, and abandoning the contest only during its short-lived Great Proletarian Cultural Revolution. The United States had tried to supplant waning European influence on the rimlands of Eurasia, in order to keep Russia from moving in. It failed in numerous areas, and Russia did move in, but the United States found that Russian influence was aimed more at China than at the United States. And China, in return, looked to the United States as a balance. And in the meantime many of the new states, whatever course they chose, showed that they really meant to belong to neither camp.

The bipolar structure remained bipolar in terms of nuclear capabilities, but politically it was fractured into several groups and major states, and it was hard to draw analogies from past balance-of-power systems. What, for example, could one make of a Japan, the third industrial power in the world (one that might well become the second)—but that had only a small self-defense force and, because of its import necessities, was still vulnerable to economic forces it could not control? In addition to the complications of this militarily bipolar and politically multipolar system, there existed regional subsystems whose members might try to isolate themselves from the overall system, but could do so only for particular issues. African states, for example, could try to solve conflicts between African states within the confines of the Organization of African Unity. But when it came to economic development, issues of trading links with the EEC or other powers came to the fore; when the issue of southern Africa was treated, the trade relations of the southern areas with Europe or the United States were all-important; the Middle East constantly intruded on the consciousness of African states. A few countries, like Burma, tried to isolate themselves. It was a fruitless endeavor. But it was certain that the regionalism endemic in Latin America represented an effort to detach the area from undue influence by the United States, now that, presumably, there was nothing to fear from other outside influences.

It took time for leaders to see and react to these changes in the structure of the system. Stalin, trying to keep his bloc intact, failed in his attempt to overthrow Tito in 1948. Later, when Khrushchev was in power and tried to build domestic support through relaxation of Stalinist repression, he faced disaster in the bloc as the virus of Titoism spread to Poland and Hungary. He resorted to force, and won. But 12 years later his successors had to do the same thing again in Czechoslovakia. And in the meantime all hopes that China would remain a partner in the bloc were lost; the use of force threatened again, but both states drew back from the prospect. All of this meant that, Stalin's control over Communist parties gone, the dynamism of a single world Communist movement was lost. Communist leaders found friendly relations with capitalist states possible; in December 1972 Rumania joined the International Monetary Fund and the World Bank. Khrushchev and then Brezhnev continued to talk of intensifying the ideological struggle; but Russia needed allies and Russia needed to trade. In so doing—in Asia, the Middle East, and Latin America—it buttressed in power bourgeois nationalist governments. It was all pretty dismaying to people who had seen victory in World War II as one great step in the march of world Communism, and the breakup of empires and the triumph of Communism in China another. But somehow it was hard to bring new members into the bloc when there was no bloc— and new "People's Republics" did not want to come into a bloc anyway.

Western leaders may have been correct in assessing many of the horrors of Stalinism; Khrushchev—to the discomfiture of Western Communists—more than confirmed all they had claimed, although much of his de-Stalinization was self-serving and some of what he said about Stalin suspect. But it took until the mid-sixties for American leaders to accept generally the diversity that had grown within Communism and to act on the slow realization that there was no longer a single Communist bloc. It all made diplomacy a far more complicated matter; there was no longer a rule that the first step must always be to block Communism because it was an extension of Russian power. In South Asia, for example, in the disputes between India and Pakistan, if one sided with India one was on the Russian side, if with Pakistan, on the Chinese side. Anti-Communism had never *really* been enough. Now, finally, it was *clearly* not enough.

Both major powers, then, had come to a realization that their early guidelines to policy were no longer valid. By the same token, they had also come to a realization that they would have a hard time breaking up what did exist of the others' sphere. Stalin was perhaps the first to realize that intervening in the West was fruitless—or at least he gave some evidence of this. Khrushchev relearned it in 1962 during the missile crisis. The United States was perhaps slower to learn, insisting in 1952 that "liberation" must still be the aim of foreign policy. It was not: 1953 and East German revolt and 1956 and Hungarian revolt proved it. But the idea colored American policy for a long time. It was a part of the Wilsonian heritage, reinforced by the experience of World War II, when people concluded that had the world taken heed of what Nazism really implied and acted to block it earlier, rather than appeasing it, the world might have been spared World War II. When Ernest Hemingway wrote *For Whom the Bell Tolls* about the Spanish Civil War, he took the title from poet John Donne: "—therefor, do not ask for whom the bell tolls, it tolls for thee." The idea was incorporated into the United Nations Charter. The United States took it over, Truman used it in announcing the Truman Doctrine, and in 1961 John F. Kennedy could still say, "We shall pay any price, bear any burden, meet any hardship, support any friend, oppose any foe to assure the survival and the success of liberty." By the end of the Vietnam War the Nixon administration had retreated to a less moralistic position, accepting that it could not protect freedom everywhere and that such an attempt would, in fact, lead to the evils that analysts like Morgenthau and Kennan had foreseen 25 years earlier. The debate would never end, however. Just as Brezhnev had to argue for the intensification of the ideological struggle (while establishing trade relations with fascist Greece), so in the United States people who had condemned it for its "interventionism" wanted it to act to help overthrow racism in South Africa. But neither side displayed much of the concern that had existed in the 1950s about whether the less developed countries would end up in one camp or the other.

It seemed, then, that a new view had come to prevail about the structure of the international system. It was embodied, also, in the arms control agreements so painfully negotiated in the decade after the missile crisis. They were far from satisfactory in guaranteeing a real stability, but they did accept and embody the ideas that neither side could afford to use the weapons and that stability was in fact, the major aim. And so, although the Soviet Union sided strongly with the Arabs in their struggle with Israel, it disappointed the more militant Arabs because it would not back them into an allout war that would bring it into open conflict with the United States.

With the possibility of major war virtually eliminated, attention had turned to other forms of struggle. The United Nations had been able to bring about a major form of political change in helping to dismantle empires, aided by pressures from the United States and the Soviet Union alike. But it was not a world legislature, and force remained a chief means both for bringing about change and trying to block it. At first, because of prevailing bipolar views, guerrilla warfare was viewed by the United States primarily as a new means to carry on the struggle for Communism, and Khrushchev and others did much to foster the view. But in other parts of the world, force in the form of guerrilla war or terrorism was regarded as a legitimate means to bring about desired change, with no thought as to its effect upon the bipolar structure. And so the world saw such struggle legitimized in the United Nations, which had originally been conceived of as an organization that would do away with all use of force. Even more, overt armed intervention by one state in another's affairs came to be accepted if the ends were generally acceptable. Thus, although the United States might be condemned for Vietnam and the Dominican Republic, India's liberation of Goa and its intervention in Pakistan on behalf of Bangla Desh were widely approved. After World War II, when it seemed that such remote actions as Japan's seizure of Manchuria in 1931 or Hitler's intervention in the Spanish Civil War of the mid 1930s had led directly to the wider conflict, the common view, reflected in quotations from John Donne and in the Charter, was that conflict anywhere was of concern to the international community as a whole and must be stopped. Now, 30 years later, there might still be concern, but in the cases of "just" wars, the concern would be either to localize them or to get support for them—not to prevent them.

The evolution of the international political system over these 30 years, with its concomitant changes in attitudes, also saw an evolution of the international economic system, and it became obvious that international economics could not be even conceptually separated from international politics. In fact, by the beginning of the 1970s, many analysts saw economic problems and conflicts as the main subject matter for international political maneuvering. The dollar crisis of the previous five years was but a reflection that the United States had overreached itself in the world at large and had to retrench politically, seeking out more cooperative arrangements that might be granted only grudgingly and in return for many American concessions. But all states had become subject to similar limitations: England joined the Common Market against the wishes of its populace because it could no longer compete, and this necessitated a wholesale rearrangement of its relations with the old Commonwealth and with the United States. Brezhnev might talk of ideological struggle, but the Soviet Union had to import wheat. Communists might talk about how capitalists had to search for markets, but for Communist countries to import—as they had to do—they had to export and, therefore, search for markets. Once the People's Republic of China had recaptured an export market for its goods after the end of the Great Cultural Revolution, it promptly raised the price of the goods. Whether or not less-developed countries received capital aid on the terms they wanted depended more and more on the balance-of-payments situations of developed countries and this depended in part on the structure of the international monetary system—a system that had fallen into considerable dissarray. It was for this reason that they had successfully pressed to be included in the negotiations for the new monetary system. Radical and revisionist historians in the United States argued that the United States had foisted the International Monetary Fund and other such agencies on other countries at the end of World War II in an effort to create the system that the United States wanted. But in late 1971 newly independent Western Samoa became the 120th member of the IMF just one year before Communist Rumania joined: all found it a useful and necessary organization if they were to engage in the trade essential to their economies.

Economic pressures and inducements had always been a component of foreign policy in the form of blockades, aid, or trade pressures. In a more interdependent world the possibilities multiplied, but the power relationships were no clearer than those created by the presence of nuclear weapons. It was common to think of economic power as wielded by the wealthy, creditor states. But with gunboat diplomacy by the great powers largely a thing of the past, debtor states found it easier to insist on renegotiation or scaling down of debts in return for good relations. The possibility that control over scarce resources might give great leverage was finally acted upon by the oil-rich states in the early 1970s, as oil scarcity loomed; some of the Arab states saw it also as a means of influencing the United States to use genuine pressure upon Israel to withdraw from the occupied territories, or at least to reduce support for the Jewish state. Throughout the world matters such as exchange rates, trade deals, nationalizations and compensation agreements, the operations of multinational corporations, preferential trading agreements, all made headlines and engaged corps of diplomats and produced international conferences. Economic development had long become a subject of international concern, with only the means at issue. Now the underlying ecological crisis, population expansion, and the problem of exhaustion of nonrenewable

resources began to put all the assumptions in doubt. Western political institutions had been rejected in many parts of the world, although the scientific culture and administrative concepts might be accepted as necessary adjuncts to modernization. But the very issue of whether modernization was desirable or possible began to be raised, complicated by the fact
that population increase—the consequence of Western-introduced public
health measures and transportation improvements—meant that it seemed
impossible to simply go back to traditional society. As these issues engaged international society, providing a new and unmapped environment
for international politics, the international political system would never
be the same. A greater degree of international cooperation and coordination seemed imperative, but the weak international organizations hardly
looked as though they could provide the means toward these.

The world had fractured into several great trading groups: the North
Atlantic, the Communist, the semi-industrialized, the less-developed. Despite all the questions about what constituted development, relations between the first two groups and the second two had become, over the decades, a central world political problem. Early in the 1960s the solutions
—such as in the Alliance for Progress in Latin America, or the Aswan
Dam in Egypt—still looked relatively easy, and the first United Nations
Conference on Trade and Development met in Geneva in 1964 with high
hopes. A massive reorientation in trade would stimulate the necessary
massive economic growth in what had been dubbed by the General Assembly the "Decade of Development." By the time of the third UNC-
TAD in Santiago, Chile in 1972, hopes and aims were both lower, states
looked more to their own efforts and to a variety of strategies—many of
them more nationalist. But underlying all efforts lay the grim fact of continued almost unchecked population growth in the less-developed countries. Unless limited by artificial and social means, it would ultimately be
checked by famine and disease. To people in the last two groups of countries, the Cold War had been only a foolish exercise, having little to do
with the world's real problems, and much of international politics had
been mere shadow play.

Throughout the world there was a turning away, often, from the international realm, and a reassertion of national, regional, or local concerns.
But the pattern of international affairs, determined by the foreign policies of some 135 semisovereign, semi-independent states, would still do
much to create the framework and limits within which, on a local level,
individual human beings would work out their own lives.

BIBLIOGRAPHY

The area covered by this book necessitates a highly selective bibliography. It consists mainly of nontechnical and relatively general works in English which in themselves can lead the reader to other, more specialized sources. No attempt has been made to include books in the more specialized areas of international relations such as international law, economics, or finance, since the focus of the book is political history. With isolated exceptions, textbooks have not been included. Numerous works are included which are dated from the point of view of history or policy recommendation, but which serve as sources for how events and developments were viewed at the time the books were written.

The bibliography should serve, therefore, primarily as a useful source for works that will take the reader more deeply into the events summarized in this book, and to other, more analytical and technical works. The divisions in it are necessarily somewhat arbitrary. In general, works on relations of a major power and a particular area are listed under the area, although books on the second Indochina war are listed under "United States."

For the reader who wants to keep abreast of the development of world events and go beyond the too often shortsighted reporting in his daily newspaper, numerous periodicals and yearbooks exist that provide useful summaries and articles. A number of them are listed below. All readers should also be familiar with several major bibliographical sources: the volumes published at ten-year intervals of the *Foreign Affairs Bibliography,* New York: Bowker (for the Council on Foreign Relations), and the yearly and quarterly volumes of the *Public Affairs Information Service Bulletin,* which lists periodical articles and pamphlets as well as books.

The heavily annotated *Foreign Affairs Fifty-Year Bibliography* (Ann Arbor: Bowker, 1972), edited by Byron Dexter, is invaluable; *International Organization: an Interdisciplinary Bibliography* (Stanford: Hoover Institution Press, 1971), edited by Michael Haas, is not annotated, but is a useful guide. For ready reference on names, places, dates, and excellent summaries of events, *Keesing's Contemporary Archives* (London: Keesing Publications) is indispensable.

PERIODICALS

Carnegie Endowment for International Peace, *International Conciliation Pamphlets* (now discontinued).
Current History.
Foreign Affairs.
Foreign Policy.

Foreign Policy Association *Headline* Series.
International Affairs.
International Organization.
Problems of Communism.
U. N. Monthly Chronicle.
World Politics.
    There are also numerous excellent periodicals on the politics of various regions of the world.

YEARBOOKS

Année Politique. Paris: Presses Universitaires.
Annuaire Européen—European Yearbook. The Hague: Nijhoff.
Annual Register of World Events. New York: Longmans.
Chronologie Internationale. Paris: Documentation Française.
Stebbins, Richard P., et al., *The United States in World Affairs.* New York: Harper (for the Council on Foreign Relations) .
Survey of International Affairs. New York: Oxford University Press (for the Royal Institute of International Affairs) .

GENERAL

Aron, Raymond, *The Century of Total War.* Garden City: Doubleday, 1954.
Fontaine, André, *History of the Cold War.* New York: Pantheon Books, 1968–69, 2 vols.
Herz, John, *International Politics in the Atomic Age.* New York: Columbia University Press, 1952.
Kaplan, Morton A. (ed.) , *The Revolution in World Politics.* New York: Wiley, 1962.
Lichtheim, George, *Imperialism.* New York: Praeger, 1971.
Lukacs, John A., *New History of the Cold War.* Garden City: Doubleday, 3d ed., 1973.
Macridis, Roy (ed.) , *Foreign Policy in World Politics.* New York: Prentice-Hall, 4th ed., 1972.
Martin, Laurence, *Arms and Strategy: The World Power Structure Today.* New York: McKay, 1973.
Meadows, D. H., et al. *The Limits to Growth.* New York: Universe Books, 1972.
Sakharov, Andrei D., *Progress, Coexistence and Intellectual Freedom.* New York: Norton, 1968.
Seton-Watson, Hugh, *Neither War nor Peace: The Struggle for Power in the Post-War World.* New York: Praeger, 1960.
Snyder, Louis L., *The New Nationalism.* Ithaca: Cornell University Press, 1968.
Vernon, Raymond, *Sovereignty at Bay: The Multinational Spread of U.S. Enterprises.* New York: Basic Books, 1971.
Ward, Barbara and René Dubos, *Only One Earth.* New York: Norton, 1972.

Wilson, Thomas W., Jr., *International Environmental Action: A Global Survey*. New York: Dunellen, 1971.

UNITED NATIONS

Annual Review of United Nations Affairs. New York: New York University Press.

Boyd, Andrew, *United Nations: Piety, Myth and Truth*. Baltimore: Penguin, 1962.

Burns, Arthur Lee and Nina Heathcote, *Peace Keeping by United Nations Forces: From Suez to the Congo*. New York: Praeger, 1963.

Claude, Inis L., Jr., *Swords into Plowshares*. New York: Random House, 4th ed., 1971.

Everyman's United Nations. New York: United Nations Sales section.

Gardner, Richard N., *In Pursuit of World Order*. New York: Praeger, rev. ed., 1966.

_____ and Max Millikan, *The Global Partnership: International Agencies and Economic Development*. New York: Praeger, 1968.

Holcombe, Arthur N., et al., *Strengthening the United Nations*. New York: Harper, 1957.

James, Alan, *The Politics of Peacekeeping*. New York: Praeger, 1971.

Kay, David, *The New Nations in the United Nations*. New York: Columbia University Press, 1970.

Lash, Joseph P., *Dag Hammarskjold: Custodian of the Brushfire Peace*. Garden City: Doubleday, 1961.

Lie, Trygve, *In the Cause of Peace*. New York: Macmillan, 1954.

Luard, Evan, *The Evolution of International Organizations*. New York: Praeger, 1966.

Nicholas, Herbert, *The United Nations as a Political Institution*. New York: Oxford University Press, 3d ed., 1967.

O'Brien, Conor Cruse, *To Katanga and Back*. New York: Simon & Schuster, 1963.

Stoessinger, John G., *The United Nations and the Superpowers: China, Russia, and America*. New York: Random House, 3rd ed., 1973.

_____, et al., *Financing the United Nations System*. Washington, D.C.: Brookings Institution, 1963.

Urquhart, Brian, *Hammarskjold: The Diplomacy of Crisis*. New York: Knopf, 1972.

Wilson, Thomas W., Jr., *International Environmental Action: A Global Survey*. New York: Dunellen, 1971.

Yearbook of the United Nations. New York: United Nations, Office of Public Information.

WEAPONS, STRATEGY, AND ARMS CONTROL

Amrine, Michael, *The Great Decision: The Secret History of the Atomic Bomb*. New York: Putnam, 1959.

Aron, Raymond, *The Great Debate: Theories of Nuclear Strategy*. Garden City: Doubleday, 1965.

Barnet, Richard J., *Who Wants Disarmament?* Boston: Beacon Press, 1960.

Bloomfield, Lincoln P., et al., *Khrushchev and the Arms Race: Soviet Interests in Arms Control and Disarmament, 1954–1964*. Cambridge: MIT Press, 1966.

Bottome, Edgar M., *The Balance of Terror: A Guide to the Arms Race*. Boston: Beacon Press, 1971.

Brennan, Donald G. (ed.), *Arms Control, Disarmament, and National Security*. New York: Braziller, 1961.

Brodie, Bernard (ed.), *The Absolute Weapon*. New York: Harcourt, 1946.

Darby, Philip, *British Defense Policy East of Suez, 1947–68*. New York: Oxford University Press, 1973.

Eckstein, Harry (ed.), *Internal War: Problems and Approaches*. New York: Free Press of Glencoe, 1964.

Epstein, William, *Disarmament: Twenty-five Years of Effort*. Toronto: Canadian Institute of International Affairs, 1971.

Gavin, James M., *War and Peace in the Space Age*. New York: Harper, 1958.

Halperin, Morton H., *Contemporary Military Strategy*. Boston: Little, Brown, 1967.

Kahn, Herman, *On Thermonuclear War*. Princeton: Princeton University Press, 1960.

———, *Thinking About the Unthinkable*. New York: Horizon Press, 1962.

Kecskemeti, Paul, *Strategic Surrender: The Politics of Victory and Defeat*. Stanford: Stanford University Press, 1958.

Kohl, Wilfrid, *French Nuclear Diplomacy*. Princeton: Princeton University Press, 1971.

Moulton, Harland B., *From Superiority to Parity: The United States and the Strategic Arms Race, 1961–1971*. Westport (Conn.): Greenwood Press, 1973.

Newhouse, John, *Cold Dawn: The Story of SALT*. New York: Holt, Rinehart & Winston, 1973.

———, et al., *US Troops in Europe: Issues, Costs, and Choices*. Washington: Brookings Institution, 1971.

Paret, Peter and John W. Shy, *Guerrillas in the 1960's*. New York: Praeger (for the Center of International Studies), 1962.

Spanier, John W. and Joseph L. Nogee, *The Politics of Disarmament: A Study in Soviet-American Gamesmanship*. New York: Praeger, 1962.

WORLD WAR II AND AFTERMATH

Calvocoressi, Peter and Guy Wint, *Total War: The Story of World War II*. New York: Pantheon, 1972.

Churchill, Sir Winston, *The Second World War*. Boston: Houghton, 1948–1953 (6 vols.).

Command Decisions. New York: Harcourt (prepared by the Office of the Chief of Military History, Department of the Army, under the general editorship of Kent Roberts Greenfield) , 1959.

de Gaulle, Charles, *War Memoirs*, Vols. II and III. New York: Simon and Schuster, 1959 and 1960.

Feis, Herbert, *Between War and Peace: The Potsdam Conference*. Princeton: Princeton University Press, 1960.

———, *Churchill-Roosevelt-Stalin: The War They Waged and the Peace They Sought*. Princeton: Princeton University Press, 1957.

———, *The Atomic Bomb and the End of World War II*. Princeton: Princeton University Press, 1966.

———, *From Trust to Terror: The Onset of the Cold War, 1945–1950*. New York: Norton, 1970.

Herring, George C., Jr., *Aid to Russia, 1941–1946: Strategy, Diplomacy, and the Origins of the Cold War*. New York: Columbia University Press, 1973.

Morison, Samuel Eliot, *Strategy and Compromise*. Boston: Atlantic (Little, Brown) , 1958.

Opie, Redvers, et al., *The Search for Peace Settlements*. Washington: Brookings Institution, 1951.

Rozek, Edward J., *Allied War-Time Diplomacy: A Pattern in Poland*. New York: Wiley, 1958.

Wheeler-Bennett, John and Anthony Nicholls, *The Semblance of Peace: The Political Settlement After the Second World War*. New York: St. Martin's Press, 1972.

Young, Peter, *World War 1939–45*. New York: Crowell, 1966.

UNITED STATES

Abel, Elie, *The Missile Crisis*. New York: Bantam Books, 1956.

Acheson, Dean, *Present at the Creation*. New York: Norton, 1969.

Alperovitz, Gar, *Atomic Diplomacy: Hiroshima and Potsdam*. New York: Vintage Books, 1967.

Brandon, Henry, *The Retreat of American Power*. Garden City: Doubleday, 1973.

Brown, Seyom, *The Faces of Power: Constancy and Change in United States Foreign Policy from Truman to Johnson*. New York: Columbia University Press, 1968.

Brown, William A., Jr. and Redvers Opie, *American Foreign Assistance*. Washington: Brookings Institute, 1953.

Bundy, McGeorge, *The Pattern of Responsibility*. Boston: Houghton, 1951.

Burnham, James, *Containment or Liberation: An Inquiry Into the Aims of U.S. Foreign Policy*. New York: Day, 1953.

Byrnes, James F., *Speaking Frankly*. New York: Harper, 1947.

Cooper, Chester L., *The Lost Crusade*. New York: Dodd, Mead, 1970.

Donovan, Robert J., *Eisenhower: The Inside Story*. New York: Harper, 1956.

Dulles, Foster Rhea, *American Policy Toward Communist China, 1949–1969*. New York: Crowell, 1972.

Eisenhower, Dwight D., *The White House Years: Mandate for Change, 1953–1956*. Garden City: Doubleday, 1963.

Fleming, Denna Frank, *The Cold War and Its Origins, 1919–1960*. Garden City: Doubleday, 1961.

Fox, William T. R. and Annette B. Fox, *NATO and the Range of American Choice*. New York: Columbia University Press, 1967.

Fulbright, William J., *The Arrogance of Power*. New York: Vintage Books, 1967.

Gaddis, John Lewis, *The United States and the Origins of the Cold War, 1941–1947*. New York: Columbia University Press, 1972.

Gelber, Lionel, *America in Britain's Place: The Leadership of the West and Anglo-American Unity*. New York: Praeger, 1961.

Halberstam, David, *The Best and the Brightest*. New York: Randon House, 1972.

Hoffmann, Stanley, *Gulliver's Troubles, or the Setting of American Foreign Policy*. New York: McGraw-Hill, 1968.

Hoopes, Townsend, *The Devil and John Foster Dulles*. Boston: Little, Brown, 1973.

____, *The Limits of Intervention*. New York: David McKay, 1969.

Jones, Joseph, *The Fifteen Weeks*. New York: Viking Press, 1955.

Kennan, George F., *American Diplomacy, 1900–1950*. Chicago: University of Chicago Press, 1951.

Kennedy, Robert F., *Thirteen Days: A Memoir of the Cuban Missile Crisis*. New York: Norton, 1971.

Kolko, Gabriel, *The Politics of War*. New York: Random House, 1968.

____, and Joyce Kolko, *The Limits of Power*. New York: Harper and Row, 1972.

Lippmann, Walter, *The Cold War: A Study in United States Foreign Policy*. New York: Harpers, 1947.

Lowenthal, Abraham F., *The Dominican Intervention*. Cambridge: Harvard University Press, 1972.

Maddox, Robert James, *The New Left and the Origins of the Cold War*. Princeton: Princeton University Press, 1973.

Millis, Walter (ed.), *The Forrestal Diaries*. New York: Viking Press, 1951.

Osgood, Robert E., et al., *America and the World. Vol. II: Retreat from Empire? The First Nixon Administration*. Baltimore: Johns Hopkins University Press, 1973.

Paige, Glenn D., *The Korean Decision: June 24–30, 1950*. New York: Free Press, 1968.

The Pentagon Papers. New York: Bantam Books, 1971.

Reitzel, William, et al., *United States Foreign Policy, 1945–55*. Washington: Brookings Institute, 1956.

Ridgeway, Matthew B., with Harold H. Mastin, *Soldier: The Memoirs of Matthew B. Ridgeway*. New York: Harper, 1956.

Rose, Lisle A., *After Yalta*. New York: Scribner's, 1973.

Rostow, W. W., *The United States in the World Arena: An Essay in Recent History.* New York: Harper, 1960.

Schlesinger, Arthur M., Jr., *The Bitter Heritage.* New York: Crest Books, 1967.

——, *The Thousand Days.* New York: Crest Books, 1967.

Siracusa, Joseph M., *New Left Diplomatic Histories and Historians: The American Revisionists.* Port Washington (New York) : Kennikat Press, 1973.

Spanier, John W., *American Foreign Policy Since World War II.* New York: Praeger, 6th ed., 1973.

——, *The Truman-McArthur Controversy and the Korean War.* New York: Norton, rev. ed., 1965.

Stevenson, Charles A., *The End of Nowhere: American Policy Toward Laos Since 1954.* Boston: Beacon Press, 1972.

Truman, Harry S., *Memoirs.* Garden City: Doubleday, 1955–56 (2 vols.) .

Tucker, Robert W., *Nation or Empire?* Baltimore: Johns Hopkins University Press, 1968.

United States Relations With China: With Special Reference to the Period 1944–1949. Based on the files of the Department of State. Washington: Department of State, 1949.

Van Alstyne, Richard W., *The United States and East Asia.* New York: Norton, 1973.

Williams, William A., *The Tragedy of American Diplomacy.* Cleveland: World, 1959.

USSR

Allen, Robert L., *Soviet Economic Warfare.* Washington: Public Affairs Press: 1960.

Aspaturian, Vernon V., *Process and Power in Soviet Foreign Policy.* Boston: Little, Brown, 1971.

Au, Tai Sung, *The Sino-Soviet Territorial Dispute.* Philadelphia: Westminster Press, 1973.

Brumberg, Abraham (ed.) , *Russia Under Khrushchev.* New York; Praeger, 1962.

Dallin, Alexander, *The Soviet Union at the United Nations.* New York: Praeger, 1962.

Dallin, David J., *Soviet Espionage.* New Haven: Yale University Press, 1955.

——, *Soviet Foreign Policy After Stalin.* Philadelphia: Lippincott, 1961.

Dinerstein, Herbert S., *War and the Soviet Union.* New York: Praeger, (rev. ed.) , 1962.

Fairhall, David, *Russian Sea Power.* Boston: Gambit, 1971.

Garthoff, Raymond L., *Soviet Military Policy: A Historical Analysis.* New York: Praeger, 1966.

Goldman, Marshall I., *Soviet Foreign Aid.* New York: Praeger, 1967.

Hudson, G. F., et al., *The Sino-Soviet Dispute.* New York: Praeger, 1961.

Laqueur, Walter Z., *The Soviet Union and the Middle East.* New York: Praeger, 1959.

Moseley, Philip E., *The Kremlin and World Politics*. New York: Vintage, 1960.

Ra'anan, Uri, *The USSR Arms the Third World: Case Studies in Soviet Foreign Policy*. Cambridge: MIT Press, 1969.

Shulman, Marshall, *Stalin's Foreign Policy Reappraised*. Cambridge: Harvard University Press, 1963.

Sokolovskii, Vasilii, *Soviet Military Strategy in the Nuclear Age*. Englewood Cliffs, N.J.: Prentice- Hall, 1963.

Ulam, Adam B., *Expansion and Coexistence*. New York: Praeger, 1968.

____, *The Rivals*. New York: Viking Press, 1971.

Zagoria, Donald S., *The Sino-Soviet Conflict, 1956–1961*. Princeton: Princeton University Press, 1962.

EASTERN EUROPE

Armstrong, Hamilton Fish, *Tito and Goliath*. New York: Macmillan, 1951.

Bromke, Adam and Teresa Rakowska-Harmstone, *The Communist States in Disarray, 1965–1971*. Minneapolis: University of Minnesota Press, 1972.

Brzezinski, Zbigniew K., *The Soviet Bloc: Unity and Conflict*. Cambridge: Harvard University Press, 2nd ed., 1967.

Dedijer, Vladimir, *Tito*. New York: Simon and Schuster, 1953.

Kaser, Michael, *Comecon: Integration Problems of the Planned Economies*. New York: Oxford University Press, 1967.

Kecskemeti, Paul, *The Unexpected Revolution: Social Forces in the Hungarian Uprising*. Stanford: Stanford University Press, 1961.

Korbel, Josef, *The Communist Subversion of Czechoslovakia, 1939–1948: The Failure of Coexistence*. Princeton: Princeton University Press, 1959.

Kovrig, Bennett, *The Myth of Liberation: East Central Europe in U.S. Diplomacy and Politics since 1941*. Baltimore: Johns Hopkins University Press, 1973.

Laqueur, Walter Z. and Leopold Labedz, *Polycentrism: The New Factor in International Politics*. New York: Praeger, 1962.

Lukacs, John A., *The Great Powers and Eastern Europe*. New York: American Book, 1953.

Seton-Watson, Hugh, *The East European Revolution*. New York: Praeger, 3rd ed., 1956.

Tigrid, Pavel, *Why Dubcek Fell*. London: Macdonald, 1971.

Toma, Peter (ed.), *The Changing Face of Communism in Eastern Europe*. Tucson: Arizona University Press, 1970.

Ulam, Adam B., *Titoism and the Cominform*. Cambridge: Harvard University Press, 1952.

Vàli, Ferenc, *Rift and Revolt in Hungary: Nationalism Versus Communism*. Cambridge: Harvard University Press, 1961.

Zinner, Paul E., *Revolution in Hungary*. New York: Columbia University Press, 1962.

EUROPE: GENERAL, EUROPEAN UNION, AND ATLANTIC ALLIANCE

Ball, M. Margaret, *NATO and the European Union Movement*. New York: Praeger (for the London Institute of World Affairs), 1959.

Beaufre, André, *NATO and Europe*. New York: Knopf, 1967.

Bell, Coral, *Negotiation from Strength*. New York: Knopf, 1963.

Beloff, Nora, *The General Says "No"*. Baltimore: Penguin, 1964.

Benoit, Emile, *Europe at Sixes and Sevens*. New York: Columbia University Press, 1961.

——, *Britain in Western Europe*. New York: Royal Institute of International Affairs, 1956.

Buchan, Alastair, *Europe's Futures, Europe's Choices*. New York: Columbia University Press, 1969.

Calleo, David P., *The Atlantic Fantasy*. Baltimore: Johns Hopkins University Press, 1970.

Camps, Miriam, *Britain and the European Community, 1955–1963*. Princeton: Princeton University Press, 1964.

Clay, Lucius, *Decision in Germany*. Garden City: Doubleday, 1950.

Defense in the Cold War. New York: Royal Institute of International Affairs, 1950.

Diebold, William, Jr., *Trade and Payments in Western Europe*. New York: Harper (for the Council on Foreign Relations), 1952.

Feld, Werner, *The European Common Market and the World*. Englewood Cliffs: Prentice-Hall, 1967.

Haas, Ernst B., *The Uniting of Europe*. Stanford: Stanford University Press, 1958.

Hallstein, Walter, *United Europe: Challenge and Opportunity*. Cambridge: Harvard University Press, 1962.

Holborn, Hajo, *The Political Collapse of Europe*. New York: Knopf, 1951.

Kissinger, Henry, *The Troubled Alliance*. New York: McGraw-Hill, 1965.

Kitzinger, Uwe, *Diplomacy and Persuasion: How Britain Joined the Common Market*. London: Thames and Hudson, 1973.

Kraft, Joseph, *The Grand Design: From Common Market to Atlantic Partnership*. New York: Harper and Row, 1962.

Mander, John, *Berlin, Hostage for the West*. Baltimore: Penguin, 1962.

Neustadt, Richard, *Alliance Politics*. New York: Columbia University Press, 1970.

Pfaltzgraff, Robert, *The Atlantic Community*. New York: Van Nostrand, 1969,

Price, Harry Bayard, *The Marshall Plan and Its Meaning*. Ithaca: Cornell University Press, 1955.

Reynaud, Paul, *Unite or Perish: A Dynamic Program For a United Europe*. New York: Simon and Schuster, 1951.

Robertson, A. H., *The Council of Europe*. New York: Praeger (for the London Institute of World Affairs), 2nd ed., 1961.

Steel, Ronald, *The End of Alliance*. New York: Delta, 1966.

Vali, Ferenc, *The Quest for a United Germany*. Baltimore: Johns Hopkins Press, 1967.

Van der Beugel, Ernst H., *From Marshall Aid to Atlantic Partnership: European Integration as a Concern of American Foreign Policy*. New York: Elsevier, 1966.

Ward, Barbara, *The West at Bay*. New York: Norton, 1948.

Willis, F. Roy, *France, Germany, and the New Europe, 1945–1967*. New York: Oxford University Press, rev. ed., 1968.

WESTERN EUROPEAN COUNTRIES

Brandt, Willy, *A Peace Policy for Europe*. New York: Holt, Rinehart and Winston, 1969.

Davison, W. Phillips, *The Berlin Blockade: A Study in Cold War Politics*. Princeton: Princeton University Press, 1958.

de Gaulle, Charles, *Memoirs of Hope: Renewal and Endeavor*. New York: Simon and Schuster, 1972.

Eden, Anthony, *Full Circle: The Memoirs of Anthony Eden*. Boston: Houghton, 1960.

Epstein, Leon, *Britain—Uneasy Ally*. Chicago: University of Chicago Press, 1954.

Fitzsimons, Matthew A., *The Foreign Policy of the British Labour Government, 1945–1951*. Notre Dame: University of Notre Dame Press, 1953.

Freund, Gerald, *Germany Between Two Worlds*. New York: Harcourt, 1961.

Furniss, E.S., Jr., *France, Troubled Ally: de Gaulle's Heritage and Prospects*. New York: Harper (for the Council on Foreign Relations), 1960.

Grosser, Alfred, *La IVème République et Sa Politique Extérieure*. Paris: Colin, 1960.

——, *French Foreign Policy Under de Gaulle*. Boston: Little, Brown, 1967.

Hanrieder, Wolfram, *The Stable Crisis: Two Decades of German Foreign Policy*. New York: Harper and Row, 1970.

Litchfield, E. H., et al., *Governing Post-War Germany*. Ithaca: Cornell University Press, 1953.

Montgomery, John D., *Forced to Be Free: The Artificial Revolution in Germany and Japan*. Chicago: University of Chicago Press, 1957.

Tint, Herbert, *French Foreign Policy Since the Second World War*. New York: St. Martin's Press, 1972.

Vandenbosch, Amry, *Dutch Foreign Policy Since 1815*. The Hague: Nijhoff 1959.

Walker, Patrick Gordon, *The Commonwealth*. London: Secker and Warbury, 1962.

Werth, Alexander, *France: 1940–1955*. New York: Holt, 1956.

Whetten, Lawrence L., *Germany's Ostpolitik: Relations Between the Federal Republic and the Warsaw Pact Countries*. New York: Oxford University Press, 1971.

Whitaker, Arthur P., *Spain and the Defense of the West: Ally and Liability*. New York: Harper (for the Council on Foreign Relations), 1961.

Williams, Francis, *Twilight of Empire: Memoirs of Prime Minister Clement Attlee*. New York: Barnes, 1962.

Woodhouse, Christopher, *British Foreign Policy Since the Second World War*. New York: Praeger, 1962.

DECOLONIZATION AND NEW STATES

Buss, Claude A., *The Arc of Crisis*. Garden City: Doubleday, 1961.

Calvocoressi, Peter, *World Order and New States: Problems of Keeping the Peace*. New York: Praeger (for the Institute of Strategic Studies, London), 1962.

Duroselle, Jean-Baptiste and Jean Meyriat (eds.), *Les Nouveaux Etats dans les Relations Internationales*. Paris: Colin, 1962.

Easton, Stewart, *The Twilight of European Colonialism: A Political Analysis*. New York: Holt, Rinehart and Winston, 1960.

Emerson, Rupert, *From Empire to Nation*. Cambridge: Harvard University Press, 1960.

Kahin, George McT., *The Asian-African Conference*. Ithaca: Cornell University Press, 1956.

―――― (ed.), *Major Governments of Asia*. Ithaca: Cornell University Press, 1958.

Martin, Lawrence W. (ed.), *Neutralism and Nonalignment: The New States in World Affairs*. New York: Praeger (for the Washington Center of Foreign Policy Research, School of Advanced International Studies, Johns Hopkins University), 1962.

Miller, J.D.B., *The Politics of the Third World*. New York: Oxford, 1967.

MIDDLE EAST

Badeau, John S., *The American Approach to the Arab World*. New York: Harper and Row, 1968.

Bar-Zohar, Michael, *Embassies in Crisis: Diplomats and Demagogues Behind the Six-Day War*. Englewood Cliffs: Prentice-Hall, 1971.

Bullard, Sir Reader William (ed.), *The Middle East: A Political and Economic Survey*. New York: Royal Institute for International Affairs, 3rd ed., 1958.

Campbell, John C., *Defense of the Middle East: Problems of American Policy*. New York: Harper (for the Council on Foreign Relations), rev. ed., 1960.

Cohen, Aharon, *Israel and the Arab World*. New York: Funk and Wagnalls, 1970.

Cremeans, Charles D., *The Arabs and the World: Nasser's Arab Nationalist Policy*. New York: Praeger (for the Council on Foreign Relations), 1963.

Ford, Alan W., *The Anglo-Iranian Oil Dispute of 1951–1952*. Berkeley: University of California Press, 1954.

Hurewitz, J. C., *Middle East Politics: The Military Dimension*. New York: Praeger, 1969.

―――― , *The Struggle for Palestine*. New York: Norton, 1950.

Kerr, Malcolm, *The Arab Cold War, 1958–1964*. New York: Oxford University Press, 1965.

Khouri, Fred J., *The Arab-Israeli Dilemma*. Syracuse: Syracuse University Press, 1968.

Kirk, George E., *Contemporary Arab Politics: A Concise History*. New York: Praeger, 1961.

Laqueur, Walter Z. (ed.), *The Middle East in Transition: Studies in Contemporary History*. New York: Praeger, 1958.

——, *The Struggle for the Middle East: The Soviet Union in the Mediterranean, 1958–1968*. New York: Macmillan, 1969.

Lenczowski, George, *The Middle East in World Affairs*. Ithaca: Cornell University Press, 3rd ed., 1962.

——, *Soviet Advances in the Middle East*. Washington: American Enterprise Institute for Policy Research, 1972.

Longrigg, Stephen H., *Oil in the Middle East*. New York: Oxford University Press, 3rd ed., 1968.

Monroe, Elizabeth, *Britain's Moment in the Middle East, 1914–1956*. Baltimore: Johns Hopkins University Press, 1963.

Nasser, Gamal Abdul, *The Philosophy of the Revolution*. Buffalo: Smith, Keynes, and Marshall, 1959.

Nutting, Anthony, *Nasser*. New York: Dutton, 1972.

——, *No End of a Lesson*. New York: Potter, 1967.

O'Ballance, Edgar, *The War in the Yemen*. Hamden (Conn.) : Archon, 1971.

Pryce-Jones, David, *The Face of Defeat: Palestinian Refugees and Guerrillas*. New York: Holt, Rinehart and Winston, 1973.

Safran, Nadav, *From War to War: The Arab-Israeli Confrontation, 1948–1967*. New York: Pegasus, 1969.

Shwadran, Benjamin, *Jordan: A State of Tension*. New York: Council for Middle Eastern Affairs Press, 1959.

——, *The Middle East, Oil and the Great Powers*. New York: Council for Middle Eastern Affairs Press, 3rd ed., 1974.

Thomas, Hugh, *Suez*. New York: Harper and Row, 1967.

Wheelock, Keith, *Nasser's New Egypt: A Critical Analysis*. New York: Praeger, 1960.

ASIA

Brecher, Michael, *The New States of Asia: A Political Analysis*. New York: Oxford University Press, 1963.

Clubb, Oliver E., Jr., *The United States and the Sino-Soviet Bloc in Southeast Asia*. Washington: Brookings Institute, 1962.

Fifield, Russell H., *The Diplomacy of Southeast Asia: 1945–1958*. New York: Harper, 1958.

——, *Southeast Asia in United States Policy*. New York: Praeger (for the Council on Foreign Relations) , 1963.

Jukes, Geoffrey, *The Soviet Union in Asia*. Berkeley: University of California Press, 1973.

Kahin, George McT. (ed.), *Government and Politics of Southeast Asia*. Ithaca: Cornell University Press, 2nd ed., 1964.

Modelski, George (ed.), *SEATO: Six Studies*. Melbourne: Cheshire (for the Australian National University), 1962.

Rosinger, Lawrence K., et al., *The State of Asia: A Contemporary Survey*. New York: Knopf (for the Institute of Pacific Relations), 1951.

Thorp, Willard L. (ed.), *The United States and the Far East*. Englewood Cliffs, N.J.: Prentice-Hall (for the American Assembly), 2nd ed., 1962.

Vinacke, Harold M., *Far Eastern Politics in the Postwar Period*. New York: Appleton, 1956.

ASIAN COUNTRIES

Ball, William McMahon, *Japan: Enemy or Ally?* New York: Day (for the Institute of Pacific Relations), 1949.

Barnds, William J., *India, Pakistan and the Great Powers*. New York: Praeger, 1972.

Barnett, A. Doak, *A New U.S. Policy Toward China*. Washington: Brookings Institute, 1971.

Berkes, Ross N. and Mohinder S. Bedi, *The Diplomacy of India*. Stanford: Stanford University Press, 1958.

——, *Japan's Modern Century*. New York: Ronald, 1955.

Boyd, R.G., *Communist China's Foreign Policy*. New York: Praeger, 1962.

Brecher, Michael, *Nehru: A Political Biography*. New York: Oxford University Press, 1959.

Brzezinski, Zbigniew, *The Fragile Blossom: Crisis and Change in Japan*. New York: Harper and Row, 1972.

Buttinger, Joseph, *A Dragon Embattled*. New York: Praeger, 1967, 2 vols.

Chakravarti, Prithwis Chandra, *India's China Policy*. Bloomington: Indiana University Press, 1962.

Clubb, O. Edmund, *China and Russia*. New York: Columbia University Press, 1971.

Elegant, Robert S., *The Dragon's Seed: Peking and the Overseas Chinese*. New York: St. Martin's Press, 1959.

Fall, Bernard B., *Street Without Joy: Indochina at War, 1946–1954*. Harrisburg: Stackpole, 1961.

——, *The Two Viet-Nams*. New York: Praeger, 2nd ed., 1967.

Feis, Herbert, *The China Tangle*. Princeton: Princeton University Press, 1953.

Galbraith, John K., *Ambassador's Journal*. Boston: Houghton, 1969.

Hammer, Ellen J., *The Struggle for Indochina. 1940–1955*. Stanford: Stanford University Press, 1966.

Higgins, Trumbull, *Korea and the Fall of MacArthur: A Précis in Limited War, 1950–1953*. New York: Putnam, 1962.

Hinton, Harold, *China's Turbulent Quest*. New York: Macmillan, 1970.

Hodson, H. V., *The Great Divide: Britain—India—Pakistan*. New York: Atheneum, 1971.

Hsieh, Alice Langley, *Communist China's Strategy in the Nuclear Era*. Englewood Cliffs, N.J.: Prentice-Hall, 1962.

Kahn, Herman, *The Emerging Japanese Superstate: Challenge and Response*. Englewood Cliffs, N. J.: Prentice-Hall, 1970.

Kautsky, John H., *Moscow and the Communist Party of India*. Cambridge: Technology Press; New York: Wiley, 1956.

Korbel, Josef, *Danger in Kashmir*. Princeton: Princeton University Press, 1954.

Langdon, F. C., *Japan's Foreign Policy*. Vancouver: University of British Columbia Press, 1973.

Mende, Tibor, *China and Her Shadow*. New York: Coward-McCann, 1962.

Moraes, Frank, *Revolt in Tibet*. New York: Macmillan, 1960.

Pye, Lucian, *Guerrilla Communism in Malaya*. Princeton: Princeton University Press, 1956.

Ridgeway, Matthew B., *The Korean War*. Garden City: Doubleday, 1967.

Sihanouk, Norodom, *My War with the CIA: The Memoirs of Prince Norodom Sihanouk*. New York: Pantheon, 1973.

Simmonds, J.D., *China's World: The Foreign Policy of a Developing State*. New York: Columbia University Press, 1971.

Simon, Sheldon, *The Broken Triangle: Peking, Djakarta, and the PKI*. Baltimore: Johns Hopkins Press, 1968.

Stein, Arthur, *India and the Soviet Union*. Chicago: University of Chicago Press, 1969.

Van Ness, Peter, *Revolution and Chinese Foreign Policy*. Berkeley: University of California Press, 1970.

Warner, Denis, *The Last Confucian: Vietnam, Southeast Asia, and the West*. New York: Macmillan, 1963.

Watt, Alan, *The Evolution of Australian Foreign Policy. 1938–1965*. New York: Cambridge University Press, 1967.

Whiting, Allen S., *China Crosses the Yalu: the Decision to Enter the Korean War*. New York: Macmillan, 1960.

Wildes, Harry Emerson, *Typhoon in Tokyo: The Occupation and Its Aftermath*. New York: Macmillan, 1964.

Zagoria, Donald S., *Vietnam Triangle: Moscow, Peking, Hanoi*. New York: Pegasus, 1967.

AFRICA

Cohn, Helen D., *Soviet Policy Toward Black Africa: The Focus On National Integration*. New York: Praeger, 1972.

DuBois, W.E.B., *The World and Africa*. New York: Viking, rev. ed., 1965.

Gordon, King, *The United Nations in the Congo: A Quest for Peace*. New York: Carnegie Endowment for International Peace, 1962.

Grundy, Kenneth W., *Confrontation and Accomodation in Southern Africa: The Limits of Independence.* Berkeley: University of California Press, 1973.

Gutteridge, William, *The Military in African Politics.* London: Methuen, 1969.

Hall, Richard, *The High Price of Principles: Kaunda and the White South.* London: Hodder, 1969.

Hodgkin, Thomas, *Nationalism in Colonial Africa.* London: Muller, 1956.

Hovet, Thomas, Jr., *Africa in the United Nations.* Evanston: Northwestern University Press, 1963.

Kraft, Joseph, *The Struggle for Algeria.* Garden City: Doubleday, 1961.

Legum, Colin (ed.), *Africa: A Handbook to the Continent.* New York: Praeger, 1962.

_____, *Pan-Africanism: A Short Political Guide.* New York: Praeger, 1962.

Mazrui, Ali A., *Toward A Pax Africana.* London: Werdenfeld, 1967.

McKay, Vernon, *Africa in World Politics.* New York: Harper, 1963.

_____, (ed.), *African Diplomacy: Studies in the Determinants of Foreign Policy.* New York: Praeger, 1966.

Nkrumah, Kwame, *Africa Must Unite.* New York: Praeger, 1963.

Nielsen, Waldemar A., *The Great Powers and Africa.* New York: Praeger (for the Council on Foreign Relations), 1969.

Padelford, Norman J. and Rupert Emerson (eds.), *Africa and World Order.* New York: Praeger, 1963.

Rivkin, Arnold, *Africa and the West: Elements of a Free-World Policy.* New York: Praeger, 1962.

St. Jorre, John de, *The Brother's War: Biafra and Nigeria.* Boston: Houghton, 1972.

Thiam, Doudou, *The Foreign Policy of African States.* New York: Praeger, 1965.

Tillion, Germaine, *Algeria: The Realities.* New York: Knopf, 1958.

Wallerstein, Immanuel, *Africa: The Politics of Independence.* New York: Vintage Books, 1961.

Welch, Claude E., Jr., *Dream of Unity: Pan Africanism and Political Unification in West Africa.* Ithaca: Cornell University Press, 1966.

Zartman, William I., *International Relations in the New Africa.* Englewood Cliffs, N.J.: Prentice-Hall, 1966.

THE AMERICAS

Arevalo, Juan José, *The Shark and the Sardines.* New York: Lyle Stuart, 1961.

Berle, Adolf A., Jr., *Latin America: Diplomacy and Reality.* New York: Harper and Row (for the Council on Foreign Relations), 1962.

Bonsal, Philip W., *Cuba, Castro, and the United States.* Pittsburgh: University of Pittsburgh Press, 1971.

Dobell, Peter C., *Canada's Search for New Roles: Foreign Policy in the Trudeau Era.* New York: Oxford University Press, 1972.

Dreier, John C. (ed.), *The Alliance for Progress: Problems and Perspectives.* Baltimore: Johns Hopkins Press, 1962.

——, *The Organization of American States and the Hemisphere Crisis.* New York: Harper and Row (for the Council on Foreign Relations), 1962.

Eayrs, Ames, *Northern Approaches: Canada and the Search for Peace.* New York: St. Martin's Press, 1962.

Gil, Federíco, *Latin American—United States Relations.* New York: Harcourt, 1971.

Goldhamer, Herbert, *The Foreign Powers in Latin America.* Princeton: Princeton University Press, 1972.

Grunwald, Joseph, et al., *Latin American Economic Integration and U.S. Policy.* Washington: Brookings Institution, 1972.

Hanson, Simon G., *Dollar Diplomacy Modern Style: Chapters in the Failure of the Alliance for Progress.* Washington: Inter-American Press, 1970.

Lieuwen, Edwin, *Arms and Politics in Latin America.* New York: Praeger (for the Council on Foreign Relations), rev. ed., 1961.

Meyer, Karl and Tad Szulc, *The Cuban Invasion: The Chronicle of a Disaster.* New York: Praeger, 1962.

Pachter, Henry M., *Collision Course: The Cuban Missile Crisis and Coexistence.* New York: Praeger, 1963.

Sheer, Robert and Maurice Zeitlin, *Cuba: Tragedy in Our Hemisphere.* New York: Grove Press, 1963.

Schneider, Ronald M., *Communism in Guatemala: 1944–1954.* New York: Praeger, 1958.

Slater, Jerome, *Intervention and Negotiation: The United States and the Dominican Revolution.* New York: Harper and Row, 1970.

Suaréz, Andés, *Cuba: Castroism and Communism, 1959–1966.* Cambridge: MIT Press, 1967.

Szulc, Tad, *The Winds of Revolution: Latin America Today, and Tomorrow.* New York: Praeger, rev. ed., 1965.

Tannenbaum, Frank, *Ten Keys to Latin America.* New York: Knopf, 1962.

Whitaker, Arthur P., *The Western Hemisphere Idea: Its Rise and Decline.* Ithaca: Cornell University Press, 1954.

INDEX